D1716369

LAW FOR SOCIETY

NATURE, FUNCTIONS, AND LIMITS

ASPEN PUBLISHERS

LAW FOR SOCIETY

NATURE, FUNCTIONS, AND LIMITS

KEVIN M. CLERMONT
Ziff Professor of Law
Cornell University

ROBERT A. HILLMAN
Woodruff Professor of Law
Cornell University

SHERI LYNN JOHNSON
Professor of Law
Cornell University

ROBERT S. SUMMERS
McRoberts Research Professor of Law
Cornell University

Wolters Kluwer
Law & Business

AUSTIN   BOSTON   CHICAGO   NEW YORK   THE NETHERLANDS

Aspen Publishers
Attn: Permissions Department
76 Ninth Avenue, 7th Floor
New York, NY 10011-5201

To contact Customer Care, e-mail customer.care@aspenpublishers.com, call 1-800-234-1660, fax 1-800-901-9075, or mail correspondence to:

Aspen Publishers
Attn: Order Department
PO Box 990
Frederick, MD 21705

Printed in the United States of America.

1 2 3 4 5 6 7 8 9 0

ISBN 978-0-7355-6853-2

Library of Congress Cataloging-in-Publication Data

Law for society : nature, functions, and limits / Kevin M. Clermont ... [et al.].
  p. cm.
Includes index.
ISBN 978-0-7355-6853-2
1. Law—United States. I. Clermont, Kevin M.

KF385.A4L39 2010
349.73—dc22

2009054119

About Wolters Kluwer Law & Business

Wolters Kluwer Law & Business is a leading provider of research information and workflow solutions in key specialty areas. The strengths of the individual brands of Aspen Publishers, CCH, Kluwer Law International and Loislaw are aligned within Wolters Kluwer Law & Business to provide comprehensive, in-depth solutions and expert-authored content for the legal, professional and education markets.

CCH was founded in 1913 and has served more than four generations of business professionals and their clients. The CCH products in the Wolters Kluwer Law & Business group are highly regarded electronic and print resources for legal, securities, antitrust and trade regulation, government contracting, banking, pension, payroll, employment and labor, and healthcare reimbursement and compliance professionals.

Aspen Publishers is a leading information provider for attorneys, business professionals and law students. Written by preeminent authorities, Aspen products offer analytical and practical information in a range of specialty practice areas from securities law and intellectual property to mergers and acquisitions and pension/benefits. Aspen's trusted legal education resources provide professors and students with high-quality, up-to-date and effective resources for successful instruction and study in all areas of the law.

Kluwer Law International supplies the global business community with comprehensive English-language international legal information. Legal practitioners, corporate counsel and business executives around the world rely on the Kluwer Law International journals, loose-leafs, books and electronic products for authoritative information in many areas of international legal practice.

Loislaw is a premier provider of digitized legal content to small law firm practitioners of various specializations. Loislaw provides attorneys with the ability to quickly and efficiently find the necessary legal information they need, when and where they need it, by facilitating access to primary law as well as state-specific law, records, forms and treatises.

Wolters Kluwer Law & Business, a unit of Wolters Kluwer, is headquartered in New York and Riverwoods, Illinois. Wolters Kluwer is a leading multinational publisher and information services company.

Summary of Contents

Contents

Chapter 3

Law as an Instrument for Administering the Regulatory State

Looking at the longish list of authors of this book should suggest to the college or university teacher that a number of law teachers share a firm conviction that law is an unjustly neglected part of general education—and that these new teaching materials fill a true need.

Indeed we have long found it striking that most of even the best-educated students leave college in unblemished ignorance of the concept of law and with little idea of the legal system under which they have lived and will live. The would-be educated citizen, and surely the graduate beginning any of many specialized disciplines, cannot justify such ignorance. A survey course on introduction to law provides a ready cure, while not only enriching the mind but also usually providing a lot of fascinating fun. But we are getting ahead of ourselves by addressing this question of why even a generalist should take a survey course on law. Section Three of the General Introduction, which begins the book, makes, to the students, what turns out to be the easy case for including law in the program of general education.

The harder question is how a teacher should try to introduce law. Certainly a survey of the contents of law, studying contracts in a nutshell and then torts and so on, makes little educational sense. Leaping instead to the abstract level of legal philosophy, without first providing students with sufficient concrete information, results in conveying little. Worse yet and perhaps even detrimental is the popular but ineffective approach of reprinting selected interdisciplinary readings that deliver strong opinions about particular aspects of law to an audience of novices who know too little about the subject to engage it. In brief, the shortcomings of all three of these approaches reflect the oft-noted difficulty of trying to teach anything about law without somehow managing to teach all of law.

The correct approach must be more analytic, breaking law down into a manageable number of comprehensible units that students can assemble into a coherent concept of law. This approach would put natural bounds on and give a sense of direction to an introductory book and course, affording students a perceptible sense of concrete but significant learning. However, the most common analytic approach divides law into its principal institutions of the judiciary, legislature, executive, and administrative agency. This parochial division distorts the operation of law. Law actually performs its social tasks by collaborative effort, with roles for private persons as well as for players such as courts, legislators, and other official actors.

A sounder and more comprehensive breakdown, we think, would look at the means and ends of social ordering through law. We therefore try to get at what law is by examining, first, how law does what it does and, second, what it can and cannot do. We present law as a set of five basic techniques for addressing many problems of any society. That is to say, the essential *nature* of law lies for us in its problem-solving *functions*, subject to the critical concession that law has very real and serious *limits* on what it can accomplish. We believe this approach is the most productive and accurate way to learn and think about law. But again we are getting ahead of ourselves. Section Four of the General Introduction further outlines this instrumentalist conception of law.

As to the book's structure, the focus will fall first on the variety of law's available techniques and their limits. See especially the Introductory Note to Part One. The focus will then shift to the subsidiary matter regarding the basic social functions on which the law's techniques are commonly put to work. See especially the Introductory Note to Part Two.

Both of these two major parts of the book subdivide into chapters. Part One comprises Chapters 1 through 5. These chapters respectively treat the five basic legal instruments for social ordering by studying how law acts through remedying grievances, imposing punishment, regulating administratively, conferring public benefits, and facilitating private arrangements. The first of these chapters is by far the longest, because it provides the background invoked in the subsequent chapters. Each of the chapters contains eight sections that flesh out the particular instrument in a logical and comprehensive manner, encouraging comparative analysis along those lines of the instruments' principal differentiating characteristics. Together these five chapters offer an overview of the means at law's disposal.

After Part One so treats the instruments of law in order to show how law does what it does, Part Two applies them to a few selected social tasks. Sketching the law in action there elaborates what the law can do and cannot do. Although we divide the book into Part One on the means of law and Part Two on the ends of law, our hope throughout is to convey a sense of the nature, functions, and limits of law.

Thus, our analytic approach dictates a highly structured book. Its parts, chapters, and sections follow a pattern. For the most part they need not be taught in the order they appear, but conveying the pattern will remove much of the confusion from whatever route is taken through the book.

Our approach is not untried. In 1965 Charles G. Howard & Robert S. Summers produced Law: Its Nature, Functions, and Limits. In 1972 Professor Summers revamped the book into its successful second edition. In 1986, Doris Marie Provine, John J. Barceló III, Sheri Lynn Johnson, Robert A. Hillman, and Kevin M. Clermont turned out its third and final edition. Years of teaching experience with it only heightened our appreciation of that book and our resolve to sustain it. We therefore produced this revamped set of materials. We built on the 1986 book, including the excellent contributions to Chapters 3 and 4 by Marie Provine and Jack Barceló, who were unable to continue on the project. Our aim was to turn out an even more provocative, readable, and teachable book.

Robert S. Summers is a distinguished senior professor at Cornell Law School. Among his areas of great strength is jurisprudence, where he has carefully developed the framework of his ideas by a prodigious flow of books and articles. We owe the conceptual structure of this book to him. See, e.g., Robert S. Summers, The Technique Element in Law, 59 Cal. L. Rev. 733 (1971); cf.

Kevin M. Clermont & Robert A. Hillman, Why Law Teachers Should Teach Undergraduates, 41 J. Legal Educ. 289 (1991). Unfortunately, his heavy research commitments precluded active participation in the new book. The traditional acknowledgment accordingly is particularly appropriate here: he deserves much of the credit for this book but absolutely none of the blame for those passages where we wandered from the path. We collaborated on much of the work, but the following paragraphs describe the allocation of ultimate responsibility.

Sheri Lynn Johnson has a B.A. from the University of Minnesota and a J.D. from Yale Law School. After a practice in criminal law, she turned to teaching and writing in both criminal and constitutional law. She prepared Chapters 2 and 7.

Robert A. Hillman, with a B.A. from the University of Rochester and a J.D. from Cornell Law School, followed a federal clerkship with New York City practice and then a teaching career. He specializes in contracts and commercial law, and he has written extensively in those fields. He prepared Chapters 3, 5, and 6.

Kevin M. Clermont, with an A.B. from Princeton University and a J.D. from Harvard Law School, also followed a federal clerkship with New York City practice and then a teaching career. He specializes and writes in civil procedure. He acted as coordinating author, and he also prepared the General Introduction, Chapters 1 and 4, and the book's connective materials.

We three would like to take this opportunity to thank our students Emily Derr, Mark Grube, Meli Maccurdy, Kelly Mellecker, Matthew O'Connor, and Dana Westberg for their excellent research assistance—and indeed to thank generations of undergraduate students and teaching assistants for their reactions to our previous materials. In the publication phase, Susan Boulanger's editing and Troy Froebe's production skills proved invaluable.

Finally, as to conventions in preparing this book, note that we used the original numbers for footnotes by judges in judicial opinions and by authors in quoted materials, when we retained their footnotes. We omitted other such footnotes without any indication. We lettered rather than numbered our own footnotes. We also omitted many case and statutory citations by courts and commentators without so indicating. On those mundane notes we close, but with the grand hope that teachers and their students will come to agree that this book usefully fills a gap in general education.

Kevin M. Clermont
Robert A. Hillman
Sheri Lynn Johnson

January 2010

LAW FOR SOCIETY

NATURE, FUNCTIONS, AND LIMITS

*Law is probably the most neglected phase of our
culture in the liberal arts curriculum.*
PAUL A. FREUND

*[T]he method . . . by which an end was obtained was of
more consequence than the nature of the end itself.*
SIR HENRY SUMNER MAINE

This book derives from the conviction that study of law is a valuable and even necessary part of a general education. We propose in this introduction to explain, partly through demonstration, our conviction. The rest of this book then tries to fill that critical gap in students' education.

To begin at the very beginning, though, we refer here to the study of law at a very general level: *what is law, and what can it do and not do?* This book presents law as a set of varied but limited techniques for resolving conflicts and addressing many other social problems. That is to say, the essential nature of law lies for us in its problem-solving functions, subject to the critical concession that law has very real and serious limits on what it can accomplish.

Say a bridge catastrophically collapses in Minneapolis. How should society, through its federal or state government, deploy law to address this problem? First, the victims or their survivors could turn to the courts for compensation from any suable persons who were to blame. Of course, the inefficiency and incompleteness of this remedy are legendary, and it is not the ideal way to prevent the next bridge collapse. Second, the law could more directly pursue deterrence by criminally prosecuting the blameworthy persons. But experience has taught not only that the criminal law is a cumbersome tool but also that a fair society uses it with meticulous restraint. Third, the state and federal administrative agencies with oversight responsibility could step up their inspection functions. Regulatory bureaucracies, though, prove very difficult to keep trim and effective. Fourth, the people could just resolve to spend more money in building and maintaining safe highways and bridges. But the natural forces of politics will impede optimal public works. Fifth, the law could facilitate or even require people to protect themselves, perhaps through obtaining insurance policies. Yet many of us would be dissatisfied with the thought, as we enter onto a bridge, that our well-being is up to ourselves.

This illustration suffices to show that to treat the nature, functions, and limits of law, even at a general level, this book must go beyond legal philosophy and interdisciplinary perspectives. It must provide a more descriptive foray into our legal system. If students have not acquired concrete and comprehensive information about law, any attempt to leap into abstract legal philosophy or to use some other discipline as a perspective from which to view law is apt to confuse and frustrate. Consequently, our approach will teach some actual law, while exposing students to some original legal sources. Nonetheless, this is not a casebook. It admittedly includes some cases. It even intends incidentally to develop the skill of insightful reading of judicial opinions. Yet in presenting primary legal materials, this book's constant intention is to enhance students' general education, not to serve a prelaw program of study.

Let you and us begin. This introduction is divided into four sections. To demonstrate the educational worth of actual cases, the first section contains an exemplar chosen for its pedagogic value—but happening to be one of the most debated free-speech cases in history, as well as one that will trigger difficult debate over the wisdom of preserving old freedoms in today's age of terrorism. The second section consists of a sample analysis of the case accompanied by our observations—which analysis should make this first case much more comprehensible, but which mainly aims at demonstrating how an inside view of legal particulars can develop general insights and perspectives. Stepping back, the third section of these introductory materials comprises secondary sources expanding on why law is indeed an appropriate subject for the generalist's study. The fourth section concludes with commentary on how best to engage and use this book.

Section One
INTRODUCTORY CASE

VILLAGE OF SKOKIE v. NATIONAL SOCIALIST PARTY OF AMERICA
Supreme Court of Illinois, January 27, 1978
69 Ill. 2d 605, 373 N.E.2d 21

David Goldberger and Barbara O'Toole, of Roger Baldwin Foundation of ACLU, Inc., Chicago, [lawyers for the Nazis].

Harvey Schwartz, Corp. Counsel, Skokie (Gilbert Gordon, Chicago, of counsel), for [the Village].

PER CURIAM ["By the Court"]:

Plaintiff, the village of Skokie, filed a complaint in the circuit court of Cook County seeking to enjoin defendants, the National Socialist Party of America (the American Nazi Party) and 10 individuals as "officers and members" of the party, from engaging in certain activities while conducting a demonstration within the village. The circuit court issued an order enjoining certain conduct during the planned demonstration. The appellate court modified the injunction order [so as to enjoin only display of the swastika]. We allowed defendants' petition for leave to appeal.

> An "injunction" is a court order to do or refrain from doing some act.

The pleadings and the facts adduced at the hearing are fully set forth in the appellate court opinion, and only those matters necessary to the discussion of the issues will be repeated here. The facts are not disputed.

It is alleged in plaintiff's complaint that the "uniform of the National Socialist Party of America consists of the storm trooper uniform of the German Nazi Party embellished with the Nazi swastika"; that the plaintiff village has a population of about

> Here are the facts.

2

70,000 persons of which approximately 40,500 persons are of "Jewish religion or Jewish ancestry" and of this latter number 5,000 to 7,000 are survivors of German concentration camps; that the defendant organization is "dedicated to the incitation of racial and religious hatred directed principally against individuals of Jewish faith or ancestry and non-Caucasians"; and that its members "have patterned their conduct, their uniform, their slogan and their tactics along the pattern of the German Nazi Party ...."

... In an affidavit ..., defendant Frank Collin, who testified that he was "party leader," stated that on or about March 20, 1977, he sent officials of the plaintiff village a letter stating that the party members and supporters would hold a peaceable, public assembly in the village on May 1, 1977, to protest the Skokie Park District's requirement that the party procure $350,000 of insurance prior to the party's use of the Skokie public parks for public assemblies. The demonstration was to begin at 3 p.m., last 20 to 30 minutes, and consist of 30 to 50 demonstrators marching in single file, back and forth, in front of the village hall. The marchers were to wear uniforms which include a swastika emblem or armband. They were to carry a party banner containing a swastika emblem and signs containing such statements as "White Free Speech," "Free Speech for the White Man," and "Free Speech for White America." The demonstrators would not distribute handbills, make any derogatory statements directed to any ethnic or religious group, or obstruct traffic. They would cooperate with any reasonable police instructions or requests.

At the hearing on plaintiff's motion for an "emergency injunction" a resident of Skokie testified that he was a survivor of the Nazi holocaust. He further testified that the Jewish community in and around Skokie feels the purpose of the march in the "heart of the Jewish population" is to remind the two million survivors "that we are not through with you" and to show "that the Nazi threat is not over, it can happen again." Another resident of Skokie testified that as the result of defendants' announced intention to march in Skokie, 15 to 18 Jewish organizations, within the village and surrounding area, were called and a counterdemonstration of an estimated 12,000 to 15,000 people was scheduled for the same day. There was opinion evidence that defendants' planned demonstration in Skokie would result in violence.

The circuit court entered an order enjoining defendants from "marching, walking or parading in the uniform of the National Socialist Party of America; marching, walking or parading or otherwise displaying the swastika on or off their person; distributing pamphlets or displaying any materials which incite or promote hatred against persons of Jewish faith or ancestry or hatred against persons of any faith or ancestry, race or religion" within the village of Skokie. The appellate court, as earlier noted, modified the order so that defendants were enjoined only from intentional display of the swastika during the Skokie demonstration.

Here is the ruling of the trial court, which Illinois calls a circuit court.

Then comes the intermediate appellate court's modification, which enjoined the defendants from "[i]ntentionally displaying the swastika on or off their persons, in the course of a demonstration, march, or parade."

The appellate court opinion adequately discussed and properly decided those issues arising from the portions of the injunction order which enjoined defendants from marching, walking, or parading, from distributing pamphlets or displaying materials, and from wearing the uniform of the National Socialist Party of America. The only issue remaining before this court is whether the circuit court order enjoining defendants from displaying the swastika violates the first amendment rights of those defendants.

Here is the sole issue presented to the state's supreme court by the Nazis' appeal.

In defining the constitutional rights of the parties who come before this court, we are, of course, bound by the pronouncements of the United States Supreme Court in its interpretation of the United States Constitution. The decisions of that court, particularly Cohen v. California (1971), 403 U.S. 15, 91 S. Ct. 1780, in our opinion compel us to permit the demonstration as proposed, including display of the swastika.

Here is the sate supreme court's reasoning based on the First Amendment rule.

"It is firmly settled that under our Constitution the public expression of ideas may not be prohibited merely because the ideas are themselves offensive to some of their hearers" (Bachellar v. Maryland (1970), 397 U.S. 564, 567, 90 S. Ct. 1312, 1315), and it is entirely clear that the wearing of distinctive clothing can be symbolic expression of a thought or philosophy. The symbolic expression of thought falls within the free speech clause of the first amendment (Tinker v. Des Moines Independent Community School District (1969), 393 U.S. 503, 89 S. Ct. 733), and the plaintiff village has the heavy burden of justifying the imposition of a prior restraint upon defendants' right to freedom of speech (Carroll v. President of Princess Anne County (1968), 393 U.S. 175, 89 S. Ct. 347; Organization for a Better Austin v. Keefe (1971), 402 U.S. 415, 91 S. Ct. 1575).

The Village fails to fit within the "fighting words" exception to the rule.

The village of Skokie seeks to meet this burden by application of the "fighting words" doctrine first enunciated in Chaplinsky v. New Hampshire (1942), 315 U.S. 568, 62 S. Ct. 766. That doctrine was designed to permit punishment of extremely hostile personal communication likely to cause immediate physical response, "no words being 'forbidden except such as have a direct tendency to cause acts of violence by the persons to whom, individually, the remark is addressed.'" In *Cohen* the Supreme Court restated the description of fighting words as "those personally abusive epithets which, when addressed to the ordinary citizen, are, as a matter of common knowledge, inherently likely to provoke violent reaction." Plaintiff urges, and the appellate court has held, that the exhibition of the Nazi symbol, the swastika, addresses to ordinary citizens a message which is tantamount to fighting words. Plaintiff further asks this court to extend *Chaplinsky*, which upheld a statute punishing the use of such words, and hold that the fighting-words doctrine permits a prior restraint on defendants' symbolic speech. In our judgment we are precluded from doing so.

In *Cohen*, defendant's conviction stemmed from wearing a jacket bearing the words "Fuck the Draft" in a Los Angeles County courthouse corridor. The Supreme Court for reasons we believe applicable here refused to find that the jacket inscription constituted fighting words. That court stated

These four paragraphs are a quotation from the Cohen *case. We wonder whether we have to explain that case's facts: "You have probably been in your job too long when ... You have to explain to half of your Constitutional Law students why someone might have been offended by the message on the back of Cohen's jacket and, to the other half, what the political message was." Paul A. LeBel, Diagnosing Posttenure Slump Syndrome: A Guide to the Aging of Law Professors, 39 J. Legal Educ. 49, 49 (1989).*

The constitutional right of free expression is powerful medicine in a society as diverse and populous as ours. It is designed and intended to remove governmental restraints from the arena of public discussion, putting the decision as to what views shall be voiced largely into the hands of each of us, in the hope that use of such freedom will ultimately produce a more capable citizenry and more perfect polity and in the belief that no other approach would comport with the premise of individual dignity and choice upon which our political system rests. See Whitney v. California, 274 U.S. 357, 375–377, 47 S. Ct. 641 (1927) (Brandeis, J., concurring).

To many, the immediate consequence of this freedom may often appear to be only verbal tumult, discord, and even offensive utterance. These are, however, within established limits, in truth necessary side effects of the broader enduring values which the process of open debate permits us to achieve. That the air may at times seem filled with verbal cacophony is, in this sense not a sign of weakness but of strength. We cannot lose sight of the fact that, in what otherwise might seem a trifling and annoying instance of individual distasteful abuse of a privilege, these fundamental societal values are truly implicated. . . . "so long as the means are peaceful, the communication need not meet standards of acceptability," Organization for a Better Austin v. Keefe, 402 U.S. 415, 419, 91 S. Ct. 1575 (1971).

Against this perception of the constitutional policies involved, we discern certain more particularized considerations that peculiarly call for reversal of this conviction. First, the principle contended for by the State seems inherently boundless. How is one to distinguish this from any other offensive word [emblem]? Surely the

State has no right to cleanse public debate to the point where it is grammatically palatable to the most squeamish among us. Yet no readily ascertainable general principle exists for stopping short of that result were we to affirm the judgment below. For, while the particular four-letter word [emblem] being litigated here is perhaps more distasteful than most others of its genre, it is nevertheless often true that one man's vulgarity is another's lyric. Indeed, we think it is largely because governmental officials cannot make principled distinctions in this area that the Constitution leaves matters of taste and style so largely to the individual. . . .

Finally, and in the same vein, we cannot indulge the facile assumption that one can forbid particular words without also running a substantial risk of suppressing ideas in the process. Indeed, governments might soon seize upon the censorship of particular words [emblems] as a convenient guise for banning the expression of unpopular views. We have been able, as noted above, to discern little social benefit that might result from running the risk of opening the door to such grave results.

The display of the swastika, as offensive to the principles of a free nation as the memories it recalls may be, is symbolic political speech intended to convey to the public the beliefs of those who display it. It does not, in our opinion, fall within the definition of "fighting words," and that doctrine cannot be used here to overcome the heavy presumption against the constitutional validity of a prior restraint.

The Village also fails to fit within any "offensive speech" or "hostile audience" exception.

Nor can we find that the swastika, while not representing fighting words, is nevertheless so offensive and peace threatening to the public that its display can be enjoined. We do not doubt that the sight of this symbol is abhorrent to the Jewish citizens of Skokie, and that the survivors of the Nazi persecutions, tormented by their recollections, may have strong feelings regarding its display. Yet it is entirely clear that this factor does not justify enjoining defendants' speech. The *Cohen* court spoke to this subject:

Finally, in arguments before this Court much has been made of the claim that Cohen's distasteful mode of expression was thrust upon unwilling or unsuspecting viewers, and that the State might therefore legitimately act as it did in order to protect the sensitive from otherwise unavoidable exposure to appellant's crude form of protest. Of course, the mere presumed presence of unwitting listeners or viewers does not serve automatically to justify curtailing all speech capable of giving offense. See, e.g., Organization for a Better Austin v. Keefe, 402 U.S. 415, 91 S. Ct. 1575 (1971). While this Court has recognized that government may properly act in many situations to prohibit intrusion into the privacy of the home of unwelcome views and ideas which cannot be totally banned from the public dialogue, e.g., Rowan v. Post Office Dept., 397 U.S. 728, 90 S. Ct. 1484 (1970), we have at the same time consistently stressed that "we are often 'captives' outside the sanctuary of the home and subject to objectionable speech." Id., at 738, 90 S. Ct. at 1491. The ability of government, consonant with the Constitution, to shut off discourse solely to protect others from hearing it is, in other words, dependent upon a showing that substantial privacy interests are being invaded in an essentially intolerable manner. Any broader view of this authority would effectively empower a majority to silence dissidents simply as a matter of personal predilections.

See also Kunz v. New York (1951), 340 U.S. 290, 71 S. Ct. 312; Street v. New York (1969), 394 U.S. 576, 89 S. Ct. 1354.

Similarly, the Court of Appeals for the Seventh Circuit, in reversing the denial of defendant Collin's application for a permit to speak in Chicago's Marquette Park, noted that courts have consistently refused to ban speech because of the possibility of unlawful conduct by those opposed to the speaker's philosophy.

Starting with Terminiello v. City of Chicago, 337 U.S. 1, 69 S. Ct. 894 (1949), and continuing to Gregory v. City of Chicago, 394 U.S. 111, 89 S. Ct. 946 (1969), it has become patent that a hostile audience is not a basis for restraining otherwise legal First Amendment activity. As with many of the cases cited herein, if the actual behavior is not sufficient to sustain a conviction under a statute, then certainly the anticipation of such events cannot sustain the burden necessary to justify a prior restraint.

Collin v. Chicago Park District (7th Cir.1972), 460 F.2d 746, 754.

Rockwell v. Morris (1961), 12 A.D.2d 272, 211 N.Y.S.2d 25, aff'd mem. (1961), 10 N.Y.2d 721, 749, 219 N.Y.S.2d 268, 605, 176 N.E.2d 836, 177 N.E.2d 48, cert. denied (1961), 368 U.S. 913, 82 S. Ct. 194, also involved an American Nazi leader, George Lincoln Rockwell, who challenged a bar to his use of a New York City park to hold a public demonstration where anti-Semitic speeches would be made. Although approximately $2\frac{1}{2}$ million Jewish New Yorkers were hostile to Rockwell's message, the court ordered that a permit to speak be granted, stating:

> A community need not wait to be subverted by street riots and storm troopers; but, also, it cannot, by its policemen or commissioners, suppress a speaker, in prior restraint, on the basis of news reports, hysteria, or inference that what he did yesterday, he will do today. Thus, too, if the speaker incites others to immediate unlawful action he may be punished—in a proper case, stopped when disorder actually impends; but this is not to be confused with unlawful action from others who seek unlawfully to suppress or punish the speaker.
>
> So, the unpopularity of views, their shocking quality, their obnoxiousness, and even their alarming impact is not enough. Otherwise, the preacher of any strange doctrine could be stopped; the anti-racist himself could be suppressed, if he undertakes to speak in "restricted" areas; and one who asks that public schools be open indiscriminately to all ethnic groups could be lawfully suppressed, if only he choose to speak where persuasion is needed most.

In summary, as we read the controlling Supreme Court opinions, use of the swastika is a symbolic form of free speech entitled to first amendment protections. Its display on uniforms or banners by those engaged in peaceful demonstrations cannot be totally precluded solely because that display may provoke a violent reaction by those who view it. Particularly is this true where, as here, there has been advance notice by the demonstrators of their plans so that they have become, as the complaint alleges, "common knowledge" and those to whom sight of the swastika banner or uniforms would be offensive are forewarned and need not view them. A speaker who gives prior notice of his message has not compelled a confrontation with those who voluntarily listen.

As to those who happen to be in a position to be involuntarily confronted with the swastika, the following observations from Erznoznik v. City of Jacksonville (1975), 422 U.S. 205, 95 S. Ct. 2268, are appropriate:

> The plain, if at all times disquieting, truth is that in our pluralistic society, constantly proliferating new and ingenious forms of expression, "we are inescapably captive audiences for many purposes." Rowan v. Post Office Dept., [397 U.S. 728,] 736, 90 S. Ct. 1484. Much that we encounter offends our esthetic, if not our political and moral, sensibilities. Nevertheless, the Constitution does not permit government to decide which types of otherwise protected speech are sufficiently offensive to require protection for the unwilling listener or viewer. Rather, absent the narrow circumstances described above [home intrusion or captive audience], the burden normally falls upon the viewer to "avoid further bombardment of [his] sensibilities simply by averting [his] eyes." Cohen v. California [403 U.S. 15,] 21, 91 S. Ct. 1780.

Thus by placing the burden upon the viewer to avoid further bombardment, the Supreme Court has permitted speakers to justify the initial intrusion into the citizen's sensibilities.

We accordingly, albeit reluctantly, conclude that the display of the swastika cannot be enjoined under the fighting-words exception to free speech, nor can anticipation of a hostile audience justify the prior restraint. Furthermore, *Cohen* and *Erznoznik* direct the citizens of Skokie that it is their burden to avoid the offensive symbol if they can do so without unreasonable inconvenience. Accordingly, we are constrained to reverse that part of the appellate court judgment enjoining the display of the swastika. That judgment is in all other respects affirmed.

Affirmed in part and reversed in part.

CLARK, JUSTICE, dissenting.

Here, finally, is the state supreme court's "reluctant" decision.

Section Two
SAMPLE ANALYSIS WITH ANNOTATIONS

Reading one's first law case can be a bit of a shock. If you had trouble understanding *Skokie*, we recommend your trying the online exercise on case reading. We based that exercise on this very case. Go to http://www2.cali.org//autopublish/lessons/9000343/.

Also, the following is a sample analysis of the *Skokie* case, annotated with our comments and a few questions. Our analysis could serve as a sample of the notes you bring to any class that will discuss a case. Although our accompanying annotations are much longer than any written material you would prepare, they should at least give you an idea of the kind of queries you should pose to yourself while tackling a case.

Sample Analysis	Annotations
Facts: The American Nazi party wanted to conduct a demonstration, peacefully but in uniform with swastika, to protest a local requirement that insurance be procured prior to public assemblies in the public parks. The Village of Skokie, which has a large Jewish population including many survivors of Nazi concentration camps, wanted to restrict the demonstration that the Nazis planned for May 1, 1977, in front of the village hall.	(1) In this first part of your notes, you should state who the parties are and what happened to them before reaching the courthouse. Limit yourself to the legally relevant facts. For example, this particular Nazi group had its headquarters in Chicago, and Skokie is a suburb of Chicago. These facts are not relevant and so should be omitted from your notes, just as they were omitted from the court's opinion itself. In our case, the Supreme Court of Illinois expressly limited the facts it presented to the narrow issue being considered on review. To get a fuller version of the events in suit, as we have done for some of our comments, you would have to consult the appellate opinion in the court below or even the documents that constitute the record in the case. Sometimes, however, judicial opinions will include a great many irrelevant facts, and you will have to sift through them for the essence in order to write this part of your notes. Write the "Facts" (and the other entries) in your own words. Nothing is gained by merely transcribing the opinion. By recording the case in your own language, you will be less likely to assume mistakenly that you understand what some judge has written. (2) In summarizing a case, you should follow a logical and set format. As to choice of format, many possibilities are defensible. We choose to begin with the out-of-court facts in the interest of chronology and as an indication of their enormous importance in shaping the decision. However, under "Facts" we do not record the fruits of some abstract historical inquiry. Instead, we record the facts as they are accepted by the court for the purpose of its imminent decision. The court's set of facts depends on the procedural posture of the case at the time. For example, in the *Skokie* case,

Sample Analysis	Annotations
	there had been no trial. The court never got further than holding a quick hearing on whether to grant an emergency injunction to keep things fixed while the case progressed. So the facts before the court at this point were far from fully developed.
	Fixing the correct version of the facts will sometimes prove difficult for you. You will be unable to write this first part of your notes until you determine how the facts fit into the entire case or, in other words, until you have thought about the rest of your notes. This warning reveals that such notetaking should serve not only as a record of completed reading and study but also as a stimulus to further investigation and analysis.
Prior Proceedings: Plaintiff, the Village of Skokie, sued the defendants (the American Nazi party and ten individuals as officers and members) in order to keep the peace and to prevent offensive conduct.	(3) This very important portion of your notes should be detailed, covering everything that happens from crossing the threshold of the trial court to the moment as of which the opinion before you speaks. Often impossible is knowing precisely what or why a court is deciding without knowing the procedural background in the case. For example, appellate review of a decision on the pleadings will raise different issues from those on review of a jury verdict. Put a better way, "Now a case never reaches a court of review until it has first been through a tribunal of trial—else there would be nothing to review. But the cases, so-called, in your case-books are almost exclusively chosen from courts of review. To understand them, therefore, you must get at least some quick picture of what has gone on before they got there." Karl N. Llewellyn, The Bramble Bush 20 (7th printing 1981).
Brought in the Circuit Court of Cook County, this civil suit sought an injunction against certain activities by the defendants while demonstrating in the village.	(4) To initiate the lawsuit, the village filed a complaint on April 28, 1977, in a circuit court. This first court is a trial court. It is in this forum that pleadings are filed and evidence taken. Although the parties will have an opportunity to renew their legal arguments in courts of appeal, usually through both oral arguments and written briefs, the nature of the claims and defenses and the factual record are determined at this initial trial-court stage. Crucial, therefore, is that a party raise all potential grounds and present its facts fully at the trial level.
	(5) One question you must ask in considering a case is whether it is within state or federal jurisdiction. Unlike state courts of general jurisdiction, federal courts are courts of limited jurisdiction. This means that federal courts normally have the power to hear only those kinds of cases that are within the constitutional grant of federal judicial power (see Article III, Section 2 of the United States Constitution, which appears in the Appendix of this book) and that have also been entrusted by congressional enactment to the federal courts. State courts normally have wider jurisdiction. They will hear cases that federal courts cannot.
	The plaintiff brought this case in a trial court of the state of Illinois. This meant that Illinois law would govern the lawsuit,

Sample Analysis	Annotations

Skokie, Ill.

although any applicable federal laws including the Constitution would be binding in the state court.

(6) A second question you should address is whether the case is a criminal case. The answer is not always obvious. The *Skokie* case is potentially confusing because a governmental body, the village, was a party. Although the government is always a party in criminal proceedings, not every case involving the government is a criminal one.

In truth, this case was noncriminal, or civil, in nature because the village did not function as a prosecutor, it alleged no specific criminal violation by the Nazis, and the village was not attempting to punish the Nazis. Instead, the plaintiff alleged a threatened civil wrong and sought civil relief from the court.

(7) A third question to consider is the particular type of relief that the plaintiff requests. Most forms of civil relief fall into two major categories: money damages and injunctions. Here, the village was not suing for money damages as compensation, but rather it requested the court to order the defendants not to do something. The village wanted to invoke this injunctive power to restrain the Nazis' march.

The courts' exercise of their power to grant injunctions is sometimes highly controversial. Some scholars argue that courts abuse this power, and infringe on the function and power of the legislature, by making policy decisions best left to representative bodies. Other scholars hail the courts' use of this power as the only practical way to safeguard constitutional rights. Indisputably, injunctive remedies have formed the core of the most far-reaching decisions of the modern day, such as mandatory school busing to achieve integration.

Plaintiff moved for a preliminary injunction, in connection with which the circuit court considered the plaintiff's complaint, a defendant's affidavit, and oral testimony.

(8) A motion is an application to the court for an order. A preliminary injunction is a provisional order, often intended to preserve the status quo until the trial court can decide on permanent relief. Before issuing a preliminary injunction, the trial court will conduct a hearing but not a full trial.

The circuit court preliminarily enjoined the defendants from demonstrating in Nazi uniform, displaying the swastika, and distributing or displaying materials that promoted racial or religious hatred.

(9) The circuit judge, sitting alone, issued the preliminary injunction on April 29, 1977. Any injunction is a powerful remedy, with the court ready to enforce its order with its drastic contempt powers. The defendants here obeyed.

Defendants appealed the circuit court's decision to the Appellate Court of Illinois.

(10) The defendants now had a right to appeal to the next highest court, here the First District, First Division, of the Appellate Court of Illinois. By taking an appeal the defendants

Sample Analysis	Annotations
	became the so-called appellants, while the plaintiff became the so-called appellee.
	On an appeal, the appellant asserts that the trial court, over the appellant's objection, committed some prejudicial error in rendering its decision. The appellee defends that decision. Courts of appeal give great deference to the facts (what happened out in the real world?) as found by the trial court below. In questions of legal interpretation (what is the prevailing law?), however, courts of appeal feel free to reexamine the lower court's conclusions.
The appellate court modified the circuit court's injunction to prohibit only intentional display of the swastika.	(11) In reality, a good deal of procedural jockeying occurred at this stage of the case. The Nazis desperately tried to get immediate review by the higher courts and to suspend the injunction in the meantime. The outcome of their efforts was the intermediate appellate court's decision, under an expedited schedule, on July 12, 1977. This court acts by decision of a three-judge panel.
	Although the appellate court agreed with the circuit court that some limitation on the Nazi protest was appropriate, the appellate court obviously felt that the circuit court had gone too far in restricting the Nazis' activity. The opinion before you does not explicitly present the reasoning behind the appellate court's decision. To find out exactly why the appellate court permitted the Nazis to demonstrate in uniform, for instance, you would have to read the appellate court's opinion. Courts of appeal normally act by written decision and opinion, and many of these are printed. This one appears officially in volume 51 of the Illinois Appellate Reports, Third Series, at page 279. It also appears in volume 366 of the parallel, unofficial regional reporter called North Eastern Reporter, Second Series, at page 347. The citation is therefore 51 Ill. App. 3d 279, 366 N.E.2d 347 (1977).
Defendants petitioned for leave to appeal the appellate court's decision to the Supreme Court of Illinois.	(12) Neither party had fully attained its stated goal. Either party, or both, could have sought further review. The defendants were still sufficiently unhappy with the swastika ban to desire an appeal to the Supreme Court of Illinois.
	The Illinois Supreme Court is mainly a court of discretionary review. No party normally has an automatic right to this second tier of review. Like the United States Supreme Court, the Illinois Supreme Court decides which cases it wants to hear. It chooses in accordance with Illinois Supreme Court Rule 315(a): "The following, while neither controlling nor fully measuring the court's discretion, indicate the character of reasons which will be considered: the general importance of the question presented; the existence of a conflict between the decision sought to be reviewed and a decision of the Supreme Court, or of another division of the Appellate Court; the need for the

Sample Analysis	Annotations
	exercise of the Supreme Court's supervisory authority; and the final or interlocutory character of the judgment sought to be reviewed."
The supreme court granted leave to appeal.	(13) The Supreme Court of Illinois is the highest court of the state. It comprises seven justices, who sit together on each case.
	Why do you think the Illinois Supreme Court agreed to hear this case? We think it was because of the "general importance" of the case, as this dispute was receiving major attention from the public and the Illinois court knew that the United States Supreme Court was looking over its shoulder.
Issue: Did the court order enjoining the Nazis from displaying the swastika during their planned demonstration in Skokie violate their First Amendment rights?	(14) In this part of your notes, you should list the precise question or questions the court is to decide. In our case, the court focused the question explicitly. Often, however, the issues are far from obvious, and this entry in your notes may require much digging on your part.
Decision: Yes.	(15) Here you should give the decision on each one of the prior-listed issues.
The supreme court therefore reversed on this point.	Also indicate the disposition of the case. Although the supreme court agreed with most of the appellate court's decision, it rejected the remaining ban on the swastika. Thus, the supreme court affirmed the appellate court's decision in part and reversed in part.
	The supreme court's opinion was by the whole court, or per curiam, which means that all the justices (except the one dissenter) agreed but no individual justice was credited with authoring the opinion. Justice Clark did not write an opinion, so his reasons for dissenting are unknown.
	(16) The defendants now had what they wanted. The plaintiff chose not to pursue this particular lawsuit any further, either in the United States Supreme Court or in the lower courts. However, the Skokie controversy had not ended.
	On May 2, 1977, the village had enacted a series of three ordinances intended to prohibit the Nazis' planned demonstration and specifying *criminal* penalties for violation. In other words, the village had begun to invoke a different instrumentality of the law to help in achieving its ends. But now the Nazis sued civilly to enjoin enforcement of the ordinances, suing this time in federal court by alleging unconstitutional infringement of their civil rights. The United States District Court for the Northern District of Illinois struck down the ordinances, the United States Court of Appeals for the Seventh Circuit affirmed, and the Supreme Court of the United States eventually declined to review the case. Smith v. Collin, 439 U.S. 916, 99 S. Ct. 291 (1978).

Sample Analysis	Annotations
	Ironically, with all legal obstacles to a Skokie demonstration removed, Collin canceled that demonstration three days before its rescheduled date of June 25, 1978. Relying on the Skokie rulings, the Nazis had obtained a federal court order overcoming Chicago's attempt to block Nazi demonstrations in Chicago. "Collin explained that the aim of the Nazis' Skokie efforts had been 'pure agitation to restore our right to free speech.' He stated that 'he had used the threat of the Skokie march to win the right to rally in [Chicago].' No serious violence occurred when about 25 Nazis held a rally in a Chicago park on July 9, 1978." Kathleen M. Sullivan & Gerald Gunther, Constitutional Law 1078 (15th ed. 2004). The resulting mob scene was, however, the occasion for seriously offensive conduct. See Susan Stamberg, Every Night at Five 32–38 (1982) (transcript of National Public Radio's report on the Nazi rally).
	What of Frank Joseph Collin, seated in the picture, who was born in 1944 as the half-Jewish son of a Holocaust survivor actually named Cohn? In 1979, the Nazis ousted him as leader, and he left the party. In 1980, he was convicted of molesting young boys and served three years in prison. Later, he became a self-described neo-pagan and now, by the name of Frank Joseph, is a published "expert" on Atlantis.
Reasons: The state supreme court began with the premise that the First Amendment, which applies to the states through the Fourteenth Amendment, protects *speech* from most governmental *restrictions*. This freedom of speech extends to the expression of even repugnant messages; and, according to prior case law, it also extends to so-called symbolic speech, which is nonverbal conduct intended to be and which is primarily communicative. The forms of possible governmental restrictions are (1) prior restraints, or censorship, and (2) subsequent sanctions, which could be civil or criminal in nature. Prior restraints are particularly suspect, and so are treated as presumptively unconstitutional.	(17) In this part of your notes, you should state the gist of the court's reasoning. Sometimes a great deal of work is necessary to perceive the court's reasoning, especially because some opinions are expressed in the form of free association. Moreover, even when clearly reasoned and crisply written, an opinion may not be easy to follow if it assumes a basic knowledge that the reader does not possess. This particular case is not a model of clarity, and it requires careful attention to First Amendment principles and case law with which you may be somewhat unfamiliar.
	When you trace the court's reasoning, another difficult task is separating, as well as possible, that reasoning directly involved in and necessary to the decision (holding) from asides unnecessary to the decision (dicta).
	As a doctrinal matter, the court's holding here was that the swastika ban came within no exception to the First Amendment and so had to fall. At least in this case, it adopted technical pigeonholing as its approach to First Amendment cases, rather than more freely balancing benefits, harms, and other equities in the particular case to decide whether to restrict speech. Nevertheless, it used a wide-ranging and malleable line of reasoning to guide its pigeonholing.

This means that the supporter of the restriction bears the considerable burden of justifying it, as by showing that a content-based prior restraint falls clearly within one of the limiting exceptions to the First Amendment, such as obscenity.

Accordingly, in this case the village tried to justify a prior restraint on certain speech by getting within the previously established exception for fighting words or perhaps some exception for a hostile audience.

First, the court ruled that the swastika ban did not fit within the fighting words exception (1) because prior cases had narrowly defined fighting words, and indeed had seemingly used this exception to permit only subsequent sanctions, and (2) because an analysis of the benefits and harms of both the speech and its restriction argued against an exception to the First Amendment here, especially where the audience was not truly captive. Second, the court ruled that the ban did not fit within any exception for speech that is likely to provoke a hostile audience to unlawful action, with the court using those same two supporting arguments to avoid this supposed exception that looks more to the public risks deriving from the subjective reaction of the particular crowd. Third, along the way, the court refused to recognize any First Amendment exception for offensive speech, hostile audience, or any other exception arguably applicable to this case's facts.

Village Hall of Skokie, Illinois
Courtesy of Skokie Historical Society

Frank Collin
Courtesy of Chicago Sun-Times

Sample Analysis	Annotations
Hence, the court struck down the swastika ban.	(18) In this course, the "Reasons" part of your notes represents the key component of your study. Unlike the law student, who may be misled by a compulsion to memorize the "black letter" or bottom-line rule (e.g., in our case, the swastika may be displayed), you should feel freer to concentrate on the process of legal reasoning. The justifications of a court's decision are even more crucial to understanding the role of law in our society than is the actual legal rule itself.
	We do not intend our sample analysis to be complete or definitive. Although it contains more background than you would ordinarily include, our otherwise short entry under "Reasons" conveys merely one way of analyzing and distilling the holding. Try your hand at composing your own version of the court's reasoning.
	(19) In doing so, you should attempt to identify the types of reasons that the court finds persuasive.
	This might lead you to consider the fundamental question of *who* really shapes the law. If, for example, you believe that judges act on their own behalf or for a socioeconomic elite, you may dismiss most legal reasoning as mere rhetoric. If you take a more sophisticated view of the tensions among the competitors for this role, you will give careful attention to legal reasoning for the light it sheds on who wields ultimate power.
	Analysis of legal reasoning should lead you to consider the critical questions of *why* we have law. Why is law necessary? Why do we have the law that we have? Here the judges' different types of reasons should be directly instructive.
	To analyze the reasoning of a judicial opinion, it is useful to identify four basic, albeit overlapping, types of reasons: authoritative, institutional, goal, and rightness reasons. These kinds of reasons have counterparts in daily-life decision making, but considering them systematically in a legal context is desirable here.
	(20) Authoritative, or formal, reasons relate to a court's obligation to follow any applicable law previously established by a competent lawmaker. For instance, a court might deny an injunction because of some provision in the federal Constitution forbidding judicial action. Other such reasons include those based on applicable and valid federal statutes, state constitutions, and state statutes.
	An important example of an authoritative reason lies in a court's reference to precedent. The Anglo-American legal system has traditionally relied heavily on judge-made law, as opposed to statutory codes like the modern Internal Revenue Code. An important corollary of that system is the doctrine of stare decisis. This doctrine dictates that a court normally must

Sample Analysis	Annotations

follow relevant holdings of its own prior decisions and those of higher courts. Stare decisis tends to restrain the judges' exercise of power and also to enhance the efficiency and fairness of the legal system.

What role did precedent play in the *Skokie* case? How did the court distinguish the *Chaplinsky* case, which upheld the criminal conviction of a street proselytizer who had called the city marshal "a damned Fascist" and said other fighting words to him? Was precedent dispositive, or did other kinds of reasons influence this court's decision? Precedent played a big role verbally. But more realistically, we think that the court found it fairly easy to distinguish *Chaplinsky* as not involving a prior restraint, and so escaped the constraint of that precedent and allowed other kinds of reasons to come into play.

(21) Institutional reasons relate to a court's concerns with observing the bounds on its proper governmental role and following proper processes. For instance, a court might deny an injunction because of the impracticality of supervising and enforcing it. Other institutional reasons include those based on the proper division of legal labor among institutions, the efficient operation of the judicial machinery, values inherent in fair processes, and limitations on law's efficacy.

An actual example of an institutional reason appears in the *Skokie* court's reference to the difficulties of line drawing that issuing an injunction would impose. That is, distinguishing impermissible from permissible speech in future cases would be impractical; also, such distinctions would offend a generally accepted notion that courts should draw only principled and not arbitrary distinctions.

From where does the *Skokie* court derive this institutional reason? It appears in the court's long quotation from the *Cohen* case. But there the court seems to be adopting *Cohen*'s reasoning, because of the persuasiveness of the substantive reasons underlying that earlier decision, rather looking to *Cohen* as formally binding precedent on this institutional point. That is, the court seems to us to be forwarding its own reasons by means of quotations of other courts. The quoted institutional reasons thus derive from some judicially shared concept of the role of courts. The persuasiveness of those reasons is open to debate.

(22) The third type of reason is the goal reason. Such a reason derives its justificatory force from the prediction that the decision it supports will have future effects that serve a good social goal. For example, a court might deny an injunction because enjoining the defendant would impede the free flow of information and hence debilitate democracy. Other goal reasons include those based on social equality, general safety, public health, and family harmony.

Sample Analysis	Annotations
	Goal reasons are often difficult to work with. They are sometimes difficult to construct, exposing judges to various errors such as mispredicting effects or misjudging the goodness of a social goal. There is sometimes more than one applicable goal reason, and they may point toward opposite decisions. The goal reasons sometimes conflict with apparent rightness in the present case, as where a fear that "hard cases make bad law" prompts a court to render a harsh decision in order to create a precedent that will more justly handle the stream of future cases.
	What do you think of the *Skokie* court's use of goal reasons? Were there competing goal reasons, mentioned or unmentioned? What other kinds of reasons should have influenced the court's decision? You should think about such questions, but the main point is the subjectivity of the answers. The law has thereby decided to value the marketplace of ideas, better citizenry, and the individual's self-fulfillment over public order and the audience's sensitivity, and the *Skokie* court conforms to that view.
	(23) Rightness reasons, the last type of reason, derive their force from the decision's accord with sociomoral norms of rightness as applied to the parties' past actions. For example, a court might deny an injunction because the plaintiff was more to blame for creating the present situation than was the defendant. Other such reasons include those based on requiring compensation for lack of due care, protecting justified reliance, and imposing punitive desert.
	Of the four types of reasons, rightness reasons may seem the most intuitively obvious. However, in similar ways rightness reasons prove to be complex, too, and so require careful analysis.
	What rightness reasons can you construct to support the denial or grant of a swastika ban? Did the *Skokie* court invoke any rightness reasons to support its decision? Not really. Did the court seem happy with its decision, so that it was simply packaging a result that it wanted? Not really. Apparently the "just" decision, which would rest on all four kinds of reasons, does not always coincide with what seems intuitively to be the right decision.
	(24) Ultimately, by the process of legal reasoning, the court must combine its reasons into a decision, yielding what will henceforth be the law under the doctrine of stare decisis.
	More specifically, the court held inapplicable the fighting-words exception. When the court has finished narrowing that exception, does its continued existence make any sense? Indeed, does it still exist—if *Skokie* does not come within that exception, what case would? See Note, The Demise of the *Chaplinsky* Fighting Words Doctrine: An Argument for its Interment, 106 Harv. L. Rev. 1129 (1993) (observing that the U.S. Supreme Court has since struck down restrictions on cross-burnings, and

Sample Analysis	Annotations
Remarks:	concluding: "By overruling *Chaplinsky*, the Court not only would eliminate a legal doctrine that manifests an anachronistic male bias, but also would eradicate a device that enables officials to use their discretionary power to harass minorities or to suppress the dissident speech."). Would an injunction against the Nazis pass muster if the Nazis already had repeatedly demonstrated in Skokie, many times with disruption? Under the post-*Skokie* law, that would be a very close case to call. (25) Here you should jot down your comments on and criticisms of the case. You might make a preliminary attempt before class, but this should be supplemented during and after class. Emphasize the validity of the reasoning. Jot down what kind of job you think the court did overall, that is, whether you find its reasoning compelling. This is, after all, a tough case. As Justice Blackmun said in dissenting from the United States Supreme Court's denial of leave to seek review in *Smith* v. *Collin*: "On the one hand, we have precious First Amendment rights vigorously asserted and an obvious concern that, if those asserted rights are not recognized, the precedent of a 'hard' case might offer a justification for repression in the future. On the other hand, we are presented with evidence of a potentially explosive and dangerous situation, enflamed by unforgettable recollections of traumatic experiences in the second world conflict.... I also feel that the present case affords the Court an opportunity to consider whether, in the context of the facts that this record appears to present, there is no limit whatsoever to the exercise of free speech. There indeed may be no such limit, but when citizens assert, not casually but with deep conviction, that the proposed demonstration is scheduled at a place and in a manner that is taunting and overwhelmingly offensive to the citizens of that place, that assertion, uncomfortable though it may be for judges, deserves to be examined." Try to think beyond the confines of the case, too. For example, what would you think of a city ordinance that outlaws, as a form of sex discrimination, the dissemination of "pornography," which it defines not in narrow terms of obscenity but as "the graphic sexually explicit subordination of women, whether in pictures or in words"? Compare American Booksellers Association v. Hudnut, 598 F. Supp. 1316 (S.D. Ind. 1984), aff'd, 771 F.2d 323 (7th Cir. 1985), aff'd mem., 475 U.S. 1001, 106 S. Ct. 1172 (1986) (striking down such an Indianapolis ordinance), with New York v. Ferber, 458 U.S. 747, 102 S. Ct. 3348 (1982) (upholding legislation outlawing dissemination of child pornography). See also Note, Anti-Pornography Laws and First Amendment Values, 98 Harv. L. Rev. 460 (1984).

Section Three
GENERAL EDUCATION AND THE LAW

General education is to be distinguished from a specialist's education. General education is broad and "liberal," in the dictionary sense of covering all subjects befitting a free person. Specialist education is technical, preparing the student for a specific vocation or profession.

In American law schools, law is studied as a specialist's subject—as preparation for a professional pursuit. As a consequence, many people misconceive law as a vast collection of unconnected rules, fit to be memorized by law students only. Even if that were true, it would not follow that law cannot also be a subject for general education. A fallacious argument is that any subject studied vocationally is automatically disqualified as a subject for general education. As Alfred North Whitehead pointed out: "Again, there is not one course of study which merely gives general culture, and another which gives special knowledge. The subjects pursued for the sake of a general education are special subjects specially studied . . . ." A.N. Whitehead, The Aims of Education and Other Essays 18 (1929).

Nevertheless, not all subjects that specialists pursue necessarily qualify for a place in general education. Does law qualify?

Interestingly, in the good old days, law was very much a part of a generalist's education. Harold J. Berman, On the Teaching of Law in the Liberal Arts Curriculum 9–12 (1956), explained:

> An imposing array of distinguished men—most of them, to be sure, lawyers— have said that it is not only proper but very important that "every gentleman and scholar," as Blackstone put it in 1758, should have "a competent knowledge of the laws of that society in which we live." Such a knowledge, Blackstone added, is "an highly useful, I had said almost essential, part of liberal and polite education."
>
> The famous Commentaries on the Laws of England comprise Blackstone's lectures given at Oxford University not primarily to prospective lawyers but to students of the liberal arts. Their influence upon the thinking of generations of Englishmen and Americans, laymen as well as lawyers, is well known. Edmund Burke referred to their impact on the American colonists in a well-known passage in his Speech on Conciliation with America. "In no country perhaps in the world," Burke said, "is the law so general a study. . . ."
>
> The colonists' zeal for the study of law, Burke added, gave them a capacity to "snuff the approach of tyranny in every tainted breeze." . . .
>
> Unquestionably the professional law school as it has developed in the United States has been an extremely important instrument for improving not only the character of the Bar but also the quality of the legal system itself. Yet a price has been paid for this gain, in that by and large general education in law for non-lawyers has been sacrificed. With the emergence of professional graduate schools of law it seems simply to have been taken for granted by most people that the nature of our legal system is a subject beyond the ken or the interest of the undergraduate and the non-specialist.

This is not to suggest that law has today disappeared from undergraduate education. Quite the opposite is true, and has been true for quite some time. As John D. Appel, Law as a Social Science in the Undergraduate Curriculum, 10 J. Legal Educ. 485, 485 (1958), observed:

> To be sure, law is, at present, the partial or total subject matter of many college courses. Some of these can only with difficulty be termed general liberal arts courses, but rather are technical, and primarily devised as necessary adjuncts to a specialized vocational program. Examples, which might be multiplied, are courses in law of the press (and other communications media) for journalism students, and law of business organization and finance for students of accounting or business administration. Other law courses on the college level are less obviously vocational in purpose and content, and these include labor law, jurisprudence, and constitutional law—commonly found in the undergraduate (or graduate) departments of economics, philosophy, and history or political science. Although this latter group might properly be considered part of a liberal arts curriculum, the courses are nevertheless, specialized in approach, and their value is considered to lie in the light they may shed on a particular field of study.

Unfortunately, colleges frequently confine the study of law to such vocational preparation, so that even the best liberal education typically leaves the student in ignorance of the central concept of law and with little idea of the practical workings of the system under which he or she lives.

Thus, we are not advocating another technical course (like communications law or business law) with a specific focus that serves as an adjunct to a vocational program, nor a narrow course on one area of law (labor law or constitutional law, for example) open to those who desire that specific knowledge. Instead, what we are advocating is the reintroduction of an independent general course about law that claims its own rightful place in the liberal arts curriculum. So, does law qualify for a place in general education?

One way for a course to qualify for a place in general education is to have a core of humanistic content. Does law have a core of humanistic content? Harry Kalven, Jr. & Hans Zeisel, Law, Science, and Humanism, in The Humanist Frame 329, 331–33 (Julian Huxley ed., 1961), thought so:

> Humanism appears to involve at least two related notions: respect for human values, notably those of dignity and individuality, and a concern with the aesthetic side of life, as reflected in art and literature. In both these senses the law is deeply humanistic. It is not an accident that the most revered American legal heroes such as Justice Holmes or Judge Learned Hand have been cultural heroes also. They have not only been distinguished as judges but have style as men and in particular as writers. If one wanted to locate the best image law has of itself he might well study the values implicit in the law's extraordinary admiration for Justice Holmes. For the American lawyer he is the beau ideal, and the lawyer quotes his aphorisms as the literate layman quotes Hamlet. This fascination with wit, style, felicity of phrase suggests that for those who have made it their life-work, law has a strong aesthetic appeal, and is at its best a kind of literature. . . .

Finally and foremost law is always engaged in translating the values of society into legal norms. All laws involve the resolution of issues of policy, and under the American system of a written constitution and judicial review, adjudication of constitutional issues brings the larger issues of the day into dramatic focus. The law is thus a remarkable repository of dramatic debate over values. At its best, this debate will be as good as anything written on these themes.

One might further argue that we use law as an instrument to serve human purposes. Legal resources are means to social ends. The faith that we can affect our destiny is one of the most enduring tenets of humanism. From this it follows that law is fundamentally humanistic in character.

Nevertheless, a surer way to justify the study of law as part of a general education is directly to fashion the subject of law, properly conceived and taught, as a social science. Then the reasons flow. In that same portion of his excerpted book, Professor Berman continued by starting a list of some reasons for introducing courses in law into the liberal arts curriculum:

1. that an understanding of the nature of the legal order and of legal reasoning is of significant cultural value in itself;
2. that an understanding of law is essential to an understanding of the political values of American society and of the international community; and that it illuminates not only political science but also other disciplines such as philosophy, history, economics, sociology, and anthropology;
3. that the diffusion of an understanding of law to wider segments of the scholarly community will result in a greater illumination of legal science, as scholars of other disciplines come to give more attention to legal data;
4. that the study of law is an important means of developing the student's sense of justice and his capacity for responsible judgment;
5. that the study of law is an important foundation in the training of students for the responsibilities of social, economic and political activity.

Let us continue building that list by careful consideration of the following excerpt.

A. BARTLETT GIAMATTI, THE LAW AND THE PUBLIC

97 F.R.D. 545, 608–11 (1982), reprinted in 38 Rec. A.B. City N.Y. 34, 35–40 (1983)*

The question is: Why do the American people know and understand so little about the law?

Consider the circumstances of the question. We Americans care deeply about the law. The Constitution has a sacred place in our culture and its framers constitute a shadowy pantheon, the Olympians at the beginning. From the perception of a revealed text whose interpretation is entrusted to the least understood and most mystified branch of our government comes the American reverence for the law, a reverence bordering on obsession, revealed in innumerable ways.

Some of these ways paradoxically entail criticisms or what we may call negative tributes. The courts are too slow or too soft; the Constitution is incomplete: we need an amendment to produce fiscal balance or equal rights for women or a proper regard for the sacredness of life. Other ways are simply part of daily speech. We hear every day on all sides: someone's "rights" are assured or abridged; the law is too weak or too strong; there are too many lawyers; they are too powerful; they are clearly indispensable. (Americans go to lawyers as in other times and places humankind went to shamans or wise elders, constantly and cautiously.) The fact remains that the lay public is endlessly concerned with the law. From the level of that most American of catch phrases—"there oughta be a law"—to the insight that, in legal processes consented to by a free people, a people may guard its several freedoms and thus insure a free Republic in diversity, Americans chafe under and kick against, but finally worship every day at, the law.

Whatever the law means. And that is how my question arises. Why the ignorance? The beginnings of an answer to that question may reside in the fact that the institutions and people best fitted to tell them do not tell them. By institutions and people, I mean us. I believe a large share of the responsibility for educating the public in the nature and purposes of the law resides with your [legal] profession and with the press. I think, however, the first responsibility to educate about the law obviously lies with the centers of education.

It is remarkable how small a role the law plays in our undergraduate curricula or in our view of a liberal education. We have various theories and practices regarding general education, areas of concentration, required courses, "core" curricula and so forth to insure breadth and depth in undergraduate education. We construct a general grounding in values and skills with specific foci, all meant to instill a love of learning for its own sake and intended to fashion the intensely practical capacities to think clearly and to express oneself cogently. But learning about the law is almost completely absent.

The study of the law is a complex, technical and professional discipline, not appropriate to a liberal education for undergraduates, one is told. I agree. But the study of economics or mathematics or Greek in college is also complex and must be pursued in postgraduate school in order to become professionally adept. We teach mathematics,

economics and Greek, yet we do not believe that the law has a place, and I do not understand such an omission. . . .

In our success in encouraging the necessary specialities we have forgotten two things: the lesser being, that specialists can only communicate with other specialists; the greater being, that if no one communicates the principles and purposes upon which the specialists depend to the larger society, the larger society will continue to be dependent but, without any understanding of broad principles or purposes, will only grow resentful and suspicious. It will increasingly come to distrust the specialist. What is far worse, the lay public will deepen in ignorance and indifference regarding the essential goals of the law about which no one has deigned to speak publicly and clearly. The cynicism about lawyers, the suspicions about courts, the lust to supplant law with decree that one hears on all sides worries me a great deal and it should worry you. While one may, as I have, argue that such reactions are often negative tributes by the American people to law and legal process, the force of the reactions begins to pass into a sentiment corrosive of those values and processes you are sworn to uphold and I, like you, cherish.

I look, therefore, to the academy, as part of a liberal education, to educate the society of the future about the law. Were such courses to be created, they should not be for those who plan to devote themselves professionally to the law. They should be for the future lay people without which your profession cannot exist—not in the easy sense that the layman is the client pool but in the larger sense that uninformed consent is no consent at all but simply the subscription to myth. And that is no basis for a just society.

After the academy, I look to your profession to educate the public. . . . At the present, the lay American of almost any social or economic condition knows the names of three or four gorgeously notorious lawyers; has a negative view of "palimony" and the insanity defense; thinks well of Associate Justice O'Connor; cannot name more than two other Justices and believes the First and Fifth Amendments do most of the work—for good or ill. The "law" in everyday thought means the police and the court system—both viewed as either overreacting or overworked. Books by members of the bar about famous cases they have won do not bring the full light of the profession to bear on the stresses, responsibilities, intricacies, decisions or deep pleasures that practice engages. Between Perry Mason, "The Paper Chase," and idealized public defenders the entertainment industry continues to do what it always does, sell stereotypes created by itself to advertisers. . . .

. . . Lawyers and judges on their lay, community rounds, teachers of law in their popular writings, the associations of the Bar, the various members of the profession in public forums of many kinds, all must do an immense amount, now not done and necessary to do, to foster an understanding of the principles and purposes of the law. Even more to the point, you must educate us in the limits of the law. This last is especially important.

Someone is obliged to convince the American people that if they ask everything of legal process, it will not be able to do much of anything; someone is obliged to say, clearly and persuasively, that if the means for the resolution of conflict is asked only to legitimize every form of contention, paralysis will result; someone is obliged to say what the law *cannot do*; and what lawyers are not good for; what courts ought neither to consider nor to control. It is the obligation of your profession to say these things because you alone have standing sufficient to increase the public's understanding.

Finally, some among you ought to be seized of the need to shape self-criticism of a responsible and knowledgeable sort. Otherwise the position of privileged trusteeship you now rightly enjoy will be increasingly viewed as an interest only in private prerogatives unaware of public obligations. You must believe it is worth educating the public or your profession will lose the respect without which neither the profession nor the law can function. I ask you not to be publicists in some narrow sense. I ask you to clarify and to communicate the broad limits of your profession in the interest of furthering the effectiveness of your essential efforts.

NOTES

1. Bart Giamatti, father of movie actors, had quite the career himself. He was President of Yale University and, later, Commissioner of Major League Baseball.

2. As part of his justifying the generalist's study of law, Giamatti scores the American ignorance of the nature and functions of law. But he especially censures ignorance of the limits of law. The public ignores the plain fact that law cannot do everything. Indeed, it cannot do a lot of things. Most often, the observation of "there oughta be a law" is deeply ignorant.

3. To be somewhat more specific for purposes of illustration, consider the importance to a student of policy, specializing perhaps in economics or political science, of studying the limits on social ordering. Isolating policy aims for study, without regard to the methods of the policies' implementation, is not even

possible. The means through which we pursue ends define the very character of our realization of those ends. And limits on the means impose limits on the ends. Thus, the study of limits on means to social ends is essential.

4. Means to social ends describes tools that include the law, does it not? Thus, the study of the limits of law is essential.

Section Four
PEDAGOGIC NOTES

A. Themes This Book Seeks to Develop

So, law can, should, and even must be studied by anyone who wishes to become a liberally educated person. This book embraces that premise. Then, hewing to the purposes of general education, it seeks to convey an understanding of law in and for society.

Although the book's concerns accordingly are broad, entry into any subject demands an analytic breakdown into understandable components that reflect the subject's essential nature. A book on law for generalists should treat a manageable number of comprehensible units that the students can eventually reconstruct into an intelligible concept of law. Therefore, this book chooses to break law down into a manageable number of techniques for resolving conflicts and addressing other social problems.

As the book conveys a sense of what law is and what it can and cannot do, certain major themes emerge as natural consequences. Three of them may usefully be listed as follows:

1. The *nature* of law is essentially instrumental in character, in the sense of serving as one of the tools that any organized society may use to deal with social problems. As means to those ends, society has at its disposal a set of basic legal techniques for addressing social problems:

    (a) remedying grievances,
    (b) imposing punishment,
    (c) regulating administratively,
    (d) conferring public benefits, and
    (e) facilitating private arrangements.

    That is, the available resources of law break down into five basic modes of legal activity by the government (the remedial instrument, the penal instrument, the administrative instrument, the public-benefit instrument, and the private-arrangement instrument), with possible variants of each and possible combinations of several. For some social problems, only one of these instruments may prove appropriate, but for many others more than one or all five may contribute, each in its own way, toward solving the problem.

2. Societies typically apply their legal resources to a wide variety of important *functions* that range from ensuring general safety to redressing social inequality. But of course legal resources are more effective at some tasks than at others. Even where law is useful, certain of its instruments that societies have applied to the particular end may be inappropriate for the task, and certain others may not have been applied in their most effective form.

3. This way of looking at the nature of law naturally highlights the functions of law in social ordering, but one must not overlook the *limits* of law. Law is not omnicompetent.

These three themes allow imposing reasonable bounds on, and giving a sense of direction to, the book's coverage. However, this analytic approach dictates a highly structured book. Its parts, chapters, and sections follow a pattern. For the most part they need not be read in the order they appear, but an awareness of the pattern will remove much of the confusion from whatever route is taken through the book. Readers should examine the whole book at the outset to perceive that pattern.

B. Methods This Book Seeks to Employ

As already demonstrated, this book proceeds in the belief that showing is better than merely telling. Therefore, it includes some primary legal materials, such as cases, statutes, regulations, programs, and contracts. The book's inclusion of primary documents, some types of which will be new to the student, should help to make it more engaging as well as effective.

Also, this book reflects the belief that insight and perspective most effectively develop from close examination of particulars, rather than from reading generalized text. Thus, we intend the primary sources not only to show by way of illustration but also to serve as vehicles for developing general insights and perspectives. A glance from inside of any subject is necessary before one can think profitably about it, even if, as a good generalist, one's goal is to acquire an outside view of the subject as a whole. For example, the materials on negligence law in Chapter 1 aim not at providing instruction on negligence law as such, but instead serve to teach about the makers and appliers of law, improving the law, limitations of law, and more.

Surprisingly, this approach does not require much of a technical perspective from the book's authors or a technical orientation from its readers. If you find yourself preoccupied with an inadvertently unexplained legal technicality in any of the pages ahead, you may not be approaching the materials in the proper spirit. We also observe that if in the years to come these materials no longer fully reflect the current state of the law, their utility should remain largely intact because their mission does not involve conveying the precise state of the law at any given time. The shared object of teacher and student is general insight and perspective.

What this approach does, however, require is careful, critical, and active thinking about the subject matter. You cannot stand ready as a mere passive recipient of information, but instead must read and reread with word-by-word care and must analyze with critical faculties in high gear. You should be constantly asking yourself significant questions and trying to answer them, always actively thinking beyond the confines of the instant case or illustration, and continually summarizing and synthesizing the materials. Good students engage not in the process of receiving information but instead in the process of creating understanding. The materials reflect this approach in their dialectic emphasis, the juxtaposition of conflicting views, the court cases full of argument, and the authors' questions.

In sum, hard work lies ahead. Although the sole aspiration is the big picture, you will not get there by passive and uncritical skimming. Such skimming may work to give the gist in some courses. But because a book containing primary legal materials is no ordinary textbook, skimming such a book will yield nothing more than a collection of meaningless fact patterns from unrelated illustrations and perhaps a few legal rules that by themselves have little or no importance or accuracy. Instead, only your studying a series of painstaking microscopic views will reveal the big picture. The work is hard, but exciting.

THE
MEANS
OF LAW

Each of the foregoing chapters breaks down into eight sections: (1) introduction, (2) methods, (3) lawmakers, (4) structures and processes for applying law, (5) roles of private citizens and their lawyers, (6) improvements, (7) limitations, and (8) summary.

INTRODUCTORY NOTE TO PART ONE
What is the nature of law? In an account of the nature of a complex form of social organization such as law, it is possible and fruitful to consider a

variety of questions, including: (1) What are its characteristic minimal substantive contents? (2) What are its characteristic normative dimensions? (3) What are its basic institutional features? (4) What are its relationships to cognate phenomena, for example, politics, morality, and various social means to ends? (5) What are the range, efficacy, and limits of its methodology?

In this book, all the foregoing questions are considered. Obviously, considering each in depth would not be possible. Of all these questions, the one selected for most intensive treatment concerns law's methodology. This selection results from our belief that the most productive and accurate way to introduce law is to convey an instrumentalist conception of law, in the sense of exploring the way law can serve as one of the tools that society may use to address social problems. Accordingly, our focus will fall first on the variety of law's available techniques and their limits. See especially Part One. That focus will raise a subsidiary question: what are the basic social functions on which the law's methodology is commonly put to work? See especially Part Two.

Both of these two major parts of the book subdivide into chapters. Part One comprises Chapters 1 through 5. These chapters respectively treat the five basic legal instruments for social ordering by studying how law acts through remedying grievances, imposing punishment, regulating administratively, conferring public benefits, and facilitating private arrangements. The first of these chapters is by far the longest, because it provides the background invoked in the subsequent chapters. Together these five chapters offer an overview of the means at law's disposal.

Each of the instruments differs in primary thrust: one is reparative, one prohibitive, one regulative, one distributive, and one facilitative of choice. But they differ in many other ways, such as in the peculiar combination of legal resources they each deploy. Additionally, some partially differentiating characteristics are common to only a few of the instruments, and thus help distinguish them from the other instruments.

Accordingly, each of the chapters contains eight sections that flesh out the particular instrument in a logical and comprehensive manner. For example, using negligence law to illustrate the remedial instrument, Chapter 1 introduces the subject, examines the method of money damages to remedy negligently inflicted injuries, explores the roles of courts and legislatures in making negligence law, demonstrates the application of that method and that law by tracing an actual case from accident to appeal, and so on through the list of eight sections. We repeat those same eight sections in each of the first five chapters to encourage comparative analysis of the principal differentiating characteristics. By comparing, say, the varying roles of private citizens and their lawyers, and by observing that in regards to such characteristics some instruments conform and others differ, you can acquire a deeper understanding of the five distinct instruments.

After Part One so treats the instruments of law in order to show how law does what it does, Part Two applies them to a few selected social tasks. Sketching the law in action there elaborates what the law can and cannot do. Thus, although we divide the book into Part One on the means of law and Part Two on the ends of law, our hope throughout is to convey a sense of the nature, functions, and limits of law.

Chapter 1

LAW AS AN INSTRUMENT FOR

REMEDYING WRONGS

If a plaintiff has a right, he must of necessity have a . . . remedy.
LORD CHIEF JUSTICE HOLT

Such words as "right" are a constant solicitation to fallacy.
JUSTICE OLIVER WENDELL HOLMES

Section One
INTRODUCTION TO THE REMEDIAL INSTRUMENT

Materials Drawn Mainly from Negligence Law

Jones hits Smith. Brown carelessly crashes his car into Olson's, killing him. Carlson overirrigates his land and floods Bright's property. Gye entices a highly valued employee away from his competitor, Brooks. Harper defames Joseph. Thomas infringes Cooper's trademark. Events of this kind, which might be enumerated endlessly, occur daily in any society.

Should society do anything about such events (or about the threat of their occurrence)? One possible technique of the law would be the provision of remedies for grievances, threatened as well as actual. Our law in fact so acts in many circumstances, as this chapter will explain.

The pedagogic vehicles set out in this chapter to show law operating as a remedial instrument consist mainly of primary source materials from the law of negligence. In studying these materials, you should bear in mind three things.

First, law as used here has significance beyond that of providing remedies for grievances, actual or threatened. For example, its mere availability can and does influence the Joneses of the world not to hit the Smiths in the first place, or the Browns of the world to drive more carefully. And, as we shall show, its availability allows for the possibility of rational dispute settlement of a private kind vitally significant to society.

Second, the general remedial instrument leaves room for much variety of legal method and process and the like. We shall be focusing on a particular scheme: the basic remedial methodology of Anglo-American legal systems. Its general combination of legal resources is not the only one possible. This combination, however, is not mere happenstance either.

Third, the remedial instrument may or may not be put into use alone, so to speak. People may or may not use it together with any or all of the four other basic legal instruments considered respectively in Chapters 2 through 5. Take the social problem of slaughter on the highways as an example. People might content themselves with using the law merely to provide monetary compensation for those injured or bereaved. But then the law, too, might punish reckless drivers (Chapter 2), test drivers for proficiency and license only those qualified, and inspect cars to make sure they are sound (Chapter 3), build safer highways (Chapter 4), or encourage and facilitate some forms of private transportation instead of others (Chapter 5).

In presenting the remedial instrument, Chapter 1 will proceed through the following sections:

- Section Two, Remedial Methods, introduces various remedies that the law provides to grievants, but focuses on money damages.
- Section Three, Making Remedial Law, studies how courts and legislatures create negligence law.
- Section Four, Applying Remedial Law, demonstrates the application of remedial law by tracing an actual case from accident through appeal.
- Section Five, Roles of Private Citizens and Their Lawyers, shows how private parties and their lawyers participate in the making and applying of remedial law.
- Section Six, Improving the Remedial Instrument, identifies and discusses some of the ways the law could better remedy grievances.
- Section Seven, Limitations of Law as a Remedial Instrument, stresses inherent limitations in the law's use of the remedial instrument, taking a look at the specific problems of imposing a duty to rescue and of giving damages for unwanted birth.
- Section Eight, Summary, will look backward—but also forward by providing additional readings.

Section Two
REMEDIAL METHODS

Law has a variety of methods to remedy grievances. One of the less obvious methods is the injunction against the occurrence of a threatened grievance, which we saw at work in the *Skokie* case. We shall introduce other remedies throughout this book.

Of remedial methods, however, the most common is what lawyers call money damages. Damages are a form of "substitutional" redress. Because the law cannot replace a victim's lost hand, restore lost time at work as such, or undo pain and suffering, some substitute is necessary. But this idea of using money as the substitute is not always easy to implement. Moreover, the procedural means chosen to implement the idea may significantly limit the character of what the law can achieve in particular cases.

A. Historical Background of Damages

In any event, the idea of requiring the loss causer to pay money has ancient and interesting antecedents in Anglo-American law. The following excerpt traces those long roots. We include it not only for its intrinsic interest and instructiveness, but also to introduce the role of history in shaping our law.

CHARLES T. McCORMICK, HANDBOOK ON THE LAW OF DAMAGES
21–24, 64–65 (1935)*

The practice of assessing damages, that is, of finding rationally a measure in money for a loss or injury not directly connected with money, is so familiar to us, that it seems an inherent and necessary part of our procedure. Nevertheless, this practice, in anything like its present form, came as a fairly late development in English remedial law.

It is true that long before the Norman Conquest we find among the Anglo-Saxon peoples a system of money compensation for wrongs of violence. This was a step in the gradual substitution of judicial redress for the vengeance of the blood feud. To make it easier for the parties to reach a compromise or settlement of the feud, the state published a schedule of payments, fixing the prices at which the wrongdoer should make *bot*, or compensation for various kinds of injuries. The following items are selected from a long list contained in the Laws of Ethelbert, of about 600 A.D.

34. If there be an exposure of the bone, let bot be made with III shillings.

39. If an ear be struck off, let bot be made with XII shillings.

40. If the other ear hear not, let bot be made with XXV shillings. . . .

51. For each of the four front teeth, VI shillings; for the tooth which stands next to them, IV shillings; for that which stands next to that, III shillings; and then afterwards, for each a shilling. . . .

The particularity of the classification and the rigid tariff of payments are evidently designed to lessen possibility of dispute over the amount to be paid. While compensation for loss is one of the ends in view, the payments thus fixed in advance are not closely comparable to awards of damages made by a tribunal which is allowed to use its judgment in assessing an equivalent in money for an injury brought to its attention.

This system of compromise, compelled by custom and the courts, or by the threat of clan vengeance in the offing, and aided by the published tariffs of standardized prices for wrongdoing, seems to have remained through the Saxon era the everyday method of redress and to have made unnecessary the development of a practice of awarding damages until more than a hundred years after the Norman Conquest. The scarcity of coined money in England in the period before the Conquest must likewise have operated to delay the emergence of a flexible remedy of money damages. . . .

It seems, then, a substantial probability that the remedy of damages came first into English practice at about the same time that English courts began to use juries [in the late twelfth century]. . . . At all events, from the beginnings of the *practice* of giving damages in the King's Court, the jurors are normally called upon to assess the damages. As long as the jurors are left free to fix the amount by their own lights, no *law* of damages is needed. The development of that law is the by-product of the widening control by the judges over the action of the jurors. . . .

In cases where the claim is for unliquidated damages, where the law furnishes no rule for precise measurement in money of the loss or injury, it will often be a difficult process for twelve men to reach an agreement upon the sum to be awarded. Nevertheless, they must somehow agree if a verdict is to be reached, and this can only be done through individual concessions, and a final adoption by all of a figure mutually satisfactory. While this is

---

* Copyright © 1935 by West Publishing Co. Reprinted by permission.

recognized in the opinions, the courts have made certain pronouncements disapproving the use by the jurors of certain expedients for reaching agreement. Drawing lots, tossing a coin, or other resort to chance is, of course, forbidden. The courts go further and announce the doctrine that the jurors must not make a compromise which entails the abandonment by one group of their convictions as to one vital point, in return for a similar sacrifice of the convictions held by another group upon a different issue. An illustration is an award which represents a compromise of the issues of liability and amount. In a leading case, a young man under 21 was injured through the negligence, as he claimed, of the defendant, so that it was necessary to remove one of his eyes by an operation. The injury was conceded, but the negligence was hotly contested at the trial. The jury returned a verdict for the plaintiff for $200. It was held that the verdict, in view of these circumstances, must have been the result of an improper compromise, and that a new trial should be ordered.

B. Award of Damages Today

The preceding excerpt by McCormick (dean of the University of Texas School of Law and a procedure expert) invokes the useful distinction between *procedural* law and *substantive* law. The latter is the body of enforceable rights and duties that concern day-to-day conduct in private and public life transpiring essentially outside the courthouse or other dispute-settlement forum. The former comprises society's processes for submitting and resolving factual and legal disputes over those substantive rights and duties.

As to the procedural law of remedies, a big difference is between *judge* and *jury*. Judges are the ones who issue injunctions, as in *Skokie*. But either the plaintiff or the defendant can request to have a jury decide the facts and award the remedy in an action for money damages, as in the upcoming *Butterfield* case. In such a jury trial, a judge still sits to run the proceedings and to decide any questions of law that arise, but the jury will decide all the questions of fact and then apply the law to the facts by producing a verdict that awards any damages. To enable the jurors to perform their task, the judge will instruct (or "charge" or "direct") them on what the law is.

The general approach, then, is for a jury to award a lump-sum for all losses suffered already from the wrong and expected to be suffered in the future. Reconsider the example given at the end of the passage from McCormick's treatise. The damages for loss of an eye should have been huge, but the showing of a wrongful act was iffy. So the jurors who felt there was no negligence compromised with those jurors who felt there was, agreeing on a small amount of damages. Trying to understand this example forces one to distinguish between the issues of *liability* and of *damages*, the two basic parts of the relevant substantive law.

Under our law, the remedy of money damages is not available for just any grievance, however great the injury might be. The remedy is available only when the law says the remedy is available. As part of the steps in making a remedy available, the substantive law must recognize the particular grievance, which the law does by creating liability for it. We now turn to that subject of liability, using the first of our selections from negligence law as a vehicle for developing the relevant understandings.

Section Three
MAKING REMEDIAL LAW

A. Origin of a Doctrine

Remedies must be premised on substantive law. For an example, the legal rule that one who negligently harms another must compensate the victim serves as a premise for countless claims to money damages in our law of today. More specifically, the rule provides that if the defendant owed the plaintiff a *duty* to use reasonable care and if the defendant *breached* that duty so as to *cause* the plaintiff *injury*, then the plaintiff is entitled to a court judgment that the plaintiff recover money damages from the defendant.

This rule on negligence constitutes the most important branch of the law of torts, or civil wrongs. The rule slowly evolved from ancient origins, emerging with some clarity in fourteenth-century England. It is a good rule in general, serving the rightness, or fairness, reason that defendants should pay for their lack of due care, and also serving the goal, or efficiency, reason that each defendant should have the incentive to take an appropriate number of precautionary steps. Fairness is not a simple concept, of course, but here it implies the corrective justice notion of making a person, who has done wrong, compensate the injured victim. Efficiency does not call for creating a perfectly safe world, but it would want to deter inefficient risk-taking by fixing the legal standard of care to require taking all steps whose expected benefits in safety exceed its costs to society.

As we shall now illustrate, this generally good rule on negligence nevertheless came to be modified by counter, or qualifying, rules, first in England and later in the United States. The following is the initial step in developing the defense of contributory negligence, which barred recovery from a negligent defendant by a plaintiff who had failed to be careful. As you read the case—and search out its facts, prior proceedings, issue, decision, and reasons—you will have the most trouble with the prior proceedings. So let us explain a few things.

Mr. Butterfield went to court on the back of the negligence rule, complaining of injuries and asking for damages. In other words, he chose not to accept the grievance as a matter of fate, or to exact money from Mr. Forrester by force or privately settle their dispute.

Despite appearances, this case represents the decision by an important English *trial* court called the King's Bench, not an *appellate* court. A trial court initially resolves disputes over issues of fact and law. At the end of a trial, a trial court may undertake to correct its own errors as by granting a new trial. A modern appellate court reviews certain trial-court decisions for prejudicial errors. But, at the time in England, the trial-court decisions in this case were not subject to appeal.

In the *Butterfield* case, the trial court consisted of four judges. A single judge had been sent to the locality, Derby, as the court's delegate to try the *facts* with a local jury. The defendant won the jury's verdict, by having defended that the plaintiff was at fault. The plaintiff's lawyer thought that the presiding judge, Justice Bayley, had erred in stating the applicable law to the jury in part of his instructions. Afterward, upon a motion for a new trial, this *legal* issue was referred back to the central courthouse at Westminster for the whole trial court to consider. The judges then orally rendered their opinions on the legal issue. A couple of their reported opinions appear below after the privately published report's summary of the case's allegations, evidence, and instructions.

BUTTERFIELD v. FORRESTER
King's Bench, 1809
103 Eng. Rep. 926

This was an action . . . for obstructing a highway, by means of which obstruction the plaintiff, who was riding along the road, was thrown down with his horse, and injured, etc. At the trial before Bayley, J., at Derby, it appeared that the defendant, for the purpose of making some repairs to his house, which was close by the roadside at one end of the town, had put up a pole across part of the road, a free passage being left by another branch or street in the same direction. That the plaintiff left a public house not far distant from the place in question at 8 o'clock in the evening in August, when they were just beginning to light candles, but while there was light enough left to discern the obstruction at one hundred yards distance; and the witness who proved this, said that if the plaintiff had not been riding very hard he might have observed and avoided it; the plaintiff, however, who was riding violently, did not observe it, but rode against it, and fell with his horse and was much hurt in consequence of the accident; and there was no evidence of his being intoxicated at the time. On this evidence, Bayley, J., directed the jury, that if a person riding with reasonable and ordinary care could have seen and avoided the obstruction; and if they were satisfied that the plaintiff was riding along the street extremely hard, and without ordinary care, they should find a verdict for the defendant, which they accordingly did.

[The plaintiff's attorney moved for a new trial, arguing that the judge's instruction to the jury was improper. He cited a textbook for the proposition that if the defendant lays logs across a highway, the plaintiff can recover whether or not he was exercising due care for his own safety.]

BAYLEY, J. The plaintiff was proved to be riding as fast as his horse could go, and this was through the streets of Derby. If he had used ordinary care he must have seen the obstruction; so that the accident appeared to happen entirely from his own fault.

LORD ELLENBOROUGH, C.J. A party is not to cast himself upon an obstruction which has been made by the fault of another, and avail himself of it, if he do not himself use common and ordinary caution to be in the right. In cases of persons riding upon what is considered to be the wrong side of the road, that would not authorize another purposely to ride up against them. One person being in fault will not dispense with another's using ordinary care for himself. Two things must concur to support this action: an obstruction in the road by the fault of the defendant, and no want of ordinary care to avoid it on the part of the plaintiff.

[There were no reported opinions of the other judges. But the court as a whole refused a new trial, and so the plaintiff lost.]

NOTES

1. Here the *Butterfield* court plainly made law, approving the jury instruction's new exception to the general negligence rule, which exception would henceforth apply as law. A common fallacy about law is that courts, especially trial courts, do not make any law. But given our doctrine of stare decisis, courts will make law, no matter how rabidly the system opposes judicial activism. A court must decide cases coming before it; new cases will arise; the court's decisions in the new cases will become law by virtue of stare decisis; hence, courts make law.

2. You should note a number of characteristics of the lawmaking process here. Consider that court-made law is announced in the course of resolving a disputed grievance. One meaning of the old maxim *ex facto jus oritur* is that "law grows out of fact." The *Butterfield* case show this nicely.

3. Consider the different roles played by a number of people other than judges, including most prominently the parties and their lawyers, in the law-making process in *Butterfield.*

4. Lon L. Fuller, The Morality of Law 48 (rev. ed. 1969), argued that the nature of law requires general rules. Fuller suggested that it is characteristic of legal systems to function largely through general rules rather than through specific orders. Law is not, in his words, merely "a series of patternless exercises of political power." The *Butterfield* court might simply have denied the new trial without announcing any generalities. Consider the disadvantages this practice would involve, especially if all courts adopted it.

5. The judges' explanations revealed the kinds of considerations that influenced the court, which were similar to the reasons that motivated the *Skokie* supreme court. The *Butterfield* court, by putting together the general rule with its new exception, was surely thinking of fairness, but may also have had efficiency in the back of its mind. After all, the plaintiff should have the incentive to take an appropriate number of precautionary steps too—or were the judges perhaps trying to protect growing industries from the pro-plaintiff inclinations of juries?

6. But wait a minute. We are reading this case to say that a negligent defendant pays, *unless the plaintiff's negligence contributed to causing the harm.* Yet the judges do not say that exactly, do they? Justice Bayley resorts to the fiction of sole causation, saying that the plaintiff's negligence acted alone. Lord Chief Justice Ellenborough speaks of an intentionally acting plaintiff, which the case did not involve. Accordingly, future cases would have to figure out what *Butterfield* was to mean.

DAVIES v. MANN
Exchequer, 1842
152 Eng. Rep. 588

Case for negligence. The declaration [complaint] stated that the plaintiff theretofore, and at the time of the committing of the grievance . . . was lawfully possessed of a certain donkey, which said donkey of the plaintiff was then lawfully in a certain highway, and the defendant was then possessed of a certain wagon and of certain horses drawing the same, which said wagon and horses of the defendant were then under the care, government, and direction of a certain then servant of the defendant, in and along the said highway; nevertheless the defendant, by his said servant, so carelessly, negligently, unskilfully, and improperly governed and directed his said wagon and horses, that by and through the carelessness, negligence, unskilfulness, and improper conduct of the defendant, by his said servant, the said wagon and horses of the defendant then ran and struck with great violence against the said donkey of the plaintiff, and thereby then wounded, crushed, and killed the same, &c.

The defendant pleaded not guilty [in other words, made a general denial].

At the trial, before Erskine, J., at the last Summer Assizes for the county of Worcester, it appeared that the plaintiff, having fettered the fore feet of an ass belonging to him, turned it into a public highway, and at the time in question the ass was grazing on the off side of a road about eight yards wide, when the defendant's wagon, with a team of three horses, coming down a slight descent, at what the witness termed a smartish pace, ran against the ass, knocked it down, and the wheels passing over it, it died soon after. The ass was fettered at the time, and it was proved that the driver of the wagon was some little distance behind the horses. The learned Judge told the jury, that though the act of the plaintiff, in leaving the donkey on the highway so fettered as to prevent his getting out of the way of carriages travelling along it, might be illegal [you should read this to mean "negligent"], still, if the proximate cause of the injury was attributable to the want of proper conduct on the part of the driver of the wagon, the action was maintainable against the defendant; and his Lordship directed them, if they thought that the accident might have been avoided by the exercise of ordinary care on the part of the driver, to find for the plaintiff. The jury found their verdict for the plaintiff, damages 40s [about a month's wages].

[The defendant's attorney] moved for a new trial, on the ground of misdirection. The act of the plaintiff in turning the donkey into the public highway was an illegal one, and, as the injury arose principally from that act, the plaintiff was not entitled to compensation for that injury which, but for his own unlawful act, would never have occurred. [The reporter tells us that the famously persnickety Baron Parke here orally interrupted: The declaration states that the ass was lawfully on the highway, and the defendant has not specifically denied that allegation in its plea, or answer; therefore, it must be taken to be admitted.] The principle of law, as deducible from the cases, is, that where an accident is the result of faults on both sides, neither party can maintain an action. Thus, in Butterfield v. Forrester, 11 East, 60, it was held that one who is injured by an obstruction on a highway, against which he fell, cannot maintain an action, if it appear that he was riding with great violence and want of ordinary care, without which he might have seen and avoided the obstruction. So, in Vennall v. Garner, 1 C. & M. 21 [(Exch. 1832)], in case for running down a ship, it was held, that neither party can recover when both are in the wrong; and Bayley, B. [who had become a judge of the Court of Exchequer], there says, "I quite agree that if the mischief be the result of the combined negligence of the two, they must both remain in statu quo, and neither party can recover against the other." Here the plaintiff, by fettering the donkey, had prevented him from removing himself out of the way of accident; had his fore feet been free, no accident would probably have happened. [The defendant's attorney here cited a few other cases.]

LORD ABINGER, C.B. I am of opinion that there ought to be no [new trial] in this case. The defendant has not denied that the ass was lawfully in the highway, and therefore we must assume it to have been lawfully there; but even were it otherwise, it would have made no difference, for as the defendant might, by proper care, have avoided injuring the animal, and did not, he is liable for the consequences of his negligence, though the animal may have been improperly there.

PARKE, B. This subject was fully considered by this Court in the case of Bridge v. The Grand

36

Junction Railway Company, 3 M. & W. 246 [(Exch. 1838)], where, as appears to me, the correct rule is laid down concerning negligence, namely, that the negligence which is to preclude a plaintiff from recovering in an action of this nature, must be such as that he could, by ordinary care, have avoided the consequences of the defendant's negligence. I am reported to have said in that case, and I believe quite correctly, that "the rule of law is laid down with perfect correctness in the case of *Butterfield v. Forrester*, that, although there might have been negligence on the part of the plaintiff, yet unless he might, by the exercise of ordinary care, have avoided the consequences of the defendant's negligence, he is entitled to recover; if by ordinary care he might have avoided them, he is the author of his own wrong." In that case of *Bridge v. Grand Junction Railway Company*, there was a plea imputing negligence on both sides; here it is otherwise; and the Judge simply told the jury, that the mere fact of negligence on the part of the plaintiff in leaving his donkey on the public highway, was no answer to the action, unless the donkey's being there was the immediate cause of the injury; and that, if they were of opinion that it was caused by the fault of the defendant's servant in driving too fast or, which is the same thing, at a smartish pace, the mere fact of putting the ass upon the road would not bar the plaintiff of his action. All that is perfectly correct; for although the ass may have been wrongfully there, still the defendant was bound to go along the road at such a pace as would be likely to prevent mischief. Were this not so, a man might justify the driving over goods left on a public highway, or even over a man lying asleep there, or the purposely running against a carriage going on the wrong side of the road.

[The other judges, Barons Gurney and Rolfe, concurred in denying a new trial.]

NOTES

1. The *Davies* case came from another English trial court, the Exchequer, which was staffed by judges entitled barons. This court helped explain *Butterfield*, but also laid down new law beyond that of *Butterfield.* For that reason, or perhaps another, *Davies* has received lots of attention, as exemplified by The Case of Mr. Davies' Donkey, 9 Canadian Law Times 95, 95–96 (1889):

LORD ABINGER, C.B. loq.

> *Davies possessed an ass: no doubt*
> *   Trained to the horticultural load;*
> *One day he turned his donkey out,*
> *   Its fore-feet fettered, on the road.*
> *Here one remark seems necessary—*
> *   'Twas very wrong of Davies—very!*

CHORUS OF BARONS.

> *Oh fair judicial harmony!*
> *   In this great truth we all agree.*

LORD ABINGER, C.B.

> *While thus the ingenuous creature fed,*
> *   Mann's man came driving, all too fast.*
> *O'er the mild brute the roadsters sped,*
> *   And Davies' donkey breathed its last.*
> *We dwell not on the owner's sense*
> *   Of loss—it's not in evidence.*

CHORUS OF BARONS.
> *Davies, thy grief, thy bosom's rents,*
>> *Thy groans—are not in evidence!*

LORD ABINGER, C.B.
> *Who caused this crisis asinine?*
>> *Mann's man—and Mann must foot the bill:*
> *Had his man passed the road's decline*
>> *With ordinary caution, still,*
> *Still might the rich unstinted strain*
>> *Of Davies' donkey shake the plain.*

CHORUS OF BARONS.
> *Wisdom hath given sentence! though*
>> *The donkey was not rightly there,*
> *Was Mann's rude man excused? Oh, no!*
>> *He ought to drive with proper care.*
> *Wherefore we do adjudge and say,*
>> *For Davies' donkey Mann must pay!*

ALL, STERNLY.
> *For DAVIES' donkey MANN must pay!*
> (*He pays*)

2. *Butterfield* and *Davies* are similar cases in terms of facts, prior proceedings, and issue, but the decision was different: in *Butterfield*, the plaintiff lost; in *Davies*, the plaintiff won. That obviously raises the question whether the *Davies* case was decided consistently with the law of the *Butterfield* case. They were if they can be distinguished, which one does by identifying a factor or factors present in this case but not in *Butterfield*, or absent in this case but present in *Butterfield*, that would justify a different view of the merits of the two cases. Here the difference was that the *Davies* defendant's servant, for whose acts the defendant was liable, was present at the scene of the accident and had a chance to avoid it—while the plaintiff was the one with the last chance in *Butterfield*. This factor altered the balance of fairness, efficiency, and other reasons.

3. Recall that *Butterfield* ruled that a plaintiff cannot recover if the negligent defendant alleges and proves, as a defense, the plaintiff's contributory negligence. The *Davies* case originated the so-called last clear chance rule, according to which a contributorily negligent plaintiff will not fail *where the defendant negligently failed to take advantage of a last clear chance to avoid the accident.* Thus, the last clear chance rule modifies the *Butterfield* rule.

STARE DECISIS

Given the modern doctrine of stare decisis, today's judges are very concerned about whether their present decision is consistent with decisions previously made on similar facts, unless appropriate grounds exist for distinguishing the prior decisions. But why does the stare decisis doctrine exist? The following excerpt from a book by a U.S. Supreme Court Justice tries to explain. But then the next excerpt adds a note of realism from one of the major legal scholars of modern times.

ARTHUR J. GOLDBERG, EQUAL JUSTICE

75–76 (1971)

The doctrine of stare decisis has been called "a natural evolution from the very nature of our institutions." Lacking a comprehensive statement of legal rules, the common law system reiied instead upon the courts to rationally develop preexisting, general principles. The aim was uniformity of decision over time and throughout the judicial system. Realization of the aim necessitated narrowing of the judges' discretion to modify the preexisting principles, and this came to be accomplished by the strong presumption against overruling prior decisions that we call stare decisis.

The desire for uniformity was not based solely or even primarily on theoretical grounds; it was sought for some very practical reasons, of which I offer you five familiar ones. First, stare decisis fostered public confidence in the judiciary and public acceptance of individual decisions by giving the appearance of impersonal, consistent, and reasoned opinions. Second, while the respect shown old decisions thus buttressed courts against the world, such respect also induced in fact a

greater impersonality of decision and thereby buttressed the judges against their own natural tendencies and prejudices. This pushed us a giant step away from a government of men toward a government of laws. Third, a rule against overruling facilitates private ordering, since settled law encourages reliance at the stage of primary private activity and also helps lawyers in the counseling of that activity. Fourth, stare decisis eases the judicial burden by discouraging suits—potential litigants cannot expect to get a different view from a different judge—and also by facilitating decision once suits are brought. As Justice Cardozo put it:

> The labor of judges would be increased almost to the breaking point if every past decision could be reopened in every case, and one could not lay one's own course of bricks on the secure foundation of . . . [those] laid by others.

Fifth and last, justice in the case at hand is served by eliminating the injustices of unfair surprise and unequal treatment.

KARL N. LLEWELLYN, THE BRAMBLE BUSH

72–76 (7th printing 1981)*

We turn first to what I may call the orthodox doctrine of precedent . . . . Every case lays down a rule, the rule of the case. The express ratio decidendi is prima facie the rule of the case, since it is the ground upon which the court chose to rest its decision. But a later court can reexamine the case and can invoke the canon that no judge has power to decide what is not before him, can, through examination of the facts or of the procedural

issue, narrow the picture of what was actually before the court and can hold that the ruling made requires to be understood as thus restricted. In the extreme form this results in what is known as expressly "confining the case to its particular facts." This rule holds only of redheaded Walpoles in pale magenta Buick cars. And when you find this said of a past case you know that in effect it has been overruled. Only a convention, a

---

somewhat absurd convention, prevents flat over-ruling in such instances. It seems to be felt as definitely improper to state that the court in a prior case was wrong, peculiarly so if that case was inthe same court which is speaking now. It seems to be felt that this would undermine the dogma of the infallibility of courts. So lip service is done to that dogma, while the rule which the prior court laid down is disembowelled. The execution proceeds with due respect, with mandarin courtesy.

Now this orthodox view of the authority of precedent—which I shall call the *strict* view—is but *one of two views* which seem to me wholly contradictory to each other. It is in practice the dogma which is applied to *unwelcome* precedents. It is the recognized, legitimate, honorable technique for whittling precedents away, for making the lawyer, in his argument, and the court, in its decision, free of them. It is a surgeon's knife.

It is orthodox, I think, because it has been more discussed than is the other. Consider the situation. It is not easy thus to carve a case to pieces. It takes thought, it takes conscious thought, it takes analysis. There is no great art and no great difficulty in merely looking at a case, reading its language, and then applying some sentence which is there expressly stated. But there is difficulty in going underneath what is said, in making a keen reexamination of the case that stood before the court, in showing that the language used was quite beside the point, as the point is revealed under the lens of leisured microscopic refinement.... The strict doctrine, then, is the technique to be learned. *But not to be mistaken for the whole.*

For when you turn to the actual operations of the courts, or, indeed, to the arguments of lawyers, you will find a totally different view of precedent at work beside this first one. That I shall call, to give it a name, the *loose view* of precedent. That is the view that a court has decided, and decided authoritatively, *any* points or all points on which it chose to rest a case, or on which it chose, after due argument, to pass. No matter how broad the statement, no matter how unnecessary on the facts or the procedural issues, if that was the rule the court laid down, then that the court has held. Indeed, this view carries over often into dicta, and even

into dicta which are grandly obiter. In its extreme form this results in thinking and arguing exclusively from *language* that is found in past opinions, and in citing and working with that language wholly without reference to the facts of the case which called the language forth.

Now it is obvious that this is a device not for cutting past opinions away from judges' feet, but for using them as a springboard when they are found convenient. This is a device for *capitalizing welcome precedents.* And both the lawyers and the judges use it so. And judged by the *practice* of the most respected courts, as of the courts of ordinary stature, this doctrine of precedent is like the other, recognized, legitimate, honorable.

What I wish to sink deep into your minds about the doctrine of precedent, therefore, is that it is two-headed. It is Janus-faced. That it is not one doctrine, nor one line of doctrine, but two, and two which, *applied at the same time to the same precedent, are contradictory of each other.* That there is one doctrine for getting rid of precedents deemed troublesome and one doctrine for making use of precedents that seem helpful. That these two doctrines exist side by side. That the same lawyer in the same brief, the same judge in the same opinion, may be using the one doctrine, the technically strict one, to cut down half the older cases that he deals with, and using the other doctrine, the loose one, for building with the other half. Until you realize this you do not see how it is possible for law to change and to develop, and yet to stand on the past....

Nor, until you see this double aspect of the doctrine-in-action, do you appreciate how little, in detail, you can predict *out of the rules alone*; how much you must turn, for purposes of prediction, to the reactions of the judges to the facts and to the life around them....

People—and they are curiously many—who think that precedent produces or ever did produce a certainty that did not involve matters of judgment and of persuasion, or who think that what I have described involves improper equivocation by the courts or departure from the court-ways of some golden age—such people simply do not know our system of precedent in which they live.

The English Common Law and Its Reception in the United States

Law of the kind laid down in *Butterfield* and in *Davies* is called common law. (1) This name originally implied a uniform or common law for the entire country of England on the legal points involved, in place of diverse local customs. (2) The name then came to distinguish the characteristic Anglo-American legal system from other legal systems, such as the civil-law regimes of France and Germany with their comprehensive codes (incidentally, "civil law" in this sense refers to those countries' legal systems based on comprehensive written codes derived from Roman law, and has nothing whatever to do with the civil/criminal distinction in our system). (3) But today common law frequently means judge-made law, as opposed to statutory law.

Adoption of the rules of the common law, meant in all three senses, has been a familiar feature of American legal experience in all the states except Louisiana, which kept the French Civil Code. Indeed, most states, in their beginnings, passed so-called reception statutes. The one enacted by Illinois upon statehood in 1819 and still on the books is illustrative: "The common law of England, so far as the same is applicable and of a general nature . . . , shall be the rule of decision, and shall be considered as of full force until repealed by legislative authority." 5 Ill. Comp. Stat. 50/1. One scholar has commented on such statutes as follows:

> One aspect of the constitutional and statutory provisions by which the common law was continued in effect deserves particular emphasis. Because of the terms in which such provisions were written, the American courts exercised powers far more extensive than those possessed by judges

in England administering the common law. For under [these provisions] the American judges were bound to enforce the common law of England only if it was applicable to American circumstances. As a consequence, they were quick to discard an English doctrine if, in the language of our own time, it seemed "un-American."

Mark DeWolfe Howe, The Migration of the Common Law: The United States of America, 76 L.Q. Rev. 49, 51 (1960); see also Ford W. Hall, The Common Law: An Account of Its Reception in the United States, 4 Vand. L. Rev. 791 (1951).

Butterfield and *Davies*, however, were widely adopted throughout the Anglo-American legal world. This included the United States, as explained by Judge McLain in Fuller v. Illinois Central R.R., 100 Miss. 705, 717–18, 56 So. 783, 786 (1911):

> The groans, ineffably and mournfully sad, of Davies' dying donkey, have resounded around the earth. The last lingering gaze from the soft, mild eyes of this docile animal, like the last parting sunbeams of the softest day in spring, has appealed to and touched the hearts of men. There has girdled the globe a band of sympathy for Davies' immortal "critter." Its ghost, like Banquo's ghost, will not down at the behests of the people who are charged with inflicting injuries, nor can its groanings be silenced by the rantings and excoriations of carping critics. The law as enunciated in that case has come to stay.

BRITISH COLUMBIA ELECTRIC RAILWAY v. LOACH
Privy Council, 1915
[1916] 1 A.C. 719 (B.C.)

[This case arose in Canada. We see it on appeal. A train had killed Sands. Loach, as administrator of Sands' estate, sued the railway in a trial court for negligence. He lost, and then he appealed on error of law. The court of appeal reversed. The railway then appealed—to an English court! The English Privy Council then had some power to review Canadian court decisions. The Privy Council, as you will now read, affirmed the reversal, issuing this written and more modern opinion. Incidentally, as to the name of the case, the railway company's name appears first because it is the appellant.]

LORD SUMNER:

This is an appeal from a judgment of the Court of Appeal of British Columbia in favor of the administrator of the estate of Benjamin Sands, who was run down at a level crossing by a car of the appellant railway company and was killed. One Hall took Sands with him in a cart, and they drove together on to the level crossing, and neither heard nor saw the approaching car till they were close to the rails and the car was nearly on them. There was plenty of light and there was no other traffic about. The [special verdict, an unusual procedure comprising a set of specific questions submitted to the jury], though rather curiously expressed, clearly finds Sands guilty of negligence in not looking out to see that the road was clear. It was not suggested in argument that he was not under a duty to exercise reasonable care, or that there was not evidence for the jury that he had disregarded it. Hall, who escaped, said that they went "right on to the track," when he heard Sands, who was sitting on his left say "Oh," and looking up saw the car about fifty yards off. He says he could then do nothing, and with a loaded wagon and horses going two or three miles an hour he probably could not. It does not seem to have been suggested that Sands could have done any good by trying to jump off the cart and clear the rails. The car knocked cart, horses, and men over, and ran some distance beyond the crossing before it could be stopped. It approached the crossing at from thirty-five to forty-five miles an hour. The driver saw the horses as they came into view from behind a shed at the crossing of the road and the railway, when they would be ten or twelve feet from the nearest rail, and he at once applied his brake. He was then 400 feet from the crossing. If the brake had been in good order it should have stopped the car in 300 feet. Apart from the fact that the car did not stop in time, but overran the crossing, there was evidence for the jury that the brake was defective and inefficient and that the car had come out in the morning with the brake in that condition. The jury found that the car was approaching at an excessive speed and should have been brought under complete control, and although they gave as their reason for saying so the presence of possible passengers at the station by the crossing, and not the possibility of vehicles being on the road, there can be no mistake in the matter, and their finding stands. It cannot be restricted, as the trial judge and the [defendant] sought to restrict it, to a finding that the speed was excessive for an ill-braked car, but not for a properly-braked car, or to a finding that there was no negligence except the "original" negligence of sending the car out ill-equipped in the morning.

Clearly if the deceased had not got on to the line he would have suffered no harm, in spite of the excessive speed and the defective brake, and if he had kept his eyes about him he would have perceived the approach of the car and would have kept out of mischief. If the matter stopped there, his administrator's action must have failed, for he would certainly have been guilty of contributory negligence. He would have owed his death to his own fault, and whether his negligence was the sole cause or the cause jointly with the railway company's negligence would not have mattered.

It was for the jury to decide which portions of the evidence were true, and, under proper direction, to draw their own inferences of fact from such evidence as they accepted.... If the jury accepted the facts above stated, as certainly they well might do, there was no further negligence on the part of Sands after he looked up and saw the car, and then there was nothing that he could do. There he was, in a position of extreme peril and by his own fault, but after that he was guilty of no fresh fault. The driver of the car, however, had seen the horses some perceptible time earlier, had duly applied his brakes, and if they had been effective he could, as the jury found, have pulled up in time. Indeed, he would have had 100 feet to spare. If the car was 150 feet off when Sands looked up and said "Oh," then each had the other in view for fifty feet before the car reached the point at which it should have stopped. It was the motorman's duty, on seeing the peril of Sands, to make a reasonable use of his brakes in order to avoid injuring him, although it was by his own negligence that Sands was in danger. Apparently he did his best as things then were, but partly the bad brake and partly the excessive speed, for both of which the [defendant was] responsible, prevented him from stopping, as he could otherwise have done. On these facts, which the jury were entitled to accept and appear to have accepted, only one conclusion is possible. What actually killed Sands was the negligence of the railway company, and not his own, though it was a close thing.

Some of the judges in the Courts below appear to have thought that because the equipment of the car with a defective brake was the original cause of the collision, and could not have been remedied after Sands got on the line, no account should be taken of it in considering the motorman's failure to avoid the collision after he knew that Sands was in danger. . . .

These considerations were again urged at their Lordships' bar under somewhat different forms. It was said . . . that the negligence relied on as an answer to contributory negligence must be a new negligence, the initial negligence which founded the cause of action being spent and disposed of by the contributory negligence. . . .

This matter was much discussed in Brenner v. Toronto Ry. Co., 13 Ont. L.R. 423, when Anglin J. delivered a valuable judgment in the Divisional Court. . . .

The facts of that case were closely similar to those in the present appeal, and it was much relied on in argument in the Court below. Anglin J., . . . observed as follows: ". . . If, notwithstanding the difficulties of the situation, efforts to avoid injury duly made would have been successful, but for some self-created incapacity which rendered such efforts inefficacious, the negligence that produced such a state of disability is not merely part of the inducing causes—a remote cause or a cause merely sine qua non—it is, in very truth, the efficient, the proximate, the decisive cause of the incapacity, and therefore of the mischief. . . . Negligence of a defendant incapacitating him from taking due care to avoid the consequences of the plaintiff's negligence, may, in some cases, though anterior in point of time to the plaintiff's negligence, constitute 'ultimate' negligence, rendering the defendant liable notwithstanding a finding of contributory negligence of the plaintiff. . . ."

Their Lordships are of opinion that, on the facts of the present case, the above observations apply and are correct. Were it otherwise the defendant company would be in a better position, when they had supplied a bad brake but a good motorman, than when the motorman was careless but the brake efficient. If the superintendent engineer sent out the car in the morning with a defective brake, which, on seeing Sands, the motorman strove to apply, they would not be liable, but if the motorman failed to apply the brake, which, if applied, would have averted the accident, they would be liable.

. . . The object of the inquiry is to fix upon some wrong-doer the responsibility for the wrongful act which has caused the damage. . . .

In the present case their Lordships are clearly of opinion that, under proper direction, it was for the jury to find the facts and to determine the responsibility, and that upon the answers which they returned, reasonably construed, the responsibility for the accident was upon the [defendant] solely, because, whether Sands got in the way of the car with or without negligence on his part, the [defendant] could and ought to have avoided the consequences of that negligence, and failed to do so, not by any combination of negligence on the part of Sands with [its] own, but solely by the negligence of [its] servants in sending out the car with a brake whose inefficiency operated to cause the collision at the last moment, and in running the car at an excessive speed, which required a perfectly efficient brake to arrest it.

Their Lordships will accordingly humbly advise His Majesty that the appeal should be dismissed with costs.

NOTES

1. In cases like *Butterfield* and *Davies*, courts developed a body of common-law rules that served as premises for the remedy of money damages. Prior to *Loach*, this law might have been stated in sort of a decision-tree: a defendant who negligently harmed another is liable, unless the plaintiff's negligence contributed to causing the harm, except where the defendant negligently failed to take advantage of the last clear chance to avoid the accident. The question then is how *Loach* overruled or added to this law.

2. A persuasive argument can be made that the *Loach* decision was inconsistent with the last clear chance rule. Among other things, note that the railway had no *last* clear chance to avoid the accident. Any contrary description would be a fiction. As events reached a climax, the railway could do nothing to prevent the accident. Indeed, all of the railway's negligence occurred *before* the cart's emerging from behind the shed, when Sands' contributory negligence began and persisted for some four seconds. It was therefore Sands who had the last clear chance. Yet the plaintiff wins. (Note that the court instead says that the negligence was "solely" that of the railway. You might construe this as an effort to square its result with the dictates of the last clear chance rule. But this statement too was pure fiction, a way for the court to stick its head in the sand, or to mislead the reader.)

3. A better argument can be made that the new decision in *Loach* simply added to the law, by grafting an alternative exception onto the end of the decision-tree: *or where the defendant had earlier negligently incapacitated itself from taking advantage of any chance to avoid the accident.* The decision-tree is thus becoming quite a complicated cluster of doctrine. (Note also that in the United States, each state came to adopt one or another *variant* of this cluster of doctrine.)

4. When all this is said and done, the question remains whether the cluster of negligence doctrine is satisfactory. It does not appear to be dictating results so much as summarizing results. If what is really driving the courts is the search on the particular facts for the more blameworthy party—or for the party who could more efficiently have taken the needed precautionary step—and if the courts' desire to express the result in a general rule leads to ever more doctrinal refinement, as in *Loach*'s creation of the "self-created incapacity rule," then other factual settings will obviously require still further refinements. A ready example would involve a defendant's behavior that is not merely negligent, but is willful, wanton, or reckless: in such case today, contributory negligence is not available as a defense. In other words, the decision-tree may not only be a charade, but be forever an incomplete version of the charade.

COMPARATIVE NEGLIGENCE

The law of liability for negligence was becoming ever more complicated, a condition that always prompts criticism. Another source of dissatisfaction, however, lay in the all-or-nothing system of money damages, whereby one party must lose and the other win, even though both were at fault. Accordingly, some called for changing this system. For example, William L. Prosser, dean of Berkeley's School of Law and the leading torts scholar of his time, argued the following in Comparative Negligence, 51 Mich. L. Rev. 465, 469, 472–74 (1953):

> The attack upon contributory negligence has been founded upon the obvious injustice of a rule which visits the entire loss caused by the fault of two parties on one of them alone, and that one the injured plaintiff, least able to bear it, and quite possibly much less at fault than the defendant who goes scot free. No one ever has succeeded in justifying that as a policy, and no one ever will. Its outrageousness became especially apparent in the cases of injuries to employees, where a momentary lapse of caution after a lifetime of care in the face of the employer's negligence might wreck a man's life and leave him uncompensated as a charge upon society; and the demand for some modification of the rule became an integral part of the movement which finally led to the workmen's compensation acts. . . .
>
> The real explanation [of the last clear chance rule] would appear to be nothing more than a dislike for the defense of contributory negligence, and a rebellion against its application in a group of cases where its hardship is most apparent. The last clear chance has been called a "transitional doctrine," a way station on the road to apportionment of damages; but its effect has been to freeze the transition rather than to speed it. Actually the last clear chance cases present one of the worst tangles known to the law. In some jurisdictions the application of the rule has been limited to cases where the plaintiff is helpless and the defendant has in fact discovered the situation; in others it is extended to cases where the defendant might have discovered it by the exercise of reasonable care. In still others it is applied to situations where the plaintiff is not helpless at all and continues to be negligent, but is unaware of his danger, while the defendant has discovered it. In still others it is applied to cases where the defendant's antecedent negligence, as in driving a car with defective brakes, has rendered him unable to take advantage of the "last clear chance" he would otherwise have had. . . .
>
> Quite apart from all this confusion, the real objection to the last clear chance is that it seeks to alleviate the hardships of contributory negligence by shifting the entire loss due to the fault of both parties from the plaintiff to the defendant. It is still no more reasonable to charge the defendant with the plaintiff's share of the consequences of his fault than to charge the plaintiff with the defendant's; and it is no better policy to relieve the negligent plaintiff of all responsibility for his injury than it is to relieve the negligent defendant.

This kind of thinking put on the table the institution of some sort of scheme for apportionment of damages. Would such a "comparative-negligence" scheme be desirable (and how would it work)? According to economists, apportionment is just as efficient in terms of incentives for the parties to act safely, so the desirability arguments turn on fairness. And fairness prodded the English Parliament to adopt the statute of 8 & 9 Geo. 6, ch. 28 in 1945. The scholar Glanville Williams explained it, in The Law Reform (Contributory Negligence) Act, 1945, 9 Mod. L. Rev. 105, 105–06 (1946):

> Thus
> Was justice ever ridiculed in Rome:
> Such be the double verdicts favoured here
> Which send away both parties to a suit
> Nor puffed up nor cast down—for each a crumb
> Of right, for neither of them the whole loaf.
>   (The Ring and the Book, ii, 747–752.)

Thus Robert Browning: and from his lines we may perhaps gather what he would have thought of the Law Reform (Contributory Negligence) Act, 1945. But then, Browning was not a lawyer, or he could not have supposed that one party to a suit must necessarily be wholly in the right and the other wholly in the wrong....

In general terms the object of the Act is to enable the Judge in cases of contributory negligence to apportion the damages between the parties according to the respective degrees of responsibility for the damage. Thus if either sues the other he will get such damages as are attributable to the other party's portion of the responsibility.

A simple illustration will make this clear. Suppose that A and B are involved in an accident, through the negligence of both, and A suffers £500 damage while B suffers £100 worth of damage. It is held that A's responsibility for the damage amounts to four-fifths and B's to one-fifth of the total, that is to say, that A's responsibility is four times that of B's. Then A will recover from B one-fifth of his damages, amounting to £100, and B will recover from A four-fifths of his damages, amounting to £80. Thus on balance B will owe A £20 in respect of damages. Reviewing the situation, and leaving [legal] costs out of account, it will be seen that A suffers his original £500 damage less the £20 received from B, = £480 while B suffers his original £100 damage plus the sum of £20 paid to A, = £120. Thus A's loss is four times that of B, which reflects the Court's assessment of the responsibility for the situation....

The operative provision of the Act...runs as follows:—

> Where any person suffers damage as the result partly of his own fault and partly of the fault of any other person or persons, a claim in respect of that damage shall not be defeated by reason of the fault of the person suffering the damage, but the damages recoverable in respect thereof shall be reduced to such extent as the Court thinks just and equitable having regard to the claimant's share in the responsibility for the damage.

In the United States, the move to comparative negligence had begun even earlier, in 1908, but progressed slowly thereafter. In the 1960s and 1970s, however, the movement snowballed to leave only a tiny handful of states, then and today, still adhering to the rule that contributory negligence is a complete bar to the plaintiff's recovery. This particular reform merits a closer look, from an institutional perspective.

B. Reform of the Doctrine

Anglo-American lawmakers over the centuries have, in the fashion illustrated here, developed a great mass of remedial common law. In evaluating the important work of courts, distinguishing several different kinds of criticism is useful. Thus, of a given decision, or series of decisions, it may or may not be possible to say: (a) "These results (or reasons) are unsound," or (b) "These results (or reasons) are inconsistent." That sort of inquiry has been our focus thus far. But for certain legal changes, a different line of inquiry becomes relevant. Of such a decision, or series of decisions, it may or may not be possible to say: (c) "It is inappropriate for courts to make law of this kind at all," or (d) "Though it is not inappropriate for courts to make such law, it is, relatively speaking, more appropriate for legislatures to make it."

Assuming the desirability of reforming the common-law negligence decision-tree, and assuming that some kind of comparative-negligence formula for apportioning damages in accordance with the respective fault of the parties is the best overall solution, those further questions arise: Would it be inappropriate for a court to make this reform, leaving the legislature as the only appropriate body to do so? If it would not be inappropriate for a court so to act, still, would it be more appropriate for the legislature to act?

Contrary to a common fallacy about law, courts and legislatures are not equivalent as lawmakers. What factors are relevant in deciding which institution or body ought to have primary responsibility for originating or evolving the governing precepts? Relevant factors of appropriateness and comparative appropriateness will now be canvassed.

LEGISLATURES

Legislatures are generally thought of as lawmakers par excellence in modern societies. They embody the voice of the demos, constituting the supreme lawmaker within constitutional limits but answering to the people. And they are well equipped to make certain kinds of law.

First, unlike courts as we traditionally know them, a legislature can set up committees and commissions to investigate social problems in depth and in breadth, preparatory to making law. Such an apparatus for "legislative" fact-finding is unavailable to a court, which normally must rely on what the contending parties want to put before it, some of which may not even be admissible under rules of evidence.

Second, a legislature can act on its own initiative, and it can deal with more aspects of a social problem at one time than can a court. A court cannot take the initiative but must wait until two parties present a case to it for decision before it can make law at all. Even when a case is presented to a court, the decision will always address only part of the underlying social problem. Often not until a number of cases have arisen will a court even be able to see what the whole problem entails, and sometimes this sporadic approach masks the general pattern altogether. For these reasons, it will at best take a court longer to work out a comprehensive and sound solution.

Third, when a court does act definitively, this will usually have a retroactive effect, whereas a legislature may better secure fairness by acting prospectively.

Fourth, in general a court's decision coercively binds only the parties, whereas a legislature can speak directly to the populace as a whole.

Fifth, what a court decides to do about a social problem might be buried in a mass of arcane law reports, whereas a legislature can adopt methods of promulgation and publicity better designed to get the word around and thus to allow the citizenry to conform their primary conduct.

Sixth, courts do not have all the methods for dealing with a social problem that legislatures have. A court cannot allocate more funds to prosecutors. A court cannot set up a licensing system. A court cannot impose a tax. A court cannot start giving weather reports. Some things remain beyond the innovative powers of courts.

Seventh, legislatures can act without the restrictions of the theoretical expectations we impose on courts. As a society we feel, for example, that courts should draw only principled distinctions and that courts should not work obviously major social changes—at least as we traditionally conceive of the courts' role.

COURTS

Yet, as makers of certain other kinds of law, courts have important advantages over legislatures.

First, in dissecting and elaborating statutory pronouncements in particular cases, courts make a kind of interpretational law that legislators are distinctly unsuited to make. Specific questions of legal right arising under statutory law ought not to be subject to the influence of political pressures and considerations extrinsic to the statutorily defined merits. If legislatures were to decide such questions, keeping such pressures and considerations out of the picture would be far more difficult. Legislatures are not set up to deal with such questions anyway. Many of their personnel do not have the requisite training. And their procedures are not appropriate for careful definition of issues of fact between particular opponents, nor for the requisite dispassionate "adjudicative" fact-finding in particular cases, and so on. Also, legislatures simply could not take on such work. They would not have time.

Second, statutes do not and indeed cannot foresee and provide for all eventualities. Gaps abound in the statutory law. To do justice, courts should sometimes generate law on such interstitial matters rather than await the possibility of the legislature returning to the subject.

Third, even as a wholly original matter, if neither legislature nor court has had much prior experience with a social problem, letting the courts wrestle with the problem on a case-by-case basis may be best. Courts operate on a level that enables them to test general propositions against the reality of concrete situations. And courts can more readily modify basic law of their own making as necessity arises than bend statutory language supposedly applicable.

Fourth, even when legislatures do not lack relevant knowledge of the field, courts may still be better suited to originate the basic governing law. The factors relevant to sound solution may vary so much from case to case within the field as to defy statutory formulation. Or the issues arising within the field may call for commonsense solutions in terms of familiar everyday moral concepts such as "blame." Judges have more relevant experience in formulating law of this kind than have legislators. This has not gone unrecognized. Our law of negligence, for example, is largely judge-made.

Fifth, if the courts have done much of the original work in developing an area of the law, allowing them to continue the evolutionary task of clarifying and reshaping that law may be preferable. Legislatures might lack either the aptitude or the time for this task, which has traditionally been performed by the courts. Indeed, legislative enactments overriding the common law might prove quite disruptive in the law's development.

Sixth, when the issue is not one on which political parties divide, there is less reason for insisting that it be resolved in the first instance by a legislative body. Consider questions such as what the measure of damages should be for breach of contract. Generally speaking, these are relatively apolitical matters. Courts can thrash them out in the context of relevant particulars under enhanced conditions of institutional impartiality.

Seventh, the issue may instead be one that has become a political football within the legislative body, but clearly ought not to be left that way. Another possibility is that the majoritarian process of legislatures would fail to protect the interests of certain small groups within society. Again, the matter might be best left to courts. (An alternative is the more-or-less independent administrative body empowered to make governing regulations within a basic framework hewn out by the legislature. The desire to remove a matter from politics has often prompted the establishment of such bodies. On this, more later in Chapter 3.)

INSTITUTIONAL CONSIDERATIONS IN TORT REFORM

Now, we need to apply these considerations to the reform of moving from a contributory-negligence regime to a comparative-negligence scheme. Should courts or legislatures act? Professor Cornelius J. Peck, in his article, The Role of the Courts and Legislatures in the Reform of Tort Law, 48 Minn. L. Rev. 265, 304–07 (1963),* saw a clear answer:

> The doctrine of comparative negligence should replace the absolute bar imposed by the contributory negligence rule, and this substitution should be made by the judiciary. . . . In Illinois, a limited form of comparative negligence, based on a distinction between gross and slight negligence [so that relatively slight contributory negligence would not completely bar plaintiff's recovery], was judicially adopted in 1858 and ultimately abandoned, also by judicial

---

* Copyright © 1963 by the Minnesota Law Review Foundation. Reprinted by permission.

decision, in 1894. The significance of the abandonment is not that comparative negligence is unsound . . . but that such changes were made by courts, rather than legislatures, at a time when the creative role of the judiciary was not as well understood as at the present time.

It is unlikely that sufficient support for a comparative negligence rule could be organized to obtain its passage through a state legislature. As in other areas appropriate for judicial reform, lobby and pressure groups are active and successful in preventing bills incorporating comparative negligence principles from obtaining full legislative consideration. . . .

Moreover, empirical data bearing upon the subject is as available to courts as it is to legislatures and their committees. Probably the most important consideration is the effect that such a change would have upon the operations of insurance companies. Few others could justifiably claim to have made commitments and taken action in reliance upon the existence of a rule by which contributory negligence bars recovery. What evidence there is indicates that a change in the rule would have a minimal and perhaps undiscernible effect on the total operations of insurers. The apparent explanation of this fact is that comparative negligence is in fact the standard by which parties negotiate settlements. The proportion of cases controlled by a judgment, which may involve as little as two percent of all claims, is too small to affect the overall result even if juries did conscientiously follow the instructions given them. . . .

Finally, the involved and convoluted features of the last clear chance doctrine seem to ameliorate what would otherwise appear to be the harsh consequences of a rule barring recovery on the basis of contributory negligence. They provide for the layman the appearances of a system carefully designed to work justice between the parties to accident litigation. To judges and members of the legal profession, of course, the doctrine represents nothing more than an illogical scheme, difficult to apply, and frequently impossible to justify, the existence of which is tolerated only because it permits courts to escape the harsh consequences of the contributory negligence rule. As elsewhere, such doctrinal complications not only establish the need for reform; they also establish the propriety of judicial action.

But others disagreed, including the modern Illinois Supreme Court, which we last saw in *Skokie*. The next case was one for "wrongful death." A wrongful-death act allows a representative of the decedent to sue for negligence or tort resulting in death. Such a statute was necessary to change the old common-law rule that the cause of action died with the victim.

MAKI v. FRELK

Supreme Court of Illinois, 1968
40 Ill. 2d 193, 239 N.E.2d 445

KLINGBIEL, JUSTICE:

On this appeal we are presented with a question arising solely on the pleadings. In 1965 Minnie Maki, as administrator of the estate of her deceased husband, filed a complaint under the Wrongful Death Act against Calvin Frelk in the circuit court of Kane County. The complaint is in three counts. Defendant answered as to the allegations of counts I and II, and moved to strike count III. The court granted the motion, striking count III for failing to state a cause of action. In its order the court recited that there was no just reason for delaying enforcement or appeal.

The plaintiff thereupon sought review.... The appellate court reversed and remanded (Maki v. Frelk, 85 Ill. App. 2d 439, 229 N.E.2d 284), and we granted petitions by both the plaintiff and the defendant for leave to appeal from the appellate court judgment. The National Association of Independent Insurers and a group of trial lawyers called "Illinois Defense Counsel" have appeared as amici curiae ["friends of the court," or nonparties who submit advisory briefs].

The complaint alleges that on October 16, 1964, at about 9 P.M. the plaintiff's decedent was driving his car in a westerly direction on Plato Road near the intersection with Illinois Route 47, in Kane County, and the defendant was driving a car in a northerly direction along Illinois Route 47 near the intersection, that defendant was guilty of driving too fast, failing to yield the right of way, failing to keep a proper lookout for other cars, failing to keep his own car under control, failing to stop so as to avoid a collision, otherwise improperly operating the vehicle, and operating it without sufficient brakes, and that as a direct and proximate result of one or more of such acts his car collided with the car operated by plaintiff's decedent, causing the latter's death. The third count, stricken for failure to state a cause of action, did not allege due care on the part of the plaintiff and the decedent. Instead it alleged that "if there was any negligence on the part of plaintiff or plaintiff's decedent it was less than the negligence of the defendant, Calvin Frelk, when compared."

There is no dispute that under the rule as it now exists a plaintiff must be free from contributory fault in order to recover, and that contributory negligence of the deceased is a bar to recovery under the Wrongful Death Act. (Howlett v. Doglio, 402 Ill. 311, 83 N.E.2d 708.) In contending the third count nevertheless states a cause of action, plaintiff urges that the rule ought now be changed in favor of a form of comparative negligence. The appellate court agreed. It reviewed the history of contributory negligence, considered arguments generally advanced for and against the adoption of a comparative negligence rule, and concluded that contributory negligence shall no longer bar recovery if it is not as great as the negligence of the person against whom recovery is sought but that any damages allowed shall be diminished in proportion to the amount of negligence attributable to the person recovering....

After full consideration we think, however, that such a far-reaching change, if desirable, should be made by the legislature rather than by the court. The General Assembly is the department of government to which the constitution has entrusted the power of changing the laws.

Where it is clear that the court has made a mistake it will not decline to correct it, even though the rule may have been re-asserted and acquiesced in for a long number of years. No person has a vested right in any rule of law entitling him to insist that it shall remain unchanged for his benefit. But when a rule of law has once been settled, contravening no statute or constitutional principle, such rule ought to be followed unless it can be shown that serious detriment is thereby likely to arise prejudicial to public interests. The rule of stare decisis is founded upon sound principles in the administration of justice, and rules long recognized as the law should not be departed from merely because the court is of the opinion that it might decide otherwise were the question a new one.

Counsel on both sides have argued this case at length, supplying the court with a comprehensive review of many authorities. But we believe that on the whole the considerations advanced in support of a change in the rule might better be addressed to the legislature. As amici have pointed out, the General Assembly has incorporated the present doctrine of contributory negligence as an integral part of statutes dealing with a number of particular subjects (see, e.g., provisions imposing liability for injuries caused by the negligence of firemen "without the contributory negligence of the injured person..."...), and the legislative branch is manifestly in a better position than is this court to consider the numerous problems involved. We recently observed, with regard to a contention that exculpatory clauses in residential leases ought to be declared void, that "In our opinion the subject is one that is appropriate for legislative rather than judicial action." (O'Callaghan v. Waller & Beckwith Realty Co., 15 Ill. 2d 436, 441, 155

N.E.2d 545, 547.) We think the same must be said with respect to the change urged in the case at bar.

The circuit court was correct in striking count III of the complaint in the case at bar, and the appellate court erred in reversing its order. The judgment of the appellate court will therefore be reversed, the order of the circuit court affirmed, and the cause remanded to the circuit court for further proceedings not inconsistent with the views herein expressed.

[Of the seven justices (all of whom, incidentally, are elected), Justice Ward, joined by Justice Schaefer, dissented. His dissenting opinion is omitted.]

JUDICIAL REACTION TO LEGISLATIVE REFORM

Despite Professor Peck's prediction, many state legislatures (but not Illinois's) soon stepped in to adopt comparative negligence. He later explained this rapid development thus: "It appears, however, that in most of the cases of legislative action the change was made to avoid adoption of no-fault auto accident reparation plans. There was a united lobbying effort of plaintiffs' attorneys, defense attorneys, and the insurance industry, not because they believed in the justice of comparative negligence, but because they wanted an amelioration of tort law that they could explain made unnecessary the adoption of no-fault automobile accident reparation plans. . . . The legislative adoption of comparative negligence thus stands as an illustration of how interested lobbyists can achieve action that did not occur solely upon consideration of reform on its merits." Cornelius J. Peck, Comments on Judicial Creativity, 69 Iowa L. Rev. 1, 19-20 (1983); see Comments on *Maki v. Frelk*—Comparative v. Contributory Negligence: Should the Court or Legislature Decide?, 21 Vand. L. Rev. 889 (1968).

At any rate, lots of legislative reform came. But legislative contributions to the growth of common law are not without risks, and some of these risks can be compounded by judicial attitudes toward the interpretation of legislative enactments.

One kind of risk is that the legislature may become preoccupied with only one context in which the problem arises and as a result come up with a statute that incorporates terms referring only to the particular context, when in fact the statute ought to apply to other contexts as well. Such an enactment may stunt the growth of the law, for the legislature may be slow to return to the problem, and the courts may insist on reading the statute narrowly rather than extending it by analogy. For example, suppose that the English apportionment statute expressly applied only "in all actions brought for personal injuries, or where such injuries have resulted in death," as some such statutes did. Further suppose that a case like *Davies v. Mann* then arises, but with the plaintiff suing for damage to his *property*. By the literal language of the statute, would the court be empowered to apportion damages, extending the statute by analogy? Unfortunately, Anglo-American courts have not always been so bold. Indeed, they have frequently read statutes of the kind quite restrictively. This phenomenon has been described by Justice Walter V. Schaefer (who dissented in *Maki*) in his article, Precedent and Policy, 34 U. Chi. L. Rev. 3, 19–20 (1966):

> The contrast between the impact of a statute and that of a common law decision upon the body of the law is graphically shown in Dean Landis' description of the effect of *Rylands v. Fletcher* upon Anglo-American law. There the House of Lords decided that one who artificially accumulated water upon his land was absolutely liable for damage caused by its escape. The decision was based upon the analogy drawn from earlier cases which had dealt with the liability of the man who kept wild animals upon his land. The doctrine of *Rylands v. Fletcher* has been important in our law since 1868, and the rule there announced has been applied in many situations. Dean Landis says:
>
>> Had Parliament in 1868 adopted a similar rule, no such permeating results to the general body of Anglo-American law would have ensued. And this would be true, though the act had been preceded by a thorough and patient inquiry by a Royal Commission into the business of storing large volumes of water and its concomitant risks, and even though the same Lords who approved Mr. Fletcher's claim had in voting "aye" upon the measure given reasons identical with those contained in their judgments. Such a statute would have caused no ripple in the processes of adjudication either in England or on the other side of the Atlantic, and the judicial mind would have failed to discern the essential similarity between water stored in reservoirs, crude petroleum stored in tanks, and gas and electricity confined and maintained upon the premises.

Thus, whether to extend a statute by analogy is one kind of question judges must face once legislators have made their own imprint on the common law. However, there is a more fundamental question: how should judges determine the meaning of such a statute in the first place?

Observe, for example, that the English apportionment statute in fact begins: "Where any person suffers damage as the result partly of his own fault and partly of the fault of any other person...." The clearest kind of case to which this language applies is one where plaintiff and defendant are simultaneously negligent in causing the injury, as for example where plaintiff and defendant both enter an intersection against a four-way stop and run into each other. But instead consider a case like *Davies v. Mann* again, and ask whether the English act applies. Lord Justice Asquith made the following argument in Henley v. Cameron, 118 L.J.K.B. (n.s.) 989, 996 (C.A. 1948) (dissenting opinion): "The rule of 'last clear opportunity' is based on causation and assumes that where the last opportunity resided definitely with X (who failed to use it), the damage was suffered *not* partly as the result of X's fault and partly as the result of some other person's, but wholly and solely as the result of that of X." On this view, the words of the statute would not be satisfied. Yet, a court could feel that the literal meaning of words alone should not be decisive, and that the proper statutory interpretation would be the one that produces the most desirable result. Accordingly, the English courts have construed the statute to apply to cases like *Davies v. Mann*, so burying the last clear chance rule.

Nevertheless, there are limits on how far a court should run with the "spirit" of a statute like the English apportionment statute. If the defendant acted intentionally in inflicting injury, should the statute still work to reduce the damages for a contributorily negligent plaintiff? Most courts have said no. But what of willful, wanton, or reckless behavior by the defendant, rather than intentional infliction of harm? The courts have split on this issue. There will be many other issues on which the "letter" of the statute seems at odds with good policy. At some point, the unambiguous words of a statute should come to control decision.

One view of this difficult task of statutory interpretation—giving appropriate effect to both the spirit and the letter of a statute—is summarized in these terms by William L. Reynolds, Judicial Process in a Nutshell 225 (3d ed. 2003): "The legislature has the primary voice when it acts within the Constitution. The court's job, then, is to give effect to what the legislature has passed. In doing so, the most important factor is the language of the statute, the manner in which the legislature expressed its desires. The touchstone of this process is purpose: the aim or goal of the statute. In understanding purpose the court must set the statute in context; context is found by looking at the circumstances that surrounded its passage. Useful in this process is legislative history, especially committee and conference reports.... Finally, the court's obligation to engage in principled and consistent decision making does not cease because it is dealing with statutes."

ALVIS v. RIBAR
Supreme Court of Illinois, 1981
85 Ill. 2d 1, 421 N.E.2d 886

MORAN, JUSTICE:

These two cases, consolidated for appeal, present a question which arises solely from the pleadings. In each, plaintiff's complaint included a count based on the doctrine of comparative negligence, which count was dismissed by the trial court on motion by the defendants. In *Alvis* v. *Ribar*, the appellate court affirmed summarily, stating, "...it is not for this court to attempt to reverse the many cases and opinions of the Illinois Supreme Court in this area." (78 Ill. App. 3d 1117, 1119, 398 N.E.2d 124.) This court allowed leave to appeal. [A description of the case consolidated with *Alvis* is omitted, but it was brought under the Wrongful Death Act.]

Plaintiffs ask this court to abolish the doctrine of contributory negligence and to adopt in its place the doctrine of comparative negligence as the law in Illinois.

In *Alvis* v. *Ribar*, a motor vehicle operated by defendant Ribar skidded out of control and collided with a metal barrel which anchored an official intersection stop sign. The sign had been temporarily placed at the intersection while construction work on the intersecting road was being done by the defendant contractor, Milburn Brothers, Inc., under the supervision of defendant Cook County. Plaintiff Alvis, who was a passenger in defendant Ribar's vehicle, sustained injuries as a result of the collision. He filed a multicount personal injury complaint seeking damages from all three defendants....

I
The History of Contributory Negligence

...Case law developed the doctrine of contributory negligence in Illinois. In Aurora Branch R.R. Co. v. Grimes (1852), 13 Ill. 585, 587–88, this court followed the *Butterfield* case and added the requirement that the burden of proof is upon the plaintiff to show not only negligence on the part of the defendant, but also that plaintiff himself exercised proper care and circumspection. In the next few years the decisions involving "last clear chance" (Moore v. Moss (1852), 14 Ill. 106, 110 . . .), degrees of negligence (Chicago & Mississippi R.R. Co. v. Patchin (1854), 16 Ill. 198, 203), and proximate cause (Joliet & Northern Indiana R.R. Co. v. Jones (1858), 20 Ill. 221, 227) created confusion. Mr. Justice Breese reviewed these decisions in Galena & Chicago Union R.R. Co. v. Jacobs (1858), 20 Ill. 478, a case which involved a $4\frac{1}{2}$-year-old boy who had been run over by a railroad locomotive. There the court ultimately disagreed with the *Butterfield* holding and adopted a form of comparative negligence in its place.

This, and all the cases subsequent, to which we have referred, have one common basis, and that is found in the old law maxim that "no man shall take advantage of his own wrong or negligence" in his prosecution or defense against another.

The court concluded that liability does not depend absolutely on the absence of all negligence on the part of the plaintiff but upon the relative degrees of care or want of care manifested by both parties.

[A]ll care or negligence is at best but relative, the absence of the highest possible degree of care showing the presence of some negligence, slight as it may be. The true doctrine, therefore, we think is, that in proportion to the negligence of the defendant, should be measured the degree of care required of the plaintiff—that is to say, the more gross the negligence manifested by the defendant, the less degree of care will be required of the plaintiff to enable him to recover. Although these cases do not distinctly avow this doctrine in terms, there is a vein of it very perceptible, running through very many of them, as, where there are faults on both sides, the plaintiff shall recover, his fault being to be measured by the defendant's negligence, the plaintiff need not be wholly without fault . . . .

We say, then, that in this, as in all like cases, the degrees of negligence must be measured and considered, and wherever it shall appear that the plaintiff's negligence is comparatively slight, and that of the defendant gross, he shall not be deprived of his action.

Thus, in 1858, Illinois became a State which followed the doctrine of comparative negligence. . . .

. . . No attempt was made to divide the damages under this "comparative negligence" rule, and where it was applied the effect was full recovery by the plaintiff. The injured person was required to show not only that his negligence was slight and that the defendant's negligence was gross, but also that they were so when compared with each other, since the element of comparison was the essence of the doctrine.

During the next 27 years, the rule stated in *Jacobs* was followed and then abandoned by this court in Calumet Iron & Steel Co. v. Martin (1885), 115 Ill. 358, 368–69, 3 N.E. 456, and City of Lanark v. Dougherty (1894), 153 Ill. 163, 165–66, 38 N.E. 892, where it unequivocally made any contributory negligence on the part of the plaintiff a complete bar to recovery. Dean Green summarized the reasons for abandonment: the formula was not complete in that the "degrees of negligence" did not mitigate the damages which the plaintiff could recover; the "degrees of negligence" resulted in doctrinal conflict and confusion; and the *Jacobs* case had not overruled the *Grimes* case . . . . Green, Illinois Negligence Law, 39 Ill. L. Rev. 36, 47–51 (1944).

Other jurisdictions found problems in the doctrine of contributory negligence. Criticism of the harshness of the doctrine came as swiftly as did its acceptance into the law, and courts found exceptions [such as the "last clear chance" rule] to soften that harshness. . . .

Comparative negligence made its first permanent entry into American law in 1908 in the form of the Federal Employers' Liability Act (45 U.S.C. sec. 53). The Act applied to all negligence cases for injuries sustained by railroad employees engaged in interstate commerce, whether such cases were brought in a State or a Federal court. The concept of comparative negligence provided that the contributory negligence of the employee would not act as a bar to recovery, but that recovery would be diminished in proportion to the amount of negligence attributable to him. The introduction of the Federal Employers' Liability Act was the catalyst for a flood of State statutes which established a comparative negligence standard for injuries to laborers, and, especially, for railroad employees....

In 1910, Mississippi became the first State to adopt a comparative negligence statute applicable to negligence cases generally. (Miss. Code Ann. sec. 11-7-15 (1972).) The statute adopted the "pure" form of comparative negligence under which each responsible party would pay for the injuries sustained according to the relative percentage of his fault. Another form of comparative negligence was enacted by Wisconsin in 1931. (Wis. Stat. Ann. sec. 895.045 (West 1966).) This "modified" form allowed a negligent plaintiff to recover for his injuries [in proportion to the defendant's share of negligence, but only if the plaintiff's] negligence was "not as great as that of the defendant."

Today, a total of 36 States have adopted comparative negligence....

Twenty-three States have adopted the Wisconsin "modified" approach. Ten States have adopted the Mississippi "pure" comparative negligence approach. Two States, Nebraska and South Dakota, have a system which allows the plaintiff to recover only if his negligence is "slight" and that of defendant's is "gross." Georgia has its own unique system. It is important to note that 29 of these 36 States have adopted comparative negligence in the last 12 years.

In England, the birthplace of *Butterfield* v. *Forrester*, the concept of contributory negligence was long ago abandoned and replaced by a system of comparative negligence. Similarly, in many jurisdictions outside the United States the rule of contributory negligence has been abandoned in favor of comparative negligence. (Canada, the Canal Zone, Switzerland, Spain, Portugal, Austria, Germany, France, the Philippines, Japan, Russia, New Zealand, West Australia, Poland, and Turkey. See H. Woods, The Negligence Case:

Comparative Fault 17 (1978).) In light of these changes the Supreme Court of Michigan, in Placek v. City of Sterling Heights (1979), 405 Mich. 638, 653, 275 N.W.2d 511, 515, stated:

> This precedent is so compelling that the question before remaining courts and legislatures is not whether but when, how and in what form to follow this lead.

II
Contributory Negligence v. Comparative Negligence

The contributory negligence defense has been subject to attack because of its failure to apportion damages according to the fault of the parties. Under a comparative negligence standard, the parties are allowed to recover the proportion of damages not attributable to their own fault. The basic logic and fairness of such apportionment is difficult to dispute.

The defendants herein claim that no change of circumstances has been shown which would call for a change from the established doctrine of contributory negligence. The Illinois Defense Counsel, in its amicus curiae brief, relies on the words of Mr. Justice Powell for the proposition that change is not demanded by the public.

> [T]here is little evidence that the public generally is concerned. If indeed the present rule is as "archaic" and "unjust" as is contended, one would normally expect much greater support for the organized efforts being made to abolish it. (Powell, Contributory Negligence: A Necessary Check on the American Jury, 43 A.B.A. J. 1005, 1008 (1957).)

It must be noted, however, that at the time of Mr. Justice Powell's quoted assessment, only six States had adopted the doctrine of comparative negligence. That 30 additional States have since adopted the doctrine evidences that the basis for the assessment has changed and that today there is, indeed, a compelling public demand to abolish the old rule. Certainly, the concern which prompted the adoption of the rule can no longer support its retention. There is no longer any justification for providing the protective barrier of the contributory negligence rule for industries of the nation at the expense of deserving litigants. It must be pointed out that today most cases against industrial defendants are brought under the Worker's Compensation Act, under which plaintiff's negligence is not an issue. (Ill. Rev. Stat. 1979, ch. 48, par. 138.1 et seq.) ... We believe that the concept of comparative negligence which produces a more just and socially desirable distribution of loss is demanded by today's society.

Defendants contend that the apportionment of relative fault by a jury cannot be scientifically done, as such precise measurement is impossible. The simple and obvious answer to this contention is that in 36 jurisdictions of the United States such apportionment is being accomplished by juries. The Supreme Court of California, in responding to a similar contention, stated:

> These inherent difficulties are not, however, insurmountable. Guidelines might be provided the jury which will assist it in keeping focussed upon the true inquiry [citation], and the utilization of special verdicts or jury interrogatories can be of invaluable assistance in assuring that the jury has approached its sensitive and often complex task with proper standards and appropriate reverence. (Li v. Yellow Cab Co. (1975), 13 Cal. 3d 804, 824, 119 Cal. Rptr. 858, 872, 532 P.2d 1226, 1240.)

We agree that such guidelines can assist a jury in making apportionment decisions and view the necessary subtle calculations no more difficult or sophisticated for jury determination than others in a jury's purview, such as compensation for pain and suffering. Although it is admitted that percentage allocations of fault are only approximations, the results are far superior to the "all or nothing" results of the contributory negligence rule. "Small imperfections can be disregarded, small inequities tolerated, if the final result is generally satisfactory." Turk, Comparative Negligence on the March, 28 Chi.-Kent L. Rev. 189, 341–42 (1950).

Defendants assert that the contributory negligence rule should be retained in that the comparative negligence doctrine rewards carelessness and ignores the value of requiring prudent

behavior. ... Contrary to defendants' assertion, we believe that the need to deter negligent parties supports the adoption of the comparative negligence doctrine in which each party would be liable for damages in direct proportion to his degree of carelessness.

Defendants claim that the change to comparative negligence will cause administrative difficulties due to an increase in claims, a decrease in settlements, and a resulting overcrowded docket. An Arkansas study showed that, there, the adoption of comparative negligence prompted no drastic change in court burden; that the change increased potential litigation but promoted more pretrial settlements. The report concluded that concern over court congestion should not be a factor in a State's decision to adopt comparative negligence. Rosenberg, Comparative Negligence in Arkansas: A "Before and After" Survey, 13 Ark. L. Rev. 89, 108 (1959).

... We believe that the defendants' fears concerning the judicial administrative problems attendant upon the adoption of comparative negligence are exaggerated. But were defendants' fears well founded, we could nevertheless not allow the contributory negligence rule to remain the law of this State in the face of overwhelming evidence of its harsh and unjust results.

Defendants claim that the adoption of comparative negligence would escalate insurance rates to an unbearable level. This has not been found to be the case. Effects, in fact, have been found to be minimal. Rosenberg, Comparative Negligence in Arkansas: A "Before and After" Survey, 13 Ark. L. Rev. 89, 108 (1959).

The amicus curiae brief submitted by the Illinois Defense Counsel suggests that, under the contributory negligence rule, the jury has sufficient flexibility to do substantial justice and that this flexibility negates the necessity for the adoption of comparative negligence. In essence, the Illinois Defense Counsel alludes to the oft-observed phenomenon that, once inside the jury room, juries often ignore the harshness of the contributory negligence rule and, instead, dole out justice by a common sense approach according to the relative culpability of the litigants. We agree that such may be the case and, in fact, find the proclivity of juries to ignore the law to be a compelling reason for the abolition of that law. The Supreme Court of Florida addressed this concern.

> [T]here is something basically wrong with a rule of law that is so contrary to the settled convictions of the lay community that laymen will almost always refuse to enforce it, even when solemnly told to do so by a judge whose instructions they have sworn to follow. . . .
>
> The disrespect for law engendered by putting our citizens in a position in which they feel it is necessary to deliberately violate the law is not something to be lightly brushed aside; and it comes ill from the mouths of lawyers, who as officers of the courts have sworn to uphold the law, to defend the present system by arguing that it works because jurors can be trusted to disregard that very law. (Hoffman v. Jones (Fla. 1973), 280 So. 2d 431, 437.)

There is something inherently wrong with a rule of law so repulsive to a jury's common sense of justice that veniremen feel compelled to ignore the law.

III
Judicial v. Legislative Change

It is urged by defendants that the decision to replace the doctrine of contributory negligence with the doctrine of comparative negligence must be made by the legislature, not by this court. In each of the States that have judicially adopted comparative negligence, the court addressed the propriety of judicial versus legislative adoption. In each, the court found that contributory negligence is a judicially created doctrine which can be altered or totally replaced by the court which created it. (Claymore v. City of Albuquerque (N.M. Ct. App., Dec. 8, 1980), Nos. 4804, 4805, slip op. at 77–78; Placek v. City of Sterling Heights (1979), 405 Mich. 638, 657, 275 N.W.2d 511, 517; Bradley v. Appalachian Power Co. (W. Va. 1979), 256 S.E.2d 879, 881; Li v. Yellow Cab Co. (1975), 13 Cal. 3d 804, 813–14, 119 Cal. Rptr. 858, 864–65, 532 P.2d 1226, 1232–33; Kaatz v. State (Alaska 1975), 40 P.2d 1037, 1049; Hoffman v. Jones (Fla. 1973), 280 So. 2d 431, 434.) . . .

The Illinois Defense Counsel has, in its brief, urged that the legislature is better equipped to enact comparative negligence, asserting that "the legislative process . . . involves a broad examination of the entire problem without emphasis on a particular fact situation." The Defense Counsel and defendants claim that judicial adoption of comparative negligence would result in a piecemeal approach that would leave for future cases many ancillary questions. They claim that the law would be left in confusion and turmoil.

An examination of the States from which comparative negligence statutes have emerged reveals that such statutes are very general and brief and do not address collateral issues. Rather, the legislators apparently deemed it wise to leave the solution of collateral issues to the courts.

Defendants point out that, since 1976, six bills were introduced in the Illinois legislature to abolish the doctrine of contributory negligence. They interpret the failure of each bill to pass as a sign of the General Assembly's desire to retain the present status of the rule. Another conclusion may be drawn, however, as pointed out by Mr. Justice Ward in his dissenting opinion in Maki v. Frelk (1968), 40 Ill. 2d 193, 203, 239 N.E.2d 445:

> It can be argued that the legislature's inaction in this area is attributable to its feeling that it is more appropriate, considering the history of the question in Illinois, for the judiciary to act.

In support of their view that the legislature intends to retain the rule, defendants point to various statutes which have incorporated the contributory negligence defense. They claim that these statutes act as a legislative ratification of the doctrine of contributory negligence. We do not agree. We believe that in enacting such statutes the legislature did not focus on the merits of the contributory negligence rule, but, rather, conformed the statutes to the then-existing law as announced by the court.

We believe that the proper relationship between the legislature and the court is one of cooperation and assistance in examining and changing the common law to conform with the ever-changing demands of the community.

There are, however, times when there exists a mutual state of inaction in which the court awaits action by the legislature and the legislature awaits guidance from the court. Such a stalemate is a manifest injustice to the public. When such a stalemate exists and the legislature has, for whatever reason, failed to act to remedy a gap in the common law that results in injustice, it is the imperative duty of the court to repair that injustice and reform the law to be responsive to the demands of society.

IV
Stare Decisis

Defendants urge us to abide by the doctrine of stare decisis and follow the holding in Maki v. Frelk (1968), 40 Ill. 2d 193, 239 N.E.2d 445. They contend that it is crucial to the due administration of justice, especially in a court of last resort, that a question once deliberately examined and decided be closed to further scrutiny. It must first be pointed out that the *Maki* decision, filed 13 years ago, did not, as claimed by defendants, address the merits of the case. On the contrary, the court avoided the merits by holding that the problem was one for the legislature.

It is interesting to observe that if Illinois courts had, in fact, rigidly adhered to the stare decisis rule throughout this State's legal history, the comparative standard could not have been adopted in Galena & Chicago Union R.R. Co. v. Jacobs (1858), 20 Ill. 478. Similarly, the comparative rule could not have been later discarded in Calumet Iron & Steel Co. v. Martin (1885), 115 Ill. 358, 3 N.E. 456, and City of Lanark v. Dougherty (1894), 153 Ill. 163, 38 N.E. 892.

The tenets of stare decisis cannot be so rigid as to incapacitate a court in its duty to develop the law. Clearly, the need for stability in law must not be allowed to obscure the changing needs of society or to veil the injustice resulting from a doctrine in need of reevaluation. This court can no longer ignore the fact that Illinois is currently out of step with the majority of States and with the common law countries of the world. We cannot continue to ignore the plight of plaintiffs who, because of some negligence on their part, are forced to bear the entire burden of their injuries. Neither can we

condone the policy of allowing defendants to totally escape liability for injuries arising from their own negligence on the pretext that another party's negligence has contributed to such injuries. We therefore hold that in cases involving negligence the common law doctrine of contributory negligence is no longer the law in the State of Illinois, and in those instances where applicable it is replaced by the doctrine of comparative negligence.

V
The "Pure" Versus the "Modified" Form of Comparative Negligence

There remains the question of the form of comparative negligence to be adopted. Under a "pure" form, the plaintiff's damages are simply reduced by the percentage of fault attributable to him. Under a "modified" form, a negligent plaintiff may recover so long as the percentage of his fault does not exceed 50% of the total.

Defendants argue that should this court decide to adopt comparative negligence, the modified approach should be selected. They point to the basic unfairness of the "pure" system by example: A plaintiff who is 90% negligent has suffered $100,000 in damages. A defendant who is only 10% negligent has suffered only $10,000 in damages. Defendants here point out the basic unfairness of requiring the 10% negligent defendant to pay $10,000 to a plaintiff who was 90% at fault. . . . In a suit under a "pure" form of comparative negligence in which the defendant counterclaims for his own damages, each party must bear the burden of the percentage of damages of all parties in direct proportion to his fault. In the example above, the 90% negligent plaintiff will bear 90% of his own damages as well as 90% of defendant's. On the other hand, the 10% negligent defendant will be made to bear 10% of his own damages as well as 10% of plaintiff's. Neither party is unjustly enriched. Neither party escapes liability resulting from his negligent acts or omissions. It is difficult to see unfairness in such a distribution of liability.

Opponents of the "pure" form of comparative negligence claim that the "modified" form is superior in that it will increase the likelihood of settlement and will keep down insurance costs. However, studies done comparing the effects of the "pure" versus the "modified" forms show the differences in insurance rates to be inconsequential. (V. Schwartz, Comparative Negligence 346 (1974).) Fears as to the likelihood of settlement are not supported in fact or logic. It is argued that the negligent plaintiff will refuse to settle knowing that, under the "pure" system he will be able to recover "something" in court. The converse can as easily apply: the defendant may be encouraged to settle knowing that he cannot rely on the "modified" 50% cut-off point to relieve him of liability. . . .

Wisconsin's "modified" system has been criticized because a large number of cases appealed focused on the narrow question of whether plaintiff's negligence amounted to 50% or less of the aggregate. (Prosser, Comparative Negligence, 41 Cal. L. Rev. 1, 23 (1953).) This, in fact, caused the Wisconsin Supreme Court to examine the question of whether the "modified" system should be replaced with the "pure" form of comparative negligence. (Vincent v. Pabst Brewing Co. (1970), 47 Wis. 2d 120, 177 N.W.2d 513.) There, as in Maki v. Frelk (1968), 40 Ill. 2d 193, 239 N.E. 445, the merits of the case were not addressed, for the majority of the court ruled that the determination should be left to the legislature, which had originally adopted the "modified" form by statute. One dissenting and three concurring justices, however, expressed their intent to judicially adopt the "pure" form if the legislature failed to do so.

The "pure" form of comparative negligence is the only system which truly apportions damages according to the relative fault of the parties and, thus, achieves total justice. We agree with the *Li* court that "the '50 percent' system simply shifts the lottery aspect of the contributory negligence rule to a different ground." (Li v. Yellow Cab Co. (1975), 13 Cal. 3d 804, 827, 119 Cal. Rptr. 858, 874, 532 P.2d 1226, 1242.) There is no better justification for allowing a defendant who is 49% at fault to completely escape liability than there is to allow a defendant who is 99% at fault under the old rule to escape liability.

Mindful of the facts stated and that the vast majority of legal scholars who have studied the area recommend the "pure" approach, we are persuaded that the "pure" form of comparative negligence is preferable, and we therefore adopt it as the law of Illinois.

. . . We have already noted that the doctrine of "last clear chance" was created to escape the harshness of the contributory negligence rule. As the need for it disappears in the face of this decision, the vestiges of the doctrine of "last clear chance" are hereby abolished.

We believe that the use of special verdicts and special interrogatories will serve as a guide to assist the jury in its deliberations. We leave the resolution of other collateral issues to future cases.

VI
Application

Finally, we address the question of the applicability of the rule here announced. We hold that this opinion shall be applied to the parties before us on appeal, and to all cases in which trial commences on or after June 8, 1981, the date on which the mandate in this case shall issue. This opinion shall not be applicable to any case in which trial commenced before that date—except that if any judgment be reversed on appeal for other reasons, this opinion shall be applicable to any retrial.

For the reasons stated, we hereby abolish the common law doctrine of contributory negligence and adopt in its place the doctrine of comparative negligence in its pure form. The judgments of the appellate court and circuit courts are reversed and the causes are remanded to the respective circuit courts for further proceedings in accordance with the views expressed herein.

UNDERWOOD, JUSTICE, dissenting:

While I acknowledge the court's power to radically change a rule of law which has existed in this State for nearly a century, I still believe, as I did when Maki v. Frelk (1968), 40 Ill. 2d 193, 239 N.E.2d 445, was decided, that the decision to change is best left to the General Assembly.

...One of the major problems with a judicially decreed change of this magnitude is its effect upon a great many other, related areas of law. What modifications, for example, are now to be made in the doctrines of...wilful and wanton misconduct...and many others? While the newly decreed rule of comparative negligence may ultimately affect all of these situations to a now unknown degree, the court can consider only one case at a time. Unless the legislature acts, it will in all probability be years before these questions can be judicially answered. Meanwhile, litigants and the trial courts must attempt to predict the manner in which this court will eventually resolve these now unresolved questions. The fact that the General Assembly could, if it considered a change desirable, adopt one of the comprehensively drafted bills with which it has been presented and resolve these related questions simultaneously is, to me, a persuasive reason for this court to exercise a greater degree of judicial restraint....

While I do not totally disagree with the proposition that modification of our heretofore existing contributory negligence rule is desirable, I am not at all certain that the pure form of comparative negligence is the preferred substitute. If it is, it seems odd that of the 36 States which have adopted some form of comparative negligence approximately two thirds have chosen a modified form. And, while the majority says the pure form "achieves total justice," the fact that this form permits a grossly negligent but severely injured plaintiff to recover substantial damages from a slightly negligent defendant with only minor injuries certainly represents a radical departure from the concept of individual responsibility which has heretofore underlain our system of tort law. Despite the assertion by the majority that the pure form produces a utopian form of justice, most of the States adopting a comparative negligence rule have preferred to deny recovery to one whose own negligence was the principal cause of his injuries.

Whether a change is desirable, and, if so, what that change should be, are major policy questions. Their resolution will have a substantial effect upon the people of this State. Recovery will henceforth be possible for conduct of a significantly less reprehensible nature than heretofore. Litigation will surely increase, thus augmenting the burden upon our already overburdened courts, and insurance rates will likely rise in unknown amounts. Policy choices such as those involved here are, it seems to me, best left to the judgment of a General Assembly staffed and equipped to explore, consider, and resolve simultaneously these many-faceted questions.

The majority emphasizes as justification for its action the cliche that courts which created a rule can modify it, and cites cases from some six States which have adopted comparative negligence. There are a greater number, including *Maki*, to the contrary....

It is to me anomalous for the majority to cite the introduction, consideration, and rejection of six bills in the legislature in less than five years as support for the proposition that there has been legislative "inaction" on the subject. Rather, it seems to me, the introduction of so many bills indicates a considerable amount of activity, and an additional bill, House Bill 0142, providing a system of comparative negligence, is presently pending. The General Assembly has been well aware from our annual reports to it that the large majority of the judges of Illinois were in favor of legislative adoption of some form of comparative negligence. There is no reason to believe, as the majority suggests, that the absence of legislation doing so should now be viewed as indicating the legislature is awaiting action by this court. Rather, I would have thought the substantial volume of proposed legislation on the subject which had failed to pass indicated the General Assembly's considered judgment that no change should be made. If that assumption is correct, my colleagues are simply overruling the judgment of the members of our General Assembly on a major question of public policy because they "believe that the concept of comparative negligence which produces a more just and socially desirable distribution of loss is demanded by today's society" and "it is the imperative duty of the court to repair that injustice [contributory negligence] and reform the law to be responsive to the demands of society." I would respectfully suggest that the 236 members of the General Assembly are far better situated than the members of this court to determine what is "socially desirable" and to gauge the "demands of society." In a republic in which law-making power is vested, at least theoretically, in our elected representatives, I would have thought a greater degree of judicial self-restraint desirable. The willingness of the judiciary to invade the legislative realm simply encourages additional resort to the courts for resolution of difficult questions of public policy better left to the legislative branch. . . .

RYAN, JUSTICE, dissenting:

I join in the dissent of Mr. Justice Underwood. . . .

For the sake of stability, if for no other reason, it would appear preferable to have such a radical change as this made by the legislature. . . . Now, just 12 years later, with only two members of the *Maki* court still serving [Justices Underwood and Ward], this court has reversed itself and has held that this court and not the legislature should reject contributory negligence in favor of comparative negligence. Conceivably in a few years, when the present members of this court will no longer be serving and when their replacements may be less enthusiastic about comparative negligence, this court could reject the judge-made law of this case. If we were to adhere to the holding of *Maki* and accept the action or inaction of the legislature, as the case may be, as the policy of this State, the law would be free from this possible uncertainty and we would either follow the doctrine of contributory negligence or comparative negligence free from judicial tinkering. . . .

Contributory negligence is, of course, based upon the fault concept of tort law. Comparative negligence, while ostensibly involving the fault concept, is, in reality, a product of that school of tort law which has held that it was unjust for one who is injured not to be compensated for his loss. This is particularly true of "pure," as compared with "modified," comparative negligence. Thus the focus of pure comparative negligence is on compensation and the distribution of the loss and retains only a semblance of the fault basis as a means of accomplishing its main purpose. In other words, in my opinion, pure comparative negligence is another fiction in the law which those who refuse to accept the no-fault theory of recovery have promoted to accomplish essentially no-fault recovery. . . .

To say that a jury will discount a plaintiff's recovery by his degree of negligence is not realistic. Just as sympathetic juries operating under limitations of contributory negligence apply a form of comparative negligence, juries operating under pure comparative negligence will, in effect, compensate a plaintiff for his injuries, regardless of the degree of his fault. . . .

NOTES

1. The preceding version of *Alvis* is a sharply edited version of a much longer report of the case, which also included many citations. Worth noting is that American judicial opinions are written, in contrast to the oral tradition of the English.

2. Another common fallacy about law is that "law is nothing but politics." But what is meant by "politics"? Generally true is that law rests on political power. Generally true is that questions for lawmakers such as courts and legislatures are questions of policy and in that sense political. Also generally true is

"THE OPPORTUNITY TO BE FAIR AND JUST IS REWARDING — BUT WHAT I ESPECIALLY LIKE IS TAKING THE LAW INTO MY OWN HANDS."

that the content of even judge-made law is, over the long run, influenced to some extent by political considerations: the specific wants of political pressure groups, the specific wants of political parties, the specific wants of political creditors and constituents. But making too much of these general truths is easy. For instance, is it wholly appropriate to say that the courts in the *Butterfield*, *Davies*, and *Loach* cases were responding to political wants? Not solely. Consider, too, the proper interpretation of remedial-law statutes. When courts interpret these, are they responding merely to such wants? And what of the usual judicial deference to stare decisis? Whether or not one case is decided consistently with another is a political question only in a special sense.

3. Nevertheless, the *Maki* and *Alvis* cases would seem to destroy the opposing fallacious view of the judiciary as an ivory tower, do they not?

LEGISLATIVE REACTION TO JUDICIAL REFORM

In *Alvis*, we saw that the Illinois Supreme Court tired of waiting for the legislature to act. But remember that in our system, the legislature has the last word on nonconstitutional matters. The legislature can always come in and change the common law.

In 1986, the Illinois General Assembly reentered the arena, enacting what now stands as 735 Ill. Comp. Stat. 5/2-1116(c):

> In all actions on account of death, bodily injury or physical damage to property in which recovery is predicated upon fault, the contributory fault chargeable to the plaintiff shall be compared with the fault of all tortfeasors whose fault was a proximate cause of the death, injury, loss, or damage for which recovery is sought. The plaintiff shall be barred from recovering damages if the trier of fact finds that the contributory fault on the part of the plaintiff is more than 50% of the proximate cause of the injury or damage for which recovery is sought. The plaintiff shall not be barred from recovering damages if the trier of fact finds that the contributory fault on the part of the plaintiff is not more than 50% of the proximate cause of the injury or damage for which recovery is sought, but any economic or non-economic damages allowed shall be diminished in the proportion to the amount of fault attributable to the plaintiff.

Section Four
APPLYING REMEDIAL LAW

Remedial methods and the general rules specifying the conditions for their application would not alone be sufficient to constitute an effective remedial instrument. We have yet to show why and how this is so. Indeed, we have not yet even shown the origin of the felt need for courts. After all, remedial law might have been formulated solely by legislatures. Therefore, here we shall turn to the necessity of authoritatively applying the law to particular facts—and thereby show the need for courts.

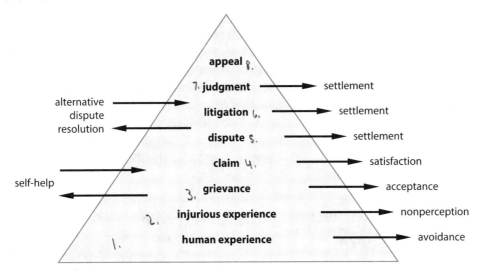

Before considering authoritative structures and processes for applying law to facts of particular cases, however, we must stress that law is most often applied by private parties on their own, without any resort to authoritative schemes set up by the legal system. A common fallacy about law is that occasions to apply it arise only after a dispute arises, and yet another is that law is something only authorized officials can and do apply. Well in advance of disputes, many private persons seek legal advice from lawyers about how to avoid grievances in the first place. And when disputes do arise, many private persons are able to settle these disputes on their own, in light of what they are told by their lawyers about the relevant law. Much more significantly, most private persons similarly act without the aid of lawyers at all.

Another way to make the same point is to introduce you to the so-called grievance pyramid. This image represents, as one progresses up the steps of the pyramid, how the whole realm of experiences significantly narrows to disputes, a small subset that produces in turn those selected cases you have read so far in this book. Infinite experiences produce countless disputes, which yield few lawsuits. For example, only a small percentage of grievances ripen into claims, by the aggrieved's voicing the grievance to the injurer; most aggrieved persons accept their injury as part of life or just figure that there is no remedy available; tellingly, the theorists in this subject sometimes refer to acceptance as "lumping it." Similarly, most disputants never make it to a lawyer, much less to a courthouse. Injured persons abandon or settle the overwhelming majority of grievances at some point along the line.

Still, even if its concern is only the tiny tip of a huge iceberg, the authoritative scheme for applying remedial law matters a lot to society and to citizens. By litigation, courts act as the default enforcer of law and resolver of disputes. Litigation not only produces singular decisions that restructure society but also serves as a major vehicle for lawmaking in our government and for articulation of societal values. And the legal system's adjudication enunciates the law that sets the standards under which potential litigants alternatively resolve their disputes by nonlitigation processes, "bargaining in the shadow of the law" to reach outcomes that generally conform to the law and thereby further the law's purposes.

In the materials that follow, we shall use *Brown v. Hayden Island Amusement Co.*, an actual litigated case only somewhat altered for pedagogic purposes, as the vehicle for presenting an inside view of structures and processes widely used in Anglo-American countries for authoritatively applying law to facts. This "Swimming Pool" case is a simple negligence case, arising in a state that had not yet adopted an apportionment approach to contributory negligence. So you can readily apply your new knowledge to it. But in what follows, the emphasis will be on the process through which the remedial instrument has traditionally functioned, and no longer on whether the legal system does or does not provide a remedy. This process-oriented emphasis is deliberate, for a main aim of this chapter is to show the law in action in one of its most important operational instruments.

Why trace an actual case from beginning to end, even a simple one that we have slightly simplified further? If you are truly to understand the basics of the remedial instrument, you must be able to visualize the relevant occurrences during its application. The most satisfactory way to help you visualize that process is by exposure to the events as they occur in the concrete. Moreover, although the process itself breaks down into stages, you can adequately grasp them only in relation to each other. You must study the whole interdependent process through an overview of what occurs at sequential stages and why these stages are as they are. Finally, what follows will serve as useful background for understanding the appellate decisions that appear later in this book because such decisions always concern something that happened "below" during one of the stages in the trial court.

Before finally plunging into the case at hand, several caveats are appropriate. *First*, there are other uses of the remedial instrument besides its use to redress personal injuries negligently caused by others. Nevertheless, such a use is nicely representative. You will encounter some of those other uses in later chapters of this book. *Second*, there are other processes for resolving disputed issues of fact and law besides a compulsory adjudicative process (run by an umpire-like judge) that is adversarially initiated and informed (by active lawyers acting for parties). Such a process has, however, been so dominant in our legal evolution that many people assume it to be intrinsic to the remedial instrument. In Section Six of this chapter, we explore some possible alternatives. *Third*, the particular version of the general adjudicative-adversarial process reflected in the upcoming case is by no means the only version in use in our country. Thus, for example, important differences exist between it and the version in federal courts governed by the so-called Federal Rules of Civil Procedure. Systematically taking account of such differences lies beyond the purposes of this book.

A. Occurrence of Injury

Once upon a time the City of Portland, in the State of Oregon, had a population of 350,000. It also had nineteen swimming areas open to the public. On the evening of June 7, 1958, Sharon Ann Brown, a fifteen-year-old high school student, bought a ticket to swim at a public swimming area located at the huge Jantzen Beach Amusement Park, owned and operated by the Hayden Island Amusement Company on a Columbia River island at the northern outskirts of Portland. The swimming area included four pools: two for wading, one "shallow pool," and one "deep pool."

Ms. Brown was admitted to the pool area. After changing into her swimsuit, she walked to the edge of the shallow pool and dove in, striking her head on the bottom. As a result, she was hospitalized for 31 days with a broken neck, and she thereafter suffered from other ailments, which she traced to the accident. In other words, she had begun her travel upwards through the grievance pyramid.

B. Retaining a Lawyer

Today, the United States has a fast-growing body of well over a million lawyers. Of these, about 700,000 are in private practice, or more than 2 per 1,000 people. Most such lawyers now work as partners or associates in law firms, although many still work as solo practitioners.

Arrangements for the retention of a private-practice lawyer by a client vary considerably. In cases where the plaintiff retains a lawyer to assert a claim for damages for personal injuries, lawyer and client frequently sign a so-called contingent fee agreement whereby the lawyer receives nothing if he recovers nothing but receives a percentage (fixed or variable) of whatever he does recover. In many states, contingent fees of one-third of the recovery are common. By contrast, a lawyer defending against such a personal injury claim would, in many cases, be retained on an hourly basis by an insurance company that had insured the defendant against such liability. Stating a meaningful average fee is difficult, but fees in the range of several hundred dollars per hour are most common.

In America, each party usually pays her own lawyer the agreed fee. At the conclusion of litigation, the court normally awards "costs," to be paid by the losing party to the prevailing party. Costs include relatively small, direct expenses of litigation, such as filing fees, but they ordinarily do not include the large item of counsel fees. (Note that in most of the rest of the world, including England, the losing party also pays the attorneys' fees of the prevailing party.)

In a fairly large city like Portland, how is the typical citizen to locate a good lawyer when she has a need for one? It is not particularly easy. The citizen may know or learn of an attorney through informal contacts or a legal directory or sometimes through the lawyer's advertising or a lawyer referral program sponsored by a bar association.

In the Swimming Pool case, Paul R. Brown, Ms. Brown's father and a worker in a manufacturing plant, considered seeing a lawyer about his daughter's injury but put the idea out of his mind after mulling over "all the difficulties of getting involved with the courts and with lawyers." Over two years later, however, he changed his mind when he became acquainted at a church picnic with a young lawyer named Alonzo P. Stiner. A University of Oregon graduate and an associate in a firm of 15 lawyers, he had been in practice only a year and a half. He had never tried a case entirely on his own, because the senior members of the firm were reluctant to turn over such responsibility to a new associate. But Lon Stiner was eager to try a case alone and knew his chances would be better with his seniors if he brought in a client.

On December 18, 1960, the Browns went to Mr. Stiner's office where, among other things, they signed a contingent fee agreement, calling for the lawyer's firm to receive 30 percent of whatever recovery he secured from the Hayden Island Amusement Company, whether via settlement or via litigation.

C. Lawyer's Preliminary Determinations of Relevant Facts and Law

As we indicated earlier, facts, for purposes of litigation, are not facts as such. Some adjudicative body has to decide what they are, on the basis of what the lawyers put before it. In many cases, much time is wasted because of inadequate factual investigations by a lawyer—and many of those cases are lost.

The good lawyer will seldom make up his mind about the probable facts merely on the basis of an interview with his own client. But in that interview, he will try to be thorough about the facts. On December 18, 1960, the day the Brown family went to Mr. Stiner's office, Stiner interviewed mother, father, and daughter thoroughly, and then they all visited the pool area where the accident had occurred. That evening before going home, Stiner dictated detailed memoranda on the interview and visit.

Here is a puzzle: On the one hand, can a lawyer know what facts are relevant to the legal validity of a claim before he researches the relevant law? (He cannot be expected to carry all such law in his head.) On the other hand, can the lawyer know what law to research before he has determined all the relevant facts? (To complicate things further, not all questions will divide neatly into either questions of pure fact or questions of pure law. In the Swimming Pool case, we shall encounter an important example of a mixed question of fact and law, viz., the question whether a party's conduct in the given case was negligent conduct.) The puzzle's solution lies in approaching the facts and the law as an iterative process: the lawyer's investigation of the facts prompts some research on the law, which induces more and different investigation of the facts, and so on.

It is sometimes said that many claimants' lawyers commence legal proceedings without first investigating the facts and the law very thoroughly. They then need to state their clients' claims generally and in several versions so as not to foreclose the possibility that at least some facts will turn up before or at trial on which some branch of law will allow their clients to recover. We shall have occasion to evaluate this kind of practice at a later point. It may be not all bad.

Other claimants' lawyers at the outset try to be specific in thinking about the facts and about the substantive rules of liability and defense with which they will have to contend. We shall assume that Mr. Stiner is of this ilk.

The first thing such a lawyer will have to concern himself with is whether he can, with some expectation of being able to prove them, allege facts that, if proved, would constitute a *cause of action*. What is a cause of action? You may view it as a legal rule that gives a right to a remedy in specified circumstances, and in the absence of any defense. To ascertain this right, the claimant's lawyer must consult the substantive law. That law will lay down the *elements* of the relevant cause of action—the minimal set of facts the claimant must establish to prevail lawfully. Recall the four elements of the cause of action for negligence: if the defendant owed the plaintiff a *duty* to use reasonable care and if the defendant *breached* that duty so as to *cause* the plaintiff *injury*, then the plaintiff is entitled to a court judgment that plaintiff recover money damages from defendant.

But a good cause of action (or, in modern terminology, a claim) will not, in many cases, be enough, for it is only a prima facie right to a remedy. The defendant may have a good defense, such as contributory negligence. The plaintiff's counsel will do well to check into the facts and the law on this, too. Counsel is bound by the rules of professional conduct not to stir up baseless litigation. Also, he could not afford to waste his time.

Let us assume that Mr. Stiner has turned up probable facts that lead him to conclude that (1) he can justifiably allege facts constituting a cause of action against the Hayden Island Amusement Company for negligence in operating its pool and (2) he can justifiably meet a possible defense by the Hayden Island Amusement Company that Ms. Brown was contributorily negligent and therefore not entitled to recover anything. We may assume, then, that Stiner has dug up two general rules of substantive law of potential relevance, ones you are familiar with: in rough-and-ready terms, these rules are that (1) a defendant who negligently harmed another is liable, (2) unless the plaintiff's negligence contributed to causing the harm.

You should not assume that Mr. Stiner would stop his digging on facts and law at this point. To now we have spoken of preliminary determinations. Through discovery devices and other means to be explained below, he will inform himself further, given that he has decided on the basis of his preliminary determinations that his client appears to have a good case. Incidentally, he knew that it was not too late because, for actions for negligent injury to person or property, Oregon has a ten-year statute of limitations, which is the statute that sets a time limit after an event for commencing a lawsuit.

D. Efforts at Private Settlement

On January 20, 1961, Ms. Brown, on the advice of her parents, agreed to authorize Mr. Stiner to settle the claim for anything at or over two thousand dollars, which would cover medical bills and other related expenses. Stiner then got in touch with the Hayden Island Amusement Company and learned which firm represented the company. After Stiner discussed the claim with a lawyer from that firm on two occasions, it emerged that no settlement could be had, at least none at the two-thousand-dollar figure. Thus, litigation loomed.

You should not assume that settlement efforts always precede steps in litigation. Often the two proceed concurrently. Often neither side makes any effort at settlement until many steps toward trial have been taken. This is not hard to explain. A claimant who starts formal proceedings may lead a doubting potential defendant to take her seriously for the first time, because the defendant will at the very least suffer the expense of having to respond. Furthermore, by starting formal proceedings, the claimant can gain access to those compulsory discovery devices for learning more facts about the case, should she be in the dark.

E. Commencing Legal Proceedings

We have already drawn the distinction between trial courts and appellate courts. In a governmental system such as the American one, each *state* has both these kinds of courts, and the *federal* government itself has both trial and appellate courts as well. Mr. Stiner could bring Ms. Brown's case only in a state court, because there was no basis for federal jurisdiction.

In a typical state judicial system, one finds trial courts of limited jurisdiction (for example, courts handling the probate of wills) and trial courts of general jurisdiction, and also possibly one or more intermediate appellate courts and certainly one ultimate appellate court (usually called the supreme court of the state). Mr. Stiner had to determine in which state trial court he should bring Ms. Brown's case. He properly decided upon the trial court of general jurisdiction named the Circuit Court of the State of Oregon for the County of Multnomah.

How would Mr. Stiner actually commence proceedings against the Hayden Island Amusement Company in that court? He did so on January 26, 1961, by filing with the clerk of the court a *complaint*—a document that stated his client's grievance and asked for an appropriate remedy, and which we shall set out in the next subsection. More precisely, Stiner had to get the court to appoint his minor client's father as her guardian for the purposes of the litigation, and have him make complaint on her behalf.

Next, on February 2, 1961, Mr. Stiner had a copy of the complaint and a *summons* he had prepared served by the Multnomah County sheriff on Ruth Turpin, who was an agent of the Hayden Island Amusement Company registered to receive legal papers. When the complaint and summons are delivered to a defendant, it has a certain number of days in which to respond to the complaint. The actual summons—a document that formally asserts power over the defendant and notifies it of the need to respond to the lawsuit—was addressed to the corporation and read in part as follows.

SUMMONS

You are hereby required to appear and answer the Complaint filed against you . . . within ten days from the date of service of this Summons upon you . . . ; and if you fail so to answer, for want thereof, the plaintiff will take judgment against the defendant in the amount of $1116.35 special damages and $10,000.00 general damages and for costs . . . incurred herein.

F. Pretrial

Lay people are unaware that exceedingly few trials take place today. Most time and money in litigation are expended in pretrial proceedings, which can be quite complicated.

DEFINING AND SEPARATING DISPUTED ISSUES OF FACT AND LAW

After the plaintiff has properly haled the proper defendant before the proper adjudicative body, the next step has traditionally been for the lawyers to go to work *defining* the issues of fact and law to be adjudicated. And this would indeed seem to be the natural next step. If the issues are defined at this stage, the lawyers will not waste time and money preparing for presentation of evidence or argument on matters they really agree on. They will know what they do have to prepare for and can go right to work. Accordingly, many devisers of adjudicative procedure have provided that this next stage in the process would be one of defining issues, largely through *pleadings.*

Because this approach has been so influential, and because the Swimming Pool case proceeded via this approach, we shall here take up, as the next stage in the process, getting the basic issues of fact and law defined. But note that the Federal Rules of Civil Procedure take a different approach. They reflect a belief that expecting the pleadings to define the issues, or do much more than give notice of the parties' opposing positions, is expecting too much and opens the door to abusive practice and inefficient squabbling. So the Federal Rules rely heavily on the use of devices such as discovery, rather than on pleadings, to get the issues defined. Among other things, this means that under the Federal Rules, the two stages of issue definition and of preparation for deciding issues are not so clear-cut and tend to merge.

You may be wondering why we also speak of *separating* issues of fact from issues of law. For now, suffice it to say that in our system, a jury frequently resolves issues of fact, whereas a judge resolves issues of law. And in the Swimming Pool case, a jury was to sit. The system must separate the issues so that each ends up before the proper adjudicator.

Getting back to defining the issues, we have already seen that the plaintiff's lawyer, Mr. Stiner, filed a complaint to which the defendant had to respond within ten days from the date of service. Stiner had drafted the complaint to read basically as follows (you should not assume that we offer any of the pleadings in this case as a model of perfection).

COMPLAINT
IN THE CIRCUIT COURT OF THE STATE OF OREGON
FOR THE COUNTY OF MULTNOMAH

Sharon Ann Brown
by Paul R. Brown, her Guardian ad litem,

Plaintiff,

vs.   No. 271230

Hayden Island Amusement Co.,

Defendant.

COMES NOW Sharon Ann Brown by her Guardian ad litem, Paul R. Brown, and for complaint against the defendant alleges:

I.

That Sharon Ann Brown was at all times mentioned herein and is at the present time a minor child born April 10, 1943.

II.

That Paul R. Brown is her father and the duly appointed Guardian ad litem.

III.

That on June 7, 1958, plaintiff was a paying guest at the swimming pool operated by defendant on Hayden Island, Multnomah County, Oregon.

IV.

That on the above date she, upon arrival at the pool and after changing into her swimming suit, attempted to join her friends in the pool and dived into the pool at the side, gauging the depth of the water at the point where she dived in by the position of the top of the water on the bodies of her friends standing together in the pool at a point near the center of the pool crosswise and approximately even with the point on the side of the pool from which she dived.

V.

That plaintiff reasonably assumed that the depth of the water in the pool was the same from side to side in accordance with the type of construction used generally in the construction of swimming pools; that is, deep in one end and shallow at the other, with a uniform depth from side to side.

Setting up elements of a negligence claim.

VI.

That unknown to plaintiff the depth of the water was not uniform across the pool but was much shallower near the edge from which she dived than at the point even therefrom where her friends were standing.

VII.

That when plaintiff dived into the water her head struck the bottom of the pool, resulting in injuries as hereinafter described.

VIII.

That the sole and proximate cause of said injuries was the negligence of the defendant in the following particulars, to-wit:

(a) In misleading the plaintiff as to the depth of the swimming pool at the place where she dived.

(b) In failing to warn the plaintiff that the bottom of this pool was not constructed in the same manner as other swimming pools in the vicinity of Portland, Oregon, in regard to depth of water near the sides of the pool.

(c) In failing to properly care for the plaintiff by calling a doctor and ambulance after the defendant knew of the accident and injury and the nature thereof.

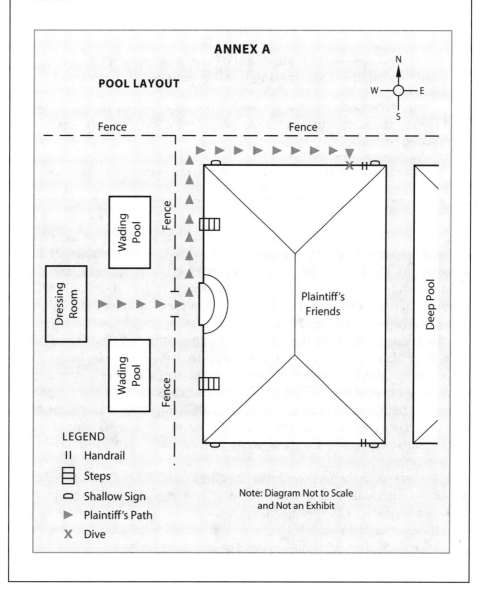

ANNEX A

POOL LAYOUT

Note: Diagram Not to Scale and Not an Exhibit

LEGEND

II   Handrail

     Steps

     Shallow Sign

▶   Plaintiff's Path

X   Dive

IX.

That as a direct and proximate result of the defendant's negligence, the plaintiff's neck was crushed, broken and dislocated; the ligaments, muscles and soft tissues were torn and stretched; her head was cut to a length necessarily requiring approximately fourteen stitches. That on account of such injuries she was necessarily required to have medical attention and on account of her broken neck she was necessarily required to be hospitalized for a period of approximately 31 days; all of which she became obligated to pay in the amount of $1116.35 special damages, the same being a reasonable amount for the services rendered. That plaintiff's injuries are permanent and she has had considerable pain and suffering, all to her general damages of $10,000.00.

X.

That the above medical attention and hospitalization were reasonable necessities furnished to said minor plaintiff in treatment of the aforesaid injuries.

WHEREFORE, plaintiff prays judgment against defendant in the amount of $1116.35 special damages and $10,000.00 general damages and for costs incurred herein.

[Mr. Stiner's signature]

[The diagram Annex A was attached to the foregoing complaint.]

Observe that the complaint includes no explicit references to any rules of law that might support Ms. Brown's claim. In drafting the complaint, it was necessary for Ms. Brown's lawyer only to allege facts that, if proved, would constitute a valid cause of action under the law. But to do this, of course, he had to know the rule of law that entitled a person to compensation for negligently caused harm, and he had to know how this rule had been applied in similar cases.

Observe also that the complaint does not purport to constitute proof of any facts. Instead, it alleges that certain facts occurred, on which Ms. Brown bases her claim. It does not merely allege raw facts, but also alleges some facts in the nature of conclusions, like negligence and causation. In sum, it gives a somewhat particularized mention of each of the elements of the cause of action and their factual circumstances—and it should try to avoid saying anything else, because extra stuff can only cause trouble later on, such as by boxing the pleader in.

If the defendant should deny any of the allegations of fact, then and only then would it be necessary to determine what the facts were. This might be done in a trial, at a later stage of the proceedings.

If the complaint does not set forth the law on which it is based, and if it does not prove facts, then what does it do? For one thing, it informs the defending party that the plaintiff is asserting against him a claim based on those allegations of fact. A fundamental principle of procedural justice is that a person need not satisfy the claim of another if he has not received notice of that claim and had an opportunity to defend against it.

Suppose the defendant simply ignores the service of the complaint and summons? A plaintiff has the power, by properly commencing a legal action, to require the defendant to choose between (1) responding to the complaint and (2) having a judgment entered against him. That is, if the defendant should choose not to respond, the plaintiff would become entitled to a *default* judgment in her favor. And the effect of having a default judgment entered against the defendant for a sum of money would be that the sheriff could lawfully sell enough of the defendant's property to satisfy the judgment.

The legal system thereby gives the plaintiff a significant power. So, normally, the defendant, through his lawyer, responds in some timely fashion to the plaintiff's complaint. On the one hand, his response might conceivably be to *admit* his liability for the relief requested. Upon payment, the proceedings would end. On the other hand, he might choose to *defend*. In so doing, he might take one or more of the following three courses of action.

First, he might say to the plaintiff: "So what? The facts you allege—even if proved—would not constitute a valid legal cause of action." Second, he might say: "I deny the facts you allege. Your side of the story is quite different from mine." Third, he might say: "The facts you allege do not tell the whole story. Other facts afford me a good defense to your cause of action." We shall now take up each of these three basic types of defenses in order.

Consider the first basic defense. Under many systems of adjudicative procedure, including the procedure applicable in the Swimming Pool case, the appropriate pleading for the defendant to use to contest the legal validity of the plaintiff's stated cause of action is called a *demurrer*. In other systems of adjudicative procedure, that issue would be raised by other means, for example, by a "motion to dismiss" under Federal Rule 12(b)(6).

Any rational adjudicative process for resolution of disputed claims in accordance with preexisting general substantive rules would provide some means to test the legal validity of such a claim at some stage in advance of trial. It makes no sense to go to the trouble of determining disputed facts if upon their determination favorably to the claimant she would still not, under the relevant legal rules, be entitled to a remedy. So, a demurrer says, let us assume for the time being that all that the plaintiff alleges is true, and then ask whether the law would give relief.

In common-law systems, the rendering of such preliminary trial-court rulings on the legal validity of causes of action is an important avenue for the growth of the law. A common fallacy about law, already refuted, is that only appellate judges have a hand in lawmaking. Another common fallacy is that general rules already exist by which to test the legal validity of all causes of action. At any given time, various as yet unrecognized causes of action lie just around the corner. By refusing to sustain a demurrer, a trial judge may recognize the validity of a wholly new kind of cause of action. If the judge's action survives any appeal, the judge will have had a hand in making significant new law.

This kind of procedural device generally provided the way much of negligence law developed. Here is a different example: A student sues for breach of contract, alleging that this introductory law course does not live up to its catalog description. The proper response by the lawyer for the defendant university would be a demurrer. And the demurrer would succeed—because as a matter of law, rather than fact, the course description does not form part of the contract between student and university.

Anyway, after arranging for a small delay, Robert T. Mautz, one of the lawyers for the Hayden Island Amusement Company, filed a demurrer to Ms. Brown's complaint on February 27, 1961. The demurrer read in effect as follows, with appropriate heading and signature.

DEMURRER

Defendant demurs to the complaint on the ground that it fails to state a cause of action on which relief can be granted.

The court set March 17, 1961, as the date for the hearing on this demurrer. Commonly, the opposing lawyers will support their respective positions by filing *memoranda of law* with the court around the time for oral argument on the demurrer.

After the hearing on the demurrer, Judge Arlie G. Walker struck paragraph VIII(c) of Ms. Brown's complaint, but otherwise overruled the demurrer. He did so on April 28, 1961. This ruling represented a holding that the defendant had no duty under Oregon law to care for a plaintiff who injured herself. This ruling did not involve any finding of fact, because we know that the procedural device of demurrer temporarily assumes the facts alleged by the plaintiff to be true.

The lawyer for Ms. Brown then amended the complaint, primarily to conform to the ruling of the judge. The amended complaint withstood a new demurrer. Under Oregon law, the defendant did have a duty to avoid negligently injuring the plaintiff. Thus, the court's decision meant that, if at a trial she could prove her remaining allegations, and nothing else was proved, she would be entitled to compensation.

But must there necessarily be a trial? No, a trial is not necessary unless some facts are in dispute between the parties. And only the other two kinds of defenses can produce factual disputes.

The second basic defense that a defendant may raise against the plaintiff's complaint is not that it fails to allege facts constituting a valid legal claim but that the facts alleged are not true. When a defendant so offers a *denial* of some or all of the allegations of the complaint, factual issues arise.

The third basic defense that the defendant may interpose says in effect that the facts alleged do not tell the whole story and that, even if those facts are true, other facts afford a good defense to the cause of action. Such a defense is called an *affirmative defense.* An example is contributory negligence.

The defendant can both deny the plaintiff's allegations and raise affirmative defenses in a pleading called an *answer.* An affirmative defense can also give rise to issues of fact. If the plaintiff denies the defendant's additional facts, further factual issues will arise. In states like Oregon at that time, such a denial would be set forth by the plaintiff in yet another pleading, which is called a *reply.* Also, the plaintiff could use a demurrer to challenge the legal sufficiency of any affirmative defense.

In Ms. Brown's case, the defendant company, through its lawyer Mautz, not only denied most of the allegations in Ms. Brown's complaint but also alleged other facts that, if proved, would constitute a good defense. These denials and also the allegations supporting the affirmative defense were embodied in the defendant's answer. The answer, filed with the court on June 30, 1961, read basically as follows.

ANSWER

In answer to plaintiff's amended complaint, defendant admits, denies and alleges as follows:

I.

Denies the allegations thereof generally and specifically and the whole thereof, except admits the allegations of paragraphs I and II thereof.

For an affirmative defense, defendant alleges:

I.

Any injuries or damages suffered by the plaintiff at the time and place referred to in her amended complaint and herein were proximately caused by her own carelessness and negligence in diving into a swimming pool without ascertaining the depth of the water at the place where she was diving and in failing to take heed of the "shallow" signs at said pool and in making an improper type of dive into the pool in view of the depth of the water at the place where plaintiff dived.

WHEREFORE, defendant prays judgment herein.

The defendant's affirmative defense thus was contributory negligence. Unlike in Illinois at the time of *Alvis*, Oregon's law gave to the defendant the burdens of allegation and of proof as to the failure of the plaintiff to exercise due care.

In response to the answer, and after yet a little more procedural maneuvering, Mr. Stiner filed a reply on August 21, 1961. There were no further pleadings in the case. The reply read in part as follows.

REPLY

COMES NOW plaintiff and for reply to defendant's answer denies each and every allegation and the whole thereof.

WHEREFORE, having fully replied to defendant's answer, prays that plaintiff be given judgment for the relief prayed for in the complaint.

These pleadings are typical of those used in many cases. Looking back, what are the functions of these written documents called pleadings? The complaint tells the defendant why he is being sued. The defendant's demurrer challenges the complaint's sufficiency in law. The defendant's answer denies facts alleged in the complaint and sets forth any affirmative defenses. The reply of the plaintiff denies the allegations constituting any affirmative defenses.

At the conclusion of the pleading stage, what has the system accomplished? In some cases, the court may have decided that the plaintiff had no valid legal cause of action (or the defendant may have admitted all alleged facts but lost on the legal sufficiency of claim and affirmative defense, or the plaintiff may have admitted all alleged facts of an affirmative defense and unsuccessfully challenged its legal sufficiency). That would end the case. Most disputed claims, however, do not so end on the pleadings. Ordinarily, a factual dispute will arise and persist, so that a trial of the facts will appear necessary—and will indeed occur unless the parties themselves reach some settlement before trial (which most often happens).

What, in theory, are these pleadings supposed to accomplish as far as a prospective trial is concerned? The pleadings usually do not go to the jury. But they do serve a number of purposes with respect to trial. First, they disclose whether any facts are in dispute. Thus the parties can determine whether a trial is appropriate. Second, when facts are in dispute, they define what those disputed facts are. As a result, the parties know how to prepare for the trial. Presumably, the parties will not waste time and money on unnecessary preparation. Third, because a party generally cannot introduce evidence at the trial to prove facts not alleged, the pleadings put bounds on the proof and help protect against surprise attacks. Fourth, because the party who alleges facts normally has the burden of proving them, at the end of the pleading stage each party will know what her or his burden of proof is. Fifth, these pleadings separate disputes over fact, which will go to the jury, from disputes over the applicable law, which are for the judge to decide.

Cutting against the pleadings' accomplishing a great deal is the parties' power to amend their pleadings. During the pleading stage or later, even at trial, a party can move to amend a pleading that has proved confining or otherwise troublesome. The judge will allow such an amendment when justice so requires—meaning that the judge will discretionarily balance (1) the fault of the movant for the delay in finally stating her position, less the prejudice to her interests in a full presentation on the merits that would unavoidably be caused by denying the amendment, against (2) any fault of the opponent in inducing the delay, less the delay's prejudice to him that would unavoidably be caused by allowing the amendment, with the judge also throwing onto the balance (3) any considerations of public interest, which usually favor amendment. The judge may allow the amendment subject to conditions, such as a postponement, or continuance, of proceedings to give the opponent time to prepare anew.

At any rate, in Ms. Brown's case, the pleading activity has pared down the complaint. We also know that a jury will have to decide the disputed four elements of the two negligent acts, as well as the elements of the affirmative defense.

The pleading stage has been the subject of this subsection. Any rational system of procedure for resolving claims must provide for pleadings of some kind. Much controversy has arisen in our law over the kind of pleadings that should be required and how much they should be expected to accomplish. Further discussion of this controversy is, however, beyond the scope of an introductory book.

PREPARING FOR TRIAL (AND SEEKING SETTLEMENT OR OTHER DISPOSITION WITHOUT TRIAL)

After the pleading stage, normally a considerable lapse of time occurs before the trial takes place. During this period, the lawyers for plaintiff and defendant will prepare for the trial. They will also usually try to work out a compromise settlement. They attempted to settle Ms. Brown's case, but without success.

In modern procedural systems, pleadings do not do all the official procedural work of getting a case into shape for trial or disposing of the case short of trial. Three other important mechanisms share the burden during this pretrial period: discovery, motion for summary judgment, and pretrial conference. We should take a look at each. Note that the three are not used in all cases or in any fixed order.

Discovery.   The principal problem for the lawyer preparing for trial is to find out how he can best prove his case. This will require an investigation to determine possible witnesses and other sources of evidence that may be presented at the trial. The lawyer who prepares well not only will investigate his own side of the case but also will try to learn as much as possible about the way the opposing lawyer proposes to prove her side of the case.

In preparing for trial, the lawyers do much of this investigation by private means. But because no one is bound to talk with or display papers to an investigator, American law now provides a machinery called discovery, which the lawyer can choose to use in order to compel his target to respond. It allows the lawyer to expand on the notice given by the pleadings. He thereby can clarify and narrow the issues and, especially, can investigate the facts and explore the evidence before trial. This permits him to build his own case and feel out his opponent's case. The system's primary motive behind allowing this pretrial airing of the case is to avoid an inaccurate or unfair outcome determined by the parties' relative capacities for pursuing private investigation and for surviving a blind trial. Discovery might also facilitate settlement; and it might even allow the tried case to proceed more efficiently, as the trial stage becomes more predictable and orderly (and dull).

Discovery can perform these functions better than elaborate pleadings would. Still, questions persist regarding the desirability of the system's trying to perform these functions at all, at least when one moves out of the world of theory and into the reality of litigation. That is, doubts remain whether the benefits of discovery outweigh its costs. Surprise at trial might sometimes act as a promoter of truth, and the discovery weapons sometimes allow browbeating of the opponent. The time and money involved certainly can be staggering, consuming years and millions of dollars in big cases. Nevertheless, most commentators agree that discovery is, and should be, here to stay. In any event, the machinery of discovery, although largely hidden from lay people, has profoundly transformed our procedural system.

Discovery is meant to work almost wholly by action of the parties, without intervention by the court. Nevertheless, to remedy abuse or recalcitrance, anyone involved in the process should be able to invoke the court's assistance in a situation of need. Discovery comprises a variety of specific devices. Oregon law then relied primarily on the two discovery devices called *inspection* and *deposition.*

Inspection is a simple enough concept. A written request to a party for production of any designated documents or other tangible things (or for entry upon land or other property) within that party's possession, custody, or control provides a route for the discovering party to inspect, copy, test, or sample them. The responding party must serve a written response, either agreeing to comply or objecting with good reasons. Similarly, the lawyer may compel a nonparty to produce by using a subpoena.

A deposition is a bit more startling device. A deposition is a proceeding initiated by any party for taking anyone's testimony, in a private setting but otherwise similar to trial—with oral direct examination, cross-examination, and so on. The party can depose any party or any other person, which is, when you think about it, an extraordinary power to bestow on a private person.

In the usual case, leave of court is not needed to initiate the deposition procedure. The discovering party gives reasonable notice in writing to the other parties to the action, specifying the time and place of the deposition and naming the deponent. A nonparty deponent is officially summoned to appear at the deposition, and perhaps to bring and produce documents and other things, by the service upon her of a subpoena. If the deponent is a party, a subpoena need not be used, because the notice of examination itself suffices as a command, and the notice to a party deponent may be accompanied by an inspection request to produce documents and other things at the taking of the deposition.

Typically, the actual oral deposition involves a sworn deponent, a reporter, and a bunch of lawyers sitting around a table in some lawyer's office. Unlike trial, there is no judge, which necessitates recording evidentiary objections. The idea is that the deponent should answer, under any appropriate objection, all questions, except the deponent may refuse to answer particular questions thought to be irrelevant and to call for an answer that would infringe on some privilege or otherwise be damaging or offensive.

Largely because of all the attorneys' time involved, a deposition is very expensive to conduct. But there is no substitute for pinning down a respondent or reaping other fruits of oral testimony.

Observe that a lawyer can use the foregoing procedures to "force" information from people who may otherwise refuse to cooperate. Parties and nonparty witnesses generally cannot keep documents secret or remain silent. This is a vital power given a lawyer preparing for trial. You should consider whether the administration of justice would suffer if lawyers could not compel inspection or testimony prior to trial.

Motion for Summary Judgment.   After the lawyers have completed preparation for trial, and one of them has concluded that the other has insufficient evidence to prove her side of the case, should there be some method of avoiding a trial?

Some legal systems have recognized that a rational system of procedure not only should provide some means of testing the legal basis of a claim or defense in advance of trial, like the demurrer, but also should provide a means of testing its factual basis, like the motion for summary judgment. The latter device is the important tool for determining whether trial is necessary. Providing for summary judgment is a good idea, especially in today's strained procedural system, as it allows weeding out those cases that do not require trial at all. There should be a way to show that an opponent, perhaps a plaintiff trying to extort a settlement or a defendant seeking to delay the day of reckoning, has pleaded allegations with no support whatsoever.

Summary judgment nicely complements the prevailing scheme of bare pleading and extensive discovery. It is broadly available: (1) Either a claimant or a defending party may move, at almost any time in the pretrial period. (2) The motion may concern all or part of any claim. (3) The motion may be made on the pleadings alone, or it may be supported by sworn statements called affidavits, by products of discovery, and by other factual materials, all of which can be used to pierce the pleadings. The procedure aims at revealing whether factual disputes truly exist after all.

Summary judgment will be given to a movant "entitled to a judgment as a matter of law" if "there is no genuine issue as to any material fact." Summary judgment thus allows the judge to decide legal disputes, without trial, when there are no genuine and material factual disputes. The principal inquiry on the motion is whether factual disputes truly exist—it is never how to resolve factual disputes that do exist. If there is a real factual dispute, the judge must deny the motion. In determining whether there is a genuine issue as to any fact, the judge construes all factual matters in the light reasonably most favorable to the party opposing the motion and then asks whether reasonable minds could differ. That is, the judge can grant summary judgment if, looking only at all the evidence that is favorable to the opponent of the motion and also any unquestionable evidence that is favorable to the movant, the judge believes that a reasonable fact-finder could not find for the opponent. Under this standard, disputes on the papers as to objective fact can sometimes be resolved by overwhelming evidence that removes all reasonable doubt, but disputes that turn on credibility cannot. In sum, the prevailing standard is tough to satisfy, in that it will knock out cases only when the opponent would be taking an irrational position in disputing the facts.

Pretrial Conference.   Some legal systems have also recognized that a rational system of procedure should provide a means to propel the case through the pretrial process or to refocus the case just before trial. Such a procedure is the modern judicially supervised pretrial conference.

At any time after commencement of the action, the court in its discretion may direct the attorneys and unrepresented parties to appear before it for one or more pretrial conferences. The key feature (and perhaps the secret strength) of this procedure is that there is no uniform practice, but instead the practice varies from judge to judge, and especially from case to case.

In the piddling case, the court may not hold any pretrial conference. In selected, more difficult cases—typically—the court will call one pretrial conference after discovery and shortly before trial; local rules might require the litigants to engage in an extensive written exchange of views beforehand, and they will have to attend the conference further to reveal fully and fairly their positions and plans; but that conference will properly tend—with some courts' practices in notable disagreement—to be otherwise voluntary in tone and relatively uncomplicated, informal, and nonbinding in format. In the "big case," the court today is likely to be much more active through a series of conferences, all being held in open court and on the record.

A pretrial conference allows the court and the litigants to confer about the case, so moving it along to disposition and molding it for trial. Such a conference may lead to settlement. It should condense and shape the case, as by amending the pleadings, formulating and simplifying the issues, streamlining the proof, or handling any other of a wide variety of pretrial matters. After a pretrial conference, the court must enter a binding order reciting the action taken at the conference, although the order is amendable.

Ms. Brown's Pretrial Experience.   The lawyers had only about two months after the end of the pleading stage in which to prepare for trial. During this time, they made various private investigations, and both visited the scene of Ms. Brown's accident. On August 25, 1961, at the instance of the lawyer for the defendant, Ms. Brown's deposition was taken before an officer, who transcribed the entire proceeding. Although lawyers for both sides were present, the defendant's lawyer asked nearly all of the questions. These related to Ms. Brown's background, the way in which the swimming pool accident happened, and the consequences of the accident. The transcript numbered 37 pages. Remember that this was a simple sort of case.

Oregon procedure at the time was quite rudimentary. It provided neither for a motion for summary judgment nor for a routine pretrial conference. (Today, the Oregon Rules provide for summary judgment, and any trial court has the power to hold a pretrial conference.) Nothing else was to be done in the pretrial period of Ms. Brown's case. Accordingly, on September 7, 1961, the court set October 25, 1961, as the date for the trial.

G. Trial

Much of what the nonlawyer knows of the law has been learned from watching trials or from reading descriptions of trials. For that person, the trial is the heart of the law. But this view is distorted. First, litigation is only one of the many places where the law plays a big role. Second, relatively few litigated cases, even among those in which factual disputes arise, ever reach trial. In the vast majority of cases, the parties, sometimes through their lawyers, are able to negotiate a satisfactory compromise settlement. Perhaps, then, negotiation should be thought of as the heart of the law.

Yet, the law of the courtroom—the law governing the way in which an adjudicator determines the facts of a civil case—is a critical part of that important body of law called civil procedure. An adjudicative process that did not provide a means of resolving factual as well as legal disputes would be unsatisfactory because often there is no dispute as to the applicable law but there is a vigorous dispute as to the facts. Moreover, the law of the courtroom influences the application of law in many other formal and informal contexts. Let us therefore look in some detail at what transpires in the courtroom.

In the United States, the factual basis of a money claim may be tried—at the choice of either party's lawyer—before a jury of six to twelve persons, who will listen to the evidence and at the close of the trial render their decision. A judge will preside throughout the proceedings. (If the parties do not desire a jury, then the judge will decide the facts.) What are the steps in a jury trial of an ordinary case in which one party is asserting a claim against another? There are eight, which we shall then run through for Ms. Brown's trial.

1. As **the trial begins**, the lawyers will each present to the selected jurors a sort of introductory road map of the case entitled an *opening statement*, with which the lawyers help the jury follow the proceedings by outlining

their respective sides of the case and explaining how they propose to prove their allegations of fact.

2. The plaintiff will then present the **case in chief**, introducing her *evidence*. We shall illustrate the way to introduce evidence at a later point in this subsection. After the plaintiff has finished, or *rested*, the defendant's lawyer may think that the plaintiff has not introduced sufficient evidence for a jury to reasonably find that the plaintiff's allegations have been proved. The defendant's lawyer may then move that the judge dismiss the case by granting a *judgment of involuntary nonsuit,* or make an equivalent motion with a different name. He is saying in effect that the plaintiff has put forward her best case and it is not enough to prove negligence or whatever, so there is no need for me to go forward by presenting my case. If that motion is successful, the plaintiff's lawyer might scramble to cure the defect by moving to amend the plaintiff's complaint or reopen her case in order to introduce more evidence.

3. If the judge denies the defendant's motion, the defendant will then present his **case in defense**, introducing evidence either trying to meet the plaintiff's allegations or trying to prove new matter on which the defendant has the burden of proof.

4. To meet new facts put in evidence by the defendant, the plaintiff can next offer **rebuttal** evidence. Conceivably, the defendant could then introduce rebutting evidence, and so on.

5. After all of the evidence has been introduced, if either lawyer thinks that the thrust of the entire evidence of both parties is so strong in his client's favor that no reasonable jury could find for his opponent, he may then make a **motion** for a *directed verdict.* When the judge directs a verdict, she in effect decides the facts herself, for she renders a judgment in favor of the moving party. Is this an invasion of the province of the jury? No, jurors are supposed to decide only genuine issues of fact, issues over which reasonable persons could differ. If the overwhelming weight of the evidence is on one side, then reasonable jurors could not differ, and the judge should withdraw the case from the jury. However, this standard is stringent, so that a directed verdict is proper only in very lopsided cases.

6. If the motion or motions for a directed verdict are denied, the time has come for **arguments**. Each lawyer will then, in turn, make a *closing argument* to the jury, in which he will review the evidence and advance reasons why the jury should return a verdict in favor of his client.

7. The trial judge will then give **instructions** to the jury, in which she will state the applicable law and tell the jury what findings they would have to make in order to render a verdict for the plaintiff and what findings they would have to make in order to render a verdict for the defendant.

8. Thereafter, the jury, after retiring to deliberate in the jury room, will return a *verdict.* The judge will then entertain motions to render *judgment notwithstanding the verdict* (for example, on the ground that the judge

should have granted a motion for a directed verdict) or to grant a *new trial* (for example, on the ground that the judge committed some error of law during the trial), and she will rule thereon. As **the trial stage ends**, the clerk of the court will enter a *judgment.* From it, an appeal will then be possible.

Ms. Brown's Trial Begins

Ms. Brown's case went to trial before a twelve-person jury on October 25, 26, and 27, 1961. After selecting a jury, the lawyers, Mr. Stiner for the plaintiff and Mr. Bruce Spaulding for the defendant, made their opening statements. The presiding judge, Judge Ralph M. Holman, then told the jury that they, along with the judge and the lawyers, would take a bus to the scene of the accident. This visit to the swimming pool provided the jurors with background for understanding the testimony to follow.

Plaintiff's Case in Chief

Upon returning from the scene, the presiding judge asked Mr. Stiner to call his first witness to the witness stand. This witness, a Dr. E.G. Chuinard, who had treated Ms. Brown, testified as to the nature and the extent of the injuries she had suffered as a result of diving into the defendant's pool. The questions by Stiner, and the answers by Chuinard, follow in part:

Q: What did you find in your examination? Did you find any fractures?

A: Yes. On the physical examination, the patient had marked spasm and guarding of the neck against all motion. She also had a laceration on the scalp, which is about two inches long and which had been sutured. The X rays showed that she had a fracture of the first cervical vertebra and another fracture of the fifth cervical vertebra. The fracture of the first one, which is the first vertebra in the neck directly under the head, was comminuted or compressed. And the fifth vertebra had a fracture out of it, out of the body of the vertebra, and was dislocated forward on the vertebra below it.

Q: I assume they are the X rays that were taken?

A: Yes.

    MR. STINER: May I have these marked for identification, your Honor?

    THE COURT: I believe they are already marked.

    MR. SPAULDING: There will be no objection to admitting them into evidence.

    THE COURT: One through seven are received.

    (Whereupon Plaintiff's Exhibits Nos. 1 to 7 inclusive were received in evidence. X rays.)

Q: (By Mr. Stiner) At this time, doctor, I would like to hand you Plaintiff's Exhibits 1 through 7 so you may use those and explain the injuries that the plaintiff sustained.

. . . .

Q: Doctor, did you feel the injuries that Sharon had sustained were of a permanent nature?

A: Yes, definitely. These X-ray findings will never change. I think that it is reasonable that the things that she complains of now, such as fatigue, tiring, aching with the fatigue, are due to the accident. She certainly disclaimed having them before. And, very reasonably, this degree of injury would be the cause of these symptoms.

Q: In other words, the dislocation is something of a permanent nature; the bone that you showed dislocated—

A: The dislocation is not there. That has been reduced. But the defect in the bone is there.

Mr. Spaulding then briefly cross-examined the doctor, along these lines:

Q: Doctor, you said that the dislocation had been reduced. By that do you mean that it has been eliminated?

A: There is no dislocation now.

Q: And is the motion in her neck now back to normal?

A: It is within normal range, yes.

. . . .

Q: Could you tell what the direction of force was that caused these injuries to her neck? Would it be straight down?

A: Well, of course, I had the benefit of this patient's history; that she dove into a tank. And putting that together with the laceration on her scalp, I felt that she probably had a blow directly on the top of her head. This I would accept without question as being a reasonable producing cause of the neck fractures.

Q: She was apparently diving straight down?

A: Yes.

The next witness called to the stand by Mr. Stiner, on the next day, was the plaintiff, Sharon Brown. We present part of her testimony given in response to questions by Stiner, followed by part of her testimony given in response to cross-examination by Mr. Spaulding. Then follows further testimony in response to questions by Stiner, and so on.

Note that all this testimony is still part of the plaintiff's case in chief. In other words, as the plaintiff's lawyer presents his case, the defendant's lawyer is not totally passive but instead participates in the presentation of evidence, primarily by cross-examination.

Direct Examination

By Mr. Stiner:

Q: Would you state your name and address for the record?

A: Sharon Brown, 11525 Southeast Powell, Portland, Oregon.

Q: That's your home address. What is your temporary address at the present time?

A: At the present time I am living at Lausanne Hall, which is at the campus at Willamette University.

Q: Where did you live in June of 1958?

A: In June, 1958, I lived on 71st and Harold in Southeast Portland.

Q: And where did you go to school? Let's start with grade school.

A: I went to two grade schools: I went to Buckman Grade School for the first and second grades and then I transferred to Arleta Grade School where I completed grade school.

Q: Where did you go to high school?

A: I went two years to Franklin High and then my junior and senior years I went to David Douglas High School.

. . . .

Q: Do you want to tell us a little bit about your swimming, what experience you have had, when you started swimming, and so forth?

A: Well, we lived at—when we lived at 71st and Harold we lived right across from the Mount Scott Pool and so for about six years I was swimming almost every day of the summer and I hadn't swum before that time. But as soon as we moved there I began swimming and I swam for six years steadily.

. . . .

Q: . . . Were you an average swimmer or better than average swimmer?

A: I was a better than average swimmer. I had had quite a bit of experience.

Q: Had you ever done any diving?

A: Yes.

Q: Would you tell us about your diving?

A: Well, I had done diving off of a board and the side and was doing some kinds of trick diving that you just fool around with.

Q: So, in other words, you did all types of diving?

A: Yes.

Q: When did you start your diving . . . ?

A: Oh, I started diving about a year after I first started to swim, about the fourth grade.

Q: Can you explain to us briefly what the Mount Scott Pool is like?

A: The Mount Scott Pool is only composed of two pools—a shallow pool and a deeper pool. The shallow pool was towards the dressing rooms as you come out of the dressing room. The shallow pool is before you and beyond that is the deeper pool. Facing in this direction the diving board is in the left-hand side of the deeper pool, and so the deepest side of the deep pool is in the left and so it gets shallower towards the right. . . .

. . . .

Q: ...Now, you say, Sharon, you had been accustomed of diving in the shallow pool at Mount Scott. Was that a common practice?

A: Yes, it was.

Q: For both yourself and other people?

A: Yes.

Q: In other words, your friends would dive in that pool?

A: That's right. And I have a brother who's two years younger than I am and who is also a swimmer and did that diving.

Q: And I assume there are other people besides you and your brother?

A: Oh, yes, definitely.

Q: What type of diving did you do?

A: Oh, from the side, shallow diving.

MR. SPAULDING: You are now talking about the Mount Scott Pool, aren't you?

MR. STINER: Yes.

. . . .

Q: And you mentioned the depth of the Mount Scott shallow pool was what?

A: At that spot in the pool it's approximately four to five feet deep.

Q: Was it deeper in any other parts?

A: In any other or than any—

Q: No, no, in any other parts what was the depth?

A: That was the deepest part of the shallow pool.

Q: Four to five feet?

A: Yes.

Q: And people commonly dived in this pool?

A: Yes.

Q: And now, on June 7th did you go to Jantzen Beach to go swimming?

A: Yes, I did.

. . . .

Q: Now, when you came around the pool what did you see, other than what you described so far, let's say when you came around the corner there?

A: Well, I saw what I thought was the same kind of arrangement as the Mount Scott Pool, a shallow pool and a deep pool; and I took it for granted that this spot where I dove in would be deeper, as it was at the Mount Scott Pool.

Q: Did you see your friends in the pool?

A: Yes, I did.

Q: How deep was the water where they were?

A: Approximately chest deep.

Q: About how tall were your friends?

A: They varied in height from about, oh, five-eleven to six, six-three.

Q: In other words, they were fairly tall?

A: Yes.

Q: When you saw the water on your friends did you draw any conclusions as to the depth of the water in the pool where you were to dive?

A: Yes, I did. I figured if it was that deep on them, then it must be even deeper towards this end, since I figured that was a gradual deepening of the water towards where I was standing so I assumed it would be deep enough for a dive.

Q: Did you see any signs at all indicating the depth of the pool?

A: No, I didn't.

Q: Did you look for them?

A: I glanced around before I dove in but there were no signs that I could see.

Q: Did you see any other signs of any nature indicating that you should not dive in this pool?

A: No, I didn't.

Q: When you came upon the pool was there any question in your mind that this was not what is termed the shallow pool?

A: No, I knew that it was a shallow pool....

. . . .

Q: What type of a dive did you do? Would you describe that to us?

A: I did a shallow dive.

Q: Well, would you describe what is a shallow dive?

A: It's rather hard to describe; at an angle, at—about a forty-five degree angle to the pool.

. . . .

Q: Did you stop stationary at the pool before you dove in or was it a running dive, or what kind of a dive?

A: I paused just before I came to the edge and I took about two steps before I dove.

Q: Well, would you term that a running dive?

A: It's kind of in-between.

. . . .

Q: Would you describe what happened, now, when you dove into the pool?

A: Well, I dove into the pool and my hands hit the bottom and jerked back and my head hit and I realized I had obviously hit the bottom of the pool and I stood up and I was pretty dizzy, although I wasn't unconscious, and the kids around me asked me if I was all right and I said yes, I was. The only thing that was abnormal about me at that time was that I couldn't turn my head from side to side in that direction like that (indicating). And they suggested that I go back into the warmer water of the deep pool because the warmer water might make my neck feel better. They kind of assumed that I just wrenched it. No one had thought that I had broken my neck, none of us did, so I got into the deeper pool, which had warmer water, thinking that it might help a little bit.

Q: What did you do then?

A: I breast stroked across the pool, up to the middle wall between the deep and shallow pool, to that point, where a few of my friends were standing and the girls started massaging my neck hoping that it would help, which of course it didn't, and since that didn't help one of the girls told me I had blood on my lip so I went into the dressing room and took off my bathing cap; and when I took off my bathing cap that blood came cascading down and I realized I had cut my head and the bathing cap had not split but it had been holding the blood up there all this time and I was pretty shocked. . . .

. . . .

Q: . . . I want to ask you when you stood up in the water after you dove in and hit your head, how deep was the water upon you then?

A: My recollection is rather hazy. I think it was about waist deep, as I can remember, on me.

. . . .

Q: How deep would that be in terms of feet?

A: About three feet deep.

. . . .

Q: . . . I want to go back and ask you one more question about the Jantzen Pool. Had you ever been to the Jantzen Pool before this time?

A: No, I hadn't.

Q: Had you ever heard of anybody talking about it with regard to the construction of the pool?

A: No, I had never heard anybody talk about it in regards to construction.

Q: How had you heard people talk about it?

A: Well, I knew there was a pool at Jantzen Beach and that's where we were going. That's all I heard about it.

Q: Before you went did you have knowledge of how pools are built, in other words, the shallow pool and a deep pool, this two-pool setup?

A: Well, my knowledge as to how swimming pools in general were built was based on my previous experiences with the Mount Scott Pool and pools around that area where I had gone swimming.

. . . .

Q: When you went out to the Jantzen Pool— now, back to the 7th of June—was there anything to indicate to you that you should not dive into this pool?

MR. SPAULDING: We object to that question, your Honor, as calling for a conclusion.

THE COURT: Objection sustained.

Q: (By Mr. Stiner) Were there any signs indicating you should not dive into the pool?

A: No.

Q: Did anyone tell you or indicate to you that you should not dive into the pool?

MR. SPAULDING: Your Honor, I object to the question as leading and—

THE COURT: Objection overruled. Go ahead.

Q: (By Mr. Stiner) Was anything said to you? Do you want to answer that last question?

A: No, there was nothing said to me.

Q: Did you see anything indicating that you should not dive into the pool?

MR. SPAULDING: I object to that question again, your Honor, as calling for a conclusion.

THE COURT: You may ask her if she saw any signs, or anything of that kind, but you are getting pretty general.

MR. STINER: I have no further questions, your Honor.

Cross-Examination

By Mr. Spaulding:

Q: You say you arrived out there at Jantzen Beach between six and seven?

A: Approximately between six and seven.

Q: And in June that's broad daylight, isn't it?

A: I'd say it's dusk.

. . . .

Q: Well, could you see, for instance, to read outdoors there where you were by the pool? Was it that light?

A: I guess I probably could read. We didn't have to have headlights coming down to Jantzen Beach.

Q: Now, I understand you had been doing some substantial swimming and diving for, what, ten years or—no, seven or eight years before this?

A: Six or seven years.

Q: You mentioned that you did some trick diving. What kinds of trick diving have you done?

A: Well, things like diving backwards and doing sailor dives and—

Q: What is the sailor dive?

A: Oh, that's diving with your hands down at your side, just diving in. You don't do this sort of dive in a shallow pool.

. . . .

Q: Now, when you went there to that pool, you say you knew before you went in that it was a shallow pool?

A: I knew when I saw the way the pools were arranged that it was a shallow pool.

Q: And that's before you went in the water?

A: Before I went in the water, yes, sir.

Q: And then you said you looked around, or you said you glanced around before you dove. What were you glancing around for?

A: Well, any indication that it might be dangerous to dive.

Q: Well, you already knew that the water was shallow?

A: Yes, sir.

Q: And there were a lot of other people in that shallow pool besides your friends, were there not?

A: I really don't remember.

Q: Don't you remember on your deposition that you took you told us about other people being there?

A: I said there could have been and there more than likely would have been. It was on a weekend and—

Q: Well, when you glanced around to see if there was any indication of anything, did you look around to see how far the water came up on people in various parts of that pool?

A: No, I just looked at my friends.

Q: Oh? Well, on your deposition, with reference to other people around there, was this your testimony? This is page fourteen:

> Q: Was there anybody else in the shallow pool at the time you dove in?
>
> A: Yes, sir.
>
> Q: And were they all over the pool or in any particular spot?
>
> A: They were scattered throughout the pool. There were a few in this place and a few in this other place. They weren't all grouped together.
>
> Q: So people generally scattered around throughout the pool?
>
> A: Yes, sir.

Was that your testimony on your deposition?

A: Yes, sir, it was.

Q: And does that refresh your memory now with reference to people being scattered all around the pool?

A: What I meant by that, I knew that there weren't any grouped around my friends.

Q: That you what?

A: That there weren't any people grouped around my friends. My friends were in a general group around the pool. If there were any other people around in the pool they weren't in a central group, they were scattered around.

Q: That's what you meant here, that there were people scattered all around but you weren't paying any particular attention to them?

A: I wasn't paying attention to them, yes.

. . . .

Q: The Mount Scott Pool you had swum in hundreds of times, probably?

A: Yes, sir.

Q: And so the thing that the difficulty arose over, you assumed that this—pool out here was constructed the same as the Mount Scott Pool?

A: Yes, sir.

Q: And that is, would have a deep place in the same corner as the Mount Scott Pool had a deep place?

A: Yes, sir.

. . . .

Q: Now, have you on occasion ever scraped the bottom when you dove at Mount Scott?

A: By "scraped the bottom" do you mean brush your nose against the bottom?

Q: No, anything.

A: Yes, I have done that. I have skinned my nose a few times.

. . . .

Q: ...Now, the water was clear out there at Jantzen Beach so that you could see the bottom, wasn't it?

A: Yes, sir.

. . . .

Q: And you knew, I take it from your testimony, that all pools would have different depths at different parts of the pool?

A: I don't quite understand your question.

Q: Well, like you knew at the Mount Scott shallow pool that it was deeper in some places than it was at others.

A: Yes, sir.

Q: And you knew that all pools have places in them that are deeper than other places in the pools?

A: Yes, sir.

Q: You say you had no information about where it was deeper or where it was shallower at Jantzen excepting that you supposed it was like Mount Scott?

A: That's right.

Q: Now, you say that at the place where you dove, your best estimate is that the water was about three feet deep there?

A: Yes, and that's a rough estimate.

Q: I understand that, doing the best you can as in your condition after you were hurt?

A: That's right.

Q: And about how many feet of water would you say would be required to safely make the type of dive that you did make?

A: I would say that I had been used to doing this type of a dive in four feet of water.

MR. SPAULDING: I think that's all.

THE COURT: Anything further?

MR. STINER: I have a few, your Honor....

. . . .

Redirect Examination

By Mr. Stiner:

Q: Sharon, there were some questions at the first part of the cross-examination regarding the light problem. Was there any problem in seeing?

A: No.

Q: There was also some talk about sailor dives. Had you ever been injured doing a sailor dive?

A: No.

. . . .

Q: With reference to your deposition and the number of people in the pool, in the area where you dived, in the immediate area, were there any other people?

A: No.

Q: Was anybody standing along the wall?

A: No.

Q: That would be the north wall.

A: No, sir.

. . . .

Q: ...Is there any indication of the depth of the water where you dove in?

A: Not that I could see.

Q: You saw the boys in the middle of the pool?

A: Yes, sir.

Q: Where was the water upon them?

A: About chest deep.

Q: Did you notice the railing there before you dove in?

MR. SPAULDING: What's that?

MR. STINER: The rail before you get out of the pool at the north end.

Q: (By Mr. Stiner) I assume, then, before you dove into the pool there was something more than just your knowledge of the Mount Scott Pool regarding the depth here, is that right?

A: Yes, sir.

Q: And what was that?

A: Well, I assumed that it must be deep enough to require one of those handrailing things to get out of the water.

Q: Anything else?

A: Other than the fact that I assumed it must be at least as deep as approximately chest deep on my friends.

MR. STINER: I have no further questions, your Honor.

Recross-Examination

By Mr. Spaulding:

Q: You mean when you went around there and walked over towards the place where you took two steps and a partial running dive you considered all those things, that they would not construct a handrail and a ladder unless it was chest deep on you? You considered—

A: In considering these things I didn't stand there and say, "Now, it's chest deep on my friends and there's a handrail there so it must be at least as deep on me." I just kind of generally took in the whole situation and drew a conclusion, I guess.

Q: You looked at the bottom? You could see the bottom through the water?

A: Yes.

Q: You saw some steps that went down, didn't you, into the shallow pool, steps that you'd walk into the pool as distinguished from how it is over here where you dive in (indicating)?

A: Yes, sir.

Q: What did you think they meant, though, when you were considering these things before you dove?

A: That it must be pretty shallow in that part.

MR. SPAULDING: That's all.

MR. STINER: Two more questions, then.

Redirect Examination

By Mr. Stiner:

Q: Can you tell how deep the pool is by looking at the bottom?

A: No.

Q: Where were the steps that counsel is referring to?

A: On the right-hand side and the left-hand side of the circular steps in the front of the pool.

. . . .

MR. STINER: No further questions.

THE COURT: You may step down.

In completing his case, Mr. Stiner called three additional witnesses to testify, each of whom Mr. Spaulding cross-examined. These were Mr. and Mrs. Paul Brown (Ms. Brown's parents) and Mr. Harold E. Milliken (assistant chief sanitary engineer for the state board of health). Mr. Brown testified, in part, that he had viewed the Jantzen Beach pool several times, but the first time, sometime probably in July 1958, he saw only faintly imprinted "shallow" signs. Mrs. Brown supported that testimony. Mr. Milliken testified, in part, that he knew of no pools other than the $165' \times 100'$ Jantzen Beach pool that were shallow all around and sloped toward the middle, and that no purpose other than drainage was served by having a pool deep at one end and shallow at the other.

At the close of the plaintiff's case, the following events occurred:

MR. STINER: Plaintiff will rest, your Honor.

THE COURT: Defendant may proceed.

MR. SPAULDING: I have a matter we ought to take up in chambers, I suppose.

THE COURT: Very well. We will have a recess. The court reporter and counsel in chambers.

(Whereupon the Court and counsel for the respective parties retired to the Court's chambers out of the presence of the jury and the following proceedings were had, to-wit:)

MR. SPAULDING: The defendant moves to the Court for a judgment of involuntary nonsuit in favor of the defendant and against the plaintiff for the reason that there is no evidence in the case to show any negligence on the part of the defendant that was the proximate cause of the injury to the plaintiff; and for the further reason that the evidence affirmatively shows that plaintiff was negligent as a matter of law proximately contributing to her injury.... I am not going to argue unless you want me to.

....

THE COURT: ...I will deny defendant's motion for involuntary nonsuit. Exception allowed.

An "exception" is a party's formal objection to a legal decision, recorded at trial and intended to preserve the point for possible appeal. Next, sensing a weakness in the plaintiff's case, Mr. Stiner took a protective step:

MR. STINER: Comes now the plaintiff and moves this Court to amend Paragraph VIII, Subsection (a) to read in the place of that portion stricken the following: "In failing to provide adequate markings showing the depth of the water in the pool." And this motion is made so as to conform with the evidence.

THE COURT: Do you have any objection, Mr. Spaulding?

MR. SPAULDING: Yes, we object to it. In the first place, it doesn't conform to the evidence and it brings in a new element in the case without adequate notice to the defendant so the defendant can properly prepare for trial. It is not sufficiently definite and certain as to what we have failed to provide in the way of markings, and it takes us by surprise.

THE COURT: The motion will be allowed and exception allowed to the defendant.

MR. SPAULDING: Will we be permitted a time to reinvestigate our case?

THE COURT: How much time do you want, Mr. Spaulding?

MR. SPAULDING: Probably one day.

THE COURT: You mean until tomorrow morning. That will give you all afternoon now being a quarter to three.

MR. SPAULDING: I just can't tell how long it would take me, but I would hope that I can do it by tomorrow afternoon.

THE COURT: Off the record.

(Whereupon an off-the-record discussion was had.)

MR. SPAULDING: I have announced that I am unable to find anybody to go get my witness and I am willing to go ahead.

THE COURT: All right. I want the record to show that I am willing to give you additional time if you desire.

MR. SPAULDING: Yes, you told me that and I said that I am willing to go ahead.

THE COURT: All right, let's go.

Defendant's Case in Defense

The only witness called by Mr. Spaulding to testify on behalf of the defendant company was Mr. J.F. Turpin, manager of Jantzen Beach Amusement Park, whom Mr. Stiner cross-examined. Mr. Turpin testified on direct examination in part as follows:

Q: ...Mr. Turpin, are there markings around that pool showing the various depths of the water?

A: You are talking about the shallow pool?

Q: Yes, the shallow pool?

....

A: Yes, there are figures that show the depth of the pool.

Q: How long have they been there?

A: Well, they have been there for six years that I know of.

Q: And you say six years because that's the length of time you have been manager?

A: That's right, that's right.

Q: Well, just describe where those markings are and what they say.

A: Well, they are a set of steps on either side of the fountain as you come out of the dressing room and on either side there are markings of the depth of the water.

Q: And what does it say?

A: Two feet.

Q: And then what about on the north end of the shallow pool?

A: When the pools were built on the north side, on either side, more or less about twenty-five per cent of the end in from either side, they are embedded in tile and it says "Shallow." They are embedded, as I remember, in white tile with red markings signifying shallow.

....

Q: ...What time of the year do you repaint these markings?

A: Well, we opened the pool the 15th of May this year and they were painted previous to our opening.

Q: Well, that's this year. How about '58?

A: The same. I can't remember what date we opened in '58, to be very frank with you, but they were painted before we opened the pool.

Q: And what color of paint?

A: Red.

Q: Red?

A: Red.

. . . .

Q: ...Now, has there ever been any complaint about your pool from any authority?

MR. STINER: Objection to it, your Honor.

THE COURT: Objection sustained. It doesn't make any difference whether there was or not.

MR. SPAULDING: I think that's all....

Rebuttal

Mr. Stiner recalled Mr. Paul Brown to the stand and asked more about the signs seen at the pool in July 1958. Then Mr. Spaulding cross-examined, concluding:

Q: You didn't particularly look all around, did you?

A: We walked all along the wire there.

Q: But you never got inside the pool?

A: No, there was the wires.

Q: And you didn't ask to get inside?

A: No, there was nobody around there, sir.

Q: Nobody around there in July?

A: Well, I don't know. There wasn't anybody at the fence.

MR. STINER: Object to the question. It's improper cross-examination.

THE COURT: Objection overruled.

Q: (By Mr. Spaulding) You say there was nobody by the fence?

A: There was nobody there, that's right, by the fence. We parked the car outside there and went to the gate out by the parking lot.

Q: And you didn't go in the office to see if you could get a view right there?

A: No, we didn't.

Q: And you didn't do that either on the second occasion you were there?

A: No, we didn't, sir.

Q: And that fence is quite a high fence there that's several feet from the edge of the pool?

A: As near as I could estimate I'd say about eight, nine feet, sir.

MR. SPAULDING: I think that's all.

THE COURT: You may step down.

(Witness excused.)

MR. STINER: Plaintiff will rest, your Honor.

Motion

THE COURT: We will have a short recess prior to argument, gentlemen. The jury can retire.

(Whereupon the midafternoon recess was taken.)

MR. SPAULDING: At this time the defendant moves for a directed verdict in favor of defendant and against plaintiff for the same reasons and upon the grounds as stated with reference to the motion for involuntary nonsuit.

THE COURT: Motion denied, exception allowed.

MR. SPAULDING: Very well.

Arguments

THE COURT: You may proceed with your argument, Mr. Stiner.

(Whereupon counsel for the respective parties presented their closing arguments to the jury.)

THE COURT: Ladies and gentlemen of the jury, we are going to recess now until tomorrow morning when I will instruct you. It is not proper that you discuss this case with anybody, not even among yourselves, and until such time as you have been instructed and have retired to the jury room to deliberate. When you are back in the jury room deliberating, you can discuss it to your heart's content, but prior to that time with no one.

Now we are switching courtrooms tomorrow, and tomorrow morning we will be in Courtroom 540 down on the fifth floor....

Instructions

THE COURT: Ladies and gentlemen of the jury, it is now my duty to instruct you upon the law of this case and it is your duty to follow my instructions. Your determination of the facts and as to what actually happened and what the circumstances were is final and I can't interfere with that. But those facts, before they can be interpreted in the form of a judgment, must first have the law applied to them as I give it to you and you have to take that as I say it is.

Now, the plaintiff in this case is Sharon Ann Brown. She comes into court and she says that she suffered certain personal injuries as the result of the negligence of the defendant. . . .

. . . .

To this the defendant files an answer and defendant denies the contentions that plaintiff makes in her complaint. The defendant denies that it is in any way responsible for the accident, denies that it was negligence and denies that it owes any money to the plaintiff; and, as a matter of fact, they say that the plaintiff herself was contributorily negligent in these three particulars: 1, in diving into a swimming pool without ascertaining the depth of the water at the place where she was diving and, 2, in failing to take heed of the shallow sign at said pool and, 3, in making an improper type of dive into the pool in view of the depth of the water at the place where plaintiff dived. And then defendant says that this was the cause of plaintiff's injuries, was her own negligence. Then in turn the plaintiff comes back and denies everything that the defendant has said in its answer about her being negligent.

Now, these make up the issues in this case. Before plaintiff is entitled to recover, she must recover on these issues and the issues that are made in these pleadings alone and not otherwise.

Now to start out with, the slate is clear. The presumption is that persons are not negligent and are not careless; therefore, the presumption is in this case that neither the plaintiff nor the defendant was negligent or at fault in any way. So, when plaintiff charges in her complaint that the defendant was guilty of negligence, the burden of proof is upon her to prove such claims by a preponderance of the evidence and in the absence of such proof she cannot recover; likewise, when defendant in its answer claims the plaintiff was guilty of negligence, the burden of proof is upon it to prove such claims by a preponderance of the evidence.

By preponderance of the evidence is meant the outweighing of the evidence. It doesn't necessarily mean the greater number of witnesses nor the greater volume of evidence; it is that evidence which is more convincing, more worthy of belief, and which makes out the better case. It means that the facts asserted must have been proved more probably true than false.

If after consideration you cannot make up your minds who has made the better case upon a particular point, the burden of proof has not been carried as regards this point.

Now, the defendant has charged negligence against the plaintiff in three particulars. It isn't necessary for the defendant to prove all three of the acts of negligence charged to prove that the plaintiff was negligent, but it is necessary that one or more be proved before the burden of proof is sustained in this regard.

Now, what is negligence? Negligence is the doing of that or the failure to do that which a reasonably careful person would or would not have done under the same or similar circumstances. It's just a common-sense rule. In other words, in this case the law requires that the plaintiff take due care to keep from injuring herself and that is such care as a reasonably prudent person of her age and her experience would have taken under the same and similar circumstances to prevent injury to herself.

Now, what is the duty of the landowner in this particular case? In this particular case, the plaintiff being a paying customer at defendant's place of business, the plaintiff is known at law what we call an invitee. And what I am going to read to you now is the responsibility which the invitor has to his invitee in the conduct of his premises and his business. The possessor, and when I say possessor in this particular case, I mean the defendant in this particular case, is required to exercise reasonable care and to warn the invitee, that is, the plaintiff in this case, or to make the premises safe for her as to conditions of which the possessor knows or those which he could discover with reasonable care.

Now, when you decide whether or not this defendant has complied with that duty which the law lays upon it, you should consider that in considering whether the defendant has complied with this standard of care, that the rules should be applied to them: What would have a reasonably prudent person done under the same and similar circumstances? In other words, that standard of care is the standard of care which is put up to the defendant in deciding whether or not it has complied with this duty which the law lays upon it.

Now, should you find from the evidence that the defendant was negligent....Before plaintiff may recover, such negligence must be the proximate cause of the accident and her injuries.

What do we mean by proximate cause? By proximate cause is meant the thing which actually caused the injury. It need not be the only cause but it must be one of them and such as might have been reasonably foreseen as leading to injury. A person may do a negligent act but unless that negligence directly causes an injury it is not the proximate cause and such person is not responsible; likewise, if you should find from the evidence that plaintiff was guilty of negligence in one or more of the particulars claimed in defendant's answer, before such negligence will prevent a recovery by plaintiff it must be the proximate cause of the accident and her injuries under the rule of proximate cause which I have just given.

A party asserting that certain claimed negligence was the proximate cause of the accident has the burden of proving it by a preponderance of the evidence the same as any other claim that they make. Now, the defendant in charging the plaintiffs negligence caused or contributed to the accident and her injuries has thereby raised the defense of contributory negligence. Contributory negligence consists of acts or omissions charged by the defendant amounting to negligence on the part of the person injured which were a proximate cause of her injuries. If you find from all the evidence in this case that plaintiff was guilty of such negligence, even though the defendant might be negligent also, there could be no recovery. Now, that's just a nice way of saying that if they were both at fault in this matter and that fault contributed to the happening of the accident, then there could be no recovery.

Now, if you find from the evidence that defendant was guilty of negligence in one or more of the particulars set out in plaintiff's complaint which was the proximate cause of the injuries to plaintiff, and that plaintiff was free from negligence which was the proximate cause of the accident and her injuries, then and only then would you have a right to go to the question of damages....

. . . .

You ladies and gentlemen can just remain seated while I retire into chambers with counsel so they may take an opportunity to take exceptions to the instructions I may or may not have given.

(Whereupon the Court and counsel for the respective parties retired to the Court's chambers out of the presence of the jury and the following proceedings were had, to-wit:)

THE COURT: Are there any exceptions on instructions as given, by the plaintiff?

. . . .

MR. STINER: The only other exception I have is that the Court referred to the question of coming down to negligence and contributory negligence as determining if parties were at fault.

THE COURT: And that fault contributed to the accident, I added.

MR. STINER: And I believe this is misleading as it does not distinguish between the duties of the parties regarding the defendant's part to a business invitee.

THE COURT: You don't contend that I didn't in another part of my instruction, and just previous to this, state what their duties were and apply the rules to it?

MR. STINER: Yes, but I did not hear it stated that the girl was to be considered in the light of a reasonably prudent fourteen-year-old girl.

THE COURT: I am sure that I did say that. I—

MR. SPAULDING: Of her age and experience.

THE COURT: A person of her age and experience, but you are allowed an exception. Anything else?

MR. STINER: Nothing further, your Honor.

THE COURT: I presume the defendant has no exceptions at all. Normally the defendant has none.

. . . .

MR. SPAULDING: With reference to the third instruction on contributory negligence, that contributory negligence is nothing more nor less than if both parties were at fault; then the defense of contributory negligence would be available. That amounts to a statement that by setting forth contributory negligence, defendant admits that it was negligent. The defendant is entitled to rely on contributory negligence and does not thereby necessarily admit negligence.

And, in connection with that, we take exception to the Court's failure to give the Defendant's Requested Instruction No. 11 which states the rule—which I believe is the rule in Oregon that by setting up the defense of contributory negligence in its answer in this case, the defendant is not deemed to admit that it was negligent in the matter under consideration.

THE COURT: You've got me. You've got me in that I did exclude from that a statement to

that effect. What I should have said and, of course, that is what I get for ad-libbing and trying to make it plain for those people. Whenever you make it plain that's understandable to them it's always a mistake. And when I ad-libbed I made a mistake. What I should have said, "What this means is that it means if the plaintiff was solely at fault, or they were both at fault, and that contributed to the happening of the accident then she is not entitled." That's what I should have said. I will go back and say it because I did exclude the possibility that she could be solely at fault. So I will go back and tell the jury if she's solely at fault she can't recover.

. . . .

MR. SPAULDING: The defendant excepts to the refusal of the Court to give Defendant's Requested Instruction No. 7 which has to do with the duties of the plaintiff where she knew, as she admitted as she did, that this was a shallow pool; that she has a duty to do something to ascertain the depth of the water before making the type of dive that she did and I don't think the jury was properly instructed on that subject.

THE COURT: I think the thing that you stated now is a complete defense to your lawsuit, in all probability, and is the reason I contemplate I will set this plaintiff's judgment aside.

MR. SPAULDING: In other words, that you couldn't have given that without giving me a directed verdict?

THE COURT: In effect, yes.

. . . .

THE COURT: . . . I think I would like to say in the record I think I adequately covered it when I told the jury the duty that she was under; in other words, that of a reasonably prudent girl of her age and experience. . . . I just happened to think that as a matter of law she was guilty of contributory negligence and not doing other things for her own safety. And, as I say, that's why I contemplated setting aside the judgment if and when it is returned.

. . . .

The Trial Stage Ends

Verdict. After Judge Holman gave additional instructions to the jury, the jury retired, elected a foreman, deliberated, and returned a unanimous verdict in favor of the plaintiff for $10,000 on October 27, 1961.

The verdict was a general one, which said only that the plaintiff won and how much. Thus, it was the jury's job to find facts and to apply the law to the facts it found. The latter task presupposed understanding the law—understanding, for example, that contributory negligence is a complete bar. It would have been possible, as in the *Loach* case, to have the jury find detailed facts by a special verdict, leaving the judge to apply the law to the facts as found. But here, as in almost all cases, the verdict was a general verdict.

Observe that the jury merely rendered a verdict in the form of a conclusion without reasons. Observe, too, that the court reporter did not go into the jury room and transcribe what occurred there. There was no way of knowing, or even investigating, whether the jury decided on the basis of some utter irrelevancy. Contrast the other aspects of the trial. And reflect on the following comment of Lord Devlin, a noted British jurist, in Trial by Jury 13–14 (1956):

> Judges give their reasons, either so as to satisfy the parties or because they themselves want to justify their judgments. . . . The jury just says yes or no. Indeed, it is not allowed to expand upon that and its reasons may not be inquired into. It is the oracle deprived of the right of being ambiguous. The jury was in its origin as oracular as the ordeal [a predecessor form of trial]: neither was conceived in reason: the verdict, no more than the result of the ordeal, was open to rational criticism. This immunity has been largely retained and is still an essential characteristic of the system.

In any event, the *Brown* jury's general verdict for the plaintiff meant that the jurors had found the defendant negligent and the plaintiff not contributorily negligent. They found these facts by applying a standard of more-likely-than-not true.

The diagram represents the internal thought process of the fact-finder. The plaintiff (π) starts at the left edge on the issue of negligence. The grid measures the jury's view of the evidential probability that the disputed fact exists, with probability increasing from 0 percent on the left to 100 percent on the right. On all the evidence, she must show that likelihood lies beyond the midpoint to win. That is, she must show that it is more likely than not that negligence exists.

The defendant (Δ) starts on the right as to contributory negligence at 0 percent probability, and must end up to the left of the midpoint to succeed on that affirmative defense. Thus, we know from the verdict that the jury found the likelihood of negligence to lie to the right of the midpoint and the likelihood of contributory negligence to lie on or to the right of the midpoint.

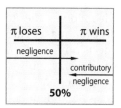

Motion for Judgment. On November 3, 1961, Mr. Spaulding moved that the court set this verdict aside and render judgment for the defendant notwithstanding the verdict, in effect renewing his directed verdict motion. Mr. Stiner naturally resisted. The date of November 17 was set for argument on the merits of this motion. On November 27, Judge Holman granted the defendant's motion. The clerk of the court then entered judgment for the defendant, including $48 in costs.

Judge Holman set aside the plaintiff's verdict. Yet, at the trial, he was unwilling to direct a verdict (or grant an involuntary nonsuit) for the defendant on the same grounds. Are these positions consistent, given that the standard of decision for these different motions is the same? First, observe that if the trial judge had not allowed the jury to return a verdict—that is, if he had directed a verdict for the defendant—and later the appellate court determined that this was an error, a whole new trial would be necessary. However, if the appellate court determined that entering judgment notwithstanding the verdict was an error, it would be necessary only to reinstate the jury verdict for the plaintiff. So, the latter route may be an economical way to proceed. Second, if the case is so lopsided as to warrant a directed verdict for the defendant, it is perhaps likely that the jury will find for the defendant. And if the jury does so find, then there will be no need to deal further with the legal question posed by the motion for a directed verdict, and also the judge will have avoided any appearance of intruding into the jury's sphere. Again, denying the directed verdict motion, but possibly later granting the same party's motion for judgment notwithstanding the verdict, may be a sound course for the judge to follow.

What is the standard a judge employs to take a case away from the jury in this way? On any of these judgments as a matter of law, including summary judgment, the standard is basically the same and is extremely high. It is important to understand, because it involves the key idea of how an overseeing decision maker can set outer limits on the primary decision maker's operation.

The standard allows granting only if, viewing the opponent's evidence in the light reasonably most favorable to the opponent, a reasonable jury could not find for the opponent. In hypothesizing the jury's function, the judge should draw all inferences in the opponent's favor to the limits of reasonableness, although this approach still requires discarding any of the opponent's evidence that is so incredible that a reasonable jury could not believe it. The granting judge then must think not merely that a verdict for the opponent would be wrong or even that it would be clearly wrong, but that it would be irrational.

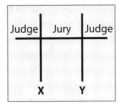

Imagine a single disputed issue of typical fact on which the plaintiff bears the burden of proof. Then imagine a grid representing the judge's disagreement with a potential verdict for the plaintiff, or equivalently the judge's view of probability of error in such a verdict, with disagreement or probability decreasing from one on the left to zero on the right. It is important to realize that such a diagram represents the probability of jury error in finding that the disputed fact exists, not the judge's view of the evidential probability that the disputed fact exists. In other words, this diagram represents the judge's thought process in externally overseeing the jury as fact-finder, not the judge's thought process if the judge were finding facts.

The plaintiff in our imagined case starts at the left of the diagram. If she presents no evidence, the judge would ordinarily grant a motion for a judgment as a matter of law against her. She is consequently bound to go forward with evidence until she satisfies the judge that a reasonable jury would be warranted in finding for her. That is, by presenting evidence she must get beyond line X to make a jury question of the imagined single issue of fact. The plaintiff's getting to or beyond line X means that although the judge might still disagree with a verdict for the plaintiff, the judge thinks a reasonable jury could find that the plaintiff sustained her burden of proof. If the plaintiff does not get to line X, that means that the judge would so vehemently disagree with a verdict for the plaintiff as to consider the jury irrational, and so the judge can grant the motion for a judgment as a matter of law. Line X, again, represents the judge's view on the limit of rationality in the jury's finding for the plaintiff, rather than the judge's view of the evidential probability that the disputed fact exists. For example, the judge might disbelieve all of the plaintiff's abundant evidence, but still acknowledge that a reasonable jury could believe it; the judge should then rule that the plaintiff has produced enough to get to the jury because a reasonable jury could find for the plaintiff.

Given a sufficiently strong body of evidence, even the party bearing the burden of proof can sometimes properly obtain judgment as a matter of law. The same standard of decision applies to both parties' motions. In terms of the above X-Y diagram, a moving plaintiff would be contending that the case had progressed to the right of line Y and stayed there even after the defendant's evidence, so that no reasonable jury could fail to find for the plaintiff. If the plaintiff is correct as to this, then the defendant had to have produced enough evidence to get back into the jury zone between Y and X, where a reasonable jury could find either for the defendant or for the plaintiff in deciding whether the fact is more probable than not to exist. Because the defendant failed to push back sufficiently, the judge can enter judgment against it. Thus, the judge sets outer limits on the jury's operation.

In sum, Judge Holman set aside the plaintiff's verdict apparently because he believed she had been contributorily negligent as a matter of law. That meant that he saw the evidence in such a way that the contributory negligence line on this diagram extended from the right edge all the way to the left of line X.

NOTES

1. The *remedy* the plaintiff sought in this Swimming Pool case was monetary compensation. You should reflect, using the materials from the preceding sections of this chapter, on whether her losses were reasonably measurable in money. Pain and suffering is particularly difficult to measure.

2. The plaintiff based her *grievance* on the principle that one who negligently causes harm to another must compensate therefor. The defendant defended against the claim in part on the basis of the principle that a contributorily negligent plaintiff loses. As we have seen, courts rather than legislatures first laid down these principles, and courts continue to play a role in laying down such principles today. Contrast a law requiring all swimming pool owners to mark their pools in certain ways. A legislature would be better qualified than a court to make such a law, and an administrative agency might be best.

3. Now, in this section, we have come to *applying the remedial law.* In many societies, law as a remedial instrument functions (a) to influence behavior before the fact so that harms and losses do not occur in the first place, (b) to settle disputes between private parties, and (c) to provide for the redress of such harms and losses when they do occur. Each of these has its own independent value. Law as an influencer of behavior before the fact can be driven home with reference to the Swimming Pool case and the process reflected therein. Consider the role of this process as a determinant of behavior beyond that of the immediate parties. The Hayden Island Amusement Company was insured by an independent insurer against liability to the Ms. Browns of the world. Had the insured company lost on the ground that its warning signs were inadequate, the insurer would instruct it and other pool owners whom it insures on how to provide adequate warning signs. Absent an insurer in the picture, potential defendants on their own or an administrative agency might so act.

4. In retrospective application of remedial law, if the supposed loss causer does not voluntarily pay but instead disputes the legal or factual premises of the aggrieved's claim, the legal systems must provide an authoritative process to resolve the disputed issues of law and fact. This takes us into the realm of *civil procedure.* The law must cover the many steps in processing a case and, on each, must decide between specifying a general rule or formulating a discretionary standard for ad hoc decision. Suffice it to say that the making and application of procedural law turn out to be much more contentious than a lay person would ever guess. Although the procedure is designed to isolate and sharpen the issues

Truth and Justice

In some cases, the actual facts are found. And striving to find the truth is usually laudable. But truth does not equate to justice. Let us try to explain why.

Initially, even when truth is the proper aim, how much certainty is possible anyway? Consider, for example, what the sources of proof are in a court of law. Testimony of witnesses predominates. Such testimony can be somewhat unreliable. The Swimming Pool case can help to illustrate (1) that witnesses do not always perceive events accurately in the first place, (2) that they do not always remember well, (3) that they do not always communicate what they experienced, (4) that they sometimes, even in good faith, distort their experience, and (5) that they may lie. While fact-finding is therefore a very human endeavor, the humans who undertake it are additionally subject to significant institutional limitations on their efforts. For example, the court does not have a subpoena power broad enough to bring in witnesses from anywhere in the world. Moreover, even if all this were not so, how much certainty is optimal? Time and money are not unlimited resources.

Yet something more profound is afoot: Truth is not the only aim. Consider the following from Sir Frederick Pollock's Essays in the Law 275 (1922): "Perhaps the greatest of all the fallacies entertained by lay people about the law is one which, though seldom expressed in terms, an observant lawyer may quite commonly find lurking not far below the surface. This is that the business of a court of justice is to discover the truth. Its real business is to pronounce upon the justice of particular claims, and incidentally to test the truth of the assertions of fact made in support of the claim in law, provided that those assertions are relevant in law to the establishment of the desired conclusion; and this is by no means the same thing."

Surely a reader could ask, "How can there be any inconsistency between truth and justice? Indeed, justice can only be done on the basis of the facts. Justice cannot be done in the dark." But Pollock may have been considering

procedural justice. For example, giving each side an equal chance to present his case may, in a particular case, lead to substantive injustice—one side, the weaker side factually, may be able to demonstrate a better case factually than can the other side. Nonetheless, recognition of this risk has not induced courts to deny each side an equal opportunity to be heard.

Pollock's remark can be generalized: Society makes and applies laws in a way to maximize the net total of its deepest underlying values, and so society may, in an adjudicative process, subordinate the pursuit of truth to other social aims. One of these aims is that of offering the parties a day in court, a forum in which to have it out. In the end, the court may lose sight of the truth, but the parties will have had their say against each other, and this will have served as a substitute for disorderly forms of self-help. For another example, any society would favor a process that saves time and money. For yet another example, an adjudicator may have to apply rules of evidence that limit or close off relevant lines of factual inquiry altogether. Evidentiary privileges, like the husband-wife privilege, may frustrate the pursuit of truth. A rule that privileges a witness not to testify because her testimony would violate a confidential relation may operate to keep the adjudicator in the dark in the particular case. When this happens, society has sacrificed substantive justice, insofar as it is necessarily premised on truth, to the aim of inducing and protecting confidential relations. That aim is not so much procedural justice as a conflicting substantive aim.

Accordingly, legal actors (i.e., private citizens, their lawyers, and public officials) must take account of much law of a process-oriented character (i.e., law other than the basic substantive law governing the availability of remedies for grievances). This law, if well designed, will reflect a variety of important values. These values generate standards or criteria for judging the goodness or badness of processes such as adjudication, legislation, and administration. The important point here is that one has not exhaustively accounted for the total significance of such values merely by stressing their relationship to quality of outcome. Some processes have significance quite apart from their impact on outcome, and some indeed lead to a negative impact on outcome. This point is overlooked by some contemporary reformers who have their tunnel vision focused on result and result alone.

There is independent worth, for example, in having processes in which those most vitally affected can be meaningfully heard and in having processes free of the taint of undue influence. The kinds of values reflected thereby, in contrast to *outcome values*, we shall call *process values*. To speak somewhat more carefully, then, we shall use the phrase "process values" to refer to values by which we can judge a legal process to be good as a process, apart from any good outcome it may yield in the case at hand. We might use the phrase "outcome-value efficacy" to refer to the tendency of a legal process to favor the desired winner.

We do not mean to suggest that process values are beyond argument. Indeed, the word "value" suggests just the opposite. They are latent and subtle. Moreover, much room remains for debate as to what they mean precisely (think particularly of equality) and how much weight they deserve relatively (think generally of process versus outcome values) and also as to whose values they are and how they come

into play. Nevertheless, process values do seem to exist, independent of outcome values. One proof of the independent importance of process values is that we all know from experience that we would condemn public processes that did not reflect such values even if the processes' decisional output were invariably good. That is, for reasons independent of outcome, we want processes in which affected parties are heard and in which decision makers are free of undue influence. All that ends well is not well after all.

Now we want to look at the remedial instrument from this angle. However, there is no such thing as a unitary "remedial process." Rather, the remedial instrument breaks down into many different processes, including the various processes for creating the basic substantive rules; processes of negotiation and settlement of disputed claims that avoid the necessity of formal adjudication; processes of adjudication of both law and fact; various processes for enforcing adjudicative outcomes against unwilling parties; and processes of surveillance of adjudication, including appellate review. Most of these processes reflect many of the same process values, though not always in the same form. For a final example of a value common to most processes, we previously referred to the principle that a person should not have to satisfy the claim of another without receiving notice of that claim at the outset. This procedural principle surely serves outcome values, it being a generally efficacious means to proper results in lawsuits. But this fundamental principle also serves process values, such as participatory governance and procedural fairness. Consequently, a huge body of law has grown up to ensure adequacy of notice to the defendant, and it applies even where society is otherwise assured of the "justice" of the plaintiff's claim.

A way to summarize is to say that the remedial instrument, with its elaborate procedures for resolving disputes over the factual premises of particular remedies, is a multipurpose institutional scheme, only one of the purposes of which is the pursuit of truth, with other purposes thereof either cooperatively or antagonistically involving themselves in the combined pursuit of justice.

in dispute and thus to simplify the controversy, the uncertainties of the procedure often serve to inject a further disputatious ingredient into a lawsuit.

5. Speaking of the most basic features of procedure, Anglo-American legal systems have traditionally offered an *adjudicative process adversarially initiated and informed* to resolve the disputed issues of law and fact. Except for the appeal, we have now seen the remedial instrument operate from beginning to end in a representative case. The judge resolved some of the disputed issues, and the jury others. Were judge and jurors alike adjudicators? Yes. Note also that in the very typical Swimming Pool case, a private person took the original initiative to put the law in motion, not some public official. Moreover, the adjudicators were adversarially informed. What does this mean? Did the judge go out and look up the law on the legal issues raised? Did the jury go out and dig up the evidence on the factual issues involved? No, nearly all this informing was done through the efforts of the opposing lawyers. How did the legal issues arise in the first place? The factual issues? Again, not through the initiative of judge or jury, but through the initiative of lawyers and parties.

6. Notice how the plaintiff, the defendant, the lawyers, the jury, and the judge all shared in administering the remedial instrument in the Swimming Pool case, albeit by playing differing *roles*. From this case it can be seen that, in general, legal issues are presented to the judge by the lawyers and are resolved on the basis of argument as a matter of judgment as to which has the stronger side. By contrast, the factual issues here are resolved by the jury on the basis of the parties' evidence and in accord with the preponderance of the evidence.

7. This is not to say that there is no *judicial power to control the jury*. On the contrary, one of the beauties of the Swimming Pool case is that it also illustrates so-called judicial controls on so-called jury irrationality. But you must not assume that the jury's work is fully and effectively reviewable by the trial judge (or appellate judges). Suppose, for example, that in the jury room, the jury in the Swimming Pool case felt that Ms. Brown was contributorily negligent but decided to make some law of its own. That is, suppose it (as have some legislatures) rejected the law that proof of contributory negligence constitutes a complete bar and substituted a comparative negligence principle, deciding that the defendant should bear half of the plaintiff's $10,000 loss because the defendant had been in good part negligent too and therefore giving the plaintiff a general verdict for $5,000. When the jury returned such a verdict, the verdict would not be perceptible or vulnerable as being lawless, because such a verdict is consistent with underlying findings that the defendant was negligent, the plaintiff was not contributorily negligent, and the damages were only $5,000 and not $10,000.

H. Post-Trial

ENFORCEMENT OF JUDGMENTS

After a jury returns a verdict in favor of the plaintiff in a civil action, and the court enters judgment for the plaintiff, the defendant must satisfy the judgment unless he appeals. If the judgment calls for money, and the defendant does not voluntarily pay, the plaintiff can obtain a *writ of execution* from the clerk of the court. This writ is addressed to the local sheriff and orders him to seize property owned by the defendant, sell it, and pay the plaintiff the amount of her judgment. By obtaining a judgment in her favor, the plaintiff thus becomes entitled to invoke the strong arm of the law in her behalf. However, if the defendant appeals from the entry of judgment against him, he can normally *stay* satisfaction of this judgment until the end of the appeal.

In Ms. Brown's case, although the jury returned a verdict in her favor, the trial judge refused to permit a judgment for her. Instead, he set aside the verdict and rendered judgment for the defendant. In circumstances such as these, the plaintiff may appeal to an appellate court, and this is what Ms. Brown, through her lawyer, did.

APPELLATE REVIEW

The appeal idea is firmly entrenched in modern systems of law, so that nearly all such systems have appellate as well as trial courts. Unlike trial courts, which now seldom consist of more than one judge, appellate courts normally consist of several judges. The chief business of appellate judges is to decide appeals from rulings made by the trial-court judge, and in so doing appellate judges perform two distinct functions. First, they keep the law uniform and sound. Second, they correct, or provide for the correction of, prejudicial errors made by trial judges in particular cases.

Without appellate judges to perform that first institutional function, the law applied by trial judges might vary from trial judge to trial judge throughout the territory over which the appellate court has jurisdiction. Appellate judges have primary responsibility for the development of the common law and for sound interpretational law. Many of their decisions, unlike most decisions of trial judges, are published and bound in volumes accessible to lawyers and, theoretically, to the public. These decisions constitute case law binding in all similar cases that later arise in the same court or in its lower courts.

As to the second of the two functions performed by appellate judges in deciding appeals, we said that appellate judges correct, or provide for the correction of, prejudicial errors made by trial judges. Of all officials who make decisions in our legal system, trial judges in their rulings are subject to the closest scrutiny. Indeed, civil procedure provides for the rather merciless exposure of the errors made by trial judges.

Should the rulings of trial judges be subject to such intensive scrutiny? The decisions of other officials in the legal system are not similarly subject to scrutiny. Why single out trial judges in this way? The merciless exposure and correction of trial judges' errors might lead people to disrespect these judges and also might diminish those judges' sense of responsibility. Further, appeals are time-consuming and costly. The justification for them should therefore be clear. Most people quickly conclude that the system of appellate review of a trial judge's rulings is appropriate. But they pause when considering whether they would extend the appeal idea. Should the statutory enactments of a legislature be subject to appeal to a higher legislature? Should the policy decisions of an administrator be subject to appeal? Should nonpolicy decisions of the administrator be subject to appeal? Should appellate courts themselves review not only the trial judge's conclusions on legal questions but also the findings of fact of the jury? Should the appellate court itself hear witnesses and, in effect, conduct a second full trial of a case? The correctness function of appeal turns out not so easy to justify, and it very obviously has limits:

1. Observe that upon review of the trial court's outcome, only mistakes made by the trial judge himself are subject to correction, and these are usually mistakes of law. The nature of the questions on which a trial judge may be required to rule before, during, and after a trial is highly varied. For example, he may have to rule whether the plaintiff has alleged facts constituting a valid legal claim; whether the defendant has alleged facts constituting a valid affirmative defense to the plaintiff's claim; whether one of the parties or some witness should be compelled to make various disclosures prior to trial; whether evidence offered at trial is legally admissible; whether a party has introduced sufficient evidence to justify a verdict in her favor; whether particular instructions should be given to the jury; whether a verdict for one of the parties should be set aside and judgment rendered notwithstanding the verdict; whether a new trial should be granted to correct some mistake; or whether the victor has established the essential facts in a nonjury trial. The trial judge's rulings on all such questions are subject to appeal. But they are subject to different standards of review: on questions of law, the appellate court will substitute its view for the trial judge's conclusions; but on factual findings, the appellate court will defer to the trial judge's view and will overturn only when it rather strongly disagrees with him, reversing not for error but only for clear error.

2. A lawyer in proceedings before a trial court normally must record an immediate objection to any and all judicial rulings that she thinks erroneous in order to appeal successfully from such rulings at a later time. This requirement exists to ensure that the trial judge will have every opportunity to correct his own errors when they are made. But an effect of imposing the requirement is that the client is the one who suffers if her lawyer fails to object to an erroneous ruling.

3. Appellate courts normally do not correct errors they see on their own, but instead require lawyers to assert them specifically on appeal. This refusal to correct unasserted errors is another reflection of our adversary system.

How do our appellate courts operate? The losing party may appeal within a prescribed period of time after the entry of a judgment. The rules usually allow an appeal only from the final judgment in the trial court, at which time the losing party can assert a complete list of prejudicial errors appearing in the trial court's records and duly objected to. However, an immediate appeal may lie from certain important orders issued during the course of trial-court proceedings, such as injunctions.

"I didn't make a conscious career decision to go into appellate work -- it's just that I kept losing all of my trials."

The law requires the losing party to file a notice of appeal, as well as to serve it on the opposing party so that he, too, can make necessary preparations. The appealing party is called the appellant or petitioner, and the other party the appellee or respondent. With the help of counsel, the clerk of the trial court will assemble and transmit to the clerk of the appellate court all papers necessary for the appellate judges to understand what the appeal is about. In some cases, the clerk transmits a transcript of the entire trial. The ensemble is called the *record.*

In most courts, the parties to an appeal must file *briefs* on the law relating to the questions to be considered in the appeal. The briefs are almost always prepared by lawyers. The appellant's brief will state the facts of the case, list the asserted errors to be corrected, present arguments that these are truly errors deserving correction, and discuss cases or statutes that presumably support these arguments. The appellee will then prepare and file a similar brief presenting her side of the case. The appellant might submit a reply brief.

Ordinarily, lawyers for both sides will also have an opportunity to appear together before the appellate court and orally argue their respective sides of the case. They will hit the highlights of their briefs, while trying to get the judges intellectually and emotionally involved.

After the appellate court has heard these arguments, deliberated on the case, and decided by majority vote, it will typically prepare an opinion stating its decision and the reasoning on which the decision is based. If the appellate court decides that the trial judge erred, the appellate court will, unless the error was not prejudicial, require its correction. This may involve a new trial with its expenditures of time and money, or it may require much less.

Ms. Brown's Appeal

Recall that the trial judge who presided in Ms. Brown's case set aside her verdict and rendered judgment for the Hayden Island Amusement Company notwithstanding the verdict, chiefly because he thought that as a matter of law she had been contributorily negligent. On December 18, 1961, Ms. Brown's lawyer filed a notice of appeal to the appropriate appellate court, which at the time was an appeal directly to the supreme court of the state (Oregon now has an intermediate Court of Appeals). He assigned as error the granting of judgment notwithstanding the verdict. Thereafter, the clerk transmitted the record, and the lawyers for both sides prepared and filed briefs. On October 5, 1962, Messrs. Stiner and Spaulding presented their oral arguments before the supreme court. On February 20, 1963, the seven justices of the court handed down its decision.

The following excerpts are from the eighty-seven pages of briefs filed by the lawyers for both sides. Several different issues of law were considered in these briefs. However, the following excerpts are addressed to only one issue: whether the evidence showed overwhelmingly that Ms. Brown's own actions constituted contributory negligence so that she could not prevail. If the only reasonable view was that her actions constituted contributory negligence, then, even though a jury had decided that her actions did not constitute contributory negligence, the defendant should prevail—"as a matter of law."

Extracts from Plaintiff's Brief

In order to find plaintiff contributorily negligent as a matter of law, the court must find, considering all the evidence in the light most favorable to the plaintiff, that reasonable men would all agree and conclude that she failed to use reasonable care and it would be impossible for a jury of reasonable men to conclude otherwise. Jensen v. Salem Sand and Gravel Co., 192 Or. 51, 58, 233 P.2d 237 (1951). In the *Jensen* case, the court stated:

> Ordinarily, the question of contributory negligence is a jury question, and rarely will courts find that contributory negligence exists as a matter of law. When a given state of facts is such that reasonable men may fairly differ upon the question as to whether a plaintiff is guilty of contributory negligence, the matter becomes a jury question. Whether or not the given act may be negligence or not negligence depends upon the circumstances, for, as said in 1 Beven on Negligence (3rd ed.) at p. 9, "it is not the acts that connotes the negligence, but the circumstances."

The circumstances in the case at bar do not warrant the conclusion the plaintiff was contributorily negligent as a matter of law.

Extracts from Defendant's Brief

Defendant of course concedes the well-known general rules pointed out by plaintiff for determination of the question of contributory negligence

as a matter of law. In other words, it is defendant's position that under the facts conceded by plaintiff's own evidence reasonable men could not differ in this case.

What were the circumstances?

Plaintiff was an intelligent, athletically inclined young lady. She was a "better than average swimmer," an experienced swimmer with years of experience in performing "all types of diving".... She was experienced in diving in a shallow pool ... and knew what the dangers thereof were if not done properly, as she had hit bottom before when diving in a shallow pool.... She knew the pool was shallow before she dove into it.... However, before she dove she could not see "any indication of the depth of the water where you dove in".... It was daylight ... and there was no problem in seeing.... She knew how to dive in a shallow pool.... Although there were numerous other people standing in various parts of the pool (other than her friends in one place) she made no attempt to measure the water on them.... The water was clear.... She could plainly see the bottom of the pool....

Taking plaintiff at her word, as we must, that, although she could plainly see the bottom of the pool, still she could not see "any indication of the depth of the water where you dove in" ..., we submit that no reasonable man could possibly differ that she was not exercising the degree of care and prudence to be expected of a reasonably prudent, intelligent, fifteen-year-old, experienced swimmer and diver when she dove into this water onto the top of her head ... under those circumstances, that is, without having "any indication of the depth" ..., except her knowledge that it was shallow.

This case is basically the same as Johnson v. Hot Springs Land & Improvement Co., [76 Or. 333, 148 P. 1137 (1915)], excepting in *Johnson* defendant provided a diving board at the place where plaintiff dove and such diving board was an invitation to use it for diving. In *Johnson* plaintiff was told upon entering the pool that the water was shallow, and was 3 to 3½ feet deep, but was coming in fast, and it would not be long until the tank was full. "They were neither told that the pool was safe for diving nor warned that it was unsafe." Plaintiff thereupon waited "about twenty minutes" and then apparently made his own assumptions as to the depth of the water at that time. Plaintiff was nineteen years old, of ordinary intelligence, and was a good swimmer and diver. Apparently, without having any precise information as to how much deeper the water had gotten, he dove off the diving board and sustained injury, for which he sued, making a similar allegation as that upon which plaintiff relies in this case, that "defendant failed to warn (him) that on account of the shallowness it was dangerous to dive into the water." He claimed that he was unfamiliar with the premises and did not know the risk of diving, and that he had a right to rely upon the assurances of the defendant arising from the fact that defendant had rented him a bathing suit and charged him an admission. The Supreme Court stated as follows:

> One of the objects of the rule requiring the owner of a place of amusement like the one maintained by defendant to warn patrons of danger is to acquaint the patron with the hazard so that he may avoid injury. If the deceased had knowledge of the shallowness of the water and the danger incident to diving from the springboard, then he knew all and no less than he could have known had defendant expressly warned him of the risk. If the defendant had, in fact, cautioned Johnson against the peril, and, notwithstanding such warning, the latter dived off the springboard, then, on the facts of the instant case, the defendant would not be liable because of the knowledge imparted to Johnson; and so, too, the same result follows if Johnson did, in fact, know of the danger, even though not told by the defendant. *If with knowledge of the danger, Johnson placed himself in peril, and, on account thereof, was injured, he was chargeable with contributory negligence.* (Emphasis supplied)

We submit that this holding in *Johnson* is apropos to our case because in our case plaintiff knew that the water was shallow, although there is evidence that she did not know the precise depth. She appreciated the consequences of diving into a shallow pool and she dove anyway....

... By the exercise of the slightest care, such as [merely] jumping into the [water] feet first, or simply looking at the bottom, or by looking "around to see how far the water came up on people in various parts of that pool" ... where "they were scattered around," ... to whom she "wasn't paying any attention" ... she would have been accurately advised of the precise depth of the pool.

Extracts from Plaintiff's Reply Brief

Defendant concedes that in determining if the plaintiff was contributorily negligent or not, reasonable men must all conclude she failed to use reasonable care. However, the defendant has apparently overlooked the well-established rule of law that in order to reach this conclusion all evidence must be considered in the light most favorable to the plaintiff.

The defendant states "she had hit bottom before when diving into a shallow pool" when in fact the plaintiff testified she had brushed her nose against the bottom.... Also, it is stated the plaintiff made no attempt to measure the water on other people in the pool when in fact the transcript states she wasn't paying any particular attention to them ... and nobody was near the north wall .... Defendant takes the plaintiff's statement that she looked at the bottom of the pool, leaving out the fact she could not tell the depth by looking at the bottom, seizes upon a statement by the plaintiff relating to depth markings and argues all reasonable men would agree she was contributorily negligent as a matter of law "when she dove into this water on top of her head"....

... Also, the defendant omitted the plaintiff's testimony that she "generally took in the whole situation and drew a conclusion".... The defendant must have necessarily overlooked ... the evidence that prior to making a 45° angle dive the plaintiff noted a handrail to her immediate left, the depth of the water on her friends in the pool ..., the steps going into shallow water across the pool ..., and she looked but did not see anything indicating she should not dive into the pool ... or that it would be dangerous to dive into the pool ....

In Johnson v. Hot Springs Land Co., 76 Or. 333, 338, 148 P. 1137 (1915), the decedent knew exactly how deep the water was or at least reasonable men would all agree he should have known. He and his friends had been swimming and diving into a half filled pool for fifteen minutes. In reviewing the evidence, the court said:

> Arthur Johnson was a good diver; he had been in the plunge at least on two prior occasions when the water was at its usual depth of about seven feet; he and his friends were told, upon making inquiry, that the water was between 3 and $3\frac{1}{2}$ feet deep, and that it was shallow, but that the water was coming in fast; he and his companions sat around and waited "for the water to fill up" because the shallowness was apparent; he could not well have avoided seeing his friends standing up in the water; and consequently he must have known the depth of the water. It is also clear that he realized the danger of diving off the spring-board into the water at the same time because, as Halvorsen said, Johnson was going "to make a long dive to make it shallow in the water," and his feet slipped, or he lost his balance in the air, and he came down straight.
>
> The evidence has been narrated, and considered in a light most favorable to the plaintiff, and the conclusion is inevitable not only that Johnson knew the depth of the water, but that he also appreciated the danger. The fact that he attempted "to make a long dive to make it shallow in the water" reflects the knowledge then had by the deceased.

Defendant argues since the case at bar involves a shallow pool and the plaintiff failed to measure the "precise depth," she was contributorily negligent as a matter of law based upon the holding of *Johnson*. Counsel ignores the fact the defendant did nothing to warn the plaintiff of the depth of the water in the case at bar and argues everything the plaintiff did to ascertain the depth of the water short of "merely jumping into the water feet first" was unreasonable or did not fulfill her "duty."

The plaintiff was entitled to rely upon what she observed to indicate the depth of the water. Unlike the *Johnson* case, this was the plaintiff's first visit to defendant's pool. Unlike the *Johnson* case, there was no warning given regarding the depth of the water, nor was there any warning she should not dive into the defendant's shallow pool or that she did so at her own risk. In the *Johnson* case, the court reviewed the decedent's knowledge with respect to the depth of the water as follows:

> Murphy, Peck and Halvorsen each testified that after entering the water and by standing up in it the depth was found to be between 3 and $3\frac{1}{2}$ feet, but no one remembered having seen Johnson standing up in the water, although they were together in plain view of each other all the time. They had been swimming and diving about 15 minutes. Peck and Halvorsen each had dived off the bank three or four times, *and Johnson had done the same thing twice.* (Emphasis added)

The plaintiff did not have any knowledge of the actual depth as the decedent must have had in the *Johnson* case, since she had not been in the water. She did everything possible to ascertain the depth of the water but actually measure the "precise depth" with a yardstick which the defendant didn't even bother to do and mark on the side of the pool. It is hard to see how defendant can argue that all men would agree the plaintiff failed to act in a reasonable manner to ascertain the depth of the water. Plaintiff submits she certainly acted in a reasonable manner which, of course, is what twelve reasonable persons concluded in this case. . . .

Defendant argues if the plaintiff had looked around "she would have been accurately advised of the precise depth of the pool". . . . However, she did look around and there were no markings to indicate the precise depth of the pool and there were no people in the water along the north wall or in the area where she dove.

NOTES

1. Recall that the lawyers, through the pleading process, had defined the issues of fact to be resolved at the trial. Likewise, through the entire pretrial, trial, and post-trial process, the lawyers defined issues of law, which they might possibly present later to appellate judges for decision on appeal. Thus, lawyers are very much in control.

2. Consider the strength of the lawyers' arguments. The plaintiff's reply brief said, "Plaintiff submits she certainly acted in a reasonable manner which, of course, is what twelve reasonable persons concluded in this case." But as a matter of pure logic, the jury verdict was not relevant in deciding the question before the appellate court. That question was whether such a verdict would be irrational. Next observe that in the foregoing briefs, the lawyers argued over whether the prior *Johnson* decision was "in point." Do you think that the decision cited was in point or that it was distinguishable, as lawyers say?

3. The chief reason why Judge Holman set aside the plaintiff's verdict was that he believed the plaintiff had been contributorily negligent as a matter of law. The plaintiff's lawyer challenged as error the grant of judgment notwithstanding the verdict, and both lawyers naturally devoted a large part of their briefs to this contributory negligence issue. Another issue was whether, as a matter of law, the defendant had been negligent at all, and each brief included several pages on this issue. This issue arose from the trial-court proceedings because it was the alternative ground for the defendant's motions, and its lawyer argued it on appeal. How would you expect the appellate court to decide these two issues on appeal?

BROWN v. HAYDEN ISLAND AMUSEMENT CO.

Supreme Court of Oregon, 1963
233 Or. 416, 378 P.2d 953

LUSK, J.:

The plaintiff, a girl fifteen years of age, brought this action to recover damages for personal injuries sustained by her when she dived into a swimming pool owned and maintained by the defendant and struck her head on the bottom of the pool. She alleged that the defendant was negligent (a) in failing to provide adequate markings showing the depth of the water in the pool and (b) in failing to warn the plaintiff that the bottom of this pool was not constructed in the same manner as other swimming pools in the vicinity of Portland, Oregon, in regard to depth of water near the sides of the pool. There was a jury trial and at the conclusion of the testimony the court denied a motion for a directed verdict made by the

defendant. . . . The jury returned a verdict for the plaintiff. Thereafter the court, on motion of the defendant, entered judgment for the defendant notwithstanding the verdict and the plaintiff has appealed.

[The supreme court's recital of the trial-court evidence is omitted.]

In Johnson v. Hot Springs Land & Imp. Co., 76 Or. 333, 337–338, 148 P. 1137, 1139, where the plaintiff, who was injured in diving from a springboard into a pool maintained by the defendant, was denied recovery because of contributory negligence, Mr. Justice Harris, speaking for the court, stated the rule applicable to a case of this kind as follows:

> Stating the law with reference to, and as limited by, the facts in the instant case, it may be said that the defendant was not an insurer of the safety of Arthur Johnson. . . .

Where a person, however, provides accommodations of a public nature, that person is required to use reasonable care and diligence in furnishing and maintaining such accommodations in a reasonably safe condition for the purpose for which they are apparently designed and to which they are adapted. If for any reason the accommodations are not reasonably safe and suitable for the purposes for which they are ordinarily used in a customary way, then the public should be excluded entirely, or appropriate notice of the unsafe and unsuitable condition should be given, and persons warned of the dangers in using them. The springboard and the water beneath it constituted the accommodations which the defendant furnished to the deceased, who was a patron for hire, and, as such, was using them for diving purposes, to which they were adapted, and in the way in which they were customarily used. Persons patronizing the natatorium have a right to assume that the defendant has performed its duty, and that reasonably safe and suitable accommodations have been furnished. 38 Cyc. 268; Barrett v. Lake Ontario Beach Imp. Co., 174 N.Y. 310, 66 N.E. 968.

This language has been cited and quoted with approval by many courts throughout the country.

In applying it to the present case, it is to be borne in mind that, as the plaintiff knew, the defendant maintained for the use of its patrons two pools, one, the shallow pool in which she received her injury and which was not equipped with a diving board, and the other the deep pool which was so equipped. There is no evidence that the shallow pool was "ordinarily used in a customary way" for diving or indeed that anyone had ever dived into it before. The plaintiff did not allege in her complaint that the defendant was negligent in failing to warn her by signs or otherwise against diving into this pool, but she did allege that it was negligent in failing to mark the depth of the water. What this actually comes to is a claim that the defendant should have given notice not only that the pool was shallow, but how shallow it was. We think that no such duty rested upon the defendant and that notice to its patrons that the pool was shallow was sufficient notice to a reasonably prudent person that it was a pool of a particular character maintained for certain limited uses, one of which was not diving. The deep pool with its diving board was an invitation to dive. The shallow pool by contrast carried a warning that it was intended to serve a different purpose.

In this connection it is worthy of note, since the case of the plaintiff is largely built on her experience at the Mount Scott pool, where she had swum hundreds of times, that there is no evidence that the depth of the water at that pool was marked, and that in testifying to its depth the plaintiff resorted to approximations.

The defendant was not charged with knowledge that the plaintiff would assume that the water at the place where she dived was of sufficient depth for diving with safety to herself. She was not warranted in assuming that the pool was deeper at one end than another or, if this were the case, that she was at the deep end; for in going to the spot from which she dived she passed one marker indicating that the water was shallow at the north end of the pool and she decided to dive from a spot only a few feet from a similar marker. She did not testify that she saw the markers, but neither did she deny that she saw them. They were there to be seen and the defendant could rightly assume that they would be seen. The defendant was entitled to assume "that patrons would act as reasonable men act" and that they "would possess such perception of the surrounding circumstances as a reasonable man would have, that they would possess such knowledge of other pertinent matters as a reasonable man would have, and that they would correlate such perception and knowledge with reasonable intelligence and judgment...." Glaze v. Benson, 205 Md. 26, 33, 106 A.2d 124, 128. See, also, Restatement, Torts §289.

The evidence on behalf of the plaintiff as to the faded appearance of one of the markers at some undetermined time is not sufficiently substantial to show that this was the condition of the marker on the day of the accident....

The plaintiff seems to have assumed that because people dive from a particular spot in the Mount Scott pool it would be safe for her to dive at a correspondingly located spot at the Jantzen pool. The defendant was not charged with knowledge of the construction of the Mount Scott pool, nor of the manner in which it was used by the plaintiff and others. The defendant was under no duty to maintain a pool constructed as are other pools in the Portland area so long as its pool, as constructed and maintained, was reasonably safe, considering the purpose for which it was built and its customary use. . . .

The mere fact that a pool of the kind in question is not deep at one end and shallow at the other is no evidence of negligence. There must be something in addition which might mislead a reasonable person as to the depth of the water. It is necessary that a pool be deeper at some point than at others for drainage, but beyond this no purpose is served by having a "shallow" pool deep at one end and shallow at the other. The plaintiff's witness Milliken so testified.

The plaintiff testified that she judged the depth of the water by the fact that it was breast high on her friends in the pool some seventy feet distant from her. She thought that it must be even deeper where she dived, but here again she indulged the unwarranted assumption that the Jantzen pool was built like the Mount Scott pool. Moreover, if, as she testified, she "took in the whole situation" and saw people "scattered throughout the pool" (though not in "the immediate area" where she dived) it must have occurred to her as a reasonably prudent person that this was not a pool the floor of which sloped gradually from the south end to the north end. . . .

We have examined the cases cited by the plaintiff involving diving accidents in public swimming pools or at bathing beaches in which the courts have held that the questions of negligence and contributory negligence were for the jury, and others collected in the Annotation, 48 A.L.R.2d 104, but we see no occasion to discuss these cases in this opinion. Of necessity, the decision in each case must depend on its own particular facts and circumstances. The governing principles, as stated in Johnson v. Hot Springs Land & Imp. Co., supra, are clear and well established. The task of the court is simply to apply those principles to the evidence. The plaintiff sustained serious injuries in this unfortunate accident which befell her, but the defendant was not an insurer of her safety, and, since there is no evidence of a departure from the standard of care which the law imposes upon the defendant, the court rightly allowed the motion for judgment [notwithstanding the verdict]. The judgment is affirmed [with another $198 imposed as costs].

Sloan, J., dissenting:

Defendant solicits people of all ages and experience to use its pools. Some are acquainted with the peculiar design of the pools, others, like plaintiff, are not. It seems to me that we are not justified in judging plaintiff's actions from the caution of mature years blessed with a measurable degree of hindsight.

The jury should decide if defendant had given adequate warning to unwary patrons of the hazards inherent in this pool.

NOTES

1. Students sometimes read appellate opinions as if they were short essays on some branch of the law. This is not the best approach. It is best to read such opinions as efforts to resolve particular issues—as problems to be solved in a specific context. Does the appellate court here decide the defendant was, as a matter of law, not negligent, or did it decide the plaintiff was, as a matter of law, contributorily negligent, or both? It appears to us that the court decided on the basis of the defendant's lack of negligence.

Fact and Law

The distinction between fact and law is obviously a key one, both for separating issues between jury and judge and for fixing the standard of review, but is it a clear one? No. Moreover, the line is not the same for jury and appeal purposes. Consider this from Richard H. Field, Benjamin Kaplan & Kevin M. Clermont, Materials for a Basic Course in Civil Procedure 1373–74 (9th ed. 2007):

> Among the questions of "fact" assigned to the jury, there may be two types of questions: (1) determining what happened, that is, what the parties did and what the circumstances were; and (2) evaluating those facts in terms of their legal consequences, for instance, whether the conduct of the defendant in the circumstances was not that of a reasonable person. But the court always sets the outside limits within which the jury may perform its function. Sometimes such judicial interceding invokes only the rationality limit on the jury's application of law . . . , but at other times what the court is actually doing is specifically formulating a substantive rule of law. For example, with respect to the latter type of question the Court, in Railroad Co. v. Stout, 84 U.S. (17 Wall.) 657, 663 (1874), said: "So if a coach-driver intentionally drives within a few inches of a precipice, and an accident happens, negligence may be ruled as a question of law. On the other hand, if he had placed a suitable distance between his coach and the precipice, but by the breaking of a rein or an axle, which could not have been anticipated, an injury occurred, it might be ruled as a question of law that there was no negligence and no liability." The court is saying that in certain circumstances there is or is not liability. Note that the court could formulate the law in such a detailed fashion as to reduce greatly the role of the jury.

This point is pursued in Fleming James, Jr., Geoffrey C. Hazard, Jr. & John Leubsdorf, Civil Procedure 433–34 (5th ed. 2001):

> It is clear that rules of law could be formulated and administered so as to exclude the jury altogether from making these evaluations. A court could decide, for instance, that under a given set of circumstances motorists must blow their horns and that under a different set of circumstances they need not do so. Under such a pair of rules, the theoretical function of the jury would be to decide only whether the circumstances existed and whether the horn was blown, the question whether it should have been blown being decided by the court. By the same token, the rule could be formulated such that the jury decides not only whether the horn was blown but also whether the horn should have been blown.
>
> Whether rules of law shall be administered in either of these two ways is of great importance in many cases; when the facts are not disputed it is, of course, decisive. In deciding whether an issue will be regarded as one of fact or law, courts are deciding whether they think it calls for the community judgment of a jury or for the presumably detached expertise of a judge. The measure of "reasonableness," which recurs at so many points in our law, usually is construed as invoking the community standard of what the reasonably prudent person would do in the circumstances; the application of this standard is committed to the community's representatives on the jury. This is the prevailing rule today in negligence cases. . . .
>
> The policy considerations underlying the characterization of an issue as one of fact or law go beyond the roles of jury and trial judge: They also involve the role of the appellate courts. If an issue is treated as one of law, the decision of the issue is finally determinable by the appellate courts, whereas a fact issue as determined in the trial court is conclusive unless the appellate court can say there was insufficient evidence to sustain the finding.

2. In discharging its surveillance function—that of helping to ensure that prejudicially erroneous rulings of law made by the trial judge and properly appealed by one of the parties do not go uncorrected—the appellate court does not take new evidence to go behind the fact-findings. But this appellate court nevertheless was fairly active in reconsidering the evidence below.

3. Appellate judges typically, and traditionally, give reasons for their decisions. How many different reasons did Justice Lusk give, and how good were they? Was justice done in the *Brown* case? That is, did you agree with the appellate-court decision?

4. As a postscript, the Jantzen Beach Amusement Park closed on Labor Day, 1970. Hayden Island now is home to the Jantzen Beach SuperCenter, a shopping mall located on the grounds formerly occupied by the park. See Jantzen Beach Amusement Park, http://www.pdxhistory.com/html/jantzen_beach.html.

Section Five
ROLES OF PRIVATE CITIZENS AND THEIR LAWYERS

Now is an appropriate time to start exploring another common fallacy about law: the top-and-bottom fallacy. In this view, the law divides people in a society into the public officials (judicial, legislative, administrative) and the private citizens; the officials are on the top, and the citizens are at the bottom; and the officials dictate in various ways to the citizens below. This picture of law operating as a remedial instrument is dramatically false. And its falsity does not depend on any distinction between dictatorships and democracies. One can imagine a dictatorship making use of law as a remedial instrument in ways that call upon private citizens and their lawyers to perform important roles. Certainly in our system, these actors perform important roles.

First, in standard instances of the operation of the remedial instrument, the decision whether to put the law in motion is in private hands. As a rule, we have no public prosecutor of private claims to money damages, injunctions, and the like.

Second, the private litigant also functions as a lawmaker. Who was Butterfield? Davies? Loach? Appropriately, their names appear on cases, each of which made some new law. Private parties typically assert remedial claims and defenses and then advance arguments in support of their legality, all through lawyers who are professionally trained for such purposes. Thus, private citizens and their lawyers work together to help make law. Courts declare the law, yes, but they do not do so in a vacuum. They do not do so in the absence of a specific case. Without actual private litigants, there would be no occasion for courts to declare any law. Further, when courts do declare law, this is on the basis of contentions and arguments put before them by the opposite sides in the case. You might profitably review the *Butterfield, Davies,* and *Loach* cases with the thought of identifying some of the very contentions and arguments in those cases that the courts were either rejecting or accepting. These contentions and arguments did not spring solely from the judges themselves. Most of them were urged upon the courts by the lawyers for the parties.

Third, as for determining the facts of particular disputes and applying law thereto, whether in the course of alternative dispute resolution or within the public court system, private citizens and their lawyers are thoroughly active from beginning to end, as we demonstrated in depth in the Swimming Pool case. Consider whether you agree with this argument concerning that case: "Ms. Brown's lawyer actually lost the case by his own mishandling of it. He should have emphasized from the outset the failure of the defendant to post adequate warning signs against diving rather than the fact that the pool was oddly constructed. With the evidence structured in accordance with this theory, the jury would have properly found the defendant negligent. And, equally important, Ms. Brown's own negligent failure to look around carefully would not, on this view, have constituted contributory negligence, because the defendant blew the last clear chance to avoid the accident by failing to give adequate warning. Ms. Brown's lawyer mishandled her case in other ways as well. This was his first trial all alone, whereas defense counsel was a seasoned professional."

Fourth, once the plaintiff secures judgment, this is by no means equivalent to satisfaction of judgment. We saw that in the remedial instrument as we know it, the citizen, through his lawyer, again must often take further steps to bring the strong arm of the law into play. In short, the whole process is in large part privately propelled.

Fifth, private persons dissatisfied with the basic remedial methods, law, structures, or processes can always turn to legislators to seek reforms. The initiative for legislative action commonly comes from outside the legislature—from private citizens and their lawyers. For example, in getting the law changed from a contributory negligence approach to an apportionment approach, private persons have played significant roles.

A. Attorney's Zealousness

Let us now look more closely at the roles of the lawyer. At this stage of the book, an appropriate step is to narrow the focus to the lawyer's role as advocate in court, but we shall eventually consider the lawyer's other roles such as negotiator and adviser. The best general statement on the advocate's role, as ideally conceived, is probably that adopted by a joint conference of the American Bar Association and the Association of American Law Schools. That statement, which follows, also offers the classic rationale for the adversary system.

We follow that excerpt with one of the most famous attacks on the adversary system and the lawyer's role within it. The author was a very prominent judge and critic of the American legal system. His arguments and examples are powerful. As you read him, try your hand at formulating appropriate limits on cross-examination.

JOINT CONFERENCE ON PROFESSIONAL RESPONSIBILITY, REPORT
44 A.B.A. J. 1159, 1160–61 (1958)*

The lawyer appearing as an advocate before a tribunal presents, as persuasively as he can, the facts and the law of the case as seen from the standpoint of his client's interest. It is essential that both the lawyer and the public understand clearly the nature of the role thus discharged. Such an understanding is required not only to appreciate the need for an adversary presentation of issues, but also in order to perceive truly the limits partisan advocacy must impose on itself if it is to remain wholesome and useful.

In a very real sense it may be said that the integrity of the adjudicative process itself depends upon the participation of the advocate. This becomes apparent when we contemplate the nature of the task assumed by any arbiter who attempts to decide a dispute without the aid of partisan advocacy.

Such an arbiter must undertake, not only the role of judge, but that of representative for both of the litigants. Each of these roles must be played to the full without being muted by qualifications derived from the others. When he is developing for each side the most effective statement of its case, the arbiter must put aside his neutrality and permit himself to be moved by a sympathetic identification sufficiently intense to draw from his mind all that it is capable of giving—in analysis, patience and creative power. When he resumes his neutral position, he must be able to view with distrust the fruits of this identification and be ready to reject the products of his own best mental efforts. The difficulties of this undertaking are obvious. If it is true that a man in his time must play many parts, it is scarcely given to him to play them all at once.

It is small wonder, then, that failure generally attends the attempt to dispense with the distinct roles traditionally implied in adjudication. What generally occurs in practice is that at some early point a familiar pattern will seem to emerge from the evidence; an accustomed label is waiting for the case and, without awaiting further proofs, this label is promptly assigned to it. It is a mistake to suppose that this premature cataloguing must necessarily result from impatience, prejudice or mental sloth. Often it proceeds from a very understandable desire to bring the hearing into some order and coherence, for without some tentative theory of the case there is no standard of relevance by which testimony may be measured. But what starts as a preliminary diagnosis designed to direct the inquiry tends, quickly and imperceptibly, to become a fixed conclusion, as all that confirms the diagnosis makes a strong imprint on the mind, while all that runs counter to it is received with diverted attention.

An adversary presentation seems the only effective means for combatting this natural human tendency to judge too swiftly in terms of the familiar that which is not yet fully known. The arguments of counsel hold the case, as it were, in suspension between two opposing interpretations of it. While the proper classification of the case is thus kept unresolved, there is time to explore all of its peculiarities and nuances.

These are the contributions made by partisan advocacy during the public hearing of the cause. When we take into account the preparations that must precede the hearing, the essential quality of the advocate's contribution becomes even more apparent. Preceding the hearing, inquiries must be instituted to determine what facts can be proved or seem sufficiently established to warrant a formal test of their truth during the hearing. There must also be a preliminary analysis of the issues, so that the hearing may have form and direction. These preparatory measures are indispensable whether or not the parties involved in the controversy are represented by advocates.

Where that representation is present there is an obvious advantage in the fact that the area of dispute may be greatly reduced by an exchange of written pleadings or by stipulations of counsel. Without the participation of someone who can act responsibly for each of the parties, this

---

essential narrowing of the issues becomes impossible. But here again the true significance of partisan advocacy lies deeper, touching once more the integrity of the adjudicative process itself. It is only through the advocate's participation that the hearing may remain in fact what it purports to be in theory: a public trial of the facts and issues. Each advocate comes to the hearing prepared to present his proofs and arguments, knowing at the same time that his arguments may fail to persuade and that his proofs may be rejected as inadequate. It is a part of his role to absorb these possible disappointments. The deciding tribunal, on the other hand, comes to the hearing uncommitted. It has not represented to the public that any fact can be proved, that any argument is sound, or that any particular way of stating a litigant's case is the most effective expression of its merits.

The matter assumes a very different aspect when the deciding tribunal is compelled to take into its own hands the preparations that must precede the public hearing. In such a case the tribunal cannot truly be said to come to the hearing uncommitted, for it has itself appointed the channels along which the public inquiry is to run. If an unexpected turn in the testimony reveals a miscalculation in the design of these channels, there is no advocate to absorb the blame. The deciding tribunal is under a strong temptation to keep the hearing moving within the boundaries originally set for it. The result may be that the hearing loses its character as an open trial of the facts and issues, and becomes instead a ritual designed to provide public confirmation for what the tribunal considers it has already established in private. When this occurs adjudication acquires the taint affecting all institutions that become subject to manipulation, presenting one aspect to the public, another to knowing participants.

These, then, are the reasons for believing that partisan advocacy plays a vital and essential role in one of the most fundamental procedures of a democratic society. But if we were to put all of these detailed considerations to one side, we should still be confronted by the fact that, in whatever form adjudication may appear, the experienced judge or arbitrator desires and actively seeks to obtain an adversary presentation of the issues. Only when he has had the benefit of intelligent and vigorous advocacy on both sides can he feel fully confident of his decision.

Viewed in this light, the role of the lawyer as a partisan advocate appears not as a regrettable necessity, but as an indispensable part of a larger ordering of affairs. The institution of advocacy is not a concession to the frailties of human nature, but an expression of human insight in the design of a social framework within which man's capacity for impartial judgment can attain its fullest realization.

When advocacy is thus viewed, it becomes clear by what principle limits must be set to partisanship. The advocate plays his role well when zeal for his client's cause promotes a wise and informed decision of the case. He plays his role badly, and trespasses against the obligations of professional responsibility, when his desire to win leads him to muddy the headwaters of decision, when, instead of lending a needed perspective to the controversy, he distorts and obscures its true nature.

JEROME FRANK, COURTS ON TRIAL
80–85 (1949)*

When we say that present-day trial methods are "rational," presumably we mean this: The men who compose our trial courts, judges and juries, in each law-suit conduct an intelligent inquiry

* Jerome Frank, *Courts on Trial: Myth and Reality in American Justice*. Copyright 1949 by Jerome Frank; copyright renewed © 1976 by Princeton University Press. Excerpt pgs. 80–85, reprinted by permission of Princeton University Press.

into all the practically available evidence, in order to ascertain, as near as may be, the truth about the facts of that suit. That might be called the "investigatory" or "truth" method of trying cases. Such a method can yield no more than a guess, nevertheless an educated guess....

... Our mode of trials is commonly known as "contentious" or "adversary." It is based on what I would call the "fight" theory, a theory which derives from the origin of trials as substitutes for private out-of-court brawls.

Many lawyers maintain that the "fight" theory and the "truth" theory coincide. They think that the best way for a court to discover the facts in a suit is to have each side strive as hard as it can, in a keenly partisan spirit, to bring to the court's attention the evidence favorable to that side. Macaulay said that we obtain the fairest decision "when two men argue, as unfairly as possible, on opposite sides," for then "it is certain that no important consideration will altogether escape notice."

Unquestionably that view contains a core of good sense. The zealously partisan lawyers sometimes do bring into court evidence which, in a dispassionate inquiry, might be overlooked. Apart from the fact element of the case, the opposed lawyers also illuminate for the court niceties of the legal rules which the judge might otherwise not perceive. The "fight" theory, therefore, has invaluable qualities with which we cannot afford to dispense.

But frequently the partisanship of the opposing lawyers blocks the uncovering of vital evidence or leads to a presentation of vital testimony in a way that distorts it....

What is the role of the lawyers in bringing the evidence before the trial court? As you may learn by reading any one of a dozen or more handbooks on how to try a law-suit, an experienced lawyer uses all sorts of stratagems to minimize the effect on the judge or jury of testimony disadvantageous to his client, even when the lawyer has no doubt of the accuracy and honesty of that testimony. The lawyer considers it his duty to create a false impression, if he can, of any witness who gives such testimony. If such a witness happens to be timid, frightened by the unfamiliarity of courtroom ways, the lawyer, in his cross-examination,

plays on that weakness, in order to confuse the witness and make it appear that he is concealing significant facts. Longenecker, in his book Hints on the Trial of a Law Suit (a book endorsed by the great Wigmore), in writing of the "truthful, honest, over-cautious" witness, tells how "a skilful advocate by a rapid cross-examination may ruin the testimony of such a witness." The author does not even hint any disapproval of that accomplishment. Longenecker's and other similar books recommend that a lawyer try to prod an irritable but honest "adverse" witness into displaying his undesirable characteristics in their most unpleasant form, in order to discredit him with the judge or jury. "You may," writes Harris, "sometimes destroy the effect of an adverse witness by making him appear more hostile than he really is...." Taft says that a clever cross-examiner, dealing with an honest but egotistic witness, will "deftly tempt the witness to indulge in his propensity for exaggeration, so as to make him 'hang himself.' And thus," adds Taft, "it may happen that not only is the value of his testimony lost, but the side which produces him suffers for seeking aid from such a source"— although, I would add, that may be the only source of evidence of a fact on which the decision will turn.

... Anthony Trollope, in one of his novels, indignantly reacted to these methods. "One would naturally imagine," he said, "that an undisturbed thread of clear evidence would be best obtained from a man whose position was made easy and whose mind was not harassed; but this is not the fact; to turn a witness to good account, he must be badgered this way and that till he is nearly mad; he must be made a laughing-stock for the court; his very truths must be turned into falsehoods, so that he may be falsely shamed; he must be accused of all manner of villainy, threatened with all manner of punishment; he must be made to feel that he has no friend near him, that the world is all against him; he must be confounded till he forget his right hand from his left, till his mind be turned into chaos, and his heart into water; and then let him give his evidence. What will fall from his lips when in this wretched collapse must be of special value, for the best talents of practiced forensic heroes are daily used to bring it about; and no member of the Humane Society interferes to protect the wretch. Some sorts of torture are as it were tacitly allowed even among humane people. Eels are skinned alive, and witnesses are sacrificed, and no one's blood curdles at the sight, no soft heart is sickened at the cruelty." This may be a somewhat overdrawn picture. Yet, referring to this manner of handling witnesses, Sir Frederic Eggleston recently said that it prevents lawyers from inducing persons who know important facts from disclosing them to lawyers for litigants. He notes, too, that "the terrors of cross-examination are such that a party can often force a settlement by letting it be known that a certain … counsel has been retained."

The lawyer not only seeks to discredit adverse witnesses but also to hide the defects of witnesses who testify favorably to his client. If, when interviewing such a witness before trial, the lawyer notes that the witness has mannerisms, demeanor-traits, which might discredit him, the lawyer teaches him how to cover up those traits when testifying: He educates the irritable witness to conceal his irritability, the cocksure witness to subdue his cocksureness. In that way, the trial court is denied the benefit of observing the witness's actual normal demeanor, and thus prevented from sizing up the witness accurately.

Lawyers freely boast of their success with these tactics. They boast also of such devices as these: If an "adverse," honest witness, on cross-examination, makes seemingly inconsistent statements, the cross-examiner tries to keep the witness from explaining away the apparent inconsistencies. "When," writes Tracy, counseling trial lawyers, in a much-praised book, "by your cross-examination, you have caught the witness in an inconsistency, the next question that will immediately come to your lips is, 'Now, let's hear you explain.' Don't ask it, for he may explain and, if he does, your point will have been lost. If you have conducted your cross-examination properly (which includes interestingly), the jury will have seen the inconsistency and it will have made the proper impression on their minds. If, on re-direct examination the witness does explain, the explanation will have come later in the case and at the request of the counsel who originally called the witness and the jury will be much more likely to look askance at the explanation than if it were made during your cross-examination." Tracy adds, "Be careful in your questions on cross-examination not to open a door that you have every reason to wish kept closed." That is, don't let in any reliable evidence, hurtful to your side, which would help the trial court to arrive at the truth. …

In short, the lawyer aims at victory, at winning in the fight, not at aiding the court to discover the facts. He does not want the trial court to reach a sound educated guess, if it is likely to be contrary to his client's interests. Our present trial method is thus the equivalent of throwing pepper in the eyes of a surgeon when he is performing an operation. …

However unpleasant all this may appear, do not blame trial lawyers for using the techniques I have described. If there is to be criticism, it should be directed at the system that virtually compels their use, a system which treats a lawsuit as a battle of wits and wiles. As a distinguished lawyer has said, these stratagems are "part of the maneuvering … to which [lawyers] are obliged to resort to win their cases. Some of them may appear to be tricky; they may seem to be taking undue advantage; but under the present system it is part of a lawyer's duty to employ them because his opponent is doing the same thing, and if he refrains from doing so, he is violating his duty to his client and giving his opponent an unquestionable advantage. …" These tricks of the trade are today the legitimate and accepted corollary of our fight theory.

ALVIN B. LEBAR, SHADOWS IN THE COURTROOM

Case & Com., Nov.-Dec. 1975, at 49, 51–53*

Louis J, at 38 years of age was such a physical specimen that after meeting him, you would go home and start doing push-ups. A college tennis champ and all around "comer," he had married well and things had been on the rise ever since. His wife, Adeline, "my Addie" as Lou liked to say, was a svelte campus queen from a high placed social family and a fine sportswoman herself. She was also a straightforward and likeable person.

Although it's been many years, I cannot think of the old Monterey Hotel in Asbury Park without seeing Lou and Addie. In 1949 the Monterey was the "in" spot at Asbury. A huge, bluish tinted cement building with white ornamental woodwork, the place dominated the maze of hotels pressed against the colorful boardwalk. The Monterey, like all such grand ladies was to fall on hard times but it was then a place of grace and luxury. Lou was part owner of a heavy equipment company in New York and on the verge of closing an important business deal in South Jersey. To be certain of the details, he decided to come out and finalize the transaction. He arranged to stay at the Monterey. On a Friday evening in August he drove a shiny white Cadillac up to the entrance of the Hotel. The car was less than a week old. After signing the register, he turned the keys of the car over to the bellhop to park. In those days, many of the bellhops were farm boys from surrounding rural Monmouth County with an inordinate interest in motor cars. In any event, the bellhop took the car for a joy ride, instead of the parking lot, and late that evening—smashed it into a utility pole. The Caddie was a total wreck as was the bellhop, although the boy survived to tell the tale. A cash purchase, for some reason the comprehensive insurance on the car was not operative at the time of the accident. The company denied coverage.

I had known Lou only slightly, meeting him as a co-member of an interstate charity board but he was really out of my league. At the time we filed suit against the hotel for the value of the car

(having failed to collect from the insurance company) he was a fast rising political star and prime candidate for a major appointment in New York. Our suit alleged that the Hotel Monterey was responsible for the negligence of its employee, the badly battered bellhop. A simple matter ... only the value of the car was in issue. The answering pleadings admitted that Lou was a guest at the hotel and had paid his bill. In response to my client's pointed inquiries over the ensuing months, I stated that the case had been narrowed to the matter of auto damages.

The trial was scheduled for a hot July morning in the old County Courthouse on Main Street in Freehold, New Jersey. A special summer date was assigned the hearing so that Lou might attend a business convention in Brussels. Outside the dusty parking lot, the temperature seemed cool compared to the heat of the courtroom. The air hung heavy, sliced quietly by the circling overhead ceiling fan. Other than the judge and jury, the only persons in attendance were a little knot of principals who sat close to the counsels' bench during the trial. Just before opening, we tried to settle the case for a bit under book value but to no avail. By the time we broke for lunch at 1 P.M., we had proved the accident through the local police; the employment relationship between hotel and bellhop, and other details.

Lou had driven to Freehold with his wife, Addie and both were in high spirits during our lunch at the American Restaurant and Bar across the street. We were having such a good time, that it was downright unpleasant returning to the sweltering courtroom. In the afternoon, our first witness was Lou himself. We whizzed through the direct examination, Lou proving a sharp, articulate and impressive witness. Under cross-examination, the defendant's counsel spoke quietly ... barely audible. Lou fenced the opening questions nicely and then it happened. Opening his briefcase, the lawyer produced the hotel registry

---

Monterey Hotel, Asbury Park, N.J.

book and, with voice rising, asked that it be marked for identification. I objected, noting lightly that registration had *already* been admitted in the hotel's answering pleading but the lawyer persisted in placing the book in evidence anyway. He was allowed to pursue the matter. At this point I should have noticed that Lou's perennial tan was turning chalky white well before the crucial question by counsel: "Is this your signature in the registry for Mr. and *Mrs.* Louis J?" *MRS.* LOUIS J? Mrs. J, Addie, that is, shot up straight and stared at her husband. She told me at lunch she had never been to Asbury Park ... certainly not that night, anyway. In the meantime, before I could object further, Lou was turning increasingly pallid, his solid confidence fading fast. Words weren't coming out ... just sounds. I started to mumble something about the Fifth Amendment and self-incrimination but Lou wasn't listening. He was busy just cracking up. We asked for and received a halt in the trial so that my client might regain his composure but by 4 P.M. he was still unable to return to the witness stand forcing us to settle the case for less than half its worth. I still regret it. The question of possible adultery, while it might bear on credibility, was really irrelevant to the issue. I doubt if it would have made any difference even before a rural jury of that day. But it was no longer of consequence.

I watched Lou and Addie spin away from the parking lot in yet another new Cadillac heading towards Route #9 and New York City. She was sitting in the back. They would never be the same.

It was more than a year later that I read of their marital separation and property settlement. *This* story was widely covered by the New York press. I doubt if any of the reporters ever heard of the Monterey Hotel. Lou wished he hadn't either.

B. Attorney's Competence

The book has by now introduced you to the historically influential English courts. It has also dealt with the numerically significant state court cases. Now you are ready to see the systemically important federal courts. *Reizakis*

Adverse Fact and Law

Although a lawyer is under a general duty of truthfulness that proscribes outright lying, it is accepted that a lawyer need not volunteer facts known to her but adverse to her client's interests, except in certain special circumstances. No general duty of candor exists. Quite to the contrary, in her proper role as a zealous representative, a lawyer is under a duty not to reveal voluntarily any adverse facts, unless her client consents. Thus, an ethics committee approved the conduct of the defendant's attorney in the following circumstances:

> In an action on behalf of an infant three years of age, for injuries sustained by falling off a porch owned by the defendant, due to the alleged negligence of the defendant, where there is no eyewitness known to the plaintiff's attorney, and thereafter when the case came to trial, the infant's case was dismissed on motion of the defendant's attorney on the ground that the infant plaintiff was unable to make out a sufficient case of circumstantial evidence. During the presentation of the plaintiff's case, said attorney for the defendant had an eyewitness to said accident actually present in court, and did not mention said fact, either to the plaintiff's attorney or to the Court and kept the Court in ignorance of the fact that a person did exist who actually saw said accident, and was present in court.

New York County Lawyers' Association Comm. on Professional Ethics, Op. 309 (1933).

Strangely enough, the prevailing ethical rules, which are adopted by the American Bar Association as a model for binding rules within the several states, provide that a lawyer shall not knowingly "fail to disclose to the tribunal legal authority in the controlling jurisdiction known to the lawyer to be directly adverse to the position of the client and not disclosed by opposing counsel." Model Rules of Professional Conduct Rule 3.3(a)(3) (1983).

These contrasting commands present many problems of interpretation and application. But let us cut to the heart of the matter: Why do you think that there is a duty to disclose adverse law but not fact?

On the one hand, perhaps the need for disclosure is greater for law than for fact. Which is the court more likely to learn on its own: law or fact? But which, if nondisclosed, holds a greater potential for eventually embarrassing the judge? Which would lawyers more likely disclose, if obligated to? Which is more important to society, as opposed to the parties, to resolve accurately? Law seems to be the answer, assuming law is always readily distinguishable from fact in this context. "A common-law tradition where individual decisions strongly affect the development of legal doctrine for future cases almost necessarily implies a reasoning together of bench and bar and a candid and thorough exploration of the legal issues and precedents." Jack B. Weinstein, Judicial Notice and the Duty to Disclose Adverse Information, 51 Iowa L. Rev. 807, 810 (1966).

On the other hand, even if the need for disclosure is greater for law than for fact, the inconsistency could imply that either the disclosure rule for law or the nondisclosure rule for fact is wrong. Which, then, should be reformed? Disclosure of adverse law appears to be both a beneficial exception to adversary behavior and an exception that the system can sustain. This exception suggests more broadly that there may be structural reforms (e.g., alleviating lawyer mismatches) or new limits on the advocate's behavior (e.g., tempering cross-examination) that could be implemented with beneficial effect but without endangering or abandoning the system itself. Other changes, however, may be basically at odds with the system. Could disclosure of adverse fact, then, be instituted without undermining the spirit of partisan advocacy essential to the adversary system? At any rate, would such a disclosure rule discourage private factual investigation, give unethical lawyers a big advantage, or damage the attorney-client relationship? In the long run and in a practical sense, would truth, procedural justice, and party satisfaction be served thereby? Perhaps not.

is an ordinary negligence case that could be brought in a federal trial court because of the parties' diversity of citizenship. The action proceeded pursuant to the previously mentioned Federal Rules of Civil Procedure. We encounter it on appeal by the plaintiff from the dismissal of his case, a dismissal that raises interesting questions regarding the role of lawyers as well as the role of judges in policing lawyers.

REIZAKIS v. LOY
United States Court of Appeals, Fourth Circuit, 1974
490 F.2d 1132

Thomas J. Harrigan, Arlington, Va. (Harrigan, Morris & Artz, Arlington, Va., on brief), for appellant.

Richard H. Lewis, Fairfax, Va. (Brault, Lewis, Geschickter & Palmer, Fairfax, Va., on brief), for appellee.

Before BOREMAN, SENIOR CIRCUIT JUDGE, and BUTZNER and RUSSELL, CIRCUIT JUDGES.

BUTZNER, CIRCUIT JUDGE:

Paris Reizakis appeals from an order dismissing his action against Albert E. Loy with prejudice.[1] Because the circumstances disclosed by this record do not justify the sanction imposed by the district court, we reverse.

[This personal injury action arose from an automobile accident on Monday, April 13, 1970, on U.S. Route 50 in Fairfax County, Virginia. The Canadian plaintiff-pedestrian sued the American defendant-driver on April 16, 1971, in the United States District Court for the Eastern District of Virginia. During the discovery phase, the plaintiff's counsel engaged in some minor foot-dragging.]

During these proceedings, Reizakis was represented by Peter A. Chaconas, of Washington, D.C., and Rudolph N. D'Agaris, of Maryland. Because neither were [locally qualified], they were prohibited by a local rule of the district court from representing Reizakis without being associated with a Virginia attorney who had been admitted to practice in the court. Reizakis' Virginia attorney was Robert C. Watson. In the latter part of May [1972], Watson, with Reizakis' consent, prepared an order to permit D'Agaris and him to withdraw. At the June [15th] pretrial conference, the court denied withdrawal until Watson was replaced by another Virginia lawyer and set the case for trial on

Tuesday, September 12, 1972. Notwithstanding the denial of his motion to withdraw, Watson took the position that Reizakis had released him in May. He notified Reizakis of the trial date, but apparently neither he nor D'Agaris did anything further to prepare for trial.

Sometime after the middle of August, Chaconas satisfied himself that the doctors who were to be Reizakis' witnesses would be available for the September trial. However, he did not obtain subpoenas for them. In the meantime, acting on behalf of Reizakis, he made several unsuccessful attempts to engage local counsel to replace Watson, but not until the first week of September did he succeed in obtaining a new Virginia associate.

On Thursday, September 7, five days before the scheduled trial, Thomas J. Harrigan, the replacement for Watson, and Richard H. Lewis, attorney for Loy appeared before the district court. They were accompanied by Watson who moved for a continuance of the trial so that Harrigan could have a reasonable time to prepare the case. The record does not indicate that Lewis offered any objection at this time. The court, however, denied the continuance, and Harrigan declined to enter a formal appearance because he believed he could not prepare adequately in

---

1. The court acted under Fed. R. Civ. P. 41(b), which provides in part:

   For failure of the plaintiff to prosecute or to comply with these rules or any order of court, a defendant may move for dismissal of an action or of any claim against him.... Unless the court in its order for dismissal otherwise specifies, a dismissal under this subdivision ... operates as an adjudication upon the merits.

   The statute of limitations also bars reassertion of Reizakis' claim.

the short time remaining. Harrigan promptly told Chaconas of the court's ruling, and although he had not entered a formal appearance, he nevertheless said that if the witnesses were available he would attempt to prepare the case. The next day, Friday, Chaconas told Harrigan that the doctors were available and that the case was ready. Harrigan studied the file over the week end, but when he telephoned the doctors on Monday, September 11, he learned that none of them could be present. By this time it was too late to subpoena them.

On the day of trial, Tuesday, September 12, Reizakis, Chaconas, Watson, D'Agaris, and Harrigan appeared in the district court. Chaconas, citing the absence of the doctors, moved for a continuance. Lewis, noting the inconvenience to Loy's witnesses, objected, and the court denied the motion. Chaconas then stated that the witnesses who were to testify on the issue of liability were present, and he moved to have the trial proceed on this issue and for a continuance of the damage issue only. Again, Lewis objected, and the court denied the motion. Chaconas then conceded that in view of the court's rulings it was impossible to proceed, and Lewis moved to dismiss the case for lack of prosecution. The court granted the motion and assessed the costs, including jury fees, mileage, and per diem against Reizakis. It then granted Watson's and D'Agaris' motion to withdraw.

A district court unquestionably has authority to grant a motion to dismiss for want of prosecution. Fed. R. Civ. P. 41(b). Indeed, as the Supreme Court held in Link v. Wabash R.R., 370 U.S. 626, 82 S. Ct. 1386 (1962), the trial court can take such action on its own motion. But courts interpreting the rule uniformly hold that it cannot be automatically or mechanically applied. Against the power to prevent delays must be weighed the sound public policy of deciding cases on their merits. Consequently, dismissal "must be tempered by a careful exercise of judicial discretion." Durgin v. Graham, 372 F.2d 130, 131 (5th Cir. 1967). While the propriety of dismissal ultimately turns on the facts of each case, criteria for judging whether the discretion of the trial court has been soundly exercised have been stated frequently. Rightfully, courts are reluctant to punish a client for the

behavior of his lawyer. Therefore, in situations where a party is not responsible for the fault of his attorney, dismissal may be invoked only in extreme circumstances. Indeed, it has been observed that "[t]he decided cases, while noting that dismissal is a discretionary matter, have generally permitted it only in the face of a clear record of delay or contumacious conduct by the plaintiff." Durham v. Florida East Coast Ry. Co., 385 F.2d 366, 368 (5th Cir. 1967). Appellate courts frequently have found abuse of discretion when trial courts failed to apply sanctions less severe than dismissal. And generally lack of prejudice to the defendant, though not a bar to dismissal, is a factor that must be considered in determining whether the trial court exercised sound discretion.

It is in the light of the foregoing interpretation of Rule 41(b) that we must consider the circumstances of this case. The facts do not depict "a drawn out history" of "deliberately proceeding in dilatory fashion," as in Link v. Wabash R.R., 370 U.S. 626, 633, 82 S. Ct. 1386, 1390 (1962). Moreover, Reizakis was not shown to be personally responsible for any of the incidents that delayed the case. While he knew that Watson wished to withdraw, he not unreasonably expected his principal counsel, Chaconas, to arrange for a local associate to comply with the rules. Furthermore, he apparently knew nothing about the failure to subpoena the doctors. To the contrary, it appears that he advanced money for witness fees and expected the case to be tried as scheduled. His attorneys were unable to proceed either because they failed to give the doctors adequate notice, or because Chaconas relied on his understanding that the doctors would be available without taking the precaution of subpoenaing them. In selecting an appropriate sanction for this dereliction, the district court did not consider measures less drastic than dismissal, such as imposing a fine or costs against Reizakis' attorneys. Finally, it does not appear that a continuance would have prejudiced Loy's defense. Of course, Loy, his witnesses, and his attorney would have been subjected to extra expenses and inconvenience if the case had been rescheduled, but monetary sanctions were available to rectify this harm as well. Moreover, inconvenience to some of the witnesses could have been prevented by trying the issue of liability as suggested by Reizakis' counsel.

The District Court for the Eastern District of Virginia is exceptionally busy, and the demands on the time of its judges and its jurors are great. Its judges properly are diligent in bringing litigation to trial without delay. But the interpretation of Rule 41(b) found in the well reasoned cases cited above bars dismissal for the circumstances disclosed by this record. Available to the district court were lesser sanctions sufficient to assure prompt disposition of this case and to discourage similar conduct in the future. Additionally, the liability issue could have been tried, and if Reizakis lost, the case would have ended without further delay.

The judgment is reversed, and this case is remanded with directions that it be reinstated.

BOREMAN, SENIOR CIRCUIT JUDGE (dissenting):

With all due regard and respect for the opinion of my brothers, somewhat reluctantly I state this note of disagreement. Naturally, our sympathies are with any litigant who suddenly discovers that the results of his counsel's inattention, indifference, lack of diligence, or negligence, are visited upon him in terms of the dismissal of his case and the loss of an opportunity to be compensated in damages for personal injuries; but sympathy can have no place in the decision process. Each case properly is to be considered on its own peculiar facts and circumstances. . . .

[The following] excerpt [is] from the transcript of the proceedings before the court when the case was called for trial.

> MR. CHACONAS: At this moment, Your Honor, I would like to make a motion.
> THE COURT: All right, sir.
> MR. CHACONAS: I would like to make an oral motion to ask for a continuance in this case due to the fact that our expert witnesses are not available at this moment. We do not know when they will be, and if your Honor does not grant us the motion, therefore, I ask that the case will not be submitted to this Court at this time.
> THE COURT: The case has been set for trial since June 15. Ample time has been

had to prepare the case. If there was a question of the unavailability of any witnesses, that should have been ascertained from depositions taken. There was ample time for those depositions.
> MR. CHACONAS: For the record, I would like also to state that these Doctors are not available because they are performing their duties in the medical profession as we are attempting here to perform our duties in the legal profession.

> I do respect the Court's opinion in denying me the motion for a continuance, but I want the record to clearly show that there was an attempt by the Attorneys for the Plaintiff to obtain and retain these Doctors to appear here today, and I want the record to clearly state that.
> THE COURT: Were subpoenas issued?
> MR. CHACONAS: There were no subpoenas issued. There were telephone conversations and telegrams to ascertain the presence of these Doctors, but unfortunately, apparently, their emergencies were above their presentation here for the purposes of their patients, I suppose.
> THE COURT: Can you tell me when you first ascertained that they would not be available?
> MR. CHACONAS: Well, we began three and four weeks ago and as of Friday we ascertained that one of the Doctors would be available today, but he is out of town, and through secretaries or answering service or whatever it may be, but the point is that they were contacted through their agencies or agents or through the answering bureau or the Medical Bureau, and they were put on notice and we have taken our position that they were put on notice.
> THE COURT: Three or four weeks ago when you ascertained that some of them might be unavailable was any effort made—
> MR. CHACONAS: No, your Honor, we were not put on that notice. We were put on notice that they would be in contact

and be available, and that is where we stand. I don't think that a legal profession should be running around on a horse looking for Tonto or something like that. These people are owed money. They have for two years been taking care of Mr. Reizakis. I don't know what it is. It is just a situation that is difficult for our profession, and I do hope you sympathize with our position that we just cannot put these people in line to just come in sometimes, and it is not a question that they are being denied their fee because the fees are available; they are income, and I do believe that the client—and the client is not a citizen of this country. This is the unfortunate part about it.

Your Honor, the client has a right to be represented and he has a right to be represented in the sense that we do have available people to testify for him, and the surety of the situation is with professionalism, whatever it may be.

I am not trying to put on a speech. They are just not here, and we did our duty as officers of the court, and that is all we can do....

No citation of authority is needed to support the premise that district courts must have control of their dockets without disruption or interference in order to assure the orderly conduct of the court's business. I take judicial notice of the fact that the Eastern District of Virginia is an extremely busy district; the dockets ... are overburdened with cases involving litigants who are often anxiously and impatiently awaiting the opportunity to have their "turn at bat"—to have their day in court. The rapidly developing policy of the judicial system looks with disfavor upon counsel's lack of diligence or negligence in preparing cases for trial. The court is in position to get the "feel" of the case and to appraise the attitude of counsel toward the diligent prosecution of the litigation....

The court, in States Steamship Company v. Philippine Air Lines, 426 F.2d 803, 804 (9 Cir. 1970), had this to say:

Whether the judge misused or abused his discretion, of necessity, depends upon the facts of each case. This court has never

attempted to fix guidelines, although a good rule of thumb might be to follow Judge Magruder's oft-quoted phrase in In re Josephson, 218 F.2d 174, 182 (1st Cir. 1954), that the exercise of discretion of the trial judge should not be disturbed unless there is "a definite and firm conviction that the court below committed a clear error of judgment in the conclusion it reached upon a weighing of the relevant factors." ...

In an action for damages for personal injuries, Link v. Wabash Railroad Co., 370 U.S. 626, 82 S. Ct. 1386 (1962), it appears that after extended pretrial proceedings which delayed the maturing of the case the trial court, on September 29, 1960, scheduled a pretrial conference for one o'clock on October 12, 1960, and notified counsel for both sides. Late in the morning of October 12 plaintiff's counsel telephoned the judge's secretary that he was otherwise engaged in another city, that he could not attend the conference at the appointed hour but that he would be there on the afternoon of October 13 or anytime on October 14 if the pretrial conference could be reset. When plaintiff's counsel failed to appear on October 12 the court, sua sponte, dismissed the action for failure of counsel to appear and for failure to prosecute. The Court upheld the action of the trial court, even in the absence of a motion to dismiss, and at pages 633 and 634, 82 S. Ct. at page 1390 stated:

On this record we are unable to say that the District Court's dismissal of this action for failure to prosecute, as evidenced only partly by the failure of petitioner's counsel to appear at a duly scheduled pretrial conference, amounted to an abuse of discretion. It was certainly within the bounds of permissible discretion for the court to conclude that the telephone excuse offered by petitioner's counsel was inadequate to explain his failure to attend. And it could reasonably be inferred from his absence, as well as from the drawn-out history of the litigation, ... that petitioner had been deliberately proceeding in dilatory fashion.

There is certainly no merit to the contention that dismissal of petitioner's claim because of his counsel's unexcused conduct imposes an unjust penalty on the client. Petitioner voluntarily chose this attorney as his representative in the action, and he cannot now avoid the consequences of the acts or omissions of this freely selected agent. Any other notion would be wholly inconsistent with our system of representative litigation, in which each party is deemed bound by the acts of his lawyer-agent and is considered to have "notice of all facts, notice of which can be charged upon the attorney." Smith v. Ayer, 101 U.S. 320, 326.

Lack of diligence of plaintiff and his counsel in the preparation of the instant case and in complying with the court's orders and directions is evident. We have no satisfactory information as to the problems confronting the court with respect to granting a continuance, but I venture the statement that if every plaintiff-litigant requested a continuance on the date fixed for the trial of his case and refused to proceed any attempt by the court to maintain the orderly control of its business would be an exercise in futility. No court can succeed if it permits the lawyers, officers of the court, to control the dockets and the court's business.

In the case at bar it is argued, and the majority holds, that the negligent conduct of plaintiff's counsel should not operate to the disadvantage and prejudice of their client. However, the district court noted that the plaintiff himself was not blameless:

> THE COURT: In June when I set this case for trial Mr. Watson then said that he was then requesting to withdraw. I wouldn't let him withdraw. I told him

he would have to tell his client that the case was definitely going to be tried on September 12, and that if he had to get another counsel that there were two months left for him to get counsel at least, three months, and so the Plaintiff, insofar as counsel is concerned, is not blameless in this matter.

He has known for some time that the case was going to be tried today with or without Mr. Watson, and there was no reason that he could not have notified his Doctors as early as June and ascertained then their availability.

As the late Judge Sobeloff ... wrote in Universal Film Exchanges, Inc. v. Lust, 479 F.2d 573, 577:

> Our decision does not leave a client without remedy against the negligent attorney. Lawyers are not a breed apart. Where damages are inflicted upon innocent clients by other professionals, such as doctors or dentists, the remedy is a suit for malpractice. The same is true where damage is inflicted upon a client through an attorney's professional negligence. Indeed, the Supreme Court explicitly pointed out in Link, supra, 370 U.S. 626, 82 S. Ct. 1386 at n.10, that if the attorney's conduct was substantially below what was reasonable under the circumstances, the client's remedy was a suit for malpractice.

Upon this record I am not convinced that there was a clear abuse of the court's discretion in granting the defendant's motion to dismiss under Rule 41(b).

NOTES

1. Remedies, substantive general rules defining their availability, structures and processes for applying remedial law to facts of particular cases—all these are integral features of the anatomy and physiology of law as a remedial instrument. But what value would this instrument have if it lacked power to coerce? What if the defendant in the *Brown* case had refused to be haled into court at all? What if the court then entered a default judgment, but when the sheriff came to confiscate some of the defendant's property to pay the judgment, the defendant's agent

met him at the entrance with a shotgun? What if subpoenaed witnesses refused to show up at the actual trial? What if jurors declined to serve? Or what if someone staged a demonstration in the courtroom while the Hayden Island Amusement Company official was testifying? Plainly, law could not operate as a remedial instrument without power to apply coercive force. It uses coercive sanctions, e.g., dismissal as in *Reizakis*, which is a deprivation of the plaintiff's property interest in a cause of action. Nevertheless, such use is subject to strict controls laid out in case law, court rules, statutes, and the Constitution. Recall that the Fifth and Fourteenth Amendments prohibit the government's deprivation "of life, liberty, or property, without due process of law."

2. Dismissal for failure to prosecute is within the discretion of the trial judge. However, the appellate court can specify the procedures for exercising that discretion. First, the appellate court can reverse for failure to follow the procedural law. Second, even if the trial judge acts in accordance with all procedural requirements, the appellate court can review the outcome for abuse of discretion. As the *Reizakis* dissent explains, reversal for abuse of discretion means clear error—that the appellate court quite strongly disagrees with the trial judge's decision, not merely that as an original matter the appellate judges would have decided otherwise. Yet, it appears that the appellate court took this second route, despite the trial judge's better "feel" for what had happened.

Section Six
IMPROVING THE REMEDIAL INSTRUMENT

The resources or means of law are not static. They, like the end uses of law, change. When we think of law reform, we normally think of changes in the substantive uses of law. But the improvement of law's own resources is itself a vitally important field for reform. Accordingly, this and the next four chapters include a separate section stressing this point.

A. Improving Adversarial Adjudication

In our exploration of the remedial instrument, many reform proposals have surfaced regarding its methods, law, structures, and processes. For example, we have considered the proper role of the jury and also possible excesses of the adversary system. We could have formulated many other proposals for reform. A prerequisite to any serious proposal is careful study. But undoubtedly, room exists for significant reform of the basic remedial instrument exemplified by the Swimming Pool case.

Let us consider a representative reform proposal. You have probably heard a criticism that sounds like this: "Our system involves appalling delay. In some cities the civil calendar is several years behind. Courts are clogged with cases, principally those arising from accidents. Something must be done. Justice delayed is justice denied." Do you agree? What might be done? Is it not all quite simple?

HANS ZEISEL, HARRY KALVEN, JR. & BERNARD BUCHHOLZ, DELAY IN THE COURT
xxii–xxvi (2d ed. 1978)*

Delay in the courts is unqualifiedly bad. It is bad because it deprives citizens of a basic public service; it is bad because the lapse of time frequently causes deterioration of evidence and makes it less likely that justice be done when the case is finally tried; it is bad because delay may cause severe hardship to some parties and may in general affect litigants differentially; and it is bad because it brings to the entire court system a loss of public confidence, respect, and pride. It invites in brief the wisecrack made a few years ago in a magazine editorial: "Okay, blind, but why so slow?"

These are obvious evils and scarcely require a statement. But in addition, a delayed court system brings in its wake many not so obvious secondary evils. It produces an unhealthy emphasis on the desirability of settlement and on the impropriety of litigation. It creates a stimulus for major changes in substantive law and procedure, such as the abolition of jury trial in civil cases, or shifting large areas of tort law to compensation schemes analogous to workmen's compensation, or changing the rules as to contributory negligence as defense or payment of interest on tort damages. These proposals, whatever their merits, should not be adopted or rejected simply because of extrinsic pressures from a delayed court system. Again, extended delay may result in, indeed almost compel, departure from legal ethics, as lawyers find it necessary to provide financial support for indigent clients over the long interval between accident and trial. And a delayed calendar creates totally new issues for a court, as it seeks to determine what if any cases should be given preference and tried ahead of the others. As Judge Ulysses S. Schwartz of the Illinois Appellate Court eloquently pointed out in a recent opinion, delay in the law is an old, old evil:

The law's delay in many lands and throughout history has been the theme of

tragedy and comedy. Hamlet summarized the seven burdens of man and put the law's delay fifth on his list. If the meter of his verse had permitted, he would perhaps have put it first. Dickens memorialized it in Bleak House, Chekhov, the Russian, and Molière, the Frenchman, have written tragedies based on it. Gilbert and Sullivan have satirized it in song. Thus it is no new problem for the profession, although we doubt that it has ever assumed the proportions which now confront us. "Justice delayed is justice denied," and regardless of the antiquity of the problem and the difficulties it presents the courts and the bar must do everything possible to solve it.[6] . . .

In any study of court congestion questions of tone are important. Concern with the elimination of delay must not blind us to the distinctive nature of the judicial enterprise. The administration of a court is not simply the administration of a business, judges are not simply employees, and the values of the efficiency expert are not the only ones involved. . . .

And yet deference to the subtle values involved should not make it inadmissible to recognize that the administration of justice too involves problems of management and efficiency.

---

6. Gray v. Gray, 6 Ill. App. 2d 571, 578–579, 128 N.E.2d 602, 606 (1955). We might add to Judge Schwartz's roster the report of the law's most distinguished poet laureate on what must have been easily the world's most delayed court. Goethe, after having received his doctor juris degree, practiced law for a while before the Reichskammer Court in Wetzlar, about which he writes in the twelfth chapter of his autobiography: "An immense mountain of swollen files lay there growing every year, since the seventeen assessors were not even able to handle the current workload. Twenty thousand cases had piled up, sixty could be disposed of every year, while twice as many were added." It

was not unusual for a case to remain on the docket for more than a hundred years. One, for instance, involving the city of Gelnhausen, began in 1459 and was in 1734 still waiting for the court's decision. A dispute between the city of Nuremberg and the electorate of Brandenburg had begun in 1526 and remained for ever undecided when in 1806 the court was dissolved. The piteous state of the court created the unique profession of "solicitants" whose sole job it was to secure preferments for their clients. This custom resulted

eventually in the jailing of its leading practitioner and in the removal of three judges from the court because of bribery.

The effects of this delayed court on Goethe were profound and in the end salutary. It made him lose whatever taste he had for the law, gave him sufficient leisure (the court had 174 holidays annually) to fall into desperate love with Charlotte Buff, the heroine of Werther, the novel which was to catapult him firmly into world fame.

RICHARD A. POSNER, AN ECONOMIC APPROACH TO LEGAL PROCEDURE AND JUDICIAL ADMINISTRATION
2 J. Legal Stud. 399, 400–01, 445–48 (1973)*

An important purpose of substantive legal rules (such as the rules of tort and criminal law) is to increase economic efficiency. It follows ... that mistaken imposition of legal liability, or mistaken failure to impose liability, will reduce efficiency. Judicial error is therefore a source of social costs and the reduction of error is a goal of the procedural system. . . .

Even when the legal process works flawlessly, it involves costs—the time of lawyers, litigants, witnesses, jurors, judges, and other people, plus paper and ink, law office and court house maintenance, telephone service, etc. These costs are just as real as the costs resulting from error: in general we would not want to increase the direct costs of the legal process by one dollar in order to reduce error costs by 50 (or 99) cents. The economic goal is thus to minimize the sum of error and direct costs.

Despite its generality, this formulation provides a useful framework in which to analyze the problems and objectives of legal procedure. It is usable even when the purpose of the substantive law is to transfer wealth or to bring about some other noneconomic goal, rather than to improve efficiency. All that is necessary is that it be possible, in principle, to place a price tag on the consequences of failing to apply the substantive law in all cases in which it was intended to apply, so that our two variables, error cost and direct cost, remain commensurable. . . .

... To most experts in judicial administration, delay between the filing and final disposition of a legal claim is an unmitigated evil and the proper focus of judicial reform. This is an odd way to look at the matter. Delay is an omnipresent feature of social and economic life. It is only excessive delay that is undesirable, and what is excessive can be determined only by comparing the costs and benefits of different amounts of delay.

A major cost associated with queuing as a method of rationing goods is the opportunity cost of the time people spend in the queue. Where the parties' time is their own while they wait (as when a theatergoer is forced to "wait" for six months to see a popular musical), the queue is merely a "figurative" queue. The court queue is a literal queue for defendants incarcerated awaiting trial and for some owners of property "tied up" in litigation. Otherwise it is a figurative queue, but this does not mean that it is costless. Court delay increases error costs because the adaptation of legal rules to altered circumstances is retarded and because evidence decays over time, increasing the probability of an erroneous decision. Clearly, at some level of delay error costs would become prohibitive. Delay also increases error costs by widening the gap between damages and judgments that is created by the fact that the legal interest rate is lower than the market rate and interest is usually allowed not from the date of the event giving rise

---

to the suit but only from the date of judgment. This particular source of error cost from delay could be eliminated simply by increasing the interest rate and computing interest from the date of violation.

Delay is also a source of benefits. Presumably it enables a reduction in the number of judges and other court personnel, court houses, etc. It may increase the settlement rate. . . .

Whether existing levels of delay are optimum is very difficult to judge, in part because the usual statistics of delay do not measure the court queue—the waiting period—accurately. Delay is generally measured from the filing of the defendant's answer to the complaint to the final disposition of the case. This interval is too long because it includes time during which the parties are not waiting at all, but litigating or preparing to litigate or attempting to negotiate a settlement. It is too short because it excludes the period between the event giving rise to the legal dispute (or the earliest time when a settlement might have been made) and the filing of the answer.

In 1972, the average interval between answer and final disposition, in personal-injury cases tried before juries in state courts, was 21.7 months, an increase of only three months since 1963. Delays in other kinds of cases, and in the federal courts, appear to be substantially shorter. The situation in a few major cities, however, is a good deal worse. Statistics that actually measure either the court queue or the costs and benefits of court queues of different length are unavailable. . . .

The proposal to reduce delay by adding judges—usually considered the sovereign remedy—ignores several realistic possibilities that might undermine the effectiveness of the measure. The reduction in delay brought about by the addition of judges might be offset by the lower settlement rate in the personal-injury area, and perhaps in other areas, that can be foreseen if delay is reduced; the additional litigation would create a new source of delay. Moreover, with litigation a speedier method of dispute resolution, disputants who under existing conditions of delay substitute other methods of dispute resolution (such as arbitration) because they value prompt resolution would be attracted back to the courts, and again a new source of delay would be created. An analogy may be drawn to building a new freeway: by improving road transportation the freeway induces some people who previously used other modes of transportation to switch to driving, and this leads to new congestion.

The essential point is that minimization of delay is not an appropriate formulation of the goal of judicial reform. The goal, it has been argued in this article, is to minimize the sum of the error costs and of the direct costs of legal dispute resolution. The problem of delay must be placed within that larger framework of inquiry. Indeed, unless that is done, delay cannot even be defined in a meaningful fashion.

B. Abandonment of Adversariness

Some criticisms may require consideration of more drastic alternatives. For example, we have seen how the remedial instrument demands structures and processes for applying law to facts of particular cases, and how adversarial and adjudicative processes are deployed for this purpose in Anglo-American systems. Are there vices of the adversarial form of adjudication that tinkering cannot eliminate? Are there alternatives to *adversarial* adjudication?

Well, of course. We earlier referred to another of the world's great legal system systems, the civil-law regimes based on their comprehensive codes. First, we shall present a summary account of its set of structures and processes, which is far less adversarial than our own, though still adjudicative. Second, we shall consider whether adoption of such a setup would be likely to eliminate or minimize certain specific objections to adversarial adjudication.

1. For the summary account, we rely on Benjamin Kaplan, a great professor of procedure at Harvard Law School and later a distinguished justice of Massachusetts' highest court. In Civil Procedure—Reflections on the Comparison of Systems, 9 Buff. L. Rev. 409, 409–14 (1960),* he described an archetype of European civil law, Germany's classic system. To begin sort of in the middle, the civil law does not have our kind of trial (and has no jury, of course). Instead, it has a conference method that Kaplan colorfully describes:

> One of the leitmotifs of the German process is sounded by the Siegfried horn of the summons in the action. This invites appearance at a *Termin zur mündlichen Verhandlung*, a court-session for oral-argument, or rather for conference, since the ideal style of proceeding is less that of a contentious confrontation than a cooperative discussion. The conference is set perhaps three to four weeks after initial service of the papers—which by the way is usually accomplished by mail—and it is commonly attended by the parties as well as counsel. Now the point to be made is that the whole procedure up to judgment may be viewed as being essentially a series of such conferences, the rest of the process having a sort of dependent status. Prooftaking occurs to the extent necessary in the spaces, as it were, between conferences. Intermediate decisions are made along the way. But the conferences are the heart of the matter. Very promptly, then, the litigants are brought under the eye of the court and the case begins to be shaped; and this treatment is applied to the action at intervals until it is fully opened and finally broken. "Conference" betokens informality and this characterizes the entire German procedure. "Conference" also suggests what is the fact, that possibilities of settlement are openly, vigorously, and continually exploited.
>
> I must relate German pleadings to the conference method—I shall use the word "pleadings" although these writings are quite different from the American variety. The action starts with a complaint served together with the summons, but beyond this there is no prescribed number or sequence of pleadings. Pleadings are to be put in in such numbers and at such times as to prepare for, strengthen, and expedite the conferences and thereby the general movement of the case. They have no position independent of the conferences. Indeed the [legislature] looked to a free, oral restatement of the pleadings at conference. Such oral recapitulation no longer occurs: the court reads the pleadings in advance and the lawyers are assumed to adopt the pleadings except as they speak up to the contrary. Still no question arises as to the sufficiency of the pleadings as such, nor is there any motion practice directed to the pleadings themselves. In short, pleadings merge into, are an ingredient of the conferences. What is wanted from the pleadings as adopted and perhaps revised at conference is a narrative

---

of the facts as the parties see them at the time, with offers of proof—mainly designated witnesses and documents—and demands for relief. There is no insistence on niceties of form, and legal argumentation, though strictly out of place, is common in today's pleadings. Amendments, even drastic amendments, of the statements can be made until the end of the case, normally without any penalty for late change. This malleability of the pleadings flows from the realization and expectation that a case may change its content and color as it is repeatedly discussed and as proof is from time to time adduced.

Returning to the conduct of the conferences, we find the presiding judge highly vocal and dominant, the parties themselves often voluble, the lawyers relatively subdued. To understand the judicial attitude and contribution at conference, we must take account of two related concepts. First, there is the principle jura novit curia, the court knows and applies the law without relying on the parties to bring it forward. Second, article 139 of the code, as strengthened in recent years, imposes a duty on all courts to clarify the cause and lead the parties toward full development of their respective positions. Thus with awareness of the law implicit in the case, the court is obliged to discuss it freely with the litigants, and in that light to indicate what will be material to decision. By discussion with counsel and the parties the court completes the picture of the controversy as presented by the litigants, throwing light upon obscurities, correcting misunderstandings, marking out areas of agreement and disagreement. It spurs and guides the parties to any necessary further exploration of facts and theories, and may suggest appropriate allegations, proof offers, and demands. The court, however, is not bound to take over and commandeer the litigation, nor does it have the power to do so in an ultimate sense. To some degree—the power is greater in "family" matters than in ordinary cases—the court may call up evidence and background information. The calling of experts is basically a matter for the court. But, in general, allegations, proof offers, and demands can be made only by the parties and so in the last analysis major control of the cause-materials remains with them. Nevertheless, as the parties are likely to follow the court's suggestions, we have here a significant potential in the court which imparts a special quality to the procedure; and this is so despite the fact that clarification and leading are hardly noticeable in simpler cases where the lawyers seem to be providing competent representation. The role of the court not only at conference but throughout the proceedings is envisioned as being both directive and protective. The court as vigorous chairman is to move the case along at a good pace, stirring the parties to action on their own behalf, exercising its limited sua sponte powers where necessary, conscious of a duty to strive for the right solution of the controversy regardless of faults of advocacy.

Conferences propel the lawsuit. Most dates are set by the court in open session. It acts in discretion with due regard to the convenience of the parties: few "iron" time provisions are laid down in the code, and the parties cannot control the pace by stipulation. When discussions disclose ripe questions of law, a time will be set for decision. If they show up disputed issues of fact, there will be an order and a time set for prooftaking.

2. What about that proof of facts? In the United States, we have a distinctive system that is very dependent on efforts by the parties and their lawyers, as demonstrated in the Swimming Pool case. But German proof of facts, which takes place between the conferences, would not fit the German system if it were to proceed in our style. Again, Kaplan explains the different approach in four short paragraphs:

> To understand German prooftaking, we have first to ask what investigation of the facts a German lawyer customarily makes. He consults his client and his client's papers. But he has substantially no coercive means of "discovering" material for the purpose of preparing his proof offers or readying himself for prooftaking. Moreover he is by no means at liberty to go out and talk informally with prospective witnesses. He is hobbled by the principle that he is to avoid all suspicion of influencing those who may be later called to give evidence in court. I shall not attempt to mark the exact boundaries of this inhibition or to dredge up the possible evasive contrivances. I shall simply say that German lawyers are not prime movers with respect to the facts. The régime just described does make for unrehearsed witnesses....
>
> The court draws up the order for prooftaking, the *Beweisbeschluss*, from the nominations set out in the pleadings as they may have been revised at conference. Prooftaking need not be concentrated at a single session, and is in fact not often so concentrated. Accordingly the court may pick and choose what it wants to hear at particular sessions. It can take proof in any order—evidence on a defense ahead of evidence on the main case, even evidence on the negative of an issue ahead of the affirmative.
>
> Witnesses are sequestered, kept out of the courtroom until called. The court asks the witness to state what he knows about the proof theme on which he has been summoned. When the witness has done that in narrative without undue interruption, the court interrogates him, and this is the principal interrogation. Counsel put supplemental questions. Lawyers' participation is likely to be meager. If a lawyer puts too many questions he is implying that the court does not know its business, and that is a dubious tactic. A full stenographic transcript is not kept. Instead the court dictates a summary of the witness' testimony for the minutes which is then read back and perhaps corrected.
>
> German law has few rules excluding relevant evidence. In general relevant evidence is admissible and when admitted is freely evaluated: thus there is no bar to the admission of hearsay. But a few qualifications must be made. German law recognizes a series of privileges. It is somewhat irresolute in compelling production in court of various kinds of documentary proof. Testimony will be received from the parties themselves only in particular circumstances defined by law, and in no event may a party be compelled to testify. Party-testimony is viewed as a kind of last resort. This raises a quiddity, for parties are regularly heard in conference, nominally for purposes of clarification, not proof. I say "nominally" because German law tends to blur the line between evidence stricto sensu and other happenings in the courtroom.

3. Rather obviously, then, the German system is quite a different one for its main participants, judges and lawyers. It certainly does not prompt ideas of basing TV dramas on the courtroom. Indeed, the participants' daily professional lives seem a bit drab:

> The German court system is manned by a quite sizeable number of judges. They are career men, appointed on the basis of government examinations, modestly paid, of good but not exalted social prestige, looking primarily to ministerial departments of justice for advancement. In normal times men customarily enter into judicial service at an early age, generally without substantial experience in practice. Judges have traditionally been chided for *Lebensfremdheit*, undue detachment from the rough-and-tumble of life. We have caught a hint of their paternalistic role in the court procedure. This is not far distant from, indeed it comprises, an element of the bureaucratic. Working, many of them, in collegial courts whose judgments, stiffly authoritative in style, disclose neither individual authorship nor individual dissent, German judges live rather anonymous lives. And they are desk-bound through a large part of their working time, for files must be read in preparation for court sessions, and most decisions in actions large and small must be compendiously written up.

> As to the German lawyers, I must avoid leaving the impression that their contribution to litigation is unimportant, or that their attitude is flaccid. Despite the court's capacity for active interposition, the frame of the case is made by the lawyers and there is room for contentious striving. Still the procedural system we have outlined does not make for notably vigorous performance by counsel. Moreover the education of lawyers tends against their full identification with clients as combatants: a significant part of their post-University required training is as apprentice-judges. Most important, we must notice some economic facts. Lawyers' fees for litigation, generally corresponding with statutory scales fixed in relation to the amount in controversy, are low.

4. Nevertheless, despite these stark differences, the civil-law system works. Indeed, it seems to have some real benefits, compared to our system:

> Taking all elements of expense into consideration, German litigation is cheap by comparison with the American brand. But on the threshold a German litigant must conjure with the fact that if as plaintiff or defendant he turns out loser in the lawsuit, he will have to reimburse his opponent's expenses—counsel fees and court costs at the statutory rates together with ordinary disbursements. Let us note here that contingent-fee arrangements ... are proscribed in German practice. A comprehensive system of state-provided legal aid aims to enable not only downright paupers but any citizens of insufficient means to prosecute or defend civil cases upon a plausible showing of a prospect of success.

> Lastly I must respond to the nervous question which any American lawyer would surely want to ask: Does the German system get over its court business without undue delay? German court statistics—at least those publicly available and not held in subterranean tunnels by the

ministries—are curiously sparse; but these figures combine with the opinion of German lawyers familiar with the scene to indicate that the courts, although handling a very considerable volume of cases, are disposing of their calendars with fair speed.

5. Okay, with that background you can start to consider whether abandoning adversariness, in the civil-law spirit, would be likely to eliminate or minimize certain specific objections to Anglo-American adversarial adjudication. Consider whether adoption of a Germanic system would obviate any of the following imagined objections to our system:

a. "In an ideal remedial instrument, outcomes would not be influenced by extraneous factors but only by factors relevant to the legal and factual merits of the dispute. To the extent that we cannot devise adequate means of coping with unjust influences such as disparity in abilities of lawyers, then we are forced to consider more fundamental alterations in our processes. Therefore, for example, we should seek out alternatives that do not rely so heavily on efforts of opposing lawyers to inform decision makers." But is there any way of substantially playing down the role of lawyers? And would there be any significant costs of doing this?

b. "The adversarial atmosphere scares off witnesses and naturally repels evidence, especially testimony and things under the control of disinterested persons. Litigants then have available for use only the partisan and coerced residue after people with ingenuity have made themselves anonymous."

c. "Adversarial-adjudicative processes of the kind under consideration inherently tend to become complicated and sophisticated. Thus, they invite a multitude of procedural rules and principles of a constitutive and regulative character. These rules and principles in turn invite litigation concerning their own meaning and applicability with the consequence that the whole system tends to become litigiously incestuous. Worse yet, these rules can and sometimes do frustrate the quest for substantive justice."

d. "We must not forget the hidden social costs in adversarial adjudication. Recalling how it all got started in Anglo-American law is sobering. We have mentioned trial by ordeal. Another early mode of trial was trial by battle, in which the disputants' champions actually fought each other physically. Modern procedure is partly an outgrowth of this system. Today, we continue to pit two parties against each other. The abrasive character of this confrontation atmosphere cannot be denied. The resulting trauma to participants, particularly to the parties themselves as opposed to their lawyers, may not be measurable, but it is nonetheless real and damaging."

e. "Then there is simply the direct cost of all this in economic terms. The processes involved are highly formal and closely regimented, they call for considerable professional expertise, and they consume time voraciously. All this costs money, and lots of it. Finally, when it is recalled that many courts are way behind on their dockets, one wonders whether the whole system should not be radically revised."

This is not a purely academic exercise. The United States has taken big strides in modern times toward the civil-law style, with our adoption of pretrial conferences being only the most obvious step. Meanwhile, since the time of Kaplan's account, German procedure has somewhat evolved toward the common-law style, including a movement, based on efficiency concerns, toward greater concentration of proceedings in a single hearing. Comparative law specialists use the term "convergence" for such two-sided movement of law toward the center.

C. Abandonment of Adjudication

In the preceding passages, we offered a variety of criticisms of adversarial adjudication. It may be, though, that if a social thinker really wanted to justify abandonment of adversarial adjudication, she ought to urge abandonment of adjudication. *Adjudication*—referral of two-sided disputes to an impartial third person for decision—begets adversarial adjudication, does it not? But how could the need for adjudication itself be eliminated and aggrieved citizens still be left with something resembling a remedial instrument? This is not impossible, at least for some types of claims.

In the Swimming Pool case, the relevant rule of law might have provided that "any person suffering personal injuries caused by another in the course of leisure activity shall be entitled to compensation therefor from public funds upon application to the appropriate public official. Satisfactory proof of such injuries, of causation by another, and of nature of activity must be submitted."

Observe that an arrangement of this kind would not, in the first instance, call for adjudication at all. It would not even require the loss causer to be present at the official determination of loss and causation and activity, let alone pay out of its own pocket (or that of its insurer). Indeed, there would be no reason to permit the loss causer itself to demand an elaborate day in court, for it does not risk bearing the loss and it is not being branded a wrongdoer. The proceeding would involve the loss causer only indirectly. However, the taxpayers would have to pay, and the loss causer would feel less deterrence.

In short, here we do not have a two-sided dispute for reference to a third person. The public official would operate by unilateral inquiry, discussion, and disposition. A dispute could arise between the aggrieved and the relevant public official over facts of loss and causation and activity or over law, and *this* dispute would be of a two-sided kind that perhaps the law would then allow to be referred to a third-party adjudicative body for resolution. But absent this, no need for adjudication would arise.

Now consider the feasibility and desirability of a system of this kind to handle personal injury claims arising from automobile accidents. One such system is the no-fault insurance scheme.

A couple of law professors proposed this scheme in the 1960s. The idea was to supplement traditional liability insurance, which covers what a negligent driver has to pay in the tort system, with a new compulsory insurance

that simply covers economic losses and operates in the fashion of health insurance. The injured person—any authorized operator of or passenger in the covered car or any pedestrian it strikes—would make a claim to the insurance company covering the car, which would pay up to specified dollar limits regardless of fault. The claim could be for reasonable expenses and lost income from personal injury, less a small deductible. Coverage also extended to the insured person and household members if injured by an uninsured motorist. However, the policy could exclude benefits to a person injured while driving under the influence of alcohol or drugs, intending to cause injury, or committing a felony.

The key component of the proposal was that this no-fault coverage would be in lieu of tort damages. Only if damages were serious enough, could the injured person pursue a tort action for uncovered injuries. Proponents of no-fault argued that reducing lawsuits in this way would give us a more efficient automobile insurance system, with more victims being compensated more quickly, and that drivers have plenty of incentive to drive carefully anyway.

In 1971 a Massachusetts no-fault statute came into effect, with a dollar limit of $10,000 per accident. In the 1970s, a flurry of legislative activity brought some version of no-fault to almost half the states. Trial lawyers and also insurance companies detested the reform, and so they lobbied to block passage of good no-fault acts and to weaken or repeal enacted ones. Now, the movement has stalled. The result is that the current system is not markedly less litigious than the old tort system. (But elsewhere, in New Zealand and Quebec for example, "comprehensive" no-fault schemes have abolished all tort actions for personal injury or death in automobile accidents, with the public system compensating in moderate amounts.)

Section Seven
LIMITATIONS OF LAW AS A REMEDIAL INSTRUMENT

Under what circumstances is law most effective as a remedial instrument? Here is only the beginning of a list of those circumstances: the loss sustained (or threatened) thereby can readily be determined and remedied; the law itself that treats the availability of the remedy has already been well defined in readily understandable terms; in event of disputes between the parties over the right-fulness of the claim to a remedy under the law and the facts, a well-designed set of structures and processes has been constructed for authoritative resolution thereof, and proof of the facts in particular cases can typically be made on the basis of reliable kinds of evidence; and the aggrieved who sustained such a loss will be motivated to seek such a remedy. These, then, are some of the conditions for the maximal effectiveness of law as a remedial instrument.

It should be obvious, then, that the remedial instrument is not without its correlative limitations.

ROSCOE POUND, THE LIMITS OF EFFECTIVE LEGAL ACTION
27 Int'l J. Ethics 150, 161–66 (1917)

One set of limitations grows out of the difficulties involved in ascertainment of the facts to which legal rules are to be applied. This is one of the oldest and most stubborn problems of the administration of justice.... For example, the law is often criticised because it does not protect against purely subjective mental suffering except as it accompanies or is incident to some other form of injury and within disputed limits even then. There are obvious difficulties of proof in such cases. False testimony as to mental suffering may be adduced easily and is very hard to detect. Hence the courts, constrained by the practical problem of proof to fall short of the requirements of the logical system of rights of personality, have looked to see whether there has been some bodily impact or some wrong infringing some other interest which is objectively demonstrable, and have put nervous injuries which leave no bodily record and purely mental injuries in the same category.

Another set of limitations grows out of the intangibleness of duties which morally are of great moment but legally defy enforcement. I have spoken already of futile attempts of equity at Rome and in England to make moral duties of gratitude or disinterestedness into duties enforceable by courts. In modern law not only duties of care for the health, morals and education of children, but even truancy and incorrigibility are coming under the supervision of juvenile courts or courts of domestic relations. But note that the moment these things are committed to courts, administrative agencies have to be invoked to make the legal treatment effective. Probation officers, boards of children's guardians and like institutions at once develop. Moreover one may venture to doubt whether such institutions or any that may grow out of them will ever take the place of the old-time interview between father and son in the family woodshed by means of which the intangible duties involved in that relation were formerly enforced.

A third set of limitations grows out of the subtlety of modes of seriously infringing important interests which the law would be glad to secure effectively if it might. Thus grave infringements of individual interests in the domestic relations by tale-bearing or intrigue are often too intangible to be reached by legal machinery. Our law has struggled hard with this difficulty. But the results of our action on the case for criminal conversation and alienation of affections, which long ago excited the ridicule of Thackeray, do not inspire confidence nor does the sole American precedent for enjoining a defendant from flirting with the plaintiff's wife assure a better remedy. So also with the so-called right of privacy. The difficulties involved in tracing injuries to their source and in fitting cause to effect compels some sacrifice of the interests of the retiring and the sensitive.

A fourth set of limitations grows out of the inapplicability of the legal machinery of rule and remedy to many phases of human conduct, to many important human relations and to some serious wrongs. One example may be seen in the duty of husband and wife to live together and the claim of each to the society and affection of the other.... To-day this interest has no sanction beyond morals and the opinion of the community....

... The scope of preventive relief is necessarily narrow. In the case of injuries to reputation, injuries to the feelings and sensibilities—to the "peace and comfort of one's thoughts and emotions"—the wrong is ordinarily complete before any preventive remedy may be invoked, even if other difficulties were not involved. Specific redress is only possible in case of possessory rights and of certain acts involving purely economic advantages. A court can repossess a plaintiff of Blackacre, but it cannot repossess him of his reputation. It can make a defendant restore a unique chattel, but it cannot compel him to restore the alienated affections of a wife. It can constrain a defendant to perform a contract to convey land, but it cannot constrain him to restore the peace of mind of one whose privacy has been grossly invaded. Hence in the great majority of cases substitutional redress by way of money damages is the only resource and this has been the staple remedy of the law at all times. But this remedy is palpably inadequate except where interests of substance are involved. The value of a chattel, the value of a commercial contract, the value of use and occupation of land—such things may be measured in money. On the other hand attempt to reach a definite measure of actual money compensation for a broken limb is at least difficult; and valuation of the feelings, the honor, the dignity of an injured person is downright impossible. We try to hide the difficulty by treating the individual honor, dignity, character and reputation, for purposes of the law of defamation, as assets, and Kipling has told us what the [Indian] thinks of the result. "Is a man sad? Give him money, say the Sahibs. Is he dishonored? Give him money, say the Sahibs. Hath he a wrong upon his head? Give him money, say the Sahibs." It is obvious that the ... point is well taken. But it is not so obvious what else the law may do. If, therefore, the law secures property and contract more elaborately and more adequately than it secures personality, it is not because the law rates the latter less highly than the former, but because legal machinery is intrinsically well adapted to securing the one and intrinsically ill adapted to securing the other.

Finally, a fifth set of limitations grows out of the necessity of appealing to individuals to set the law in motion. All legal systems labor under this necessity. But it puts a special burden upon legal administration of justice in an Anglo-American democracy. For our whole traditional polity depends on individual initiative to secure legal redress and enforce legal rules. It is true, the ultra individualism of the common law in this connection has broken down. We no longer rely wholly upon individual prosecutors to bring criminals to justice. We no longer rely upon private actions for damages to hold public service companies to their duties or to save us from adulterated food. Yet the possibilities of administrative enforcement of law are limited also, even if there were not grave objections to a general regime of administrative enforcement. For laws will not enforce themselves. Human beings must execute them, and there must be some motive setting the individual in motion to do this above and beyond the abstract content of the rule and its conformity to an ideal justice or an ideal of social interest.

A. Illustration: Liability

HURLEY v. EDDINGFIELD

Supreme Court of Indiana, 1901
156 Ind. 416, 59 N.E. 1058

Baker, J.:

The appellant sued appellee for $10,000 damages for wrongfully causing the death of his intestate. The court sustained appellee's demurrer to the complaint, and this ruling is assigned as error.

The material facts alleged may be summarized thus: At and for years before decedent's death appellee was a practicing physician at Mace, in Montgomery county, duly licensed under the laws of the state. He held himself out to the public as a general practitioner of medicine. He had been decedent's family physician. Decedent became dangerously ill, and sent for appellee. The messenger informed appellee of decedent's violent sickness, tendered him his fee for his services, and stated to him that no other physician was procurable in time, and that decedent relied on him for attention. No other physician was procurable in time to be of any use, and decedent did rely on appellee for medical assistance. Without any reason whatever, appellee refused to render aid to decedent. No other patients were requiring appellee's immediate service, and he could have gone to the relief of decedent if he had been willing to do so. Death ensued, without decedent's fault, and wholly from appellee's wrongful act. The alleged wrongful act was appellee's refusal to enter into a contract of employment. Counsel do not contend that, before the enactment of the law regulating the practice of medicine, physicians were bound to render professional service to every one who applied. Whart. Neg. §731. The act regulating the practice of medicine provides for a board of examiners, standards of qualification, examinations, licenses to those found qualified, and penalties for practicing without license. Acts 1897, p. 255; Acts 1899, p. 247. The act is a preventive, not a compulsive, measure. In obtaining the state's license (permission) to practice medicine, the state does not require, and the licensee does not engage, that he will practice at all or on other terms than he may choose to accept. Counsel's analogies, drawn from the obligations to the public on the part of innkeepers, common carriers, and the like, are beside the mark. Judgment affirmed.

NOTES

1. There are similarly shocking cases, e.g., Yania v. Bigan, 397 Pa. 316, 155 A.2d 343 (1959) (no liability for defendant who invited decedent onto his land, taunted him to jump into a water-filled mining pit, and did nothing to save him from drowning). In a more recent case from Oregon (where Ms. Brown's case had encountered her opponent's successful demurrer on the ground of no duty to

rescue), the plaintiff, who was visiting the defendants' next-door neighbors, was stabbed by Simmons, who was a social guest of the defendants. Plaintiff sued to recover damages for his personal injuries, alleging that defendants failed to discourage or otherwise restrain Simmons when they knew or should have known of Simmons' intent and that they failed to warn plaintiff when Simmons' intent became known to them. The lower court granted defendants' motion for judgment on the pleadings. The appellate court affirmed, Reynolds v. Nichols, 276 Or. 597, 600, 556 P.2d 102, 104 (1976), explaining: "The allegations that defendants failed to give warning of Simmons' intent to assault plaintiff and to restrain Simmons do not state a cause of action. As we said in Cramer v. Mengerhausen, 275 Or. 223, 227, 550 P.2d 740, 743 (1976), '[t]here is no duty to aid one in peril in the absence of some special relation between the parties which affords a justification for the creation of a duty.'"

2. The idea, then, is that you could sit on a dock and watch a stranger drown, rather than tossing him the life buoy! Why does Anglo-American law not impose a duty to aid someone in peril, even when disaster is perfectly foreseeable and safe rescue would be easy? One could argue that liability for a pure failure to act in the plaintiff's interest impinges on the defendant's individual liberty. One could more persuasively argue that promulgating and administering any such duty to act would be very hard—especially in ambiguous situations or where multiple potential rescuers were present—and likely ineffective. The grievance is not readily definable, making it hard to conform behavior to the specified standard of altruism and later hard to verify a failure to conform. In any event, most states largely leave the matter to moral and social pressures (and the possibility of professional regulation, as for doctors), which are fairly effective.

3. In considering the wisdom of our law's approach, you have to realize that it is not quite as heartless as it sounds, because most states provide some very big exceptions. First, as already suggested, if the defendant has a special relationship with the plaintiff, such as innkeeper, it has a duty to aid, as held in Lundy v. Adamar of N.J., Inc., 34 F.3d 1173 (3d Cir. 1994) (casino owner owed duty to provide medical care to patron suffering heart attack, although that duty did not require having a physician available to perform intubation). Second, if the defendant caused the plaintiff's harm, even innocently, it has a duty to aid. In a case from Indiana (where *Hurley* earlier arose), the court induced "a legal obligation to take positive or affirmative steps to effect the rescue of a person who is helpless and in a situation of peril, when the one proceeded against is a master or an invitor or when the injury resulted from use of an instrumentality under the control of the defendant." L.S. Ayres & Co. v. Hicks, 220 Ind. 86, 95, 40 N.E.2d 334, 337 (1942) (liability for the aggravation of injuries suffered by a little boy in an escalator without the defendant department store's negligence).

4. Also, if a person, say a doctor, chooses to act, then she will be liable for her negligent conduct in the course of the rescue. "The result of all this is that the good Samaritan who tries to help may find himself mulcted in damages, while the priest and the Levite who pass by on the other side go on their cheerful way

rejoicing." W. Page Keeton, Dan B. Dobbs, Robert E. Keeton & David G. Owen, Prosser and Keeton on the Law of Torts 378 (5th ed. 1984). This has led most states to enact a "Good Samaritan Act" that absolves from liability for negligence any doctor who gratuitously helps in an emergency.

5. A very few states have gone further to impose a broad duty to rescue, although they very rarely enforce it. In fact, Vermont invoked a different instrument of the law by enacting a criminal statute that imposes a fine of not more than $100 for willful failure to aid, a so-called Bad Samaritan Act that appears in Vt. Stat. Ann. tit. 12, §519(a):

> A person who knows that another is exposed to grave physical harm shall, to the extent that the same can be rendered without danger or peril to himself or without interference with important duties owed to others, give reasonable assistance to the exposed person unless that assistance or care is being provided by others.

And virtually all states have criminal statutes requiring certain people, like doctors, to report certain kinds of crimes, like child abuse. California takes a different approach with its program for compensating volunteers injured during a rescue, which appears in Cal. Govt. Code §§13970–13974.

B. Illustration: Damages

The "no duty to rescue" cases represent an area where the law, in recognition of its limitations, has chosen not to impose liability. See generally Julie A. Davies & Paul T. Hayden, Global Issues in Tort Law 118-29 (2008); Thomas C. Galligan, Jr., Aiding and Altruism: A Mythopsycholegal Analysis, 27 U. Mich. J.L. Reform 439 (1994); James A. Henderson, Jr., Process Constraints in Tort, 67 Cornell L. Rev. 901 (1982); Marin Roger Scordato, Understanding the Absence of a Duty to Reasonably Rescue in American Tort Law. 82 Tul. L. Rev. 1447 (2008).

We turn now to a different set of cases on "wrongful pregnancy or birth" where the law, still in recognition of its own limitations, has chosen not to give damages for certain kinds of harm. See generally Nicolette Priaulx, The Harm Paradox: Tort Law and the Unwanted Child in an Era of Choice (2007); Amy Norwood Moore, Note, Judicial Limitations on Damages Recoverable for the Wrongful Birth of a Healthy Infant, 68 Va. L. Rev. 1311 (1982).

COCKRUM v. BAUMGARTNER
Supreme Court of Illinois, 1983
95 Ill. 2d 193, 447 N.E.2d 385, cert. denied,
464 U.S. 846, 104 S. Ct. 149 (1983)

Ward, Justice:

This appeal concerns the extent of the damages that may be recovered in a malpractice action based on a so-called "wrongful pregnancy" or "wrongful birth." The issue was raised in two medical malpractice suits that were consolidated on appeal from the circuit court of Cook County to the appellate court. In both cases, the plaintiffs had alleged that but for the negligence of the defendants each of the female plaintiffs would not have borne a child. In both actions, the plaintiffs sought to recover for the pain of childbirth, the time lost in having the child, and the medical expenses involved. The plaintiffs sought also to recover as damages the future expenses of raising the children, who, it would appear, are healthy and normal. The circuit court dismissed the counts that set out the claims for the expenses of rearing the children. The plaintiffs appealed, and the appellate court reversed those judgments. We granted the defendants leave to appeal....

... *Cockrum* v. *Baumgartner* was brought by Donna and Leon Cockrum against Dr. George Baumgartner.... The Cockrums alleged that Dr. Baumgartner negligently performed a vasectomy upon Leon Cockrum. Also, they claimed that he was negligent in telling them that a sperm test conducted by the laboratory showed no live sperm when he should have known that the laboratory report showed that the vasectomy had been medically unsuccessful. The Cockrums also alleged that after the attempted vasectomy Donna Cockrum became pregnant and gave birth to a child, and they claimed that she would not have become pregnant if the physician had not been negligent.

In *Raja* v. *Tulsky*, Edna and Afzal Raja brought an action against Dr. A. Tulsky and Michael Reese Hospital and Medical Center. The Rajas alleged that Dr. Tulsky negligently performed a bilateral tubal cauterization upon Edna Raja, which operation was designed to make her sterile. They alleged that about five years after the operation Edna Raja began to experience signs of pregnancy. She was examined at Michael Reese's gynecology clinic and advised, however, that she was not pregnant. Later, after the time in which the plaintiffs say it was medically safe to have an abortion, she learned that she was in fact pregnant. Edna Raja alleged that she suffers from hypertensive cardiac disease, and that she had been informed that it would be medically dangerous for her to have a child. The Rajas claim that Michael Reese was negligent in failing to determine that she was pregnant. They say that if Michael Reese had told her that she was pregnant, she would have elected to terminate the pregnancy. Those counts in which Dr. Tulsky was named as a defendant were dismissed as barred by the statute of limitations and are not at issue here.

... The only issue is whether the trial court erred in dismissing the counts in which the plaintiffs sought to recover as damages the future expenses of rearing the child....

The courts in the majority of States that have considered "wrongful pregnancy" or "wrongful birth" actions have recognized a cause of action against a physician where it is alleged that because of the doctor's negligence the plaintiff conceived or gave birth. (See Annot., Tort Liability for Wrongfully Causing One to be Born, 83 A.L.R.3d 15, 29 (1978).) These courts have generally held that in such actions the infant's parents may recover for the expenses of the unsuccessful operation, the pain and suffering involved, any medical complications caused by the pregnancy, the costs of delivery, lost wages, and loss of consortium. There is sharp disagreement, however, on the question involved here: whether plaintiffs may recover as damages the costs of rearing a healthy child.

There are courts which have allowed the recovery of the cost of rearing a child on the ground that such expense is a foreseeable consequence of the negligence. Those courts also have held that this recovery may be offset, however, by an amount representing the benefits received by the parents from the parent-child relationship.

In a substantially greater number of jurisdictions, however, courts have denied recovery in suits for costs of rearing a child.

Some of these courts have pointed to the speculative nature of the damages. Others have expressed concern for the child who will learn that his existence was unwanted and that his parents sued to have the person who made his existence possible provide for his support.... Courts have also stated that allowing such damages would open the door to various false claims and fraud.

Too, many courts have declared an unwillingness to hold that the birth of a normal healthy child can be judged to be an injury to the parents. That a child can be considered an injury offends fundamental values attached to human life....

Beardsley v. Wierdsma (Wyo. 1982), 650 P.2d 288, is another decision in which the court refused to permit the recovery of rearing costs. In rejecting the notion that would allow the recovery of rearing costs with an offset for the benefits of parenthood, it was observed:

> We believe that the benefits of the birth of a healthy, normal child outweigh the expense of rearing a child. The bond of affection between child and parent, the pride in a child's achievement, and the comfort, counsel and society of a child are incalculable benefits, which should not be measured by some misplaced attempt to put a specific dollar value on a child's life.
>
> The benefit or offset concept smacks of condemnation law, where the trier of fact determines the value of the land taken by the condemnor. The trier of fact then determines the benefit that results to the land owner, which benefit is deducted from the original value to determine the proper award. If the concept of benefit or offset was applied to "wrongful birth" actions, we can conceive of the ridiculous result that benefits could be greater than damages, in which event someone could argue that the parents would owe something to the tortfeasors. We think that a child should not be viewed as a piece of property, with fact finders first assessing the expense and damage incurred because of a child's life, then deducting the value of that child's life.

Similarly, in Terrell v. Garcia (Tex. Civ. App. 1973), 496 S.W.2d 124, 128, cert. denied (1974), 415 U.S. 927, 94 S. Ct. 1434, the court, not without emotion, reasoned:

> [A] strong case can be made that, at least in an urban society, the rearing of a child would not be a profitable undertaking if considered from the economics alone. Nevertheless, ... the satisfaction, joy and companionship which normal parents have in rearing a child make such economic loss worthwhile. These intangible benefits, while impossible to value in dollars and cents are undoubtedly the things that make life worthwhile. Who can place a

> price tag on a child's smile or the parental pride in a child's achievement? Even if we consider only the economic point of view, a child is some security for the parents' old age. Rather than attempt to value these intangible benefits, our courts have simply determined that public sentiment recognizes that these benefits to the parents outweigh their economic loss in rearing and educating a healthy, normal child. We see no compelling reason to change such rule at this time.

We consider that on the grounds described the holding of a majority of jurisdictions that the costs of rearing a normal and healthy child cannot be recovered as damages to the parents is to be preferred. One can, of course, in mechanical logic reach a different conclusion, but only on the ground that human life and the state of parenthood are compensable losses. In a proper hierarchy of values the benefit of life should not be outweighed by the expense of supporting it. Respect for life and the rights proceeding from it are at the heart of our legal system and, broader still, our civilization....

We would observe, too, that it is clear that public policy commands the development and the preservation of family relations. Exemplary of that policy in the tort context is the rule prohibiting suits by children against their parents for negligence. (Thomas v. Chicago Board of Education (1979), 77 Ill. 2d 165, 171, 395 N.E.2d 538.) To permit parents in effect to transfer the costs of rearing a child would run counter to that policy. As stated earlier, those jurisdictions that permit a recovery for rearing costs have recognized that the recovery should be offset by the measure by which the plaintiffs have been benefited by becoming parents.... It can be seen that permitting recovery then requires that the parents demonstrate not only that they did not want the child but that the child has been of minimal value or benefit to them. They will have to show that the child remains an uncherished, unwanted burden so as to minimize the offset to which the defendant is entitled....

We cannot on balance accept the plaintiffs' contention too that we should rigidly and unemotionally, as they put it, apply the tort concept that a tortfeasor should be liable for all of the costs he has brought upon the plaintiffs. It has been perceptively observed, by distinguished authority, that the life of the law is not logic but experience. Reasonableness is an indispensable quality in the administration of justice. The New York Court of Appeals, in rejecting a claim made in very different context, used language, however, that is not without appropriateness here:

> While it may seem that there should be a remedy for every wrong, this is an ideal limited perforce by the realities of this world. Every injury has ramifying consequences, like the ripplings of the waters, without end. The problem for the law is to limit the legal consequences of wrongs to a controllable degree. (Tobin v. Grossman (1969), 24 N.Y.2d 609, 619, 249 N.E.2d 419, 424, 301 N.Y.S.2d 554, 561.)

The reasons given for denying so-called rearing costs are more convincing than the reasons for abstractly applying a rule not suited for the circumstances in this character of case.

As we have noted, the plaintiffs themselves also rely upon considerations of public policy to temper the harshness of a proposed mechanical application of a principle of damages. In general, under the law of damages a plaintiff cannot recover for elements of damage he could reasonably have avoided. It has been said that this avoidable consequences rule might prevent recovery for rearing costs where the parents had an opportunity to avoid parenthood through abortion or adoption. In contending that the avoidable-consequences rule should not be applied, it was argued for the plaintiffs in oral argument that applying the rule here would violate a policy based on natural appreciation and affection, which favors the rearing of children by their natural parents.

The area of law we consider here is new, but there is reason to believe this question and related issues will be presented with increasing frequency. As the decisions we have cited show, courts regard the questions as matters of high social importance, transcending the individual controversies involved.

Dean Prosser recognized that considerations of public policy are of great importance in the law of torts. He commented:

> Perhaps more than any other branch of the law, the law of torts is a battleground of social theory. Its primary purpose, of course, is to make a fair adjustment of the conflicting claims of the litigating parties. But the twentieth century has brought an increasing realization of the fact that the interests of society in general may be involved in disputes in which the parties are private litigants. The notion of "public policy" involved in private cases is not by any means new to tort law, and doubtless has been with us ever since the troops of the sovereign first intervened in a brawl to keep the peace; but it is only in recent decades that it has played a predominant part. Society has some concern even with the single dispute involved in a particular case; but far more important than this is the system of precedent on which the entire common law is based, under which a rule once laid down is to be followed until the courts find good reason to depart from it, so that others now living and even those yet unborn may be affected by a decision made today. There is good reason, therefore, to make a conscious effort to direct the law along lines which will achieve a desirable social result, both for the present and for the future. (Prosser, Torts sec. 3, at 14–15 (4th ed. 1971).)

For the reasons given, the judgment of the appellate court is reversed and the judgments of the circuit court are affirmed.

CLARK, JUSTICE, dissenting:

This court today has come to the conclusion that child-rearing costs are not recoverable in a wrongful birth action in Illinois. The court relies primarily on what it sees as a necessary public policy posture in reaching the conclusion it does. However, I believe the court's opinion is internally inconsistent, and I feel that, upon a careful examination, it mischaracterizes the issues without any substantive legal foundation upon which to build. The court inconsistently has said that the birth of a normal child cannot be judged to be an injury to parents and yet, at the beginning of the opinion, the court recognizes that a cause of action exists for wrongful birth in this State, and that plaintiffs can recover for the pain of childbirth, the time lost in having the child, and the medical expenses incurred. The court in effect has found that the birth of a normal child is recognized as an injury in "wrongful birth actions" in Illinois; the issue is what damages are recoverable as a result of that injury to the parents. If, as the court hypothesizes, the birth of a normal child cannot be construed as an injury, how then can the plaintiff recover for the "pain" of childbirth? Should, then, the court characterize the time "lost in having the child" as "lost" time (which in effect is found to be compensable)? Why then allow for the medical costs of childbirth if they represent the first installment in an investment in the preservation and development of family relations? The opinion of the court contradicts itself. Once the court has agreed that the cause of action for wrongful birth can be brought in Illinois, the policy questions that the opinion grapples with are moot.

The court determines that while other jurisdictions have applied "mechanical logic" in reaching a different conclusion than this court does, such a result can only be reached "on the ground that human life and the state of parenthood are compensable losses." . . . I believe the court has mischaracterized the issue in a most unfortunate and hyperbolic way. It is not at all that human life or the state of parenthood are inherently injurious; rather it is an unplanned parenthood and an unwanted birth, the cause of which is directly attributable to a physician's negligence, for which the plaintiffs seek compensation. . . .

I would also follow those other jurisdictions where child-rearing costs, while recoverable, are offset to a certain degree by the benefits of parenthood. Potential benefits, including companionship, that the parents may derive from that parent-child relationship should be considered by the trier of fact in determining the ultimate amount of damages. I do not believe that the many benefits of having a child should be excluded as a matter of law; nor do I feel that such benefits can be held to automatically offset all expenses. Plaintiffs who choose to rear this unplanned child should be allowed to recover for damages according to the degree of the injury. That will inevitably vary. . . .

While such a computation in offsetting the benefits that accrue to the parents against the expenses to be incurred is difficult, it is no more formidable a task than determining the amount of damages to be awarded for loss of consortium in a wrongful death action.

In reaching the result arrived at today, I believe the court has taken a myopic view of prospective parents' considerations. A couple privileged to be bringing home the combined income of a dual professional household may well be able to sustain and cherish an unexpected child. But I am not sure the child's smile would be the most memorable characteristic to an indigent couple, where the husband underwent a vasectomy or the wife underwent a sterilization procedure, not because they did not desire a child, but rather because they faced the stark realization that they could not afford to feed an additional person, much less clothe, educate and support a child when that couple had trouble supporting one another. The choice is not always giving up personal amenities in order to buy a gift for the baby; the choice may only be to stretch necessities beyond the breaking point to provide for a child that the couple had purposely set out to avoid having. The court today expresses concern about putting a negative imprimatur on a child's life and yet, in denying damages for child rearing, the court may well be accomplishing the very result it seems so intent on avoiding—making a child of an unwanted birth a victim of a very real continuing financial struggle and thus a painful reminder of the obligations of parenthood to a couple who had no appetite for a parental lifestyle. Does that child then become more wanted because this court has seen fit to deny foreseeable expenses in a case where a physician's negligence is undisputed?

SIMON, J., joins in this dissent.

NOTES

1. The trick in reading this wrongful pregnancy or birth case is to keep your focus. The case does not entail, of course, the problem of recovery for prenatal injuries to a fetus. Nor does the case involve recovery for the extraordinary medical expenses of caring for a nonhealthy child whose birth, not the birth defect, was attributable to a doctor's negligence, an issue with which our old friend, the Supreme Court of Illinois, has struggled. Compare Siemieniec v. Lutheran Gen. Hosp., 117 Ill. 2d 230, 512 N.E.2d 691 (1987), with Williams v. Univ. of Chicago Hosps., 179 Ill. 2d 80, 688 N.E.2d 130 (1997). Instead, the issue in *Cockrum* is whether a doctor should pay the rearing expenses for a healthy child born as a result of the doctor's negligence.

2. The Associated Press filed this report on September 18, 2007:

> An Australian woman who gave birth to twins instead of a single baby after undergoing in-vitro fertilization has sued her doctor for the cost of bringing up the second child.
>
> The woman, who cannot be identified because of a court order, is seeking $329,000 to cover the expense of raising one child until age 21.
>
> Testifying in the Supreme Court of the Australian Capital Territory on Tuesday, the 40-year-old mother said she told her doctor that she only wanted one child.
>
> But an embryologist under the doctor's supervision implanted two embryos in her uterus, resulting in the birth of non-identical twin girls.
>
> The woman told the court that she and her female partner were devastated when they learned she was carrying twins, and even considered putting one of the babies up for adoption.
>
> The couple, whose combined income exceeds $82,875, are seeking $329,000 to cover the costs of raising one of the girls, including private school fees. They also want more than $12,000 to compensate them for time off work and medical expenses.

How would you decide the case, if it had arisen in Illinois?

Section Eight
SUMMARY

When a person thinks of law, one of the first things that comes to mind is the law's technique of remedying the citizens' grievances. See generally Dan B. Dobbs, The Law of Torts (2000). Their grievances are myriad, but a very nice example is negligence.

Available remedies include injunctions and, most importantly, damages. See generally Dan B. Dobbs, Law of Remedies (2d ed. 1993). Accordingly, we reviewed the development of the laws that give money damages for negligently inflicted injuries.

Those laws were the creation of old English courts. By the interaction of stare decisis and logic-chopping, the courts of England and its former colonies shaped an ever more complex doctrine for deciding in any situation who was more to blame and should therefore bear the loss. Later the legislatures stepped in, reforming the all-or-nothing system of damages by implementing a regime of comparative negligence. The courts reacted, and the legislatures reacted in turn. Today courts and legislatures, with their differing competencies, work together in overseeing and further developing this branch of law.

The creation and development of law would not suffice as a remedial legal instrument. An additional need is the authoritative application of law to the facts of particular cases. This, of course, is a peculiarly judicial task. Studying how the courts go about performing that task took us into the realm of civil procedure. For further references on this law, we suggest Fleming James, Jr., Geoffrey C. Hazard, Jr. & John Leubsdorf, Civil Procedure (5th ed. 2001), or the more specialized Charles Alan Wright & Mary Kay Kane, Law of Federal Courts (6th ed. 2002). For you, we chose to expose the application of law by following, rather lengthily, the progress in the legal system of a single case—the Swimming Pool case—from accident through appeal. This case-study approach is an especially effective method for learning about law. For an additional exemplar, we recommend John A. Humbach, Whose Monet? An Introduction to the American Legal System (2007). But there are many other such studies. You might read on your own (1) Joyce Bichler, DES Daughter: The Joyce Bichler Story (1981), (2) David Crump & Jeffrey B. Berman, The Story of a Civil Case (3d ed. 2001), (3) Marc A. Franklin, The Biography of a Legal Dispute (1968), (4) Sandra M. Gilbert, Wrongful Death: A Medical Tragedy (1995), (5) Brandt Goldstein, Storming the Court (2005), now elaborated in Brandt Goldstein & Rodger Citron, A Documentary Companion to *Storming the Court* (2008), (6) Jonathan Harr, A Civil Action (1995), now elaborated in Lewis A. Grossman & Robert G. Vaughn, A Documentary Companion to *A Civil Action* (4th ed. 2008), (7) Nan D. Hunter, The Power of Procedure: The Litigation of *Jones v. Clinton* (2002), (8) Jonathan Mahler, The Challenge: *Hamdan v. Rumsfeld* and the Fight over Presidential Power (2008), (9) Samuel Mermin, Law and the Legal System (2d ed. 1982), (10) Peter N. Simon, The Anatomy of a Lawsuit (rev. ed. 1996), (11) Jeffrey W. Stempel, Litigation Road: The Story of *State Farm v. Campbell* (2008), (12) Gerald M. Stern, The Buffalo Creek Disaster (1976), (13) Barry Werth, Damages: One Family's Legal Struggles in the World of Medicine (1998), or (14) William Zelermyer, The Legal System in Operation (1977).

All this talk of courts and legislatures unfortunately suggests that private citizens have a small role to play in making and applying remedial law. This is certainly untrue. As one counterexample appropriate to this opening chapter, we focused on the critical role of the private attorney as advocate. The law demands zealousness on behalf of the client, but the law simultaneously imposes significant constraints on the attorney. The law also demands competence of the attorney, although the law must find ways to remedy the incompetencies that lawyers sometimes shockingly inflict. See generally Charles W. Wolfram, Modern Legal Ethics (1986).

Such failures prompt thoughts of reforming the remedial instrument. We explored various possibilities, ranging from tweaks to speed up the process of adversarial adjudication to overhauls that would make the process drastically less adversarial or even nonadjudicative. Reform is not only possible but necessary. Nevertheless, we had to stress that many obvious reforms would be ineffective or even dangerously counterproductive, which might explain why they remain obvious yet still not implemented.

Finally, that somewhat pessimistic tone leads naturally to a consideration of the inherent limitations of the remedial instrument. As usual in this opening chapter that must set the stage for the following chapters, we began with some general observations on the limitations of law as a whole. We then turned to a study of the specific, in order to reveal a few limitations of the remedial instrument. We tried to show why Anglo-American law would allow you to sit on a dock and watch a stranger drown, rather than tossing him a life buoy. We tried to explain, maybe more convincingly, why the law does not require a doctor to pay the rearing expenses for a healthy child born as a result of the doctor's negligence. Right or wrong, these particular rules go far toward proving generally the existence of the law's limitations.

Chapter 2

LAW AS AN INSTRUMENT FOR

PUNISHING WRONGS

Whatever views one holds about the penal law, no one will question its importance in society. This is the law on which men place their ultimate reliance for protection against all the deepest injuries that human conduct can inflict on individuals and institutions. By the same token, penal law governs the strongest force that we permit official agencies to bring to bear on individuals.

HERBERT WECHSLER

Section One
INTRODUCTION TO THE PENAL INSTRUMENT

Materials Drawn from Substantive and Procedural Criminal Law

Conduct that offends public morals and social mores is extremely common. Maybe you like to gamble or use drugs; more likely you speed on the highway; possibly you will intentionally injure someone; and almost certainly you occasionally say something rude. Society will obviously be interested in these antisocial behaviors and will respond to them in some way. Not so obvious is whether that response should include punishment. The penal, or criminal, law is distinguished by its heavy reliance on punishment. Punishment has classically been defined as the deliberate infliction of pain or other unpleasant consequences for the violation of a legal rule. Of course, the most common methods of punishment today do not involve intentional infliction of physical pain so much as unpleasant consequences, such as imprisonment or fines. Nonetheless, because the infliction of suffering of any sort appears to be a bad thing, asking what justifies punishment is natural. Most people assume that the state has the power to impose punishment, but what justifies the state's use of that power? Why does the state punish criminals, and what benefit does society gain through exercising its power in such a way? Two of the most popular theories that attempt to answer these questions are retributivism and utilitarianism.

A. Retributivism

One proposed justification for punishing wrongdoers is retribution. A retributivist believes that punishment is both inherently good and morally required when it is deserved. Most retributivists also believe that an individual deserves punishment when he or she freely chooses to break society's rules. But *how much* punishment is appropriate? One central principle of retributivism is the principle of equality. A person who inflicts an undeserved evil upon another deserves a punishment equivalent to the evil he inflicted. Thus, inflicting an evil on another (whether theft, assault, murder, or any other harm) should result in the infliction of that same evil upon yourself. Proponents of pure or strict retributivism contend that only this Law of Retribution can be considered when determining what punishment must be imposed upon a wrongdoer; other factors, such as the costs or effectiveness of the punishment, should be ignored. This purity might seem to advocate a somewhat primitive form of justice, recalling the biblical injunction "an eye for an eye, and a tooth for a tooth."

A more modern version of this principle of just deserts is proportionality: the idea that punishment for various crimes should reflect their relative severity. Retributivism, whether strict or less literal, is properly characterized as backward-looking, because it looks back at the crime itself to determine punishment, without looking forward at the results of imposing the sentence.

DETERMINING THE SEVERITY OF A CRIME

Generally, retributivists determine the severity of a crime based on some combination of two factors: the degree of harm or potential for harm caused by the criminal's actions, and the mental state of the actor. Thus, homicide is worse than assault, and intentional murder worse than negligent homicide. It is difficult, however, to know how heavily to weigh either factor for any particular crime. In any event, using these factors does not always lead to a satisfying result.

With respect to the degree of harm caused, if two assailants each fire a handgun at the same person but only one hits his mark and kills the victim, usually the perpetrator whose bullet hit will be charged with murder, while the other will be charged with attempted murder. Both intended to kill the victim, and they created the same potential for harm. The only difference is that one actually caused the harm, while the other did not. The impulse of most people would be to say that the murderer should be punished more severely, but is it fair to give the other defendant a lesser sentence simply because he was lucky (or a bad shot)? Should an inept criminal get preferential treatment because he is unable to complete his crime? While these questions may seem difficult, legislatures have answered them quite uniformly: a criminal who succeeds in causing the harm he intends is punished more severely than one who fails. This may reflect society's recognition that in some cases the harm itself should be punished, not simply the actor's intent. Similarly, the law generally refuses to punish an actor who attempts to commit a crime, but who could not possibly do any harm because of an inherent factual impossibility. For example, if the actor attempts to cast a voodoo curse on his victim, fully believing it will cause death, in most jurisdictions he will not be charged with attempted murder even though he has the same malicious intent as someone who attacks his victim with a knife or gun.

With respect to the intentions of the actor, a problem arises in determining what is the most culpable mental state. On first thought, it would seem that intentionally causing the death of another human being is clearly worse than accidentally doing so. But is this always the case? If a devoted husband disconnects the breathing tube of his wife, who is terminally ill and in great pain, is this so clearly worse than a man who agrees to a drag race in the middle of a crowded neighborhood and runs over an innocent bystander? Although a retributivist might attempt to avoid this uncomfortable conclusion by making an exception for mercy killing, this is the kind of exception that risks swallowing the proportionality principle. Should the criminal law also treat leniently a parent who kills a retarded child, claiming that the life of any retarded person is intolerable? Thus, it is not easy for the retributivist to spell out in advance the rules dictating where on the continuum of evil each crime lies.

TWO PROBLEMS WITH RETRIBUTIVISM'S ASSUMPTIONS

In addition to difficulties with accurately measuring the severity of crimes, retributivist theory must confront empirical evidence relating to its underlying assumptions.

U.S. Department of Justice, Bureau of Justice Statistics, Profile of Jail Inmates, 2002

Pre-Arrest Personal Income (annually*)	Percent of Jail Inmates 1996	2002
No income	14.4%	19.3%
Less than $3,600	16.7%	10.6%
$3,600–$7,199	18.9%	15.0%
$7,200–$11,999	17.2%	14.2%
$12,000–$23,999	20.4%	24.4%
$24,000 or more	12.4%	16.4%

Retributive theory rests upon the notion that individuals who commit crimes have chosen to act wrongly, and have done so of their own free will. This is what makes them deserving of punishment. Later in this chapter, we shall see some situations in which the law may excuse a criminal act, because the actor did not or could not freely choose to commit the crime. Here, however, we consider a situation in which society itself may encourage, or even compel, individuals to commit crime. Marxist theory posits that "[C]riminality has two primary sources: (1) need and deprivation on the part of disadvantaged members of society, and (2) motives of greed and selfishness that are generated and reinforced in competitive capitalistic

---

* DOJ figures gave monthly income for the month before arrest, converted here into approximate annual income. The Poverty Threshold determined by the U.S. Census Bureau was in 1996 $7,995 for an individual and $16,036 for a family of four, and was in 2002 $9,183 for an individual and $18,392 for a family of four.

societies. Thus criminality is economically based — either directly in the case of crimes from need, or indirectly in the case of crimes growing out of motives or psychological states that are encouraged and developed in capitalistic society." Jeffrie G. Murphy, Marxism and Retribution, 2 Phil. & Pub. Aff. 217, 234 (1973). The statistics above suggest that economics has a causal connection to criminality. If you agree with Marx, you will find it difficult to justify our system of punishment through retributive notions alone. Even if you do not agree with Marx at all, you may be troubled by the idea that retribution singles out individual choice as the cause of crime, despite evidence that poverty appears to greatly influence who commits crimes.

A quite different objection to retributivism is that it assumes that the costs and benefits of punishment, both to the society and to the individual being punished, are irrelevant in determining the appropriate punishment. A pure retributivist ought not to care whether the system actually discourages crime, so long as criminals are being punished for their wrongdoing. Any reduction in the crime rate is a peripheral benefit. Moreover, the pure economic cost of punishment to society is also irrelevant to a retributivist. Thus, for example, even if probation were demonstrated to be more effective in deterring recidivism for thieves, and it were demonstrated to be significantly cheaper, a pure retributivist would not care, because the only relevant question would be what the morally appropriate punishment for theft is. To many observers, this approach is impractical.

B. Utilitarianism

The other major theory for the justification of punishment is utilitarianism. At its heart, utilitarianism expresses a desire to maximize the net happiness of society, which will normally involve minimizing pain and unpleasantness. Because punishment is unpleasant, or even painful, a utilitarian believes that punishment itself is evil, and its use can be justified only if it will exclude greater evil. The main harm that the penal law looks to exclude is, of course, crime itself, so criminal punishment is justified only if it will prevent more crime.

JUSTIFICATIONS OF UTILITARIANISM

The most obvious utilitarian justification for modern punishment, then, is deterrence. Deterrence can be divided into two categories: general and specific.

General deterrence posits that potential criminals will refrain from committing crimes because of the possibility of punishment. In other words, punishing a criminal is justified because it makes an example of that person, thereby convincing others not to act in a like manner. Under utilitarian theory, society punishes the criminal not for the purpose of causing him pain, but to instill the fear of punishment in others who, absent the example, would have committed crimes.

Specific deterrence is more narrowly focused, as it aims to convince the criminal who himself was punished not to commit further crimes, lest he suffer punishment again. But available statistics cast doubt upon the successfulness of specific deterrence. For example, 67.5 percent of released prisoners were rearrested within three years. U.S. Department of Justice, Bureau of Justice Statistics, Recidivism of Prisoners Released in 1994 (June 2002), available at http://www.ojp.usdoj.gov/bjs/pub/pdf/rpr94.pdf. This would suggest that incarceration is relatively ineffective for deterrence. Indeed, incarceration may encourage crime of some sorts, either because prior incarceration makes lawful employment more difficult to obtain or because minor offenders are socialized by more hardened criminals.

Besides deterrence, there are two additional ways in which punishment may act to prevent a specific criminal from breaking laws in the future. The first, *incapacitation*, or physical restraint of the rule breaker, is more limited than specific deterrence. At the very least, the incarceration of an offender should keep him from committing crimes during the duration of his sentence. However, even the limited goal of incapacitation is not perfectly achieved in all cases; some offenders may escape and commit further crimes; others may perpetrate crimes upon guards and inmates, such as rape, assault, or even murder; and some incarcerated members of criminal gangs continue to organize crimes committed outside of prison. The second, *rehabilitation*, or reform of the rule breaker, is more ambitious than either specific deterrence or incapacitation. Rehabilitation refers to the reform of the criminal into a citizen who wants to obey the law, and has the capacity to do so. Obviously, when punishment achieves this end, the utilitarian is very happy, for the welfare of both the individual and the society as a whole has been increased, but the data reported above suggest that this is a relatively rare result of punishment.

PROBLEMS WITH UTILITARIANISM

A pioneer of utilitarian theory, Jeremy Bentham, in An Introduction to the Principles of Morals and Legislation 170–71 (rev. ed. 1907) (1st ed. London 1789), laid out four cases in which punishment should not be inflicted. These are: (1) where it is *groundless*: where there is no harm for it to prevent, because the actor's conduct was not harmful; (2) where it will be *inefficacious*: where imposing the punishment would not deter such conduct in the future; (3) where it is *unprofitable*, or too *expensive*: where the harm or cost it would produce would be greater than the harm or cost it would prevent; and (4) where it is *needless*: where the harm may be prevented, or cease of itself, at less cost.

Now, if the Marxist view of criminality's economic underpinnings is correct, incarceration may have very little deterrent effect, because it is more likely to exacerbate a convict's economic situation than to improve it. Commentators lacking any Marxist affiliation, but possessing a strong utilitarian bent, have suggested that remedying the underlying societal factors is both more important and more efficient than incarceration. Improving education and lawful employment opportunities, for example, attacks the root causes of criminal activity, rather than focusing on an after-the-fact reaction to crime. As one former Chief Judge for the U.S. Court of Appeals for the District of Columbia Circuit put it, "It makes about as much sense to look to prisons to solve our chronic crime problem as it would be to build more funeral parlors to solve a cholera epidemic." Abner J. Mivka, The Treadmill of Criminal Justice Reform, 43 Clev. St. L. Rev. 5, 8 (1995). Thus, the first problem with the utilitarian justification of punishment would seem to be that punishment, as currently administered, may not be utilitarian at all.

A second problem is quite different and relates not to whether widely accepted prevailing punishment schemes can be justified under utilitarian theory, but whether utilitarian theory provides the correct criteria for determining the occasions on which punishment is appropriate. Many people equate retributivism with revenge and, believing that revenge is unenlightened, characterize themselves as utilitarian. However, consider the following examples — which for many people seem to cry out for punishment — and then ask how a true utilitarian would respond to these examples.

Case 1: Thomas Blanton was prosecuted and convicted on four counts of murder for the racially motivated 16th Street Church bombing in Birmingham, Alabama, in 1963. Nineteen sticks of dynamite were placed in the basement of the church, and the explosion killed four African–American children, aged 11–14. Blanton was not convicted for his role in the bombing until 2001, when he was sentenced to life in prison. Blanton v. State, 886 So. 2d 850 (Ala. 2003). What utility is served by sending a 62–year-old man (who has committed no crimes in the recent past) to jail for the rest of his life? Remember, a strict utilitarian view would not look backward at the nature or "wrongness" of the crime in question, but only at the costs and benefits that his punishment will have for society. Though one might argue that Blanton's sentence may generally deter future hate crimes, it is difficult to justify his sentence without retributive notions.

Case 2: Julius Viel was a Nazi SS commander in World War II. In April 2001, he was convicted in Germany of murdering seven Jewish prisoners in a concentration camp during the war, and sentenced to 12 years in prison. Viel suffered from cancer and died in prison in February 2002. Did his punishment serve any utilitarian purpose? As a sick, elderly man, he was extremely unlikely to commit any further crimes. Moreover, it seems even less likely that his punishment would deter others from committing government-sponsored murders. If you believe Viel's conviction and sentence are justified because he deserves punishment for what he has done, then you are endorsing a retributive rationale — at least in this case.

C. Looking Backward and Forward

Retributivism looks backward at a criminal's conduct, punishing him because he deserves it, according to the severity of his actions. Utilitarianism looks forward to the costs and benefits that will follow from imposing punishment and punishes according to the net maximum benefit to society. It appears that neither theory alone can explain or justify our current criminal justice system. Perhaps this shows the limitations of both theories, or perhaps it shows flaws in the criminal justice system. Nevertheless, the theories can provide a useful framework for evaluating aspects of that system and proposing improvements, as well as in analyzing the rest of the material in this chapter.

In presenting the penal instrument, this chapter will proceed through the same sections used for the remedial chapter:

- Section Two, Penal Methods, further explores the topic of criminal punishment by introducing two kinds of defenses, justification and excuse.
- Section Three, Making Penal Law, studies the appropriate roles of courts and legislatures in creating the criminal law.
- Section Four, Applying Penal Law, demonstrates the application of penal law by tracing the process from arrest through adjudication, with a special focus on the screening function of police, prosecutors, juries, and judges.
- Section Five, Roles of Private Citizens and Their Lawyers, shows how private parties and their lawyers participate in the making and applying of penal law.
- Section Six, Improving the Penal Instrument, identifies and discusses some of the impediments to the fair and accurate determination of the appropriate punishment for a particular offender.
- Section Seven, Limitations of Law as a Penal Instrument, stresses inherent limitations in the law's use of the penal instrument, taking a look at the specific problems of consensual sex crimes and the death penalty.

Section Two
PENAL METHODS

When the state invokes the penal instrument, individuals may lose their property, their liberty, or even their lives. Against which individuals should the government wield such powerful techniques? Punishing all who are discovered to have violated a legal rule is possible, and early English criminal law opted for this simple but harsh method of selection. As the criminal law became more sophisticated, however, its awesome reach was limited by *affirmative defenses*. When a defendant admits he violated a criminal prohibition, but claims that for some reason his punishment would be either unfair of ineffective, he is said to be offering an affirmative defense. If his claim is that the circumstance renders what he did morally correct, then his defense is a *justification* for his conduct. If he did wrong, but he claims that he was not really to blame for doing wrong, then his defense is an *excuse*. The following materials address one justification (necessity), one excuse (insanity), and one non-defense (mistake of law).

Generally speaking, the judge will determine whether the facts the defendant alleges constitute a valid justification or excuse, and the jury will determine whether the facts he alleges actually occurred. If the defendant establishes the existence of a valid affirmative defense, the defendant will escape punishment, but he may still be subject to civil legal action for his conduct.

A. Necessity

REGINA v. DUDLEY & STEPHENS
Queen's Bench Division, 1884
14 Q.B.D. 273

Indictment for the murder of Richard Parker on the high seas within the jurisdiction of the Admiralty.

At the trial before Huddleston, B., at the Devon and Cornwall Winter Assizes, November 7, 1884, the jury, at the suggestion of the learned judge, found the facts of the case in a special verdict which stated "that on July 5, 1884, the prisoners, Thomas Dudley and Edward [*sic*] Stephens, with one Brooks, all able-bodied English seamen, and the deceased also an English boy, between seventeen and eighteen years of age, the crew of an English yacht, a registered English vessel, were cast away in a storm on the high seas 1600 miles from the Cape of Good Hope, and were compelled to put into an open boat belonging to the said yacht. That in this boat they had no supply of water and no supply of food, except two 1 lb. tins of turnips, and for three days they had nothing else to subsist upon. That on the fourth day they caught a small turtle, upon which they subsisted for a few days, and this was the only food they had up to the twentieth day when the act now in question was committed. That on the twelfth day the remains of the turtle were entirely consumed, and for the next eight days they had nothing to eat. That they had no fresh water, except such rain as they from time to time caught in their oilskin capes. That the boat was drifting on the ocean, and was probably more than 1000 miles away from land. That on the eighteenth day, when they had been seven days without food and five without water, the prisoners spoke to Brooks as to what should be done if no succour came, and suggested that some one should be sacrificed to save the rest, but Brooks dissented, and the boy, to whom they were understood to refer, was not consulted. That on the 24th of July, the day before the act now in question, the prisoner Dudley proposed to Stephens and Brooks that lots should be cast who should be put to death to save the rest, but Brooks refused to consent, and it was not put to the boy, and in point of fact there was no drawing of lots. That on that day the prisoners spoke of their having families, and suggested it would be better to kill the boy that their lives should be saved, and Dudley proposed that if there was no vessel in sight by the morrow morning the boy should be killed. That next day, the 25th of July, no vessel appearing, Dudley told Brooks that he had better go and have a sleep, and made signs to Stephens and Brooks that the boy had better be killed. The prisoner Stephens agreed to the act, but Brooks dissented from it. That the boy was then lying at the bottom of the boat quite helpless, and extremely weakened by famine and by drinking sea water, and unable to make any resistance, nor did he ever assent to his being killed. The prisoner Dudley offered a prayer asking forgiveness for them all if either of them should be tempted to commit a rash act, and that their souls might be saved. That Dudley, with the assent of Stephens, went to the boy, and telling him that his time was come, put a knife into his throat and killed him then and there; that the three men fed upon the body and blood of the boy for four days; that on the fourth day after the act had been committed the boat was picked up by a passing vessel, and the prisoners were rescued, still alive, but in the lowest state of prostration. That they were carried to the port of Falmouth, and committed for trial at Exeter. That if the men had not fed upon the body of the boy they would probably not have survived to be so picked up and rescued, but would within the four days have died of famine. That the boy, being in a much weaker condition, was likely to have died before them. That at the time of the act in question there was no sail in sight, nor any reasonable prospect of relief. That under these circumstances there appeared to the prisoners every probability that unless they then fed or very soon fed upon the boy or one of themselves they would die of starvation. That there was no appreciable chance of saving life except by killing some one for the others to eat. That assuming any necessity to kill anybody, there was no greater necessity for killing the boy than any of the other three men. But whether upon the whole matter by the jurors found the killing of Richard Parker by Dudley and Stephens be felony and murder the jurors are ignorant, and pray the advice of the Court thereupon, and if upon the whole matter the Court shall be of opinion that the killing of Richard Parker be felony and murder, then the jurors say that Dudley and Stephens were each guilty of felony and murder as alleged in the indictment."

LORD COLERIDGE, C.J.:

...From these facts, stated with the cold precision of a special verdict, it appears sufficiently that the prisoners were subject to terrible temptation, to sufferings which might break down the bodily power of the strongest man, and try the conscience of the best. Other details yet more harrowing, facts still more loathsome and appalling, were presented to the jury, and are to be found recorded in my learned Brother [Huddleston]'s notes. But nevertheless this is clear, that the prisoners put to death a weak and unoffending boy upon the chance of preserving their own lives by feeding upon his flesh and blood after he was

killed, and with the certainty of depriving *him* of any possible chance of survival. The verdict finds in terms that "if the men had not fed upon the body of the boy they would *probably* not have survived," and that "the boy being in a much weaker condition was *likely* to have died before them." They might possibly have been picked up next day by a passing ship; they might possibly not have been picked up at all; in either case it is obvious that the killing of the boy would have been an unnecessary and profitless act....

There remains to be considered the real question in the case — whether killing under the circumstances set forth in the verdict be or be not murder. The contention that it could be anything else was, to the minds of us all, both new and strange, and we stopped the Attorney General in his negative argument in order that we might hear what could be said in support of a proposition which appeared to us to be at once dangerous, immoral, and opposed to all legal principle and analogy. All, no doubt, that can be said has been urged before us, and we are now to consider and determine what it amounts to. First it is said that it follows from various definitions of murder in books of authority, which definitions imply, if they do not state, the doctrine, that in order to save your own life you may lawfully take away the life of another, when that other is neither attempting nor threatening yours, nor is guilty of any illegal act whatever towards you or any one else. But if these definitions be looked at they will not be found to sustain this contention....

The one real authority of former time is Lord Bacon, who, in his commentary on the maxim, "necessitas inducit privilegium quoad jura privata," lays down the law as follows: — "Necessity carrieth a privilege in itself.... [I]f a man steal viands to satisfy his present hunger, this is no felony nor larceny. So if divers be in danger of drowning by the casting away of some boat or barge, and one of them get to some plank, or on the boat's side to keep himself above water, and another to save his life thrust him from it, whereby he is drowned, this is neither se defendendo nor by misadventure, but justifiable." ... Lord Bacon was great even as a lawyer; but it is permissible to much smaller men, relying upon principle and on the authority of others, the equals and even the superiors of Lord

Bacon as lawyers, to question the soundness of his dictum. There are many conceivable states of things in which it might possibly be true, but if Lord Bacon meant to lay down the broad proposition that a man may save his life by killing, if necessary, an innocent and unoffending neighbour, it certainly is not law at the present day. . . .

Now, except for the purpose of testing how far the conservation of a man's own life is in all cases and under all circumstances, an absolute, unqualified, and paramount duty, we exclude from our consideration all the incidents of war. We are dealing with a case of private homicide, not one imposed upon men in the service of their Sovereign and in the defence of their country. Now it is admitted that the deliberate killing of this unoffending and unresisting boy was clearly murder, unless the killing can be justified by some well-recognized excuse admitted by the law. It is further admitted that there was in this case no such excuse, unless the killing was justified by what has been called "necessity." But the temptation to the act which existed here was not what the law has ever called necessity. Nor is this to be regretted. Though law and morality are not the same, and many things may be immoral which are not necessarily illegal, yet the absolute divorce of law from morality would be of fatal consequence; and such divorce would follow if the temptation to murder in this case were to be held by law an absolute defence of it. It is not so. To preserve one's life is generally speaking a duty, but it may be the plainest and the highest duty to sacrifice it. War is full of instances in which it is a man's duty not to live, but to die. The duty, in case of shipwreck, of a captain to his crew, of the crew to the passengers, of soldiers to women and children, as in the noble case of the *Birkenhead;* these duties impose on men the moral necessity, not of the preservation, but of the sacrifice of their lives for others, from which in no country, least of all, it is to be hoped, in England, will men ever shrink, as indeed, they have not shrunk. It is not correct, therefore, to say that there is any absolute or unqualified necessity to preserve one's life. "Necesse est ut eam, non ut vivam," is a saying of a Roman officer quoted by Lord Bacon himself with high eulogy in the very chapter on necessity

to which so much reference has been made. It would be a very easy and cheap display of commonplace learning to quote from Greek and Latin authors, from Horace, from Juvenal, from Cicero, from Euripides, passage after passage, in which the duty of dying for others has been laid down in glowing and emphatic language as resulting from the principles of heathen ethics; it is enough in a Christian country to remind ourselves of the Great Example whom we profess to follow. It is not needful to point out the awful danger of admitting the principle which has been contended for. Who is to be the judge of this sort of necessity? By what measure is the comparative value of lives to be measured? Is it to be strength, or intellect, or what? It is plain that the principle leaves to him who is to profit by it to determine the necessity which will justify him in deliberately taking another's life to save his own. In this case the weakest, the youngest, the most unresisting, was chosen. Was it more necessary to kill him than one of the grown men? The answer must be "No" —

> So spake the Fiend, and with necessity,
> The tyrant's plea, excused his devilish deeds.

It is not suggested that in this particular case the deeds were "devilish," but it is quite plain that such a principle once admitted might be made the legal cloak for unbridled passion and atrocious crime. There is no safe path for judges to tread but to ascertain the law to the best of their ability and to declare it according to their judgment; and if in any case the law appears to be too severe on individuals, to leave it to the Sovereign to exercise that prerogative of mercy which the Constitution has intrusted to the hands fittest to dispense it.

It must not be supposed that in refusing to admit temptation to be an excuse for crime it is forgotten how terrible the temptation was; how awful the suffering; how hard in such trials to keep the judgment straight and the conduct pure. We are often compelled to set up standards we cannot reach ourselves, and to lay down rules which we could not ourselves satisfy. But a man has no right to declare temptation to be an excuse, though he might himself have yielded to it, nor allow compassion for the criminal to change or weaken in any manner the legal definition of the crime. It is therefore our duty to declare that the prisoners' act in this case was wilful murder, that the facts as stated in the verdict are no legal justification of the homicide; and to say that in our unanimous opinion the prisoners are upon this special verdict guilty of murder.[1]

THE COURT then proceeded to pass sentence of death upon the prisoners.[2]

1. My brother Grove has furnished me with the following suggestion, too late to be embodied in the judgment but well worth preserving: "If the two accused men were justified in killing Parker, then if not rescued in time, two of the three survivors would be justified in killing the third, and of the two who remained the stronger would be justified in killing the weaker, so that three men might be justifiably killed to give the fourth a chance of surviving." — C.

2. This sentence was afterwards commuted by the Crown to six months' imprisonment.

NOTES

1. The court obviously felt that it would be better for the Crown to exercise clemency than to itself recognize the defense of necessity for the crime of murder. Note Lord Coleridge's statement, "We are often compelled to set up standards we cannot reach ourselves, and to lay down rules which we could not ourselves satisfy." A retributivist might agree with this statement, because regardless of the "necessity," Dudley and Stevens committed a wrong by killing the boy, and therefore deserve punishment. But could a retributivist agree with the court's subsequent suggestion that the Crown should exercise clemency? If the act was wrong, and hence deserving of punishment, then a retributivist should object to clemency for the same reason he would object to a necessity defense.

2. Consider whether utilitarianism provides a more satisfactory explanation for the court's decision and its suggestion that clemency would be appropriate. On the one hand, excusing Dudley and Stevens could have the effect of reducing the deterrent effect of the law: if shipwrecked sailors knew that murder and cannibalism would be exonerated, they might be quicker to carry out the crime, even though they are not yet on the verge of death. On the other hand, punishing Dudley and Stevens, assuming they were in fact unable to survive without eating the boy, would make no sense to a utilitarian, given that men in such an extreme situation probably cannot be deterred. Thus, the compromise is to keep the law as it was, but to have the Crown exercise clemency in cases where the circumstances really were extreme. This sounds like a practical solution, until one considers the problem of equality. Cabin boys were traditionally from a lower social class than were seamen. Would the court have been equally likely to urge clemency (and the Crown equally likely to grant) clemency if the cabin boy had eaten Dudley or Stevens? One of the costs of relying upon discretion of one sort or another, rather than creating affirmative defenses, is that sympathy and prejudice have much more room to operate in discretionary systems.

3. When Dudley, Stephens, and Brooks were rescued, they willingly told of the events that led to Parker's death. If they had remained silent, no prosecution

would have been possible. Their statements to their rescuers (and later to law enforcement officials) made it clear that they did not expect to be punished. When all three were charged with murder, they expressed great surprise. (Eventually, charges against Brooks were dropped so that he could be a witness for the prosecution; in England, as in this country, no person may be compelled to be a witness against himself or herself.) To the modern reader, their attitudes seem strange, but it appears that their expectations were entirely reasonable given the custom of the time. After a detailed review of earlier instances of shipwreck and survival cannibalism, Professor Brian Simpson concluded:

> [I]t is quite clear that the situation confronting the survivors of the yacht *Mignon-ette* was one for which they were well prepared and that in a general sense, Dudley and his companions knew the proper thing to do; someone must be killed that the others might live. They also knew that to obtain blood to drink, a living victim was preferable; to wait until death occurred was unwise. They knew too the appropriate preliminary course of action, which was to draw lots, a practice viewed as legitimating killing and cannibalism, particularly if agreed upon by a council of sailors. . . . What sailors did when they ran out of food was to draw lots and eat someone.

A.W.B. Simpson, Cannibalism and the Common Law 140 (1984); see also Neil Hanson, The Custom of the Sea (2000); Note, In Warm Blood: Some Historical and Procedural Aspects of Regina v. Dudley and Stephens, 34 U. Chi. L. Rev. 387 (1967). Should the fact that the defendants clearly thought their actions proper — and that most seamen of the time would have thought them proper — exonerate them? Keep this question in mind when reviewing the materials below on mistake of law.

4. The other famous criminal case arising from a shipwreck is United States v. Holmes, 26 F. Cas. 360 (C.C.E.D. Pa. 1842) (No. 15,383), which Lord Coleridge condescendingly observed could "hardly . . . be an authority satisfactory to a court in this country." Several members of the crew threw 14 male passengers overboard in order to lighten the leaking lifeboat. One of the crew members, Holmes, was tried for manslaughter. In that case, the judge charged the jury that necessity could be a complete defense to the charges, but only if a case of necessity did exist, the slayer was faultless, he owed no duty to the victim, and he was under no obligation to make his own safety a secondary concern. The judge told the jury that it was the duty of the sailors to prefer the passengers unless the sailors were needed to work the boat, and that all on board should draw lots if circumstances permit. The jury convicted Holmes, recommending mercy. Holmes was sentenced to six months' imprisonment at hard labor plus time served. Do you think the rule given by the judge in the *Holmes* case is preferable to the *Dudley & Stephens* rule? Would the *Holmes* rule have acquitted Dudley and Stephens?

5. *Dudley & Stephens* outlines the common-law rule that murder is never justified by necessity. Other crimes, however, are justified by necessity, so long as the crime committed caused less harm than was avoided, and the harm avoided was imminent. For example, the law might justify breaking and entering

if the perpetrator was trying to take shelter from a tornado. In contrast to the common-law approach, the Model Penal Code (MPC) allows the defense of necessity to justify murder. The MPC was designed by the American Law Institute to be a comprehensive model for criminal law legislation. The majority of states have enacted portions of the code, often with some revisions. Is the MPC approach preferable to the common-law approach?

6. The justification of necessity has a close relative in the excuse of duress. Duress is an affirmative defense to crime when another person has threatened the defendant with imminent bodily harm unless he commits the crime; it requires that the defendant be unable to escape the harm without committing the crime. For example, if Dudley had held a gun to Stephens' head, saying "kill the cabin boy for us to eat, or I will kill you," then Stephens would have had a defense of duress. Thus, the most important distinction is that necessity is created by "natural" forces, while duress is intentionally created by a human actor. A second distinction is that to prevail under a defense of necessity, the defendant must show that the harm he avoided was less than the harm he caused, which is not necessary under the excuse of duress. Look back to the distinction between justification and excuse with which we began this section, and notice that this second difference makes necessity a justification, and duress an excuse.

7. The issues raised by governmental use of harsh interrogation techniques against suspected terrorists have some similarities to those raised by the necessity and duress defenses. Is torture justified or excused in the so-called ticking-bomb scenario? That is, if a detainee knows the location of a nuclear bomb set to go off in Manhattan, is it justifiable or excusable to employ torture in an interrogation to extract that information? Proponents would weigh the massive potential loss of life against the less serious evil of inflicting physical pain on the detainee and say that torture is the lesser of two evils. Some opponents of the use of torture will claim that torture is never permissible, while others will attack the scenario as unrealistic. For example, how could the torturer be sure there is a bomb? That the detainee knows where it is? That torture will elicit a response? A truthful response? In time to take action? By injecting uncertainty into the scenario, these opponents weaken the case for torture. Beyond such attacks are the fears that, if employed, torture will not be confined to ticking-bomb cases. Notice that similar arguments could be made with respect to adopting a defense of necessity for the crime of murder. Is it logically necessary to take the same position about the use of torture as it is to take about the extension of the defense of necessity to the crime of murder? You should revisit these questions after reading the materials on interrogation contained in Section Four.

B. Insanity

As with other excuses, the defendant (or more often, his lawyer) argues that, although he committed the crime, he is not a suitable subject for criminal punishment. The utilitarian rationale for the insanity defense is that punishing a criminally insane defendant will generally not deter him (specific deterrence) or other such individuals (general deterrence), as it is the nature of an insane defendant's mental disease or defect that causes him to break society's rules. A retributivist would say that a criminally insane defendant did not act of his own free will, but rather under the influence of his mental disease or defect, and thus is not deserving of punishment. Thus, utilitarians and retributivists agree that insanity should serve as an excuse.

Nonetheless, the insanity defense is one of the most controversial excuses recognized by the criminal law. Most of the controversy concerns the proper definition of insanity. What test should be used to measure whether a defendant is insane? There have been many different views on this question since courts first recognized insanity as an excuse. There is no real consensus today on which test is best. Consider the pros and cons of each test as it is presented, and then try to rank them. Some tests appeal greatly to your internal sense of justice, some are easier than others to apply, and some give more guidance (and thus less discretion) to the jury. Is this discretion a good thing? Some commentators would advocate giving juries a free hand, while others do not trust juries with too much discretion.

The "Wild Beast" Test. One early test for the insanity defense was the wild beast test, adopted in England in the early eighteenth century. This test excuses the accused wrongdoer only if he "is a man that is totally deprived of his understanding and memory, and doth not know what he is doing, no more than . . . a wild beast." S. Sheldon Glueck, Mental Disorder and the Criminal Law 139 (1925) (quoting Rex v. Arnold, 16 How. St. Tr. 695, 764 (1724)). Obviously, this sets a very high bar for the defendant looking to escape punishment. The wild beast test, and similar tests like the "raving lunatic" test, were abandoned long ago in most jurisdictions in favor of less extreme rules.

The **M'Naghten** *Rule.* "To establish a defense on the ground of insanity it must be clearly proved that, at the time of committing the act, the party accused was laboring under such a defect of reason, from disease of the mind, as to not know the nature and quality of the act he was doing, or if he did know it, that he did not know that what he was doing was wrong." M'Naghten's Case, 8 Eng. Rep. 718, 722 (H.L. 1843). This test contains two alternative prongs: cognitive incapacity (inability to know the nature and quality of the one's act) and moral incapacity (unawareness of wrongfulness of the criminal act). Thus, a defendant who, because of mental disease or defect, thought he was squeezing lemons when he was strangling a stranger is excused under *M'Naghten*, as is the defendant who believes that he is shooting someone who has been poisoning him with kryptonite. The *M'Naghten* rule was quickly adopted in the United States and remains the test of criminal insanity in many states.

The Irresistible Impulse Test. Some states modified the *M'Naghten* rule by adding a third prong, one that focuses on volition. The most common such supplement to *M'Naghten*, the irresistible impulse test, excuses criminal conduct that is the result of a delusional compulsion or overpowering urge, when that compulsion was brought about by mental disease or defect. Thus, the defendant may know what he is doing and that it is wrong, but if he is unable to control his actions, the irresistible impulse test will excuse him. Generally, this defense will be unavailable where there is sufficient evidence of planning and deliberation on the part of the defendant.

The Durham, or Product, Test. The U.S. Court of Appeals for the District of Columbia Circuit created a new test in 1954, one that was considerably broader than *M'Naghten* even supplemented by a volitional prong. Durham v. United States, 214 F.2d 862 (D.C. Cir. 1954). Under the *Durham* test, also called the product test, a defendant is excused for his criminal conduct if that conduct was the product of a mental disease or defect. In other words, if the defendant would not have committed the crime absent his mental illness, the *Durham* test would deem him not responsible for his crime. Thus, a pedophile might plausibly claim that absent his mental illness, he would not have had the desire to have sex with a child — so despite the fact that he knew what he was doing and knew sex with children was wrong and he was not impaired in his ability to control his impulse to engage in sex with children, he could be excused. The breadth of this test gave juries relatively little guidance, and many feared that jurors would simply defer to psychiatric expert testimony to determine whether the defendant's actions were the product of a mental disease or defect and thus abdicate their fact-finding responsibility. These concerns eventually led to the D.C. Circuit abandoning this test, and it is not in use anywhere today.

The Model Penal Code. Section 4.01 of the Model Penal Code excuses criminal conduct when a defendant, due to mental disease or defect, "lacks substantial capacity either to appreciate the criminality [wrongfulness] of his conduct or to conform his conduct to the requirements of law." The first prong of this test parallels the *M'Naghten* rule, while the second is similar to the irresistible impulse test. However, notice the use of the words "substantial capacity" and "appreciate." Contrast these terms with *M'Naghten*'s requirement that the defendant does not "know" that what he is doing is wrong. The MPC drafters were attempting to move toward a formulation of insanity that conformed with advances in psychology. To do so, they moved away from an absolute requirement of total incapacity. For this reason, the MPC test gained widespread approval for a time.

In 1981, John W. Hinckley attempted to assassinate President Ronald Reagan. Hinckley did not succeed, but in the attempt severely wounded Reagan and three other people. At his trial in 1982, Hinckley pled that he was not guilty because he was insane at the time of the offense. Predictably, defense psychiatric experts agreed that Hinckley was insane, either diagnosing him as schizophrenic or as suffering from severe depression, while prosecution experts said he was never insane. The defense pointed to Hinckley's obsession with actress Jodie Foster, whom he contacted and to whom he wrote numerous letters, as the reason for his attempt to kill Reagan. Hinckley believed, according to the defense, that his attempt would make him a nationally recognized figure and thereby cause Foster to notice him. The jury, instructed under the Model Penal Code definition of insanity, acquitted Hinckley.

Hinckley's acquittal sparked outrage among the populace, and legislators in many jurisdictions, under enormous public pressure, worked quickly to constrict the insanity defense. A number of states immediately returned to the *M'Naghten* rule, thus eliminating the volitional prong as well as returning to the absolute incapacity standard for the remaining cognitive and moral prongs. Four states have gone so far as to abolish the insanity defense altogether.

Guilty But Mentally Ill. Instead of, or in addition to, narrowing the definition of insanity, a number of states have enacted statutes enabling a jury to find a defendant *guilty* but mentally ill (GBMI) rather than *not guilty* by reason of insanity (NGRI). A verdict of GBMI does not excuse the defendant of the charged crime or exempt him from punishment, but it is supposed to assure that he receives treatment for his mental illness during the period of incarceration. Because the defendant is found criminally responsible, he may be sentenced as harshly as though he had been found simply guilty of the crime and, regardless of whether he or she recovers, will serve the sentence normally imposed for the crime of which he was convicted. This can include life in prison, or even the death penalty. Moreover, if and when the defendant is released from prison, he bears the stigma of a criminal conviction. In contrast, a defendant found NGRI may be released shortly after the verdict if a state psychiatric facility finds them sane, though this is rare. Because the individual was found not criminally responsible, the state cannot incarcerate him or even utilize the restrictions of probation.

RANDY BORUM & SOLOMON M. FULERO, EMPIRICAL RESEARCH ON THE INSANITY DEFENSE AND ATTEMPTED REFORMS: EVIDENCE TOWARD INFORMED POLICY
23 Law & Hum. Behav. 117, 132–33 (1999)

Advocates of the various procedural changes to the insanity defense, most of which were proposed as an indirect way of limiting the use of the insanity defense, have generally been frustrated by the lack of substantive effect that those changes were supposed to have had. Changing the substantive test or definition of insanity to what would appear to be a more restrictive one has little or no effect on the number of insanity acquittals, though the results are somewhat mixed. Changing the burden of proof and the standard of proof required has had virtually no effect. Restricting mental health expert testimony appears to have had no effect.

Later, the GBMI option appeared on its face to be an attractive alternative for those interested in limiting the insanity defense. However, GBMI does not appear to increase effective treatment options or enhance public safety. In addition, the empirical research reviewed here does not support the position that NGRI acquittals will decrease with the introduction of the GBMI option. Indeed, it appears that those found GBMI come not from the group of defendants that would formerly have been found NGRI, but instead from the population that would formerly have been found guilty. . . .

Finally, those who have advocated for the most extreme solution — the abolition of the insanity defense — appear to have little empirical support for their position. As set forth above, the arguments that form the underpinnings of the abolitionist position — that the insanity defense is overused and often successful, that it is used mostly in heinous crimes, that successful NGRI acquittees spend little or no time in custody, and that NGRI acquittees are more dangerous than other types of releasees — appear to be myths without empirical foundation. . . .

Overall, then, efforts to "fix" the insanity defense by "tinkering" or by more drastic means have generally had little effect. This, we would argue, is largely because there is no real evidence that it is broken. It is a defense that is rarely raised, and usually unsuccessful. Even when defendants raising insanity are successful, they will generally spend in confinement as much time as if or more time than if they had simply been found guilty.

In addition, the moral integrity of the criminal law would seem to necessitate at least some provision for lessening the culpability of individuals who, as a result of severe mental illness, do things that they do not know are wrong. Punishing people whose conduct is driven by mental disability, rather than wrongful intent, does not serve any legitimate objective of general deterrence.

Certainly, the specific deterrent objective of protecting the public from future harm by a mentally ill and dangerous person is a legitimate one. However, it is clearly one not best achieved by attempts to tinker with, change, or abolish the insanity defense. Instead, sound and carefully implemented conditional release programs appear to have the greatest effect on enhancing public protection, while simultaneously providing necessary treatment. These programs provide greater supervision than is generally afforded to persons on probation or parole; further, the conditions of release are rehabilitative in nature and specifically tailored to the reduction of future problematic behavior that might result from untreated mental illness.

The South Carolina Supreme Court has upheld the death sentence of James Wilson, who prior to being sentenced to death was found GBMI. Under South Carolina law, a person may be found GBMI only if he lacked *sufficient* capacity to conform his conduct to the requirements of the law. Put differently, the same judge who sentenced Mr. Wilson to death found that he was unable to control the conduct for which he was sentenced to death. Consider whether either retributive or utilitarian justifications for punishment can explain this decision. In upholding the sentence, the South Carolina Supreme Court did not claim that a deterrence rationale could support such a sentence, but held that retribution could. Do you think a retributivist would agree?

G. Mistake of Law

REX v. ESOP
Central Criminal Court, 1836
173 Eng. Rep. 203

The prisoner was indicted for an unnatural offence, committed on board of an East India ship, lying in St. Katherine's Docks. It appeared that he was a native of Bagdad.

[Attorney] for the prisoner. — In the country from which the prisoner comes, it is not considered an offence; and a person who comes into this country and does an act, believing that it is a perfectly innocent one, cannot be convicted according to the law of England. A party must know that what he does is a crime. This is the principle upon which infants, idiots, and lunatics are held not to be answerable. If a person is unconscious that he is doing a wrong act, or believes that it is a right or innocent act, he is exonerated. Where one man kills another under the persuasion that he is doing a good action, he is not liable to punishment, for he knows not the distinction between right and wrong, and upon that point is insane.

BOSANQUET, J.: I am clearly of opinion that this is no legal defence.

VAUGHAN, J.: Where is the evidence that it is not a crime in the prisoner's own country? But if it is not a crime there, that does not amount to a defence here. Numbers have been most improperly executed if it is a defence.

The prisoner, after the examination of some witnesses on his behalf, from whose statements it appeared that the witnesses for the prosecution acted under the influence of spite and ill will, was found

Not guilty.

NOTES

1. If the prospective offender does not know that an act is proscribed, or even wrong in some sense, is punishing her for ignorance either useful or fair? Punishment despite such ignorance has long been viewed as a necessary part of the criminal law, due in part to the fear that if ignorance were a defense, false claims of ignorance would be rampant and often difficult to disprove. It is therefore presumed that an individual knows the law, so that even if a person can prove beyond a shadow of a doubt that she did not, her criminal conduct is not excused. There have been very slight inroads made against this doctrine, but only in extreme cases. For example, a Los Angeles city ordinance required any previously convicted felon to register with the city if remaining for more than five days. Lambert, a woman previously convicted of felony forgery, was arrested in Los Angeles for violating this ordinance, after living there for seven years. She claimed she did not register because she was unaware of the ordinance. The Supreme Court, in a 5–4 decision, found that her conviction violated the Due Process Clause of the Fourteenth Amendment. The Court focused on the fact that the defendant's criminal conduct — failure to register — was passive in nature, since her mere presence in the city violated the ordinance. Because she did not have notice that her passive conduct was criminal, Lambert's conviction could not stand. Lambert v. California, 355 U.S. 225, 78 S. Ct. 240 (1957).

2. The criminal law treats mistakes of fact quite differently from mistakes of law. Generally speaking, if an actor makes a mistake of fact that unbeknownst to him renders his conduct unlawful, the law will generally not punish his actions unless the mistake is unreasonable. For example, if I come up behind someone who resembles my high school friend, and I slap him on the back, I am not guilty

of battery even if it turns out that it is not my friend, and instead is a stranger who resents my slap. Additionally, some crimes require specific knowledge or intent, so that even an unreasonable mistake of fact can avoid being a crime. For example, the common-law crime of larceny is the taking of another's property with the specific intent to deprive him of the use of that property. Therefore, if you pick up your classmate's book because you honestly think it is your book, even though your belief is unreasonable (perhaps because his book is blue and yours is red), you do not intend to deprive him of the use of his property, and so you are not guilty of larceny. Initially, it may seem surprising that mistakes of law are treated so much more harshly than are mistakes of fact. The key idea is that a mistake of fact can negate an element of the crime, whether that element involves an act or an intent.

3. Thus far we have considered mistakes that a defendant willingly discloses in an attempt to exculpate himself. A defendant may also make a mistake that, if detected, is inculpatory, and may form the basis of prosecution. That is, a defendant may do something that does not in fact constitute a crime or have a criminal result, but which he believed to be a crime or which he intended to have a criminal result. This is a very murky area, and one on which not all courts agree, though some cases are clear. To begin with the easiest inculpatory mistake to assess, if you try to shoot and kill someone, mistakenly thinking your empty gun is loaded, you are indeed guilty of attempted murder. At the other extreme, if you shoot a deer on December 1st believing that hunting season ended on November 30th, but in fact hunting season ends on December 1st, you are not guilty of attempting to kill a deer out of season. The first mistake looks purely factual, and inculpates you; the second looks purely legal, and does not inculpate you. But suppose you intended to steal your classmate's textbook but took your own by mistake. Are you then guilty of attempted larceny? Or suppose you bought a brownie believing that it contained marijuana, though it did not? Are you guilty of attempted possession of a controlled substance? If you place a curse on your rival, wrongly believing that it can cause his death, should you be punished for attempted murder? Notice that your answers to these questions may depend upon whether retribution or deterrence is more important to you.

"My ignorance of the law was simply appalling."

Section Three
MAKING PENAL LAW

In this section, we consider the appropriate roles of legislative bodies and judicial courts in the creation and interpretation of criminal prohibitions. In Anglo-American legal systems, legislatures have generally superseded courts as the primary source of these prohibitions, so that the earlier tradition of common-law or judge-made crimes is now widely disapproved.

There exists a constant tension between the creation of law and its application. This tension goes to the roots of our society. The framers of the Constitution gave legislative power to Congress, while empowering the judicial branch to interpret while applying those laws. State constitutions generally separate powers in the same way. Therefore, when a court interprets a statute in such a way that does not conform to the legislative intent, the court may be usurping legislative power that is supposed to be reserved to elected representatives.

In some cases, a dispute arises as to whether a court is merely *applying* a statute to a new fact situation, thus properly assuming the role of interpreting the prohibition, or whether it is *extending* the statute, thus improperly usurping the legislature's role of creating crimes.

UNITED STATES v. WILTBERGER
Supreme Court of the United States, 1820
18 U.S. (5 Wheat.) 76

MR. CHIEF JUSTICE MARSHALL delivered the opinion of the Court: . . .

The rule that penal laws are to be construed strictly, is perhaps not much less old than construction itself. It is founded on the tenderness of the law for the rights of individuals; and on the plain principle that the power of punishment is vested in the legislative, not in the judicial department. It is the legislature, not the Court, which is to define a crime, and ordain its punishment.

It is said, that notwithstanding this rule, the intention of the law maker must govern in the construction of penal, as well as other statutes. This is true. But this is not a new independent rule which subverts the old. It is a modification of the ancient maxim, and amounts to this, that though penal laws are to be construed strictly, they are not to be construed so strictly as to defeat the obvious intention of the legislature. The maxim is not to be so applied as to narrow the words of the statute to the exclusion of cases which those words, in their ordinary acceptation, or in that sense in which the legislature has obviously used them, would comprehend. The intention of the legislature is to be collected from the words they employ. Where there is no ambiguity in the words, there is no room for construction. The case must be a strong one indeed, which would justify a Court in departing from the plain meaning of words, especially in a penal act, in search of an intention which the words themselves did not suggest. To determine that a case is within the intention of a statute, its language must authorize us to say so. It would be dangerous, indeed, to carry the principle, that a case which is within the reason or mischief of a statute, is within its provisions, so far as to punish a crime not enumerated in the statute, because it is of equal atrocity, or of kindred character, with those which are enumerated. If this principle has ever been recognized in expounding criminal law, it has been in cases of considerable irritation, which it would be unsafe to consider as precedents forming a general rule for other cases. . . .

Punishment by Analogy

While Chief Justice Marshall's rejection of punishment by analogy has been long accepted in many countries, some, including Germany, China, and Russia, have not always agreed. For example, in 1935, the Government of the Reich in Germany provided:

> Whoever commits an action which the law declares to be punishable or which is deserving of punishment according to the fundamental idea of a penal law and the sound perception of the people, shall be punished. If no determinate penal law is directly applicable to the action, it shall be punished according to the law, the basic idea of which fits it best.

While many students of Anglo-American jurisprudence would decry the above provision, many Germans at the time hailed the new law, believing that it gave judges a free hand and prevented criminals from avoiding punishment through technicalities.

Many people today are outraged that our law allows criminals to use technicalities to avoid punishment. Some "technicalities," however, serve important purposes. One of these is notice, as illustrated in the following case. But there are other values that so-called technicalities serve: For example, the Fourth Amendment prohibits unreasonable searches and seizures. While this provision sometimes results in the suppression of reliable evidence, it also protects the population against random intrusions into their belongings and activities. If police could stop anyone at any time, everyone would risk interruption of their daily lives. Moreover, some groups would be more likely to be intruded upon than others; the Fourth Amendment is some assurance (though not perfect or complete assurance) against discriminatory activities by the police.

KEELER v. SUPERIOR COURT
Supreme Court of California, 1970
2 Cal. 3d 619, 470 P.2d 617, 87 Cal. Rptr. 481

Mosk, Justice:

In this proceeding for writ of prohibition we are called upon to decide whether an unborn but viable fetus is a "human being" within the meaning of the California statute defining murder (Pen. Code, §187). We conclude that the Legislature did not intend such a meaning, and that for us to construe the statute to the contrary and apply it to this petitioner would exceed our judicial power and deny petitioner due process of law.

The evidence received at the preliminary examination may be summarized as follows: Petitioner and Teresa Keeler obtained an interlocutory decree of divorce on September 27, 1968.

They had been married for 16 years. Unknown to petitioner, Mrs. Keeler was then pregnant by one Ernest Vogt, whom she had met earlier that summer. She subsequently began living with Vogt in Stockton, but concealed the fact from petitioner. Petitioner was given custody of their two daughters, aged 12 and 13 years, and under the decree Mrs. Keeler had the right to take the girls on alternate weekends.

On February 23, 1969, Mrs. Keeler was driving on a narrow mountain road in Amador County after delivering the girls to their home. She met petitioner driving in the opposite direction; he blocked the road with his car, and she pulled over to the side. He walked to her vehicle and began speaking to her. He seemed calm, and she rolled down her window to hear him. He said, "I hear you're pregnant. If you are you had better stay away from the girls and from here." She did not reply, and he opened the car door; as she later testified, "He assisted me out of the car.... [I]t wasn't roughly at this time." Petitioner then looked at her abdomen and became "extremely upset." He said, "You sure are. I'm going to stomp it out of you." He pushed her against the car, shoved his knee into her abdomen, and struck her in the face with several blows. She fainted, and when she regained consciousness petitioner had departed.

Mrs. Keeler drove back to Stockton, and the police and medical assistance were summoned. She had suffered substantial facial injuries, as well as extensive bruising of the abdominal wall. A Caesarian section was performed and the fetus was examined *in utero*. Its head was found to be severely fractured, and it was delivered stillborn. The pathologist gave as his opinion that the cause of death was skull fracture with consequent cerebral hemorrhaging, that death would have been immediate, and that the injury could have been the result of force applied to the mother's abdomen. There was no air in the fetus' lungs, and the umbilical cord was intact.

Upon delivery the fetus weighed five pounds and was 18 inches in length. Both Mrs. Keeler and her obstetrician testified that fetal movements had been observed prior to February 23, 1969. The evidence was in conflict as to the estimated age of the fetus; the expert testimony on the point, however, concluded "with reasonable medical certainty" that the fetus had developed to the stage of viability, i.e., that in the event of premature birth on the date in question it would have had a 75 percent to 96 percent chance of survival.

An information was filed charging petitioner, in Count I, with committing the crime of murder (Pen. Code, §187) in that he did "unlawfully kill a human being, to wit Baby Girl VOGT, with malice aforethought."...

Penal Code section 187 provides: "Murder is the unlawful killing of a human being, with malice aforethought." The dispositive question is whether the fetus which petitioner is accused of killing was, on February 23, 1969, a "human being" within the meaning of this statute. If it was not, petitioner cannot be charged with its "murder" and prohibition will lie....

We conclude that in declaring murder to be the unlawful and malicious killing of a "human being" the Legislature of 1850 intended that term to have the settled common law meaning of a person who had been born alive, and did not intend the act of feticide — as distinguished from abortion — to be an offense under the laws of California.

Nothing occurred between the years 1850 and 1872 to suggest that in adopting the new Penal Code on the latter date the Legislature entertained any different intent....

The People urge, however, that the sciences of obstetrics and pediatrics have greatly progressed since 1872, to the point where with proper medical care a normally developed fetus prematurely born at 28 weeks or more has an excellent chance of survival, i.e., is "viable"; that the common law requirement of live birth to prove the fetus had become a "human being" who may be the victim of murder is no longer in accord with scientific fact, since an unborn but viable fetus is now fully capable of independent life; and that one who unlawfully and maliciously terminates such a life should therefore be liable to prosecution for murder under section 187. We may grant the premises of this argument; indeed, we neither deny nor denigrate the vast progress of medicine in the century since the enactment of the Penal Code. But we cannot join in the conclusion sought to be deduced: we cannot hold this petitioner to answer for murder by reason of his alleged act of killing an unborn — even though viable — fetus. To such a charge there are two insuperable obstacles, one "jurisdictional" and the other constitutional.

[The court then held that in California the creation of crimes is a task for the legislature and that judicial enlargement of §187 would violate the separation of powers.]

The second obstacle to the proposed judicial enlargement of section 187 is the guarantee of due process of law. Assuming *arguendo* that we have the power to adopt the new construction of this statute as the law of California, such a ruling, by constitutional command, could operate only prospectively, and thus could not in any event reach the conduct of petitioner on February 23, 1969.

The first essential of due process is fair warning of the act which is made punishable as a crime. "That the terms of a penal statute creating a new offense must be sufficiently explicit to inform those who are subject to it what conduct on their part will render them liable to its penalties, is a well-recognized requirement, consonant alike with ordinary notions of fair play and the settled rules of law." (Connally v. General Constr. Co. (1926) 269 U.S. 385, 391, 46 S. Ct. 126, 127.) . . .

. . . When a new penal statute is applied retrospectively to make punishable an act which was not criminal at the time it was performed, the defendant has been given no advance notice consistent with due process. And precisely the same effect occurs when such an act is made punishable under a preexisting statute but by means of an unforeseeable *judicial* enlargement thereof. (Bouie v. City of Columbia (1964) 378 U.S. 347, 84 S. Ct. 1697.)

In *Bouie* two Negroes took seats in the restaurant section of a South Carolina drugstore; no notices were posted restricting the area to whites only. When the defendants refused to leave upon demand, they were arrested and convicted of violating a criminal trespass statute which prohibited entry on the property of another "after notice" forbidding such conduct. Prior South Carolina decisions had emphasized the necessity of proving such notice to support a conviction under the statute. The South Carolina Supreme Court nevertheless affirmed the convictions, construing the statute to prohibit not only the act of entering after notice not to do so but also the wholly different act of remaining on the property after receiving notice to leave.

The United States Supreme Court reversed the convictions, holding that the South Carolina court's ruling was "unforeseeable" and when an "unforeseeable state-court construction of a criminal statute is applied retroactively to subject a person to criminal liability for past conduct, the effect is to deprive him of due process of law in the sense of fair warning that his contemplated

conduct constitutes a crime." Analogizing to the prohibition against retrospective penal legislation, the high court reasoned "Indeed, an unforeseeable judicial enlargement of a criminal statute, applied retroactively, operates precisely like an ex post facto law, such as Art. I, §10, of the Constitution forbids. An ex post facto law has been defined by this Court as one 'that makes an action done before the passing of the law, and which was *innocent* when done, criminal; and punishes such action,' or 'that *aggravates a crime*, or makes it *greater* than it was, when committed.' Calder v. Bull, 3 Dall. 386, 390. If a state legislature is barred by the Ex Post Facto Clause from passing such a law, it must follow that a State Supreme Court is barred by the Due Process Clause from achieving precisely the same result by judicial construction. Cf. Smith v. Cahoon, 283 U.S. 553, 565, 51 S. Ct. 582, 586. The fundamental principle that 'the required criminal law must have existed when the conduct in issue occurred,' Hall, General Principles of Criminal Law (2d ed. 1960), at 58–59, must apply to bar retroactive criminal prohibitions emanating from courts as well as from legislatures. If a judicial construction of a criminal statute is 'unexpected and indefensible by reference to the law which had been expressed prior to the conduct in issue,' it must not be given retroactive effect. Id., at 61."

The court remarked in conclusion that "Application of this rule is particularly compelling where, as here, the petitioners' conduct cannot be deemed improper or immoral." In the case at bar the conduct with which petitioner is charged is certainly "improper" and "immoral," and it is not contended he was exercising a constitutionally favored right. But the matter is simply one of degree, and it cannot be denied that the guarantee of due process extends to violent as well as peaceful men. The issue remains, would the judicial enlargement of section 187 now proposed have been foreseeable to this petitioner? . . .

Turning to the case law, we find no reported decision of the California courts which should have given petitioner notice that the killing of an unborn but viable fetus was prohibited by section 187. . . .

We conclude that the judicial enlargement of section 187 now urged upon us by the People would not have been foreseeable to this petitioner, and hence that its adoption at this time would deny him due process of law.

Let a peremptory writ of prohibition issue restraining respondent court from taking any further proceedings on Count I of the information, charging petitioner with the crime of murder.

BURKE, ACTING CHIEF JUSTICE (dissenting):

The majority hold that "Baby Girl" Vogt, who, according to medical testimony, had reached the 35th week of development, had a 96 percent chance of survival, and was "definitely" alive and viable at the time of her death, nevertheless was not a "human being" under California's homicide statutes. In my view, in so holding, the majority . . . frustrate the express intent of the Legislature, and defy reason, logic and common sense. . . .

The majority opinion suggests that we are confined to common law concepts, and to the common law definition of murder or manslaughter. However, the Legislature, in Penal Code sections 187 and 192, has defined those offenses for us: homicide is the unlawful killing of a "human being." Those words need not be frozen in place as of any particular time, but must be fairly and reasonably interpreted by this court to promote justice and to carry out the evident purposes of the Legislature in adopting a homicide statute. Thus, Penal Code section 4, which was enacted in 1872 along with sections 187 and 192, provides: "The rule of the common law, that penal statutes are to be strictly construed, has no application to this Code. All its provisions are to be construed according to the fair import of their terms, with a view to effect its objects and to promote justice." . . .

The common law reluctance to characterize the killing of a quickened fetus as a homicide was based solely upon a presumption that the fetus would have been born dead. . . . Based upon the state of the medical art in the 17th, 18th and 19th centuries, that presumption may have been well-founded. However, as we approach the 21st century, it has become apparent that "This presumption is not only contrary to common experience and the ordinary course of nature, but it is contrary to the usual rule with respect to presumptions followed in this state." [People v. Chavez, 77 Cal. App. 2d 621, 626, 176 P.2d 92, 95 (1947).]

There are no accurate statistics disclosing fetal death rates in "common law England," although the foregoing presumption of death indicates a significantly high death experience. On the other hand, in California the fetal death rate in 1968 is estimated to be 12 deaths in 1,000, a ratio which would have given Baby Girl Vogt a 98.8 percent chance of survival. (California Statistical Abstract (1969) Table E–3, p. 65.) If, as I have contended, the term "human being" in our homicide statutes is a fluid concept to be defined in accordance with present conditions, then there can be no question that the term should include the fully viable fetus.

The majority suggest that to do so would improperly create some new offense. However, the offense of murder is no new offense. Contrary to the majority opinion, the Legislature has not "defined the crime of murder in California to apply only to the unlawful and malicious killing one who has been born alive." Instead, the Legislature simply used the broad term "human being" and directed the courts to construe that term according to its "fair import" with a view to effect the objects of the homicide statutes and promote justice. (Pen. Code, §4.) What justice will be promoted, what objects effectuated, by construing "human being" as excluding Baby Girl Vogt and her unfortunate successors? Was defendant's brutal act of stomping her to death any less an act of homicide than the murder of a newly born baby? No one doubts that the term "human being" would include the elderly or dying persons whose potential for life has nearly lapsed; their proximity to death is deemed immaterial. There is no sound reason for denying the viable fetus, with its unbounded potential for life, the same status.

The majority also suggest that such an interpretation of our homicide statutes would deny defendant "fair warning" that his act was punishable as a crime. Aside from the absurdity of the underlying premise that defendant consulted

Coke, Blackstone or Hale before kicking Baby Girl Vogt to death, it is clear that defendant had adequate notice that his act could constitute homicide. Due process only precludes prosecution under a new statute insufficiently explicit regarding the specific conduct proscribed, or under a preexisting statute "by means of an unforeseeable *judicial* enlargement thereof."

Our homicide statutes have been in effect in this state since 1850. The fact that the California courts have not been called upon to determine the precise question before us does not render "unforeseeable" a decision which determines that a viable fetus is a "human being" under those statutes. Can defendant really claim surprise that a 5–pound, 18–inch, 34–week-old, living, viable child is considered to be a human being? . . .

SULLIVAN, J., concurs [in dissent].

NOTES

1. Recall that when law is used as a remedial instrument, courts have served as a substantial source of governing law. Why is this judicial role acceptable in the remedial instrument but not in the penal instrument? Our Constitution demands clear forewarning and so prohibits "ex post facto" criminal laws, meaning laws that punish an action that was legal when it was committed. Civil laws, however, may be retroactively applied. Remember that the penal instrument is distinguished by its heavy reliance on punishment. It is difficult to justify punishment for crimes not defined by the legislature, whether using utilitarian or retributive theory. Punishing an actor for a undefined crime will not further deterrence, because avoiding criminal conduct is impossible when such conduct has not yet been proscribed. For a retributivist, a criminal is culpable because he chose to break the law, but if the law did not exist when the defendant made his choice, it is hard to condemn him for disobeying law. Note, however, that both a utilitarian and a retributivist might think that conduct that is obviously wrong — crimes that are *mala in se* — should be distinguished from conduct that is wrong only because it is prohibited — crimes that are *mala prohibitum*. While *mala prohibitum* crimes can be neither effectively deterred nor morally condemned absent a preexisting prohibition, one might argue that an obviously heinous offense might be morally deserving of punishment. Can you think of how a utilitarian might attempt to justify punishment of morally heinous activity that was not proscribed at the time of the offense?

2. Of course, while judges normally cannot create or extend crimes, they do frequently create and extend affirmative defenses. Occasionally, they may then reverse themselves and contract or abolish affirmative defenses. Recall the above discussion on the insanity defense. Some courts have declined to change their state's rule, leaving that decision to the legislature, while others changed the standards through judicial action. Even if one approves of judicial creation or extension of affirmative defenses, it may be that judicial contraction or abolition of those rights raises due process issues.

Section Four
APPLYING PENAL LAW

If the penal instrument consisted only of prohibitions, defenses, and prescribed penalties, it would be fundamentally deficient. The penal law is not self-executing. Rather, it requires the participation of many individuals serving as police, prosecutors, magistrates, grand jurors, judges, petit jurors, and prison officials. An individual in one of these public positions is obviously important for the role she plays in processing an offender through the criminal justice system. Equally important, however, is her decision that a particular suspect should not proceed further in the criminal justice system. Police, prosecutors, juries, and judges all perform this *screening function*. Decisions will often be based upon the suspect's apparent guilt or innocence, but they may be based on other factors as well. Some of the discretion possessed by police, prosecutors, juries, and judges is probably necessary, but ensuring that that discretion is prudently and fairly exercised is difficult. The readings in this section examine the exercise of discretion, but before we turn to them, summarizing the steps in a typical state criminal proceeding may be useful.

Cases generally enter the criminal justice system through the police. A crime may be observed by the police or reported to the police. Perhaps further investigation is needed, but perhaps not. At some point, the police make an *arrest*, and the adjudicative process begins.

Shortly after the arrest, the suspect will be taken before a judicial officer for a *preliminary hearing*, the purpose of which is to determine whether there is probable cause to believe the arrestee has committed an offense. If the judicial officer does not find probable cause to believe an offense has been committed, she will order the release of the person arrested. If, on the other hand, the prosecutor has shown probable cause, the judicial officer will decide whether the defendant should be held in jail, released on bail, or released "on his own recognizance," which means released upon his promise to appear when next summoned.

If the crime is a serious one (i.e., a felony as opposed to a misdemeanor), in many states the prosecution cannot proceed further until the defendant has also been indicted by a grand jury. The grand jury will be a body of 12 to 23 laypeople who will decide whether enough evidence has been gathered to justify putting the defendant on trial. Usually, only the prosecution's evidence is heard by the grand jury, and if the grand jury is satisfied by the evidence, it will return an *indictment* (also called a true bill), which formally charges the defendant with one or more offenses.

After indictment, or after the prosecutor prepares a so-called information if an indictment was unnecessary, the defendant will appear to plead to the charges. At this proceeding, usually called an *arraignment*, the defendant may move to quash the indictment or information. Like the defendant's demurrer in a civil case, this motion challenges the legal sufficiency of the charges.

If the motion is denied, the defendant will plead either guilty or not guilty. If he pleads guilty, he will be held for sentencing.

If he pleads not guilty, he will be held for trial. At trial, the defendant may represent himself or may be represented by an attorney. If he cannot afford an attorney, the court will appoint one for him or assign the case to the public defender's office. *Opening statements*, first by the prosecutor and then by the defense attorney, begin the trial. The prosecutor then presents her evidence, attempting to prove the defendant's guilt beyond a reasonable doubt. When the prosecutor has finished her presentation, the defendant's lawyer can move to have the case dismissed because of the *insufficiency of the evidence*. If the court grants this motion, the trial will be over and the defendant will be released. If the defendant's motion is not granted, the defendant's lawyer will then present the defendant's evidence, if any. The defendant need not testify, and no adverse inference may be drawn from his decision not to testify. After all the evidence has been presented, the defendant's lawyer can move for a *directed verdict* of not guilty. If the court grants this motion, the trial will be over and the defendant will be released.

If the defendant's motion is not granted, the prosecution and defense will make *closing arguments*. The judge will then *instruct* the jury on the law relevant to the case. The judge will explain the elements of the crime charged and tell the jurors that to convict the defendant, they must find that each and every element of the crime has been proved beyond a reasonable doubt. If the jury returns a *verdict* of not guilty, the trial will be over and the defendant will be released.

If the jury returns a verdict of guilty, the defendant will later receive a *sentence*. Unless the case is one in which a death sentence might be imposed, the judge rather than the jury will usually sentence the defendant. Usually, she is guided by a presentence report written by a probation officer who has interviewed the defendant, the defendant's family and employer, if any, the victim, and sometimes other people who have information concerning the offense or the defendant.

After the defendant is convicted and sentenced, his lawyer may *appeal* to a higher court. If the appellate court finds prejudicial error in the conduct of the defendant's trial, it will reverse and remand; if the appellate court finds the evidence insufficient, it will reverse and dismiss the indictment. Otherwise, it will affirm the defendant's conviction.

The decision of the highest court of the state is usually final. If, however, the defendant claims that his federal rights have been violated, he can ask the United States Supreme Court to review his case. It is unlikely that the United States Supreme Court will decide to review the defendant's case, but if it does so, reversal is possible after convincing the Supreme Court that the state has violated a federal right. If the Supreme Court does not grant review and relief, the defendant may file a petition in state court for post-conviction relief; such petitions generally allege facts not contained within the trial record and often focus on misconduct by the defense attorney, the prosecutor, or the jury. Finally, the defendant may file a *habeas corpus petition* in a federal district court, and if that court finds a violation of federal rights, it may order the state to either retry the defendant or release him.

A. The Police

ARREST

Police officers exercise discretion on a daily basis. For example, an officer may choose to give a speeding driver a warning rather than a ticket. Even more commonly, the officer may choose not to pull over a driver at all, rather waiting for someone who may be going even faster. Police officers make such choices constantly, and these choices are an exercise of discretion. They occur in more serious situations, as well. An officer responding to a domestic disturbance may simply break up the altercation, declining to make any arrests. She may make an arrest with no thought of prosecution, but only to get one of the combatants off the street and out of harm's way. In doing so, the officer is performing a function that, while often overlooked by legal scholars, takes up the vast majority of an officer's time.

DAVID H. BAYLEY, POLICE FOR THE FUTURE
16-21 (1994)

Very little of the work patrol officers do has to do with crime. British and U.S. studies have consistently shown that not more than 25% of all calls to the police are about crime; more often the figure is 15–20%.... Moreover, what is initially reported by the public as crime is often found not to be crime by the police who respond ....Thus the real proportion of requests to the police that involve crime may be more like 7–10%.

Most of the genuine crime that police are called upon to handle is distinctly minor. Not unimportant necessarily — certainly not to the people involved — but a far cry from the senseless violence and mayhem that newspapers and television lead the public to expect....

If the majority of police officers are not directly fighting crime, what are they doing? The answer is that they are restoring order and providing general assistance. In the apt words of Egon Bittner, the key function of the police is to stop "something-that-ought-not-to-be-happening-and-about-which-someone-had-better-do-something-now." Police interrupt and pacify situations of potential or ongoing conflict. Typical instances are young men drinking beer on a street corner and making rude remarks; people playing rock music at a high volume late at night in an apartment; kids turning on a fire hydrant to provide a shower on a hot summer day; homeless people begging and sleeping in the corridors of a busy bus terminal....

Most of the time the police do not use the criminal law to restore calm and order. They rarely make arrests, although the threat of doing so always exists. Research into the handling of domestic disputes in the United States has shown that police routinely pursue eight different courses of action. Most commonly, they simply leave after listening, without doing anything at all (23.7% of cases). Next, they give friendly advice about how to avoid a repetition of the incident (16.1%). Arrest is the third most frequently used action, occurring in 13.9% of incidents.... Police also pointedly warn people about what will happen if they are called back; promise future help if it is needed; give explicit advice to one or the other about what they should do to extricate themselves from the conflict; make sure that one party leaves the scene; or suggest referral to third parties, professional or otherwise.

The infrequency of arrests is not just true of police responses to disputes. In general, patrol officers, who are responsible for most contacts with the general population, rarely make arrests. In the United States in 1990, police officers made an average of 19 arrests a year. That is less than one arrest per officer every 15 working days, and it includes arrests of all sorts. . . .

Although police rarely enforce the law in their manifold encounters with people, it would be wrong to suggest that the power of arrest is not important. The threat is potent, whatever the outcome of particular encounters. The power to arrest gives the police tremendous leverage. It is what makes their intervention authoritative. Police *can* forcibly stop people from doing what they are doing. Police *can* legally throw people on the ground and cuff their hands behind their back; they *can* shackle them to iron benches in police stations; they *can* order people to kneel on sidewalks with their faces pressed against brick walls; they *can* force them to lie prone on dirty sidewalks while police dogs stand guard; and they *can* push people into bare cells with wet concrete floors and slam shut the heavy barred door behind them. As U.S. police officers sometimes say, "Maybe I can't give 'em the rap [a conviction], but I sure can give 'em the ride."

While there is no question that police officers exercise considerable discretion in utilizing their power of arrest, it is uncertain whether that discretion is a good thing. For example, when a police officer arrests a suspect for a minor crime, such as drinking in public, she is then allowed to search that suspect. This search may lead to evidence of more serious crimes, such as possession of a handgun or of narcotics. While initially this would seem to be a desirable result, the potential for abuse is serious. What if an officer decided only to arrest black suspects for such minor offenses, believing that they are more likely to possess serious contraband? While such racial profiling is not officially advocated by any police department, it may continue unofficially so long as officers have discretion in making arrests. Such conduct is difficult to deter, because it is virtually invisible to oversight. Without records of those situations in which an officer did not take action, it is impossible to determine whether her conduct was driven by impermissible motives.

For another example, the order-maintenance goal of policing is often a source of friction between police and prosecutors. An officer making an arrest for purposes of defusing a situation may not be concerned with getting a conviction in court, and thus will not be concentrating on the nuances of proper criminal procedure. If a violation has occurred, when the prosecutor takes over the case, she may be hampered in her prosecution of the crime by the consequent loss of important evidence. The police officer achieved her objective of preventing immediate disorder, but the prosecutor's objectives are frustrated. Of course, prosecutors may fail to understand the urgency with which police must make decisions and take action in difficult situations.

By contrast, discretion in making arrests can be quite useful, especially for police forces pursuing the somewhat more recently developed methods of order-maintenance policing. Recently, many municipal police forces, most notably the New York Police Department, have subscribed to community policing theories. These theories prescribe a community-based approach, in which officers develop a working relationship with the citizens in a neighborhood, responding to their concerns. Each neighborhood in a city may have different aspects, and the officer must exercise discretion to respond to her assigned neighborhood's specific concerns and preferences about the character of police action. The responsible exercise of discretion can help relieve the tension that has existed between the police and many communities. An officer may build a relationship with community members by using her discretion to decline to enforce some misdemeanors. In this way, she may build up goodwill and respect that can benefit her more than use of force. In one notable example, when an officer in Chicago was being punched by a suspect resisting arrest, neighborhood gang members rushed to her defense and helped her get the man under control. See Johnathan Eig, Eyes on the Street: Community Policing in Chicago, Am. Prospect, Nov.–Dec. 1996, at 63.

INTERROGATION

For those cases that will be prosecuted, the manner in which evidence is gathered after arrest is extremely important. The accused may be a very good source of information, but he may also be reluctant to provide information. Here we consider what methods police may use to elicit information from suspects and what safeguards should be required to ensure that police do not place undue pressure on the accused to provide incriminating information.

BROWN v. MISSISSIPPI
Supreme Court of the United States, 1936
297 U.S. 278, 56 S. Ct. 461

MR. CHIEF JUSTICE HUGHES delivered the opinion of the Court:

The question in this case is whether convictions, which rest solely upon confessions shown to have been extorted by officers of the state by brutality and violence, are consistent with the due process of law required by the Fourteenth Amendment of the Constitution of the United States.

Petitioners were indicted for the murder of one Raymond Stewart, whose death occurred on March 30, 1934. They were indicted on April 4, 1934, and were then arraigned and pleaded not guilty. Counsel were appointed by the court to defend them. Trial was begun the next morning and was concluded on the following day, when they were found guilty and sentenced to death.

Aside from the confessions, there was no evidence sufficient to warrant the submission of the case to the jury. After a preliminary inquiry, testimony as to the confessions was received over the objection of defendants' counsel. Defendants then testified that the confessions were false and had been procured by physical torture. The case went to the jury with instructions, upon the request of defendants' counsel, that if the jury had reasonable doubt as to the confessions having resulted from coercion, and that they were not true, they were not to be considered as evidence. On their appeal to the Supreme Court of the State, defendants assigned as error the inadmissibility of the confessions. The judgment was affirmed....

... There is no dispute as to the facts upon this point, and as they are clearly and adequately stated in the dissenting opinion of Judge Griffith (with whom Judge Anderson concurred), showing both the extreme brutality of the measures to extort the confessions and the participation of the state authorities, we quote this part of his opinion in full, as follows:

The crime with which these defendants, all ignorant negroes, are charged, was discovered about 1 o'clock p.m. on Friday,

March 30, 1934. On that night one Dial, a deputy sheriff, accompanied by others, came to the home of Ellington, one of the defendants, and requested him to accompany them to the house of the deceased, and there a number of white men were gathered, who began to accuse the defendant of the crime. Upon his denial they seized him, and with the participation of the deputy they hanged him by a rope to the limb of a tree, and, having let him down, they hung him again, and when he was let down the second time, and he still protested his innocence, he was tied to a tree and whipped, and, still declining to accede to the demands that he confess, he was finally released, and he returned with some difficulty to his home, suffering intense pain and agony. The record of the testimony shows that the signs of the rope on his neck were plainly visible during the so-called trial. A day or two thereafter the said deputy, accompanied by another, returned to the home of the said defendant and arrested him, and departed with the prisoner towards the jail in an adjoining county, but went by a route which led into the state of Alabama; and while on the way, in that state, the deputy stopped and again severely whipped the defendant, declaring that he would continue the whipping until he confessed, and the defendant then agreed to confess to such a statement as the deputy would dictate, and he did so, after which he was delivered to jail.

The other two defendants, Ed Brown and Henry Shields, were also arrested and taken to the same jail. On Sunday night, April 1, 1934, the same deputy, accompanied by a number of white men, one of whom was also an officer, and by the jailer, came to the jail, and the two last named defendants were made to strip and they were laid over chairs and their backs were cut to pieces with a leather strap with buckles on it, and they were likewise made by the said deputy definitely to understand that the whipping would be continued unless and until they confessed, and not only confessed, but confessed in every matter of detail as demanded by those present; and in this manner the defendants confessed the crime, and, as the whippings progressed and were repeated, they changed or adjusted their confession in all particulars of detail so as to conform to the demands of their torturers. When the confessions had been obtained in the exact form and contents as desired by the mob, they left with the parting admonition and warning that, if the defendants changed their story at any time in any respect from that last stated, the perpetrators of the outrage would administer the same or equally effective treatment.

Further details of the brutal treatment to which these helpless prisoners were subjected need not be pursued. It is sufficient to say that in pertinent respects the transcript reads more like pages torn from some medieval account than a record made within the confines of a modern civilization which aspires to an enlightened constitutional government.

All this having been accomplished, on the next day, that is, on Monday, April 2, when the defendants had been given time to recuperate somewhat from the tortures to which they had been subjected, the two sheriffs, one of the county where the crime was committed, and the other of the county of the jail in which the prisoners were confined, came to the jail, accompanied by eight other persons, some of them deputies, there to hear the free and voluntary confession of these miserable and abject defendants. The sheriff of the county of the crime admitted that he had heard of the whipping, but averred that he had no personal knowledge of it. He admitted that one of the defendants, when brought before him to confess, was limping and did not sit down, and that this particular defendant then and there stated that he had been strapped so severely that he could not sit down, and, as already stated, the signs of the rope on the neck of another of the defendants were plainly visible to all. Nevertheless the solemn farce of hearing the free and voluntary confessions was gone through with, and these two sheriffs and one other person then present were the three witnesses used in court to establish the so-called confessions, which were received by the court and admitted in evidence over the objections of the defendants duly entered of record as each of the said three witnesses delivered their alleged testimony....

...The evidence upon which the conviction was obtained was the so-called confessions. Without this evidence, a peremptory instruction to find for the defendants would have been inescapable. The defendants were put on the stand, and by their testimony the facts and the details thereof as to the manner by which the confessions were extorted from them were fully developed, and it is further disclosed by the record that the same deputy, Dial, under whose guiding hand and active participation the tortures to coerce the confessions were administered, was actively in the performance of the supposed duties of a court deputy in the courthouse and in the presence of the prisoners during what is denominated, in complimentary terms, the trial of these defendants. This deputy was put on the stand by the state in rebuttal, and admitted the whippings. It is interesting to note that in his testimony with reference to the whipping of the defendant Ellington, and in response to the inquiry as to how severely he was whipped, the deputy stated, "Not too much for a negro; not as much as I would have done if it were left to me." Two others who had participated in these whippings were introduced and admitted it — not a single witness was introduced who denied it....

The state is free to regulate the procedure of its courts in accordance with its own conceptions of policy, unless in so doing it "offends some principle of justice so rooted in the traditions and conscience of our people as to be ranked as fundamental." Snyder v. Massachusetts, [291 U.S. 97, 105, 54 S. Ct. 330, 332 (1934)].... [The state] may dispense with indictment by a grand jury and substitute complaint or information. Walker v. Sauvinet, 92 U.S. 90; Hurtado v. California, 110 U.S. 516, 4 S. Ct. 111, 292; Snyder v. Massachusetts, supra. But the freedom of the state in establishing its policy is the freedom of constitutional government and is limited by the requirement of due process of law....The rack and torture chamber may not be substituted for the witness stand. The state may not permit an accused to be hurried to conviction under mob domination — where the whole proceeding is but a mask — without supplying corrective process. Moore v. Dempsey, 261 U.S. 86, 91, 43 S. Ct. 265. The state may not deny to the accused the aid of counsel. Powell v. Alabama, 287 U.S. 45, 53 S. Ct. 55. Nor may a state, through the action of its officers, contrive a conviction through the pretense of a trial which in truth is "but used as a means of depriving a defendant of liberty through a deliberate deception of court and jury by the presentation of testimony known to be perjured." Mooney v. Holohan, 294 U.S. 103, 112, 55 S. Ct. 340, 342. And the trial equally is a mere pretense where the state authorities have contrived a conviction resting solely upon confessions obtained by violence. The due process clause requires "that state action, whether through one agency or another, shall be consistent with the fundamental principles of liberty and justice which lie at the base of all our civil and political institutions." Hebert v. Louisiana, 272 U.S. 312, 316, 47 S. Ct. 103, 104. It would be difficult to conceive of methods more revolting to the sense of justice than those taken to procure the confessions of these petitioners, and the use of the confessions thus obtained as the basis for conviction and sentence was a clear denial of due process....

...The court thus denied a federal right fully established and specially set up and claimed, and the judgment must be reversed.

Torture and Terrorism

The practice of "waterboarding" has crystalized the once-abstract questions raised in Note 7 of Section One. Waterboarding is a form of torture that consists of immobilizing a person on his or her back with the head inclined downwards, and then pouring water over his or her face and into his or her breathing passages. This causes the person to experience intense sensations of drowning, and generally creates a belief that death is imminent. In 2007, it was revealed that the CIA had used — and was using — waterboarding on extrajudicial prisoners, and that the United States Department of Justice had approved use of the procedure. This produced outraged protests from many groups across the globe, but President Bush's administration defended the practice as not being "torture," relying on the fact that it (normally) does not cause permanent damage.

In January 2009, newly elected President Obama banned the use of waterboarding, though in April of the same year, the Department of Defense refused to say whether it was still being used for training purposes. Al-Qaeda suspects whom the CIA waterboarded include high profile defendants Khalid Sheikh Mohammed, Abu Zubaydah, and Abd al-Rahim al-Nashir. If these men were tried in ordinary courts, Brown v. Mississippi would seem to make it clear that any confessions that resulted from waterboarding would not be admissible. However, at this time it is unclear whether these men will instead be tried by military tribunals, where the constitutional requirements of due process may — or may not — be applied.

Notice that even if one endorsed the proposition that the use of waterboarding *to prevent future terrorist activity* is justified, this would not resolve the question of whether confessions stemming from waterboarding should be admissible to convict the defendants against whom the technique had been used.

The *Brown* Court relied upon the Fourteenth Amendment guarantee of due process to decide the case. A later case, *Miranda v. Arizona*, with which most Americans are now familiar, relied upon the Fifth Amendment privilege against compelled self-incrimination. At the time *Brown* was decided, it appeared that the Fifth Amendment did not constrain state officials but only federal officials, and it was also unclear whether the Self-Incrimination Clause had any application outside of the courtroom. In between *Brown* and *Miranda*, the Supreme Court had determined that the Fifth Amendment did apply to the states, and *Miranda* itself determined that the privilege extended to compulsion exerted outside the courtroom. Because the *Miranda* majority was convinced that custodial interrogation was inherently coercive, it concluded that procedural safeguards designed to dispel that coercion were necessary. These safeguards include the now-familiar *Miranda* warnings, which provide that the defendant must be informed "that he has the right to remain silent, that anything he says can be used against him in a court of law, that he has the right to the presence of an attorney, and that if he cannot afford an attorney one will be appointed for him prior to any questioning if he so desires." Miranda v. Arizona, 384 U.S. 436, 479, 86 S. Ct. 1602, 1630 (1966).

Although the *Miranda* Court was concerned with the coercive pressure that police could bring to bear against a suspect subjected to custodial interrogation, it permitted police to continue to use deception and trickery while attempting to extract a confession, provided that the suspect was first made aware of those rights and that any invocation of his rights was scrupulously honored. Because it was custodial interrogation that, according to *Miranda*, created inherent coercion, whether the *Miranda* safeguards apply depends upon whether both "custody" and "interrogation" are present when the accused made the statement that the government wishes to introduce against him.

In a subsequent case, the Court defined "interrogation" as "not only express questioning, but also . . . any words or actions on the part of the police (other than those normally attendant to arrest and custody) that the police should know are reasonably likely to elicit an incriminating response from the suspect." Rhode Island v. Innis, 446 U.S. 291, 301, 100 S. Ct. 1682, 1689–90 (1980) (finding no interrogation in that case).

Later, the Court held that a suspect is in "custody" for purposes of triggering *Miranda*'s protection when his "freedom of action is curtailed to a degree associated with formal arrest." Berkemer v. McCarty, 468 U.S. 420, 440, 104 S. Ct. 3138, 3151 (1984) (internal quotation marks omitted). In *Berkemer*, the defendant was pulled over for suspicion of driving under the influence. At the scene of the traffic stop, the police officer asked the defendant if he had been using intoxicants, and the defendant stated that he had consumed two beers and several joints of marijuana. After subsequently failing a field sobriety test, the officer arrested the defendant and transported him to the county jail. There, a blood test did not detect any alcohol in the suspect's system, but further questioning prompted him to admit again that he had been drinking and smoking marijuana. The Court held that the statements made before the actual arrest were admissible, because the suspect was not in custody during the traffic stop until the formal arrest was made. The statements made after the arrest, however, were inadmissible because the defendant had not been advised of his rights.

NOTES

1. Studies comparing the rate of confessions prior to the *Miranda* decision with the rate of confessions after the *Miranda* rules were in effect show little change. Do these findings suggest that the *Miranda* rules should be abandoned because they are unnecessary? Alternatively, do they suggest that *Miranda* does not go far enough, perhaps because *Miranda* assigns the dispelling of coercion to the very person (the police officer) who creates that coercion? Would it be preferable to require that a judge or defense lawyer inform the defendant of his rights?

2. As to applying the *Miranda* standards, consider the facts of *Innis*: The defendant was arrested at 4:30 A.M. on suspicion of robbery, after a taxi driver

identified him in a photo lineup as the man who robbed him with a sawed-off shotgun. Another taxi driver had recently been killed by a shotgun in an apparent robbery. After arresting the suspect and advising him of his *Miranda* rights, and after his requesting to see a lawyer, the officers began transporting him to the police station. En route, one of the officers began a conversation with another about the shotgun, which had not yet been found. The officer stated that there was a school for handicapped children nearby, and he hoped that the police found the gun soon, because he was worried that a handicapped child might find the gun and maybe accidentally kill herself. At this point, the suspect, who could hear the officer's conversation, interrupted the conversation and told the officers to go back so he could show them where the gun was, which he then did. At trial, both the gun and the defendant's statements concerning the gun's location were introduced as evidence against him. Should the police officers have known that their conversation was reasonably likely to elicit an incriminating response from the suspect? It is not much of a stretch to assume that the officers' conversation was designed to elicit just such a response. Justice Marshall's dissent in the case points out, "One can scarcely imagine a stronger appeal to the conscience of a suspect — *any* suspect — than the assertion that if the weapon is not found an innocent person will be hurt or killed. And not just any innocent person, but an innocent little child — a little girl — a helpless, handicapped little girl on her way to school." Did the majority follow the interrogation standard that they had created?

B. The Prosecutor

"We set out to learn about police operations by posing the question: What happens after arrest? What happens after arrest, most often, is that the prosecutor drops the case." Brian Forst, Judith Lucianovic & Sarah J. Fox, What Happens After Arrest? 89 (1977).

Perhaps the most important aspect of prosecutorial discretion lies in the charging function. The prosecutor has (virtually) sole authority to decide whether or not to charge a suspect with a crime. If she decides to charge the suspect, she then gets to decide the type and number of charges to bring. These decisions have an enormous impact on the severity of the suspect's potential punishment. Generally, courts and legislatures have left the prosecutor with a huge amount of discretion in making these decisions, thus affording very little opportunity for courts to review them. Justifications for this autonomy include: constitutional separation of powers, based on the belief that the prosecution of crimes is a duty of the executive branch; deference to prosecutorial expertise; administrative convenience; need to make deals with offenders in exchange for their testimony against others; and individualized justice, based on the view that the criminal law regulates conduct generally, and prosecutors must therefore have the ability to take individual circumstances into account.

Prosecutors and the Adversary System

Prosecutors may be influenced by public opinion or outcries for justice in high-profile cases. Consider the following newspaper account, written just after prosecutor Michael B. Nifong was disbarred for his conduct in prosecuting players on the Duke University lacrosse team accused of rape (after Nifong had been removed from the case, the charges were dropped):

> The Duke case also has some striking resemblances to the trial of the so-called Scottsboro Boys. This case of prosecutorial abuse stemmed from a fight on the evening of March 25, 1931, in which a group of black youths threw a group of white boys off a freight train in northern Alabama. When police pulled the black boys off the train, they found two white girls dressed in men's clothing also riding the train. The girls claimed that they had been held against their will, beaten and raped by the black youths.

> Like Nifong, the Scottsboro prosecutors ignored the conspicuous absence of forensic and medical evidence supporting the rape charges — particularly the lack of bruises or torn clothing. (One girl later admitted that they had made up the story in order to avoid getting in trouble with the law themselves.) All nine Scottsboro defendants were convicted in one-day trials and sentenced to death, with the exception of a 13–year-old boy who was spared death by one holdout juror. (After the Supreme Court intervened and after multiple trials and pardons, the accused were released years later.)

> This abuse occurred because the critical safeguard of prosecutorial discretion — the decision whether to pursue a case — didn't protect the suspects. Despite what you see on television, the chances of being convicted in a criminal case are extremely high. Grand juries are said to be willing to "indict a ham sandwich," and it's not uncommon for prosecution offices to have conviction rates of 90 percent or higher. Some prosecutors grow callous and cavalier about their role. When told that he had secured the death penalty against an innocent man, a Texas prosecutor once reportedly boasted that "any prosecutor can convict a guilty man; it takes a great prosecutor to convict an innocent man."

> History is rife with such "great prosecutors" convicting the innocent to satisfy the public. In the 1913 Leo Frank trial, Atlanta Chief prosecutor Hugh Dorsey pursued a Jewish factory owner for the rape and murder of 13–year-old factory worker Mary Phagan. It was a period of intense anti-Semitism, with crowds chanting "Kill the Jew" outside the courtroom. Prosecutors ignored the fact that all the evidence pointed to a janitor, Jim Conley, as the killer. Instead, they repeatedly rewrote Conley's conflicting statements to help him manufacture a coherent account for trial. Conley was identified years later as the killer by a witness, but it was too late for Frank. He was kidnapped from prison by vigilantes (including many leading lawyers) and hanged near Mary's grave.

> Prosecutors are sworn to protect the rights of the accused as well as the accuser, to refuse to pursue cases that would not serve the interests of justice. Yet in today's environment, it appears that prosecutors can never be too tough, the way models can never be too skinny.

Johnathan Turley, Lots of Prosecutors Go Too Far. Most Get Away with It, Wash. Post, June 24, 2007, at B03.

Once a prosecutor has made a charging decision, courts will rarely intervene. One limit on a prosecutor's charging discretion is the requirement of probable cause. In order for a prosecutor to bring a case to trial, she must have sufficient evidence supporting the belief that the suspect committed a crime. If a judge finds no probable cause to believe that the suspect committed a crime, the charges will be dismissed. Note, however, that this limit on a prosecutor's discretion seeks only to prevent abusive or unfounded prosecutions. If there is sufficient evidence, the prosecutor then has almost total autonomy in deciding whether to press and maintain formal charges. Challenges to a decision, whether charges are filed or not, are rarely upheld.

Where a prosecutor decides to bring charges, and has sufficient evidence, the only judicial remedy is to have the charges dismissed for denial of equal protection or on due process grounds, and these challenges must meet very high standards. The prosecution must be purposefully and invidiously selective (i.e., based on grounds such as race or religion) or vindictive (e.g., retaliatory for the defendant's decision to exercise a constitutional right). Also, prosecutors themselves have general immunity from civil lawsuits for such prosecutions. This protection was put in place to prevent suspects from harassing prosecutors through civil process.

Few courts or legislatures have rules requiring prosecutors to file charges, so prosecutors may decide *not* to prosecute for virtually any reason. If a prosecutor decides not to charge, some avenues exist for individuals to compel the prosecutor to bring charges, but these attempts rarely succeed. Of course, this lack of formal coercion does not mean that public officials or the people themselves have no influence. Most chief prosecutors are elected officials, who in turn appoint their assistants. Should a prosecutorial office fail to press charges too often, or in a high-profile case, it could mean that the composition of the office will change with the next election.

C. The Jury

In Chapter 1 we saw how a trial judge instructs the jury on the applicable law. If the jury obviously fails to follow these instructions, the verdict may be set aside and a new trial held. Similarly, if the jury finds facts "contrary to the weight of the evidence," its verdict may be set aside and a new trial held. When the law is used as a penal instrument, however, judicial control is more limited.

The judge at trial will instruct the jury that it may convict the defendant only if the evidence proves his guilt "beyond a reasonable doubt." If the jury convicts the defendant even though the evidence of guilt was weak, the judge (or an appellate court) will overturn the conviction and dismiss the charges. But if the jury acquits the defendant, even in the face of overwhelming evidence of guilt, the courts cannot touch the verdict. An acquittal in a criminal case is final.

Jurors may acquit an obviously guilty defendant for a number of reasons. They may be confused about the law. They may feel sympathy or affection for the defendant. They may dislike the statute the accused is being tried under — or even the prosecutor trying the case. What values are threatened by the jury's unqualified power to acquit in a criminal case? Are other values protected by that power?

Recall the discussion of process values versus outcome values in Chapter 1. Our system of criminal law cannot be understood without an appreciation for the constant tension between these values. Outcome values refer to the desire to reach the right result in each individual case. Process values reflect a desire to guarantee the protections of the law to all defendants, to ensure fair application of the law. Both of these values are fundamental to our system of laws, but process values are often served at the expense of outcome values, and vice versa. The right to a trial by a jury of by one's peers is a protection designed to serve process values, and it is considered absolutely fundamental.

D. The Judge

Generally, trial judges have discretion in many of the decisions they make. Rulings on procedural motions, decisions determining the admissibility of evidence, and the making of factual findings all can involve some degree of discretion. These exercises of discretion, however, are limited by a system of appellate court review. If a trial court makes a ruling contrary to the law or the weight of evidence, other than acquittal, it may be overturned on appeal. The sentencing phase of the trial, however, has historically been subject to a large amount of judicial discretion, and hence to very limited appellate review.

The trial judge is normally responsible for sentencing convicted defendants and may select any sentence within the statutory ranges outlined for each offense. The judge may hold a hearing, at which she would hear arguments from both sides as to the sentence they believe appropriate, after which the judge would make her decision. After the trial, appellate courts are very reluctant to make any changes to the sentence imposed by the trial judge. The appellate courts give great deference to the trial judge's decision, as she was in the best position to make an objective, reasoned, transparent decision on the facts of the case. Also, the judge, rather than a legislature, is able to individualize the sentence imposed, as she has access to more facts and can take into account factors that the legislature might not have foreseen.

Nevertheless, some legislatures have attempted to limit the trial judge's discretion in sentencing, sometimes due to public outcries alleging discriminatory sentencing tendencies, either through mandatory minimum sentencing or through the use of sentencing guidelines.

Mandatory minimum statutes require a judge to sentence the defendant to at least a specified minimum term. This may be mandated for a certain charge, or for a case in which certain designated facts are established at sentencing. One well-known example of such a statue is the "three strikes" law, which at least half of the states have enacted in some form. These statutes generally require that a defendant who is convicted of a third felony (or, in some jurisdictions, a third violent felony) receive a lengthy sentence, sometimes life in prison. Such statutes limit a judge's discretion, sometimes with harsh results. In Ewing v. California, 538 U.S. 11, 123 S. Ct. 1179 (2003), Ewing had stolen three golf clubs, valued at $399 each, and was convicted of felony grand theft of personal property. It was this conviction, along with his prior criminal history of two felonies, that triggered California's mandatory minimum sentencing statute. The sentence was 25 years to life in prison. Was the sentence appropriate? A utilitarian might say that Ewing had proven himself to be a habitual felon, and rehabilitation was clearly not effective in his case, thus justifying his sentence. Is there a retributive argument justifying such a sentence? It is difficult to see Ewing's sentence as proportional to his crime, at least in the sense that retributivists use that word. The Supreme Court upheld the sentence, holding that it did not violate the Eighth Amendment's prohibition on cruel and unusual punishment.

A number of legislatures have attempted to curb judicial discretion in sentencing by promulgating sentencing guidelines. Generally, the guidelines consist of a sentencing table or grid, which starts with the sentence range for an offense. The grid will then incorporate criminal history, severity of offense, and other aggravating factors to guide the judge toward a particular narrow range. Thus, where an offense has a statutory range of 10 to 20 years in prison, the judge's discretion may be limited to deciding between 15 and 17 years. In some states the guidelines are not binding, and a judge may go outside the recommendation without providing a justification for doing so. In other states, however, the guidelines are mandatory, and a judge may depart from them only for a limited number of specified reasons. The most complex system of guidelines was created by a federal commission for criminal sentencing.

Since the inception of mandatory sentencing guidelines, a number of challenges have been raised. One notable problem in the federal guidelines was that the judge was permitted to find facts for sentencing purposes after a conviction, and even though the facts need not be found beyond a reasonable doubt, they could cause the defendant's sentence to be longer than it otherwise would have been. The case below is the Supreme Court's response to this challenge.

UNITED STATES v. BOOKER

Supreme Court of the United States, 2005
543 U.S. 220, 125 S. Ct. 738

Justice Stevens delivered the opinion of the court in part: . . .

I

Respondent Booker was charged with possession with intent to distribute at least 50 grams of cocaine base (crack). Having heard evidence that he had 92.5 grams in his duffel bag, the jury found him guilty of violating 21 U.S.C. §841(a)(1). That statute prescribes a minimum sentence of 10 years in prison and a maximum sentence of life for that offense. §841(b)(1)(A)(iii).

Based upon Booker's criminal history and the quantity of drugs found by the jury, the Sentencing Guidelines required the District Court Judge to select a "base" sentence of not less than 210 nor more than 262 months in prison. See United States Sentencing Commission, Guidelines Manual §§2D1.1(c)(4), 4A1.1 (Nov. 2003) (USSG). The judge, however, held a post-trial sentencing proceeding and concluded by a preponderance of the evidence that Booker had possessed an additional 566 grams of crack and that he was guilty of obstructing justice. Those findings mandated that the judge select a sentence between 360 months and life imprisonment; the judge imposed a sentence at the low end of the range. Thus, instead of the sentence of 21 years and 10 months that the judge could have imposed on the basis of the facts proved to the jury beyond a reasonable doubt, Booker received a 30-year sentence. Over the dissent of Judge Easterbrook, the Court of Appeals for the Seventh Circuit held that this application of the Sentencing Guidelines . . . violated the Sixth Amendment [guaranteeing jury trial], and remanded with instructions to the District Court either to sentence respondent within the sentencing range supported by the jury's findings or to hold a separate sentencing hearing before a jury. . . .

II

It has been settled throughout our history that the Constitution protects every criminal defendant "against conviction except upon proof beyond a reasonable doubt of every fact necessary to constitute the crime with which he is charged." In re Winship, 397 U.S. 358, 364, 90 S. Ct. 1068 (1970). It is equally clear that the "Constitution gives a criminal defendant the right to demand that a jury find him guilty of all the elements of the crime with which he is charged." United States v. Gaudin, 515 U.S. 506, 511, 115 S. Ct. 2310 (1995). These basic precepts, firmly rooted in the common law, have provided the basis for recent decisions interpreting modern criminal statutes and sentencing procedures. . . .

In Apprendi v. New Jersey, 530 U.S. 466, 120 S. Ct. 2348 (2000), the defendant pleaded guilty to second-degree possession of a firearm for an unlawful purpose, which carried a prison term of 5-to-10 years. Thereafter, the trial court found that his conduct had violated New Jersey's "hate crime" law because it was racially motivated, and imposed a 12-year sentence. This Court set aside the enhanced sentence. We held: "Other than the fact of a prior conviction, any fact that increases the penalty for a crime beyond the prescribed statutory maximum must be submitted to a jury, and proved beyond a reasonable doubt." Id., at 490, 120 S. Ct. 2348. . . .

In Blakely v. Washington, 542 U.S. 296, 124 S. Ct. 2531 (2004), we dealt with a determinate sentencing scheme similar to the Federal Sentencing Guidelines. There the defendant pleaded guilty to kidnaping, a class B felony punishable by a term of not more than 10 years. Other provisions of Washington law, comparable to the Federal Sentencing Guidelines, mandated a "standard" sentence of 49-to-53 months, unless the judge found aggravating facts justifying an exceptional sentence. Although the prosecutor recommended a sentence in the standard range, the judge found that the defendant had acted with "'deliberate cruelty'" and sentenced him to 90 months. Id., at 300, 124 S. Ct., at 2534. . . . The application of Washington's sentencing scheme violated the defendant's right to have the jury find the existence of "'any particular fact'" that the law makes essential to his punishment. 542 U.S., at 301, 124 S. Ct., at 2536. That right is implicated whenever a judge seeks to impose a sentence that is not solely based on "facts reflected in the jury verdict or admitted by the defendant." Id., at 303, 124 S. Ct., at 2537 (emphasis deleted). We rejected the State's argument that the jury verdict was sufficient to authorize a sentence within the general 10-year sentence for class B felonies, noting that under Washington law, the judge was *required* to find additional facts in order to impose the greater 90-month sentence. Our precedents, we explained, make clear "that the 'statutory maximum' for *Apprendi* purposes is the maximum sentence a judge may impose *solely on the basis of the facts reflected in the jury verdict or admitted by the defendant.*" *Ibid.* at 303, 124 S. Ct., at 2537 (emphasis in original). The determination that the defendant acted with deliberate cruelty, like the determination in *Apprendi* that the defendant acted with racial malice, increased the sentence that the defendant could have otherwise received. Since this fact was found by a judge using a preponderance of the evidence standard, the sentence violated Blakely's Sixth Amendment rights. . . .

If the Guidelines as currently written could be read as merely advisory provisions that recommended, rather than required, the selection of particular sentences in response to differing sets of facts, their use would not implicate the Sixth Amendment. We have never doubted the authority of a judge to exercise broad discretion in imposing a sentence within a statutory range. See *Apprendi*, 530 U.S., at 481, 120 S. Ct. 2348; Williams v. New York, 337 U.S. 241, 246, 69 S. Ct. 1079 (1949).... For when a trial judge exercises his discretion to select a specific sentence within a defined range, the defendant has no right to a jury determination of the facts that the judge deems relevant.

The Guidelines as written, however, are not advisory; they are mandatory and binding on all judges. While subsection (a) of §3553 of the sentencing statute lists the Sentencing Guidelines as one factor to be considered in imposing a sentence, subsection (b) directs that the court "*shall* impose a sentence of the kind, and within the range" established by the Guidelines, subject to departures in specific, limited cases. (Emphasis added.) Because they are binding on judges, we have consistently held that the Guidelines have the force and effect of laws....

...The Guidelines permit departures from the prescribed sentencing range in cases in which the judge "finds that there exists an aggravating or mitigating circumstance of a kind, or to a degree, not adequately taken into consideration by the Sentencing Commission in formulating the guidelines that should result in a sentence different from that described." 18 U.S.C. §3553(b)(1) (Supp. 2004). At first glance, one might believe that the ability of a district judge to depart from the Guidelines means that she is bound only by the statutory maximum. Were this the case, there would be no *Apprendi* problem. Importantly, however, departures are not available in every case, and in fact are unavailable in most. In most cases, as a matter of law, the Commission will have adequately taken all relevant factors into account, and no departure will be legally permissible....

Booker's case illustrates the mandatory nature of the Guidelines. The jury convicted him of possessing at least 50 grams of crack in violation of 21 U.S.C. §841(b)(1)(A)(iii) based on evidence that he had 92.5 grams of crack in his duffel bag. Under these facts, the Guidelines specified an offense level of 32, which, given the defendant's criminal history category, authorized a sentence of 210–to–262 months. See USSG §2D1.1(c)(4). Booker's is a run-of-the-mill drug case, and does not present any factors that were inadequately considered by the Commission. The sentencing

judge would therefore have been reversed had he not imposed a sentence within the level 32 Guidelines range.

Booker's actual sentence, however, was 360 months, almost 10 years longer than the Guidelines range supported by the jury verdict alone. To reach this sentence, the judge found facts beyond those found by the jury: namely, that Booker possessed 566 grams of crack in addition to the 92.5 grams in his duffel bag. The jury never heard any evidence of the additional drug quantity, and the judge found it true by a preponderance of the evidence....

In his dissent, ... Justice Breyer argues on historical grounds that the Guidelines scheme is constitutional across the board. He points to traditional judicial authority to increase sentences to take account of any unusual blameworthiness in the manner employed in committing a crime, an authority that the Guidelines require to be exercised consistently throughout the system. This tradition, however, does not provide a sound guide to enforcement of the Sixth Amendment's guarantee of a jury trial in today's world.

It is quite true that once determinate sentencing had fallen from favor, American judges commonly determined facts justifying a choice of a heavier sentence on account of the manner in which particular defendants acted. *Apprendi*, 530 U.S., at 481, 120 S. Ct. 2348. In 1986, however, our own cases first recognized a new trend in the legislative regulation of sentencing when we considered the significance of facts selected by legislatures that not only authorized, or even mandated, heavier sentences than would otherwise have been imposed, but increased the range of sentences possible for the underlying crime. See McMillan v. Pennsylvania, 477 U.S. 79, 87–88, 106 S. Ct. 2411 (1986). Provisions for such enhancements of the permissible sentencing range reflected growing and wholly justified legislative concern about the proliferation and variety of drug crimes and their frequent identification with firearms offenses.

The effect of the increasing emphasis on facts that enhanced sentencing ranges, however, was to increase the judge's power and diminish that of the jury. It became the judge, not the jury, who determined the upper limits of sentencing, and the facts determined were not required to be raised before trial or proved by more than a preponderance.

As the enhancements became greater, the jury's finding of the underlying crime became less significant. And the enhancements became very serious indeed. . . .

. . . The new sentencing practice forced the Court to address the question how the right of jury trial could be preserved, in a meaningful way guaranteeing that the jury would still stand between the individual and the power of the government under the new sentencing regime. . . .

IV

All of the foregoing supports our conclusion that our holding in *Blakely* applies to the Sentencing Guidelines. We recognize . . . that in some cases jury factfinding may impair the most expedient and efficient sentencing of defendants. But the interest in fairness and reliability protected by the right to a jury trial — a common-law right that defendants enjoyed for centuries and that is now enshrined in the Sixth Amendment — has always outweighed the interest in concluding trials swiftly. *Blakely*, 542 U.S., at 313, 124 S. Ct., at 2542-43. As Blackstone put it:

[H]owever *convenient* these [new methods of trial] may appear at first, (as doubtless all arbitrary powers, well executed, are the most *convenient*) yet let it be again remembered, that delays, and little inconveniences in the forms of justice, are the price that all free nations must pay for their liberty in more substantial matters; that these inroads upon this sacred bulwark of the nation are fundamentally opposite to the spirit of our constitution; and that, though begun in trifles, the precedent may gradually increase and spread, to the utter disuse of juries in questions of the most momentous concerns.

4 Commentaries on the Laws of England 343–344 (1769).

Accordingly, we reaffirm our holding in *Apprendi*: Any fact (other than a prior conviction) which is necessary to support a sentence exceeding the maximum authorized by the facts established by a plea of guilty or a jury verdict must be admitted by the defendant or proved to a jury beyond a reasonable doubt.

JUSTICE BREYER dissented in part and filed an opinion in which CHIEF JUSTICE REHNQUIST and JUSTICES O'CONNOR and KENNEDY joined.

NOTES

1. The Court did not strike down the entire body of the sentencing guidelines, but rather only those portions of the guidelines that made them mandatory. Thus, while the discretion a judge had in finding facts relevant to sentencing was reduced, in some ways and in some cases the judge was able to exercise *more* discretion in sentencing, as the guidelines became advisory only. This, the Court noted, would solve the Sixth Amendment problem, while restoring the broad discretion in sentencing that judges used to have.

2. In one sense, the actor with the most discretion in our system of criminal law is the legislature. State legislatures are generally empowered to pass any criminal laws that they see fit, provided the laws pass muster under the state and federal constitutions. What other checks exist upon the discretion of the legislature? Popular elections are one. Based upon the discussions above, what checks upon the legislature may be exercised by other actors in the criminal-justice system?

3. Some scholars note that discretion in the criminal-justice system cannot be extinguished. Rather, efforts to constrain only serve to shift discretion to another actor. The sentencing guidelines, for example, were decried as an impermissible increase in prosecutorial discretion, because prosecutors may choose what charges to bring, while judges were quite limited in choosing sentences. *Booker* may have shifted some discretionary power back to the judge by making the guidelines simply advisory, but mandatory minimum sentences and largely unlimited prosecutorial discretion keep the power balance firmly in the prosecutor's favor.

Section Five
ROLES OF PRIVATE CITIZENS AND THEIR LAWYERS

Private citizens who are the victims of crime play less of a role in the penal instrument than do victims of wrong seeking a remedy through the remedial instrument. Seekers of private remedies typically must shoulder the entire burden of litigation, whereas crime victims may — indeed must — rely upon public prosecutors to enforce the criminal law. This does not mean that the private citizen's cooperation is unimportant. If she fails to report a crime, neglects to appear for a scheduled court proceeding, refuses to testify truthfully, or testifies apathetically, the case often will be dropped or lost.

Private citizens are also involved in shaping the penal instrument. Reform in the criminal law often results from public pressure. For example, in many states increased penalties for drunk driving were the culmination of lobbying efforts by citizen groups, as were changes in rape laws that eliminated earlier requirements that the victim had put forth "utmost resistance" before the defendant could be convicted.

Finally, private persons are involved in the penal instrument as the alleged wrongdoer and the wrongdoer's lawyer. The proper role of defense lawyers is a subject of some complexity. It encompasses questions concerning when lawyers should be provided for the accused, how lawyers for the poor should be selected and compensated, what the ethical limits on defense lawyers' conduct are, and whether erroneous advice from a lawyer should constitute an excuse for criminal conduct. The following material addresses these last two questions.

A. Ethical Issues Concerning Defense Counsel's Role

The American Bar Association (ABA) promulgates rules of professional conduct for lawyers, which many states adopt. Defense attorneys must defend their clients to the best of their abilities while abiding by these rules, which can sometimes create difficult ethical questions.

The lawyer must generally abide by her client's decisions as to the objectives of the lawyer's representation, and must consult with the client on how to achieve those objectives. Also, the client decides whether to accept a plea offer, waive jury trial, or testify. The lawyer may advise the client, but cannot advise or assist the client to engage in criminal or fraudulent conduct. The lawyer may, however, discuss legal consequences of any proposed course of conduct.

An attorney may not reveal information regarding her client's representation unless the client consents. Attorneys are prohibited from revealing information about past crimes. For example, an attorney whose client has confided in her that he committed a murder may not testify in the defense of an innocent person who is being tried for the crime.

There are, however, some exceptions to this confidentiality. Where the attorney reasonably believes that the client intends to commit a crime in the future, there is no confidentiality. In fact, the attorney may have a duty to take action to prevent death or serious bodily injury. An attorney may also disclose confidences if necessary to defend herself from litigation, such as in a suit for malpractice.

Apart from their duty to clients, lawyers have a duty to the court to not knowingly make false statements of material fact or law to the court, or fail to disclose a material fact to the court when it is necessary to avoid assisting a criminal or fraudulent act by the client, or offer evidence that the lawyer knows to be false. The ABA rules state that these duties outweigh the duty to not reveal information about a client.

The requirement of confidentiality is well-known. Many commentators believe it encourages clients to fully disclose the facts to their attorneys. This presumably helps an attorney prepare her client's best defensive strategy. It may also put the attorney in an ethical dilemma, however, if the client decides to tell the attorney the truth but lie on the stand.

The exceptions to the confidentiality rules are not necessarily known by many clients. In fact, many clients believe that disclosures to an attorney are absolutely protected by confidentiality. Should attorneys have a duty to warn clients that confidentiality is not absolute, before any disclosures are made? Commentators worry that such a duty could cause clients to be less forthcoming in their conversations with attorneys, making it more difficult for the attorney to present an effective defense.

MONROE H. FREEDMAN, PROFESSIONAL RESPONSIBILITY OF THE CRIMINAL DEFENSE LAWYER: THE THREE HARDEST QUESTIONS
64 Mich. L. Rev. 1469, 1469 (1966)*

In almost any area of legal counseling and advocacy, the lawyer may be faced with the dilemma of either betraying the confidential communications of his client or participating to some extent in the purposeful deception of the court. This problem is nowhere more acute than in the practice of criminal law, particularly in the representation of the indigent accused. The purpose of this article is to analyze and attempt to resolve three of the most difficult issues in this general area:

1. Is it proper to cross-examine for the purpose of discrediting the reliability or credibility of an

---

* Reprinted from Michigan Law Review, June 1966, Vol. 64, No. 8. Copyright 1966 by Monroe H. Freedman. Professor Freedman has expanded on the views in this article, and modified them somewhat, in his book, *Lawyers' Ethics in an Adversary System* (1975), and in subsequent law review articles.

adverse witness whom you know to be telling the truth?

2. Is it proper to put a witness on the stand when you know he will commit perjury?

3. Is it proper to give your client legal advice when you have reason to believe that the knowledge you give him will tempt him to commit perjury?

Professor Freedman's questions illustrate the tension between a defense attorney's obligations to zealously defend her client and to not assist a client in committing a crime or fraud. This tension is exacerbated by the principle of confidentiality, which prevents an attorney from damaging her client's interests because of knowledge received as a confidential disclosure.

For example, in the first scenario, if an attorney knows or believes her client to be innocent, but a witness's testimony places him near the scene of the crime, is it proper for the defense attorney to attack that witness's credibility even though she knows the witness is telling the truth? The testimony is true, and damaging, but may give an incomplete picture of events. Should the attorney attack the vision or memory of the witness even though the identification was accurate? The ethical problem is compounded because the lawyer would not have known that the witness was telling the truth if the client had not disclosed this information. Thus, if the attorney refrains from attacking the credibility of the testimony, this course of action punishes the client for the confidential disclosures he made.

In the second situation, assume that the lawyer would not know that the client was going to commit perjury if the client had not informed the attorney of his guilt. Preventing the client from testifying could seriously harm his case, and this would be in response to the confidential disclosures he made to the attorney. However, the attorney has a duty to the court not to offer evidence that the lawyer knows is false. Compounding the problems raised by this scenario is the fact that the lawyer is not in a position to withdraw from the case. Anyway, she should know that the client would simply go to another attorney and refrain from informing this new one of his guilt, so that the court would still end up hearing false testimony. Instead of withdrawing, the lawyer should attempt to convince the client not to lie, but realistically she is unlikely to succeed.

The third question may arise when an accused client asks his attorney about the possible implications of statements he may make while testifying. For example, if an accused murderer testifies that he never usually carried a weapon, but had one when the crime was committed, this implies premeditation. Conversely, if he testifies that he regularly carries a weapon, this may help negate an inference of premeditation. Should an attorney explain to her client the effect that testimony may therefore have? If the attorney believes that the client did not normally carry a weapon, explaining the ramifications of this testimony may induce the client to lie under oath. However, leaving the client ignorant is unacceptable, as it prevents the client from making an informed decision on whether or not to testify at all as well as preventing the client from fully understanding the charges being brought against him.

Unfortunately, there is no truly satisfactory answer to any of the questions that Freedman poses. The ABA's ethical rules attempt to guide attorneys in their conduct, but the conflict between zealous advocacy and duty to the system all but ensures that there never will be.

Some commentators suggest that our adversary system of representation should be modified, to make a criminal trial more of a "search for the truth" than a confrontation between the parties. This modification would make confidentiality itself undesirable, as the advocate should be assisting the trier of fact search for the truth rather than assisting an admittedly guilty client to hide it. This solution, however, has not gained widespread support, as it seems to conflict with the realities of our court system as well as with the structure imposed by the Bill of Rights.

B. Effect of Counsel's Advice on Criminal Liability

Recall the discussion of mistake, in Section Two of this chapter. What happens if an individual "innocently" violates the law, relying upon advice from an attorney? What if that attorney is a state official? The case below, from Maryland's highest court, sets out the generally accepted answer to these questions.

HOPKINS v. STATE

Court of Appeals of Maryland, 1949
193 Md. 489, 69 A.2d 456, appeal dismissed, 339 U.S. 940, 70 S. Ct. 797 (1950)

DELAPLAINE, JUDGE:

This appeal was taken by the Rev. William F. Hopkins, of Elkton, from the judgment of conviction entered upon the verdict of a jury in the Circuit Court for Cecil County for violation of the statute making it unlawful to erect or maintain any sign intended to aid in the solicitation or performance of marriages. Laws of 1943, ch. 532, Code Supp. 1947, art. 27, sec. 444A.

The State charged that on September 1, 1947, defendant maintained a sign at the entrance to his home at 148 East Main Street in Elkton, and also a sign along a highway leading into the town, to aid in the solicitation and performance of marriages. Four photographs were admitted in evidence. One photograph, taken on an afternoon in September, 1947, shows the sign in Elkton containing [only] the name "Rev. W.F. Hopkins." Another, taken at night shows the same sign illuminated at night by electricity. The third shows the other sign along the highway containing [only] the words,

"W.F. Hopkins, Notary Public, Information." The fourth shows this sign illuminated at night.

The State showed that during the month of August, 1947, thirty ministers performed 1,267 marriages in Cecil County, and of this number defendant performed 286, only three of which were ceremonies in which the parties were residents of Cecil County.

Defendant did not testify. Several witnesses, however, testified that, though he has been residing in Elkton, he has been serving as the pastor of a church with about 40 members in Middletown, Delaware, known as the First Home Missionary Church....

...Defendant contended that the judge erred in excluding testimony offered to show that the State's Attorney [for Cecil County] advised him in 1944 before he erected the signs, that they would not violate the law. It is generally held that the advice of counsel, even though followed in good faith, furnishes no excuse to a person for violating the law and cannot be relied upon as a defense in a criminal action. Forwood v. State, 49 Md. 531, 538; Miller v. United States, 4 Cir., 277 F. 721. Moreover, advice given by a public official, even a State's Attorney, that a contemplated act is not criminal will not excuse an offender if, as a matter of law, the act performed did amount to a violation of the law. State v. Foster, 22 R.I. 163, 46 A. 833, 50 L.R.A. 339; Staley v. State, 89 Neb. 701, 131 N.W. 1028, 34 L.R.A., N.S., 613; State v. Whiteaker, 118 Or. 656, 247 P. 1077. These rules are founded upon the maxim that ignorance of the law will not excuse its violation. If an accused could be exempted from punishment for crime by reason of the advice of counsel, such advice would become paramount to the law.

While ignorance of fact may sometimes be admitted as evidence of lack of criminal intent, ignorance of the law ordinarily does not give immunity from punishment for crime, for every man is presumed to intend the necessary and legitimate consequences of what he knowingly does. In the case at bar defendant did not claim that the State's Attorney misled him regarding any facts of the case, but only that the State's Attorney

advised him as to the law based upon the facts. Defendant was aware of the penal statute enacted by the Legislature. He knew what he wanted to do, and he did the thing he intended to do. He claims merely that he was given advice regarding his legal rights. If there was any mistake, it was a mistake of law and not of fact. If the right of a person to erect a sign of a certain type and size depends upon the construction and application of a penal statute, and the right is somewhat doubtful, he erects the sign at his peril. In other words, a person who commits an act which the law declares to be criminal cannot be excused from punishment upon the theory that he misconstrued or misapplied the law. Levar v. State, 103 Ga. 42, 29 S.E. 467, 470; Lewis v. State, 124 Tex. Cr. R. 582, 64 S.W.2d 972, 975. For these reasons the exclusion of the testimony offered to show that defendant had sought and received advice from the State's Attorney was not prejudicial error. . . .

Judgment affirmed, with costs.

NOTES

1. Compare this case with *Rex v. Esop*. Do the reasons in favor of punishing Esop justify punishing Hopkins? Remember, *Rex v. Esop* relied on the principle that ignorance of the law is not an excuse. To hold otherwise could encourage such ignorance, as well as interject difficult factual issues concerning the lack of knowledge. Hopkins, however, knew of the law's existence, but was not a trained lawyer, so he went to a professional for advice. This should be encouraged, it would seem. Perhaps the court did not want to sanction reliance on unofficial statements. But this advice was quite official.

2. The court seems to think that Hopkins was aware of the risk, because he was aware of the law. Also, note the court's statement that when the law is doubtful, an individual acts "at his peril." Does this seem right, despite the fact that Hopkins consulted the prosecutor?

3. Hopkins consulted a prosecutor for advice on his sign but was still held accountable. What does this suggest for a defendant who contacted his own attorney because he did not know the prosecutor? If you think that Hopkins

The Right to Counsel and Ineffective Assistance of Counsel

The Sixth Amendment guarantees criminal defendants the right to the assistance of counsel, and in Gideon v. Wainwright, 372 U.S. 335, 83 S. Ct. 792 (1963), the Supreme Court held that the state must provide counsel to defendants charged with felonies who cannot afford to retain counsel. As one might imagine, this decision had enormous impact in the short run, because inmates who had not received counsel often could not be retried due to the passage of time and had to be released outright. In the long run, Gideon transformed the day-to-day functioning of the criminal justice systems of many states, though perhaps not exactly as the Supreme Court had anticipated. The next section describes some of the problems that over-crowded public defenders and their clients face. States had to decide how to provide counsel to the majority of defendants they charged with crimes. But even when lawyers have adequate time and resources, some will perform poorly, or barely perform at all. Gideon left open the question of what should happen when counsel performed inadequately. Twenty-one years later, the Supreme Court decided Strickland v. Washington, 466 U.S. 668, 104 S. Ct. 2052 (1984), which holds that a defendant is entitled to a new trial if he can show both that his lawyer fell below a broad band of competence, and that without this deficiency in performance, there is a reasonable likelihood that the outcome of the proceeding would have been different. In practice, this standard has been very hard to meet.

should not have been punished, is this hypothetical defendant more culpable? Yet, if Hopkins had consulted his own attorney, or none at all because of lack of money, to many minds the case would have been easier. Courts have generally held that a mistake of law based upon any attorney's advice is not a defense. In some jurisdictions, however, a mistake of law is a defense if the mistake was caused by a reasonable reliance on an official statement of the law, such as a judicial opinion, a legislative act later declared invalid, or an official statement rendered by the state official in charge of interpreting, administering, or enforcing the law.

Section Six
IMPROVING THE PENAL INSTRUMENT

JAMES MILLS, ON THE EDGE
120–48 (1975)*

Martin Erdmann thinks he might be antisocial. When he was six he liked to sneak across his family's red-carpeted, spiral-staircased entrance hall to the potted palm, and spit in it. At Yankee Stadium, he rooted for the Red Sox. When he went to Dartmouth, he cheered for Yale. He didn't make a lot of friends. He says he doesn't need them. Today...he has defended more criminals than anyone else in the world.

---

* Excerpts from ON THE EDGE by James Mills. Copyright © 1971, 1972, 1975 by James Mills. Reprinted by permission of Doubleday & Company, Inc.

Because he is one of the five or ten best defense lawyers in New York, he gets those criminals turned back into the streets months or years earlier than they have any right to hope for. His clients are not Mafia bosses or bank embezzlers or suburban executives who've shot their wives. He defends killers, burglars, rapists, robbers — the men people mean when they talk about crime in the streets. Martin Erdmann's clients *are* crime in the streets.

In twenty-five years Martin Erdmann has defended more than 100,000 criminals. He has saved them tens of thousands of years in prison and in those years they have robbed, raped, burglarized and murdered tens upon tens of thousands of people. The idea of having had a very personal and direct hand in all that mayhem strikes him as boring and irrelevant. "I have nothing to do with justice," he says. "Justice is not even part of the equation. If you say I have no moral reaction to what I do, you are right."

And *he* is right. As right as our adversary judicial system, as right as jury trials, as right as the presumption of innocence and the Fifth Amendment. If there is a fault in Erdmann's eagerness to free defendants, it is not with Erdmann himself, but with the system. Criminal law to the defense lawyer does not mean equity or fairness or proper punishment or vengeance. It means getting everything he can for his client. And in perhaps 98 per cent of his cases, the clients are guilty. Justice is a luxury enjoyed by the district attorney. He alone is sworn "to see that justice is done." The defense lawyer does not bask in the grandeur of any such noble oath. He finds himself most often working for the guilty and for a judicial system based upon the sound but paradoxical principle that the guilty must be freed to protect the innocent.

And Erdmann does free them, as many as he possibly can. He works for the Legal Aid Society, a private organization with a city contract to represent the 179,000 indigent defendants who flood each year into New York City courtrooms. He heads the society's supreme court branch, has fifty-five lawyers working under him. . . . He is there at 7:30, two and a half hours before the courts open, and he is alone. In another ten or fifteen minutes Milton Adler will arrive, his boss, chief attorney in the criminal branch.

Then, one or two at a time, come the phone operator and clerks, the other lawyers, the defendants on bail, mothers of men in jail, sick-looking junkies with vomit-stained shirts, frightened people who sit quietly on the seven wooden chairs along the wall, angry people mumbling viciously, insane people dressed in costumes with feathers in their hair.

Before the rush begins, Martin Erdmann sits at his desk in a side office and goes over the folders of the day's cases. Anthony Howard, a twenty-one-year-old [African American], is accused of using a stick and knife to rob a man of his wallet. Howard's mother visits him in jail, brings clean clothes and takes out his laundry. She doesn't know that the greatest danger to her son is not the robbery charge, but the man who sleeps above him in the eight-by-six-foot cell. Robert Phillips, Howard's cellmate, escaped from a state mental hospital seven years ago, was recaptured, released, then arrested for the murder of a twenty-two-year-old girl and an infant boy. After three more years in a mental hospital, he has been declared legally sane and is now awaiting trial for the murders. Erdmann looks over the file. "Prisoners who've been in mental hospitals," he says, "tell me they keep them there until they admit the charges against them. Then they mark them sane and send them down for pleading." He decides to give the Anthony Howard case to Alice Schlesinger, a young lawyer who can still believe her clients are innocent. She's good at what Erdmann calls "hand-holding," giving a defendant and his family more time than the case might need.

Adler walks in, starts to say something, and the phone rings. Erdmann answers it. The call is from a woman out on bail on a charge of throwing lye on her husband. Now she wants Erdmann to help her get a shotgun license. She says she needs it for protection.

"Okay, Mable," he says, "but don't shoot too many people." He hangs up smiling and says to Adler, "Mable's switched from lye to shotguns."

Alice Schlesinger appears in the doorway, a small young woman, about thirty, with long black hair. She wants to know what she can do to pressure the DA to start the trial of a bailed defendant charged with robbery. "Can't we put the screws to them a little? My client is very nervous and upset. He wants to get the trial over with."

"Well," says Erdmann, "of course you can always make a motion to dismiss for lack of prosecution. Say your client is suffering great emotional stress at having this dreadfully unjust accusation hanging over his head."

"Don't *smile* like that," she says. "He *is* innocent, this time."

Erdmann gets rid of the smile. "Well, you know," he says, "maybe the DA is having a little trouble locating the complainant, and your defendant's on bail anyway, so why urge them to go right out and track him down? Because if they find the complainant and go to trial and if from some extremely unfortunate occurrence your client should be convicted, then he's going to jail and he'll be a lot worse off than just nervous."

She agrees reluctantly and leaves. Erdmann sits silently at his desk, staring into the piles of papers. Then he says, "She has a lot to learn. She'll learn. With some tears, but she'll learn."

Erdmann gathers up the folders and takes the elevator to a courtroom on the thirteenth floor. . . . A few spectators walk in and Erdmann calls the names of his bail cases. No one answers. "That's not surprising," he says, "they couldn't possibly get up this early."

A DA comes in and Erdmann asks him about a kidnapping case that's approaching trial. "The DA on that one's on trial on another case, Marty. He won't be finished for a month at least."

"Wonderful." Erdmann laughs. "I hope he stays on trial until the complainant's thirty. Then it won't look so bad. She was eight when it happened and she's already eleven." The DA shakes his head and walks away. Two more DAs arrive and Erdmann talks to them, joking with them, making gentle fun of them, establishing his presence: twice their age, more experienced, more knowledgeable, more cunning. "There's no question that my reputation is much too high," he says. "It's been carefully cultivated. Myths are very important in this business."

The judge enters: Mitchell Schweitzer, tall, thin, gray-haired, on the bench twenty-six years, sixteen of them working closely with Erdmann.

He flashes a look around the room, greeting private lawyers, Erdmann and the two assistant DAs.

The clerk calls a name: "José Santiago!"

Erdmann fumbles through his folders and pulls one out. "He's mine," he says. An assistant DA looks at the rows of folders on his table and picks one up. Erdmann and the DA walk slowly toward the judge's bench, pulling out papers as they go. Erdmann has, among other things, a copy of the complaint and a handwritten interview another Legal Aid lawyer had earlier with the defendant. The DA has a synopsis of the grand jury testimony and a copy of the defendant's record. With these documents, in the next three or four minutes, while the defendant himself sits unaware in a detention pen beneath the courtroom, the judge, DA and Erdmann will determine the likelihood of guilt and the amount of time the man will serve.

Trials are obsolete. In New York City only one arrest in thousands ends in trial. The government no longer has time and money to afford the luxury of presuming innocence, nor the belief that the truest way of determining guilt is by jury trial. Today, in effect, the government says to each defendant, "If you will abandon your unsupportable claim of innocence, we will compensate you with a light sentence." The defendant says, "How light?" — and the DA, defense lawyer and judge are drawn together at the bench. The conference there is called "plea bargaining," and it proceeds as the playing of a game, with moves and countermoves, protocol, rules and ritual. Power is in the hands of the prisoners. For as increasing crime has pushed our judicial system to the crumbling edge of chaos and collapse, the defendant himself has emerged as the only man with a helping hand. The government needs guilty pleas to move the cases out of court, and the defendants are selling their guilty pleas for the only currency the government can offer — time. But no matter what sentence is finally agreed upon, the real outcome of this bargaining contest is never truly in doubt. The guilty always win. The innocent always lose.

To play the game well, a lawyer must be ruthless. He is working within, but *against*, a system that has been battered to its knees. He must not hesitate to kick it when it's down, and to take every advantage of its weakness. No one is better at the game than Martin Erdmann.

Judge Schweitzer glances through the grand jury extract handed him by the DA, a young bespectacled man named Jack Litman. Then the judge looks up over his glasses. "What are you looking for, Marty?"

Erdmann isn't sure yet. His client is accused of robbing a man on the street after stabbing him in the face, neck, chest, stomach and back. The victim was held from behind by an accomplice. "They have a big identification problem," Erdmann says. He is looking at a copy of a police report. "The DD–5 says the complaining witness refused to look at pictures in the hospital the next day because he said he wouldn't be able to identify the assailants from photographs."

"Your honor," Litman says, "they put sixty-five stitches in him."

"Just a minute," says the judge, and proceeds to read quickly to Erdmann from the grand jury extract: "They fled into an apartment house, the cop asked the super if he'd seen them, the super said they went into apartment 3–A, the cop went in, placed them under arrest and took them to the hospital where they were identified by the victim." He looks up. Erdmann has never heard the grand jury testimony before, and it hasn't exactly made his day. "So, you see, Marty, it's not such a bad case." He leans back. "I'll tell you what. A year with credit for time served." Santiago already has been in jail for ten months. With time off for good behavior, that sentence will let him out today. Erdmann agrees. The DA nods and starts stuffing papers back into the folder. "Bring him up," he says.

Santiago's accomplice is brought in with him. Both men are twenty-one, short and defiant-looking. The accomplice, Jesus Rodriguez, has his own lawyer, who now joins Erdmann in agreeing to the sentence. The lawyers explain the offer to the defendants. They tell them that the offer can be made only if they are in fact guilty. Neither the judge nor the DA nor the lawyers themselves would permit an innocent man to plead guilty. Santiago and Rodriguez look bewildered. They say they are innocent, they did nothing. Much

mumbling and consternation at the counsel table. Then Schweitzer says, "Would you like a second call?"

"Yes, your honor," says Erdmann. "A second call." The defendants are led out and downstairs to a detention pen. Erdmann looks at Santiago's interview sheet, a mimeographed form with blanks for name, age, address, education, employer, and then at the bottom, space for his version of what happened. Santiago's statement begins, "I am not guilty. I did nothing wrong." He has never been arrested before. He says he and Rodriguez were asleep in their apartment when the police charged in and grabbed them. At his arraignment some weeks ago, he pleaded not guilty.

"Talk to them," Judge Schweitzer suggests. Erdmann and his co-counsel walk over to the door of the pen. A court officer opens it and they step from the court's dark, quiet brownness into a bright, noisy, butt-littered hallway. The door slams shut behind them. From somewhere below come voices shouting, and the clang of cell doors closing. A guard yells, "On the gate!" and precedes them down a dark stairway to a barred steel door. An inside guard unlocks the door and they walk into a yellow, men's-room-tiled corridor with windows on the left and a large bench-lined cell on the right. Twenty men are in the cell, almost all of them dirty and bearded, some young and frightened sitting alone on the benches, others older, talking, standing, as at home here as on a Harlem street corner. Suddenly the voices stop and the prisoners, like animals expecting to be fed, turn their heads toward Erdmann and his co-counsel. Three other lawyers walk in, too, and in a moment the voices begin again — prisoners and lawyers arguing with each other, explaining, cajoling, conning in the jailhouse jargon of pleas and sentences: "I can get you one and one running wild [two years consecutive]. . . . I know a guy got an E and a flat [a Class E felony with a year]. . . . So you want a bullet [a year]? You'll take a bullet?"

Erdmann walks to the far end of the cell and Santiago meets him at the bars. Erdmann puts his toe on a cross strip between the bars and balances Santiago's folder and papers on his knee.

He takes out a Lucky Strike, lights it and inhales. Santiago watches, and then a sudden rush of words starts violently from his mouth. Erdmann silences him. "First let me find out what I have to know," he says calmly, "and then you can talk as much as you want." Santiago is standing next to a chest-high, steel-plate partition. On the other side of it, a toilet flushes. A few steps away, Rodriguez is talking through the bars to his lawyer.

"If you didn't do anything wrong," Erdmann says to Santiago, "then there's no point even discussing this. You'll go to trial."

Santiago nods desperately. "I ain't done nothing! I was asleep! I *never* been in trouble before." This is the first time since his initial interview seven months ago that he has had a chance to tell his story to a lawyer, and he is frantic to get it all out. Erdmann cannot stop the torrent, and now he does not try. "I never been arrested," Santiago shouts, "never been to jail, never been in *no* trouble, *nothing*. We just asleep in the apartment and the police break in and grab us out of bed and take us, we ain't done nothing, I *never* been in trouble, I never saw this man before, and he says we did it. I don't even know what we did, and I been here ten months, I don't see no lawyer or nothing, I ain't had a shower in two months, we locked up twenty-four hours a day, I got no shave, no hot food, I ain't *never* been like this before, I can't stand it, I'm going to kill myself, I got to get out, I ain't — "

Now Erdmann interrupts, icily calm, speaking very slowly, foot on the cross strip, drawing on his cigarette. "Well, it's very simple. Either you are guilty or you're not. If you're guilty of anything you can take the plea and they'll give you a year, and under the circumstances that's a very good plea and you ought to take it. If you're not guilty, you have to go to trial."

"I'm not guilty." He says it fast, nodding, sure of that.

"Then you should go to trial. But the jury is going to hear that the cop followed you into the building, the super sent him to apartment 3–A, he arrested you there and the man identified you in the hospital. If they find you guilty, you might get fifteen years."

Santiago is unimpressed with all of that. "I'm innocent. I didn't do nothing. But I got to get out of here. I got to — "

"Well, if you *did* do anything and you are a little guilty, they'll give you time served and you'll walk."

That's more like it.

"Today? I walk today?"

"If you are guilty of something and you take the plea."

"I'll take the plea. But I didn't do nothing."

"You can't take the plea unless you are guilty of something."

"I want the year. I'm innocent, but I'll take the year. I walk today if I take the year?"

The papers start to fall from Erdmann's knee and he grabs them and settles them back. "You walk if you take the plea, but no one's going to let you take the plea if you aren't guilty."

"But I didn't *do* nothing."

"Then you'll have to stay in and go to trial."

"When will that be?"

"In a couple of months. Maybe longer."

Santiago has a grip on the bars. "You mean if I'm guilty I get out today?"

"Yes." Someone is urinating on the other side of the partition.

"But if I'm innocent, I got to stay in?" The toilet flushes.

"That's right."

It's too much for Santiago. He lets go of the bars, takes a step back, shakes his head, turns around and comes quickly back to the bars. "But, *man* — "

Back upstairs at the bench, Erdmann says to Schweitzer, "He's got no record, your honor, and I've had no admission of guilt. You know I'm very careful with people who have no records — "

"And I am, too, Marty, you know that."

"He says he hasn't had a shower in two months, he's in a twenty-four-hour-a-day lockup and he wants to get out, and I don't blame him."

"Marty, I'm not taking a guilty plea just because he wants a shower."

"Of course not."

"Do you want me to talk to them?"

"I think it might be a good idea, your honor."

Santiago and Rodriguez are brought up again and led into a small jury room adjoining the

202

courtroom. Schweitzer reads the grand jury extract to the defendants, making sure they know the case against them.

Now Rodriguez says he'll take the plea. Schweitzer asks him to tell what happened the night of the robbery. Rodriguez says he and Santiago were on the street and they ran into the complainant and spoke with him and the complainant had a knife in his pocket and ended up getting cut, "but I didn't do nothing."

This departure from the original story, the admission that they had been with the victim and that there was indeed a knife, is enough for Erdmann. He looks at Schweitzer. "Now I'm convinced he's guilty." Schweitzer and Litman go back to court. Erdmann says to Santiago, "Do you want the plea?"

"Yes, man, I *told* you that, I got to get out — "

"Then the judge will ask you certain questions and you have to give the appropriate answers." He nods towards Rodriguez. "He held him and you stabbed him. Let's go."

They return to the courtroom and stand before the bench. Schweitzer asks Santiago if he wants to change his plea. Santiago is still not buying. What if this whole routine is just a trick to extract a confession from him? "One year," he says.

Schweitzer is patient. "That's not what I asked you. Do you want to change your plea?"

"One year."

Erdmann talks with him, explains that he will get the year but first he has to answer certain questions. Santiago starts off again with just wanting to get out. Erdmann quiets him down, and they try again.

Schweitzer: "Do you now wish to change your plea?"

"I want one year."

Schweitzer is exasperated. Erdmann is angry. Santiago leans over to Erdmann and again starts talking. Erdmann says strongly, "Look, do you want the plea or not? Just yes or no. Answer him. Don't make speeches. You'll *get* the year. Just answer him."

Schweitzer asks again. Santiago turns to Erdmann and starts to talk. Erdmann grimaces and covers his ear with the folder. "I don't *want*

any more speeches. I'm losing my patience. You'll *get* the year, but *first* you have to plead."

Schweitzer gives up and moves on to Rodriguez. Rodriguez quickly pleads guilty. Schweitzer asks him to tell the truth about what really happened. Rodriguez says he held the man from behind while Santiago stabbed him. Schweitzer immediately sentences him to a year. Erdmann is leaning against the clerk's desk, his arms crossed over his chest, his eyes burning into Santiago. This ignorant, stupid, vicious kid has been offered a huge, heaping helping of the Erdmann talent, the experience, the knowledge, the myth — and has shoved it away. Erdmann's face is covered with disgust. Through his eyes, way beyond them, is fury, and unclouded, clear contempt.

The defendants are led from the courtroom. Erdmann walks to his seat in the jury box. As he passes the bench, Schweitzer looks down helplessly. "He wants me to sentence him before he pleads. How can I do that?"

Erdmann sits down in the jury box. The next few defendants have private lawyers, so he just waits there: watching, smiling, his bulging eyes gently ridiculing those around him who have failed to see as clearly as he into the depths of this charade, and to have found the joke there.

The judge is asking a defendant where he got the loaded gun. "He found it," Erdmann whispers before the man answers.

"I found it," the man says.

"Where?" asks the judge.

"Someone just gave it to him," Erdmann says.

"Someone walked by and handed it to me," says the defendant.

Erdmann smiles. "It's amazing," he says, "how often people rush by defendants and thrust things into their hands — guns, watches, wallets, things like that."

One of the two DAs is Richie Lowe, a black man. . . . Black defendants coming into court glance quickly around, and they see a white judge, white defense lawyers, white clerk, white stenographer, white guards and then, over there, at that table over there, a black, the only black in the room, and he's — the *enemy*.

In the seats next to Erdmann, a prisoner is being allowed a visit with his wife and small son. "I heard about your commotion in school," the father whispers. "Now you better be good or I'm gonna get you when I get out."

Guards bring in an old, toothless black man with wild white hair and an endless record of rapes, assaults, sodomy and armed robbery. He's accused of trying to rape a four-year-old Puerto Rican girl. Some people driving in a car saw the man sitting on a wall with the girl struggling in his lap and rescued her. Erdmann, Lowe and Judge Schweitzer talk it over. Schweitzer suggests a year. Lowe runs his eyes again over the grand jury extract. He usually goes along with Schweitzer, but this time he balks. "I can't see it, your honor. I can't see it."

Erdmann speaks a few urging words, but Lowe won't budge. "No," he says, "I just can't see it, your honor. If these people hadn't come by in the car and seen the girl, this could have been — it could have been anything."

Schweitzer, himself under great appellate division pressure to dispose of cases, now pressures Lowe, politely, gently. He points out that the girl was not injured.

"I just can't, your honor," Lowe says. "I just can't. This is abhorrent, this — "

Schweitzer breaks in. "It's abhorrent to *me*, too, and it's being discussed *only* in the light of the calendar."

"Your honor, we've been giving away the courthouse for the sake of the calendar. I can't do it. I won't do it." He stuffs his papers back in the folder. "Ready for trial, your honor."

He moves back to the prosecution table and announces for the record, "The people are ready for trial."

Erdmann has been saying nothing. As he passes Lowe's table on his way to the jury box, Lowe says, "Am I being unreasonable, Marty?"

Erdmann stops for a moment, very serious, and then shakes his head. "No, I don't think you are."

Lowe is upset. The next case has not yet been called. He moves around the table, fumbling folders. Then loudly he says, "Your honor, if he takes it *right now* I'll give him a year."

The judge fires Lowe a look. "You'll *recommend* a year. *I'll* give him a year."

Erdmann talks to the defendant at the counsel table. Lowe keeps shaking his head. He is suffering. He takes a step toward the bench. "Your honor," he says desperately, "he should get zip to three, at least."

"I *know* he should," Schweitzer says.

Erdmann now stands and for the record makes the customary speech. "Your honor, the defendant at this time wishes to withdraw his plea of not guilty, previously entered, and plead guilty to the second count of the indictment, attempted assault in the second degree, a Class E felony, that plea to cover the entire indictment."

Now it's Lowe's turn to make the speech of acceptance for the people, to accept the Class E felony, the least serious type of felony in the penal code. He stands. "Your honor, the people respectfully recommend acceptance of this plea, feeling that it will provide the court with adequate scope for punishment — " He stops. The next words should be "in the interest of justice." He sits down and pretends to write something on a folder. Then softly, as if hoping he might not be heard, he speaks down into the table, " . . . in the interest of justice."

NOTES

1. The above excerpt describes a system of *horizontal representation*, which means that one lawyer works in a given courtroom on a given day — and that defendants are represented by a different lawyer at each appearance. In New York City, Legal Aid attorneys, who are unionized, went on strike in protest against this system. They won, and a system of *vertical representation*, in which each lawyer is assigned to certain clients and represents them at every appearance, was instituted. Although vertical representation is now more common, some states, such as Rhode Island, still maintain a system of horizontal representation.

2. Many of the problems that Mr. Mills describes stem from too many cases and too little money. Problems are also created by too much money. In cases where the defense has large financial resources (either because the defendant is rich or because the case is highly political and funds have been raised on behalf of the defendant), the defendant's money may substantially decrease the likelihood of conviction. For example, social scientists are sometimes employed by the defense team to supervise jury selection so as to maximize the jury's predisposition to acquit. Or the defense may hire three expert witnesses for every one hired by the prosecution. It is often assumed that defendants with the financial capacity to hire private attorneys are likely to fare better in the criminal justice system than indigent defendants, who are forced to rely upon attorneys appointed by the court, public defenders, or legal aid societies. Consider these statistics from the U.S. Department of Justice, Bureau of Justice Statistics, Report (Nov. 2000), and make your own assessment of the effect that one's ability to retain private counsel may have on the outcome of criminal proceedings:

> Almost all persons charged with a felony in Federal and large State courts were represented by counsel, either hired or appointed. . . . Indigent defense involves the use of publicly financed counsel to represent criminal defendants who are unable to afford private counsel. At the end of their case approximately 66% of felony Federal defendants and 82% of felony defendants in large State courts were represented by public defenders or assigned counsel. In both Federal and large State courts, conviction rates were the same for defendants represented by publicly financed and private attorneys. Approximately 9 in 10 Federal defendants and 3 in 4 State defendants in the 75 largest counties were found guilty, regardless of type of attorney. However, of those found guilty, higher percentages of defendants with publicly financed counsel were sentenced to incarceration. Of defendants found guilty in Federal district courts, 88% with publicly financed counsel and 77% with private counsel received jail or prison sentences; in large State courts 71% with public counsel and 54% with private attorneys were sentenced to incarceration.

3. While this section has focused on the problems faced by indigent defendants, there are many other areas of the penal law in which changes and improvements might be suggested. Recall the previous section in this chapter that discussed the distribution of discretion among actors in the system. Also, it is a common complaint that our system of incarceration has led to overcrowded prisons, inhumane or unsanitary conditions, and extreme expense.

4. Indeed, every aspect of the penal instrument can be challenged as ineffective or insufficient, and such challenges can stir great debate. When studying such disputes, recall the opening section of this chapter, which laid out the theories justifying the state's use of punishment. Although some suggested improvements may reflect a shift from utilitarianism to retributivism, or vice versa, many reflect different views within utilitarian or retributive theory. Also recall the discussion of the tension between process values and outcome values. Many suggested changes to our system would serve one of these, generally at the expense of the other. Looking at such problems in these terms will generally not yield a clear answer, but can help to clarify the debate.

Section Seven
LIMITATIONS OF LAW AS A PENAL INSTRUMENT

A. Limitations on Its Subjects

We began this chapter by noting that conduct offending public morals and social mores is extremely common. Not all of this offensive conduct is best handled by the criminal law, however. Some of it is better managed by private institutions or by social disapproval. In particular, "morals legislation" frequently raises questions about limits on the legitimate and effective use of the penal instrument.

One traditional view on the limits of the criminal law is called the harm principle. According to the harm principle, the only valid justification for the criminal law's interference with an individual's liberty is the protection of society or other individuals from harm. A fundamentally utilitarian argument, the harm principle states that a person cannot be compelled to act or refrain from acting for his or her own good. This principle stems from the belief that the ultimate goal of human rights concepts should be complete individual autonomy. An individual should be permitted to govern her own thoughts and actions in all things, so long as she does not interfere with the autonomy of another.

Modern criminal codes often contain laws, however, that are difficult to justify under the harm principle. Laws against drug use generally fall into this category. Prohibiting drug use ostensibly protects those who would otherwise harm themselves. While there is certainly an argument that widespread drug use harms society indirectly, by promoting lawless behavior and by causing unemployment, homelessness, and medical costs that society often must absorb, these harms are indirect. They could be addressed directly instead. The sheer magnitude of harm done indirectly to society by some drugs may be compelling enough to justify their prohibition, but many acts can be said to indirectly harm others. Also, the indirect-harm argument is easy to make for some drugs like methamphetamine, but what about marijuana? Should an adult's use of marijuana, alone in her own home, be criminal? Those who oppose legalization of marijuana sometimes justify its criminalization with appeals to marijuana's status as a gateway drug, but here we are beginning to stretch the indirect-harm argument. Perhaps it is moral disapproval that drives the criminalization of marijuana, rather than prevention of social harm. The question to be answered is whether moral disapproval of a certain behavior is sufficient to support its criminalization. This question, debated for centuries, is unlikely to be resolved soon.

Even more difficult to justify based upon the harm principle are laws against certain forms of consensual sexual activity by adults in private. For a time, many states had laws against certain forms of consensual sex, such as sodomy. At one point, the famous Kinsey report estimated that 95 percent of Americans were potentially criminals under these laws. Whether this statistic was accurate or not, it was widely recognized that many sexual conduct laws were unenforced. While this policy of nonenforcement may have its own negative effects on the public's view of the criminal law, what about the justification for the laws themselves? The "victimless crimes" of consensual sex acts are difficult to justify by an indirect-harm argument and impossible to justify as preventing direct harm to others or society. Unless one accepts that homosexual sodomy is immoral, that decriminalizing it will cause moral degradation in society, and that this degradation will be harmful, there is no indirect harm to society prevented by a prohibition on sodomy. Even if one does accept that sodomy is immoral, where the conduct is consensual between adults and occurs in the privacy of one's own home, how can this cause harm anyway?

JOHN STUART MILL, ON LIBERTY
68–69 (1974) (1st ed. London 1859)

The object of this essay is to assert one very simple principle, as entitled to govern absolutely the dealings of society with the individual in the way of compulsion and control, whether the means used be physical force in the form of legal penalties or the moral coercion of public opinion. That principle is that the sole end for which mankind are warranted, individually or collectively, in interfering with the liberty of action of any of their number is self-protection. That the only purpose for which power can be rightfully exercised over any member of a civilized community, against his will, is to prevent harm to others. His own good, either physical or moral, is not a sufficient warrant. He cannot rightfully be compelled to do or forbear because it will be better for him to do so, because it will make him happier, because, in the opinions of others, to do so would be wise or even right. These are good reasons for remonstrating with him, or reasoning with him, or persuading him, or entreating him, but not for compelling him or visiting him with any evil in case he do otherwise. To justify that, the conduct from which it is desired to deter him must be calculated to produce evil to someone else. The only part of the conduct of anyone for which he is amenable to society is that which concerns others. In the part which merely concerns himself, his independence is, of right, absolute. Over himself, over his own body and mind, the individual is sovereign.

It is, perhaps, hardly necessary to say that this doctrine is meant to apply only to human beings in the maturity of their faculties. We are not speaking of children or of young persons below the age which the law may fix as that of manhood or womanhood. Those who are still in a state to require being taken care of by others must be protected against their own actions as well as against external injury.

Some commentators disagree with Mill's assertion that self-protection is the only acceptable justification for criminal laws. The Supreme Court, in Bowers v. Hardwick, 478 U.S. 186, 106 S. Ct. 2841 (1986), upheld a law prohibiting consensual sodomy, holding that morality alone is a sound basis upon which to create criminal law. Seventeen years later, however, the Court overruled its decision.

LAWRENCE v. TEXAS
Supreme Court of the United States, 2003
539 U.S. 558, 123 S. Ct. 2472

Justice KENNEDY delivered the opinion of the Court:

Liberty protects the person from unwarranted government intrusions into a dwelling or other private places. In our tradition the State is not omnipresent in the home. And there are other spheres of our lives and existence, outside the home, where the State should not be a dominant presence. Freedom extends beyond spatial bounds. Liberty presumes an autonomy of self that includes freedom of thought, belief, expression, and certain intimate conduct. The instant case involves liberty of the person both in its spatial and in its more transcendent dimensions.

I

The question before the Court is the validity of a Texas statute making it a crime for two persons of the same sex to engage in certain intimate sexual conduct....

We granted certiorari, 537 U.S. 1044, 123 S. Ct. 661 (2002), to consider three questions:

1. Whether petitioners' criminal convictions under the Texas "Homosexual Conduct" law — which criminalizes sexual intimacy by same-sex couples, but not identical behavior by different-sex couples — violate the Fourteenth Amendment guarantee of equal protection of the laws.

2. Whether petitioners' criminal convictions for adult consensual sexual intimacy in the home violate their vital interests in liberty and privacy protected by the Due Process Clause of the Fourteenth Amendment.

3. Whether Bowers v. Hardwick, supra, should be overruled. See Pet. for Cert. i.

The petitioners were adults at the time of the alleged offense. Their conduct was in private and consensual.

II

We conclude the case should be resolved by determining whether the petitioners were free as adults to engage in the private conduct in the exercise of their liberty under the Due Process Clause of the Fourteenth Amendment to the Constitution. For this inquiry we deem it necessary to reconsider the Court's holding in Bowers....

The Court began its substantive discussion in Bowers as follows: "The issue presented is whether the Federal Constitution confers a fundamental right upon homosexuals to engage in sodomy and hence invalidates the laws of the many States that still make such conduct illegal and have done so for a very long time." Id., at 190, 106 S. Ct. 2841. That statement, we now conclude, discloses the Court's own failure to appreciate the extent of the liberty at stake. To say that the issue in Bowers was simply the right to engage in certain sexual conduct demeans the claim the individual put forward, just as it would demean a married couple were it to be said marriage is simply about the right to have sexual intercourse. The laws involved in Bowers and here are, to be sure, statutes that purport to do no more than prohibit a particular sexual act. Their penalties and purposes, though, have more far-reaching consequences, touching upon the most private human conduct, sexual behavior, and in the most private of places, the home. The statutes do seek to control a personal relationship that, whether or not entitled to formal recognition in the law, is within the liberty of persons to choose without being punished as criminals.

This, as a general rule, should counsel against attempts by the State, or a court, to define the meaning of the relationship or to set its boundaries absent injury to a person or abuse of an institution the law protects. It suffices for us to acknowledge that adults may choose to enter upon this relationship in the confines of their homes and their own private lives and still retain their dignity as free persons. When sexuality finds overt expression in intimate conduct with another person, the conduct can be but one element in a personal bond that is more enduring. The liberty protected by the Constitution allows homosexual persons the right to make this choice.

Having misapprehended the claim of liberty there presented to it, and thus stating the claim to be whether there is a fundamental right to engage in consensual sodomy, the *Bowers* Court said: "Proscriptions against that conduct have ancient roots." Id., at 192, 106 S. Ct. 2841. In academic writings, and in many of the scholarly amicus briefs filed to assist the Court in this case, there are fundamental criticisms of the historical premises relied upon by the majority and concurring opinions in *Bowers*. We need not enter this debate in the attempt to reach a definitive historical judgment, but the following considerations counsel against adopting the definitive conclusions upon which *Bowers* placed such reliance.

[The Court reviewed the history of laws against homosexual sodomy, which the *Bowers* Court had in part relied upon to uphold the law.]

In summary, the historical grounds relied upon in *Bowers* are more complex than the majority opinion and the concurring opinion by Chief Justice Burger indicate. Their historical premises are not without doubt and, at the very least, are overstated.

It must be acknowledged, of course, that the Court in *Bowers* was making the broader point that for centuries there have been powerful voices to condemn homosexual conduct as immoral. The condemnation has been shaped by religious beliefs, conceptions of right and acceptable behavior, and respect for the traditional family. For many persons these are not trivial concerns but profound and deep convictions accepted as ethical and moral principles to which they aspire and which thus determine the course of their lives. These considerations do not answer the question before us, however. The issue is whether the majority may use the power of the State to enforce these views on the whole society through operation of the criminal law. "Our obligation is to define the liberty of all, not to mandate our own moral code." Planned Parenthood of Southeastern Pa. v. Casey, 505 U.S. 833, 850, 112 S. Ct. 2791 (1992).

. . . In all events we think that our laws and traditions in the past half century are of most relevance here. These references show an emerging awareness that liberty gives substantial protection to adult persons in deciding how to conduct their private lives in matters pertaining to sex.

"[H]istory and tradition are the starting point but not in all cases the ending point of the substantive due process inquiry." County of Sacramento v. Lewis, 523 U.S. 833, 857, 118 S. Ct. 1708 (1998) (Kennedy, J., concurring).

This emerging recognition should have been apparent when *Bowers* was decided. In 1955 the American Law Institute promulgated the Model Penal Code and made clear that it did not recommend or provide for "criminal penalties for consensual sexual relations conducted in private." ALI, Model Penal Code §213.2, Comment 2, p. 372 (1980). It justified its decision on three grounds: (1) The prohibitions undermined respect for the law by penalizing conduct many people engaged in; (2) the statutes regulated private conduct not harmful to others; and (3) the laws were arbitrarily enforced and thus invited the danger of blackmail. ALI, Model Penal Code, Commentary 277–280 (Tent. Draft No. 4, 1955). In 1961 Illinois changed its laws to conform to the Model Penal Code. Other States soon followed. . . .

In our own constitutional system the deficiencies in *Bowers* became even more apparent in the years following its announcement. The 25 States with laws prohibiting the relevant conduct referenced in the *Bowers* decision are reduced now to 13, of which 4 enforce their laws only against homosexual conduct. In those States where sodomy is still proscribed, whether for same-sex or heterosexual conduct, there is a pattern of nonenforcement with respect to consenting adults acting in private. The State of Texas admitted in 1994 that as of that date it had not prosecuted anyone under those circumstances. . . .

The stigma this criminal statute imposes, moreover, is not trivial. The offense, to be sure, is but a class C misdemeanor, a minor offense in the Texas legal system. Still, it remains a criminal offense with all that imports for the dignity of the persons charged. The petitioners will bear on their record the history of their criminal convictions. Just this Term we rejected various challenges to state laws requiring the registration of sex offenders. Smith v. Doe, 538 U.S. 84, 123 S. Ct. 1140 (2003); Connecticut Dept. of Public Safety v. Doe, 538 U.S. 1, 123 S. Ct. 1160 (2003). We are advised that if Texas convicted an adult for private, consensual homosexual conduct under the statute here in question the convicted person would come within the registration laws of at least four States were he or she to be subject to their jurisdiction.... This underscores the consequential nature of the punishment and the state-sponsored condemnation attendant to the criminal prohibition. Furthermore, the Texas criminal conviction carries with it the other collateral consequences always following a conviction, such as notations on job application forms, to mention but one example....

The rationale of *Bowers* does not withstand careful analysis. In his dissenting opinion in *Bowers* Justice Stevens came to these conclusions:

> Our prior cases make two propositions abundantly clear. First, the fact that the governing majority in a State has traditionally viewed a particular practice as immoral is not a sufficient reason for upholding a law prohibiting the practice; neither history nor tradition could save a law prohibiting miscegenation from constitutional attack. Second, individual decisions by married persons, concerning the intimacies of their physical relationship, even when not intended to produce offspring, are a form of "liberty" protected by the Due Process Clause of the Fourteenth Amendment. Moreover, this protection extends to intimate choices by unmarried as well as married persons.

478 U.S., at 216, 106 S. Ct. 2841 (footnotes and citations omitted). Justice Stevens' analysis, in our view, should have been controlling in *Bowers* and should control here.

Bowers was not correct when it was decided, and it is not correct today. It ought not to remain binding precedent. *Bowers v. Hardwick* should be and now is overruled....

The judgment of the Court of Appeals for the Texas Fourteenth District is reversed, and the case is remanded for further proceedings not inconsistent with this opinion.

It is so ordered.

JUSTICE O'CONNOR, concurring in the judgment:
The Court today overrules Bowers v. Hardwick, 478 U.S. 186, 106 S. Ct. 2841 (1986).

I joined *Bowers*, and do not join the Court in overruling it. Nevertheless, I agree with the Court that Texas' statute banning same-sex sodomy is unconstitutional. Rather than relying on the substantive component of the Fourteenth Amendment's Due Process Clause, as the Court does, I base my conclusion on the Fourteenth Amendment's Equal Protection Clause.

The Equal Protection Clause of the Fourteenth Amendment "is essentially a direction that all persons similarly situated should be treated alike." Cleburne v. Cleburne Living Center, Inc., 473 U.S. 432, 439, 105 S. Ct. 3249 (1985). Under our rational basis standard of review, "legislation is presumed to be valid and will be sustained if the classification drawn by the statute is rationally related to a legitimate state interest." Cleburne v. Cleburne Living Center, supra, at 440, 105 S. Ct. 3249....

The statute at issue here makes sodomy a crime only if a person "engages in deviate sexual intercourse with another individual of the same sex." Tex. Penal Code Ann. §21.06(a) (2003). Sodomy between opposite-sex partners, however, is not a crime in Texas. That is, Texas treats the same conduct differently based solely on the participants....

Texas attempts to justify its law, and the effects of the law, by arguing that the statute satisfies rational basis review because it furthers the legitimate governmental interest of the promotion of morality. In *Bowers*, we held that a state law criminalizing sodomy as applied to homosexual couples did not violate substantive due process. We rejected the argument that no rational basis existed to justify the law, pointing to the government's interest in promoting morality. 478 U.S., at 196, 106 S. Ct. 2841. The only question in front of the Court in *Bowers* was whether the substantive component of the Due Process Clause protected a right to engage in homosexual sodomy. Id., at 188, n.2. *Bowers* did not hold that moral disapproval of a group is a rational basis under the Equal Protection Clause to criminalize homosexual sodomy when heterosexual sodomy is not punished.

This case raises a different issue than *Bowers*: whether, under the Equal Protection Clause, moral disapproval is a legitimate state interest to justify by itself a statute that bans homosexual sodomy, but not heterosexual sodomy. It is not. Moral disapproval of this group, like a bare desire to harm the group, is an interest that is insufficient to satisfy rational basis review under the Equal Protection Clause. See, e.g., Department of Agriculture v. Moreno, 413 U.S., at 534, 93 S. Ct. 2821; Romer v. Evans, 517 U.S., at 634–635, 116 S. Ct. 1620. Indeed, we have never held that moral disapproval, without any other asserted state interest, is a sufficient rationale under the Equal Protection Clause to justify a law that discriminates among groups of persons.

Moral disapproval of a group cannot be a legitimate governmental interest under the Equal Protection Clause because legal classifications must not be "drawn for the purpose of disadvantaging the group burdened by the law." Id., at 633, 116 S. Ct. 1620. Texas' invocation of moral disapproval as a legitimate state interest proves nothing more than Texas' desire to criminalize homosexual sodomy. But the Equal Protection Clause prevents a State from creating "a classification of persons undertaken for its own sake." Id., at 635, 116 S. Ct. 1620. And because Texas so rarely enforces its sodomy law as applied to private, consensual acts, the law serves more as a statement of dislike and disapproval against homosexuals than as a tool to stop criminal behavior. The Texas sodomy law "raise[s] the inevitable inference that the disadvantage imposed is born of animosity toward the class of persons affected." Id., at 634, 116 S. Ct. 1620. . . .

A State can of course assign certain consequences to a violation of its criminal law. But the State cannot single out one identifiable class of citizens for punishment that does not apply to everyone else, with moral disapproval as the only asserted state interest for the law. . . .

That this law as applied to private, consensual conduct is unconstitutional under the Equal Protection Clause does not mean that other laws distinguishing between heterosexuals and homosexuals would similarly fail under rational basis review. Texas cannot assert any legitimate state interest here, such as national security or preserving the traditional institution of marriage. Unlike the moral disapproval of same-sex relations — the

asserted state interest in this case — other reasons exist to promote the institution of marriage beyond mere moral disapproval of an excluded group.

A law branding one class of persons as criminal based solely on the State's moral disapproval of that class and the conduct associated with that class runs contrary to the values of the Constitution and the Equal Protection Clause, under any standard of review. I therefore concur in the Court's judgment that Texas' sodomy law banning "deviate sexual intercourse" between consenting adults of the same sex, but not between consenting adults of different sexes, is unconstitutional.

JUSTICE SCALIA, with whom THE CHIEF JUSTICE [REHNQUIST] and JUSTICE THOMAS join, dissenting: . . .

I

I begin with the Court's surprising readiness to reconsider a decision rendered a mere 17 years ago in *Bowers v. Hardwick*. I do not myself believe in rigid adherence to stare decisis in constitutional cases; but I do believe that we should be consistent rather than manipulative in invoking the doctrine. Today's opinions in support of reversal do not bother to distinguish — or indeed, even bother to mention — the paean to stare decisis coauthored by three Members of today's majority in *Planned Parenthood v. Casey*. There, when stare decisis meant preservation of judicially invented abortion rights, the widespread criticism of *Roe* was strong reason to *reaffirm* it:

> Where, in the performance of its judicial duties, the Court decides a case in such a way as to resolve the sort of intensely divisive controversy reflected in *Roe*[,] . . . its decision has a dimension that the resolution of the normal case does not carry. . . . [T]o overrule under fire in the absence of the most compelling reason . . . would subvert the Court's legitimacy beyond any serious question.

505 U.S., at 866–867, 112 S. Ct. 2791. Today, however, the widespread opposition to *Bowers*, a decision resolving an issue as "intensely divisive"

as the issue in *Roe*, is offered as a reason in favor of overruling it. Gone, too, is any "enquiry" (of the sort conducted in *Casey*) into whether the decision sought to be overruled has "proven 'unworkable,'" *Casey*, supra, at 855, 112 S. Ct. 2791.

Today's approach to stare decisis invites us to overrule an erroneously decided precedent (including an "intensely divisive" decision) if: (1) its foundations have been "ero[ded]" by subsequent decisions; (2) it has been subject to "substantial and continuing" criticism; and (3) it has not induced "individual or societal reliance" that counsels against overturning. The problem is that *Roe* itself — which today's majority surely has no disposition to overrule — satisfies these conditions to at least the same degree as *Bowers*....

...State laws against bigamy, same-sex marriage, adult incest, prostitution, masturbation, adultery, fornication, bestiality, and obscenity are likewise sustainable only in light of *Bowers'* validation of laws based on moral choices. Every single one of these laws is called into question by today's decision; the Court makes no effort to cabin the scope of its decision to exclude them from its holding. See ante ... (noting "an emerging awareness that liberty gives substantial protection to adult persons in deciding how to conduct their private lives *in matters pertaining to sex*" (emphasis added)). The impossibility of distinguishing homosexuality from other traditional "morals" offenses is precisely why *Bowers* rejected the rational-basis challenge. "The law," it said, "is constantly based on notions of morality, and if all laws representing essentially moral choices are to be invalidated under the Due Process Clause, the courts will be very busy indeed." 478 U.S., at 196, 106 S. Ct. 2841....

II

Having decided that it need not adhere to stare decisis, the Court still must establish that *Bowers* was wrongly decided and that the Texas statute, as applied to petitioners, is unconstitutional....

Our opinions applying the doctrine known as "substantive due process" hold that the Due Process Clause prohibits States from infringing fundamental liberty interests, unless the infringement is narrowly tailored to serve a compelling state interest. Washington v. Glucksberg, 521 U.S.[702], 721, 117 S. Ct. 2258 [(1997)]. We have held repeatedly, in cases the Court today does not overrule, that only fundamental rights qualify for this so-called "heightened scrutiny" protection — that is, rights which are "'deeply rooted in this Nation's history and tradition,'" ibid. All other liberty interests may be abridged or abrogated pursuant to a validly enacted state law if that law is rationally related to a legitimate state interest.

Bowers held, first, that criminal prohibitions of homosexual sodomy are not subject to heightened scrutiny because they do not implicate a "fundamental right" under the Due Process Clause, 478 U.S., at 191–194, 106 S. Ct. 2841. Noting that "[p]roscriptions against that conduct have ancient roots," id., at 192, 106 S. Ct. 2841, that "[s]odomy was a criminal offense at common law and was forbidden by the laws of the original 13 States when they ratified the Bill of Rights," ibid., and that many States had retained their bans on sodomy, id., at 193, *Bowers* concluded that a right to engage in homosexual sodomy was not "'deeply rooted in this Nation's history and tradition,'" id., at 192, 106 S. Ct. 2841.

The Court today does not overrule this holding. Not once does it describe homosexual sodomy as a "fundamental right" or a "fundamental liberty interest," nor does it subject the Texas statute to strict scrutiny. Instead, having failed to establish that the right to homosexual sodomy is "'deeply rooted in this Nation's history and tradition,'" the Court concludes that the application of Texas's statute to petitioners' conduct fails the rational-basis test, and overrules *Bowers'* holding to the contrary, see id., at 196, 106 S. Ct. 2841. "The Texas statute furthers no legitimate state interest which can justify its intrusion into the personal and private life of the individual."

I shall address that rational-basis holding presently. First, however, I address some aspersions that the Court casts upon *Bowers'* conclusion that homosexual sodomy is not a "fundamental right" — even though, as I have said, the Court does not have the boldness to reverse that conclusion.

III

The Court's description of "the state of the law" at the time of *Bowers* only confirms that *Bowers* was right....

After discussing the history of antisodomy laws, the Court proclaims that, "it should be noted that there is no longstanding history in this country of laws directed at homosexual conduct as a distinct matter." This observation in no way casts into doubt the "definitive [historical] conclusio[n]," on which *Bowers* relied: that our Nation has a longstanding history of laws prohibiting sodomy in general — regardless of whether it was performed by same-sex or opposite-sex couples .... It is (as *Bowers* recognized) entirely irrelevant whether the laws in our long national tradition criminalizing homosexual sodomy were "directed at homosexual conduct as a distinct matter." Whether homosexual sodomy was prohibited by a law targeted at same-sex sexual relations or by a more general law prohibiting both homosexual and heterosexual sodomy, the only relevant point is that it was criminalized — which suffices to establish that homosexual sodomy is not a right "deeply rooted in our Nation's history and tradition." The Court today agrees that homosexual sodomy was criminalized and thus does not dispute the facts on which *Bowers* actually relied.

Next the Court makes the claim, again unsupported by any citations, that "[l]aws prohibiting sodomy do not seem to have been enforced against consenting adults acting in private." The key qualifier here is "acting in private" — since the Court admits that sodomy laws were enforced against consenting adults (although the Court contends that prosecutions were "infrequen[t]"). I do not know what "acting in private" means; surely consensual sodomy, like heterosexual intercourse, is rarely performed on stage. If all the Court means by "acting in private" is "on private premises, with the doors closed and windows covered," it is entirely unsurprising that evidence of enforcement would be hard to come by. (Imagine the circumstances that would enable a search warrant to be obtained for a residence on the ground that there was probable cause to believe that consensual sodomy was then and there occurring.) Surely

that lack of evidence would not sustain the proposition that consensual sodomy on private premises with the doors closed and windows covered was regarded as a "fundamental right," even though all other consensual sodomy was criminalized. There are 203 prosecutions for consensual, adult homosexual sodomy reported in the West Reporting system and official state reporters from the years 1880–1995. See W. Eskridge, Gaylaw: Challenging the Apartheid of the Closet 375 (1999) (hereinafter Gaylaw). There are also records of 20 sodomy prosecutions and 4 executions during the colonial period. J. Katz, Gay/Lesbian Almanac 29, 58, 663 (1983). *Bowers'* conclusion that homosexual sodomy is not a fundamental right "deeply rooted in this Nation's history and tradition" is utterly unassailable.

Realizing that fact, the Court instead says: "[W]e think that our laws and traditions in the past half century are of most relevance here. These references show *an emerging awareness* that liberty gives substantial protection to adult persons in deciding how to conduct their private lives *in matters pertaining to sex*" (emphasis added). Apart from the fact that such an "emerging awareness" does not establish a "fundamental right," the statement is factually false. States continue to prosecute all sorts of crimes by adults "in matters pertaining to sex": prostitution, adult incest, adultery, obscenity, and child pornography. Sodomy laws, too, have been enforced "in the past half century," in which there have been 134 reported cases involving prosecutions for consensual, adult, homosexual sodomy. Gaylaw 375. In relying, for evidence of an "emerging recognition," upon the American Law Institute's 1955 recommendation not to criminalize "'consensual sexual relations conducted in private,'" the Court ignores the fact that this recommendation was "a point of resistance in most of the states that considered adopting the Model Penal Code." Gaylaw 159.

In any event, an "emerging awareness" is by definition not "deeply rooted in this Nation's history and tradition[s]," as we have said "fundamental right" status requires. Constitutional entitlements do not spring into existence because some States choose to lessen or eliminate criminal sanctions on certain behavior. Much less do they spring into existence, as the Court seems to believe, because foreign nations decriminalize conduct.... The Court's discussion of these foreign views (ignoring, of course, the many countries that have retained criminal prohibitions on sodomy) is therefore meaningless dicta....

IV

I turn now to the ground on which the Court squarely rests its holding: the contention that there is no rational basis for the law here under attack....

The Texas statute undeniably seeks to further the belief of its citizens that certain forms of sexual behavior are "immoral and unacceptable," *Bowers*, supra, at 196, 106 S. Ct. 2841 — the same interest furthered by criminal laws against fornication, bigamy, adultery, adult incest, bestiality, and obscenity. *Bowers* held that this was a legitimate state interest. The Court today reaches the opposite conclusion. The Texas statute, it says, "furthers *no legitimate state interest* which can justify its intrusion into the personal and private life of the individual" (emphasis added). The Court embraces instead Justice Stevens' declaration in his *Bowers* dissent, that "'the fact that the governing majority in a State has traditionally viewed a particular practice as immoral is not a sufficient reason for upholding a law prohibiting the practice.'" This effectively decrees the end of all morals legislation. If, as the Court asserts, the promotion of majoritarian sexual morality is not even a legitimate state interest, none of the above-mentioned laws can survive rational-basis review....

One of the most revealing statements in today's opinion is the Court's grim warning that the criminalization of homosexual conduct is "an invitation to subject homosexual persons to discrimination both in the public and in the private spheres." It is clear from this that the Court has taken sides in the culture war, departing from its role of assuring, as neutral observer, that the democratic rules of engagement are observed. Many Americans do not want persons who openly engage in homosexual conduct as partners in their business,

as scoutmasters for their children, as teachers in their children's schools, or as boarders in their home. They view this as protecting themselves and their families from a lifestyle that they believe to be immoral and destructive. The Court views it as "discrimination" which it is the function of our judgments to deter. So imbued is the Court with the law profession's anti-anti-homosexual culture, that it is seemingly unaware that the attitudes of that culture are not obviously "mainstream"; that in most States what the Court calls "discrimination" against those who engage in homosexual acts is perfectly legal; that proposals to ban such "discrimination" under Title VII have repeatedly been rejected by Congress; that in some cases such "discrimination" is mandated by federal statute, see 10 U.S.C. §654(b)(1) (mandating discharge from the Armed Forces of any service member who engages in or intends to engage in homosexual acts); and that in some cases such "discrimination" is a constitutional right, see Boy Scouts of America v. Dale, 530 U.S. 640, 120 S. Ct. 2446 (2000).

Let me be clear that I have nothing against homosexuals, or any other group, promoting their agenda through normal democratic means. Social perceptions of sexual and other morality change over time, and every group has the right to persuade its fellow citizens that its view of such matters is the best. That homosexuals have achieved some success in that enterprise is attested to by the fact that Texas is one of the few remaining States that criminalize private, consensual homosexual acts. But persuading one's fellow citizens is one thing, and imposing one's views in absence of democratic majority will is something else. I would no more require a State to criminalize homosexual acts — or, for that matter, display any moral disapprobation of them — than I would forbid it to do so. What Texas has chosen to do is well within the range of traditional democratic action, and its hand should not be stayed through the invention of a brand-new "constitutional right" by a Court that is impatient of democratic change. It is indeed true that "later generations can see that laws once thought necessary and proper in fact serve only to oppress"; and when that happens, later generations can repeal those laws. But it is the premise of our system that those judgments are to be made by the people, and not imposed by a governing caste that knows best.

One of the benefits of leaving regulation of this matter to the people rather than to the courts is that the people, unlike judges, need not carry things to their logical conclusion. The people may feel that their disapprobation of homosexual conduct is strong enough to disallow homosexual marriage, but not strong enough to criminalize private homosexual acts — and may legislate accordingly. The Court today pretends that it possesses a similar freedom of action, so that we need not fear judicial imposition of homosexual marriage . . . . At the end of its opinion — after having laid waste the foundations of our rational-basis jurisprudence — the Court says that the present case "does not involve whether the government must give formal recognition to any relationship that homosexual persons seek to enter." Do not believe it. More illuminating than this bald, unreasoned disclaimer is the progression of thought displayed by an earlier passage in the Court's opinion, which notes the constitutional protections afforded to "personal decisions relating to *marriage*, procreation, contraception, family relationships, child rearing, and education," and then declares that "[p]ersons in a homosexual relationship may seek autonomy for these purposes, just as heterosexual persons do" (emphasis added). Today's opinion dismantles the structure of constitutional law that has

permitted a distinction to be made between heterosexual and homosexual unions, insofar as formal recognition in marriage is concerned. If moral disapprobation of homosexual conduct is "no legitimate state interest" for purposes of proscribing that conduct; and if, as the Court coos (casting aside all pretense of neutrality), "[w]hen sexuality finds overt expression in intimate conduct with another person, the conduct can be but one element in a personal bond that is more enduring"; what justification could there possibly be for denying the benefits of marriage to homosexual couples exercising "[t]he liberty protected by the Constitution"? Surely not the encouragement of procreation, since the sterile and the elderly are allowed to marry. This case "does not involve" the issue of homosexual marriage only if one entertains the belief that principle and logic have nothing to do with the decisions of this Court. Many will hope that, as the Court comfortingly assures us, this is so.

The matters appropriate for this Court's resolution are only three: Texas's prohibition of sodomy neither infringes a "fundamental right" (which the Court does not dispute), nor is unsupported by a rational relation to what the Constitution considers a legitimate state interest, nor denies the equal protection of the laws. I dissent.

[Justice Thomas also filed a short dissent noting that while he agreed with Justice Scalia, he thought the Texas law was "silly."]

ARNOLD H. LOEWY, MORALS LEGISLATION AND THE ESTABLISHMENT CLAUSE
55 Ala. L. Rev. 159, 159–66 (2003)*

I. The Need for a Standard

If morality simpliciter were enough to justify legislation as *Bowers* wrongly asserted, this Essay would not be necessary. However, as *Lawrence* rightly holds, such is not the case. Nevertheless, that is hardly a unanimous view on the Court. In his *Lawrence* dissent, among other places, Justice

Scalia maintains that morality, without more, can justify legislation. Let us test this hypothesis with some hypotheticals.

(1) Alan truly believes that it is immoral for anybody to fail to attend Sunday services at the town's Methodist church. Assume that he persuades the town council, most of whom are also Methodists, to enact an ordinance requiring such attendance. Barbara intentionally refrains from

* Reprinted from Alabama Law Review, Fall 2003, Vol. 55, No. 1. Copyright 2003 by Arnold H. Loewy.

attending church and is convicted of violating the ordinance. The town defends the ordinance on the ground that its legislators believe that it is immoral to refrain from attending the ∘Methodist church's weekly service absent some sort of medical or personal emergency, which Barbara does not have.

Presumably, Justice Scalia would invalidate the hypothesized ordinance on the ground that it violates the Establishment Clause and possibly the Free Exercise Clause. He would say that morality is a rational basis for a statute, but rationality is insufficient to justify a violation of the First Amendment. So let us try a slightly less obvious hypothetical.

(2) Cantu is a devout Moslem who believes that eating pork is morally wrong and should be forbidden in his community. He persuades the town council, most of whom are also Moslem, to enact an ordinance forbidding the sale, purchase, or consumption of pork in his community. Doris serves bacon and eggs to Ed for breakfast at her restaurant. Frances buys three pounds of pork chops from George's butcher shop and consumes them at home the next day. Neither Doris, Ed, Frances, nor George believe that eating pork is immoral. All are convicted under the statute. Once more the town defends the statute on the ground that eating, serving, and selling pork is immoral.

This one might not be so easy for Justice Scalia. Nobody is being required or forbidden to worship in any particular way. Of course, he could say that the rationale for the legislation is religious, but that would prove too much. The rationale for much moral legislation is religious, including laws against consenting adult homosexual sodomy. And that is precisely the point. If morality simpliciter can qualify as a rational basis, a community can punish religious dissidents for straying from the straight and narrow.

In assessing an appropriate test, one should first consider the core purpose of the religion clauses. Without attempting to be overly nuanced, it seems basic that, to the greatest extent possible, persons should be free from compulsion to exercise another's religious beliefs in lieu of or in addition to their own. For that reason, I assume that most readers would agree that the anti-pork legislation is unconstitutional. But given that so much of our legislation is based on Judeo–Christian morality, how can we distinguish legitimate from illegitimate moral legislation?

I propose a test that looks to the purpose of legislating against the particular activity. If the activity involves morality simpliciter, i.e., the legislature simply condemns the activity because it is immoral, the law should be held to violate the Establishment Clause. On the other hand, if the legislation is predicated on purposive morality, i.e., morality that serves a secular function, the law should be sustained.

Some may argue that non-believers could support morals legislation. For example, Helen, an agnostic, may believe that homosexual sodomy should be punished because it is morally wrong. She does not believe in God and concedes that more often than not, participants in homosexual sodomy are benefited by the act. Nevertheless, she thinks that it is morally wrong and should be forbidden. Although I suspect that the number of agnostics sharing Helen's view is small, I concede that they may exist. However, I contend that the non-purposive morality that Helen supports occupies a place in her life parallel to that of God in the mind of the more traditional believer. This is so because of her concurrent beliefs in both the moral imperative and social disutility of the statute.

To test whether legislation meets my proposed test, I would ask whether a substantial number of religious skeptics would support the legislation. In the pork hypothetical, it is possible that a few non-Moslems (or non-Orthodox Jews) would support the legislation. For example, Ian, an animal rights activist who would like to ban the slaughter of all animals, might be willing to start with pigs until he can persuade others to forbid the sale of beef and lamb as well. Assuming that Ian represents a tiny minority of the community, I would not uphold the statute. If we did, we effectively would have permitted a religious majority to make criminals out of their dissident fellow citizens simply because a tiny minority of dissidents approved. Thus, I would require support by skeptics in substantial numbers to ensure that a majority's religious beliefs are not dictating the minority's lifestyle.

In the next section, I will apply my proposed test to the Ten Commandments.

II. The Ten Commandments

The Ten Commandments can be divided into three categories: those that government clearly can enforce, those that government clearly cannot enforce, and those that are partially enforceable. Obviously, the first two categories are less controversial than the third, so I shall dispose of them first.

The three Commandments forbidding murder, theft, and false testimony against one's neighbor are clearly permissible. Each of them protects a governmental interest quite independent of abstract morality. The importance to all, believer and nonbeliever alike, of not being victimized by any of these activities is too obvious to require extended defense. So, in the absence of any serious argument to the contrary, I simply assert that these Commandments are governmentally enforceable.

Quite clearly, the state cannot enforce prohibitions against non-belief in God, making graven images of God, or taking the Lord's name in vain. To the extent that these provisions also forbid blasphemy, it is quite clear that both the Establishment Clause and the Freedom of Speech Clause preclude punishment for such behavior. The Commandment against coveting is also unenforceable. One need not go so far as the Wall Street "greed is good" aphorism to recognize that a government has no power to limit a person's aspirations. Even Jimmy Carter confessed to lusting in his heart. Our traditions of not punishing a person for her thoughts, i.e., the requirement of actus reus, coupled with the difficulties of proof would render such a charge fanciful at best. To illustrate the absurdity of such a prosecution, suppose a policeman attending a party overheard Jane say: "I just love my neighbor Kevin's Mercedes. I wish I owned it." Could we even imagine the policeman saying: "Okay Jane, you're under arrest for coveting"?

Having discussed the clearly constitutional and clearly unconstitutional enforcement of the Ten Commandments, let me focus on the three that probably should be deemed partially enforceable: the Commandments concerning Sabbath, parental respect, and adultery.

The Supreme Court has had an opportunity to consider a secular version of Sabbath in McGowan v. Maryland[, 366 U.S. 420, 81 S. Ct. 1101 (1961)]. Its analysis was quite consistent with that proposed herein. In upholding laws of religious origin, the Court focused on the current secular support for the law. Noting that labor unions support Sunday closing laws, and that the value of having the same day each week as a quiet recreational day benefited all families, regardless of religious convictions, the Court upheld the Sunday closing laws as consistent with Establishment Clause principles.

Now let us vary the situation. Assume that a community with the autonomy to make its own Sabbath laws is composed of sixty percent Orthodox Jews. Assume that this community chooses to compel business closure for the period from sundown Friday through sundown Saturday. Presumably this statute would be sustained for the same reasons as the Maryland statute in *McGowan*. But suppose the community added a provision forbidding driving in the community during that timeframe.

Now, let us suppose that Laura, a non-Orthodox Jew, drove on a Friday night from her home in the community to another home three miles away to attend a party. While en route, she received a ticket for driving on Friday night. Should the courts uphold her ticket? The answer may depend on which of three rationales are offered for the "no driving ordinance."

The easiest ground for invalidating the ordinance would be if it was predicated upon the religious duty not to work, including drive, on the Sabbath. Obviously, no reasonable skeptic could support legislation enacted on such a ground, and it should therefore be unconstitutional. Suppose, however, that the ordinance was based on the desire to add to the quiet of the day. The entire community would know that from sundown Friday to sundown Saturday, there would be no vehicular traffic. The day would be quiet, unlike any other. Although a somewhat similar rationale upheld the Sunday closing laws, this seems to carry the analogy too far. Undoubtedly a few nonbelievers would like the advantage of a quieter community. But most would not. Many of those that would support a quieter day probably would prefer to eliminate automobile traffic generally. The end result would be a great inconvenience to the automobile driving public in the service of a majority religion — probably an unconstitutional result.

The strongest ground for upholding the ordinance might be safety. The presence of a vastly larger-than-normal number of pedestrians (including children) on the surface seems like a good non-religious reason for limiting vehicular traffic. If, during the year preceding passage of this ordinance, a significant number of vehicular/pedestrian accidents or near-accidents had occurred during the twenty-four hour Sabbath period, a powerful case could be made for forbidding vehicular traffic at that time. If, on the other hand, accidents were not significantly higher at that time, in part because fewer residents chose to drive in violation of the Lord's Commandment, the safety rationale would not seem very powerful.

On balance, it seems unlikely, but not impossible, that a legitimate rationale for sustaining Laura's traffic ticket can be found. The important thing is that, as in *McGowan*, any limitation on what the populace can do on the Sabbath must be justified by secular concerns, lest a religious majority coopt its dissidents into being reluctant participants in a religious ritual.

The Commandment that compels parental honor is obviously not completely enforceable. If Mike hates his father, Norman, and wants to publicize that hatred to both his father and the world, it is hard to see what governmental interest could stop him. On the other hand, suppose that Mike's home state enacts legislation compelling adult children to care for their aging parents under some circumstances. Suppose further that Norman is sufficiently needy that Mike's duty to support falls within the statutory prescription. Could Mike simply say: "I'm sorry, but I hate my father and I refuse to honor him no matter what the Fifth Commandment says"?

Mike should lose. Of course, he cannot be compelled to honor his father in the biblical sense of the term, but he can be compelled to support his father. While religious groups may be pleased to have a law compelling tangible support toward those that the Commandment compels honor, that is not where all, or even most, of the support for such legislation emanates. Reasonable skeptics in substantial numbers would likely support such legislation because it is designed to reduce welfare roles by forcing individuals, rather than the state, to care for relatives. So, while Mike can't be forced to honor Norman in his heart, he can be forced to honor him by providing sufficient support to keep him off the welfare roles.

Finally, the Commandment against adultery is partially, but not completely, enforceable by the state. Assume that Olivia, while married to Paul, engages in sexual intercourse with Quincy. Surely, the state can, if it chooses, create a divorce law that would allow Paul a larger share of the marital property in a divorce proceeding than that to which he would be entitled if Olivia had not committed adultery. This is because Olivia has breached a very special contract with Paul (marriage) in a manner that warrants a financial penalty.

Once more, one need not be a religious insider to accept this conclusion. Monogamous marriages are sufficiently fundamental to our society that, at least where the parties agree to them, the law can punish their breach. Criminalizing adultery, as some states still do, should be constitutionally sustainable. Although a breach of contract does not ordinarily give rise to criminal liability, marriage is no ordinary contract. Adultery can devastate people of all religious beliefs, as well as people bereft of religion. Whether the state does more harm than good in punishing adultery is a separate question. But even assuming that employing the criminal law is unwise, it does not follow that it is unconstitutional.

The Commandment, however, is broader than the state's interest. Under the Commandment, even adultery committed with the permission or active connivance of the supposedly injured spouse would be subject to punishment. So in my hypothetical, if Paul had actively encouraged Olivia to be intimate with Quincy, Olivia would be guilty anyway. Indeed, Paul could well be guilty of aiding and abetting. It is difficult to see any non-religious justification for such liability. Consequently, the Establishment Clause should preclude liability (criminal or civil) in those circumstances.

In sum, three of the Commandments are fully enforceable by government, four are unenforceable, and three are partially enforceable. But most importantly, enforcement must be predicated on something other than morality simpliciter.

NOTES

1. The *Lawrence* opinion is unique in several ways. Previous substantive due process cases followed a set line of reasoning, wherein the court would analyze the right being infringed upon, determine if it is a "fundamental" right, and then examine the challenged legislation under the applicable standard. If the right was determined to be fundamental, the legislation needed to be narrowly tailored to achieve a compelling government interest. If the right was not fundamental, the legislation needed merely to be rationally related to a legitimate state interest. In *Lawrence*, however, the Court never declared whether or not a fundamental right was at stake. Therefore, the Justices could not adequately describe the appropriate standard of review. Why was this case's approach different? Some commentators believe that a majority of Justices would not have signed onto the Court's opinion had it declared homosexual sodomy to be a fundamental right.

2. While the majority based its decision on the Due Process Clause of the Fourteenth Amendment, Justice O'Connor based her concurrence on its Equal Protection Clause. Why does the rest of the Court not do so as well? Perhaps it is because basing this decision on equal protection could lay the groundwork for striking down laws prohibiting gay marriage. That is, if the majority had simply banned the unequal treatment of homosexuals, the prohibition against gay marriage would be much more difficult to distinguish. The Court in *Lawrence* tries to dodge the marriage issue by focusing on an individual's liberty interest in private consensual sexual relations. The Court so leaves itself more room to distinguish gay marriage. Of course, the language and reasoning of the opinion can still be used to support an attack on laws prohibiting gay marriage. Such laws can easily be construed as casting a stigma upon homosexuality, or privileging heterosexuals, for no other reason than moral disapproval of homosexuality.

3. Professor Loewy introduces a third constitutional constraint — the Establishment Clause of the First Amendment — on the power of the legislature to enact "morals legislation." How do you think Justice Scalia would respond to Loewy's arguments? If you liked Loewy's analysis, you might wonder why no one on the Court explored the Establishment Clause as a source of constraint on legislation criminalizing homosexual conduct. A short answer is that this question was not one upon which the petitioners relied or upon which certiorari was granted. But this answer only raises another question: why did the petitioners not raise this attack on the statute as well?

B. Limitations on Its Methods

Authority and capacity to use force are obviously integral to the use of law as a penal instrument. The criminal law is designed to coerce individuals, at least those individuals it fails to persuade. The issue, then, is not whether force should be used but how much force should be used. In earlier times, torture and mutilation were generally accepted as appropriate punishment. Most societies now condemn these practices, which is not to say that they no longer exist.

In the United States, the Eighth Amendment's prohibition of "cruel and unusual punishment" is interpreted to bar most forms of corporal punishment, including torture. The notable exception is the death penalty. The Supreme Court has struck down mandatory death penalty statutes; it has also struck down statutes that fail to provide the jury with any guidelines for the imposition of the death penalty. Death penalty statutes between these two extremes (usually setting out aggravating and mitigating circumstances for the jury to consider) have been upheld by the Supreme Court.

These decisions permit each state to make its own determination of whether the death penalty furthers the goals of the criminal law. Proponents of the death penalty, who are sometimes called retentionists, argue that it increases *deterrence* of crime. Although comparative statistical studies have not proved the existence of a deterrent effect, proponents contend that common sense tells us that some people who would not be deterred by a life sentence would be deterred by the death penalty. In particular, they say that someone who has already committed a crime for which a life sentence will be imposed has no reason to refrain from further crimes if there is no death penalty. Opponents of the death penalty, or abolitionists, counter that (1) people who have already committed crimes for which life sentences will be imposed are not very susceptible to deterrence, either because they are acting irrationally or because they do not believe they will get caught, and (2) for some people, the death penalty may act as an incentive to commit crime, either because the prospect of life imprisonment seems worse than death or because they desire the publicity attendant to an execution.

Death penalty proponents also argue that *incapacitation* is more complete with the death penalty than with life imprisonment — and sometimes assert that it is cheaper as well. Opponents point out that the increased cost of death penalty cases actually exceeds the cost of life imprisonment. Proponents often answer that the greater cost of death penalty litigation could be eliminated if only opponents would end their exhaustive and frivolous litigation. To which opponents may respond that swift executions would greatly increase the number of mistakes made, as it typically takes ten years to exonerate a wrongfully convicted defendant.

Opponents object that the death penalty is contrary to the goal of *rehabilitation*. Proponents would agree but contend that some people have shown themselves to be incapable or undeserving of reform.

The apparent stalemate on these issues leaves us with the rationale of *retribution*. Proponents claim that retribution requires the death penalty. Some

Death Row Exonerations

Since 1973, 133 men on death row have been exonerated (where exoneration is defined as release from death row due to acquittal on retrial or the prosecutor's decision to drop all charges after the reversal of the death row inmate's conviction). Twenty-two men from Florida's death row have been exonerated. Illinois had 19 death row exonerations, and those exonerations played a major role in the Governor George Ryan's 2003 decision to commute the death sentences of the entire Illinois death row. Twenty-six states have had at least one death row exoneration. Exonerees are disproportionately African American.

opponents believe that retribution is not a legitimate justification of the penal law. Other opponents would argue that the death penalty is too inhumane to be just retribution and that this injustice is increased by the arbitrary selection of its victims and the possibility of error. In light of these conflicting views, consider whether a logical resolution of this issue will ever be reached. Why was it possible to gain a consensus about mutilation — which might be viewed as a partial death penalty — but not about the death penalty? One answer is aesthetic: It offends the public to *see* mutilation, or persons who have been mutilated by the state; executions, in contrast, do not occur in public. This explanation, however, does not seem a satisfactory justification to most people. Another answer is that it demeans the state to mutilate offenders, but this answer, too, seems unsatisfactory, since it raises the further question of why it does not demean the state to kill. A third possibility is provided by considering an analogy to war: It is permissible to kill, but not to torture the enemy. However, this analogy is also of dubious helpfulness, for the reason that under international law it is not permissible to either torture or to kill enemy prisoners. Consider whether there are better explanations available, or whether corporal punishment of all sorts should be viewed in the same way.

THEORETICAL AND PRACTICAL VIEWS ON THE DEATH PENALTY

One major difficulty that prevents formulating a consensus on the death penalty is the tension between theoretical and practical views on the death penalty. For example, some commentators believe that the state must have the power to condemn criminals to death as a way of expressing society's belief that some crimes are horrible enough that those who commit them deserve death. Of course, others argue that a modern civilized society should not execute criminals, no matter the crime. Other theoretical points of contention are outlined above. Complicating the debate, however, are those arguments focusing on the practicalities of the administration of the death penalty.

Should capital punishment be abolished if, even assuming that it is theoretically desirable, it is not fairly administered? For example, what if for every

100 convicts executed, one were actually innocent? What if the ratio were ten to one? The Liebman study, released in 2000, surveyed capital punishment cases from 1973 to 1995 and made a number of findings. First, it found that in almost seven out of ten capital sentence cases reviewed during the period, reviewing courts found serious, reversible error. Second, of the defendants whose cases contained such error, 82 percent were subsequently found to deserve a sentence less than death, and 7 percent were found to be innocent of the capital crime. These statistics represent the errors that were eventually caught in the multi-layered review process. A serious concern, of course, is that if so many errors find their way deep into that process, some may get through it altogether. Also, the existence of such a high error rate necessitates the extensive review process employed for capital sentencing cases, which is incredibly expensive.

Wrongful convictions aside, one of the most contentious issues in law today involves the effects of race upon capital sentencing. The now-famous Baldus study, which examined over 2000 murder cases in Georgia in the 1970s, revealed that of all the factors that might influence a jury's capital sentencing decision, the race of the victim was the most powerful predictor of a death sentence. Baldus found that defendants convicted of murdering white victims were 11 times more likely to be sentenced to death than those convicted of murdering black victims. After attempting to control for possible nonracial variables in the statistics, the study concluded that a defendant who killed a white person was 4.3 times more likely to be condemned to death based upon the victim's race alone. Baldus also found a smaller race-of-defendant effect. Faced with this data, the Supreme Court, in McCleskey v. Kemp, 481 U.S. 279, 107 S. Ct. 1756 (1987), nevertheless held that without a specific showing of purposeful improper racial bias in the case at bar, the sentence must stand. Despite the Court's rejection of the study as a demonstration of discrimination per se in homicide cases where the victim was white, the study raises serious questions about the fairness of jury-determined death sentences.

Because of the difficulties in fairly and practically administering capital punishment, it is not uncommon for individuals to agree with the death penalty in principle but decry the current system of administration as unjustifiable. The question then becomes whether there is any way to fix the system, or if the costs will always outweigh the benefits, assuming there are benefits, of having the death penalty as a sentencing option.

NOTES

1. Our emphasis on fines, imprisonment, and execution does not necessarily mean that such sanctions are the principal mechanisms of the penal instrument. That instrument relies heavily on presanction control devices, such as the deterrent effect of police patrols, the fear of conviction and its associated opprobrium, and the threat rather than the experience of punishment. Should

proponents of the death penalty rely on the argument that the threat of death, rather than its actual imposition, justifies the continued existence of such punishment? Some might say that this approach shies away from confronting the harder moral question of whether the state can ever justify killing as punishment? Think about whether retributivists and utilitarians would respond the same way to this question.

2. As this is written, 35 states and the federal government have death penalty statutes. Several death penalty states have not executed anyone for many years, however, and even in states which continue to perform executions, the number of death sentences imposed each year has fallen.

3. Among those who agree that the death penalty should remain an option, there is disagreement about whether it should be limited to murderers, or available to punish perpetrators of other serious crimes. In Kennedy v. Louisiana, 128 S. Ct. 2641 (2008), the Supreme Court held that the cruel and unusual punishment clause bars imposition of the death penalty for the crime of rape, or for other non-homicide crimes against the individual. The Court left open the question of whether the death penalty could be imposed for crimes against the state, such as treason or airplane hijacking. Both the Republican and Democratic 2008 candidates for President announced their disagreement with this decision.

Section Eight
SUMMARY

We began this chapter by considering the two primary justifications for punishment: retribution and utilitarianism. A retributivist assumes that individuals who commit crimes have chosen to do so, and therefore *deserve* punishment; a utilitarian wishes to maximize the cumulative happiness of society's members, and punishes only to the extent that punishment avoids greater harms, such as later crimes. We have seen that neither pure retributivism nor pure utilitarianism can explain our criminal justice system — or the intuitions about punishment that most of us hold.

By examining the affirmative defenses of necessity and insanity, we have considered the difference between justification and excuse and observed that even when courts agree that some affirmative defense is appropriate, they often disagree over the exact contours of the defense. We learned that even when there is agreement that conduct is morally wrong, and should be criminally sanctioned, it is, under our legal system, inappropriate for a court to broaden criminal liability to cover conduct that was not previously forbidden.

We then looked at the criminal process, considering the discretion exercised by police, prosecutors, juries, and judges. We considered the troublesome example of interrogation and looked at two quite different methods of regulating misconduct: rules prohibiting the use of coercive tactics, and rules requiring that suspects be informed of their rights to remain silent and consult with an attorney. Turning to the role of defense counsel, we learned of the debate about the proper balance between zealous advocacy on the part of a client and the duties incumbent on all officers of the court, then we considered what should happen when a client relies on erroneous advice from his or her lawyer, and we took a sobering look at the realities of attorney-client relationships in large cities.

Finally, we considered whether the penal law reaches too far when it attempts to enforce morals, or when it employs the ultimate sanction of capital punishment. With respect to the question of enforcing morals, we learned that much of criminal law has its origins in (and is supported by) morality, and yet, that moral condemnation and criminal prohibition must not be coextensive. With respect to capital punishment, we returned to the question of the justification of punishment, observing that retributivists are more likely to view the death penalty with favor than are utilitarians.

For an attempted synthesis of the substantive criminal law that is accessible to the lay reader, see George Fletcher, Rethinking Criminal Law (1978). For the fascinating story behind the Supreme Court's decision that indigent defendants are entitled to counsel, see Anthony Lewis, Gideon's Trumpet (1964). To examine the issue of wrongful convictions, see Barry Scheck, Peter Neufeld & Jim Dwyer, Actual Innocence: When Justice Goes Wrong and How to Make It Right (2003). For the stories behind the most celebrated capital punishment cases, see John H. Blume & Jordan M. Steiker, Death Penalty Stories (2009).

Chapter 3

LAW AS AN INSTRUMENT FOR

ADMINISTERING THE

REGULATORY STATE

The rise of administrative bodies probably has been the most significant legal trend of the last century and perhaps more values today are affected by their decisions than by those of all the courts....

JUSTICE ROBERT H. JACKSON

Section One
INTRODUCTION TO THE ADMINISTRATIVE INSTRUMENT

Materials Drawn Mainly from Federal Agency Law

The law achieves its purposes not only by remedying grievances (Chapter 1) and punishing bad behavior (Chapter 2), but in several additional ways as Chapters 3 through 5 demonstrate. This chapter addresses how *administrators* use law to *regulate* people's activities. Activities subject to regulation include the marketing of electricity and natural gas; the treatment of endangered species; radio and television broadcasting; commercial fishing; and processing and distribution of meat, poultry, and other foodstuffs. Regulated activities also include activities such as the purchase and sale of stocks and bonds by individuals; provision of medical services by doctors; construction of residences by local builders; and ownership and operation of motor vehicles by ordinary citizens.

Unlike the antisocial behavior with which the penal instrument deals, and unlike the wrongs targeted by the remedial instrument, the activities mentioned above are positively desirable. Why, then, does a legal system become concerned with such activities? Particularly, how can such activities generate legal needs that are best met neither through the use of law as a remedial instrument nor through the penal mode, but rather through administrative activity?

A. Reasons for Government Intervention

We need high-quality medical services, reliable transportation, and safe electricity. We want high-quality television programming and useful manufactured goods. The private activities that produce these and other goods and services are obviously very beneficial to society. But these activities may not be performed properly. An incompetent medical doctor might remove a person's pancreas instead of her appendix. An unqualified commercial airline pilot might cause an air disaster. A spinach farmer or distributor, without appropriate quality-control measures, might poison consumers. Overzealous lobstermen might harvest lobsters to the point of extinction. Improper or excessive waste discharge into air and water from manufacturing and transport activities might destroy parklands and injure health. Apart from incompetence or carelessness, conscious abuses are possible, too. A person might lose her entire savings after buying corporate stock from a fraudulent seller. An electricity retail distributor might abuse its monopoly position and charge exorbitant rates. An owner of a television station might pander to the public by showing indecent movies. Private activity can thus cause harm—avoidable harm.

The best result, of course, is the prevention of harm before it occurs. Can the affected citizen protect herself so that no legal intervention is required? Often the citizen cannot identify the risks in advance. For example, she cannot normally determine very well whether a surgeon is incompetent. She cannot normally determine whether food is contaminated or whether an airplane is safely constructed. Even when the affected citizen does know something is wrong, she may be unable to protect herself. For example, a consumer of electricity may understand that her retail supplier is charging exorbitant prices. A television viewer may have no recourse when stations jam frequencies to disrupt a competitor's programs. The affected citizen is often powerless to prevent such occurrences. There are several explanations:

MARKET FAILURE

The theory of market failure is one way of explaining why society cannot rely on the private consumer's exercise of self-help in the marketplace to obtain the degree of safety she wants in medical services, food, and airliners or to buy electricity at an unregulated price. A perfectly competitive economy with no market failures would theoretically produce the optimal amount of goods and services with the inherent risk characteristics desired by consumers. But under market failure conditions, this ideal is not reached, and government intervention is justified to correct the failure. What follows are some examples of market failures arguably justifying governmental regulation.

INADEQUATE INFORMATION

A commonly cited example of market failure is the problem of inadequate information. Businesses sometimes supply inadequate or misleading information to consumers. Sometimes the subject matter of a sale or service is so complex that consumers would need an expert's opinion for proper evaluation. But that information may be too costly for any one consumer, and consumers as a group may be unwilling to pay the cost of an expert to police misinformation or to evaluate complex products and services. Group inaction follows in part because consumers are unaware of the importance of further information (they lack the information needed to evaluate their need for further information) and in part because of what economists call the free-rider problem (each consumer is unwilling to pay for an expert opinion that will be freely available once others have paid for the opinion). To correct inadequate information, the government intervenes to supply the information, either directly or indirectly. It may do so directly, for example, by labeling food (the Agriculture Department's food labeling program) or by requiring producers to supply information (the Securities and Exchange Commission's financial reporting requirements). Or it may do so indirectly through rules against misinformation (the Federal Trade Commission's regulation of deceptive advertising), by licensing pilots and inspecting airplanes (Federal Aviation Administration), and by testing food additives and drugs (Food and Drug Administration).

NATURAL MONOPOLY

Another example of market failure is the existence of a natural monopoly, such as the retail distribution of gas and electricity. According to economic theory, perfect competition assures that suppliers will produce the quantity of a good at which the incremental cost of producing the last unit equals the price consumers are willing to pay for it. Under monopoly conditions, however, producers restrict output, raise the price, and earn supernormal profits. The antitrust laws attempt to preserve competition in markets generally, but in some industries monopoly conditions are natural. For example, it would be foolishly wasteful for several companies, each operating its own pipe or power lines, to compete with one another in supplying gas and electricity to the individual household. So, to prevent the single retail supplier from charging monopoly prices, the government intervenes to regulate the price that the supplier can charge.

COMMON POOL

The common-pool, or scarcity, problem arises when a resource, such as whales or fish, is available in limited supply and no individual harvester has an incentive to restrict harvesting to allow sufficient natural reproduction. Each harvester knows that individual conservation efforts would simply give some other harvester a larger harvest. Thus, whales and fish could be harvested to extinction if the government did not intervene to restrict the size of the catch through game or fishing commissions.

EXTERNAL COSTS

The problem of air or water pollution is a good example of external costs, or spillover effects. The manufacturer who burns sulfur-laden fuel contributes to the damage suffered in distant park and recreation areas through the effects of acid rain, formed from the sulfur dioxide particles spewed into the air and combining with natural rain. Manufacturing plants may also discharge chemical and other toxic wastes into local rivers and lakes, causing health hazards to humans, fish, and birds. The cost of this damage is generally not borne by the many manufacturers who cause it. Hence, manufacturers have no market incentive to limit the damage, because they would gain nothing from incurring costly changes in production processes to reduce toxic discharges. Government regulation deals with these problems by setting air and water quality standards, such as the rules promulgated by the Environmental Protection Agency.

B. Reasons for Resort to the Administrative Instrument

The theory of market failure helps explain the need for government intervention, but not the form that intervention should take. If the situation calls for legal intervention, why is the remedial or penal instrument insufficient? The following excerpt offers insights into some of the factors that explain the need for the administrative instrument.

ATTORNEY GENERAL'S COMMITTEE ON ADMINISTRATIVE PROCEDURE, ADMINISTRATIVE PROCEDURE IN GOVERNMENT AGENCIES
S. Doc. No. 8, 77th Cong., 1st Sess. 13–14 (1941)

If administrative agencies did not exist in the Federal Government, Congress would be limited to a technique of legislation primarily designed to correct evils after they have arisen rather than to prevent them from arising. The criminal law, of course, operates in this after-the-event fashion. Congress declares a given act to be a crime. The mere declaration may act as a deterrent. But if it fails to do so the courts can only punish the wrongdoer; they cannot wipe out or make good the wrong. Traditional noncriminal, private law operates for the most part in the same after-the-event fashion. A statute or the common law gives one individual a right to go into court and sue another. This procedure is likely to be expensive. It is uncertain. At best, in the ordinary action for money damages, it leads only to compensation for the injury, which is seldom as satisfactory as not having been injured at all. To be sure, courts of equity administer a substantial measure of preventive justice by giving injunctions against

threatened injuries. But it is necessary to prove the threat, and other limitations confine the scope of this mode of relief. The desire to work out a more effective and more flexible method of preventing unwanted things from happening accounts for the formation of many (although by no means all) Federal administrative agencies.

The rate-making powers of the Interstate Commerce Commission afford an apt illustration. The common law, from time immemorial, recognized a right of action against a common carrier on account of an unreasonable rate. The shipper or the passenger could pay the charge and then sue to recover the unreasonable excess. Preference for a mechanism whereby reasonable rates could be established in advance was a principal factor leading to the Commission's establishment. A more recent example is the Securities and Exchange Commission. Within rather severe limits, the common law recognized a right in a purchaser of securities to recover damages from the seller resulting from false statements made in effecting the sale. The importance of truth in securities led to a demand that honest statements, as well as fuller and more informative statements, be assured so far as possible in advance. If this end were to be accomplished, it could only be done by creating an administrative agency. A similar purpose, effected in a great variety of ways, underlies the formation of many other agencies. Thus, licensing is one of the most significant of all preventive agencies. It would be possible to permit anyone to act as the pilot of a ship or a plane and then to punish those whose incompetence led to accidents or to prohibit them from acting as pilots again. People have preferred, however, to attempt by a licensing method to assure competence in advance; and administrative agencies have had to be created to carry out the licensing system.

NOTES

1. The excerpt above explains that the administrative instrument normally achieves its purposes by enacting general prescriptive rules (rules that regulate conduct) in advance of anticipated harm, instead of waiting for a problem to develop as in after-the-fact adjudication of disputes between particular individuals. We return to this theme in Section Two.

2. Consider the problem of controlling air pollution. Assume that a manufacturer burns sulfur-laden fuel that produces acid rain causing $10 in property damage to each of 100 people in a tri-state area. Assume that the added cost to the manufacturer of burning sulfur-free fuel, which would eliminate the acid rain, is $500. Assume that the cost of a lawsuit against the manufacturer, seeking either damages or an injunction, is $300.

(a) Why would society want the manufacturer to switch to sulfur-free coal? Social welfare would improve because the manufacturer would have to spend only $500 to eliminate $1000 in acid rain damage.

(b) Would the remedial instruments effectively produce the socially desirable outcome? No, because no individual has a sufficient stake to justify the $300 cost of litigation, and each would wait for someone else to bring a suit in order to gain the benefit without paying for it.

(c) Is use of the administrative instrument a better solution? This is a chapter about this instrument, so the answer may be obvious. An expert agency could study the problem of air pollution and set appropriate air quality standards, including the percentage of sulfur that is permissible. The agency could adjust the standards as technology and other circumstances change. The public, who receive the benefits of the regulation, would pay for the costs of the agency action in the form of taxes.

3. Consider the problem of natural monopoly in the retail distribution of gas and electricity. The social goal is to prevent monopoly prices. Without regulation, the monopolist can charge exorbitant prices. Individuals would not sue, even if there were a basis for the suit, again because of the free-rider problem. If the monopoly is natural, meaning there are no objectionable practices by the monopolist that could be prohibited by federal antitrust laws, society

needs public utility commissions with expertise to evaluate utilities' costs and return on capital and to set reasonable rates.

4. Assume that Maine lobsters have become a more popular food and demand is growing. But the supply is limited and lobsters reproduce slowly. In fact, the danger is very real of overexploitation by lobstermen leading to extinction of the Maine lobster.

(a) Would the remedial or penal instrument effectively deal with this problem? No, again. The remedial instrument would be ineffective because no one owns the lobsters, and therefore no one could bring a suit. Similarly, without ownership rights to enforce, defining criminal conduct would be difficult. Criminalizing the harvesting of lobsters beyond some optimal amount would be problematic because of the difficulty of defining that amount and of policing the amount of harvesting.

(b) What features of the administrative instrument make it especially appropriate for this task? An agency, with specialized knowledge of the lobstering industry, could license lobster harvesters. The agency could control harvesting by limiting the number of licenses and the length of the harvesting season.

(c) Beef is also in high demand as a table food and commands a high price in the market. Why is there not a similar threat of overexploitation of cattle? Cattle ranchers own the cattle and have a strong self-interest in not over-exploiting them. Also, because of the law's recognition of ownership rights, theft of cattle can be punished criminally.

Los Angeles Times photo by Rick Loomis, © *2006. Reprinted with Permission.*

C. A Recurring Illustration: The Endangered Species Act

To protect and conserve endangered species, Congress passed the Endangered Species Act (ESA), 16 U.S.C. §§1531–1544 (enacted Dec. 28, 1973). The Act "provide[s] a means whereby the ecosystems upon which endangered species and threatened species depend may be conserved." Such conservation benefits society, according to the Act, because of the "esthetic, ecological, educational, historical, recreational, and scientific value" of endangered species. The legislative history elaborates:

> It has become increasingly apparent that some sort of protective measures must be taken to prevent the further extinction of many of the world's animal species.... [T]he rate of extinction has increased to where on the average, one species disappears per year. Consideration of this need to protect endangered species goes beyond the aesthetic. In hearings before the Subcommittee on the Environment it was shown that many of these animals perform vital biological services to maintain a 'balance of nature' within their environments. Also revealed was the need for biological diversity for scientific purposes. The two major causes of extinction are hunting and destruction of natural habitat.

S. Rep. 93-307, at 1–2 (1973).

The effects of employing the ESA can be rather dramatic. For example, in a landmark case, the U.S. Supreme Court enjoined the use of a huge dam on the Tennessee River, after Congress had expended over $100 million on its construction, because its use threatened the extinction of a small fish, the snail darter. The Court stated:

> It may seem curious to some that the survival of a relatively small number of three-inch fish, among all the countless millions of species extant would require the permanent halting of a virtually completed dam for which Congress has expended more than $100 million.... We conclude, however, that the explicit provisions of the Endangered Species Act require precisely that result.

Tennessee Valley Authority v. Hill, 437 U.S. 153, 172, 98 S. Ct. 2279, 2290 (1978).

We shall utilize the ESA as a recurring (although not the sole) example in this chapter of the administrative instrument at work. In the meantime, begin to think about the following question: are the remedial and penal instruments capable of dealing effectively with the problem of endangered species?

In considering this and other questions, Chapter 3, as the other chapters in Part One do, includes the following sections:

- Section Two, Administrative Methods, introduces the various methods used by agencies to achieve their purposes.
- Section Three, Making Administrative Law, studies the roles of legislatures, courts, and agencies in making administrative law.
- Section Four, Applying Administrative Law, sets forth examples of rules for applying and enforcing administrative law.

- Section Five, Roles of Private Citizens and Their Lawyers, focuses on private citizens' resort to courts to secure appropriate regulatory action.
- Section Six, Improving the Administrative Instrument, identifies and discusses methods for improving access to and participation in agency action.
- Section Seven, Limitations of Law as an Administrative Instrument, focuses on the limitations of administrative regulation in achieving its goals, such as the inevitability of conflicting purposes and policies.

Section Two
ADMINISTRATIVE METHODS

You should already see that a primary function of the administrative instrument is to prescribe standards with the goal of warding off harm. But the administrative instrument has other functions and utilizes many additional methods to achieve its purposes. This section accounts for many of these methods.

Agencies receive their various powers described in this section from the legislature through laws that create the agencies and enumerate their functions and powers. In the rest of this chapter, we will have a lot more to say about this division of labor and, for that matter, about many of the following enumerated methods.

A. Setting Substantive Regulatory Standards

Agencies often action as quasi-legislatures, establishing regulatory standards through administrative rulemaking. They also establish rules through administrative adjudication, which consists of judicial-like proceedings before an administrative law judge, but the former has dramatically grown in importance. Perhaps the most important reason for the growth of rulemaking is the host of laws promulgated by Congress that protect the public, both businesses and individuals, but that defer to agencies the responsibility of creating substantive standards. We shall see samples of such statutes and the resulting agency rules in this chapter.

Another reason for the growth of rulemaking is that it may produce clearer and more encompassing rules than adjudication. As with legislation, agencies engaged in rulemaking can examine a wider set of related issues and investigate the circumstances more fully than an agency engaged in a singe-issue adjudication.

B. Licensing

The power to require licenses is a classic regulatory device. Through licensing, the law can achieve many regulatory purposes. For example, licensing can limit entrance into a field in the interest of efficiency. As already suggested, allowing several electricity suppliers to string lines side by side and to serve customers in the same area would be wasteful and inefficient. In addition, licensing can restrict entry because of scarcity of resources, as the lobstering example pointed out. Licensing also can set and enforce basic qualifying standards. Doctors and lawyers, for example, must first demonstrate some capability before they can qualify for licenses to practice.

Licensing is not the same as prohibiting conduct, of course. The law prohibits murder and theft. These are not beneficial practices. Licensing is concerned with essentially beneficial activities that need to be regulated for society's benefit. Nevertheless, there is a connection between licensing and prohibition of conduct, mainly that a license allows conduct that would otherwise be prohibited. The various elements of licensing laws include:

- a description of when a license is necessary,
- requirements for a license,
- duties of a licensee,
- identification of and enumeration of the powers of the regulating agency, and
- a description of the grounds for revoking licenses and for other penalties.

George A. Warp, Licensing as a Device for Federal Regulation, 16 Tul. L. Rev. 111, 111–12 (1941).

C. Investigating

Whether or not an agency utilizes licensing, the administrative officials charged with regulating particular conduct need basic investigatory powers to determine whether people are complying with the regulations. The typical regulatory program therefore usually grants broad investigatory powers to the relevant officials. Investigation may be continuous or occasional. Officials may inspect food supplies continuously, but investigate buildings to determine compliance with building codes only occasionally. Either form of investigative activity serves not only to identify actual noncompliance but also to exert steady pressure for self-regulation. In addition, such investigations also provide information and data upon which the agency can make recommendations for changes in governing regulatory standards and requirements.

If a regulated party disputes facts found by an agency, the law may empower the administrator to make definitive findings of fact. If the findings are significant, the law usually calls for an administrative hearing to allow the party to contest the facts.

Even if a regulated party agrees with an agency's finding of facts, the party may disagree on whether the facts demonstrate a failure of compliance with governing regulatory law. A party may, for example, concede that processed meat contains certain ingredients that have certain effects but deny that the ingredients and effects make the meat "injurious to health." Again, when the agency's conclusions are significant, the law commonly affords the party subject to regulation an opportunity for an administrative hearing at which the party can present arguments on the meaning of the law as applied to the case.

Agencies also frequently impose specific duties of disclosure and reporting on the parties subject to regulation. Self-reporting obviously reduces the need for agency investigation. Reports on income realized by regulated electric utilities, for example, may alone offer a substantial basis for administrative action. If regulated people or entities balk at providing necessary information, administrators often have the power to compel disclosure. Many statutes delegate such power to administrators, but the laws often require that the agency exercise the power only with judicial approval.

D. Publicizing

The threat or use of adverse publicity motivates actors to comply with regulations. Publicity can come from press releases, newspaper articles, news conferences, and other media coverage of such things as failure to comply with a regulation, the initiation of a proceeding against a party, or the outcome of a case against the party. Such negative publicity is an important regulatory method. Think about the effect of a press release indicating that a food product may be contaminated. Not only does the press release warn consumers of hazards, but it also creates incentives in food manufacturers to produce safe products. Indeed, adverse publicity may play a much larger role in creating these incentives and in settlement of disputes without hearings than fines or other sanctions.

Needless to say, agencies can misuse the adverse-publicity strategy, such as by using adverse publicity to achieve goals beyond an agency's authorized powers or by disseminating information that turns out to be inaccurate or inflammatory.

E. Resorting to Informal Proceedings to Secure Compliance

In addition to adverse publicity, agencies use other informal methods to achieve compliance. For example, an agency can threaten a party with agency prosecution, issue informal advisory opinions and declarations of policy, and negotiate compromises. Agencies also can initiate proceedings with a formal complaint, but then seek an informal disposition without a hearing. Informal settlements have a lot in common with nonjudicial settlements of disputes under remedial law and even with plea bargaining in criminal law.

When informal methods are successful, they frequently result in a signed settlement agreement or a consent decree. In either, the party subject to regulation agrees to comply as required by the administrators and may even agree to stated penalties. But unlike other types of settlements, a consent decree is usually published and serves as a legal precedent. A regulated industry usually pays close attention to any such decree, using it to learn how the agency applies its standards and regulations to particular cases.

F. Resorting to Full-Scale Proceedings with Sanctions

Here is only one example of formal administrative adjudication: Recall the Endangered Species Act. Suppose a rancher shoots and kills a grizzly bear, which is an endangered animal, that he claims was threatening his flock of sheep. The Fish and Wildlife Service (FWS) serves the rancher with a Notice of Violation that charges the rancher with a "taking" in violation of the Act and proposes a civil penalty of $7000. (A "taking" includes hunting, shooting, or killing an endangered species.) The rancher files a petition seeking relief from the assessment and asserts a defense based on protecting his livestock. The FWS declines to accept the defense. Then, an administrative law judge determines that the defense is inadequate after a formal evidentiary hearing.

Is a hearing always required? The law rarely authorizes direct agency action against a party without a hearing, unless expedited action is crucial, such as the need to seize adulterated food. Agencies instead proceed through formal administrative proceedings, with sanctions as the end result of a finding adverse to a party.

Sanctions are just as necessary in administrative proceedings as in remedial and penal ones. Further, the threat of sanctions radically reduces the necessity for their use in each of these three instruments of the law. But there are important differences when sanctions result after an administrative proceeding. For example, moral blameworthiness is often not a factor in determining administrative sanctions:

> [I]t seems that the device of punishment for the violation of administrative duties is distinguishable from the type of ordinary crime. In the first place, this "administrative crime" is not the outbirth of a particular unmoral conduct, but is characterized by disobedience to administrative duties. In the second place, the function of this "administrative crime" is deterrence rather than retribution. The mere existence of the penal sanction should make the individual comply with his administrative duties.

Edmund H. Schwenk, The Administrative Crime, Its Creation and Punishment by Administrative Agencies, 42 Mich. L. Rev. 51, 85 (1943). Applying sanctions when a party is not morally blameworthy is sometimes controversial. If a party, acting reasonably, has no knowledge that the milk she is selling is adulterated and also was not negligent in allowing the milk to become adulterated, for example, on what grounds can sanctions be applied? At first blush, deterrence does not seem an applicable justification. However, if the seller is subject to strict liability,

"It's made from an endangered species for that one person
in a thousand who couldn't care less."

she will incur all reasonable costs to detect adulterated milk (so long as the costs are not greater than the gains from avoiding penalties). If blameworthiness were a factor, the milk seller would have little incentive to take such precautions as inspection to prevent unknowing sales of adulterated milk.

G. Encouraging Self-Regulation in Light of Published Standards

Devices from negative publicity and imposed sanctions create incentives for people to self-regulate, but self-regulation comes about for other reasons as well. For example, administrators may seek full participation of the targeted industry in formulating the governing regulations, which may lead to more enthusiasm for the resulting regulations. Agencies also disseminate relevant information on a regular basis, offer positive inducements to cooperation, and allow opportunities for voluntary compliance after a departure from a standard. These techniques encourage healthy attitudes toward self-regulation.

Here are some examples of how the Fish and Wildlife Service (FWS) recently encouraged self-regulation, according to Office of Law Enforcement, FWS, 2005 Annual Report 25-26 (2006):

- The Office of Law Enforcement worked with electric power companies to develop and publish a program for the protection of birds.
- The agency worked with the National Wind Coordinating Committee to address bird mortality arising from wind-power generators.
- The agency worked with eBay to develop better strategies for identifying and removing listings for the sale of endangered species.
- The agency created enforcement exhibits to educate the public about wildlife laws and regulations.

Self-regulation is often crucial to the success of agency policies. The relevant administrative agency may simply not have sufficient resources to police regulated conduct. For just one example, no agency could effectively keep an eye on all endangered species. The success of the ESA therefore depends on self-compliance.

H. Resorting to Courts for Appropriate Enforcement

The law might allow administrative bodies to enforce their own orders. But this has not been the general pattern in Anglo-American law. Rather, the agencies must resort to courts to enforce their orders, including license revocations and fines.

When an agency prosecutes a violation of its order in a court the proceedings resemble those of the penal instrument considered in Chapter 2. In addition, an agency may apply for a judicial order requiring a party to abide by a regulation or other agency action, utilizing the remedial procedures considered in Chapter 1.

Division of Labor

The regulatory techniques of administrative agencies catalogued above are analogous to the techniques used by the legislative (setting standards), executive (investigating and prosecuting), and judicial (adjudicating violations) branches of government. Critics worry that delegating responsibility to a single agency for all of these functions—lawmaker, police officer and prosecutor, and judge and jury—is improper, unfair, or even unconstitutional. After all, our Constitution is built around the idea of separation of powers to ensure adequate checks and balances in lawmaking and its application.

Concerns are somewhat ameliorated by an agency's division of labor. Different members of an agency typically perform each function, and sometimes they have little or no contact.

For example, an administrative judge that adjudicates a violation should have no contact with agency personnel that bring the case. In fact, the Administrative Procedure Act §554(d) specifically states that employees engaged in investigating or prosecuting a case cannot participate in a decision of an administrative judge (except as a witness or counsel).

Such an approach is not without its costs, of course. The agency's investigating or prosecuting employee may have greater expertise in the matter at hand than the decisionmaker. Sharing such knowledge might lead to a more just decision.

See Ernest Gellhorn & Ronald M. Levin, Administrative Law and Process 8-11, 281-82 (5th ed. 2006).

A party that violates the court order may be held in contempt of court and fined or imprisoned. As once noted with respect to licensing cases, "The machinery sometimes runs: statute, regulation, grant of license, [administrative] adjudication of violation, revocation of license, operation without license, [court] injunction, violation of injunction, [court] adjudication of contempt, imprisonment, purgation." Louis L. Jaffe & Nathaniel L. Nathanson, Administrative Law 18 (3d ed. 1968).

Section Three
MAKING ADMINISTRATIVE LAW

This section is mainly concerned with how agencies create substantive regulatory standards—the rules that govern people's activities. For example, the Consumer Product Safety Commission promulgates rules that govern the design and manufacture of consumer products. The section also examines the legislation that allocates authority to agencies to make the regulatory standards and that specifies the procedures agencies must follow for making it. First, we consider why legislatures delegate lawmaking and law applying power to agencies and whether such delegations are proper. Next, we study in more detail the adjudicating and rulemaking roles of agencies. Finally, we turn to the role of courts in reviewing agency action.

A. The Legislature's Role: Delegation of Power to Administrative Agencies

Potentially, the principal regulatory lawmakers are legislatures, administrative agencies, and courts. In practice, legislatures create the regulatory program but rarely articulate the relevant regulatory standards. Instead, the legislature delegates vast lawmaking power to the agency: "[T]he primary system...in this country...is that of broad delegation with little or no further legislative consideration unless there is a grave abuse of the delegated power." Walter F. Dodd, Administrative Agencies as Legislators and Judges, 25 A.B.A. J. 923, 925 (1939). But why this development? And what, generally speaking, are the appropriate collaborative roles of legislative and administrative bodies in making regulatory law?

The short answer to the first question is that legislative delegation is a matter of necessity. In a large industrial country, the legislature has neither the time nor the expertise to draft effective regulations for the myriad novel, complex, and technical activities impacted by market failures. Legislators thus are generalists who delegate to specialists the task of regulating particular activity. For just one example, consider the U.S. Supreme Court's discussion of Congress's broad delegation of administrative and interpretive power under the ESA: "The task of defining and listing endangered and threatened species requires an expertise and attention to detail that exceeds the normal province of Congress." Babbitt v. Sweet Home Chapter of Communities for a Great Oregon, 515 U.S. 687, 708, 115 S. Ct. 2407, 2418 (1995). The following excerpt elaborates on justifications for legislative delegation.

REGINALD PARKER, WHY DO ADMINISTRATIVE AGENCIES EXIST?
45 Geo. L.J. 331, 361–62 (1957)

"Government by Decree" is an indisputable necessity in the 20th century in a country of 170 million. If we were of the size of the Principality of Liechtenstein, most laws could be enacted by the people themselves and even regulations could be made, if not by the people, then by their elected representatives. This not being the case, we must have a division of legislative labor.

In other words, there are legislative tasks of an enormous variety that are too complex for Congress to perform. Today it is not doubted

any longer that to "write a self-executing law prohibiting the issuance of sub-standard utility securities would not only be ineffectual—it would be likely also to paralyze utility financing and cause endless private controversy over whether a proposed security conformed to statutory standards or not."[131] The same can be said of railroad safety standards, the regulation of which must be left to flexible expert agencies, or of pure food and drug standards, or of the hundreds of other fields with which the average member of Congress is but

---

131. Blair-Smith, Forms of Administrative Interpretation Under the Securities Laws, 26 Iowa L. Rev. 241, 268 (1941).

vaguely acquainted. If the legal development had been different, if the courts had insisted that delegated lawmaking is unconstitutional, the end of our legislative branch as we know it would have occurred long ago. Congress would have bogged down under a mass of legislative tasks, which of necessity would have been assigned to committees, with Congress itself a mere rubber-stamp. The committee staffs would have been just as large as the present administrative agencies, while their products, under the shield of congressional laws, would have been more remote from the control of the people and public opinion than the output of agencies are now....

Against these considerations—that some general "laws" must be made by agencies rather than Congress—no valid argument has been raised. Some critics say that administrative regulations are subject to too many changes or are enacted without prior hearing of interested parties. This does not go to the heart of the matter. Rather, it touches upon the advisability of adjusting rulemaking procedure in order to impose procedural safeguards in favor of those affected by regulation.

So far we have considered the reasons for legislative delegation from a practical perspective. But there is another important issue. The Constitution in Article I, Section 1 provides: "All legislative Powers herein granted shall be vested in a Congress of the United States...." The Supreme Court explained the basics of separation of powers in Tennessee Valley Authority v. Hill, 437 U.S. 153, 194, 98 S. Ct. 2279, 2301–02 (1978):

> Our system of government is...a tripartite one, with each branch having certain defined functions delegated to it by the Constitution. While "[i]t is emphatically the province and duty of the judicial department to say what the law is," Marbury v. Madison, 2 L. Ed. 60 (1803), it is equally—and emphatically—the exclusive province of the Congress not only to formulate legislative policies and mandate programs and projects, but also to establish their relative priority for the Nation. Once Congress, exercising its delegated powers, has decided the order of priorities in a given area, it is for the Executive to administer the laws and for the courts to enforce them when enforcement is sought.

Analysts express concern with broad delegation because agencies seemingly exercise "legislative powers" and thus collide with the constitutional principal of separation of powers. The Supreme Court struck down a broad congressional delegation of power to trade associations to create codes of fair competition in the famous case of A.L.A. Schechter Poultry Corp. v. United States, 295 U.S. 495, 55 S. Ct. 837 (1935). The delegating statute contained virtually no standards or policy guidelines; it said to the trade associations in effect, "here is the problem—you deal with it." Since that time, however, the Court has consistently upheld broad delegations of regulatory authority and has not struck down any other grant of congressional power to an administrative agency. Should the "nondelegation" doctrine be revived? Consider the following view.

A Closer Look at Delegation to the Federal Trade Commission

The Federal Trade Commission Act of 1914 empowered the Federal Trade Commission (FTC) broadly to bar unfair methods of competition. In addition, the FTC protects consumers from unfair practices by prescribing monetary remedies, promulgates rules specifying particular unfair or deceptive practices, conducts investigations, and issues reports and recommendations to Congress.

The first section of the Act, which appears as 15 U.S.C. §41, establishes the Commission and provides in part: "A commission is created and established, to be known as the Federal Trade Commission...which shall be composed of five Commissioners, who shall be appointed by the President, by and with the advice and consent of the Senate." Section 45(a) then authorizes the Commission to prevent unfair methods of competition:

> (1) Unfair methods of competition in or affecting commerce, and unfair or deceptive acts or practices in or affecting commerce, are hereby declared unlawful.

> (2) The Commission is hereby empowered and directed to prevent persons, partnerships or corporations...from using unfair methods of competition in or affecting commerce and unfair or deceptive acts or practices in or affecting commerce.

Congress essentially had three choices in establishing the Federal Trade Commission. It could have enacted (a) a detailed statute setting down regulatory standards (principles and rules) to be administered by the ordinary courts; (b) a statute with considerable policy detail and rule specificity, to be administered by an agency (thus delegating regulatory power—for example, a licensing function—to the agency, but not legislative power); or (c) a broad and general statute with few guidelines, to be administered by an agency (thus delegating legislative as well as regulatory power to the agency). Congress chose option (c) largely for the reasons enumerated by Professor Parker above.

RICHARD B. STEWART, THE REFORMATION OF AMERICAN ADMINISTRATIVE LAW
88 Harv. L. Rev. 1669, 1695–97 (1975)

[A]ny large-scale enforcement of the nondelegation doctrine would clearly be unwise. Detailed legislative specification of policies under contemporary conditions would be neither feasible nor desirable in many cases, and the judges are ill-equipped to distinguish contrary cases.

In many government endeavors it may be impossible in the nature of the subject matter to specify with particularity the course to be followed. This is most obvious when a new field of regulation is undertaken. Administration is an exercise in experiment. If the subject is politically and economically volatile—such as wage and price regulation—constant changes in the basic parameters of the problem may preclude the development of a detailed policy that can consistently be pursued for any length of time. These limitations are likely to be encountered with increasing frequency as the federal government assumes greater responsibility for managing the economy.

In addition, there appear to be serious institutional constraints on Congress' ability to specify regulatory policy in meaningful detail. Legislative majorities typically represent coalitions of interests that must not only compromise among themselves but also with opponents. Individual politicians often find far more to be lost than gained in taking a readily identifiable stand on a controversial issue of social or economic policy. Detailed legislative specification of policy would require intensive and continuous investigation, decision, and revision of specialized and complex issues. Such a task would require resources that Congress has, in most instances, been unable to muster. An across-the-board effort to legislate in detail would also require a degree of decentralized responsibility that might further erode an already weak political accountability for congressional decisions. These circumstances tend powerfully to promote broad delegations of authority to administrative agencies. . . .

Finally, there are serious problems in relying upon the judiciary to enforce the nondelegation doctrine. A court may not properly insist on a greater legislative specification of policy than the subject matter admits of. But how is the judge to decide the degree of policy specification that is possible, for example, in wage and price regulation when it is initially undertaken? How does he decide when knowledge has accumulated to the point where additional legislative specification of policy is now possible? . . . Such judgments are necessarily quite subjective, and a doctrine that made them determinative of an administrative program's legitimacy could cripple the program by exposing it to continuing threats of invalidation and encouraging the utmost recalcitrance by those opposed to its effectuation. Given such subjective standards, and the controversial character of decisions on whether to invalidate legislative delegations, such decisions will almost inevitably appear partisan, and might often be so.

NOTES

1. Professor John Hart Ely, a proponent of reviving the nondelegation doctrine, found unconvincing Professor Stewart's argument that "[i]ndividual politicians often find far more to be lost than gained in taking a readily identifiable stand on a controversial issue of social or economic policy." He has written:

> It's an argument, all right, but for which side? That legislators often find it convenient to escape accountability is precisely the reason *for* a nondelegation doctrine. Were it to turn out that legislators forced to govern wouldn't have the courage to do so energetically, that would be too bad . . . but at least it would be our system. . . . As Judge Wright put it in 1972: "An argument for letting the experts decide when the people's representatives are uncertain or cannot agree is an argument for paternalism and against democracy."

John Hart Ely, Democracy and Distrust: A Theory of Judicial Review 133–34 (1980).

2. Some analysts believe that Congress can always enact legislation altering any features of agency-developed regulatory law with which it disagrees. A legislative body can also monitor a regulatory program without continuously reentering the arena by way of actual legislation. The legislature can hold hearings in which it "invites" administrators to defend their policies. It can propose legislation without actually enacting it and thereby induce agency action. It can reduce or increase appropriations of funds to the regulatory body. In these and

other similar ways the legislature retains its lawmaking functions, thereby diminishing the concern about delegation.

B. The Agency's Role: Rulemaking and Adjudication

Agencies regulate in large part through rulemaking and adjudication. Rulemaking consists roughly of creating general directions to people about matters that can arise in the future. Rulemaking is similar to the promulgation of laws by a legislature. Adjudication instead focuses on particular parties and resembles judicial proceedings. We now look briefly at each in turn.

RULEMAKING

Agencies increasingly rely on this mode of regulation. Agencies receive their power to promulgate rules from the legislature. The Administrative Procedure Act (APA) generally empowers agencies to create rules, as do specific regulatory statutes that focus on the powers of particular agencies. The APA provides for "notice and comment" informal procedures of rulemaking, as well as for "formal" rulemaking procedures.

Notice-and-comment rulemaking, prescribed in §553(b), set forth below, requires the agency to publish a notice in the Federal Register, giving "an opportunity [for citizens] to participate in the rulemaking through submission of written data, views, or arguments," and to include in the adopted rule an explanation of its "basis and purpose." APA §553(c). Subsection 553(b)(A) and (B) exempts from these requirements "interpretive rules," which simply state an agency's view of existing policy; "general statements of policy," which announce intentions for the future; procedural rules; and instances in which notice and comment are "impracticable, unnecessary, or contrary to the public interest." An example of the latter would be when delay in promulgating the rule would defeat its purpose.

If a delegating statute requires a formal hearing, APA §§556 & 557 apply. These sections require a formal hearing, a record of all evidence submitted, and findings and conclusions based upon and supported by the record. All information and facts that form the basis of the decision are formally introduced before a presiding agency official and are made a part of the "record" of the proceeding. Section 556(e) defines the record as follows: "The transcript of testimony and exhibits, together with all papers and requests filed in the proceeding, constitutes the exclusive record for decision." The decision must then be made "on the record" and must be supported by it. Section 557(c) helps ensure that an agency makes a reasoned decision based on the record. It requires a particular ruling on each "finding, conclusion, or exception presented." Further, it requires that the rulings include reasons for the findings and conclusions.

You can see that administrative lawmaking is very different from the lawmaking you encountered in Chapters 1 and 2. In the Swimming Pool case in

Chapter 1, the only party entitled to notice and an opportunity to participate was the defendant swimming-pool owner. The penal instrument also provides for limited participation in trials. But APA §553 requires general notice and an opportunity to participate. Further, the notice must be detailed and informative. For greater detail on rulemaking, see Ernest Gellhorn & Ronald M. Levin, Administrative Law and Process 306-52 (5th ed. 2006).

United States Code, Title 5

§553. Rulemaking.

. . . .

(b) General notice of proposed rulemaking shall be published in the Federal Register, unless persons subject thereto are named and either personally served or otherwise have actual notice thereof in accordance with law. The notice shall include—

(1) a statement of the time, place, and nature of public rulemaking proceedings;

(2) reference to the legal authority under which the rule is proposed; and

(3) either the terms or substance of the proposed rule or a description of the subjects and issues involved.

Except when notice or hearing is required by statute, this subsection does not apply—

(A) to interpretative rules, general statements of policy, or rules of agency organization, procedure, or practice; or

(B) when the agency for good cause finds (and incorporates the finding and a brief statement of reasons therefor in the rules issued) that notice and public procedure thereon are impracticable, unnecessary, or contrary to the public interest.

As already noted, Congress may grant power to a particular agency to engage in rulemaking. The following is an example from the Federal Trade Commission Act, 15 U.S.C. §57a ("Unfair or deceptive acts or practices rulemaking proceedings"):

(a) Authority of Commission to prescribe rules and general statements of policy

(1) . . . [T]he Commission may prescribe—

(A) interpretive rules and general statements of policy with respect to unfair or deceptive acts or practices in or affecting commerce . . . , and

(B) rules which define with specificity acts or practices which are unfair or deceptive acts or practices in or affecting commerce . . . .

(b) Procedures applicable

(1) When prescribing a rule under subsection (a)(1)(B) of this section, the Commission shall . . .

(A) publish a notice of proposed rulemaking stating with particularity the text of the rule, including any alternatives, which the Commission proposes to promulgate, and the reason for the proposed rule;

      (B) allow interested persons to submit written data, views, and arguments, and make all such submissions publicly available;

      (C) provide an opportunity for an informal hearing . . . ; and

      (D) promulgate, if appropriate, a final rule based on the matter in the rulemaking record . . . together with a statement of basis and purpose.

      (2)(A) Prior to the publication of any notice of proposed rulemaking pursuant to paragraph (1)(A), the Commission shall publish an advance notice of proposed rulemaking in the Federal Register. Such advance notice shall—

            (i) contain a brief description of the area of inquiry under consideration, the objectives which the Commission seeks to achieve, and possible regulatory alternatives under consideration by the Commission; and

            (ii) invite the response of interested parties with respect to such proposed rulemaking, including any suggestions or alternative methods for achieving such objectives . . . .

Notice that subsection (a)(1) authorizes two different kinds of rules: "interpretive rules and general statements of policy," on the one hand, and substantive rules that define specific unfair or deceptive acts or practices, on the other.

Interpretive rules simply designate existing agency requirements, and general statements do not immediately bind parties. Subsection (b)(2) sets forth the procedure for promulgating interpretive rules or general statements. These requirements are not very rigorous and simply invite interested parties to comment on the proposed rule.

Subsection (b)(1) sets forth the procedure for promulgating substantive rules. You can see that this approach assures interested parties lots of opportunity for input by requiring notice of the proposed rulemaking, access to the text of the rule, explanation of the reasons for the rule, opportunity to submit materials on the merits of the rule, and an informal hearing on the issues.

These approaches to rulemaking roughly parallel other agency approaches. We now set forth an example of rulemaking by the Fish and Wildlife Service under the Endangered Species Act.

FISH AND WILDLIFE SERVICE, ENDANGERED AND THREATENED WILDLIFE AND PLANTS; FINAL REDEFINITION OF "HARM"
50 C.F.R. pt. 17 (1981)

ACTION: Final rule.

SUMMARY: This final rule is a redefinition of the Service regulation defining "harm" under section 9 of the Endangered Species Act, 50 CFR 17.3. "Harm" is redefined to mean any action, including habitat modification, which actually kills or injures wildlife, rather than the present interpretation which might be read to include habitat modification or degradation alone without further proof of death or injury. Habitat modification as injury would only be covered by the new definition if it significantly impaired essential behavioral patterns of a listed species.

DATE: This rule becomes effective November 4, 1981. . . .

SUPPLEMENTARY INFORMATION: On June 2, 1981, the Fish and Wildlife Service proposed to amend the definition of "harm" in its regulations under the Endangered Species Act at 50 CFR 17.3. 46 FR 29490 (June 2, 1981). That proposed rule invited public comment for a period of 60 days, ending on August 3, 1981. The notice proposed the redefinition on the grounds that the existing language could be construed as prohibiting the modification of habitat even where there was no injury to the listed endangered or threatened wildlife. The Office of the Solicitor, in a memorandum to the Director of the Fish and Wildlife Service, concluded that such application of Section 9 would go beyond the intent of Congress in the Act. Accordingly, the Associate Solicitor recommended that the definition be changed to obviate any such erroneous application. In addition, the issue had begun to appear in judicial opinions and the Service desired to clarify the definition to avoid any results which would be inconsistent with the Act. In proposing a redefinition, however, the Service did not intend to imply that significant habitat destruction which could be shown to injure protected wildlife through the impairment of its essential behavioral patterns was not subject to the Act. This misperception has been eliminated in the final rule.

The Service received numerous public comments from a variety of parties. Of the 328 comments received, 66 favored the redefinition as proposed, and 262 opposed the proposed redefinition. Approximately 30 of the comments received made substantive or analytical comments of varying degrees; the remaining letters simply voiced support or opposition for the proposed redefinition. The comments in support of the redefinition basically relied on the points contained in the Associate Solicitor's memorandum attached to the rulemaking. Some of the comments in favor of the redefinition, however, viewed the action as limiting "harm" to direct physical injury to an individual member of the wildlife species. This was not the intent of the Service and the final redefinition addresses that perception. The purpose of the redefinition was to preclude claims of a Section 9 taking for habitat modification alone without any attendant death or injury of the protected wildlife. Death or injury, however, may be caused by impairment of essential behavioral patterns which can have significant and permanent effects on a listed species. Many commenters suggested that the word

"actually" be reinserted in the definition to bulwark the need for proven injury to a species due to a party's actions. This has been done.

Congress made its intent to protect species and their habitat very clear. It did not, however, express any intention to protect habitat under section 9 where there was no appurtenant showing of death or injury to a protected species. This was made clear in the preamble to the original definition of harm: "Harm covers actions . . . which actually (as opposed to potentially), cause injury. . . ." . . .

Thus, to the extent that comments recommended further limitations, they misconstrued the intent of the rulemaking. In the opinion of the Service, the final redefinition sufficiently clarifies the restraints of section 9 so as to avoid injury to protected wildlife due to significant habitat modification, while at the same time precluding a taking where no actual injury is shown. . . .

The comments raised a number of specific objections to the proposed redefinition. The predominant comments are addressed individually below. . . .

Comment—The principal objection raised by both substantive and nonsubstantive comments was that the redefinition was inconsistent with the intent of Congress and with the findings of Congress under the Act that habitat destruction is one of the two major causes of extinction.

Response—This view was partly due to public misperception of the purpose and scope of the proposal. The Service agrees that where there is no legislative history specifically on point for a given section, the overall intent of Congress should control. . . . Of course, the Service recognizes that in some cases, there is critical need of protected wildlife for specific habitat. Significant modification or destruction of such habitat, where an actual injury occurs, including impairment of essential behavioral patterns, will still be viewed as being subject to section 9 of the Act.

Comment—Many comments also cited legislative history which showed that Congress intended the term "take" to be construed very broadly.

Response—While recognizing the Congressional intent, the Service feels that the legislative history cannot be read to prohibit habitat modification under section 9 without actual injury.

The examples given, in each instance, were in the context of injury to a species and not to habitat. As the final rule makes clear, where the habitat modification results in injury, the action is subject to section 9. . . .

Accordingly, the definition of "harm" in 50 CFR 17.3 is revised to read as follows: "Harm in the definition of 'take' in the Act means an act which actually kills or injures wildlife. Such act may include significant habitat modification or degradation where it actually kills or injures wildlife by significantly impairing essential behavioral patterns, including breeding, feeding or sheltering."

NOTES

1. Consider the process the FWS used in redefining "harm":

   (a) The FWS invited public comment; the public had 60 days to respond.

   (b) The notice to the public set forth the reasons for proposing the new definition.

   (c) The FWS issued a published decision after considering the public's written comments.

2. The FWS received 328 public comments, only 66 of which favored the new definition of harm. This does not necessarily mean that the FWS disregarded public opinion. It simply disagreed with a majority of the comments.

3. The new definition of harm includes habitat modification only if it "significantly impair[s] essential behavioral patterns" of listed species. Apparently, moderate impairment of behavioral patterns would not constitute harm under the definition.

ADJUDICATION

Although administrative adjudication takes many forms depending on the agency and applicable statutes and regulations, it roughly parallels judicial procedures in which the decision of a judge after a trial creates precedent that guides future conduct. The APA provides in express terms only for formal adjudication, in which an agency regulates by filing a complaint against a party and holding a hearing before an administrative law judge, who issues a decision that may create a new rule or approach to a problem. Nevertheless, informal adjudication is common and has never been considered prohibited under the APA. See Ernest Gellhorn & Ronald M. Levin, Administrative Law and Process 246-49 (5th ed. 2006).

In case of a settlement, in which the agency and the defendant might agree on the appropriate sanction for violating an agency rule, the agency still typically issues a release describing the complaint and the resolution of the matter. In such a situation, the order of settlement also guides future conduct. Consider one example of an adjudication that led to a settlement.

The Federal Trade Commission became concerned about regulating "negative option" terms in sales and services contracts. Negative options consist of terms by which the purchaser can agree in advance to accept products or services unless the purchaser affirmatively indicates otherwise. The FTC describes such options: "The central characteristic of a negative option offer is that the seller interprets the consumer's silence or failure to take an affirmative action to reject goods or services, or to cancel the sales agreement, as acceptance of the offer." FTC to Hold Public Workshop on Negative Option Marketing, FTC Release, Dec. 21, 2006. (You may have agreed to a negative option yourself, for example, if you downloaded virus-protection software, which, in the governing form contract, includes a term that automatically renews your annual subscription and charges your credit card!)

Pursuant to the FTC's rules that require certain disclosures of the terms of negative options, the FTC filed a complaint against a publishing house for failing adequately to inform customers about the terms of their book offers. Through telemarketing and advertising, the publishing house sent books to consumers for a "free" 30-day trial period. The publisher did not give adequate notice that if the customer decided to keep a book, the customer would automatically become enrolled in a "book club." As part of being a member of the club, the publisher would send notices of other books and charge the customer if the customer did not affirmatively reject the additional book. Instead of participating in a full-scale hearing, the publisher agreed to pay a fine of $500,000. In addition, the FTC order barred the publisher from attempting to collect for books already sent to customers.

RULEMAKING OR ADJUDICATION?

How should an agency decide whether to proceed by rulemaking or adjudication? One major consideration is how best to effectuate the very purpose of the administrative instrument, namely to regulate conduct *before* a problem develops. As the Supreme Court in SEC v. Chenery Corp., 332 U.S. 194, 202, 67 S. Ct. 1575, 1580 (1947), said: "Since the Commission, unlike a court, [has] the ability to make new law prospectively through the exercise of its rule-making powers, it has less reason to rely upon ad hoc adjudication to formulate new standards of conduct.... The function of filling in the interstices of the Act should be performed, as much as possible, through this quasi-legislative promulgation of rules to be applied in the future." Moreover, through rulemaking all interested parties have an opportunity to be heard prior to the rule having an effect on anyone:

> [B]y utilizing the rule-making procedure, the agency is able to afford all interested parties an opportunity to participate and present their views on a single question of basic policy affecting both the public at large and individual licensees or prospective licensees of the agency. In short, broad policy should be shaped by the agency members relying heavily on their expert staffs, with the views of as great a portion of the people likely to be affected taken into account.

Warren E. Baker, Policy by Rule or Ad Hoc Approach—Which Should It Be?, 22 Law & Contemp. Probs. 658, 664 (1957).

On the other hand, the Court in *Chenery* also recognized the importance of adjudication to maintain flexibility to deal with complex, unique, and unforeseeable circumstances:

> But any rigid requirement [of rulemaking] would make the administrative process inflexible and incapable of dealing with many of the specialized problems which arise.... Not every principle essential to the effective administration of a statute can or should be cast immediately into the mold of a general rule....
>
> ... [T]he agency must retain power to deal with the problems on a case-by-case basis if the administrative process is to be effective. There is thus a very definite place for the case-by-case evolution of statutory standards. And the choice made between proceeding by general rule or by individual, ad hoc litigation is one that lies primarily in the informed discretion of the administrative agency.

332 U.S. at 202-03, 67 S. Ct. at 1580. In addition, through adjudication of particular disputes, agencies can more gradually become acquainted with particular problems and concoct the most effective methods of dealing with them. This is particularly important, according to Mr. Baker, when an agency does "not know enough about the particular problem to warrant issuance of rule-making. This may be due to either the newness of the agency or the problem before it. It may, therefore, be necessary to proceed on a case-by-case basis until the necessary experience to draft an appropriate rule has been accumulated." Baker at 661.

Of course, adjudication can be costly both for the agency and for the defendant, sometimes requiring long hearings and procedures. Further, agencies may adjudicate only because of excess caution:

> The typical tendency of agencies to hold back from resort to the rule-making power is understandable and often it is justifiable. Waiting for a case to arise, then clarifying only to the extent necessary to decide the case, and then waiting for the next case is one way to build cautiously. In some circumstances, the slow process of making law only through adjudication is a necessity, for administrators may be truly unable to do more than to decide one case at a time. And sometimes, even when they can do more, they properly refrain from early rule-making. Building law through adjudication is a sound and necessary process; the great bulk of American law is the product of that process.
>
> Even so, I think that American administrators, by and large, have fallen into habits of unnecessarily delaying the use of their rule-making power. They too often hold back even when their understanding suffices for useful clarification through rule-making.

Kenneth Culp Davis, Discretionary Justice: A Preliminary Inquiry 57 (1969).

NOTES

1. Although agencies once favored adjudication over rulemaking, the pendulum has swung in the other direction. As we have already noted, today rulemaking dominates.

2. Nevertheless, an agency unsure or less than fully committed to a new policy may prefer adjudication because most people view rulemaking as a more permanent commitment to a policy. One scholar, David L. Shapiro, The Choice of Rulemaking or Adjudication in the Development of Administrative Policy, 78 Harv. L. Rev. 921, 942–58 (1965), suggested that an agency may favor case-by-case adjudication over rulemaking for several reasons related to this permanence point. For example, an agency enjoys more flexibility because it can more easily depart from prior policy when the policy emanates from a prior adjudicative decision. Further, a policy established by adjudication may more readily survive judicial challenge because a reviewing court is less likely to focus on the policy implicit in a single decision.

C. The Court's Role: Judicial Review of Agency Action

We have already discussed why legislatures largely delegate rulemaking power to agencies instead of fashioning rules themselves. Courts, too, rarely play a significant role in developing the content of an agency rule. Is the limited role of courts also wise? Another approach would have been for the legislature to establish the basic regulatory program and for the courts to fill in the details. But the accepted wisdom is that agencies are a better lawmaking body for promulgating regulatory rules:

> It is easy to make the case that complex subjects . . . should be the province of administrative agencies and not courts. Agencies enjoy advantages that go beyond technical expertise. Unlike courts, agencies can set their own agendas and are less dependent on the parties for the development of the factual record and legal arguments than are courts. Administrative processes also provide greater opportunities for public participation than do judicial processes, in which interested third parties are generally limited to filing amicus briefs. Agencies are also in a better position to take all aspects of a regulatory scheme into account than are courts, which by their nature will limit their consideration to the dispute at hand.

Daniel F. Spulber & Christopher S. Yoo, Mandating Access to Telecom and the Internet: The Hidden Side of Trinko, 107 Colum. L. Rev. 1822 (2007).

In light of the important role of the administrative process, arguably judicial review of agency action should be narrow. Courts should not substitute their judgment for that of the agency.

The test is whether the court believes the agency's decision was "arbitrary and capricious." Courts generally will examine whether an agency exercised its discretion within the bounds intended by Congress, but courts will also review the agency's decision for rationality. The next case explains and applies the arbitrary and capricious standard to a decision of the FWS that the northern spotted owl was not endangered or threatened.

NORTHERN SPOTTED OWL v. HODEL

United States District Court, Western District of Washington, 1988
716 F. Supp. 479

ZILLY, DISTRICT JUDGE:

A number of environmental organizations bring this action against the United States Fish & Wildlife Service ("Service") and others, alleging that the Service's decision not to list the northern spotted owl as endangered or threatened under the Endangered Species Act of 1973, as amended, 16 U.S.C. §1531 et seq. ("ESA" or "the Act"), was arbitrary and capricious or contrary to law.

Since the 1970s the northern spotted owl has received much scientific attention, beginning with comprehensive studies of its natural history by Dr. Eric Forsman, whose most significant discovery was the close association between spotted owls and old-growth forests. This discovery raised concerns because the majority of remaining old-growth owl habitat is on public land available for harvest.

In January 1987, plaintiff Greenworld, pursuant to Sec. 4(b)(3) of the ESA, 16 U.S.C. §1533(b)(3), petitioned the Service to list the northern spotted owl as endangered. In August 1987, 29 conservation organizations filed a second petition to list the owl as endangered both in the Olympic Peninsula in Washington and in the Oregon Coast Range, and as threatened throughout the rest of its range.

The ESA directs the Secretary of the Interior to determine whether any species have become endangered or threatened[1] due to habitat destruction, overutilization, disease or predation, or other natural or manmade factors.[2] The Act was amended in 1982 to ensure that the decision whether to list a species as endangered or threatened was based solely on an evaluation of the biological risks faced by the species, to the exclusion of all other factors. See Conf. Report 97-835, 97th Cong. 2d Sess. (Sept. 17, 1982) at 19.[3]

The Service's role in deciding whether to list the northern spotted owl as endangered or threatened is to assess the technical and scientific data in the administrative record against the relevant listing criteria in section 4(a)(1) and then to exercise its own expert discretion in reaching its decision.

In July 1987, the Service announced that it would initiate a status review of the spotted owl and requested public comment. The Service assembled a group of Service biologists, including Dr. Mark Shaffer, its staff expert on population viability, to conduct the review. The Service charged Dr. Shaffer with analyzing current scientific information on the owl. Dr. Shaffer concluded that: "the most reasonable interpretation of current data and knowledge indicate continued old growth harvesting is likely to lead to the extinction of the subspecies in the foreseeable future which argues strongly for listing the subspecies as threatened or endangered at this time."

---

1. The ESA defines an "endangered species" as "any species which is in danger of extinction throughout all or a significant portion of its range...." 16 U.S.C. §1532(6). A "threatened species" is "any species which is likely to become an endangered species within the foreseeable future throughout all or a significant portion of its range." 16 U.S.C. §1532(20).

2. Section 4(a)(1), codified at 16 U.S.C. §1533(a)(1), provides that:

   The Secretary [of Interior in the case of terrestrial species] shall...determine whether any species is an endangered species or a threatened species because of any of the following factors:

   (A) the present or threatened destruction, modification, or curtailment of its habitat or range;
   (B) overutilization for commercial, recreational, scientific, or educational purposes;
   (C) disease or predation;
   (D) the inadequacy of existing regulatory mechanisms; or
   (E) other natural or manmade factors affecting its continued existence.

3. In its only opinion construing the Act the Supreme Court declared that "[t]he plain intent of Congress in enacting [the ESA] was to halt and reverse the trend toward species extinction, whatever the cost." Tennessee Valley Authority v. Hill, 437 U.S. 153, 184, 98 S. Ct. 2279, 2297 (1978) (further construction of nearly completed dam was permanently enjoined after discovery that the completed dam would eliminate the remaining habitat of an endangered species, the snail darter).

M. Shaffer, letter of November 11, 1987, to Jay Gore, U.S. Fish and Wildlife Service, Region 1, Endangered Species, attached to Final Assessment of Population Viability Projections for the Northern Spotted Owl [Administrative Record at III.A.1].

The Service invited a peer review of Dr. Shaffer's analysis by a number of U.S. experts on population viability, all of whom agreed with Dr. Shaffer's prognosis for the owl, although each had some criticisms of his work.

The Service's decision is contained in its 1987 Status Review of the owl ("Status Review") [Administrative Record at II.C] and summarized in its Finding on Greenworld's petition ("Finding") [Administrative Record at I.D.1]. The Status Review was completed on December 14, 1987, and on December 17 the Service announced that listing the owl as endangered under the Act was not warranted at that time.[5] 52 Fed. Reg. 48552, 48554 (Dec. 23, 1987). This suit followed. Both sides now move for summary judgment on the administrative record before the Court.

In T.W. Electrical Service, Inc. v. Pacific Electrical Contractors Ass'n, 809 F.2d 626, 629-32 (9th Cir. 1987), the Court of Appeals for the Ninth Circuit rearticulated the test for summary judgment. The Court said, at 630-31:

> Thus, at this stage of the litigation, the [district] judge does not weigh conflicting evidence with respect to a disputed material fact. Anderson [v. Liberty Lobby, Inc., 477 U.S. 242,] 106 S. Ct. at 2513. Nor does the judge make credibility determinations with respect to statements made in affidavits, answers to interrogatories, admissions, or depositions. See id. These determinations are within the province of the factfinder at trial. Therefore, at summary judgment, the judge must view the evidence in the light most favorable to the nonmoving party: if direct evidence by the moving party conflicts with direct evidence produced by the nonmoving party, the judge must assume the truth of the evidence set forth by the nonmoving party with respect to that fact.... Inferences must also be drawn in the light most favorable to the nonmoving

party. Anderson, 106 S. Ct. at 2513; Matsushita [Elec. Indus. Co. v. Zenith Radio, 475 U.S. 574,] 106 S. Ct. at 1356-57.

This Court reviews the Service's action under the "arbitrary and capricious" standard of the Administrative Procedure Act ("APA"), 5 U.S.C. §706(2)(A). This standard is narrow and presumes the agency action is valid, Ethyl Corp. v. EPA, 541 F.2d 1, 34 (D.C. Cir.), cert. denied, 426 U.S. 941, 96 S. Ct. 2662 (1976), but it does not shield agency action from a "thorough, probing, in-depth review," Citizens to Preserve Overton Park v. Volpe, 401 U.S. 402, 415, 91 S. Ct. 814, 823 (1971). Courts must not "rubber-stamp the agency decision as correct." Ethyl Corp. v. EPA, supra at 34.

> Rather, the reviewing court must assure itself that the agency decision was "based on a consideration of the relevant factors ...." Moreover, it must engage in a "substantial inquiry" into the facts, one that is "searching and careful." This is particularly true in highly technical cases....

Id. at 34-35 (citations and footnotes omitted). Agency action is arbitrary and capricious where the agency has failed to "articulate a satisfactory explanation for its action including a 'rational connection between the facts found and the choice made.'" Motor Vehicle Mfrs. Ass'n v. State Farm Mut. Auto Ins., 463 U.S. 29, 43, 103 S. Ct. 2856, 2866 (1983) (citations omitted).

The Status Review and the Finding to the listing petition offer little insight into how the Service found that the owl currently has a viable population. Although the Status Review cites extensive

---

5. The Service's Finding provides as follows:

> A finding is made that a proposed listing of the northern spotted owl is not warranted at this time. Due to the need for population trend information and other biological data, priority given by the Service to this species for further research and monitoring will continue to be high. Interagency agreements and Service initiatives support continued conservation efforts. This finding will be published in the Federal Register and the petitioner will be notified.

Finding at 5 [Administrative Record at I.D.1].

empirical data and lists various conclusions, it fails to provide any analysis. The Service asserts that it is entitled to make its own decision, yet it provides no explanation for its findings. An agency must set forth clearly the grounds on which it acted. Judicial deference to agency expertise is proper, but the Court will not do so blindly. The Court finds that the Service has not set forth the grounds for its decision against listing the owl.

The Service's documents also lack any expert analysis supporting its conclusion. Rather, the expert opinion is entirely to the contrary. The only reference in the Status Review to an actual opinion that the owl does not face a significant likelihood of extinction is a mischaracterization of a conclusion of Dr. Mark Boyce:

> Boyce (1987) in his analysis of the draft preferred alternative[6] concluded that there is a low probability that the spotted owls will go extinct. He does point out that population fragmentation appears to impose the greatest risks to extinction.

Status Review at 24 (footnote added). Dr. Boyce responded to the Service:

> I did not conclude that the Spotted Owl enjoys a low probability of extinction, and I would be very disappointed if efforts to preserve the Spotted Owl were in any way thwarted by a misinterpretation of something I wrote.

M. Boyce, letter of February 18, 1988, to Rolf Wallenstrom, U.S. Fish and Wildlife Service, Region 1, exhibit 7 to Complaint.[7]

Numerous other experts on population viability contributed to or reviewed drafts of the Status Review, or otherwise assessed spotted owl viability. Some were employed by the Service; others were independent. None concluded that the northern spotted owl is not at risk of extinction. For example, as noted above, Dr. Shaffer evaluated the current data and knowledge and determined that continued logging of old growth likely would lead to the extinction of the owl in the foreseeable future. This risk, he concluded, argued strongly for immediate listing of the subspecies as threatened or endangered.

The Service invited a peer review of Dr. Shaffer's analysis. Drs. Michael Soule, Bruce Wilcox, and Daniel Goodman, three leading U.S. experts on population viability, reviewed and agreed completely with Dr. Shaffer's prognosis for the owl.

For example, Dr. Soule, the acknowledged founder of the discipline of "conservation biology" (the study of species extinction), concluded:

> I completely concur with your conclusions, and the methods by which you reached them. The more one hears about *Strix occidentalis caurina*, the more concern one feels. Problems with the data base and in the models notwithstanding, and politics notwithstanding, I just can't see how a responsible biologist could reach any other conclusion than yours.

M. Soule, letter of November 1, 1987, to Dr. Mark Shaffer [Administrative Record at III.B.4].

The Court will reject conclusory assertions of agency "expertise" where the agency spurns unrebutted expert opinions without itself offering a credible alternative explanation. Here, the Service disregarded all the expert opinion on population viability, including that of its own

---

6. Boyce had evaluated proposals by the U.S. Forest Service concerning northern spotted owl habitat management. The Forest Service is preparing a Supplemental Environmental Impact Statement (SEIS) on its northern spotted owl policy. A draft SEIS was published in July 1986. [Administrative Record at IV.C.4.] As of this writing, the Forest Service has not released a final SEIS. The draft Supplemental Environmental Impact Statement ("DSEIS") on the spotted owl evaluates a number of management options of northern spotted owl habitat. The Forest Service found that implementation of its preferred management alternative will result in a low probability of persistence of a well-distributed owl population on the Olympic Peninsula within 100 years and a medium to low probability in the rest of the owl's range. DSEIS at 4-28 to 31.

7. The court may consider, particularly in highly technical areas, substantive evidence going to the merits of the agency's action where such evidence is necessary as background to determine the sufficiency of the agency's consideration.

expert, that the owl is facing extinction, and instead merely asserted its expertise in support of its conclusions.

The Service has failed to provide its own or other expert analysis supporting its conclusions. Such analysis is necessary to establish a rational connection between the evidence presented and the Service's decision. Accordingly, the United States Fish and Wildlife Service's decision not to list at this time the northern spotted owl as endangered or threatened under the Endangered Species Act was arbitrary and capricious and contrary to law.

The Court further finds that it is not possible from the record to determine that the Service considered the related issue of whether the northern spotted owl is a threatened species. This failure of the Service to review and make an express finding on the issue of threatened status is also arbitrary and capricious and contrary to law.

In deference to the Service's expertise and its role under the Endangered Species Act, the Court remands this matter to the Service, which has 90 days from the date of this order to provide an analysis for its decision that listing the northern spotted owl as threatened or endangered is not currently warranted. Further, the Service is ordered to supplement its Status Review and petition Finding consistent with this Court's ruling.

It is so ordered.

"My lawyer finally got me on the endangered-species list!"

© *The New Yorker Collection 1996 Mick Stevens from cartoonbank.com. All Rights Reserved.*

NOTES

1. Each side in this case asked for summary judgment, a procedural technique explained in Section Four of Chapter 1.

2. Private organizations brought the *Northern Spotted Owl v. Hodel* judicial proceeding, not the agency itself. The case is a good example of how citizens can use courts to compel agencies to abide by the legislative command. But not every citizen or citizens' group can bring an action to question or compel agency action. The citizen or group must have what is called "standing" to sue. We look at this issue in Section Five of this chapter.

3. The case illustrates how agencies elicit, review, and assess comments for purposes of their informal rulemaking. The FWS initiated its status review of whether the northern spotted owl should be listed as an endangered or threatened species by a notice in the Federal Register asking for public comments. The FWS then assembled some of its biologists to conduct a review and invited a review of their conclusions by outside groups.

4. The judicial review standard of whether the agency action was "arbitrary and capricious" applies whether the agency or private parties bring the action. According to *Northern Spotted Owl*, an agency action is "arbitrary and capricious" if the agency fails to satisfactorily explain the reasons for its action, which reasons must show a "rational connection" between the facts and the decision.

Another Illustration of Judicial Review

Certain private organizations, and later the State of Massachusetts, petitioned the Environmental Protection Agency (EPA) to regulate greenhouse gas emissions pursuant to a provision of the Clean Air Act that requires the EPA to "prescribe ... standards applicable to the emission of any air pollutant from any class or classes of new motor vehicles or new motor vehicle engines, which in [the Administrator's] judgment cause, or contribute to, air pollution which may reasonably be anticipated to endanger public health or welfare." 42 U.S.C. §7521(a)(1). The EPA denied the petition, among other reasons, because a piecemeal approach to global warming would be ineffective and because the President's plan for dealing with the problem was more comprehensive.

In a 5–4 decision, the U.S. Supreme Court found that this decision was arbitrary and capricious, in part because the EPA's judgment on whether to regulate must rest on whether an emission "cause[s] or contribute[s] to, air pollution which may reasonably be anticipated to endanger public health or welfare," not on whether regulation would be piecemeal or whether the President has an alternative program. The Court stated: "[T]he use of the word 'judgment' is not a roving license to ignore the statutory text. It is but a direction to exercise discretion within defined statutory limits.... EPA has refused to comply with [the] clear statutory command [of §7521(a)(1)]. Instead, it has offered a laundry list of reasons not to regulate.... Although we have neither the expertise nor the authority to evaluate these policy judgments, it is evident they have nothing to do with whether greenhouse gas emissions contribute to climate change." Massachusetts v. EPA, 549 U.S. 497, 533, 127 S. Ct. 1438, 1462–63 (2007). Although the Court's decision "does not force the EPA to regulate greenhouse gas emissions, it does force the EPA to evaluate whether these emissions contribute to climate change and, to some extent, forces the EPA either to take regulatory action or explain its inaction by taking a position that puts it in direct opposition to the scientific consensus on this issue. That is, the EPA's only excuse for further inaction would be a determination that greenhouse gases do not contribute to global warming or a reasonable explanation as to why it will not exercise its discretion to determine whether they do contribute." Brit T. Brown & Benjamin A. Escobar Jr., Massachusetts v. EPA and Global Warming: Path to a Coherent Policy, Nat'l L.J., June 18, 2007, at 22.

5. Judicial review is more effective after formal rulemaking than informal rulemaking because Congress requires agencies to furnish only general explanations for their rules produced through informal rulemaking. But courts have required agencies, even in informal rulemaking, to offer more detailed and thorough explanations of their decisions, sometimes including rebuttal of arguments and data submitted by opponents of a rule. The APA does not expressly require an agency to give reasons for its decision in an adjudication, but due process may require giving reasons. For example, in the famous *Chenery* case decided before Congress passed the APA, the Supreme Court sent the case back to the Securities and Exchange Commission for a clearer explanation of the basis for its decision. The Court said that "the orderly functioning of the process of review requires that the grounds upon which the administrative agency acted be clearly disclosed and adequately sustained." SEC v. Chenery Corp., 318 U.S. 80, 94, 63 S. Ct. 454, 462 (1943).

6. Here scientific expertise and technical data constituted the record in the case. Yet the court overturned the FWS's decision as arbitrary and capricious. The court obviously was frustrated by the FWS's lack of explanation for its decision: "Although the Status Review cites extensive empirical data and lists various conclusions, it fails to provide any analysis.... The Court will reject conclusory assertions of agency 'expertise' where the agency spurns unrebutted expert opinions without itself offering a credible alternative explanation." Clearly the FWS did not comply with the *Chenery* requirement.

COST-BENEFIT ANALYSIS OF ENVIRONMENTAL ISSUES

Some analysts have used environmental issues to illustrate the difficulties of employing cost-benefit analysis in reaching policy decisions. For example, consider the following excerpt, which ends with a reference to the spotted-owl problem:

> At the first level...there is the conventional cost-benefit approach: What are the costs of each specific course of action, what are the benefits, and how do you achieve the optimum balance between the two?...The trouble is that this approach generally assumes that the problems are well defined, that the options are well defined, and that the political wherewithal is there, so the analysts job is simply to put numbers on the costs and benefits of each alternative.... Unfortunately for the standing theory, however, the real world is almost never that well defined—particularly when it comes to environmental issues. "The 'benefit' of having spotted owls is defined in terms of how many people visit the forest, how many will see a spotted owl, and what it's worth to them to see a spotted owl, et cetera. It's all the greatest rubbish.... By asking only what is good for human beings, they are being presumptuous and arrogant."

M. Mitchell Waldrop, Complexity: The Emerging Science at the Edge of Order and Chaos 331–32 (1992) (quoting Brian Arthur), quoted by Dave Iverson, Critiques of Cost-Benefit Analysis, Eco-Watch Dialogues, http://www.fs.fed.us/eco-watch/econcritiques.html (last accessed May 2, 2008).

This critique suggests that other values besides the costs and benefits of a decision, measured monetarily, should guide decisionmaking. Cultural, moral, and aesthetic values should play a role too. See Mark Sagoff, The Economy of the Earth 6 (1988).

Section Four
APPLYING ADMINISTRATIVE LAW

Thus far in this chapter we have focused on the roles of legislatures, courts, and agencies in *making* administrative law. But regulatory standards must be reinforced by rules for applying and enforcing them in particular situations. That is the subject of this section.

In the field of broadcasting, for example, Congress created a special agency, the Federal Communications Commission (FCC), to create regulatory standards. Congress also empowered the FCC to perform certain adjudicative functions and to enforce its regulatory law. The FCC uses both formal and informal enforcement procedures. Some of its formal enforcement authority is set forth in the following legislation. We offer these statutes not because we want you to learn the detail of this statutory scheme, but simply to illustrate how agencies and sometimes courts apply and enforce the rules promulgated by the agency.

United States Code, Title 47

§303. Powers and duties of Commission.

Except as otherwise provided in this Act, the Commission from time to time, as public convenience, interest, or necessity requires, shall—

. . . .

(m)(1) Have authority to suspend the license of any operator upon proof sufficient to satisfy the Commission that the licensee—

(A) has violated . . . any provision of any Act, treaty, or convention binding on the United States, which the Commission is authorized to administer, or any regulation made by the Commission under any such Act, treaty, or convention . . . .

(n) Have authority to inspect all radio installations associated with stations required to be licensed by any Act . . . or which are subject to the provisions of any Act [or] treaty . . . binding on the United States, to ascertain whether in construction, installation, and operation they conform to the requirements of the rules and regulations of the Commission, the provisions of any Act, the terms of any treaty . . . binding on the United States, and the conditions of the license . . . under which they are constructed, installed, or operated. . . .

§312. Administrative sanctions.

(a) Revocation of station license or construction permit. The Commission may revoke any station license or construction permit—

(1) for false statements knowingly made either in the application or [in a subsequent application for renewal or modification of the license or permit];

(2) because of conditions coming to the attention of the Commission which would warrant it in refusing to grant a license or permit on an original application;

(3) for willful or repeated failure to operate substantially as set forth in the license;

(4) for willful or repeated violation of, or willful or repeated failure to observe any provision of this Act or any rule or regulation of the Commission authorized by this Act or by a treaty ratified by the United States;

(5) for violation of or failure to observe any final cease and desist order issued by the Commission under this section . . . .

(b) Cease and desist orders. Where any person (1) has failed to operate substantially as set forth in a license, (2) has violated or failed to observe any of the provisions of this Act . . . , or (3) has violated or failed to observe any rule or regulation of the Commission authorized by this Act or by a treaty ratified by the United States, the Commission may order such person to cease and desist from such action. . . .

§401. Enforcement provisions.

. . . .

(b) Orders of Commission. If any person fails or neglects to obey any order of the Commission . . . while the same is in effect, the Commission or any party injured thereby, or the United States, by its Attorney General, may apply to the appropriate district court of the United States for the enforcement of such order. If, after hearing, that court determines that the order was regularly made and duly served, and that the person is in disobedience of the same, the court shall enforce obedience to such order by a writ of injunction or other proper process, mandatory or otherwise, to restrain such person or the officers, agents, or representatives of such person, from further disobedience of such order, or to enjoin upon it or them obedience to the same.

(c) Duty to prosecute. Upon the request of the Commission it shall be the duty of any United States attorney to whom the Commission may apply to institute in the proper court and to prosecute under the direction of the Attorney General of the United States all necessary proceedings for the enforcement of the provisions of this Act and for the punishment of all violations thereof. . . .

NOTES

1. Informal enforcement powers of the FCC include the right to conduct investigations and issue policy statements about enforcement, both of which should encourage self-regulation by broadcasters. You can see that the FCC's formal powers include the authority to suspend a license (§303(m)); revoke a license (§312(a)); order a broadcaster to stop a practice (§312(b)); and request court proceedings to enforce an order (§401(b)).

2. In Section Seven of this chapter, we shall provide an illustration of how the FCC applied its rules to a radio station.

Section Five
ROLES OF PRIVATE CITIZENS AND THEIR LAWYERS

In a variety of ways, ordinary citizens, sometimes with the help of lawyers, may help effectuate a regulatory program. One form of private action is participation directly in agency rulemaking or adjudication. We have already seen examples of this, and we shall study it more fully in Section Six.

Private claims can also supplement and assist an agency's regulatory program when the violation of an agency's rule or regulation serves as the basis, or part of the basis, for a private recovery based on another instrument of the law. Suppose, for example, the National Highway Traffic Safety Administration (NHTSA) establishes a safety standard requiring a certain kind of safety spring in the accelerator assembly of cars to prevent the accelerator from sticking. Fast-Buck Auto Manufacturing Company fails to include the spring in its cars. Smith buys one of Fast-Buck's cars, the accelerator sticks, and Smith is injured in an accident that the spring would have prevented. The NHTSA safety standard will be relevant to establish Fast-Buck's negligence in Smith's remedial lawsuit against Fast-Buck. Conversely, if the accelerator sticks even though Fast-Buck used the NHTSA-required spring, the safety standard might be some (but often not conclusive) evidence that Fast-Buck was not negligent, even though

Smith can prove that a more expensive and better-designed spring would have prevented the accident.

Another form of private participation, focused on here, consists of resort to courts to secure appropriate regulatory action when it appears that the officials or agencies charged with these responsibilities are acting or have acted contrary to applicable law. But this subject is vast, so we treat only one aspect, namely the requirement that plaintiffs have "standing" to sue. The standing doctrine can constitute an impediment to private-citizen lawsuits. Under the doctrine, plaintiffs must have a personal stake in the outcome of litigation as the result of sustaining a direct injury, not a potential or hypothetical one. The theory is that such plaintiffs will be zealous advocates and contribute to the sharpening of issues before the court. Further, the requirement of standing enables courts to maintain some control over the number of cases that come before them. You will encounter additional reasons for the standing doctrine in the materials that follow, including constitutional constraints on the judicial branch, whereby the judiciary can entertain only "cases" and "controversies." U.S. Const. art. III, §2.

The *Lujan* case that follows applies the standing doctrine to an environmental group, the Defenders of Wildlife (DOW). DOW challenged a regulation that requires agencies, before conducting any action that might jeopardize endangered or threatened species, to consult with the Secretary of the Interior only when the proposed action takes place in the United States or on the high seas, not when the actions take place in foreign countries. A portion of the opinions of the majority and the dissent in the Supreme Court follows.

LUJAN v. DEFENDERS OF WILDLIFE

Supreme Court of the United States, 1992
504 U.S. 555, 112 S. Ct. 2130

JUSTICE SCALIA delivered the opinion of the Court in part:

This case involves a challenge to a rule promulgated by the Secretary of the Interior interpreting §7 of the Endangered Species Act of 1973 (ESA), 87 Stat. 884, 892, as amended, 16 U.S.C. §1536, in such fashion as to render it applicable only to actions within the United States or on the high seas. The preliminary issue, and the only one we reach, is whether respondents here, plaintiffs below, have standing to seek judicial review of the rule.

I

The ESA, 87 Stat. 884, as amended, 16 U.S.C. §1531 et seq., seeks to protect species of animals against threats to their continuing existence caused by man. See generally TVA v. Hill, 437 U.S. 153, 98 S. Ct. 2279 (1978). The ESA instructs the Secretary of the Interior to promulgate by regulation a list of those species which are either endangered or threatened under enumerated criteria, and to define the critical habitat of these species. 16 U.S.C. §§1533, 1536. Section 7(a)(2) of the Act then provides, in pertinent part:

> Each Federal agency shall, in consultation with and with the assistance of the Secretary [of the Interior], insure that any action authorized, funded, or carried out by such agency . . . is not likely to jeopardize the continued existence of any endangered species or threatened species or result in the destruction or adverse modification of habitat of such species which is determined by the Secretary, after consultation as appropriate with affected States, to be critical.

In 1978, the Fish and Wildlife Service (FWS) and the National Marine Fisheries Service (NMFS), on behalf of the Secretary of the Interior and the Secretary of Commerce respectively, promulgated a joint regulation stating that the obligations imposed by §7(a)(2) extend to actions taken in foreign nations. 43 Fed. Reg. 874 (1978). The next year, however, the Interior Department began to reexamine its position. Letter from Leo Kuliz, Solicitor, Department of the Interior, to Assistant Secretary, Fish and Wildlife and Parks, Aug. 8, 1979. A revised joint regulation, reinterpreting §7(a)(2) to require consultation only for actions taken in the United States or on the high seas, was proposed in 1983, 48 Fed. Reg. 29990, and promulgated in 1986, 51 Fed. Reg. 19926; 50 CFR 402.01 (1991).

Shortly thereafter, respondents, organizations dedicated to wildlife conservation and other environmental causes, filed this action against the Secretary of the Interior, seeking a declaratory judgment that the new regulation is in error as to the geographic scope of §7(a)(2) and an injunction requiring the Secretary to promulgate a new regulation restoring the initial interpretation. The District Court granted the Secretary's motion to dismiss for lack of standing. The Court of Appeals for the Eighth Circuit reversed by a divided vote. On remand, the Secretary moved for summary judgment on the standing issue, and respondents moved for summary judgment on the merits. The District Court denied the Secretary's motion, on the ground that the Eighth Circuit had already determined the standing question in this case; it granted respondents' merits motion, and ordered the Secretary to publish a revised regulation. The Eighth Circuit affirmed. We granted certiorari.

II

While the Constitution of the United States divides all power conferred upon the Federal Government into "legislative Powers," Art. I, §1, "[t]he executive Power," Art. II, §1, and "[t]he judicial Power," Art. III, §1, it does not attempt to define those terms. To be sure, it limits the jurisdiction of federal courts to "Cases" and "Controversies".... One [doctrine that sets] apart the

"Cases" and "Controversies" that are of the justiciable sort referred to in Article III—"serv[ing] to identify those disputes which are appropriately resolved through the judicial process," Whitmore v. Arkansas, 495 U.S. 149, 155, 110 S. Ct. 1717, 1722 (1990)—is the doctrine of standing. Though some of its elements express merely prudential considerations that are part of judicial self-government, the core component of standing is an essential and unchanging part of the case-or-controversy requirement of Article III. See, e.g., Allen v. Wright, 468 U.S. 737, 751, 104 S. Ct. 3315, 3324 (1984).

Over the years, our cases have established that the irreducible constitutional minimum of standing contains three elements. First, the plaintiff must have suffered an "injury in fact"—an invasion of a legally protected interest which is (a) concrete and particularized, see id., at 756, 104 S. Ct., at 3327; Warth v. Seldin, 422 U.S. 490, 508, 95 S. Ct. 2197, 2210 (1975); Sierra Club v. Morton, 405 U.S. 727, 740-741, n. 16, 92 S. Ct. 1361, 1368-1369, n. 16 (1972); and (b) "actual or imminent, not 'conjectural' or 'hypothetical,'" Whitmore, supra, 495 U.S., at 155, 110 S. Ct., at 1723 (quoting Los Angeles v. Lyons, 461 U.S. 95, 102, 103 S. Ct. 1660, 1665 (1983)). Second, there must be a causal connection between the injury and the conduct complained of—the injury has to be "fairly... trace[able] to the challenged action of the defendant, and not...th[e] result [of] the independent action of some third party not before the court." Simon v. Eastern Ky. Welfare Rights Organization, 426 U.S. 26, 41-42, 96 S. Ct. 1917, 1926 (1976). Third, it must be "likely," as opposed to merely "speculative," that the injury will be "redressed by a favorable decision." Id., at 38, 43, 96 S. Ct., at 1924, 1926.

The party invoking federal jurisdiction bears the burden of establishing these elements. Since they are not mere pleading requirements but rather an indispensable part of the plaintiff's case, each element must be supported in the same way as any other matter on which the plaintiff bears the burden of proof, i.e., with the manner and degree of evidence required at the successive stages of the litigation. See Lujan v. National Wildlife Federation, 497 U.S. 871, 883-889, 110 S. Ct.

3177, 3185–3189 (1990); Gladstone, Realtors v. Village of Bellwood, 441 U.S. 91, 114–115, and n. 31, 99 S. Ct. 1601, 1614–1615, and n. 31 (1979). At the pleading stage, general factual allegations of injury resulting from the defendant's conduct may suffice, for on a motion to dismiss we "presum[e] that general allegations embrace those specific facts that are necessary to support the claim." *National Wildlife Federation*, 497 U.S., at 889, 110 S. Ct., at 3189. In response to a summary judgment motion, however, the plaintiff can no longer rest on such "mere allegations," but must "set forth" by affidavit or other evidence "specific facts," Fed. Rule Civ. Proc. 56(e), which for purposes of the summary judgment motion will be taken to be true. And at the final stage, those facts (if controverted) must be "supported adequately by the evidence adduced at trial." *Gladstone*, 441 U.S., at 115, n.31, 99 S. Ct., at 1616, n.31.

When the suit is one challenging the legality of government action or inaction, the nature and extent of facts that must be averred (at the summary judgment stage) or proved (at the trial stage) in order to establish standing depends considerably upon whether the plaintiff is himself an object of the action (or forgone action) at issue. If he is, there is ordinarily little question that the action or inaction has caused him injury, and that a judgment preventing or requiring the action will redress it. When, however, as in this case, a plaintiff's asserted injury arises from the government's allegedly unlawful regulation (or lack of regulation) of *someone else*, much more is needed. In that circumstance, causation and redressability ordinarily hinge on the response of the regulated (or regulable) third party to the government action or inaction—and perhaps on the response of others as well. . . . Thus, when the plaintiff is not himself the object of the government action or inaction he challenges, standing is not precluded, but it is ordinarily "substantially more difficult" to establish. *Allen*, supra, 468 U.S., at 758, 104 S. Ct., at 3328.

III

We think the Court of Appeals failed to apply the foregoing principles in denying the Secretary's motion for summary judgment. Respondents had not made the requisite demonstration of (at least) injury and redressability.

A

Respondents' claim to injury is that the lack of consultation with respect to certain funded activities abroad "increas[es] the rate of extinction of endangered and threatened species." Complaint ¶5, App. 13. Of course, the desire to use or observe an animal species, even for purely esthetic purposes, is undeniably a cognizable interest for purpose of standing. Sierra Club v. Morton, 405 U.S. at 734, 92 S. Ct., at 1366. "But the 'injury in fact' test requires more than an injury to a cognizable interest. It requires that the party seeking review be himself among the injured." Id., at 734–735, 92 S. Ct., at 1366. To survive the Secretary's summary judgment motion, respondents had to submit affidavits or other evidence showing, through specific facts, not only that listed species were in fact being threatened by funded activities abroad, but also that one or more of respondents' members would thereby be "directly" affected apart from their "'special interest' in th[e] subject." Id., at 735, 739, 92 S. Ct., at 1366, 1368.

With respect to this aspect of the case, the Court of Appeals focused on the affidavits of two Defenders' members—Joyce Kelly and Amy Skilbred. Ms. Kelly stated that she traveled to Egypt in 1986 and "observed the traditional habitat of the endangered nile crocodile there and intend[s] to do so again, and hope[s] to observe the crocodile directly," and that she "will suffer harm in fact as the result of [the] American . . . role . . . in overseeing the rehabilitation of the Aswan High Dam on the Nile . . . and [in] develop[ing] . . . Egypt's . . . Master Water Plan." App. 101. Ms. Skilbred averred that she traveled to Sri Lanka in 1981 and "observed th[e] habitat" of "endangered species such as the Asian elephant and the leopard" at what is now the site of the Mahaweli project funded by the Agency for International Development (AID), although she "was unable to see any of the endangered species"; "this development project," she continued, "will seriously reduce endangered, threatened, and endemic species habitat including areas that I visited . . . [, which] may severely shorten the future of these species"; that threat, she concluded, harmed her because she "intend[s] to return to Sri Lanka in the future and hope[s] to be more fortunate in spotting at least the endangered elephant and leopard." Id., at 145–146. When Ms. Skilbred was asked at a subsequent deposition if and when she had any plans to return to Sri Lanka, she reiterated that "I intend to go back to Sri Lanka," but confessed that she had no current plans: "I don't know [when]. There is a civil war going on right now. I don't know. Not next year, I will say. In the future." Id., at 318.

We shall assume for the sake of argument that these affidavits contain facts showing that certain agency-funded projects threaten listed species— though that is questionable. They plainly contain no facts, however, showing how damage to the species will produce "imminent" injury to Mses. Kelly and Skilbred. That the women "had visited" the areas of the projects before the projects commenced proves nothing. As we have said in a related context, "'Past exposure to illegal conduct does not in itself show a present case or controversy regarding injunctive relief . . . if unaccompanied by any continuing, present adverse effects.'" Lyons, 461 U.S., at 102, 103 S. Ct., at 1665 (quoting O'Shea v. Littleton, 414 U.S. 488, 495–496, 94 S. Ct. 669, 676 (1974)). And the affiants' profession of an "inten[t]" to return to the places they had visited before—where they will presumably, this time, be deprived of the opportunity to observe animals of the endangered species—is simply not enough. Such "some day" intentions— without any description of concrete plans, or indeed even any specification of *when* the some day will be—do not support a finding of the "actual or imminent" injury that our cases require.

Besides relying upon the Kelly and Skilbred affidavits, respondents propose a series of novel standing theories. The first, inelegantly styled "ecosystem nexus," proposes that any person who uses *any part* of a "contiguous ecosystem" adversely affected by a funded activity has standing even if the activity is located a great distance away. This approach, as the Court of Appeals correctly observed, is inconsistent with our opinion in National Wildlife Federation, which held that a plaintiff claiming injury from environmental damage must use the area affected by the challenged activity and not an area roughly "in the vicinity" of it. 497 U.S., at 887–889, 110 S. Ct., at 3188-3189. It makes no difference that the general-purpose section of the ESA states that the Act was intended in part "to provide a means whereby the ecosystems upon which endangered species and threatened species depend may be conserved," 16 U.S.C. §1531(b). To say that the Act protects ecosystems is not to say that the Act creates (if it were possible) rights of action in persons who have not been injured in fact, that is, persons who use portions of an ecosystem not perceptibly affected by the unlawful action in question.

Respondents' other theories are called, alas, the "animal nexus" approach, whereby anyone who has an interest in studying or seeing the endangered animals anywhere on the globe has standing; and the "vocational nexus" approach, under which anyone with a professional interest in such animals can sue. Under these theories, anyone who goes to see Asian elephants in the Bronx Zoo, and anyone who is a keeper of Asian elephants in the Bronx Zoo, has standing to sue because the Director of the Agency for International Development (AID) did not consult with the Secretary regarding the AID-funded project in Sri Lanka. This is beyond all reason. Standing is not "an ingenious academic exercise in the conceivable," United States v. Students Challenging Regulatory Agency Procedures (SCRAP), 412 U.S. 669, 688, 93 S. Ct. 2405, 2416 (1973), but as we have said requires, at the summary judgment stage, a factual showing of perceptible harm. It is clear that the person who observes or works with a particular animal threatened by a federal decision is facing perceptible harm, since the very subject of his interest will no longer exist. It is even plausible—though it goes to the outermost limit of plausibility—to think that a person who observes or works with animals of a particular species in the very area of the world where that species is threatened by a federal decision is facing such harm, since some animals that might have been the subject of his interest will no longer exist. It goes beyond the limit, however, and into pure speculation and fantasy, to say that anyone who observes or works with an endangered species, anywhere in the world, is appreciably harmed by a single project affecting some portion of that species with which he has no more specific connection.

B

[Justice Scalia's discussion of redressability is omitted.]

IV

... We have consistently held that a plaintiff raising only a generally available grievance about government—claiming only harm to his and every citizen's interest in proper application of the Constitution and laws, and seeking relief that no more directly and tangibly benefits him than it does the public at large—does not state an Article III case or controversy....

In Massachusetts v. Mellon, 262 U.S. 447, 43 S. Ct. 597 (1923), we dismissed for lack of Article III standing a taxpayer suit challenging the propriety of certain federal expenditures. We said:

> The party who invokes the power [of judicial review] must be able to show not only that the statute is invalid but that he has sustained or is immediately in danger of sustaining some direct injury as the result of its enforcement, and not merely that he suffers in some indefinite way in common with people generally.... Here the parties plaintiff have no such case.... [T]heir complaint ... is merely that officials of the executive department of the government are executing and will execute an act of Congress asserted to be unconstitutional; and this we are asked to prevent. To do so would be not to decide a judicial controversy, but to assume a position of authority over the governmental acts of another and co-equal department, an authority which plainly we do not possess.

Id. at 488-89, 58 S. Ct. at 601....

More recent cases are to the same effect. In United States v. Richardson, 418 U.S. 166, 94 S. Ct. 2940, we dismissed for lack of standing a taxpayer suit challenging the Government's failure to disclose the expenditures of the Central Intelligence Agency, in alleged violation of the constitutional requirement, Art. I, §9, cl. 7, that "a regular Statement and Account of the Receipts and Expenditures of all public Money shall be published from time to time." We held that such a suit rested upon an impermissible "generalized grievance," and was inconsistent with "the framework of Article III" because "the impact on [plaintiff] is plainly undifferentiated and 'common to all members of the public.'" Richardson, supra, at 171, 176-177, 94 S. Ct., at 2944, 2946.... And only two Terms ago, we rejected the notion that Article III permits a citizen suit to prevent a condemned criminal's execution on the basis of "'the public interest protections of the Eighth Amendment'"; once again, "[t]his allegation raise[d] only the 'generalized interest of all citizens in constitutional governance' ... and [was] an inadequate basis on which to grant ... standing." Whitmore, 495 U.S., at 160, 110 S. Ct., at 1725....

We hold that respondents lack standing to bring this action and that the Court of Appeals erred in denying the summary judgment motion filed by the United States. The opinion of the Court of Appeals is hereby reversed, and the cause is remanded for proceedings consistent with this opinion.

It is so ordered.

[Justice Kennedy, joined by Justice Souter, concurred in Justice Scalia's opinion, except part III–B. Justice Stevens concurred only in the judgment.]

JUSTICE BLACKMUN, with whom JUSTICE O'CONNOR joins, dissenting:

I part company with the Court.... I believe that respondents have raised genuine issues of fact—sufficient to survive summary judgment....

Article III of the Constitution confines the federal courts to adjudication of actual "Cases" and "Controversies." To ensure the presence of a "case" or "controversy," this Court has held that Article III requires, as an irreducible minimum, that a plaintiff allege (1) an injury that is (2) "fairly traceable to the defendant's allegedly unlawful conduct" and that is (3) "likely to be redressed by the requested relief." Allen v. Wright, 468 U.S. 737, 751, 104 S. Ct. 3315, 3324 (1984).

To survive petitioner's motion for summary judgment on standing, respondents need not prove that they are actually or imminently harmed. They need show only a "genuine issue" of material fact as to standing. Fed. Rule Civ. Proc. 56(c). This is not a heavy burden. A "genuine issue" exists so long as "the evidence is such that a reasonable jury could return a verdict for the nonmoving party [respondents]." Anderson v. Liberty Lobby, Inc., 477 U.S. 242, 248, 106 S. Ct. 2505, 2510 (1986). This Court's "function is not [it]self to weigh the evidence and determine the truth of the matter but to determine whether there is a genuine issue for trial." Id., at 249, 106 S. Ct., at 2511. . . .

Were the Court to apply the proper standard for summary judgment, I believe it would conclude that the sworn affidavits and deposition testimony of Joyce Kelly and Amy Skilbred advance sufficient facts to create a genuine issue for trial concerning whether one or both would be imminently harmed by the Aswan and Mahaweli projects. In the first instance, as the Court itself concedes, the affidavits contained facts making it at least "questionable" (and therefore within the province of the factfinder) that certain agency-funded projects threaten listed species.[1] The only remaining issue, then, is whether Kelly and Skilbred have shown that they personally would suffer imminent harm.

I think a reasonable finder of fact could conclude from the information in the affidavits and deposition testimony that either Kelly or Skilbred will soon return to the project sites, thereby satisfying the "actual or imminent" injury standard. The Court dismisses Kelly's and Skilbred's general statements that they intended to revisit the project sites as "simply not enough." But those statements did not stand alone. A reasonable finder of fact could conclude, based not only upon their statements of intent to return, but upon their past visits to the project sites, as well as their professional backgrounds, that it was likely that Kelly and Skilbred would make a return trip to the project areas. Contrary to the Court's contention that

Kelly's and Skilbred's past visits "prov[e] nothing," the fact of their past visits could demonstrate to a reasonable factfinder that Kelly and Skilbred have the requisite resources and personal interest in the preservation of the species endangered by the Aswan and Mahaweli projects to make good on their intention to return again. . . .

I fear the Court's demand for detailed descriptions of future conduct will do little to weed out those who are genuinely harmed from those who are not. More likely, it will resurrect a code-pleading formalism in federal court summary judgment practice, as federal courts, newly doubting their jurisdiction, will demand more and more particularized showings of future harm.

Just to survive summary judgment, for example, a property owner claiming a decline in the value of his property from governmental action might have to specify the exact date he intends to sell his property and show that there is a market for the property, lest it be surmised he might not sell again. A nurse turned down for a job on grounds of her race had better be prepared to show on what date she was prepared to start work, that she had arranged daycare for her child, and that she would not have accepted work at another hospital instead. And a Federal Tort Claims Act plaintiff alleging loss of consortium should make sure to furnish this Court with a "description of concrete plans" for her nightly schedule of attempted activities.

---

1. The record is replete with genuine issues of fact about the harm to endangered species from the Aswan and Mahaweli projects. For example, according to an internal memorandum of the Fish and Wildlife Service, no fewer than eight listed species are found in the Mahaweli project area (Indian elephant, leopard, purple-faced langur, toque macaque, red face malkoha, Bengal monitor, mugger crocodile, and python). App. 78. The memorandum recounts that the Sri Lankan Government has specifically requested assistance from the Agency for International Development (AID) in "mitigating the negative impacts to the wildlife involved." Ibid. In addition, a letter from the Director of the Fish and Wildlife Service to AID warns: "The magnitude of the Accelerated Mahaweli Development Program could have massive environmental impacts on such an insular ecosystem as the Mahaweli River system." Id., at 215. . . .

The Court also concludes that injury is lacking, because respondents' allegations of "ecosystem nexus" failed to demonstrate sufficient proximity to the site of the environmental harm. To support that conclusion, the Court mischaracterizes our decision in Lujan v. National Wildlife Federation, 497 U.S. 871, 110 S. Ct. 3177 (1990), as establishing a general rule that "a plaintiff claiming injury from environmental damage must use the area affected by the challenged activity." In *National Wildlife Federation*, the Court required specific geographical proximity because of the particular type of harm alleged in that case: harm to the plaintiff's visual enjoyment of nature from mining activities. 497 U.S., at 888, 110 S. Ct., at 3188. One cannot suffer from the sight of a ruined landscape without being close enough to see the sites actually being mined. Many environmental injuries, however, cause harm distant from the area immediately affected by the challenged action. Environmental destruction may affect animals traveling over vast geographical ranges, see, e.g., Japan Whaling Assn. v. American Cetacean Society, 478 U.S. 221, 106 S. Ct. 2860 (1986) (harm to American whale watchers from Japanese whaling activities), or rivers running long geographical courses, see, e.g., Arkansas v. Oklahoma, 503 U.S. 91, 112 S. Ct.

1046 (1992) (harm to Oklahoma residents from wastewater treatment plant 39 miles from border). It cannot seriously be contended that a litigant's failure to use the precise or exact site where animals are slaughtered or where toxic waste is dumped into a river means he or she cannot show injury.

The Court also rejects respondents' claim of vocational or professional injury. The Court says that it is "beyond all reason" that a zoo "keeper" of Asian elephants would have standing to contest his Government's participation in the eradication of all the Asian elephants in another part of the world. I am unable to see how the distant location of the destruction *necessarily* (for purposes of ruling at summary judgment) mitigates the harm to the elephant keeper. If there is no more access to a future supply of the animal that sustains a keeper's livelihood, surely there is harm. . . .

In conclusion, I cannot join the Court on what amounts to a slash-and-burn expedition through the law of environmental standing. In my view, "[t]he very essence of civil liberty certainly consists in the right of every individual to claim the protection of the laws, whenever he receives an injury." Marbury v. Madison, 1 Cranch 137, 163 (1803).

I dissent.

NOTES

1. We have omitted the portions of the *Lujan* opinions dealing with "redressability." This part of the test of standing deals with whether a court can fashion a remedy that will actually help the party asserting standing. Justice Scalia argued that the Court could only order the Secretary of Interior to require consultation by agencies doing foreign projects. But he pointed out that whether "agencies [would be] bound by the Secretary's regulation" was an "open question," in part because other agencies were not a party to the lawsuit. So, the remedy might not do the private parties any good. The dissent thought, however, that the Secretary had "officially and publicly . . . taken the position that his regulations regarding consultation . . . are binding on action agencies." Although the redressability issue is thus debatable in this case, you can see that, in a court's deciding whether to entertain a lawsuit, considering whether it can fashion an appropriate remedy makes a lot of sense.

2. The Supreme Court had previously held that organizations such as Defenders of Wildlife could protect a general interest (such as protecting wildlife) by

representing the common interests of their members. See Warth v. Seldin, 422 U.S. 490, 511, 95 S. Ct. 2197, 2211-12 (1975):

> There is no question that an association may have standing in its own right to seek judicial relief from injury to itself and to vindicate whatever rights and immunities the association itself may enjoy. Moreover, in attempting to secure relief from injury to itself the association may assert the rights of its members, at least so long as the challenged infractions adversely affect its members' associational ties....
>
> Even in the absence of injury to itself, an association may have standing solely as the representative of its members.... The possibility of such representational standing, however, does not eliminate or attenuate the constitutional requirement of a case or controversy. The association must allege that its members, or any one of them, are suffering immediate or threatened injury as a result of the challenged action of the sort that would make out a justiciable case had the members themselves brought suit. So long as this can be established, and so long as the nature of the claim and of the relief sought does not make the individual participation of each injured party indispensable to proper resolution of the cause, the association may be an appropriate representative of its members, entitled to invoke the court's jurisdiction.

See also Patricia Wald, The D.C. Circuit: Here and Now, 55 Geo. Wash. L. Rev. 718, 720 (1987):

> [I]t is my experience that there is usually no real dispute that a genuine case or controversy exists about the effects of a regulatory policy on certain segments of the citizenry, i.e., that certain types of persons will arguably be hurt by the policy, and even that the national organizational plaintiff has among its members some such citizens.

3. In *Lujan*, DOW also claimed that the ESA's citizen-suit provision expressly granted the right to sue regardless of a direct injury. The citizen-suit provision states in part that "any person may commence a civil suit on his own behalf to enjoin any person, including the United States and any ... agency ... who is alleged to be in violation of any provision of this Act." However, the Court held that the Constitution barred Congress from eliminating the injury-in-fact requirement, based on the Constitution's Case or Controversy Clause. Consider the thoughts of William A. Fletcher, The Structure of Standing, 98 Yale L.J. 221, 223-24, 231-33 (1998), on the meaning of "injury in fact":

> If a duty is statutory, Congress should have essentially unlimited power to define the class of persons entitled to enforce that duty, for congressional power to create the duty should include the power to define those who have standing to enforce it....
>
> If we put to one side people who lie about their states of mind, we should concede that anyone who claims to be injured is, in fact, injured if she can prove the allegations of her complaint. If this is so, there can be no practical significance to the Court's "injury in fact" test because all people sincerely claiming injury automatically satisfy it. This should be so because to impose additional requirements under the guise of requiring an allegation of "injury in fact" is not to require a neutral, "factual" showing, but rather to impose standards of injury derived

from some external normative source. There is nothing wrong with a legal system imposing such external standards of injury; indeed, that is what a legal system must do when it decides which causes of action to recognize as valid legal claims. However, in employing such standards, we measure something that is ascertainable only by reference to a normative structure. . . .

Another example can be used, this time from law. Imagine someone who is seriously concerned about federal government cutbacks in welfare payments, but who is not himself a welfare recipient. He feels so strongly about the matter that he occasionally loses sleep after walking past homeless people sleeping in the streets, and he spends money he would not otherwise spend to support a private charity providing aid to the homeless. If such a person brings suit challenging the cutback as contrary to the governing statute, we might be inclined to say that he is not "injured in fact." We are wrong here, too. The person is injured "in fact." We may be led to see this if we imagine a case in which my neighbor's dog is chained in his back yard, close to my bedroom window, and barks all night. I lose sleep, and I spend money on earplugs and a double glazed window. In other words, my injuries are comparable to those of the person in the homeless example, for I lose sleep and spend money. In this context, we say quite readily that I have been injured "in fact." Indeed, the law agrees with the assessment of injury and protects me with a cause of action for nuisance. . . .

. . . For the Court to limit the power of Congress to create statutory rights enforceable by certain groups of people—to limit, in other words, the power of Congress to create standing—is to limit the power of Congress to define and protect against certain kinds of injury that the Court thinks it improper to protect against.

4. You can see that "standing" constitutes a significant impediment to private lawsuits contesting agency action or inaction. Arguably, however, private lawsuits brought by organizations are best suited to counter the influence of the regulated industries. Not surprisingly, then, standing is a controversial and much debated issue. This may be especially so in the context of environmental protection. The Supreme Court addressed this subject again in *Massachusetts v. EPA*, a case we discussed briefly in Section Three. Recall that private organizations and the state of Massachusetts petitioned the Environmental Protection Agency to regulate greenhouse gas emissions pursuant to the Clean Air Act, which requires the EPA to regulate automobile air pollution. The EPA denied the petition. On appeal, one issue was the standing of the plaintiffs. In a 5–4 decision, the Court found that the State of Massachusetts had standing. A portion of the opinion on the standing issue follows.

MASSACHUSETTS v. EPA

Supreme Court of the United States, 2007
549 U.S. 497, 127 S. Ct. 1438

Justice Stevens delivered the opinion of the Court:

. . . The parties' dispute turns on the proper construction of a congressional statute, a question

eminently suitable to resolution in federal court. Congress has moreover authorized this type of challenge to EPA action. See 42 U.S.C. §7607(b)(1) ["A petition for review of action of the Administrator in promulgating any . . . standard under section 7521 . . . , or final action taken, by the Administrator under this chapter may be filed only in the United States Court of Appeals for the District of Columbia."]. That authorization is of critical importance to the standing inquiry: "Congress has the power to define injuries and articulate chains of causation that will give rise to a case or controversy where none existed before." *Lujan*, 504 U.S., at 580, 112 S. Ct. 2130 (Kennedy, J., concurring in part and concurring in judgment). "In exercising this power, however, Congress must at the very least identify the injury it seeks to vindicate and relate the injury to the class of persons entitled to bring suit." Ibid. We will not, therefore, "entertain citizen suits to vindicate the public's nonconcrete interest in the proper administration of the laws." Id., at 581, 112 S. Ct. 2130.

EPA maintains that because greenhouse gas emissions inflict widespread harm, the doctrine of standing presents an insuperable jurisdictional obstacle. We do not agree. At bottom, "the gist of the question of standing" is whether petitioners have "such a personal stake in the outcome of the controversy as to assure that concrete adverseness which sharpens the presentation of issues upon which the court so largely depends for illumination." Baker v. Carr, 369 U.S. 186, 204, 82 S. Ct. 691 (1962). As Justice Kennedy explained in his *Lujan* concurrence:

> While it does not matter how many persons have been injured by the challenged action, the party bringing suit must show that the action injures him in a concrete and personal way. This requirement is not just an empty formality. It preserves the vitality of the adversarial process by assuring both that the parties before the court have an actual, as opposed to professed, stake in the outcome, and that the legal questions presented...will be resolved, not in the rarified atmosphere of a debating society, but in a concrete factual context conducive to a realistic appreciation of the consequences of judicial action.

504 U.S., at 581, 112 S. Ct. 2130 (internal quotation marks omitted)....

Only one of the petitioners needs to have standing to permit us to consider the petition for review. We stress here, as did Judge Tatel below, the special position and interest of Massachusetts. It is of considerable relevance that the party seeking review here is a sovereign State and not, as it was in *Lujan*, a private individual....

When a State enters the Union, it surrenders certain sovereign prerogatives. Massachusetts cannot invade Rhode Island to force reductions in greenhouse gas emissions, it cannot negotiate an emissions treaty with China or India, and in some circumstances the exercise of its police powers to reduce in-state motor-vehicle emissions might well be pre-empted.

These sovereign prerogatives are now lodged in the Federal Government, and Congress has ordered EPA to protect Massachusetts (among others) by prescribing standards applicable to the "emission of any air pollutant from any class or classes of new motor vehicle or new motor vehicle engines, which in [the Administrator's] judgment cause, or contribute to, air pollution which may reasonably be anticipated to endanger public health or welfare." 42 U.S.C. §7521(a)(1). Congress has moreover recognized a concomitant procedural right to challenge the rejection of its rulemaking petition as arbitrary and capricious. §7607(b)(1). Given that procedural right and Massachusetts' stake in protecting its quasi-sovereign interests, the Commonwealth is entitled to special solicitude in our standing analysis.

With that in mind, it is clear that petitioners' submissions as they pertain to Massachusetts have satisfied the most demanding standards of the adversarial process. EPA's steadfast refusal to regulate greenhouse gas emissions presents a risk of harm to Massachusetts that is both "actual" and "imminent." *Lujan*, 504 U.S., at 560, 112 S. Ct. 2130 (internal quotation marks omitted). There is, moreover, a "substantial likelihood that the judicial relief requested" will prompt EPA to take steps to reduce that risk. Duke Power Co. v. Carolina Environmental Study Group, Inc., 438 U.S. 59, 79, 98 S. Ct. 2620 (1978).

The Injury

The harms associated with climate change are serious and well recognized. Indeed, the NRC Report itself—which EPA regards as an "objective and independent assessment of the relevant science," 68 Fed. Reg. 52930—identifies a number of environmental changes that have already inflicted significant harms, including "the global retreat of mountain glaciers, reduction in snow-cover extent, the earlier spring melting of rivers and lakes, [and] the accelerated rate of rise of sea levels during the 20th century relative to the past few thousand years . . . ." NRC Report 16.

Petitioners allege that this only hints at the environmental damage yet to come. According to the climate scientist Michael MacCracken, "qualified scientific experts involved in climate change research" have reached a "strong consensus" that global warming threatens (among other things) a precipitate rise in sea levels by the end of the century, MacCracken Decl. ¶15, Stdg. App. 207, "severe and irreversible changes to natural ecosystems," id., ¶5(d), at 209, a "significant reduction in water storage in winter snowpack in mountainous regions with direct and important economic consequences," ibid., and an increase in the spread of disease, id., ¶28, at 218-219. He also observes that rising ocean temperatures may contribute to the ferocity of hurricanes. Id., ¶¶23-25, at 216-217.

That these climate-change risks are "widely shared" does not minimize Massachusetts' interest in the outcome of this litigation. See Federal Election Comm'n v. Akins, 524 U.S. 11, 24, 118 S. Ct. 1777 (1998) ("[W]here a harm is concrete, though widely shared, the Court has found 'injury in fact' "). According to petitioners' unchallenged affidavits, global sea levels rose somewhere between 10 and 20 centimeters over the 20th century as a result of global warming. MacCracken Decl. ¶5(c), Stdg. App. 208. These rising seas have already begun to swallow Massachusetts' coastal land. Id., at 196 (declaration of Paul H. Kirshen ¶5), 216 (MacCracken Decl. ¶23). Because the Commonwealth "owns a substantial portion of the state's coastal property," id., at 171 (declaration of Karst R. Hoogeboom ¶4), it has alleged a particularized injury in its capacity as a landowner. The severity of that injury will only increase over the course of the next century: If sea levels continue to rise as predicted, one Massachusetts official believes that a significant fraction of coastal property will be "either permanently lost through inundation or temporarily lost through periodic storm surge and flooding events." Id., ¶6, at 172. Remediation costs alone, petitioners allege, could run well into the hundreds of millions of dollars. Id., ¶7, at 172; see also Kirshen Decl. ¶12, at 198.

Causation

EPA does not dispute the existence of a causal connection between man-made greenhouse gas emissions and global warming. At a minimum, therefore, EPA's refusal to regulate such emissions "contributes" to Massachusetts' injuries.

EPA nevertheless maintains that its decision not to regulate greenhouse gas emissions from new motor vehicles contributes so insignificantly to petitioners' injuries that the agency cannot be haled into federal court to answer for them. For the same reason, EPA does not believe that any realistic possibility exists that the relief petitioners seek would mitigate global climate change and remedy their injuries. That is especially so because predicted increases in greenhouse gas emissions from developing nations, particularly China and India, are likely to offset any marginal domestic decrease.

But EPA overstates its case. Its argument rests on the erroneous assumption that a small incremental step, because it is incremental, can never be attacked in a federal judicial forum. Yet accepting that premise would doom most challenges to regulatory action. Agencies, like legislatures, do not generally resolve massive problems in one fell regulatory swoop. . . .

And reducing domestic automobile emissions is hardly a tentative step. Even leaving aside the other greenhouse gases, the United States transportation sector emits an enormous quantity of carbon dioxide into the atmosphere—according to the MacCracken affidavit, more than 1.7 billion metric tons in 1999 alone. ¶30, Stdg. App. 219. That accounts for more than 6% of worldwide carbon dioxide emissions. Id., at 232 (Oppenheimer Decl. ¶3); see also MacCracken Decl. ¶31, at 220. To put this in perspective: Considering just emissions from the transportation sector, which represent less than one-third of this country's total carbon dioxide emissions, the United States would still rank as the third-largest emitter of carbon dioxide in the world, outpaced only by the European Union and China. Judged by any standard, U.S. motor-vehicle emissions make a meaningful contribution to greenhouse gas concentrations and hence, according to petitioners, to global warming.

The Remedy

While it may be true that regulating motor-vehicle emissions will not by itself *reverse* global warming, it by no means follows that we lack jurisdiction to decide whether EPA has a duty to take steps to *slow* or *reduce* it. Because of the enormity of the potential consequences associated with man-made climate change, the fact that the effectiveness of a remedy might be delayed during the (relatively short) time it takes for a new motor-vehicle fleet to replace an older one is essentially irrelevant. Nor is it dispositive that developing countries such as China and India are poised to increase greenhouse gas emissions substantially over the next century: A reduction in domestic emissions would slow the pace of global emissions increases, no matter what happens elsewhere.

We moreover attach considerable significance to EPA's "agree[ment] with the President that 'we must address the issue of global climate change,'" 68 Fed. Reg. 52929 (quoting remarks announcing Clear Skies and Global Climate Initiatives, 2002 Public Papers of George W. Bush, Vol. 1, Feb. 14, p. 227 (2004)), and to EPA's ardent support for various voluntary emission-reduction programs, 68 Fed. Reg. 52932....

In sum—at least according to petitioners' uncontested affidavits—the rise in sea levels associated with global warming has already harmed and will continue to harm Massachusetts. The risk of catastrophic harm, though remote, is nevertheless real. That risk would be reduced to some extent if petitioners received the relief they seek. We therefore hold that petitioners have standing to challenge the EPA's denial of their rulemaking petition....

CHIEF JUSTICE ROBERTS, with whom JUSTICE SCALIA, JUSTICE THOMAS, and JUSTICE ALITO join, dissenting:

Global warming may be a "crisis," even "the most pressing environmental problem of our

time." Pet. for Cert. 26, 22. Indeed, it may ultimately affect nearly everyone on the planet in some potentially adverse way, and it may be that governments have done too little to address it. It is not a problem, however, that has escaped the attention of policymakers in the Executive and Legislative Branches of our Government, who continue to consider regulatory, legislative, and treaty-based means of addressing global climate change.

Apparently dissatisfied with the pace of progress on this issue in the elected branches, petitioners have come to the courts claiming broad-ranging injury, and attempting to tie that injury to the Government's alleged failure to comply with a rather narrow statutory provision. I would reject these challenges as nonjusticiable. Such a conclusion involves no judgment on whether global warming exists, what causes it, or the extent of the problem. Nor does it render petitioners without recourse. This Court's standing jurisprudence simply recognizes that redress of grievances of the sort at issue here "is the function of Congress and the Chief Executive," not the federal courts. Lujan v. Defenders of Wildlife, 504 U.S. 555, 576, 112 S. Ct. 2130 (1992). I would vacate the judgment below and remand for dismissal of the petitions for review.

I

...Our modern framework for addressing standing is familiar: "A plaintiff must allege personal injury fairly traceable to the defendant's allegedly unlawful conduct and likely to be redressed by the requested relief." DaimlerChrysler [Corp. v. Cuno, 547 U.S. 332, 342, 126 S. Ct. 1854, 1861 (2006)] (quoting Allen v. Wright, 468 U.S. 737, 751, 104 S. Ct. 3315 (1984) (internal quotation marks omitted)). Applying that standard here, petitioners bear the burden of alleging an injury that is fairly traceable to the Environmental Protection Agency's failure to promulgate new motor vehicle greenhouse gas emission standards, and that is likely to be redressed by the prospective issuance of such standards.

Before determining whether petitioners can meet this familiar test, however, the Court changes the rules. It asserts that "States are not normal litigants for the purposes of invoking federal jurisdiction," and that given "Massachusetts' stake in protecting its quasi-sovereign interests, the Commonwealth is entitled to *special solicitude* in our standing analysis" (emphasis added).

Relaxing Article III standing requirements because asserted injuries are pressed by a State, however, has no basis in our jurisprudence, and support for any such "special solicitude" is conspicuously absent from the Court's opinion. The general judicial review provision cited by the Court, 42 U.S.C. §7607(b)(1), affords States no special rights or status. . . .

Nor does the case law cited by the Court provide any support for the notion that Article III somehow implicitly treats public and private litigants differently. . . .

II

It is not at all clear how the Court's "special solicitude" for Massachusetts plays out in the standing analysis, except as an implicit concession that petitioners cannot establish standing on traditional terms. But the status of Massachusetts as a State cannot compensate for petitioners' failure to demonstrate injury in fact, causation, and redressability.

When the Court actually applies the three-part test, it focuses, as did the dissent below, see 415 F.3d 50, 64 (C.A.D.C. 2005) (opinion of Tatel, J.), on the State's asserted loss of coastal land as the injury in fact. If petitioners rely on loss of land as the Article III injury, however, they must ground the rest of the standing analysis in that specific injury. That alleged injury must be "concrete and particularized," Defenders of Wildlife, 504 U.S., at 560, 112 S. Ct. 2130, and "distinct and palpable," *Allen*, 468 U.S., at 751, 104 S. Ct. 3315 (internal quotation marks omitted). Central to this concept of "particularized" injury is the requirement that a plaintiff be affected in a "personal and individual way," *Defenders of Wildlife*, 504 U.S., at 560, n.1, 112 S. Ct. 2130, and seek relief that "directly and tangibly benefits him" in a manner distinct from its impact on "the public at large," id., at 573-574, 112 S. Ct. 2130. Without "particularized injury, there can be no confidence

of 'a real need to exercise the power of judicial review' or that relief can be framed 'no broader than required by the precise facts to which the court's ruling would be applied.'" Warth v. Seldin, 422 U.S. 490, 508, 95 S. Ct. 2197 (1975) (quoting Schlesinger v. Reservists Comm. to Stop the War, 418 U.S. 208, 221-222, 94 S. Ct. 2925 (1974)).

The very concept of global warming seems inconsistent with this particularization requirement. Global warming is a phenomenon "harmful to humanity at large," 415 F.3d, at 60 (Sentelle, J., dissenting in part and concurring in judgment), and the redress petitioners seek is focused no more on them than on the public generally—it is literally to change the atmosphere around the world.

If petitioners' particularized injury is loss of coastal land, it is also that injury that must be "actual or imminent, not conjectural or hypothetical," *Defenders of Wildlife*, supra, at 560, 112 S. Ct. 2130 (internal quotation marks omitted), "real and immediate," Los Angeles v. Lyons, 461 U.S. 95, 102, 103 S. Ct. 1660 (1983) (internal quotation marks omitted), and "certainly impending," Whitmore v. Arkansas, 495 U.S. 149, 158, 110 S. Ct. 1717 (1990) (internal quotation marks omitted).

As to "actual" injury, the Court observes that "global sea levels rose somewhere between 10 and 20 centimeters over the 20th century as a result of global warming" and that "[t]hese rising seas have already begun to swallow Massachusetts' coastal land." But none of petitioners' declarations supports that connection. One declaration states that "a rise in sea level due to climate change is occurring on the coast of Massachusetts, in the metropolitan Boston area," but there is no elaboration. Petitioners' Standing Appendix in No. 03-1361, etc. (CADC), p. 196 (Stdg. App.). And the declarant goes on to identify a "significan[t]" *non*-global-warming cause of Boston's rising sea level: land subsidence. Id., at 197; see also id., at 216. Thus, aside from a single conclusory statement, there is nothing in petitioners' 43 standing declarations and accompanying exhibits to support an inference of actual loss of Massachusetts coastal land from 20th century global sea level increases. It is pure conjecture.

The Court's attempts to identify "imminent" or "certainly impending" loss of Massachusetts coastal land fares no better. [The opinion discusses the lack of clarity of computer models.] But even placing that problem to the side, accepting a century-long time horizon and a series of compounded estimates renders requirements of imminence and immediacy utterly toothless. "Allegations of possible future injury do not satisfy the requirements of Art. III. A threatened injury must be *certainly impending* to constitute injury in fact." *Whitmore*, supra, at 158, 110 S. Ct. 1717 (internal quotation marks omitted; emphasis added).

III

Petitioners' reliance on Massachusetts's loss of coastal land as their injury in fact for standing purposes creates insurmountable problems for them with respect to causation and redressability. To establish standing, petitioners must show a causal connection between that specific injury and the lack of new motor vehicle greenhouse gas emission standards, and that the promulgation of such standards would likely redress that injury. As is often the case, the questions of causation and redressability overlap. And importantly, when a party is challenging the Government's allegedly unlawful regulation, or lack of regulation, of a third party, satisfying the causation and redressability requirements becomes "substantially more difficult." *Defenders of Wildlife*, supra, at 562, 112 S. Ct. 2130 (internal quotation marks omitted).

Petitioners view the relationship between their injuries and EPA's failure to promulgate new motor vehicle greenhouse gas emission standards as simple and direct: Domestic motor vehicles emit carbon dioxide and other greenhouse gases. Worldwide emissions of greenhouse gases contribute to global warming and therefore also to petitioners' alleged injuries. Without the new vehicle standards, greenhouse gas emissions—and therefore global warming and its attendant harms—have been higher than they otherwise would have been; once EPA changes course, the trend will be reversed.

The Court ignores the complexities of global warming, and does so by now disregarding the "particularized" injury it relied on in step one, and using the dire nature of global warming itself

as a bootstrap for finding causation and redressability. First, it is important to recognize the extent of the emissions at issue here. Because local greenhouse gas emissions disperse throughout the atmosphere and remain there for anywhere from 50 to 200 years, it is global emissions data that are relevant.... [P]etitioners' desired emission standards might reduce only a fraction of 4 percent of global emissions.

This gets us only to the relevant greenhouse gas emissions; linking them to global warming and ultimately to petitioners' alleged injuries next requires consideration of further complexities. As EPA explained in its denial of petitioners' request for rulemaking,

> predicting future climate change necessarily involves a complex web of economic and physical factors including: our ability to predict future global anthropogenic emissions of [greenhouse gases] and aerosols; the fate of these emissions once they enter the atmosphere (e.g., what percentage are absorbed by vegetation or are taken up by the oceans); the impact of those emissions that remain in the atmosphere on the radiative properties of the atmosphere; changes in critically important climate feedbacks (e.g., changes in cloud cover and ocean circulation); changes in temperature characteristics (e.g., average temperatures, shifts in daytime and evening temperatures); changes in other climatic parameters (e.g., shifts in precipitation, storms); and ultimately the impact of such changes on human health and welfare (e.g., increases or decreases in agricultural productivity, human health impacts).

App. to Pet. for Cert. A-83 through A-84.

Petitioners are never able to trace their alleged injuries back through this complex web to the fractional amount of global emissions that might have been limited with EPA standards. In light of the bit-part domestic new motor vehicle greenhouse gas emissions have played in what petitioners describe as a 150-year global phenomenon, and the myriad additional factors bearing on petitioners' alleged injury—the loss of Massachusetts coastal land—the connection is far too speculative to establish causation....

IV

Redressability is even more problematic....

V

... The good news is that the Court's "special solicitude" for Massachusetts limits the future applicability of the diluted standing requirements applied in this case. The bad news is that the Court's self-professed relaxation of those Article III requirements has caused us to transgress "the proper—and properly limited—role of the courts in a democratic society." *Allen*, 468 U.S., at 750, 104 S. Ct. 3315 (internal quotation marks omitted).

I respectfully dissent.

[Justice Scalia's dissent, with whom Chief Justice Roberts and Justices Thomas and Alito join, is omitted.]

NOTES

1. The Supreme Court majority found that the State of Massachusetts had standing. On policy grounds, this approach has some appeal. After all, as the majority points out, Massachusetts surrendered certain "sovereign prerogatives" when it joined the union, which powers "are now lodged in the Federal Government." So when through a statute the federal government orders the EPA to protect the states by prescribing standards to regulate air pollution from cars, a state arguably should have a right to complain in court that the EPA is not doing its job. However, the dissent argues that the legislature gave no explicit standing rights to states, so they should be treated like any other potential litigant.

2. *Massachusetts v. EPA* may open up standing to more environmental groups, not just states. One case that environmental groups singled out as benefiting from the *Massachusetts* case is Center for Biological Diversity & Pacific Environment v. Kempthorne, 2007 WL 2023515 (N.D. Cal. July 12, 2007), in which environmental groups seek protection for polar bears under the ESA, on the ground that global warming has contributed to a polar meltdown. See A.B.A. J. e-Rep., Apr. 6, 2007.

Do animals themselves have standing to sue under the ESA? In Palila v. Hawaii Dept. of Land and Natural Resources, 852 F.2d 1106, 1107 (9th Cir. 1988), the Ninth Circuit appeared to grant standing under the ESA to a Hawaiian bird: "As an endangered species under the Endangered Species Act, the bird (*Loxioides bailleui*), a member of the Hawaiian honeycreeper family, also has legal status and wings its way into federal court as a plaintiff in its own right." A few courts followed *Palila* and granted standing to a bird and a turtle. But the Ninth Circuit reconsidered its language in Cetacean Community v. Bush, 386 F.3d 1169 (9th Cir. 1994). The "Cetacean Community" was "the name chosen by the Cetaceans' self-appointed attorney for all of the world's whales, porpoises, and dolphins." The court referred to the above language from *Palila* as simply a rhetorical flourish. Nevertheless, the court pointed out that Article III does not limit standing to humans: "It is obvious that an animal cannot function as a plaintiff in the same manner as a juridically competent human being. But we see no reason why Article III prevents Congress from authorizing a suit in the name of an animal, any more than it prevents suits brought in the name of artificial persons such as corporations, partnerships or trusts, and even ships, or of juridically incompetent persons such as infants, juveniles, and mental incompetents." The court concluded, however, that the language "any person" in all of the applicable statutes does not include animals. For example, the court said that under the ESA, "[t]here is no hint in the definition of 'person'...that the 'person' authorized to bring suit to protect an endangered or threatened species can be an animal that is itself endangered or threatened."

Section Six
IMPROVING THE ADMINISTRATIVE INSTRUMENT

The previous materials suggest many avenues for improving the administrative instrument. For example, lawmakers could improve this instrument of the law by making regulatory standards clearer and by creating better enforcement techniques.

In addition, lawmakers could provide better avenues for interest-group participation in the process of agency rulemaking and adjudication. This and other areas in need of improvement are the subject of the following article.

EDWARD RUBIN, IT'S TIME TO MAKE THE ADMINISTRATIVE PROCEDURE ACT ADMINISTRATIVE
89 Cornell L. Rev. 95, 101-02 (2003)

[T]he structure of the APA itself reveals that the statute is essentially a one-trick pony. All of its basic provisions rely on a single method for controlling the actions of administrative agencies, namely, participation by private parties. The publication provisions inform private parties of the agencies' actions. The rulemaking and adjudication provisions enable private parties to communicate their views to the agency decision makers. The judicial review provisions give private parties an opportunity to challenge the legality of those decisions....

One obvious difficulty with the APA's reliance on public participation is that it forces the statute to depend for its effectiveness on large organizations—business firms, labor unions and, most characteristically, organized interest groups. Very few people other than professional lobbyists or lawyers employed by such organizations read the Federal Register, send comments to agencies regarding proposed rules, or challenge the legality of such rules in federal court. The litigants in leading cases involving the legality of rulemaking are generally entities such as the Natural Resources Defense Council (NRDC), the Sierra Club, the Defenders of Wildlife, the Motor Vehicle Manufacturers Association, the Association of Data Processing Service Organizations, the Chocolate Manufacturers Association, and the Toilet Goods Association. Adjudications involve individuals, of course, and the APA does grant them important mechanisms for controlling the agency's decision. But even in this case, sustained challenges to general agency practices under the judicial review provisions are often mounted by large organizations.

The disadvantages of the APA's monochromatic approach to agency control goes well beyond the obvious unfairness of relying on large private organizations, however. Supervision exercised by private parties is necessarily external, and usually adversarial as well. It is external in that it comes from individuals and organizations outside the administrative apparatus and, indeed, outside the government in its entirety. This limits the effectiveness of the control, since those exercising it, however assiduous, are less likely to understand the internal operation of the agency, less likely to speak in its own language, and less capable of imposing direct sanctions for disobedience. Second, private party control is often adversarial. Adjudications and judicial review are necessarily so. Rulemaking comments may support the agency's proposal, but most private comments are motivated by disapproval. Thus,

private parties can be relied upon to tell the agency what it is doing wrong, but not how it might improve.

Perhaps the most serious limitation of private party participation, however, is that it is almost always incremental. Private parties tend to be reactive; they will review published regulations, comment on regulatory proposals, lobby for or against regulatory initiatives, and sue when they feel aggrieved, but they are less likely to generate any of these proposals or initiatives, and are even less likely to plan a long-term administrative strategy. Even if they did so, the APA provides them with no opportunities for communicating such initiatives or long-term strategies to the agency. Rather, it restricts their role to the ambit of particular agency decisions—to the rule on which they are commenting, the adjudication in which they are making an appearance, or the agency action that they are challenging in court.

FINANCING THE PARTICIPATION OF PRIVATE PARTIES

Private citizens can participate directly in agency proceedings, either by making complaints based on individual interest or by acting as members of public-interest groups that seek to influence agency actions when broad principles are at stake. In fact, private actors help to counterbalance the extensive participation of the regulated industry in agency action. But the very theory of government regulation, which we explored in Section One, exposes a layer of reasons for insufficient participation. In general, the interest of private citizens in agency action is too diffuse and unorganized to have much effect. In addition, no one person is willing to invest the large resources needed to influence agency action because of the free-rider problem. For example, Congress created the FCC to oversee the broad public interest in broadcasting. But direct citizen participation in the FCC's forging of broadcast policies has been minimal because of the same diffuseness of interest, transactions costs, and free-rider problems that helped explain the creation of the FCC in the first place.

Nevertheless, some private groups have been organized to pursue public-interest causes and often have been financed by charitable contributions from individuals and foundations. These include groups such as the American Civil Liberties Union, the Sierra Club, and the Environmental Defense Fund. Still, such private actors often do not have sufficient resources to be very effective in this role. Consider the following from 3 Staff of Senate Comm. on Governmental

Affairs, 95th Cong., 1st Sess., Study on Federal Regulation: Public Participation in Regulatory Agency Proceedings, at VII (Comm. Print 1977):

> (3) At agency after agency, participation by the regulated industry predominates—often overwhelmingly. Organized public interest representation accounts for a very small percentage of participation before Federal regulatory agencies. In more than half of the formal proceedings, there appears to be no such participation whatsoever, and virtually none at informal agency proceedings. In those proceedings where participation by public groups does take place, typically it is a small fraction of the participation by the regulated industry. One-tenth is not uncommon; sometimes it is even less than that. This pattern prevails in both rulemaking proceedings and adjudicatory proceedings, with an even greater imbalance occurring in adjudications than in rulemaking.
>
> (4) The single greatest obstacle to active public participation in regulatory proceedings is the lack of financial resources by potential participants to meet the great costs of formal participation. . . .
>
> (5) The regulated industry consistently outspends public participants by a wide margin in regulatory agency proceedings. . . . In some instances, industry committed as much as 50 to 100 times the resources budgeted by the public interest participants.

Lawmakers could improve the balance between regulated industries' and affected citizens' participation through some form of financial assistance to public-interest groups. For example, an agency could pay public-interest groups for participation in agency rulemaking or adjudicative proceedings, or an agency or court could award legal expenses and attorney's fees to public-interest groups successful in proceedings before agencies or courts. The environmental groups in the *Northern Spotted Owl* case incurred substantial legal expenses in their ultimately successful action, and the law could finance such public-interest participation by assessing those expenses against the FWS. True, such an approach contradicts the general approach in the United States that each party must bear its own legal expenses and attorney's fees. In Alyeska Pipeline Service Co. v. Wilderness Society, 421 U.S. 240, 95 S. Ct. 1612 (1975), for example, the Supreme Court required specific legislative authorization for a court to award legal expenses and attorney's fees to public-interest litigants. But this only means that a statute is necessary to authorize fee-shifting in favor of public-interest groups.

Shortly after the Supreme Court decision in *Alyeska*, Senator Kennedy introduced legislation, S. 2715, 94th Cong., 2d Sess. (1975), that would have authorized awards of participation expenses, litigation expenses, and attorney's fees to public-interest groups appearing in agency proceedings (both rulemaking and adjudication) or judicial review of agency action. The government was to be the principal payor, but in some circumstances the costs could be assessed against opposing private parties. The bill was not enacted. In 1980, Congress did pass the Equal Access to Justice Act, 28 U.S.C. §2412, which provides for such fee-shifting in many civil cases (but not just those involving public-interest groups) brought by or against the federal government (including federal agencies).

The question of funding of private participation in agency actions raises several debatable issues, including:

- Which private parties should be reimbursed? Consider the following opinion from Panel II: Standing, Participation, and Who Pays?, 26 Admin. L. Rev. 423, 449–50 (1974) (Harold L. Russell):

> [T]hose who have advocated the expenditure of taxpayers' money to support the intervention of public interest representatives in agency proceedings have generally taken a one-sided view of the problem. Usually, I have heard that such funds would be devoted to fostering the causes of consumers and users and the like, whereas it is undoubtedly true that the public interest also extends to the welfare of the investors and of the employees whose money and labor are expended in the production of the service consumed by the user. All have a right to the proper consideration of their interest, and each is as much entitled to the expenditure of public funds for the protection of his interest as any of the others.
>
> Further, if there were a tax money fund to support public interest participation in agency proceedings, I am confident that we would not lack for allegedly genuine public interests to exhaust that fund, even if it were greater in amount than the combined budgets of the federal agencies. I believe that funding public intervention with tax money would lead to the assertion of spurious interests. . . .

- Must the group represent a broad class of people or is a narrow interest-group enough? For that matter, are environmentalists, as an example, a broad or a narrow group?
- Should the government pay expenses of public-interest groups participating in rulemaking as well as adjudication?
- Should private parties whose efforts are in vain be reimbursed? How should success be defined? In the *Alyeska* case, mentioned above, the Wilderness Society, the Environmental Defense Fund, and the Friends of the Earth sued the Secretary of the Interior to prevent issuance of permits to oil companies that wanted to build an oil pipeline across Alaska. The plaintiffs argued (1) that the permits would violate the Mineral Leasing Act of 1920, 30 U.S.C. §185, which limits rights-of-way across public lands to a fifty-foot width, and (2) that the environmental impact statement prepared by the Interior Department was inadequate. The court of appeals ruled for the plaintiffs on the width of right-of-way, without reaching the environmental issue. Thereafter, Congress mooted the merits of the case by passing the Trans-Alaska Pipeline Authorization Act, 43 U.S.C. §1651, which specifically authorized construction of the pipeline, with certain conditions (including a fund financed by the oil companies to cover pipeline-caused damage), and barred further consideration of environmental issues. On these facts, should the plaintiffs be entitled to attorney's fees? The court of appeals thought so—before being reversed on other grounds by the Supreme Court. Wilderness Society v. Morton, 495 F.2d 1026 (D.C. Cir. 1974) (en banc), rev'd sub nom. Alyeska Pipeline Service Co. v. Wilderness Society,

421 U.S. 240, 95 S. Ct. 1612 (1975). If the goal is to have public-interest groups raise important issues, perhaps success should not be required at all.

- Should the narrow character of the issue matter? For example, the *Alyeska* court of appeals dealt with the issue in a way that would leave few issues as being unimportant:

> It is argued that the width limitation in Section 28 of the Mineral Leasing Act of 1920 does not amount to a congressional policy of preeminent importance. But the dispute in this case was more than a debate over interpretation of that Act. [The Interior Department's] primary argument was that, whatever the width restrictions in the Act originally meant, a settled administrative practice to evade those restrictions took precedence. In the final analysis, this case involved the duty of the Executive Branch to observe the restrictions imposed by the Legislative . . . and the primary responsibility of the Congress under the Constitution to regulate the use of public lands.

Perhaps there are other routes to increasing private participation. We now turn the focus to how electronic technology can facilitate access to agencies and, at the same time, the flow of helpful information to agencies. The excerpt that follows usefully documents the various ways that technology can improve the administrative process.

CARY COGLIANESE, E-RULEMAKING: INFORMATION TECHNOLOGY AND THE REGULATORY PROCESS
56 Admin. L. Rev. 353, 354-55, 356, 358-59, 362-63, 372-78 (2004)

Crafting government regulations imposes significant information demands on regulatory agencies, from completing scientific, engineering, and economic analyses to processing and responding to extensive public comments. Information is vital for understanding complex problems, identifying the need for regulation, and analyzing alternative regulatory designs. Electronic rulemaking, or e-rulemaking, offers the potential to overcome some of the informational challenges associated with developing regulations. E-rulemaking refers to the use of digital technologies in the development and implementation of regulations. The use of these technologies may help streamline and improve regulatory management, such as by helping agency staff retrieve and analyze vast quantities of information from diverse sources. By taking better advantage of advances in digital technologies, agencies may also increase the public's access to and involvement in rulemaking. . . .

Perhaps in part due to information management burdens, government regulation has come in for substantial criticism over the past few decades. For some observers, the expanding sweep of government regulation has become unacceptably incoherent and inefficient. Problems of poor data quality and inconsistent reporting are sometimes said to increase problems of regulatory incoherence. . . . In addition, in the face of resource constraints, extensive engagement with the public has not always been regulators' top priority. Yet some have argued that regulatory policy—made by unelected government officials—suffers from a democratic deficit. With more extensive and effective public participation, agencies may gain insights needed to craft better regulatory policy as well as to enhance the perceived legitimacy of government regulation. Given the controversial and significant policy choices embedded in regulatory policy, any information technologies that can improve agency management and enhance public participation seem likely to help in addressing the criticisms of rulemaking and promoting more effective, efficient, and legitimate regulatory policy. . . .

Addressing some of rulemaking's various challenges, several goals for e-rulemaking [have been identified]: increasing democratic legitimacy, improving policy decisions, reducing administrative costs, and increasing regulatory compliance....

Goal 1: Increase Democratic Legitimacy. Even though rulemaking has significant effects on society and the economy, the officials making rulemaking decisions are themselves neither elected nor otherwise immediately accountable to the larger public. Indeed, career professionals conduct the major analysis and drafting, even though the political appointees heading the agencies play a role in reviewing and approving key decisions. Yet from the standpoint of democratic legitimacy, the very significance of rulemaking combined with its distance from public scrutiny make it all the more important that regulatory officials engage the public in the process. In-person public hearings or advisory committee meetings, as well as the conventional comment period, provide the traditional means for public input into the rulemaking process. IT may broaden public outreach both by fostering greater public awareness of rulemaking as well as by simplifying the process by which citizens can add their voices to the decision making process.

Of course, without more, the goal of increasing democratic legitimacy will seem almost too general to assist information systems designers or regulatory officials. Workshop participants characterized this goal in more specific ways which should prove helpful to decisionmakers and designers. Some of those goals include: (1) increasing public understanding of rulemaking; (2) increasing both the quality and quantity of public comment on rulemaking; (3) making the public comment process more interactive and deliberative; and (4) enhancing the ability of more democratically accountable institutions, such as Congress or the President, to oversee the rulemaking process. At present, the public has relatively little understanding of both the rules that specific agencies are developing and the process by which agencies promulgate their rules. Yet such knowledge of the issues and the process are essential precursors to participating effectively in government rulemaking. IT may provide better ways of communicating the steps of the rulemaking process to the public, notifying them of rules that may affect their work or their lives, and facilitating access to information that will enable members of the public to comprehend the policy choices embedded in rulemaking....

IT could also change the manner in which members of the public share comments on rules, thereby shifting the mode of communication from a relatively unidirectional one to a more deliberative and interactive process. Citizens and government officials could interact with each other in dialogues facilitated through electronic communication technologies. In addition, members of the public could begin to comment on each other's comments as well.

Finally, IT could enable other institutions and actors to monitor what agencies are doing and seek to influence the direction of regulatory policy. Not only could information make it easier for political appointees within agencies to follow and manage the work of civil service professionals, but it could also facilitate monitoring by congressional committees, White House staff, outside interest groups, and independent analysts....

Goal 2: Improve Policy Decisions. If information technologies make it easier for rule writers to retrieve and process information needed to develop sound regulatory policy, then e-rulemaking should presumably lead to better decisions. After all, good regulatory decisionmaking generally requires extensive information about the underlying problem, its causes, and the predicted effects of different possible solutions. IT could make it easier for regulatory officials to analyze large volumes of data drawn from multiple sources....

Goal 3: Decrease Administrative Costs. Managing the rulemaking process can also be costly and at times burdensome to regulatory agencies. A third goal for e-rulemaking would be to decrease the administrative costs associated with rulemaking, that is, to lower the costs that government incurs in developing new rules. IT may allow agencies to carry out existing rulemaking responsibilities in less costly ways. For example, the DOT has reported saving more than a million dollars in storage costs each year from its investment in an online docket system....

Goal 4: Increase Regulatory Compliance. A final goal of e-rulemaking could be to increase compliance with the rules agencies promulgate. Regulation is designed to achieve social goals by bringing the behavior of businesses and individuals into alignment with the law. To the extent that IT can help increase compliance with rules, it can help in achieving the underlying social goals that the rules are intended to serve.

Of course, if those targeted by regulation do not know about or understand the rules that apply to them, compliance will be at best something that is hit or miss. Perhaps some actors will comply for reasons unrelated to the rules, but many undoubtedly will not. So the first step in increasing compliance will be to increase awareness and understanding of regulations. Compliance assistance systems may make it easier for businesses to identify rules that apply to them. For example, even though a small print shop may be unable to afford to hire an attorney, the owner or shop manager could more easily use a software package that asks a series of questions about the shop's operations and then provides information about what health and safety rules apply to the facility.

NOTES

1. Dean Coglianese discusses some of the limitations of the administrative instrument, such as the "incoherence" of its regulation, its "inefficiencies," and its anti-democratic nature, and discusses how e-rulemaking can improve the situation. As a general matter, Coglianese points out that e-rulemaking can help in the retrieval and analysis of information (thereby improving the coherence and efficiency of rulemaking) and can increase public participation (making rulemaking more democratic). Coglianese believes that e-rulemaking can improve "democratic legitimacy" by educating the public about rulemaking; increasing public input both in terms of quality and quantity; increasing the ability to monitor what agencies are doing; and increasing the "interactiveness" of the process.

An e-Rulemaking Initiative

The "Cornell e-Rulemaking Initiative," http://ceri.law.cornell.edu, comprises a group of academics from several disciplines and legal information specialists who "consult with government agencies on, and engage in theoretical and applied research" on, the benefits of e-rulemaking outlined above in the Coglianese article. The goals of the Initiative are:

1. Helping agencies use the transition to web-based rulemaking as an opportunity to improve the efficiency and quality of their rulemaking practice.

2. Facilitating public and private efforts to realize the potential of e-rulemaking to increase public understanding of, and participation in, government decisionmaking.

3. Promoting and assisting agency experimentation in web-based efforts to elicit public participation beyond just the notice-and-comment process.

4. Increasing the data available to scholars on how rulemaking actually occurs, as well as on how agencies manage, and change in light of, a significant shift in technology.

2. Coglianese also outlines additional goals, including improving the substantive quality of agency decisions, decreasing administrative costs, and increasing compliance with regulations. With the potential of e-rulemaking to improve the situation so dramatically and in so many ways, it is no wonder that officials and interested parties have begun to formulate e-rulemaking initiatives.

Section Seven
LIMITATIONS OF LAW AS AN ADMINISTRATIVE INSTRUMENT

A. Introduction

Previous sections of this chapter have suggested many limitations of the administrative process, such as the problem of agency capture by the regulated industry and the anti-democratic nature of regulation. Such problems helped instigate a deregulation movement at the end of the last century. Deregulators, who came from both political parties, sought to dismantle major parts of the administrative structure that grew up in the 1930s and continued to expand thereafter. Airline deregulation was perhaps the most visible example. Until its demise early in 1985, the Civil Aeronautics Board (CAB) was deeply enmeshed in regulating rates charged and routes flown by all commercial airlines in the country. In the Airline Deregulation Act of 1978, Congress enacted sweeping reforms that eventually abolished the CAB and left airline rates and routes to be determined largely by competition in the marketplace.

In the communications field, the FCC has itself spearheaded deregulation. It first deregulated radio. In 1976, following notice-and-comment procedures, the FCC issued a policy statement announcing that it would no longer review past and proposed changes in entertainment format (e.g., a change from classical to rock music) in radio license renewal and transfer proceedings. Instead, noting that the market had already produced lots of diversity in entertainment formats and would respond more flexibly and quickly to changing tastes than could the government, the FCC declared that it would rely on the market to ensure entertainment diversity. See In re Development of Policy re: Changes in the Entertainment Formats of Broadcast Stations, 60 F.C.C.2d 858 (1976), reconsideration denied, 66 F.C.C.2d 78 (1977). In 1981, the FCC adopted even more sweeping changes by dropping previous guidelines that had (1) required stations to carry a certain percentage of news programs; (2) limited stations in the number of commercial minutes per hour; and (3) required stations to determine community interests through polls, interviews, and demographic data. In re Deregulation of Radio, 84 F.C.C.2d 968, clarified, 87 F.C.C.2d 797 (1981).

In 1981, the FCC also included television in its deregulatory program. For both radio and TV, it changed its license renewal process by substituting a

A Reprieve for Regulation

The financial crisis of 2008 and 2009, due in no small part to the lack of regulation of banks and other financial institutions, has led to rethinking about regulation. The new sentiment perhaps is best captured in an editorial appearing in the New York Times on March 29, 2009, at C8:

Who is to carry out the reforms? Any serious call for reform has to acknowledge the severe institutional damage that has been done to the nation's regulatory agencies. For 30 years, the political tide in this country has run against regulation and for deregulation. In the last 10 years, opponents of financial regulation have been especially successful in dismantling and undermining regulation, putting their faith and the nation's future in the hands of a market discipline that turned out not to exist and can't-miss financial products that missed, big.

There is not an agency that has not suffered a diminution of expertise or reputation.

Recent examples include the Federal Reserve's repeated failures to use its consumer-protection authority to stop unfair mortgage lending; the Securities and Exchange Commission's failure to heed repeated warnings about the Madoff Ponzi scheme; the efforts by the Office of the Comptroller of the Currency, a bank regulator, to block state regulators' efforts to police lending violations; and the utter failure of the Office of Thrift Supervision, A.I.G.'s federal regulator, to understand or, even worse, care about what was going on at that company.

Unfortunately, there are many, many more examples. Advocates of deregulation point to the failures as evidence that the government has no intrinsic ability to police markets. That is incorrect. The nation's regulatory agencies have been allowed to languish, underfunded, understaffed and too often headed by political appointees who are true believers only in the dogma of deregulation and not in their agencies' missions.

If the United States is going to have meaningful reform of its out-of-control financial system, new rules will only be a first step.

postcard application for the prior lengthy form that had inquired elaborately into the station's programming. However, a station must still maintain a public file with information about its assessment of community needs, its promises to meet those needs, and its actual broadcasting performance. In re Revision of Applications for Renewal of License of Commercial and Noncommercial AM, FM, and Television Licensees, 87 F.C.C.2d 1127 (1981). This action was upheld in Black Citizens for a Fair Media v. FCC, 719 F.2d 407 (D.C. Cir. 1983). In 1984, the Commission extended to commercial television its earlier deregulation of radio (e.g., abolition of programming and commercial guidelines).

Deregulation continued in the 1990s. For example, the Telecommunication Act of 1996 deregulated the telecommunications field by relaxing restrictions on consolidation. This allowed a particular communications sector to expand its services into a previously prohibited area. For example, telephone companies could now provide cable services.

In the remaining portion of this section, we focus on another enduring limitation of the administrative instrument, which also contributed to the deregulation movement. Because society's goals are numerous and often conflicting, pursuit of one goal through regulation may result in unintended negative consequences as to another goal. In trying to resolve such problems, regulators face the question of finding the proper balance between the laudatory goals of regulation and the potential infringement of other values. To illustrate this challenge, we tell the true story of a failed FCC policy called the fairness doctrine that could not successfully accommodate conflicting goals.

The overall goal of broadcasting regulation is to enhance the quality of what listeners and viewers may hear and see. No one doubts that FCC regulation of the electromagnetic spectrum by assigning frequencies to individual radio and TV stations advances that aim. Can you imagine if people were free to set up transmitters and stations and to broadcast at will? Listeners would be treated to incomprehensible jabber produced by multiple broadcasts on the same or closely neighboring frequencies. Such regulation was especially important, of course, before the advent of cable television and the Internet.

But what about regulation of program content? Such regulation may improve content, for example, by creating rights to respond in people or groups who are attacked on the air. The public would thus have the benefit of opposing points of view. The FCC promulgated just such an equal-time regulation. But, as we shall see, such a regulation may conflict with free speech rights and also may deter broadcasters from airing controversial subjects in the first place (mainly for fear of having to grant free time for a response).

B. Brief History of a Failed Regulatory Doctrine: The Fairness Doctrine

The FCC promulgated the fairness doctrine through a series of decisions, reports, and primers. For example, although not the first utterance on the doctrine, in 1949 the FCC issued a report that focused on the importance of "providing and maintaining a climate of fairness and equal opportunity for the expression of contrary views." In re Editorializing by Broadcast Licensees, 13 F.C.C. 1246, 1254 (1949). This Editorializing Report maintained:

> In the absence of a duty to present all sides of controversial issues, overt editorialization by station licensees could conceivably result in serious abuse. But where, as we believe to be the case under the Communications Act, such a responsibility for a fair and balanced presentation of controversial public issues exists, we cannot see how the open espousal of one point of view by the licensee should necessarily prevent him from affording a fair opportunity for the presentation of contrary positions ....

In short, the public interest required that broadcasters must present all sides of controversial issues.

In 1959, Congress amended §315(a) of the Communications Act of 1934 to exclude bona fide news coverage from certain non-fairness-doctrine equal-time requirements. The legislators were careful to clarify that Congress did not intend by this legislation to affect the developing fairness doctrine. The amendment therefore included language that broadcasters must continue to "operate in the public interest and to afford reasonable opportunity for the discussion of conflicting views on issues of public importance." 47 U.S.C. §315(a). In 1964, the FCC drew together its decisions in the Fairness Primer. 29 Fed. Reg. 10,416 (1964). In 1967, the FCC issued formal rules that added meat to the bones of the doctrine, including creation of a duty that broadcasters notify people of the content of a personal attack and to offer free reply time. 47 C.F.R. 73.1910 (1967).

C. The Supreme Court Considers the Fairness Doctrine

In 1969, the U.S. Supreme Court held in Red Lion Broadcasting Co. v. FCC, 395 U.S. 367, 390, 89 S. Ct. 1794, 1806 (1969), that the fairness doctrine did not violate the First Amendment, reasoning that "[i]t is the right of the viewers and listeners, not the right of the broadcasters, which is paramount." The Court focused on the scarcity of the airwaves as a justification for regulating broadcasting in the first place. We now look at the *Red Lion* case more fully.

THE FACTS

On November 27, 1964, the Red Lion Broadcasting Company, the licensee of radio station WGCB–AM-FM, Red Lion, Pennsylvania, broadcast a 15-minute program by a Reverend Billy James Hargis as part of a program series entitled "The Christian Crusade." Reverend Hargis commented on the 1964 presidential election and among other things said:

> Who is Cook? Cook was fired from the New York World-Telegram after he made a false charge publicly on television against an unnamed official of the New York City government. New York publishers and Newsweek magazine for December 7, 1959, showed that Fred Cook and his pal Eugene Gleason had made up the whole story and this confession was made to New York District Attorney Frank Hogan. After losing his job, Cook went to work for the left-wing publication The Nation. ...Now, among other things Fred Cook wrote for The Nation was an article absolving Alger Hiss of any wrongdoing...there was a 208-page attack on the FBI and J. Edgar Hoover; another attack by Mr. Cook was on the Central Intelligence Agency...now this is the man who wrote the book to smear and destroy Barry Goldwater called "Barry Goldwater—Extremist of the Right."

Fred J. Cook learned of the foregoing and demanded that the Red Lion Broadcasting Company give him free time for a reply. Red Lion refused. Cook then filed a complaint with the FCC, alleging the foregoing facts and demanding free time. Red Lion could have insisted on a formal hearing before an FCC hearing examiner, in which the parties would have introduced evidence and presented legal arguments. The hearing examiner would have found the facts, reached conclusions of law, and prepared a proposed order disposing of the case. The FCC, after reviewing the hearing examiner's findings and conclusions, would have decided whether to issue the proposed order or to substitute a different one.

However, in the actual case, with Red Lion's consent, the FCC adjudicated informally. In a letter dated October 6, 1965, the FCC concluded that Cook had been the victim of a personal attack within the meaning of the fairness doctrine and that Cook was entitled to free use of Red Lion facilities for a response. The FCC ordered Red Lion to "advise the Commission of your plans to comply with the fairness doctrine applicable to the situation." Red Lion sent a letter on November 8 to the FCC requesting reconsideration by the FCC, but the FCC responded on December 9 by upholding its decision. As to whether the fairness doctrine violated the First Amendment, the FCC wrote:

> The ruling [in *Red Lion*] does not involve any prior restraint. The licensee is free to select what controversial issue should be covered, and whether coverage of that issue should include a personal attack. The ruling simply requires that if the licensee does choose to present a personal attack, the person attacked must be notified and given the opportunity for comparable response....
>
> A broadcaster has sought the license to a valuable public frequency, and has taken it, subject to the obligation to operate in the public interest. Valuable frequency space has been allocated to broadcasting in considerable part, so that it may contribute to an informed electorate. Report on Editorializing, 13 F.C.C. 1246–1270, par. 6. Viewed against these fundamental precepts, our ruling is, we believe, reasonably related to the public interest "in the larger and more effective use of radio" (Section 303(g) of the Communications Act). Since that is so, it is a requirement fully consistent with the Constitution.

NOTES

1. In the FCC's view, self-regulation by Red Lion failed. But this does not mean that the proceedings by the FCC were inevitable. For example, had Red Lion granted Cook's request there would have been no proceeding. We therefore should not evaluate the importance of the administrative process solely based on the frequency of coercive regulatory proceedings, but should also consider instances of self-regulation and private regulation in light of the agency's previously articulated standards.

2. The FCC learned of the alleged Red Lion violation of the fairness doctrine when Cook complained to it. This illustrates the importance of private initiative in setting the administrative instrument in motion. Unlike the remedial instrument, however, once Cook complained to the FCC, he did not have to proceed on his own.

3. Red Lion probably did not insist on formal adjudication before the FCC because the dispute was not factual in nature. No one contested what Hargis said or that Red Lion broadcast it. Instead, the dispute required the FCC to apply its legal rules to agreed facts.

4. Instead of complying with the FCC's order, Red Lion chose to seek review in the United States Court of Appeals for the District of Columbia Circuit. Through briefs and oral argument, it urged that the FCC order was unauthorized and unconstitutional. Pending this review, Red Lion was not required to comply with the FCC order. On June 13, 1967, the court of appeals decided Red Lion's appeal in favor of the FCC and thus upheld the FCC's order requiring Red Lion to give Cook free time for a reply.

5. Red Lion then took this decision to the Supreme Court of the United States. This case was argued before the Court on April 2–3, 1969, by several lawyers, including Archibald Cox, professor at the Harvard Law School, and Solicitor General Erwin Griswold, former dean of the Harvard Law School. On June 9, 1969, the Supreme Court handed down its decision.

RED LION BROADCASTING CO. v. FCC
Supreme Court of the United States, 1969
395 U.S. 367, 89 S. Ct. 1794

MR. JUSTICE WHITE delivered the opinion of the Court:

The Federal Communications Commission has for many years imposed on radio and television broadcasters the requirement that discussion of public issues be presented on broadcast stations, and that each side of those issues must be given fair coverage. This is known as the fairness doctrine, which originated very early in the history of broadcasting and has maintained its present outlines for some time. It is an obligation whose content has been defined in a long series of FCC rulings in particular cases, and which is distinct from the statutory requirement of §315 of the Communications Act that equal time be allotted all qualified candidates for public office. Two aspects of the fairness doctrine, relating to personal attacks in the context of controversial public issues and to political editorializing, were codified more precisely in the form of FCC regulations in 1967.

[The Court related the facts and concluded that the FCC did not exceed its authority in promulgating the fairness doctrine.]

The broadcasters challenge the fairness doctrine and its specific manifestations in the personal attack and political editorial rules on conventional First Amendment grounds, alleging that the rules abridge their freedom of speech and press. Their contention is that the First Amendment protects their desire to use their allotted frequencies continuously to broadcast whatever they choose, and to exclude whomever they choose from ever using that frequency. No man may be prevented from saying or publishing what he thinks, or from refusing in his speech or other utterances to give equal weight to the views of his opponents. This right, they say, applies equally to broadcasters.

A.

Although broadcasting is clearly a medium affected by a First Amendment interest, United States v. Paramount Pictures, Inc., 334 U.S. 131, 166, 68 S. Ct. 915, 933 (1948), differences in the characteristics of news media justify differences in the First Amendment standards applied to them. Joseph Burstyn, Inc. v. Wilson, 343 U.S. 495, 503, 72 S. Ct. 777, 781 (1952). For example, the ability of new technology to produce sounds more raucous than those of the human voice justifies restrictions on the sound level, and on the hours and places of use, of sound trucks so long as the restrictions are reasonable and applied without discrimination. Kovacs v. Cooper, 336 U.S. 77, 69 S. Ct. 448 (1949).

Just as the Government may limit the use of sound amplifying equipment potentially so noisy that it drowns out civilized private speech, so may the Government limit the use of broadcast equipment. The right of free speech of a broadcaster, the user of a sound truck, or any other individual does not embrace a right to snuff out the free speech of others. Associated Press v. United States, 326 U.S. 1, 20, 65 S. Ct. 1416, 1424 (1945).

... [T]he reach of radio signals is incomparably greater than the range of the human voice and the problem of interference is a massive reality. The lack of know-how and equipment may keep many from the air, but only a tiny fraction of those with resources and intelligence can hope to communicate by radio at the same time if intelligible communication is to be had, even if the entire radio spectrum is utilized in the present state of commercially acceptable technology.

It was this fact, and the chaos which ensued from permitting anyone to use any frequency at whatever power level he wished, which made necessary the enactment of the Radio Act of 1927 and the Communications Act of 1934, as the Court has noted at length before. National Broadcasting Co. v. United States, 319 U.S. 190, 210–214, 63 S. Ct. 997, 1006–1009 (1943). It was this reality which at the very least necessitated first the division of the radio spectrum into portions reserved respectively for public broadcasting and for other important radio uses such as amateur operation, aircraft, police, defense, and navigation; and then the subdivision of each portion, and assignment of specific frequencies to individual users or groups of users. Beyond this, however, because the frequencies reserved for public broadcasting were limited in number, it was essential for the Government to tell some applicants that they could not broadcast at all because there was room for only a few.

Where there are substantially more individuals who want to broadcast than there are frequencies to allocate, it is idle to posit an unabridgeable First Amendment right to broadcast comparable to the right of every individual to speak, write, or publish. If 100 persons want broadcast licenses but there are only 10 frequencies to allocate, all of them may have the same "right" to a license; but if there is to be any effective communication by radio, only a few can be licensed and the rest must be barred from the airwaves. It would be strange if the First Amendment, aimed at protecting and furthering communications, prevented the Government from making radio communication possible by requiring licenses to broadcast and by limiting the number of licenses so as not to overcrowd the spectrum.

This has been the consistent view of the Court. Congress unquestionably has the power to grant and deny licenses and to delete existing stations. FRC v. Nelson Bros. Bond & Mortgage Co., 289 U.S. 266, 53 S. Ct. 627 (1933). No one has a First Amendment right to a license or to monopolize a radio frequency; to deny a station license because "the public interest" requires it "is not a denial of free speech." National Broadcasting Co. v. United States, 319 U.S. 190, 227, 63 S. Ct. 997, 1014 (1943).

By the same token, as far as the First Amendment is concerned those who are licensed stand no better than those to whom licenses are refused. A license permits broadcasting, but the licensee has no constitutional right to be the one who holds the license or to monopolize a radio frequency to the exclusion of his fellow citizens. There is nothing in the First Amendment which prevents the Government from requiring a licensee to share his frequency with others and to conduct himself as a proxy or fiduciary with obligations to present those views and voices which are representative of his community and which would otherwise, by necessity, be barred from the airwaves.

This is not to say that the First Amendment is irrelevant to public broadcasting. On the contrary, it has a major role to play as the Congress itself recognized in §326, which forbids FCC interference with "the right of free speech by means of radio communication." Because of the scarcity of radio frequencies, the Government is permitted to put restraints on licensees in favor of others whose views should be expressed on this unique medium. But the people as a whole retain their interest in free speech by radio and their collective right to have the medium function consistently with the ends and purposes of the First Amendment. It is the right of the viewers and listeners, not the right of the broadcasters, which is paramount. It is the purpose of the First Amendment to preserve an uninhibited marketplace of ideas in which truth will ultimately prevail, rather than to countenance monopolization of that market, whether it be by the Government itself or a private licensee.... It is the right of the public to receive suitable access to social, political, esthetic, moral, and other ideas and experiences which is crucial here. That right may not constitutionally be abridged either by Congress or by the FCC.

B.

Rather than confer frequency monopolies on a relatively small number of licensees, in a Nation of 200,000,000, the Government could surely have decreed that each frequency should be shared among all or some of those who wish to use it, each being assigned a portion of the broadcast day or the broadcast week. The ruling and regulations at issue here do not go quite so far. They assert that under specified circumstances, a licensee must offer to make available a reasonable amount of broadcast time to those who have a view different from that which has already been expressed on his station. The expression of a political endorsement, or of a personal attack while dealing with a controversial public issue, simply triggers this time sharing. As we have said, the First Amendment confers no right on licensees to prevent others from broadcasting on "their" frequencies and no right to an unconditional monopoly of a scarce resource which the Government has denied others the right to use. . . .

Nor can we say that it is inconsistent with the First Amendment goal of producing an informed public capable of conducting its own affairs to require a broadcaster to permit answers to personal attacks occurring in the course of discussing controversial issues, or to require that the political opponents of those endorsed by the station be given a chance to communicate with the public. Otherwise, station owners and a few networks would have unfettered power to make time available only to the highest bidders, to communicate only their own views on public issues, people and candidates, and to permit on the air only those with whom they agreed. There is no sanctuary in the First Amendment for unlimited private censorship operating in a medium not open to all. "Freedom of the press from governmental interference under the First Amendment does not sanction repression of that freedom by private interests." Associated Press v. United States, 326 U.S. 1, 20, 65 S. Ct. 1416, 1425

(1945) [(deciding that under the antitrust laws the Associated Press, a private news-gathering association, was required to supply news to competitors of its members on a nondiscriminatory basis)].

C.

It is strenuously argued, however, that if political editorials or personal attacks will trigger an obligation in broadcasters to afford the opportunity for expression to speakers who need not pay for time and whose views are unpalatable to the licensees, then broadcasters will be irresistibly forced to self-censorship and their coverage of controversial public issues will be eliminated or at least rendered wholly ineffective. Such a result would indeed be a serious matter, for should licensees actually eliminate their coverage of controversial issues, the purposes of the doctrine would be stifled.

At this point, however, as the Federal Communications Commission has indicated, that possibility is at best speculative. The communications industry, and in particular the networks, have taken pains to present controversial issues in the past, and even now they do not assert that they intend to abandon their efforts in this regard. It would be better if the FCC's encouragement were never necessary to induce the broadcasters to meet their responsibility. And if experience with the administration of these doctrines indicates that they have the net effect of reducing rather than enhancing the volume and quality of coverage, there will be time enough to reconsider the constitutional implications. The fairness doctrine in the past has had no such overall effect.

That this will occur now seems unlikely, however, since if present licensees should suddenly prove timorous, the Commission is not powerless to insist that they give adequate and fair attention to public issues. It does not violate the First Amendment to treat licensees given the privilege of using scarce radio frequencies as proxies for the entire community, obligated to give suitable time and attention to matters of great public concern. To condition the granting or renewal of licenses on a willingness to present representative community views on controversial issues is consistent with the ends and purposes of those constitutional provisions forbidding the abridgment of freedom of speech and freedom of the press. Congress need not stand idly by and permit those with licenses to ignore the problems which beset the people or to exclude from the airways anything but their own views on fundamental questions. The statute, long administrative practice, and cases are to this effect.

Licenses to broadcast do not confer ownership of designated frequencies, but only the temporary privilege of using them. 47 U.S.C. §301. Unless renewed, they expire within three years. 47 U.S.C. §307(d). The statute mandates the issuance of licenses if the "public convenience, interest, or necessity will be served thereby." 47 U.S.C. §307(a). In applying this standard the Commission for 40 years has been choosing licensees based in part on their program proposals. . . .

E.

It is argued that even if at one time the lack of available frequencies for all who wished to use them justified the Government's choice of those who would best serve the public interest by acting as proxy for those who would present differing views, or by giving the latter access directly to broadcast facilities, this condition no longer prevails so that continuing control is not justified. To this there are several answers.

Scarcity is not entirely a thing of the past. Advances in technology, such as microwave transmission, have led to more efficient utilization of the frequency spectrum, but uses for that spectrum have also grown apace. [The Court here canvassed such uses as marine and air navigation aids and communication systems for police, ambulance, fire department, public utility, amateur, military, and common carrier users.]

The rapidity with which technological advances succeed one another to create more efficient use of spectrum space on the one hand, and to create new uses for that space by ever growing numbers of people on the other, makes it unwise to speculate on the future allocation of that space. It is enough to say that the resource is one of considerable and growing importance whose scarcity impelled its regulation by an agency authorized by Congress. Nothing in this record, or in our own researches, convinces us that the resource is no longer one for which there are more immediate and potential uses than can be accommodated, and for which wise planning is essential. . . .

. . . The judgment of the Court of Appeals in *Red Lion* is affirmed and . . . remanded for proceedings consistent with this opinion.

It is so ordered.

Not having heard oral argument in these cases, Mr. Justice Douglas took no part in the Court's decision.

The Court indicated that the outcome would have been different if the airwaves were no longer a scarce technological resource or if the fairness doctrine substantially decreased broadcasters' willingness to broadcast controversial matters. In addition, the Court would have decided for Red Lion if it believed that the First Amendment barred Congress, and therefore the FCC, from requiring stations to carry some publicly controversial programming.

In Miami Herald Publishing Co. v. Tornillo, 418 U.S. 241, 94 S. Ct. 2831 (1974), a case decided after *Red Lion*, the Supreme Court held that a Florida statute requiring newspapers to give equivalent space to a political candidate whom the newspaper had previously attacked in a political editorial violated the First Amendment. The opinion included the following discussion:

> The appellee [the political candidate] and supporting advocates of an enforceable right of access to the press vigorously argue that government has an obligation to ensure that a wide variety of views reach the public. . . .

Access advocates submit that although newspapers of the present are superficially similar to those of 1791 [when the First Amendment was adopted] the press of today is in reality very different from that known in the early years of our national existence. In the past half century a communications revolution has seen the introduction of radio and television into our lives, the promise of a global community through the use of communications satellites, and the spectre of a "wired" nation by means of an expanding cable television network with two-way capabilities. The printed press, it is said, has not escaped the effects of this revolution. Newspapers have become big business and there are far fewer of them to serve a large literate population. Chains of newspapers, national wire and news services, and one-newspaper towns, are the dominant features of a press that has become noncompetitive and enormously powerful and influential in its capacity to manipulate popular opinion and change the course of events. Major metropolitan newspapers have collaborated to establish news services national in scope. Such national news organizations provide syndicated features and commentary, all of which serve as part of the new school of "advocacy journalism."

The elimination of competing newspapers in most of our large cities, and the concentration of control of media that results from the only newspaper being owned by the same interests which own a television station and a radio station, are important components of this trend toward concentration of control of outlets to inform the public.

The result of these vast changes has been to place in a few hands the power to inform the American people and shape public opinion. Much of the editorial opinion and commentary that is printed is that of syndicated columnists distributed nationwide and, as a result, we are told, on national and world issues there tends to be a homogeneity of editorial opinion, commentary, and interpretative analysis. The abuses of bias and manipulative reportage are, likewise, said to be the result of vast accumulations of unreviewable power in the modern media empires. In effect, it is claimed, the public has lost any ability to respond or to contribute in a meaningful way to the debate on issues....

The obvious solution, which was available to dissidents at an earlier time when entry into publishing was relatively inexpensive, today would be to have additional newspapers. But the same economic factors which have caused the disappearance of vast numbers of metropolitan newspapers, have made entry into the marketplace of ideas served by the print media almost impossible. It is urged that the claim of newspapers to be "surrogates for the public" carries with it a concomitant fiduciary obligation to account for that stewardship. From this premise it is reasoned that the only effective way to insure fairness and accuracy and to provide for some accountability is for government to take affirmative action. The First Amendment interest of the public in being informed is said to be in peril because the "marketplace of ideas" is today a monopoly controlled by the owners of the market....

However much validity may be found in these arguments, at each point the implementation of a remedy such as an enforceable right of access necessarily calls for some mechanism, either governmental or consensual. If it is governmental coercion, this at once brings about a confrontation with the express provisions of the First Amendment....

Another View of *Red Lion* and the Fairness Doctrine

By the end of the *Red Lion* case, Cook said he was weary of it all and declined to reply when the station finally offered him free time. Perhaps the following explains Cook's position.

Fred Friendly, then professor of journalism at Columbia University, shed new light on the *Red Lion* case and the fairness doctrine in an article, What's Fair on the Air?, N.Y. Times, Mar. 30, 1975, §6 (Magazine), at 11, and in a subsequent book, The Good Guys, the Bad Guys, and the First Amendment: Free Speech vs. Fairness in Broadcasting (1976). Friendly reported that in the early 1960s, President Kennedy, Vice President Johnson, and the Democratic National Committee (DNC) had actively sought to utilize the fairness doctrine to obtain free air time to reply to far-right political opponents and to intimidate radio stations so that they would cancel far-right programs. According to Friendly, in 1963–1964 the DNC launched an effort to monitor extreme right-wing broadcasts and to get individuals and organizations that had been attacked in these broadcasts to request reply time. Under this campaign, the DNC apparently encouraged and helped Mr. Cook prepare his fairness doctrine demand, which was sent to over 200 stations, and counseled him on how to petition the FCC for free time if any station refused to broadcast his reply statement. According to Friendly, the DNC had earlier subsidized Mr. Cook's anti-Goldwater book by guaranteeing in advance the purchase of 50,000 copies, and a DNC staff member had supplied information for, and perhaps inspired, Mr. Cook's "Hate Clubs of the Air" piece in The Nation. Friendly reported, moreover, that some of this anti-right-wing activity was financed by a DNC-created organization with tax-exempt status, to which the DNC gave some of its own funds and to which it encouraged Democratic party supporters to contribute.

Friendly cited DNC reports claiming the fairness doctrine effort netted 1,035 letters to stations and 1,678 hours of free time from stations that carried right-wing broadcasts. Friendly quoted one DNC staff member as writing in a report to the DNC that "[e]ven more important than the free radio time was the effectiveness of this operation in inhibiting the political activity of these right-wing broadcasts," and another as writing in another report that the campaign "may have inhibited the stations in their broadcast of more radical and politically partisan programs."

Friendly concluded his article in the New York Times Magazine with the following observations:

> [T]he assumption that the problem in the *Red Lion* case was access for Fred Cook's views is, in light of what we know today, demonstrably false. Fred Cook with his Nation magazine attack on Hargis and other "Hate Clubs of the Air," and his subsidized book against Goldwater, was hardly a classical case of a man in need of access. And though the Court did not know it when it heard the case, his motivation for taking action against the Red Lion station was not just to gain access to the public air-waves in order to defend himself against an attack so much as it was the product of a carefully orchestrated program initiated by politicians to inhibit views they believed to be harmful to the country, as well as to their own political fortunes.

. . . A newspaper is more than a passive receptacle or conduit for news, comment, and advertising. The choice of material to go into a newspaper, and the decisions made as to limitations on the size of the paper, and content, and treatment of public issues and public officials—whether fair or unfair— constitutes the exercise of editorial control and judgment. It has yet to be demonstrated how governmental regulation of this crucial process can be exercised consistent with First Amendment guarantees of a free press as they have evolved to this time.

The *Tornillo* Court did not mention or cite the *Red Lion* case. The difference in treatment of broadcasting and newspapers can be explained, at least theoretically, by the lack of scarcity of print opportunities. So, if printer's ink suddenly became drastically short and the government set up a commission to ration ink, the Commission probably could do what Florida was not permitted to do in *Tornillo*, at least based on the reasoning of the *Red Lion* case.

D. Demise of a Regulatory Doctrine

The fairness doctrine was controversial from the beginning and, unsurprisingly, the doctrine got caught up in the deregulation movement of the 1980s. In 1985, the FCC issued a Fairness Report that backtracked on its factual findings in a 1974 Fairness Report that the fairness doctrine enhanced the flow of diverse viewpoints to the public. In 1985, the FCC found that the fairness doctrine created incentives for broadcasters to avoid controversial programming, so that they would not have to offer free time to opposing views or go to court to determine whether they had such a duty. In addition, the FCC relied on the "explosive growth in the various communications technologies" so that the public would be exposed to many diverse perspectives. Excerpts from the 1985 report follow.

FCC, GENERAL FAIRNESS DOCTRINE OBLIGATIONS OF BROADCAST LICENSEES
50 Fed. Reg. 35,418 (1985)

We believe the fairness doctrine is an unnecessary and detrimental regulatory mechanism. While we recognize that the fairness doctrine has been a central tenet of broadcast regulation for more than fifty years, we believe that we have a statutorily mandated duty to reassess the propriety of even long standing policies in light of changes in the broadcast marketplace and evidence that the policy may not further the public interest. After careful evaluation of the evidence of record, our experience in enforcing the fairness doctrine, and fundamental constitutional principles, we find that the fairness doctrine disserves the public interest.

Three factors form the basis for this determination. First, in recent years there has been a significant increase in the number and types of information sources. As a consequence, we believe that the public

has access to a multitude of viewpoints without the need or danger of regulatory intervention.

Second, the evidence in this proceeding demonstrates that the fairness doctrine in operation thwarts the laudatory purpose it is designed to promote. Instead of furthering the discussion of public issues, the fairness doctrine inhibits broadcasters from presenting controversial issues of public importance. As a consequence, broadcasters are burdened with counterproductive regulatory restraints and the public is deprived of a marketplace of ideas unencumbered by the hand of government.

Third, the restrictions on the journalistic freedoms of broadcasters resulting from enforcement of the fairness doctrine contravene fundamental constitutional principles, accord a dangerous opportunity for governmental abuse and impose unnecessary economic costs on both the broadcasters and the Commission....

The Record Demonstrates that the Fairness Doctrine Causes Broadcasters to Restrict Their Coverage of Controversial Issues

The record reflects that, in operation, the fairness doctrine—in stark contravention of its purpose—operates as a pervasive and significant impediment to the broadcasting of controversial issues of public importance....

Journalists who have worked in both the broadcast and print media have testified that the very existence of the fairness doctrine creates a climate of timidity and fear, unexperienced by print journalists, that is antithetical to journalistic freedom. The inhibitions resulting from the interjection of a ubiquitous and brooding governmental presence into the editorial decisionmaking process is vividly described by Mr. Dan Rather, Managing Editor and Anchor of CBS News, as follows:

> When I was a young reporter, I worked briefly for wire services, small radio stations, and newspapers, and I finally settled into a job at a large radio station owned by the Houston Chronicle. Almost immediately on starting work in that station's newsroom, I became aware of a concern which I had previously barely known existed—the FCC. The journalists at the Chronicle did not worry about it; those at the radio station did. Not only the station manager but the newspeople as well were very much aware of this Government presence looking over their shoulders. I can recall newsroom conversations about what the FCC implications of broadcasting a particular report would be. Once a newsperson has to stop and consider what a Government agency will think of something he or she wants to put on the air, an invaluable element of freedom has been lost.

The record reflects that broadcasters from television network anchors to small radio station journalists perceive the fairness doctrine to operate as a demonstrable deterrent in the coverage of controversial issues. Indeed, the record is replete with descriptions from broadcasters who have candidly recounted specific instances in which they decided not to air controversial matters of public importance because such broadcasts might trigger fairness doctrine obligations....

Equally or perhaps even more disturbing than the self-censorship of individual broadcasts is the fact that the avoidance of fairness doctrine burdens has precipitated specific "policies" on the part of broadcast stations which have the direct effect of diminishing, on a routine basis, the amount of controversial material presented to the public on broadcast stations. For example, the owner of a broadcast station and two newspapers regularly prints editorials in his newspapers but, inhibited by regulatory restrictions, is reluctant to repeat the same editorials on his radio station. Similarly, the Meredith Corporation acknowledges that one of its television stations has chosen "not to editorialize on matters of public importance, because of its concern that it does not have the resources necessary to seek out and provide exposure to opposing viewpoints in all instances." Unfortunately, the policies of these stations are not atypical. In fact, a survey conducted by NAB [National Association of Broadcasters] in 1982 found that only 45 percent of responding stations had presented editorials in the preceding two years....

Need for the Fairness Doctrine in Light of the Increase in the Amount and Type of Information Sources in the Marketplace

... The Commission's last assessment of the information marketplace, and its necessary relationship to the legal and policy underpinnings of the fairness doctrine, occurred in 1974. At that time the Commission concluded:

> The effective development of an electronic medium with an abundance of channels through the use of cable or otherwise is still very much a thing of the future. *For the present*, we do not believe that it would be appropriate—or even permissible—for a government agency charged with the allocation of the *channels now available* to ignore the legitimate First Amendment interests of the public. (emphasis added)

More than a decade has passed since this examination. During this time, we have witnessed explosive growth in various communications technologies. We find the information marketplace of today different from that which existed in 1974, as many of the "future" electronic technologies have now become contributors to the marketplace of ideas.... The growth of traditional broadcast facilities, as well as the development of new electronic information technologies, provides the public with suitable access to the marketplace of ideas so as to render the fairness doctrine unnecessary....

... [T]here has been a 44.3 percent increase in the overall number of television stations since the Supreme Court's decision in *Red Lion Broadcasting*. This represents a 13.3 percent increase in VHF stations and a dramatic 113 percent increase in UHF stations. Television growth since the Commission's 1974 Fairness Report has also been significant, amounting to a 28 percent increase in the overall number of television stations with a 66.4 percent increase in UHF stations.

The continued growth in television broadcasting has led directly to an increase in signal availability in local markets....

Conclusion

[In omitted passages, the FCC repeated its conclusion that the fairness doctrine was unnecessary and detrimental.] Notwithstanding these conclusions, we have decided not to eliminate the fairness doctrine at this time. The doctrine has been a longstanding administrative policy and a central tenet of broadcast regulation in which Congress has shown a strong although often ambivalent interest. Indeed, while Congress has not yet chosen to eliminate the doctrine legislatively, several members of Congress have recently sponsored bills seeking to abolish the fairness doctrine and its related policies. Congress also has held hearings to determine whether or not it should enact legislation to eliminate the doctrine. In addition, we recognize that the United States Supreme Court in FCC v. League of Women Voters of California[, 468 U.S. 364, 104 S. Ct. 3106 (1984),] has similarly demonstrated an interest in our examination of the constitutional and policy implications underlying the fairness doctrine. Because of the intense Congressional interest in the fairness doctrine and the pendency of legislative proposals, we have determined that it would be inappropriate at this time to eliminate the fairness doctrine. Given our decision to defer to Congress on this matter, we also believe that it would be inappropriate for us to act on the various proposals to modify or restrict the scope of the fairness doctrine. It is also important to emphasize that we will continue to administer and enforce the fairness doctrine obligations of broadcasters and to underscore our expectation that broadcast licensees will continue to satisfy these requirements.

The FCC Report, above, shows that the FCC came full circle on the appropriateness of the fairness doctrine, now calling it "an unnecessary and detrimental regulatory mechanism." But not everyone agreed with the FCC. For example, consider Lee M. Mitchell, Book Review, 37 Fed. Com. L.J. 377, 383 (1985) (reviewing Ford Rowan, Broadcast Fairness: Doctrine, Practice, Prospects (1984)). Mr. Mitchell argued that the fairness doctrine functioned essentially as a "fail safe" mechanism, affecting only the most egregious situations: "If there is to be anything left after [deregulation] runs its course, it would seem it should be this last resort protection for the public against stations which consistently exclude from the air views with which their owners disagree, exult in racial or religious bigotry or blatantly use their facilities to obtain the election of a favored candidate."

Consider also the following response, from a former FCC chairman, to the FCC's argument that broadcast channels and other information sources are no longer so scarce as to require the fairness doctrine:

The argument is disingenuous. In the last few years, The Washington Star, The Chicago Daily News and The Philadelphia Bulletin all went out of business. No new newspapers took their place. By contrast, when the F.C.C. made RKO's channels available for competitive application, it quickly got 172 applications, each applicant arguing, "Give the license to me, and turn down the other 171." And when the communications commission decided to permit new low-power television stations, it was inundated by almost 14,000 applications.

The test of scarcity cannot be measured by the number of newspapers. The proper test is the number of citizens who want a broadcast license and are unable to obtain one. At that point, a decision must be made as to who is to be allowed, and who denied, the exclusive license to use the channels. Scarcity still exists when channels are not available to all. And as long as scarcity exists, the need for some measure of regulation will exist.

Newton N. Minow, Being Fair to the Fairness Doctrine, N.Y. Times, Aug. 27, 1985, at A23.

In its 1974 Fairness Report, the FCC had expressly relied upon the First Amendment interests of the public to hear contrasting viewpoints on important issues as a valid reason for the fairness doctrine. Arguably, the FCC in its 1985 Fairness Report elevated the broadcasters' First Amendment rights over those of the public.

The following excerpt picks up the history of the fairness doctrine from the mid 1980s.

ROBERT A. HILLMAN, THE RHETORIC OF LEGAL BACKFIRE
43 B.C. L. Rev. 819, 831-34 (2002)

Although the FCC did not repeal the fairness doctrine at [the time of the 1985 Fairness Report], the handwriting was on the wall. In 1987 . . . Congress sent President Reagan a bill that would have made the doctrine federal law.[56] Reagan vetoed the bill, allowing the FCC to kill the doctrine, which is exactly what it did. In a remand from the D.C. Court of Appeals in another case that directed the FCC to consider a broadcaster's claim that the fairness doctrine impinged on its free-speech protections, the FCC concluded in part that the fairness doctrine unconstitutionally "chilled" rather than promoted speech because it discouraged broadcasters from airing controversial issues.[57] As elaborated by the FCC:

[A]lthough the [fairness] doctrine was adopted to promote robust discussion of controversial issues, the enforcement of the doctrine has actually had the net effect of reducing rather than enhancing, the discussion of controversial issues of public importance and, therefore, violated the constitutional principles announce by the Supreme Court . . . . Consequently, while the doctrine was intended to enhance First Amendment principles, the FCC determined that, in fact, it had the exact opposite result.[58]

The Commission's decision was based on the record in one case, comments from interested parties, and its 1985 Fairness Report, which the FCC termed "a comprehensive study of the administration and effects of the doctrine on broadcast journalists." Still, these materials failed to shed much light on the fairness doctrine's actual effect on stations' broadcast decisions. Much of the FCC's case against the fairness doctrine centered

---

56. S. 742, 100 Cong., 133 Cong. Rec. 8438 (1987).
57. Syracuse Peace Council v. Television Station WTVH, 2 F.C.C.R. 5043, 5049-50 (1987), reconsideration denied, 3 F.C.C.R. 2035 (1988).
58. Federal Communications Commission News Release MM-263 (Aug. 4, 1987).

on whether the increase in outlets for broadcasting diminished the problem of "spectrum scarcity" so that the First Amendment could no longer justify the regulation of broadcaster's speech. When the FCC turned to the question of whether broadcasters aired more or less controversial issues as a result of the fairness doctrine, it largely relied on the Fairness Report, which, in turn, focused not on empirical evidence but on the presumed economic incentive for broadcasters to avoid controversial views. Moreover, the FCC failed to account for the possibility that broadcasters would resist the strategy of offering bland, uninteresting program-

ming because such programming would yield lower ratings and revenues. Even less persuasive were the surveys of self-interested broadcasters, who were asked how the fairness doctrine affected them and who testified in large measure about the rather vague "climate of timidity and fear" created by the fairness doctrine....

During the mid-nineties, efforts to revive the fairness doctrine were in limbo. Proponents continued to press for reinstatement of the doctrine, with little success.... As of this writing, the possibility of the resurrection of the fairness doctrine appears slim.

As late as 2009, some senators and representatives still supported legislation that would restore the fairness doctrine, but their prospects were still poor.

The fairness doctrine story illustrates an important limitation of the administrative instrument, namely the unavoidability of regulating in an environment of conflicting rights and principles. The problem is far from unique to broadcasting. For example, consider again the ESA. It protects listed animals from injurious activity on privately owned land, including protection from land development and harvesting. For this reason, the ESA is a prime target of critics who assert that the private-land provisions unreasonably limit landowners' rights. In fact, opponents claim that this approach is actually detrimental to endangered species, because it creates incentives for private landowners, who must receive notice of impending restrictions on their land, to destroy or modify the subject species' habitat, to remove the species from their land, or to kill the species before the restrictions become effective. Even if a landowner does not commit any of these nefarious acts, government enforcement is spotty, so that landowners can destroy endangered species almost without fear of reprisal. One opponent of ESA ventured, "When landowners find an endangered animal on their property . . . the best solution under current law is to 'shoot, shovel, and shut up.'" Mark Sagoff, Muddle or Muddle Through? Takings Jurisprudence Meets the Endangered Species Act, 38 Wm. & Mary L. Rev. 825, 826 (1997) (quoting Chuck Cushman, executive director of the American Land Rights Association of Washington State). In reality, the ESA's effectiveness remains largely unknown, but the conflict between preservation goals and individual property rights remains.

Section Eight
SUMMARY

The ever-increasing complexity of our society has led to the rise of the "administrative state." In this chapter, we have looked at the reasons why government creates administrative agencies to regulate private activity. We have also reviewed the methods agencies utilize to achieve their purposes and the respective roles of agencies, courts, legislators, and private citizens. Finally, we have contemplated how the law could improve the administrative instrument and have considered some of its limitations.

In short, the government regulates private activity when private markets fail, such as when businesses do not supply sufficient information to customers, when a natural monopoly would enable an entity to charge monopoly prices, when resources are scarce and individual incentives would lead to depletion of the resource, and when some of the costs of private activity are borne by people who are not engaged in the activity. Government employs administrative agencies to remedy these market failures in part because regulation can stop harmful conduct before it occurs and because agencies have the training and enjoy the flexibility to achieve society's purposes most effectively. Methods agencies utilize for achieving their purpose include setting standards, licensing activity, investigating and agreeing to consent decrees, publicizing harmful activity, adjudicating both formally and informally cases of alleged violations of administrative standards (both before agencies and courts), and encouraging self-regulation.

We have seen that agencies, empowered by the legislature's delegation to them, make law through rulemaking and adjudication, and we have reviewed the strengths and weakness of each method of lawmaking. For example, rulemaking provides a useful forum for interested parties to present their views, but adjudication allows agencies to consider the particular context of the problem at hand.

We have also discussed the role of courts in reviewing agency action to make sure that the agency did not act arbitrarily. We have introduced the concept of "standing" to suggest one limitation on private citizens' roles in reviewing agency action in the courts. Recall that the standing doctrine means that citizens must have a real, and not just a potential, stake in the outcome of an agency determination. Standing is a controversial issue in the regulatory context because the lack of standing narrows or excludes citizen input into agency action. But improving methods of ensuring citizen access to the agency rulemaking process can mitigate the effects of the standing doctrine. These methods include financing private parties' participation in agency action and using modern technology to decrease the costs and increase the ease of citizen input.

The administrative instrument has its limitations, of course. For example, we saw how the fairness doctrine, meant to increase the dissemination of all sides of issues and ideas, in practice may have deterred broadcasters from broadcasting any controversial issues. But perhaps the demise of the fairness doctrine was caught up more in politics and the inertia of the deregulatory movement than in the merits of the doctrine itself. If so, this symbolizes another limitation of regulation.

For those who seek additional readings on the administrative instrument, two excellent general treatments are Cass Sunstein, Risk and Reason: Safety, Law, and the Environment (2004), and Jerry Mashaw, Greed, Chaos & Governance (1997). For more on the doctrine of standing, an excellent piece is Richard J. Pierce, *Lujan v. Defenders of Wildlife*: Standing as a Judicially Imposed Limit on Legislative Power, 42 Duke L.J. 1170 (1993). Finally, three older works, but still worth a look, are Alan B. Morrison, The Administrative Procedure Act: A Living and Responsive Law, 72 Va. L. Rev. 253 (1986), Robert L. Rabin, Federal Regulation in Historical Perspective, 38 Stan. L. Rev. 1189 (1986), and Stephen G. Breyer, Regulation and Its Reform (1982).

Chapter 4

LAW AS AN INSTRUMENT FOR

CONFERRING PUBLIC BENEFITS

Yet in those great state services which increase every day—educational, the poor law, public works, lighting, the postal, telegraph, and telephone systems, the railways—the state intervenes . . . in a manner that has to be . . . ordered by a system of public law.

LÉON DUGUIT

Section One
INTRODUCTION TO THE PUBLIC-BENEFIT INSTRUMENT

Materials Drawn Mainly from Public Education Law

Taxation and spending in the name of the public are the very stuff of modern government in large industrialized nations. At every level, government has authority to raise money through taxes and other charges, and to appropriate that money for various public purposes. Government spends money to build roads, airports, hospitals, dams, courtrooms, and other public structures, to restore waterfronts, historic buildings, and decaying urban mass transit systems, to make health care and other forms of assistance available to those who need help, to provide for public education, parks, museums, police protection, mail delivery, and national defense, and to promote the arts, scientific research, family farms, home ownership, and other ends deemed in the public interest.

Controversy rages over some of these objects of government spending and what forms the benefits should take, as well as where the money should come from, how much should be spent, and what level of government should raise and spend it. Debate over the substance and form of public-benefit conferral is particularly lively now, for we had been in an era of retrenchment and skepticism about the capacity of government to satisfy some social goals through public spending. Nevertheless, the United States remains firmly committed to an enormous number of programs of public-benefit conferral. We have grown comfortable with the idea of big taxes, big spending, and big government—the so-called welfare state, though much more than welfare programs is involved.

Government decisions about public-benefit conferral involve political actors responding to political pressures from lobbyists, voters, and others concerned with tax and spending decisions. So fundamental is politics to the process of allocating tax burdens and setting spending priorities that legal ordering—which involves the official development of impersonal rules of broad applicability to guide program funding, development, and administration—appears insignificant to this form of governmental activity.

That fact raises the question of whether public-benefit conferral has a significant legal dimension, as the remedial, the penal, and the administrative instruments clearly do. Or should one analyze public-benefit conferral solely or primarily in terms of political alignments, pressure groups, and political influences affecting legislators and government officials?

To answer this question, consider the kinds of issues that the government must resolve if a system of public-benefit conferral is to be effective and efficient. Assume, for example, that a county legislature decides to feed the poor within its borders. Who will bear the cost? Who qualifies as poor? What must they then do to get the food? What type of food will they get? Where will this food come from? Who will administer the program? Without rules that respond to these issues, a program cannot even get under way.

Rules are also bound to play an important role in the day-to-day administration of a program of public-benefit conferral. Think about the disputes that are sure to arise over both the imposition of burdens and the availability of benefits—disputes that would be much harder to resolve without rules as a point of reference and established processes for deciding what those rules mean. Rules serve a prophylactic function too, offering prospective guidance to officials charged with implementing programs. Equity and fairness in the allocation of burdens and benefits, widely regarded as important goals in any governmental activity in our society, will be much easier to achieve if rules exist to limit ad hoc decisionmaking and to discourage official whim and caprice.

Indeed, legal ordering—specifying constitutional guarantees that limit the reach of governmental power, rules that differentiate and define legislative and executive functions, and electoral laws—plays an important role in maintaining the very political process that sets programs for public-benefit conferral in motion. All these rules help connect public resources to public wants, while maintaining ours as a democratic nation.

Still, we can appropriately characterize public-benefit conferral as significantly legal in nature not merely if legal rules actually play a role in it, but only if that legal ordering is necessary rather than accidental, or at least has a determinative bearing on the quality of the conferral program. It certainly appears that legal rules are necessary for a minimally effective and efficient program. For example, having to formulate the guiding laws forces our legislatures to face up to the difficult questions entailed in specifying the burdens and benefits and deciding how to administer the program through the executive and judicial branches. As a result, advanced societies authorize public-benefit conferral only through laws and legal forms.

In sum, given that public-benefit conferral is undeniably an instrument for discharging social functions, and given that it is significantly legal in nature, we shall classify it as an instrument of the law—even though direct governmental action is more prominent in this instrument than in the others we have so far considered.

Including public-benefit conferral as a legal instrument does not imply that we shall ignore its high degree of direct governmental action. That feature is in fact what serves most substantially to distinguish this instrument from the remedial, the penal, and the administrative instruments, and so causes us to treat it separately. Think, for example, of the citizenry in the eighteenth century starting to agitate for a system of public schools open to all children without the payment of fees. The other three instruments offered the people little help appropriate to the introduction of a public school system. Direct governmental action was necessary. This was a task for the public-benefit instrument.

In presenting the public-benefit instrument, this chapter will draw materials mainly from that public education law, while proceeding through the following sections:

- Section Two, Public-Benefit Methods, introduces the various methods of conferring public benefits and imposing the concomitant burdens.
- Section Three, Making Public-Benefit Law, studies how state and federal legislatures, executive branches, agencies, courts, and street-level bureaucrats create most public-benefit law, as the study proceeds with a special emphasis on equal protection under education law.
- Section Four, Applying Public-Benefit Law, more briefly examines the application of education law, with a special emphasis on due process.
- Section Five, Roles of Private Citizens and Their Lawyers, shows how private parties and their lawyers participate in the making and applying of the public-benefit law on education.
- Section Six, Improving the Public-Benefit Instrument, identifies and discusses some of the ways the law could better confer public benefits.
- Section Seven, Limitations of Law as a Public-Benefit Instrument, stresses inherent limitations on the law's use of the public-benefit instrument.

You should at every stage of this chapter ask yourself how the public-benefit instrument compares and contrasts with the remedial, the penal, and the administrative instruments.

Section Two
PUBLIC-BENEFIT METHODS

A. Benefit Characteristics

Government can confer benefits by a variety of methods. As explained by Lester M. Salamon, Rethinking Public Management: Third–Party Government and the Changing Forms of Government Action, 29 Pub. Pol'y 255, 264, 268–72 (1981),* these methods merit study because each different method comes with its own

* Copyright © 1981 by the John F. Kennedy School of Government. Reprinted by permission of author.

distinctive dynamics—"a substantial amount of 'baggage' in the form of its own characteristic implementing institutions, standard operating procedures, types of expertise and professional cadre, products, degree of visibility, enactment and review processes, and relationships with other societal forces"—that substantially affect the resulting content of the governmental action.

Categorization of the forms of benefit provides a good first cut at understanding public-benefit methodology. Lawmakers' choices made along a number of basic dimensions will determine the precise form of the public benefit. Consider the following five dimensions, helpfully distinguished by Salamon:

1. Simple payment of money is one form of benefit, thought appropriate for welfare assistance, farm subsidies, disability benefits, and old-age pensions. Construction of a public facility is another type of benefit, of which examples are highways, bridges, stadiums, public auditoriums, and marinas. Continuing rendition of a service, such as provision of electricity or public school instruction, is still another form of public-benefit conferral. All of these are *direct* forms of government spending.

   Public-benefit conferral can be *indirect*, too, as when government gives tax breaks for home ownership or capital investment or wetlands preservation. Exemptions from anything that would otherwise be a legal duty, say, military service, are indirect benefits. Government also benefits groups and individuals indirectly when it guarantees, subsidizes, or underwrites loans, bank deposits, and insurance; when it adjusts interest rates to stimulate the economy; or when it places restrictions on competitors, such as tariffs and import quotas. The fact that a benefit is indirect does not reduce its significance to those who receive it.

   What motivates the lawmakers in fixing the program along the direct/indirect dimension? Politics will play a big role in the choice of form of benefits. Direct benefits are more politically suspect as a emblem of big government. But indirectness will generate difficult problems of accountability and even management. Indeed, it often seems that the harder the form is to oversee, the easier it is to enact.

   The direct or indirect way that government distributes benefits naturally depends to a certain extent on what benefit it wishes to confer and to whom. Income tax deductions for property tax payments, for example, can do little to help destitute people get adequate medical care, because the very poor seldom have taxable income or own taxable property.

   Another determinant of the direct/indirect form of benefits is the required or preferred mode of delivery. For example, our lawmakers have decided to provide education directly for the most part, and this decision has had major consequences. Staffing any public-benefit program that delivers an array of ongoing services to a broad public on a day-to-day basis is a complex and sometimes daunting task that requires much legal ordering. Public education necessitates a vast array of operational personnel who must be recruited, deployed, and retained. The effectiveness of this particular distributive program is indeed dependent on the quality of the personnel. Many factors affect the availability of good personnel, including salaries and working conditions. By what legal means should government determine salaries and working conditions? Collective bargaining is one approach. But obviously the use of collective bargaining to negotiate the terms of employment for public-sector employees as essential as schoolteachers will raise intense issues of legal ordering.

Government also faces limitations imposed by its own prior decisions regarding public-benefit conferral. For one thing, the current recipients of government spending programs, whether tobacco growers or defense contractors, will resist changes in the form of public-benefit conferral if they perceive the new standards as detrimental to their interests. Change can be difficult to effect even when the received benefits remain the same, because prior commitments limit government's flexibility. In 1971, for example, Congress passed legislation designed to make mail delivery more cost-effective. The new legislation created a government corporation for this purpose, on the theory that this form of organization would allow the service to be managed in a more businesslike way than it had as a federal department under direct congressional control. The efforts of the postal system's new managers to modernize mail delivery were stymied at first, however, not only by persistent political demands but also by the antiquated, labor-intensive, patronage-oriented system that the managers had inherited: "Clerks still stood before the familiar pigeonhole cases, sorting letters by hand at the rate of about thirty a minute. Antiquated facilities hindered mechanization; weak floors would not support heavy machinery, low ceilings ruled out overhead conveyor systems, and vertical buildings layouts defied any attempt at instituting more efficient horizontal mail-flow systems." John T. Tierney, Government Corporations and Managing the Public's Business, 99 Pol. Sci. Q. 73, 89 (1984).

Despite such determinants and limitations, experimentation and tinkering with methods for public-benefit conferral are common in America. Often the soaring costs of a program create pressure to adjust the form of benefits. Think of Social Security and the constant pressure to switch from direct payments to indirect encouragement of private retirement savings. Also, proposed adjustments will reflect beliefs about the proper balance between government and market incentives that are dominant at the time. Consider, for example, the recurrent popularity of market-oriented proposals for containing healthcare costs, such as increased cost sharing and fixed-dollar subsidies for specific healthcare services. Sometimes even the success of a program can bring forth calls for changing benefits. The success of the national park system in attracting visitors is a case in point. Millions more people now visit the national parks—enough to jam traffic, create long lines for campsites, disturb wildlife, and eliminate the possibility of solitude at the height of the season in the more popular parks. If they are to achieve their primary purposes, park officials must find some way to limit the direct benefit, whether by closing certain sites to automobiles, reducing the availability of campsites, or turning away "excess" visitors.

2. Although the direct/indirect dimension is a useful one along which to begin analyzing forms of public benefits, there are other fruitful dimensions to consider, as our few examples might have suggested. A related one is the *visibility/invisibility* dimension. The realities of legislative and budgetary processes make certain forms of benefit conferral less visible.

   Salamon expands: "Tax incentives, for example, are far less open to regular scrutiny than outright grants. 'Entitlement' programs, which establish legal rights to program benefits independent of the budget, are far less closely scrutinized than programs that are subject to yearly control. In some cases, the costs of federal action are not even known. This is the case, for example, with regulatory actions, the true impact of which appears not in the federal budget, but in the balance sheets of the regulated industries."

3. Another is the *cash/in-kind* dimension. "Cash-type programs reserve far more flexibility to recipients and are typically easier to administer. In-kind programs (e.g., food stamps, housing assistance), by tying benefits to a particular service or good, constrain recipient choices, often providing more of a particular good than a recipient would freely choose and thereby reducing the marginal value of the benefit to the recipient."

   Although recipients may prefer the cash form, politics may favor in-kind assistance. "In the first place, in-kind programs, by committing resources to the purchase of a particular good or service, can stimulate support from the producers of that good or service that would otherwise not exist. The food stamp program, for example, enjoys support from agricultural and farm interests that would not be forthcoming for a general, cash income-assistance program. Similarly, builder support for aid to the poor is much stronger for programs that tie such aid to the production of housing than for programs that make such assistance available in the form of cash. In the second place, in-kind assistance is more likely to go for the purpose intended than is outright cash. Those who make a case for assistance in terms of a particular need may therefore feel obliged to champion the delivery mechanism most certain to apply that assistance to that particular need."

4. Somewhat distinct from the form of benefits, and also from their level and target, the question of the manner of distribution of the benefits is bound to be a salient political issue. Efficiency is a perennial concern whenever government spends money, even if costs are relatively stable. Economic analysis, a strong and growing field in policy studies, can help determine which manner of distribution is most efficient, or optimal, given the goals

of the program. An economist has observed that "economic reasoning is better at helping to choose among ways to accomplish a distributional objective than at helping to choose objectives. It can help in minimizing the cost to the rich of doing something for the poor. And in case that doesn't interest you, economic reasoning can help to point out that it ought to! There is more for the poor, at any given cost to the rich, if you do it in the least wasteful way." Thomas C. Schelling, Economic Reasoning and the Ethics of Policy, 63 Pub. Int. 37, 53 (1981).

Such thoughts suggest the *automatic/administered* dimension. Salamon says: "An automatic process is one that utilizes existing structures and relationships (e.g., the tax structure or the price system) and requires a minimum of administrative decision-making. A tax credit automatically available to all firms investing in new plant or equipment, for example, would represent a largely automatic tool. A similar sum made available through grants on the basis of separately reviewed applications would represent a more highly administered tool."

Automatic processes are less costly, and they merge more smoothly into the existing social context, including our free market economy. But they have big drawbacks. "For one thing, there is far less certainty that they will have the results intended, especially when they are attached to processes with far different purposes. A program that seeks to promote worker safety by levying higher disability insurance charges on companies with poor safety records rather than by imposing detailed safety regulations, for example, may continuously be in the position of doing too little too late."

5. Questions about efficiency, important as they are, should not be the only concern when considering distributive manner, however. The manner in which the government administers the conferral of benefits can foster equality among recipients or restrict it; programs can be more or less intrusive on individuals; a program can foster the exercise of local or central authority, can encourage or discourage citizen participation, or can choose or refuse to delegate much to experts or other elites; its procedures can be more or less fair. Again, the political scientist would find these matters rich for study. For example, Salamon went on to add this nonobvious dimension for analysis of public-benefit methods:

> *Design Standards versus Performance Standards for Program Control:* Attention to the instruments of government action has implications not only for basic choices among different tools, but also for decisions about how different tools, once chosen, are managed. One of the central issues in this regard is the extent to which reliance is placed on performance standards as opposed to design standards in program operations. Design standards involve controls over detailed aspects of program operations: accounting procedures, fund transfers among different program accounts, personnel recruitment procedures, specific technological processes to adopt to reduce air pollution at particular types of sites. Performance

standards, by contrast, specify desired outputs but leave to the discretion of program managers or their third-party agents the decisions about how to design activities to achieve these outputs. Students of social regulation have faulted much of the federal government's recent regulatory effort in precisely these terms, arguing that by placing too much stress on design specifications (e.g., the location and numbers of fire extinguishers in industrial plants) rather than on performance standards (the days lost through fires), these activities end up being far less efficient economically and far more cumbersome administratively than is necessary.

Attractive as performance standards are, however, they are not without their problems. For one thing, program purposes are frequently kept deliberately vague in order to hold together the political coalition often required for passage. Moreover, programs often serve multiple purposes, and opinions can differ over the priorities to attach to each. In addition, the measurement of success and failure in terms of particular performance criteria can often be quite subjective, creating added possibilities for conflict and confusion, especially where responsibility for program decisions is split between federal authorities and their "third-party" agents. Finally, the use of performance standards involves greater uncertainty since results are not apparent for a considerable time and great opportunity exists for mistakes along the way. Those responsible for program oversight can therefore be expected to find such uncertainty exceedingly unattractive.

B. Concomitant Burdens

Certainly if any benefit is to be real, the legal system must appropriate scarce resources for its conferral. Legal systems do not themselves have those resources, so they must acquire them. But citizens will view a demand to give up scarce resources as a burden.

Such burdens come in many shapes, such as compulsory military service and eminent domain. Still, most burdens take the form of duties to pay tax, so taxes themselves deserve a few additional words here. Entire academic disciplines are devoted to tax systems and their administration. Nonetheless, we should introduce some core ideas essential to an overview of the public-benefit instrument.

Several caveats to begin: First, you must not assume that only taxes feed the public purse. User fees, borrowing, and still other sources of funds may exist. But the taxing power is central. Second, you must not think that the government exercises its taxing power solely to finance its programs in connection with the public-benefit instrument. The government has many other needs for funds. There are also other uses, ulterior uses as it were, of the taxing power in modern states, for example, to stabilize the business cycle, to reduce gross inequalities of wealth, to foster charitable activity, and so on. Third, the other instruments of law depend on taxes too. But the public-benefit instrument depends on the taxing power distinctively, for tax monies not only finance the *operations* of the distributive instrument but also pay for the *distributions* as such. The necessity of imposing large burdens poses distinctive problems of legal ordering intrinsic to public-benefit conferral.

With that said, what are the main choices involved in exercising the taxing power for specific distributive purposes?

1. Each year, the relevant officials in the distributive process could decide upon benefits and set up a tax-raising scheme to finance those benefits for that year. Alternatively, they could set up an ongoing, albeit modifiable, tax system that produces a relatively predictable level of annual income.

2. Under either such approach, revenues might come from one or more of various sources: (a) fees charged to users of particular public goods or services, (b) taxes directly on all income, (c) taxes in the context of certain income-producing relationships, for example, percentages of wages taken for retirement purposes, (d) taxes on property ownership, (e) taxes on exchange transactions, (f) taxes on inheritance transfers. These are only some of the possibilities. In legal systems that fund distributions at local, state, and national levels, the setup may provide either that the various levels will share particular sources of revenues or that one or more sources will be the exclusive province of, say, states or localities. By accident or design, the federal government has, in a sense, first call on personal and corporate incomes, and federal taxes on this prime source of revenue dwarf state taxes. States and localities have to rely on low-rate income taxes and on other sources of revenue, such as property taxes and sales taxes.

3. The possible normative principles that may influence lawmakers in deciding who will pay which taxes are several. Because the principles are not wholly consistent with each other, lawmakers must make some very basic choices. For example, the lawmakers might embrace the principle that "he or she who benefits must pay." They have invoked this beneficiary principle to make users of parklands pay for parks' establishment and maintenance through entrance and other fees, to make employers contribute to general retirement funds for employees, to make mailers pay through purchase of stamps, to make drivers on highways pay for them through tolls and gas taxes, to make local residents pay for police and fire protection through distinctly local taxes, and so on. But in fact the conditions that allow applying this beneficiary principle to public goods are of limited occurrence. It presupposes that beneficiaries can be identified, that the nature and extent of their beneficial enjoyment can be ascertained, and that a convenient means exists to make them and only them pay. And even where a situation meets these conditions, it might be pointless or self-defeating to apply the beneficiary principle to some benefits, such as welfare payments.

4. With respect to the tax burden that many benefits entail, there is another basic choice regarding the relative sizes of the burdens. Perhaps taxpayers should pay a percentage of the benefit they receive, or perhaps all taxpayers should pay regardless of their use. Perhaps all taxpayers should pay an identical share of the total cost, or perhaps taxpayers of very small

means should pay little or nothing. Perhaps all taxpayers should pay an equal percentage of their wealth, or perhaps those of greater means should pay proportionately more, those of still greater means proportionately still more, and so on, with those of the greatest means paying the highest percentage. The clash over the last approach—called a progressive tax rate—is one of the great battlegrounds of modern tax policy. The progressivity principle has been defended on such grounds as (a) the greater a taxpayer's means, the smaller is the sacrifice in giving up some of it in taxes, (b) the government should consider the more urgent needs of those of lesser means ahead of the less urgent needs of those with greater means, and (c) the government should, within limits, reduce the inequalities of wealth.

5. Again, of course, there are basic choices to be made in how to administer a tax system. The most basic choice is between a system that relies heavily on voluntary taxpayer "self-assessment" and "self-payment" and a system that relies heavily on more external means of assessment and collection. Any system that depends heavily on the former must not be too complicated and, to help preserve the taxpayer spirit required for widespread voluntary compliance, must apply to everyone of any real means, must be largely free of loopholes, and must provide effectively for exposure and punishment of evaders.

In sum, taxpayers—as well as military recruits, residents in the path of public-work projects, and other cost bearers—have reason to be concerned about the form, level, target, and manner of the government's imposition of burdens. It is a rare person who says cheerfully, as did Justice Holmes: "I like to pay taxes. With them I buy civilization." The fact that so many of us are cost bearers for government programs ensures that interest in the comparative advantages of various public-benefit methods will be widespread.

C. An Initial Illustration of Conferral Program: Public Art

All this brings us to the illustrative school of criticism captured by the phrase, "Why should *I* pay for *your* opera?" Federal aid to the arts has increased since 1970. It grew from $8 million in 1967 to $176 million in 1992, but declined to $124 million in 2006. With the availability of increased public support has come debate over, say, whether federal arts policy should encourage the widest possible dissemination of the arts *or* the highest levels of artistic achievement. See Margaret Jane Wyszomirski, Controversies in Arts Policymaking, in Public Policy and the Arts 11 (Kevin V. Mulcahy & C. Richard Swaim eds., 1982). Or which method of support is appropriate, such as direct grants to favored artists or some sort of tax-deduction scheme. Or even whether public art is a net benefit at all. See Michael Kammen, Visual Shock: A History of Art Controversies in American Culture (2006).

DOUGLAS STALKER & CLARK GLYMOUR, THE MALIGNANT OBJECT: THOUGHTS ON PUBLIC SCULPTURE

66 Pub. Int. 3, 3–4, 6–7, 10, 12, 14–15, 20 (1982)*

Millions of dollars are spent in this country on public sculpture—on sculpture that is created for the explicit purpose of public viewing, placed in public settings, and constructed generally by contemporary artists without any intention of commemorating or representing people or events associated with the site. The objects in question may be clothespins, boulders, or tortuous steel shapes. The money may sometimes come from private sources, but much of it comes from public treasuries.

One of the clearest and most general attempts to provide a justification for financing and placing these objects in public spaces is given by Janet Kardon, who is the Director of Philadelphia's Institute of Contemporary Art. "Public art," Ms. Kardon writes, "is not a style or a movement, but a compound social service based on the premise that public well-being is enhanced by the presence of large scale art works in public spaces." Large scale art works executed, to be sure, not to public taste but to the taste of the avant-garde art community. Elsewhere, she writes: "Public art is not a style, art movement or public service, but a compound event, based on the premise that our lives are enhanced by good art and that good art means work by advanced artists thrust into the public domain." The justification here is moral rather than aesthetic, phrased in terms of well-being rather than those of beauty. Public art is good for us. Her thesis is put simply and with clarity; it is perhaps the same thesis as that put forward by many writers who claim that public art "enhances the quality of life" or "humanizes the urban environment," even "speaks to the spirit."

Our view is that much public sculpture, and public art generally as it is created nowadays in the United States, provides at best trivial benefits to the public, but does provide substantial and identifiable harm. . . .

There is abundant evidence, albeit circumstantial, pointing directly to the conclusion that many pieces of contemporary public sculpture, perhaps the majority, are not much enjoyed by the public at large—even though the public firmly believes in a general way that art is a very good thing. . . .

The public distaste for today's public sculpture often goes well beyond mere words. The common responses include petitions, assemblies, litigation, and, occasionally, direct action. Enraged by what is thrust at them, the public often takes up a kind of vigilantism against contemporary public sculpture, and in community after community spontaneous bands of Aesthetic Avengers form, armed with hammers, chisels, and spraypaint cans. Jody Pinto's "Heart Chambers for Gertrude and Angelo," erected on the University of Pennsylvania campus for Ms. Kardon's own Institute of Contemporary Art, was turned into rubble overnight. . . . Of course, for any object there is some thug or madman willing or eager to destroy what he can of it, but the defacement of some pieces of public sculpture seems to enjoy a measure of community support or at least tolerance. . . .

Impressionistic evidence is rightfully mistrusted, and those who advocate public sculpture might well demand more precise evidence as to the extent and intensity of public dislike or indifference for contemporary public sculpture. But the plain fact is that there is little non-impressionistic evidence to be had, one way or the other. Remarkably, although considerable sums are spent on public sculpture in this country by government and by corporations, virtually nothing is spent to find out whether or not the public likes particular objects or dislikes them, how intense such feelings are, or, most importantly, what proportion of the affected public would prefer that the space be put to some other use. . . .

Inevitably, today's public sculpture is justified in a kind of circular way: The very fact that the public dislikes it, or even violently abhors it, is

* Reprinted with permission from: THE PUBLIC INTEREST, No. 66 (Winter, 1982), pp. 3–21. © 1982 by National Affairs, Inc.

Tilted Arc

Richard Serra, Tilted Arc 1981; weatherproof steel; cylindrical section 12' high × 120' along chord × 2½" thick; Installation: Federal Plaza, New York; Collection: U.S. General Services Administration, Washington, DC; Destroyed by the U.S. Government 1989; Photo credit: Prahn.

One of the works pictured by Professors Stalker and Glymour was "Tilted Arc" by Richard Serra. We also picture it, with the tall federal courthouse in the background. The General Services Administration had commissioned it at a cost of $175,000, under a federal policy that

half of a percent of construction budgets for federal buildings must go for art. The 12' x 120' wall of 73 tons of rusted Core-Ten steel went up in 1981, bisecting Manhattan's Federal Plaza. According to Serra, "The viewer becomes aware of himself and of his movement through the plaza. As he moves, the sculpture changes. Contraction and expansion of the sculpture result from the viewer's movement. Step by step the perception not only of the sculpture but of the entire environment changes."

However, the sculpture quickly proved wildly unpopular with local office workers, an unpopularity that grew as urban abuse turned the sculpture into an eyesore. Mounting political pressure caused the GSA to order its removal in 1985. Serra unsuccessfully argued that the art was "site-specific" and so could not be moved without destroying the piece. He then sued for $30,000,000 on numerous grounds, including that the GSA was breaking its contract with him and squelching his First Amendment rights. "The Government has to learn that art is not property," he said. "You can't move it like paper clips." He lost, before courts sitting in the pictured courthouse. Serra v. U.S. Gen. Servs. Admin., 667 F. Supp. 1042 (S.D.N.Y. 1987), aff'd, 847 F.2d 1045 (2d Cir. 1988).

Serra commented, "I don't think it is the function of art to be pleasing. Art is not democratic. It is not for the people." Federal workers dismantled the sculpture during the night of March 15, 1989, and carted it off to a scrap-metal yard. See Harriet F. Senie, The Tilted Arc Controversy (2002).

rather typically, remarked after her sculpture at the University of Pennsylvania was destroyed that "Tons of letters were written to the *Daily Pennsylvanian*, both pro and con, which is wonderful. If art can stimulate that kind of discussion and really make people think, then it's accomplished probably more than most artists could even hope for." . . .

. . . It is not for government to promote new conceptions or realizations of art. In short, the ultimate aesthetic quality of the works is not in question; their public display is.

If today's public sculpture is not much enjoyed for its aesthetic qualities, and if it carries no effective and important message which will enlighten the public, how does it improve the quality of life? How are citizens made better off by its presence? Advocates may dig in their heels and claim that those exposed to such pieces just *are* better off, whether they know it or not, for seeing and living with the things. But an inarticulable and unidentifiable benefit is no benefit at all....

A good deal of today's public sculpture offends the public eye. It offends twice: once because it is simply unsightly, as with garbage, auto salvage yards, and scrap heaps; and again because it is unsightly *art*. It is offensive to be presented with rags and scrap metal, but perhaps equally offensive to be told that an unsightly mess must be respected as art....

...And the harm is repeated and repeated and repeated. The citizen can only escape by moving his domicile or work or normal activities, or by cultivating indifference....

The harm done by public sculpture to the interests of the public is real harm, less vivid and perhaps less important than some other social harms, but real enough. To those harms we have noted, we must add the general harm, in the case of publicly financed public sculpture, of having to finance an object from which no benefit is derived, and the special exquisiteness of having to finance one's own humiliation....

Artists, critics, and art administrators may find this argument to be simply an endorsement of philistinism, but that is a grievous confusion. Philistines are people too, and, whether or not one shares their tastes, the moral point of view requires that their interests be considered.

Section Three
MAKING PUBLIC-BENEFIT LAW

A. Legislatures

Legislators are key actors in public-benefit conferral. They design and vote upon distributive policy, they authorize funding for particular programs, and they arrange to raise the revenues necessary to make the benefits possible. These are three separate types of decisions. The decision to authorize a program, for example, does not necessarily mean the legislature will fund it. Nor do votes to create and fund programs necessarily mean the legislature has solved the problems associated with generating revenues to pay for them, as critics of the congressional tendency toward deficit spending often point out.

Yet all three of these distinct powers are in the hands of the same lawmakers. Putting some of these powers in the legislature is not difficult to explain. "No taxation without representation." Moreover, there are rational reasons for not divorcing the process of deciding upon provision of benefits from the process of deciding upon concomitant burdens. Both ought to be considered together, for they are intimately interconnected in at least three ways.

First, society does not want benefits if the burdens they entail exceed the value of the benefits. On the one hand, some burdens are very severe, and they cost much to impose in terms of direct expenses and lost opportunities. It is, for example, very expensive to raise armies, especially large ones. And the competent accountant would not overlook hidden social costs. For example, controversies between taxpayer and government arise, and these take a lot out of the individual's willingness in ways that will never show up in traditional budgeting. On the other hand, measuring benefits can be exceedingly challenging. Normally the distributive instrument "converts" the subject matter of the burden into a benefit that comes in a different form. For example, money raised by taxes becomes public education. This conversion by government of tax revenues into public goods renders the application of straightforward cost-benefit analysis very difficult, although the analysis would be difficult enough even without conversion. How, for example, might one assign value to the benefit of public elementary and secondary education? Finally, public goods also often have side effects that may be good or bad and that one should take into account somehow. One must estimate and compare the monetary values of benefits and burdens, if only in very rough terms.

Second, looking at benefits and burdens together helps the lawmaker to evaluate needs more sensibly. Also, the eternal problem of priorities appears most starkly when viewed from the burden side. Furthermore, the pervasive problem of equity, which we shall soon look at in detail, often depends on regarding proposed benefits and burdens in relation to each other.

Third, giving the basic decisions on both benefits and burdens to a single lawmaker facilitates and fosters public accountability. The lawmaker that dispenses benefits cannot ignore the furor that a mounting schedule of burdens will encounter by claiming that the burdens were the fault of another lawmaker.

B. Legislative Delegatees

Legislators are thus essential for getting any program's benefits and burdens under way, but legislators are by no means the only authorized lawmakers in public-benefit conferral. Legislators routinely delegate much of the control that they otherwise could, in theory, exercise over the implementation of the programs they create. They give officials authority to make binding rules for the distribution of benefits, to resolve disputes over how those rules should apply, and to collect taxes. Whether legislators thereby improperly shirk their legislative responsibilities and violate the principle of the separation of powers is a matter of dispute among scholars. The courts, at least, have given their imprimatur to statutes delegating broad authority to administrative officials, as we saw in the preceding chapter.

Delegation by legislators proceeds in several directions. On federal matters, Congress delegates authority to state agencies and local governments as well as to federal agencies. On occasion, Congress has even delegated power over public-benefit conferral to groups of private individuals, as when it provided that marketing restrictions would apply only upon a majority vote of affected farmers. State legislators, who possess considerable independent power to design and fund public-benefit programs involving matters reserved or left to the states, also delegate much power to state officials and to local units of government like cities and school districts. The latter may delegate authority over public-benefit conferral to still smaller units, such as individual school administrators and neighborhood groups.

C. Courts

Legislators and their delegatees thus shape the program's benefits and burdens, but they can proceed in many different ways. The relationship among program objectives, rules limiting eligibility for benefits, and funding is not always straightforward. Sometimes the lawmaker simply bars certain uses for its funds, as in Congress's ban on financial assistance for abortion or its denial of research support to projects involving uninformed human subjects. But Congress also uses its power over benefits and burdens to foster policies that have little to do with the distribution per se. Congress has, for example, made the availability of federal highway funds dependent upon the willingness of the states to increase the drinking age to 21. Corporate recipients of federal aid cannot discriminate against their employees, and individuals who receive federal financial assistance must toe certain behavioral lines. The large and growing number of activities that receive some form of federal financial support means that the imposition of conditions can be a powerful tool for regulating behavior that would otherwise lie legally or politically outside the congressional domain. Here too, courts give the lawmaker a pretty free hand on the ground that the lawmaker can choose what to subsidize, although the courts hold that the lawmaker may not by conditions penalize the exercise of freedoms that constitutionally the legislature could not infringe directly.

More generally, those who implement public-benefit law usually attach a good number of strings to benefits—red tape in the eyes of those who must administer the program and those who must satisfy the conditions in order to receive the money, goods, or services. Ask a university officer about the requirements your school must satisfy as a recipient of federal or state aid, or inquire at a local social services agency about qualifications for welfare or other forms of personal assistance. (The qualifications, incentives, and prohibitions that guide and limit the availability of benefits would look even more complex if you were actually to read the legislation or regulations that authorized the program, because in them the lawmakers were writing primarily for administrative officials.)

The famous *Grove City College* case that follows involved a specific effort by Congress and the federal Department of Education to combat sex discrimination by limiting the availability of federal aid to education. But the pattern is a familiar one: the government insinuates itself by conferring benefits, its aid soon becomes indispensable, and it then starts making demands and imposing red tape that some find intrusive.

This litigation example should clarify that courts too are authorized public-benefit lawmakers, though only when justiciable controversies come their way. In this Supreme Court case, the issues involved statutory interpretation and the First Amendment rights of beneficiaries. In other cases, judges could serve as distributive lawmakers when they adjudicate conflicts between other authorized lawmakers, for example, when courts rarely set limits on legislative delegation of powers to agencies.

GROVE CITY COLLEGE v. BELL

Supreme Court of the United States, 1984
465 U.S. 555, 104 S. Ct. 1211

JUSTICE WHITE delivered the opinion of the Court:

Section 901(a) of Title IX of the Education Amendments of 1972, Pub. L. 92-318, 86 Stat. 373, 20 U.S.C. §1681(a), prohibits sex discrimination in "any education program or activity receiving Federal financial assistance," and §902 directs agencies awarding most types of assistance to promulgate regulations to ensure that recipients adhere to that prohibition....

This case presents several questions concerning the scope and operation of these provisions and the regulations established by the Department of Education. We must decide, first, whether Title IX applies at all to Grove City College, which accepts no direct assistance but enrolls students who receive federal grants that must be used for educational purposes. If so, we must identify the "education program or activity" at Grove City that is "receiving Federal financial assistance" and determine whether federal assistance to that program may be terminated solely because the College violates the Department's regulations by refusing to execute an Assurance of Compliance with Title IX. Finally, we must consider whether the application of Title IX to Grove City infringes the First Amendment rights of the College or its students.

I

Petitioner Grove City College is a private, coeducational, liberal arts college that has sought to preserve its institutional autonomy by consistently refusing state and federal financial assistance. Grove City's desire to avoid federal oversight has led it to decline to participate, not only in direct institutional aid programs, but also in federal student assistance programs under which the College would be required to assess students' eligibility and to determine the amounts of loans, work-study funds, or grants they should receive. Grove City has, however, enrolled a large number of students who receive Basic Educational Opportunity Grants (BEOGs), 20 U.S.C. §1070a, under the Department of Education's Alternate Disbursement System (ADS).

The Department concluded that Grove City was a "recipient" of "Federal financial assistance" as those terms are defined in the regulations implementing Title IX, 34 CFR §§106.2(g)(1), (h) (1982), and, in July 1977, it requested that the College execute the Assurance of Compliance required by 34 CFR §106.4 (1982). If Grove City had signed the Assurance, it would have agreed to

> [c]omply, to the extent applicable to it, with Title IX ... and all applicable requirements imposed by or pursuant to the Department's regulation ... to the end that ... no person shall, on the basis of sex, be ... subjected to discrimination under any education program or activity for which [it] receives or benefits from Federal financial assistance from the Department.

When Grove City persisted in refusing to execute an Assurance, the Department initiated proceedings to declare the College and its students ineligible to receive BEOGs. The Administrative Law Judge held that the federal financial assistance received by Grove City obligated it to execute an Assurance of Compliance and entered an order terminating assistance until Grove City "corrects its noncompliance with Title IX and satisfies the Department that it is in compliance" with the applicable regulations.

Grove City and four of its students then commenced this action in the District Court for the Western District of Pennsylvania, which concluded that the students' BEOGs constituted "Federal financial assistance" to Grove City but held, on several grounds, that the Department could not terminate the students' aid because of the College's refusal to execute an Assurance of Compliance. Grove City College v. Harris, 500 F. Supp. 253 (1980). The Court of Appeals reversed. 687 F.2d 684 (CA3 1982)....

We granted certiorari, 459 U.S. 1199, 103 S. Ct. 1181 (1983), and we now affirm the Court of Appeals' judgment that the Department could terminate BEOGs received by Grove City's students to force the College to execute an Assurance of Compliance.

II

In defending its refusal to execute the Assurance of Compliance required by the Department's regulations, Grove City first contends that neither it nor any "education program or activity" of the College receives any federal financial assistance within the meaning of Title IX by virtue of the fact that some of its students receive BEOGs and use them to pay for their education. We disagree.

Grove City provides a well-rounded liberal arts education and a variety of educational programs and student services. The question is whether any of those programs or activities "receiv[es] Federal financial assistance" within the meaning of Title IX when students finance their education with BEOGs. The structure of the Education Amendments of 1972, in which Congress both created the BEOG program and imposed Title IX's nondiscrimination requirement, strongly suggests an affirmative conclusion. BEOGs were aptly characterized as a "centerpiece of the bill," 118 Cong. Rec. 20297 (1972) (Rep. Pucinski), and Title IX "relate[d] directly to [its] central purpose." 117 Cong. Rec. 30412 (1971) (Sen. Bayh). In view of this connection and Congress' express recognition of discrimination in the administration of student financial aid programs, it would indeed be anomalous to discover that one of the primary components of Congress' comprehensive "package of federal aid," id., at 2007 (Sen. Pell), was not intended to trigger coverage under Title IX.

It is not surprising to find, therefore, that the language of §901(a) contains no hint that Congress perceived a substantive difference between direct institutional assistance and aid received by a school through its students. The linchpin of Grove City's argument that none of its programs receives any federal assistance is a perceived distinction between direct and indirect aid, a distinction that finds no support in the text of §901(a)....

With the benefit of clear statutory language, powerful evidence of Congress' intent, and a longstanding and coherent administrative construction of the phrase "receiving Federal financial assistance," we

have little trouble concluding that Title IX coverage is not foreclosed because federal funds are granted to Grove City's students rather than directly to one of the College's educational programs.

[The Court concluded that the federal assistance could be terminated solely for refusal to execute an Assurance of Compliance.]

Grove City's final challenge to the Court of Appeals' decision—that conditioning federal assistance on compliance with Title IX infringes First Amendment rights of the College and its students [to associate freely in their chosen academic community without unreasonable governmental intrusion]—warrants only brief consideration. Congress is free to attach reasonable and unambiguous conditions to federal financial assistance that educational institutions are not obligated to accept. E.g., Pennhurst State School & Hospital v. Halderman, 451 U.S. 1, 17, 101 S. Ct. 1531, 1539 (1981). Grove City may terminate its participation in the BEOG program and thus avoid the requirements of §901(a). Students affected by the Department's action may either take their BEOGs elsewhere or attend Grove City without federal financial assistance. Requiring Grove City to comply with Title IX's prohibition of discrimination as a condition for its continued eligibility to participate in the BEOG program infringes no First Amendment rights of the College or its students.

Accordingly, the judgment of the Court of Appeals is
Affirmed.

JUSTICE POWELL, with whom CHIEF JUSTICE BURGER and JUSTICE O'CONNOR join, concurring:

As I agree that the holding in this case is dictated by the language and legislative history of Title IX, and the Regulations of the Department of Education, I join the Court's decision. I do so reluctantly and write briefly to record my view that the case is an unedifying example of overzealousness on the part of the Federal Government.

Grove City College (Grove City) may be unique among colleges in our country; certainly there are few others like it. Founded more than a century ago in 1876, Grove City is an independent, coeducational liberal arts college. It describes itself as having "both a Christian world view and a freedom philosophy," perceiving these as "interrelated." At the time of this suit, it had about 2,200 students and tuition was surprisingly low for a private college. Some 140 of the College's students were receiving Basic Educational Opportunity Grants (BEOGs) .... The grants were made directly to the students through the Department of Education, and the student loans were guaranteed by the federal government. Apart from this indirect assistance, Grove City has followed an unbending policy of refusing all forms of government assistance, whether federal, state or local. It was and is the policy of this small college to remain wholly independent of government assistance, recognizing—as this case well illustrates—that with acceptance of such assistance one surrenders a certain measure of the freedom that Americans always have cherished.

This case involves a Regulation adopted by the Department to implement §901(a) of Title IX (20 U.S.C. §1681(a)). It is well to bear in mind what §901(a) provides:

> No person in the United States shall, on the basis of sex, be excluded from participation in, be denied the benefits of, or be subjected to discrimination under any education program or activity receiving federal financial assistance. . . .

The sole purpose of the statute is to make unlawful "*discrimination*" by recipients of federal financial assistance on the "basis of sex." The undisputed fact is that Grove City does not discriminate—and so far as the record in this case shows—never has discriminated against anyone on account of sex, race, or national origin. This case has nothing whatever to do with discrimination past or present. The College therefore has complied to the letter with the sole purpose of §901(a). . . .

[Other opinions dealing with another issue are omitted. That issue involved the majority's narrowing interpretation of a different aspect of Title IX, but in 1988 Congress stepped in to overturn that part of the holding.

Incidentally, conservatively idealistic Grove City College is today one of the very few colleges to refuse all federal funds. It prohibits its students from accepting federal grants or loans. It thereby escapes what is now a phenomenally extensive set of federal regulations.]

D. Street-Level Providers

Up until this point, we have taken a top-down view of the lawmaking that occurs when the government confers benefits. From the perspective of public-benefit recipients, however, the most important lawmakers may be the officials who work directly with the public on a day-to-day basis. These front-line service providers, or "street-level bureaucrats," exercise considerable discretion over the availability of benefits and their substance, as the excerpt that follows indicates. As you read it, consider what kinds of public-benefit programs depend most on street-level bureaucrats, and how lawmakers can design policies to encourage intelligent and compassionate decisionmaking at this level.

MICHAEL LIPSKY, STREET-LEVEL BUREAUCRACY
3–6 (1980)*

Typical street-level bureaucrats are teachers, police officers and other law enforcement personnel, social workers, judges, public lawyers and other court officers, health workers, and many other public employees who grant access to government programs and provide services within them. People who work in these jobs

* Lipsky, Michael. "The Critical Role of Street-Level Bureaucrats." In STREET-LEVEL BUREAUCRACY. © 1980 by Russell Sage Foundation, 112 East 64th Street, New York, NY 10021. Reprinted with permission.

tend to have much in common because they experience analytically similar work conditions.

The ways in which street-level bureaucrats deliver benefits and sanctions structure and delimit people's lives and opportunities. These ways orient and provide the social (and political) contexts in which people act. Thus every extension of service benefits is accompanied by an extension of state influence and control. As providers of public benefits and keepers of public order, street-level bureaucrats are the focus of political controversy. They are constantly torn by the demands of service recipients to improve effectiveness and responsiveness and by the demands of citizen groups to improve the efficacy and efficiency of government services. Since the salaries of street-level bureaucrats comprise a significant proportion of nondefense governmental expenditures, any doubts about the size of government budgets quickly translate into concerns for the scope and content of these public services. Moreover, public service workers have expanded and increasingly consolidated their collective strength so that in disputes over the scope of public services they have become a substantial independent force in the resolution of controversy affecting their status and position.

Street-level bureaucrats dominate political controversies over public services for two general reasons. First, debates about the proper scope and focus of governmental services are essentially debates over the scope and function of these public employees. Second, street-level bureaucrats have considerable impact on peoples' lives. This impact may be of several kinds. They socialize citizens to expectations of government services and a place in the political community. They determine the eligibility of citizens for government benefits and sanctions. They oversee the treatment (the service) citizens receive in those programs. Thus, in a sense street-level bureaucrats implicitly mediate aspects of the constitutional relationship of citizens to the state. In short, they hold the keys to a dimension of citizenship.

...They comprise a great portion of all public employees working in domestic affairs. State and local governments employ approximately 3.7 million people in local schools, more than

500,000 people in police operations, and over 300,000 people in public welfare. Public school employees represent more than half of all workers employed in local governments. Instructional jobs represent about two-thirds of the educational personnel, and many of the rest are former teachers engaged in administration, or social workers, psychologists, and librarians who provide direct services in the schools. Of the 3.2 million local government public employees not engaged in education, approximately 14 percent work as police officers. One of every sixteen jobs in state and local government outside of education is held by a public welfare worker. In this and other areas the majority of jobs are held by people with responsibility for involvement with citizens.

Other street-level bureaucrats comprise an important part of the remainder of local government personnel rolls. Although the U.S. Census Bureau does not provide breakdowns of other job classifications suitable for our purposes, we can assume that many of the 1.1 million health workers, most of the 5,000 public service lawyers, many of the employees of the various court systems, and other public employees also perform as street-level bureaucrats. Some of the nation's larger cities employ a staggering number of street-level bureaucrats. For example, the 26,680 school teachers in Chicago are more numerous than the populations of many of the Chicago suburbs.

Another measure of the significance of street-level bureaucrats in public sector employment is the amount of public funds allocated to pay them. Of all local government salaries, more than half went to public education in 1973. Almost 80 percent of these monies was used to pay instructional personnel. Police salaries comprised approximately one-sixth of local public salaries not assigned to education.

Much of the growth in public employment in the past 25 years has occurred in the ranks of street-level bureaucrats. From 1955 to 1975 government employment more than doubled, largely because of the baby boom of the postwar years and the growing number of elderly, dependent citizens increased state and local activity in education, health, and public welfare.

Street-level bureaucracies are labor-intensive in the extreme. Their business is providing service through people, and the operating costs of such agencies reflect their dependence upon salaried workers. Thus most of whatever is spent by government on education, police, or other social services (aside, of course, from income maintenance, or in the case of jails and prisons, inmate upkeep) goes directly to pay street-level bureaucrats. For example, in large cities over 90 percent of police expenditures is used to pay for salaries.

Not only do the salaries of street-level bureaucrats constitute a major portion of the cost of public services, but also the scope of public services employing street-level bureaucrats has increased over time. Charity was once the responsibility of private agencies. The federal government now provides for the income needs of the poor. The public sector has absorbed responsibilities previously discharged by private organizations in such diverse and critical areas as policing, education, and health. Moreover, in all these fields government not only has supplanted private organizations but also has expanded the scope of responsibility of public ones. This is evident in increased public expectations for security and public safety, the extension of responsibilities in the schools to concerns with infant as well as post-adolescent development, and public demands for affordable health care services.

Public safety, public health, and public education *may* still be elusive social objectives, but in the past century they have been transformed into areas for which there is active governmental responsibility. The transformation of public responsibility in the area of social welfare has led some to recognize that what people "have" in modern American society often may consist primarily of their claims on government "largesse," and that claims to this "new property" should be protected as a right of citizens. Street-level bureaucrats play a critical role in these citizen entitlements. Either they directly provide public benefits through services, or they mediate between citizens and their new but by no means secure estates.

The poorer people are, the greater the influence street-level bureaucrats tend to have over them. Indeed, these public workers are so situated that they may well be taken to be part of the problem of being poor. Consider the welfare recipient who lives in public housing and seeks the assistance of a legal services lawyer in order to reinstate her son in school. He has been suspended because of frequent encounters with the police. She is caught in a net of street-level bureaucrats with conflicting orientations toward her, all acting in what they call her "interest" and "the public interest."

E. Illustration of Program Development: Public Education

We need to broaden the focus from *who* makes public-benefit law to *what* law they make. To facilitate analysis, the implementation process can be subdivided into two tasks: (1) setting up the basic distributive structure and specifying the form of the *benefits* and (2) securing the funding to make the program operational by imposing the requisite *burdens*.

With this purpose, we return to the illustration of public education. The immensity of the undertaking is impressive: in this nation nearly 50 million students attend almost 100,000 public primary and secondary schools in now fewer than 15,000 school districts; and we spend about $500 billion annually to support those schools. The goal of educating in such numbers requires a complex mixture of legal ordering devices, and the development and administration of some of the devices inevitably create controversy. These attributes make public education an excellent vehicle for learning more about the range of issues involved in implementing distributive programs.

Nevertheless, public education is just one illustration of the public-benefit instrument. You should at every stage of this chapter ask yourself how generalizable the lessons of public education are, or how those lessons would apply to other public-benefit programs.

BENEFITS (WITH A FOCUS ON EQUALITY)

Lawmakers. Public education is a surprisingly modern idea. Earlier, people saw education as a parental responsibility, and later a concern of the church. Movements for public education began in the towns of colonial America, even before the advent of legislatures as we know them. But a heavy dose of religion remained in the mix of public education. By the end of the seventeenth century, most colonial and local legislative bodies in New England had come to accept certain ideas about public education: (1) that legislative bodies had the power to set up and administer public schools, (2) that local communities could be required to do the same, (3) that public revenues could be raised and used for this purpose, and (4) that parents could be required to educate their children, though not necessarily in public schools.

Although those ideas concerning public education would slowly migrate from New England to the Mid-Atlantic to the South, they did not make great progress until after the American Revolution. The Constitution does not mention education. Thereafter, however, the conviction began to grow that if individuals were going to govern themselves and realize their potential as individuals, then they must be educated. If one nation were to emerge, then common values, a common language, and a common literature had to be taught. If religious liberty were to become a reality in a country divided in religion, then public education had to be made available free of religious domination.

Influenced by these developing ideas, state and local legislative bodies began the task of building public educational systems. But they did not immediately set up free and universal public schools on a permanent basis. The New York state legislature, for example, experimented in 1795 with the establishment of free schools to instruct children in "English language,... English grammar, arithmetic, mathematics, and such other branches of knowledge as are most useful and necessary to complete a good English education," but the law lasted only five years. That legislature allowed local schools to charge tuition until 1867, but it at least continued to endorse the principle of public education. Steadily over the nineteenth century, the so-called common school came to be the norm, providing a free primary education to all children by teaching a common language and common values. It generally proceeded without divisions by grade. Secondary schools developed later. Even if New York City established its very first secondary school in 1825, high school attendance started to become the norm only in the

1930s. A sense of public responsibility for some post-secondary education came even later.

Congress played almost no role at all in this history. Over the years the states, while lately enjoying limited federal assistance, have remained principally in charge of public education. By state constitution and statute, each state has established a public school system.

Today, almost every state constitution addresses the matter of public education. Most state constitutions simply authorize the legislature to establish and maintain a system of free public education, but some, like New York's, actually require the legislature to create a network of public schools: "The legislature shall provide for the maintenance and support of a system of free common schools, wherein all the children of this state may be educated." N.Y. Const. art. XI, §1.

By statute, the state usually delegates much legislative power to some administrative body, such as a board of regents. The legislature also gives the regents the authority to appoint a commissioner of education who, with the help of a department of education working under him or her, must supervise the statewide system by exercising executive powers and internal judicial powers, as well as any delegated legislative powers. Among other responsibilities, the commissioner inspects schools and qualifies teachers. See, e.g., N.Y. Education Law §§101 et seq.

At the same time, the state legislature delegates most of the operational control to the local level, that is, the school district. A locally elected board of education heads up each school district and manages its educational affairs. Typically, the board is the body that decides which schools to establish for which students, that has some control over the curriculum, and that sets the rate of the property tax so critical to its schools' funding. See, e.g., N.Y. Education Law §§1501 et seq.

Nevertheless, the nonprofessional and unpaid members of the school board could hardly exercise full control. They typically defer to the expertise of the schools' administrators on major policy questions as well as on day-to-day management. Those professionals enjoy considerable control over recruiting staff, organizing the schools' internal administration, fixing the curriculum, and setting the budgetary details. By contrast, teachers and their unions traditionally have not played a big policy role, although obviously instructors shape what goes on in their classrooms. Similarly, citizen and parent groups play more of a supportive than an influential role in running the schools.

The basic structure of early American education—local schools supported by local funds, with some supervision and financing by state government, and less federal involvement—has proven remarkably resilient over time. Time has nonetheless brought with it a significant movement toward increased central control. The federal government has become involved through programs to attack certain problems, as by aiding the disabled, the disadvantaged, and other targeted groups, and so federal assistance now accounts for about 8 percent of public school revenues. The states have also become more deeply involved in funding public education, so that state aid now makes up about 49 percent of public school revenues. The remaining 43 percent still comes from local sources, while the geographical size of the school district has grown with time.

Although we still plan to move beyond this necessary background on education's lawmakers and turn to the content of the bestowed benefit, the interplay of three governmental levels is important and complicated enough, and perhaps new enough as an explicit concern for you, to warrant expansion by a fresh voice. We have sketched out that the state legislature has plenary power over education, as long as it acts without violating any constitutional provision or any federal law. But actual governance involves other lawmakers performing certain critical functions, as better explained by the project on Education and the Law: State Interests and Individual Rights, 74 Mich. L. Rev. 1373, 1375–81 (1976):*

> Only rarely have legislatures taken a broad interest in formulating and controlling educational policy. Most states have left such matters to administrative agencies and various elected bodies at the state and local levels. At the summit of the administrative hierarchy is a board that has been established in all the states. The powers of the various state boards differ. In some, the board may control all aspects of the state's educational program; in others, wide delegation to local agencies may limit the board to a very narrow range of activities. While the boards are responsible for implementing legislation and also possess policy-making discretion, out of deference to local institutions this policy-making power is rarely exercised.
>
> All states also have a superintendent of schools who typically performs such functions as the enforcement of laws, adoption of regulations, distribution of funds and financial accounting. In recent years, the state superintendents have been given greater responsibility for research and development and for general supervision of the schools. An institution at the state level, usually referred to as the "department of education," consists of supporting personnel who assist the superintendent in his administrative duties.
>
> Many of the functions performed at the state level, such as the distribution of research data and the publication of journals, merely aid the schools in their daily operations. These have little direct impact on the student and thus rarely lead to conflicts among the various interests within the educational community. Other, typically regulatory, state functions are designed, however, to serve collectivist interests in education. Most important are the controls on citizens that devolve from the legislature. Thus, socialization of all children is assured by compulsory education requirements, while the particular values and standards of achievement sought through socialization are defined by state curriculum requirements. Moreover, states have other, less direct means of defining the community norms that the educational system is designed to further. For example, all states require teachers to be certified. Licensing requirements narrow the class of individuals that will be allowed to teach to those who possess traits considered worthy of being nurtured in students. Thus, successful applicants must have a good, moral

* Reprinted from Michigan Law Review, June 1976, Vol. 74, No. 7. Copyright 1976 by Jeffrey O. Birkhold, Susan Esserman Marks, Stephen D. Anderson, James P. Blake & Stephen Godsall-Myers.

character, though what activities or traits satisfy this requirement is often uncertain. In addition, minimum education requirements for teacher's certification are typically prescribed by a state administrative agency. Such standards are intended to guarantee that teachers possess a minimum level of competence. They exemplify the state's interest in ensuring that students in *all* localities achieve a certain level of academic prowess through their exposure to teachers with adequate credentials. States also prescribe certain standards for such facilities as buildings, libraries, and equipment. This exercise of control over the quality of the student's environment is perfectly consistent with the state's interest in academic achievement. Yet the state may actually go further and impose requirements, such as the displaying of an American flag in each school, that advance the state's interest in inculcating patriotism in the young.

Despite these examples of control at the state level, the management of the educational system for the most part occurs at the local level. In recent years, state concern has been largely focused on increasing financial support for programs managed by the local communities. Great differences in wealth and resources exist among communities and some districts are unable to support an adequate system of public schools without state aid. Thus, much of the state effort in education in the past few years has been directed at these problems, but enormous discrepancies in expenditures per pupil remain.

Historically, Americans have considered schools to be an extension of the local community. Thus, although state legislatures possess plenary power over the educational system, local initiative with respect to education is so highly regarded that most states have delegated extensive authority over the actual administration of the schools to local institutions. States have divided their territory into "school districts" that perform the sole function of establishing and maintaining the public schools. Boards of education, commonly referred to as school boards, have been created as the governing body of the school district and are typically responsible for the day-to-day operation of the public schools.

Although the diversity of state statutory schemes makes it difficult to generalize about school board composition and authority, it is clear that the school board is intended to be the instrument for the public's expression of educational policy. That educational decision-making is regarded as requiring closer ties to the public than other governmental functions is demonstrated by the unique status accorded most boards. For example, school districts are usually distinct from their corresponding political units—village, city, or county—even though the boundaries may be identical. In states in which the school board is elected directly by a district's voters, the contests are held separately from those for municipal government offices and are almost always conducted on a nonpartisan basis. The severing of education from general local politics caused by these distinctions is generally respected by municipal officials, who avoid direct involvement in educational matters.

Equality.   We now turn to the content of the benefit. We do so by focusing first on what has been the most troublesome issue in the history of American education, namely, ensuring equality in the provision of the benefit. We shall continue to flesh out the content of the educational benefit in the remainder of this chapter.

Much legal ordering is necessary if government is to take seriously the fundamental tenet in all distributive programs that money, goods, and services should be distributed equitably among all potential beneficiaries. Inequity is always objectionable, but maldistribution of governmental benefits gives rise to special concern under the norm of equality under law. The offense has a double aspect: it is not simply that some are not getting their equitable share of the government pie, but that the figurative pie is itself a public product composed of compulsory contributions from taxpayers who expect equity from government.

As you read the next case, take note of who the relevant lawmakers are and what functions they perform in providing equal educational opportunity. In public education especially, the judicial system has proved necessary to make public-benefit conferral work equitably.

BROWN v. BOARD OF EDUCATION

Supreme Court of the United States, 1954
347 U.S. 483, 74 S. Ct. 686

Mr. Chief Justice Warren delivered the opinion of the Court:

These cases come to us from the States of Kansas, South Carolina, Virginia, and Delaware. They are premised on different facts and different local conditions, but a common legal question justifies their consideration together in this consolidated opinion.

In each of the cases, minors of the Negro race, through their legal representatives, seek the aid of the courts in obtaining admission to the public schools of their community on a nonsegregated basis. In each instance, they have been denied admission to schools attended by white children under laws requiring or permitting segregation according to race. This segregation was alleged to deprive the plaintiffs of the equal protection of the laws under the Fourteenth Amendment. . . .

The plaintiffs contend that segregated public schools are not "equal" and cannot be made "equal," and that hence they are deprived of the equal protection of the laws. Because of the obvious importance of the question presented, the Court took jurisdiction. Argument was heard in the 1952 Term, and reargument was heard this Term on certain questions propounded by the Court.

Reargument was largely devoted to the circumstances surrounding the adoption of the Fourteenth Amendment in 1868. It covered exhaustively consideration of the Amendment in Congress, ratification by the states, then existing practices in racial segregation, and the views of proponents and opponents of the Amendment. This discussion and our own investigation convince us that, although these sources cast some light, it is not enough to resolve the problem with which we are faced. At best, they are inconclusive. The most avid proponents of the post-War Amendments undoubtedly intended them to remove all legal distinctions among "all persons born or naturalized in the United States." Their opponents, just as certainly, were antagonistic to both the letter and the spirit of the Amendments and wished them to have the most limited effect. What others in Congress and the state legislatures had in mind cannot be determined with any degree of certainty.

An additional reason for the inconclusive nature of the Amendment's history, with respect to segregated schools, is the status of public education at that time. In the South, the movement toward free common schools, supported by general taxation, had not yet taken hold. Education of white children was largely in the hands of private groups. Education of Negroes was almost nonexistent, and practically all of the race were illiterate. In fact, any education of Negroes was forbidden by law in some states. Today, in contrast, many Negroes have achieved outstanding success in the arts and sciences as well as in the business and professional world. It is true that public school education at the time of the Amendment had advanced further in the North, but the effect of the Amendment on Northern States was generally ignored in the congressional debates. Even in the North, the conditions of public education did not approximate those existing today. The curriculum was usually rudimentary; ungraded schools were common in rural areas; the school term was but three months a year in many states; and compulsory school attendance was virtually unknown. As a consequence, it is not surprising that there should be so little in the history of the Fourteenth Amendment relating to its intended effect on public education.

In the first cases in this Court construing the Fourteenth Amendment, decided shortly after its adoption, the Court interpreted it as proscribing all state-imposed discriminations against the Negro race. The doctrine of "separate but equal" did not make its appearance in this Court until 1896 in the case of Plessy v. Ferguson, [163 U.S. 537, 16 S. Ct. 1138], involving not education but transportation. American courts have since labored with the doctrine for over half a century. In this Court, there have been six cases involving the "separate but equal" doctrine in the field of public education. In Cumming v. Board of Education of Richmond County, 175 U.S. 528, 20 S. Ct. 197, and Gong Lum v. Rice, 275 U.S. 78, 48 S. Ct. 91, the validity of the doctrine itself was not challenged. In more recent cases, all on the graduate school level, inequality was found in that specific benefits enjoyed by white students were denied to Negro students of the same educational qualifications. In none of these cases was it necessary to re-examine the doctrine to grant relief to the Negro plaintiff. And in Sweatt v. Painter, [339 U.S. 629, 70 S. Ct. 848 (1950)], the Court expressly reserved decision on the question whether *Plessy v. Ferguson* should be held inapplicable to public education.

In the instant cases, that question is directly presented. Here, unlike *Sweatt v. Painter*, there are findings below that the Negro and white schools involved have been equalized, or are being equalized, with respect to buildings, curricula, qualifications and salaries of teachers, and

other "tangible" factors. Our decision, therefore, cannot turn on merely a comparison of these tangible factors in the Negro and white schools involved in each of the cases. We must look instead to the effect of segregation itself on public education.

In approaching this problem, we cannot turn the clock back to 1868 when the Amendment was adopted, or even to 1896 when *Plessy v. Ferguson* was written. We must consider public education in the light of its full development and its present place in American life throughout the Nation. Only in this way can it be determined if segregation in public schools deprives these plaintiffs of the equal protection of the laws.

Today, education is perhaps the most important function of state and local governments. Compulsory school attendance laws and the great expenditures for education both demonstrate our recognition of the importance of education to our democratic society. It is required in the performance of our most basic public responsibilities, even service in the armed forces. It is the very foundation of good citizenship. Today it is a principal instrument in awakening the child to cultural values, in preparing him for later professional training, and in helping him to adjust normally to his environment. In these days, it is doubtful that any child may reasonably be expected to succeed in life if he is denied the opportunity of an education. Such an opportunity, where the state has undertaken to provide it, is a right which must be made available to all on equal terms.

We come then to the question presented: Does segregation of children in public schools solely on the basis of race, even though the physical facilities and other "tangible" factors may be equal, deprive the children of the minority group of equal educational opportunities? We believe that it does.

In *Sweatt v. Painter*, supra, in finding that a segregated law school for Negroes could not provide them equal educational opportunities, this Court relied in large part on "those qualities which are incapable of objective measurement but which make for greatness in a law school." In McLaurin v. Oklahoma State Regents, [339 U.S. 637, 70 S. Ct. 853 (1950)], the Court, in requiring that a Negro admitted to a white graduate school be treated like all other students, again resorted to intangible considerations: "...his ability to study, to engage in discussions and exchange views with other students, and, in general, to learn his profession." Such considerations apply with added force to children in grade and high schools. To separate them from others of similar age and qualifications solely because of their race generates a feeling of inferiority as to their status in the community that may affect their hearts and minds in a way unlikely ever to be undone. The effect of this separation on their educational opportunities was well stated by a finding in the Kansas case by a court which nevertheless felt compelled to rule against the Negro plaintiffs:

> Segregation of white and colored children in public schools has a detrimental effect upon the colored children. The impact is greater when it has the sanction of the law; for the policy of separating the races is usually interpreted as denoting the inferiority of the Negro group. A sense of inferiority affects the motivation of a child to learn. Segregation with the sanction of law, therefore, has a tendency to [retard] the educational and mental development of Negro children and to deprive them of some of the benefits they would receive in a racial[ly] integrated school system.

Whatever may have been the extent of psychological knowledge at the time of *Plessy v. Ferguson*, this finding is amply supported by modern authority.[11] Any language in *Plessy v. Ferguson* contrary to this finding is rejected.

We conclude that in the field of public education the doctrine of "separate but equal" has no place. Separate educational facilities are inherently unequal. Therefore, we hold that the plaintiffs and others similarly situated for whom the actions have been brought are, by reason of the segregation complained of, deprived of the equal protection of the laws guaranteed by the Fourteenth Amendment....

Because these are class actions, because of the wide applicability of this decision, and because of the great variety of local conditions, the formulation of decrees in these cases presents problems of considerable complexity. On reargument, the consideration of appropriate relief was necessarily subordinated to the primary question—the constitutionality of segregation in public education. We have now announced that such segregation is a denial of the equal protection of the laws. In order that we may have the full assistance of the parties in formulating decrees, the cases will be restored to the docket, and the parties are requested to present further argument on [relief. In Brown v. Board of Education, 349 U.S. 294, 75 S. Ct. 753 (1955), the Court would order the lower courts to shape and implement remedies "with all deliberate speed."]

11. K.B. Clark, Effect of Prejudice and Discrimination on Personality Development (Midcentury White House Conference on Children and Youth, 1950); Witmer & Kotinsky, Personality in the Making (1952), c. VI; Deutscher & Chein, The Psychological Effects of Enforced Segregation: A Survey of Social Science Opinion, 26 J. Psychol. 259 (1948); Chein, What are the Psychological Effects of Segregation Under Conditions of Equal Facilities?, 3 Int. J. Opinion and Attitude Res. 229 (1949); Brameld, Educational Costs, in Discrimination and National Welfare (MacIver ed., 1949), 44–48; Frazier, The Negro in the United States (1949), 674–681. And see generally Myrdal, An American Dilemma (1944).

NOTES

1. Supreme Court intervention in the name of racial equity prior to *Brown* had always rested on differences between black and white schools in educational resources, such as teachers and library books. Did the school systems challenged in the *Brown* litigation offer decidedly fewer material resources to black students

than to whites? If not, what was the unanimous Court's basis for finding a violation of the constitutional guarantee of equal protection of the law? Does the Court's reasoning suggest that the appropriate remedy for a violation is merely desegregation, or is it a more affirmative integration? Subsequent cases established an affirmative duty to integrate schools, and at least to some degree by means of various remedies such as busing, but only when the state or local officials' intentionality had caused the segregation.

2. In any event, the elimination of state statutes mandating school segregation has not eliminated racial isolation in American schools, and indeed racial isolation may be increasing. Schools that are segregated in fact by social circumstance (de facto segregation), although not intentionally by law (de jure segregation), continue to spawn lawsuits. But today many of the lawsuits contest certain steps taken voluntarily by the officials to increase their schools' diversity.

PARENTS INVOLVED IN COMMUNITY SCHOOLS v. SEATTLE SCHOOL DISTRICT NO. 1

Supreme Court of the United States, 2007
551 U.S. 701, 127 S. Ct. 2738

CHIEF JUSTICE ROBERTS:

The school districts in these cases voluntarily adopted student assignment plans that rely upon race to determine which public schools certain children may attend. The Seattle school district classifies children as white or nonwhite; the Jefferson County school district as black or "other." In Seattle, this racial classification is used to allocate slots in oversubscribed high schools. In Jefferson County, it is used to make certain elementary school assignments and to rule on transfer requests. In each case, the school district relies upon an individual student's race in assigning that student to a particular school, so that the racial balance at the school falls within a predetermined range based on the racial composition of the school district as a whole. Parents of students denied assignment to particular schools under these plans solely because of their race brought suit, contending that allocating children to different public schools on the basis of race violated the Fourteenth Amendment guarantee of equal protection. The Courts of Appeals below upheld the plans. We granted certiorari, and now reverse.

I

Both cases present the same underlying legal question—whether a public school that had not operated legally segregated schools or has been found to be unitary [which is defined below] may choose to classify students by race and rely upon that classification in making school assignments. Although we examine the plans under the same legal framework, the specifics of the two plans, and the circumstances surrounding their adoption, are in some respects quite different.

A

Seattle School District No. 1 operates 10 regular public high schools. In 1998, it adopted the plan at issue in this case for assigning students to these schools. The plan allows incoming ninth graders to choose from among any of the district's high schools, ranking however many schools they wish in order of preference.

Some schools are more popular than others. If too many students list the same school as their first choice, the district employs a series of "tiebreakers" to determine who will fill the open slots at the oversubscribed school. The first tiebreaker selects for admission students who have a sibling currently enrolled in the chosen school. The next tiebreaker depends upon the racial composition of the particular school and the race of the individual student. In the district's public schools approximately 41 percent of enrolled students are white; the remaining 59 percent, comprising all other racial groups [23.8% Asian-American, 23.1% African-American, 10.3% Latino, and 2.8% Native-American], are classified by Seattle for assignment purposes as nonwhite. If an over-subscribed school is not within 10 percentage points of the district's overall white/nonwhite racial balance, it is what the district calls "integration positive," and the district employs a tie-breaker that selects for assignment students whose race "will serve to bring the school into balance." If it is still necessary to select students for the school after using the racial tiebreaker, the next tiebreaker is the geographic proximity of the school to the student's residence.

Seattle has never operated segregated schools—legally separate schools for students of different races—nor has it ever been subject to court-ordered desegregation. It nonetheless employs the racial tiebreaker in an attempt to address the effects of racially identifiable housing patterns on school assignments. Most white students live in the northern part of Seattle, most students of other racial backgrounds in the southern part. Four of Seattle's high schools are located in the north—Ballard, Nathan Hale, Ingraham, and Roosevelt—and five in the south—Rainier Beach, Cleveland, West Seattle, Chief Sealth, and Franklin. One school—Garfield—is more or less in the center of Seattle.

For the 2000-2001 school year, five of these schools were oversubscribed—Ballard, Nathan Hale, Roosevelt, Garfield, and Franklin—so much so that 82 percent of incoming ninth graders ranked one of these schools as their first choice. Three of the oversubscribed schools were "integration positive" because the school's white enrollment the previous school year was greater than 51 percent—Ballard, Nathan Hale, and Roosevelt. Thus, more nonwhite students (107, 27, and 82, respectively) who selected one of these three schools as a top choice received placement at the school than would have been the case had race not been considered, and proximity been the next tiebreaker. Franklin was "integration positive" because its nonwhite enrollment the

previous school year was greater than 69 percent; 89 more white students were assigned to Franklin by operation of the racial tiebreaker in the 2000-2001 school year than otherwise would have been. Garfield was the only oversubscribed school whose composition during the 1999-2000 school year was within the racial guidelines, although in previous years Garfield's enrollment had been predominantly nonwhite, and the racial tiebreaker had been used to give preference to white students.

Petitioner Parents Involved in Community Schools (Parents Involved) is a nonprofit corporation comprising the parents of children who have been or may be denied assignment to their chosen high school in the district because of their race. The concerns of Parents Involved are illustrated by Jill Kurfirst, who sought to enroll her ninth-grade son, Andy Meeks, in Ballard High School's special Biotechnology Career Academy. Andy suffered from attention deficit hyperactivity disorder and dyslexia, but had made good progress with hands-on instruction, and his mother and middle school teachers thought that the smaller biotechnology program held the most promise for his continued success. Andy was accepted into this selective program but, because of the racial tiebreaker, was denied assignment to Ballard High School. Parents Involved commenced this suit in the Western District of Washington, alleging that Seattle's use of race in assignments violated the Equal Protection Clause of the Fourteenth Amendment, Title VI of the Civil Rights Act of 1964, and the Washington Civil Rights Act.

The District Court granted summary judgment to the school district, finding that state law did not bar the district's use of the racial tiebreaker and that the plan survived strict scrutiny on the federal constitutional claim because it was narrowly tailored to serve a compelling government interest. . . .

B

Jefferson County Public Schools operates the public school system in metropolitan Louisville, Kentucky. In 1973 a federal court found that Jefferson County had maintained a segregated school system, Newburg Area Council, Inc. v.

Board of Ed. of Jefferson Cty., 489 F.2d 925, 932 (CA6), vacated and remanded, 418 U.S. 918, 94 S. Ct. 3208, 3209, reinstated with modifications, 510 F.2d 1358, 1359 (C.A.6 1974), and in 1975 the District Court entered a desegregation decree. See Hampton v. Jefferson Cty. Bd. of Ed., 72 F. Supp. 2d 753, 762–764 (W.D. Ky. 1999). Jefferson County operated under this decree until 2000, when the District Court dissolved the decree after finding that the district had achieved unitary status by eliminating "[t]o the greatest extent practicable" the vestiges of its prior policy of segregation. Hampton v. Jefferson Cty. Bd. of Ed., 102 F. Supp. 2d 358, 360 (2000).

In 2001, after the decree had been dissolved, Jefferson County adopted the voluntary student assignment plan at issue in this case. Approximately 34 percent of the district's 97,000 students are black; most of the remaining 66 percent are white. The plan requires all nonmagnet schools to maintain a minimum black enrollment of 15 percent, and a maximum black enrollment of 50 percent.

At the elementary school level, based on his or her address, each student is designated a "resides" school to which students within a specific geographic area are assigned; elementary resides schools are "grouped into clusters in order to facilitate integration." The district assigns students to nonmagnet schools in one of two ways: Parents of kindergartners, first-graders, and students new to the district may submit an application indicating a first and second choice among the schools within their cluster; students who do not submit such an application are assigned within the cluster by the district. "Decisions to assign students to schools within each cluster are based on available space within the schools and the racial guidelines in the District's current student assignment plan." If a school has reached the "extremes of the racial guidelines," a student whose race would contribute to the school's racial imbalance will not be assigned there. After assignment, students at all grade levels are permitted to apply to transfer between nonmagnet schools in the district. Transfers may be requested for any number of reasons, and may be denied because of lack of available space or on the basis of the racial guidelines.

When petitioner Crystal Meredith moved into the school district in August 2002, she sought to enroll her son, Joshua McDonald, in kindergarten for the 2002–2003 school year. His resides school was only a mile from his new home, but it had no available space—assignments had been made in May, and the class was full. Jefferson County assigned Joshua to another elementary school in his cluster, Young Elementary. This school was 10 miles from home, and Meredith sought to transfer Joshua to a school in a different cluster, Bloom Elementary, which—like his resides school—was only a mile from home. Space was available at Bloom, and intercluster transfers are allowed, but Joshua's transfer was nonetheless denied because, in the words of Jefferson County, "[t]he transfer would have an adverse effect on desegregation compliance" of Young.

Meredith brought suit in the Western District of Kentucky, alleging violations of the Equal Protection Clause of the Fourteenth Amendment. The District Court found that Jefferson County had asserted a compelling interest in maintaining racially diverse schools, and that the assignment plan was (in all relevant respects) narrowly tailored to serve that compelling interest. . . .

II

As a threshold matter, we must assure ourselves of our jurisdiction. [The Court found that the plaintiffs had standing to sue.]

III

A

It is well established that when the government distributes burdens or benefits on the basis of individual racial classifications, that action is reviewed under strict scrutiny. Johnson v. California, 543 U.S. 499, 505–506, 125 S. Ct. 1141 949 (2005); Grutter v. Bollinger, 539 U.S. 306, 326, 123 S. Ct. 2325 (2003); Adarand [Constructors, Inc. v. Pena, 515 U.S. 200, 224, 115 S. Ct. 2097, 2111 (1995)]. As the Court recently reaffirmed, "'racial classifications are simply too pernicious to permit any but the most exact connection between justification and classification.'" Gratz v. Bollinger,

539 U.S. 244, 270, 123 S. Ct. 2411 (2003) (quoting Fullilove v. Klutznick, 448 U.S. 448, 537, 100 S. Ct. 2758 (1980) (Stevens, J., dissenting); brackets omitted). In order to satisfy this searching standard of review, the school districts must demonstrate that the use of individual racial classifications in the assignment plans here under review is "narrowly tailored" to achieve a "compelling" government interest. *Adarand*, supra, at 227, 115 S. Ct. 2097.

Without attempting in these cases to set forth all the interests a school district might assert, it suffices to note that our prior cases, in evaluating the use of racial classifications in the school context, have recognized two interests that qualify as compelling. The first is the compelling interest of remedying the effects of past intentional discrimination. See Freeman v. Pitts, 503 U.S. 467, 494, 112 S. Ct. 1430 (1992). Yet the Seattle public schools have not shown that they were ever segregated by law, and were not subject to court-ordered desegregation decrees. The Jefferson County public schools were previously segregated by law and were subject to a desegregation decree entered in 1975. In 2000, the District Court that entered that decree dissolved it, finding that Jefferson County had "eliminated the vestiges associated with the former policy of segregation and its pernicious effects," and thus had achieved "unitary" status. *Hampton*, 102 F. Supp. 2d, at 360. Jefferson County accordingly does not rely upon an interest in remedying the effects of past intentional discrimination in defending its present use of race in assigning students.

Nor could it. We have emphasized that the harm being remedied by mandatory desegregation plans is the harm that is traceable to segregation, and that "the Constitution is not violated by racial imbalance in the schools, without more." Milliken v. Bradley, 433 U.S. 267, 280, n.14, 97 S. Ct. 2749 (1977). Once Jefferson County achieved unitary status, it had remedied the constitutional wrong that allowed race-based assignments. Any continued use of race must be justified on some other basis.

The second government interest we have recognized as compelling for purposes of strict scrutiny is the interest in diversity in higher education upheld in *Grutter*, 539 U.S., at 328, 123 S. Ct. 2325.

The specific interest found compelling in *Grutter* was student body diversity "in the context of higher education." Ibid. The diversity interest was not focused on race alone but encompassed "all factors that may contribute to student body diversity." Id., at 337, 123 S. Ct. 2325. We described the various types of diversity that the law school sought:

> [The University of Michigan law school's] policy makes clear there are many possible bases for diversity admissions, and provides examples of admittees who have lived or traveled widely abroad, are fluent in several languages, have overcome personal adversity and family hardship, have exceptional records of extensive community service, and have had successful careers in other fields.

Id., at 338, 123 S. Ct. 2325 (brackets and internal quotation marks omitted). The Court quoted the articulation of diversity from Justice Powell's opinion in Regents of the University of California v. Bakke, 438 U.S. 265, 98 S. Ct. 2733 (1978), noting that "it is not an interest in simple ethnic diversity, in which a specified percentage of the student body is in effect guaranteed to be members of selected ethnic groups, that can justify the use of race." *Grutter*, supra, at 324–325, 123 S. Ct. 2325. Instead, what was upheld in *Grutter* was consideration of "a far broader array of qualifications and characteristics of which racial or ethnic origin is but a single though important element."

The entire gist of the analysis in *Grutter* was that the admissions program at issue there focused on each applicant as an individual, and not simply as a member of a particular racial group. The classification of applicants by race upheld in *Grutter* was only as part of a "highly individualized, holistic review," 539 U.S., at 337, 123 S. Ct. 2325. As the Court explained, "[t]he importance of this individualized consideration in the context of a race-conscious admissions program is paramount." Ibid. The point of the narrow tailoring analysis in which the *Grutter* Court engaged was to ensure that the use of racial classifications was indeed part of a broader assessment of diversity, and not simply an effort to achieve racial balance, which the Court explained would be "patently unconstitutional." Id., at 330, 123 S. Ct. 2325.

In the present cases, by contrast, race is not considered as part of a broader effort to achieve "exposure to widely diverse people, cultures, ideas, and viewpoints," ibid.; race, for some students, is determinative standing alone. The districts argue that other factors, such as student preferences, affect assignment decisions under their plans, but under each plan when race comes into play, it is decisive by itself. It is not simply one factor weighed with others in reaching a decision, as in *Grutter*; it is *the* factor. Like the University of Michigan undergraduate plan struck down in *Gratz*, 539 U.S., at 275, 123 S. Ct. 2411, the plans here "do not provide for a meaningful individualized review of applicants" but instead rely on racial classifications in a "nonindividualized, mechanical" way. Id., at 276, 280, 123 S. Ct. 2411 (O'Connor, J., concurring).

Even when it comes to race, the plans here employ only a limited notion of diversity, viewing race exclusively in white/nonwhite terms in Seattle and black/"other" terms in Jefferson County. But see Metro Broadcasting, Inc. v. FCC, 497 U.S. 547, 610, 110 S. Ct. 2997 (1990) ("We are a Nation not of black and white alone, but one teeming with divergent communities knitted together with various traditions and carried forth, above all, by individuals") (O'Connor, J., dissenting). The Seattle "Board Statement Reaffirming Diversity Rationale" speaks of the "inherent educational value" in "[p]roviding students the opportunity to attend schools with diverse student enrollment." But under the Seattle plan, a school with 50 percent Asian-American students and 50 percent white students but no African-American, Native-American, or Latino students would qualify as balanced, while a school with 30 percent Asian-American, 25 percent African-American, 25 percent Latino, and 20 percent white students would not. It is hard to understand how a plan that could allow these results can be viewed as being concerned with achieving enrollment that is " 'broadly diverse,' " *Grutter*, supra, at 329, 123 S. Ct. 2325. . . .

In upholding the admissions plan in *Grutter*, [moreover], this Court relied upon considerations unique to institutions of higher education, noting that in light of "the expansive freedoms of speech and thought associated with the university environment, universities occupy a special niche in our constitutional tradition." 539 U.S., at 329, 123 S. Ct. 2325. See also *Bakke*, supra, at 312, 313, 98 S. Ct. 2733 (opinion of Powell, J.). The Court explained that "[c]ontext matters" in applying strict scrutiny, and repeatedly noted that it was addressing the use of race "in the context of higher education." *Grutter*, supra, at 327, 328, 334, 123 S. Ct. 2325. The Court in *Grutter* expressly articulated key limitations on its holding—defining a specific type of broad-based diversity and noting the unique context of higher education—but these limitations were largely disregarded by the lower courts in extending *Grutter* to uphold race-based assignments in elementary and secondary schools. The present cases are not governed by *Grutter*.

B

[This part B disapproved of any governmental action in the mere pursuit of racial balance. Although Justices Scalia, Thomas, and Alito joined the Chief Justice's opinion in its entirety, Justice Kennedy as the critical swing vote joined it only in certain parts, declining to join in this part B and so depriving it of majority support. Although he agreed that the schools had not narrowly tailored their policies to any permissible compelling state interest, Justice Kennedy believed that sometimes government can take racial balance into account: schools could consider their racial makeup and adopt general policies to encourage a diverse student body. He wrote: "School boards may pursue the goal of bringing together students of diverse backgrounds and races through other means, including strategic site selection of new schools; drawing attendance zones with general recognition of the demographics of neighborhoods; allocating resources for special programs; recruiting students and faculty in a targeted fashion; and tracking enrollments, performance, and other statistics by race. These mechanisms are race conscious but do not lead to different treatment based on a classification that tells each student he or she is to be defined by race . . . ."]

C

The districts assert, as they must, that the way in which they have employed individual racial classifications is necessary to achieve their stated ends. The minimal effect these classifications have on student assignments, however, suggests that other means would be effective. Seattle's racial tiebreaker results, in the end, only in shifting a small number of students between schools. Approximately 307 student assignments were affected by the racial tiebreaker in 2000–2001; the district was able to track the enrollment status of 293 of these students. Of these, 209 were assigned to a school that was one of their choices, 87 of whom were assigned to the same school to which they would have been assigned without the racial tiebreaker. Eighty-four students were assigned to schools that they did not list as a choice, but 29 of those students would have been assigned to their respective school without the racial tiebreaker, and 3 were able to attend one of the oversubscribed schools due to waitlist and capacity adjustments. In over one-third of the assignments affected by the racial tiebreaker, then, the use of race in the end made no difference, and the district could identify only 52 students who were ultimately affected adversely by the racial tiebreaker in that it resulted in assignment to a school they had not listed as a preference and to which they would not otherwise have been assigned. . . .

Similarly, Jefferson County's use of racial classifications has only a minimal effect on the assignment of students. Elementary school students are assigned to their first- or second-choice school 95 percent of the time, and transfers, which account for roughly 5 percent of assignments, are only denied 35 percent of the time—and presumably an even smaller percentage are denied on the basis of the racial guidelines, given that other factors may lead to a denial. Jefferson County estimates that the racial guidelines account for only 3 percent of assignments. As Jefferson County explains, "the racial guidelines have minimal impact in this process, because they 'mostly influence student assignment in subtle and indirect ways.'"

While we do not suggest that *greater* use of race would be preferable, the minimal impact of the districts' racial classifications on school enrollment casts doubt on the necessity of using racial classifications. In *Grutter*, the consideration of race was viewed as indispensable in more than tripling minority representation at the law school—from 4 to 14.5 percent. See 539 U.S., at 320, 123 S. Ct. 2325. Here the most Jefferson County itself claims is that "because the guidelines provide a firm definition of the Board's goal of racially integrated schools, they 'provide administrators with the authority to facilitate, negotiate and collaborate with principals and staff to maintain schools within the 15–50% range.'" Classifying and assigning schoolchildren according to a binary conception of race is an extreme approach in light of our precedents and our Nation's history of using race in public schools, and requires more than such an amorphous end to justify it.

The districts have also failed to show that they considered methods other than explicit racial classifications to achieve their stated goals. Narrow tailoring requires "serious, good faith consideration of workable race-neutral alternatives," *Grutter*, supra, at 339, 123 S. Ct. 2325, and yet in Seattle several alternative assignment plans—many of which would not have used express racial classifications—were rejected with little or no consideration. Jefferson County has failed to present any evidence that it considered alternatives, even though the district already claims that its goals are achieved primarily through means other than the racial classifications.

IV

[Justice Roberts claimed that his approach was closer to the spirit of *Brown*, likewise aiming for education provided "on a nonracial basis." He wrote: "The way to stop discrimination on the basis of race is to stop discriminating on the basis of race." But Justice Kennedy chose not to join this part IV.]

The judgments of the Courts of Appeals for the Sixth and Ninth Circuits are reversed, and the cases are remanded for further proceedings.

It is so ordered.

[Before so closing, Justice Roberts in part IV also gave a detailed response to Justice Breyer's blistering and lengthy dissent, which Justices Stevens, Souter, and Ginsburg joined. Justice Breyer argued that the Court was being unfaithful to its post-*Brown* precedent. He closed: "To invalidate the plans under review is to threaten the promise of *Brown*. The plurality's position, I fear, would break that promise. This is a decision that the Court and the Nation will come to regret."

The various concurring and dissenting opinions are omitted.

Epilogue: Schools are now moving partway toward socio-economic-class-based integration, which some education experts argue might be more effective anyway. See Emily Bazelon, The Next Kind of Integration, N.Y. Times, July 20, 2008 (Magazine), at 38.]

BURDENS (WITH THE FOCUS STILL ON EQUALITY)

Public education is an expensive public benefit, second only to military defense in the costs it imposes upon taxpayers. On the one hand, the cost of supporting a large military establishment is borne through federal income taxation and is managed centrally: Congress votes upon taxes and appropriations, and depends on military and civilian officials employed by the federal government to spend that money intelligently. On the other hand, a large proportion of the costs of educating the young is borne and managed locally: local property taxes currently pay almost half of the cost of public education in most states, while local school boards usually determine how much to raise each year and how to spend that money.

How does the property tax work? Local officials assess the value of all taxable real estate in the district—residences, farms, other businesses. The school board uses its annual budgeting process to have their administrators determine how much money it needs to raise. This amount, when divided by the valuation of the district's taxable property, gives the tax rate. The tax rate is a rough measure of the district's *willingness* to support its schools. Meanwhile the property's valuation, when divided by the number of pupils in the district, is a rough measure of the district's *ability* to support its schools.

The financing aspect of local control of public education has had important consequences for the distribution of the educational benefit in the United States, because districts differ significantly in their taxable resources and in the enthusiasm with which they fund public education. The upshot is that educational spending varies greatly, sometimes tenfold, from place to place even within a given state.

State and federal educational spending tends to mitigate, but not eliminate, these differences. The federal contribution is too small to make much of a difference in local budgets, and the states have not yet committed themselves to wiping out interdistrict inequalities.

Indeed, little agreement exists among the states as to just how they at the state level should support public education, so that individual states vary considerably both in the amount they devote to public education and in the formulas they use to distribute those funds to localities. The traditional method for distributing the state aid to the districts was the so-called flat grant, which is a set amount of dollars per pupil to all school districts regardless of the district's wealth. Although even this approach for state support has some equalizing effect, persisting interdistrict inequalities pushed some states to various other formulas that increase state aid to those districts with lesser ability to support their schools.

As education grew more expensive in the 1960s, the differences between districts grew still larger, and calls to reform the traditional system became more urgent. Reformers brought their arguments for equalizing school-tax burdens and equalizing educational spending to the courts and to the state legislatures. Both responded, but not always in the ways that advocates of change favored. There is no denying, however, that the way this dispute played out over time is highly instructive.

Judicial Input. The classic case here—and we are trying to present the essential Supreme Court cases on public education—is San Antonio Independent School District v. Rodriguez, 411 U.S. 1, 93 S. Ct. 1278 (1973). See Anna Lukemeyer, Courts as Policymakers: School Finance Reform Litigation (2003), and more generally Michael A. Rebell & Arthur R. Block, Educational Policy Making and the Courts (1982).

In *Rodriguez*, the Court found the interdistrict disparities in school funding to be constitutional. Rather than imposing on you another long and complicated case, we shall use the contemporary account of the case's background, description, and assessment by Norman C. Thomas, Equalizing Educational Opportunity Through School Finance Reform: A Review Assessment, 48 U. Cin. L. Rev. 255, 278–80, 286–88, 318 (1979).* As you read it, if you lean toward thinking that the Court should have found such disparities to be unconstitutional, consider whether you would draw a distinction between education and other locally variable public benefits supported primarily by local taxes, such as fire protection or roadway expenditures.

> The initial legal test of the fiscal neutrality principle brought the reformers their first major victory. In Serrano v. Priest, [5 Cal. 3d 584, 487 P.2d 1241 (1971),] the California Supreme Court ruled that the state's school finance system violated the equal protection clauses of the state and federal constitutions because it made educational expenditures a function of community wealth. The court embraced the principle of fiscal neutrality, holding that education was a fundamental right, that school district wealth was a suspect classification and that the California school financing system based on local wealth was not necessary to the accomplishment of a compelling interest. In remanding the case to the trial court, the court stated that the "funding scheme invidiously discriminates against the poor because it makes the quality of a child's education a function of the wealth of his parents and neighbors." The court did not, however, rule out use of the property tax for educational financing, mandate the adoption of any specific remedy or

---

* Copyright © 1979 by University of Cincinnati Law Review. Reprinted by permission.

require full equalization of per-pupil expenditures. It limited the effect of its ruling to breaking the link between district wealth and school expenditures. Development of a remedy was left to the discretion of the state legislature within the parameters of the opinion....

The litigation which followed *Serrano* involved both federal and state courts. In Van Dusartz v. Hatfield, [334 F. Supp. 870 (D. Minn. 1971),] a United States district court held that Minnesota's school finance system, which made per-pupil spending a function of school district wealth, violated equal protection. The court applied the *Serrano* test of fiscal neutrality and ruled that education was a fundamental right; however, it left the formulation of the remedy to the state legislature. In doing so, it noted that the state was free "to adopt one of many optional school funding systems" and that "absolute uniformity of school expenditures" was not required. Six weeks later, in Rodriguez v. San Antonio Independent School District, [337 F. Supp. 280 (W.D. Tex. 1971), rev'd, 411 U.S. 1, 93 S. Ct. 1278 (1973),] another district court relied on *Serrano* and *Van Dusartz* in holding that the Texas school finance system, which involved local property taxes and a state-funded foundation program, violated the equal protection guarantee of the fourteenth amendment. It treated education as a fundamental right and refused to uphold the school finance system, which was based upon the suspect classification of wealth, in the absence of a showing of a compelling state interest. The Texas Board of Education appealed directly to the United States Supreme Court. The future of school finance reform through litigation based on the fourteenth amendment's equal protection clause was in limbo pending the Court's disposition of the *Rodriguez* case.

Meanwhile, state court decisions in Kansas, Michigan, New Jersey and Arizona invalidated school finance systems on the basis of state and federal constitutional provisions. Perhaps in response to the federal and state litigation, the states of California, Colorado, Florida, Illinois, Kansas, Maine, Michigan, Montana, North Dakota, Utah and Wisconsin enacted school finance reform legislation during 1972–73....

The second and current phase of the school finance reform movement began on March 21, 1973, when the United States Supreme Court handed down its long-awaited ruling in *Rodriguez*. In a 5–4 decision, the Court reversed the district court's decision invalidating the Texas school finance system. The Supreme Court's opinion, written by Justice Powell, rested on two key findings: (1) that the Texas law did not "operate to the disadvantage of any clearly identifiable suspect class" ... and (2) that education is not a fundamental right guaranteed by the Constitution. In consequence of its rejection of wealth as a suspect classification and its determination that education was not a fundamental right, the Court utilized the rational basis test rather than the more demanding standard of strict scrutiny to determine whether the Texas school finance scheme violated equal protection. The Court found the Texas school finance plan to be a reasonable means of accomplishing and protecting the state's interest in local control of and participation in educational decisions and in providing a minimum educational program in all districts.

Justice Powell emphasized the Court's reluctance to intervene in such a politically sensitive area and noted that traditional limitations on the judicial function require that ultimate solutions to social and economic problems be fashioned by legislatures responding to "democratic pressures." There was one note of encouragement for the reform movement, however, when the Court remarked that its action should not "be viewed as placing its judicial imprimatur on the status quo. The need is apparent for reform in tax systems which may well have relied too long and too heavily on the local property tax."

In the major dissent, Justice Marshall criticized the majority opinion as an abrupt departure from recent federal and state decisions invalidating state school finance systems dependent on taxable wealth and as a retreat from the Court's "historic commitment to equality of educational opportunity." Accepting the rationale of the district court and *Serrano*, Marshall concluded that education was indeed a fundamental right because it was intimately related to the exercise of first amendment freedoms and to the right to participate in the political process. Marshall believed that the Court should have applied the strict scrutiny test in judging the validity of the Texas school finance system, which, in his judgment, failed even to meet the more lenient rational basis test. It made little sense to Marshall to return the problem to "the vagaries of the political process" which has created it and proven singularly unable to remedy it.

Reaction to the *Rodriguez* decision varied widely. Some saw it as the death knell for school finance reform, and others called it a rejection of equal educational opportunity. Comment ranged from strong endorsement of Marshall's dissent, to cautious approval of the Court's position, to praise for the Court's recognition of the "limits to its own power to affect social change." Most immediate commentators expressed the opinion that the Court's refusal to invalidate the Texas school finance program did not lessen the need for reform. They were divided, however, in the degree of their optimism over the prospects for state legislative initiatives in the area.

Rodriguez removed the uncertainty over the fate of school finance reform in the federal courts. In doing so, it provided a breathing spell for states facing legal challenges on equal protection grounds, and it removed pressures for any immediate federal action to help states achieve equalization within their boundaries. The decision did not prevent state courts from hearing challenges on state constitutional grounds, which left state judges and legislators very much at liberty to implement reforms based on fiscal neutrality and the *Serrano* principle....

School finance reform is a complex issue that embodies a continuing dynamic tension between the core values of equity, equality and liberty. The strong upward surge of equality...carried through 1972 but was blunted by the *Rodriguez* decision. Since then, liberty and supportive values, such as efficiency, quality and localism, have grown in strength. Consequently, the radical restructuring of public school financing in the United States and accompanying changes in the overall pattern of public finance which appeared imminent in the early 1970's are no longer in prospect. Yet, the thrust toward reform, motivated by a desire to equalize educational opportunity in terms of per-pupil expenditures, the quest for greater equity for taxpayers as well as pupils and the attempt to make educational support more commensurate with educational needs, continue. Much has been accomplished through state courts and reform legislation in the states, and equalization remains a major concern of educational policymakers at all governmental levels.

Basics of Equal Protection

References in the preceding discussion to terms like "fundamental right," "suspect classification," and "strict scrutiny" may be confusing. A brief introduction to these concepts is in order because they figure importantly in litigation involving public schools. These terms arise in public-school litigation because of the Equal Protection Clauses of the U.S. Constitution, which promise that government will not "deny to any person within its jurisdiction the equal protection of the laws." The Fourteenth Amendment applies this restriction to state governments, and the Supreme Court has read the equivalent into the Fifth Amendment applicable to the federal government. These restrictions protect both natural persons and legal persons including corporations.

The courts have developed a more or less consistent approach for analyzing equal protection claims. The first step is to inquire: (1) Does the law or procedure in question implicate a fundamental right rooted in that Constitution, like the right to vote or procreate? and (2) Does that legal rule draw a distinction on the basis of a suspect classification, which is one based on a visible and immutable characteristic associated with historical and political disadvantage, like race or national origin? If the answer to either of these questions is yes, the court will subject the rule in question to strict scrutiny, a tough standard of judicial review. To pass constitutional muster under the strict-scrutiny standard, the rule must serve a compelling governmental interest and must be narrowly tailored to achieve that end. This was the standard that the California Supreme Court applied in *Serrano v. Priest* and the federal district court applied in *Rodriguez v. San Antonio Independent School District.*

The United States Supreme Court, as Professor Thomas noted, reversed the latter decision on the grounds that education is not a fundamental right guaranteed by the U.S. Constitution and that distinctions between poor and wealthy involve no suspect classification. Legal provisions that do not involve fundamental rights or suspect classifications receive less exacting judicial review. In many instances, it is enough that a rational basis exists for any distinctions between students or other affected individuals, so that the legal rule represents a reasonable means to a legitimate end. Only rarely would a rule fail such a lax constitutional test. In *San Antonio Independent School District v. Rodriguez*, for example, the Supreme Court applied this rational-basis test to uphold the financing law that the plaintiffs had challenged.

The stark contrast between the strict-scrutiny and rational-basis tests of constitutionality has encouraged the courts to experiment with a middle-level standard of judicial review for interests that are basic to citizens but do not receive explicit consideration in the Constitution, or for classifications by gender and other "quasi-suspect" categories. But the viability of the middle-level standard remains up in the air.

Legislative Input.   If you think that interdistrict disparities in school funding are a problem, but concede that such inequality is not unconstitutional even under the state constitution, then you would most likely address your plea for equality to the state legislature, just as Professor Thomas implied in closing. You would then encounter the surprisingly tricky question of what kind of equality the legislature should aim for (as well as how much equality we want). Should there be equal inputs or equal outcomes? Should the legislature pursue equality positively or negatively?

- A positive-input standard is one's first impulse. It would require equal expenditures per pupil throughout the state, or perhaps equal purchasing power to reflect different costs of living across the state.
- A negative-input standard would say that certain factors, such as the district's wealth or the students' race, should not cause or even correlate with different expenditures per pupil. This approach would not produce equal expenditures per pupil statewide, but would aim to eliminate any invidious differences.
- A positive-output standard would require equal educational outcomes, so that resources are available to enable each student to reach some set level or to develop to his or her fullest potential. Outcomes are, after all, the point of the public-school program, but outcome standards are hard to administer.
- A negative-output standard would say that academic achievement should not be a function of factors such as the district's wealth or the students' race. Lower achievement levels tied to such factors would necessitate greater expenditures.

This list is not exhaustive. Theorists talk also about a standard of equality of processes, which would focus on what occurs in the classroom, at the stage between inputs and outputs. And, of course, there is the constitutional standard of equal protection, which embodies more of an antidiscrimination principle for government practices.

Equality is therefore a squishy concept. David L. Kirp, an expert on education law, suggests why, in Just Schools 9 (1982):

> The specifics bespeak a larger truth: equality does not assume a single, simple, unitary, and invariant form. It is at root ambiguous, and this very ambiguity gives the concept much of its power to motivate, incite, and disappoint. Equality seems at once luminous and elusive, or perhaps luminous *because* elusive, evolving as a consequence of altered social circumstance and moral perception. It is not just that as a society we attend to smaller and smaller degrees of differentness, but also that the differences we find offensive change over time. In this sense, loyalty to equality resides not in allying oneself with a firmly settled principle but rather in the very process of pursuing the elusive, for it is the pursuit itself that counts. As Tocqueville observed: "Democratic institutions awaken and flatter the passion for equality without ever being able to satisfy it entirely. Thus complete equality is always slipping through the people's fingers at the moment when they think to grasp it." Progress entails capturing the meaning of equality in a specific setting and translating that meaning into official action, not securing a single coherent, timeless understanding.

However you define equality, the easiest way to pursue it, at least on a statewide level, would be for the state to take over the funding of public education through a statewide tax. The state could then equalize per-pupil expenditures, or it could distribute funds according to some formula aimed at another kind of equality.

Standing in the way of any such progress in the legislature is the fact that local control is our tradition (except in Hawaii, which is a single school district). See Aaron J. Saiger, Legislating Accountability: Standards, Sanctions, and School District Reform, 46 Wm. & Mary L. Rev. 1655, 1728–30 (2005). How would you summarize the principal arguments for allowing local revenues to provide prime support for public education? Should communities be able to tax themselves heavily for education if they so choose? If we allow communities the freedom to tax themselves and to enjoy the benefits of their superior revenue-raising efforts without interference from the state, should we really expect the state to "make up the difference" to districts less willing or able to raise local taxes?

Maybe there is a middle route. Here is a scheme for retaining local control while pursuing one sort of equality. It was popular with reformers, who called it district power equalizing (DPE), and a number of states adopted it. It guarantees an equal revenue yield for an equal tax rate. A 3 percent tax rate would yield, say, $1000 per pupil. A rich district taxing at 3 percent might produce more revenue than that, but it must pay its "surplus" revenues to the state. A poor district might produce less than $1000 per pupil, but the state would make up the difference. Thus, districts equally "willing" to support education would enjoy equal per-pupil expenditures, despite any differences in "ability" to raise funds.

But wait a minute. We have been focusing solely on equality from the public-school student's perspective. What about getting back to the taxpayer's perspective? What kind of equality matters there? Should it be the DPE's creation of equal capacity among taxpayers to raise education funds, or should it be imposition of equal burdens? If the latter, the legislature could impose equal taxes

New Direction

Once again, equality has proven to be an elusive goal. Because of the various roadblocks on the route to educational equality, and despite some successes in the push for that equality, many of today's reformers have redirected their efforts in a third wave of reform. Instead of pursuing equality, they now seek to compel sufficient funding to ensure "adequacy" of education, meaning that the law would guarantee to every child a minimum quality of public education rather than any financially equal education. The initial efforts focused on judicially enforcing the state constitutions' educational clauses. The ultimate efforts will, of course, be centered on the legislatures.

Others express a fear that an emphasis on adequacy could very well increase inequality, while arguing that the relative distribution of the educational benefit matters more than the absolute amount. See Mark G. Yudof, David L. Kirp, Betsy Levin & Rachel F. Moran, Educational Policy and the Law 813–27 (4th ed. 2002); William S. Koski & Rob Reich, When Adequate Isn't: The Retreat from Equity in Educational Law and Policy and Why It Matters, 56 Emory L.J. 545 (2006); see also R. Craig Wood, Educational Finance Law (3d ed. 2007); Frederick M. Wirt & Michael W. Kirst, Schools in Conflict: The Politics of Education (3d ed. 1992).

statewide, so that all pay an equal dollar amount (making no distinction between parents and nonparents, thus rejecting any pure version of a beneficiary principle, but almost necessarily making a distinction between individuals and businesses). The legislature would probably need, however, to consider ability to pay. So maybe the tax should be a percentage of wealth, as measured by income or property or by something else. But surely ability is not a linear function, so that maybe the wealthy should pay an increasingly larger percentage. And it is important to remember that expenditures on public education affect the tax-payers' property values, often in rather complicated ways. In any event, concern for taxpayer equality can conflict with the goal of student equality.

Section Four
APPLYING PUBLIC-BENEFIT LAW

A. Nature of Legal Ordering in Program Administration

A common fallacy about law is that it exists solely for purposes of immediate control over the behavior of citizens and, therefore, that it sets up all its author-itative structures and processes with the idea of securing compliance (after resolving any disputes over whether legal requirements are binding on particular facts). Securing compliance *is* a fundamental issue in designing tax legislation and other burden-imposing laws that support public-benefit conferral. But secur-ing compliance is *not* a prominent issue for the benefit-distributing parts of the program.

Distributive policies do not meet the resistance that administrative regulation or the outright prohibitions of the criminal law or even the standards of the remedial law do. As we have seen, lawmakers do put conditions on the avail-ability of public money, goods, and services. These conditions channel the flow of benefits in certain directions. Yet the primary purpose in welfare assistance, disaster relief, and other programs for public-benefit conferral remains distrib-uting benefits to people. And people are normally more than willing to receive public benefits.

Also, significant disputes over law and fact, which might arise in controver-sies over the applicability of the program to specific cases, are much less common in the public-benefit instrument than in law's other instruments. Its authoritative structures and processes are correspondingly less adjudicative.

Overall, public-benefit law is more implemental in nature, which profoundly influences its basic character and design. For example, most public-benefit law does not address the citizenry but instead addresses officials.

Nevertheless, this is not to imply that "getting organized" to confer benefits is a simple matter, legally speaking. Unless the benefit is simply an exemption from what would otherwise be a burden, such as a tax break, the act of getting organized involves, at a minimum, setting up an administrative structure, or grafting the program onto an existing structure, while specifying the scope of authority at each administrative level, and providing processes for routine agency operations.

Still, these organizational tasks pale in comparison to the complexity of the legal task of overseeing routine operations. All public-benefit programs need to be administered, which entails much legal ordering. Often, benefits depend on certain eligibility requirements set forth in the governing law. Administrators must decide whether a given individual qualifies—and thereafter whether the individual continues to qualify. Grounds may arise that justify termination of benefits. Should the administrator have the power to terminate a benefit without notice and hearing? Should the answer to that question turn on the nature of the benefit?

B. Illustration of Program Administration: Public Education

To concretize the role that law plays in ordering the conferral of public benefits, consider again the decision that government will provide free and universal education. As we have explained, the various governmental bodies in the resulting educational structure not only create public-benefit law but also must apply the law. Many questions arise whenever government administers such a program: What procedural protections should a teacher enjoy before sanctions are applied? To what extent should these protections depend on the severity of the sanction? Or how intrusive can government be in ascertaining what the students are actually doing? To what extent can government compel people to give up rights to privacy and free speech when they become beneficiaries of distributive programs? Other questions, both procedural and substantive, arise: Under what circumstances should beneficiaries have the right to force a benefit from government officials? What protections should parents and children enjoy before officials cut off educational money, goods, or services?

For a more particular illustration, way down on the retail end where things get more familiar and understandable, education officials must create rules for keeping order in the school buildings and on the school grounds. These rules, necessary to ensure the quality of the educational benefit, do in fact aim at securing control over the behavior of citizens. In that pursuit, the relevant officials may sometimes, say, suspend disorderly minors. But the public-benefit law wants to ensure that they do so fairly.

This illustration brings us back to process values. As earlier chapters have suggested, these values are fundamental to any conception of government under law. The significance of process values is clearest when government tells people what they cannot do or punishes them for violating established standards. Citizens would regard such government activities as sheer despotism if government did not, ordinarily at least, move in accordance with what they perceive to be fair procedures. But process values are no less important when government distributes goods to some and imposes burdens on others.

Three clusters of process values are particularly important in public-benefit conferral: those associated with ensuring a representative government; those guiding duly elected representatives in policymaking; and those involved in the administration of public-benefit law. Process values generate legal standards in all three areas—as outlined in our federal and state constitutions, statutes, and administrative rules. Process values generate additional standards embodied in public opinion and political tradition, although these nonlegal standards become manifest only indirectly—through elections, political contributions, polls, editorials, and other social indicators.

First, process values associated with the electoral system reveal themselves primarily through laws protecting the system against fraud, bribery, and the like and through laws ensuring that the system does not disfranchise any group or region. "No taxation without representation" was a rallying cry of the American Revolution and remains an important value in our society. Our standards have grown more stringent with time. The apportionment of legislative bodies, once virtually free of any judicial oversight, has become a significant issue in the courts and elsewhere. The law now regulates campaign contributions, political advertising, and patronage; lawmakers have even attempted to reduce the advantage that candidates with wealth or a big campaign chest enjoy by extending public financing to some electoral contests. Note also how much broader the franchise has become since the nation's founding. (Ironically, as we have developed sounder standards for the conduct of elections and extended the franchise, the percentage of those eligible who actually vote has declined. See Paul R. Abramson & John H. Aldrich, The Decline of Electoral Participation in America, 76 Am. Pol. Sci. Rev. 502 (1982).)

Second, the process values involved in policymaking center on maintaining a healthy balance of power between the levels and branches of government as they grow and change in character. Periodically, contests over the distribution of powers erupt. Sometimes the levels or branches negotiate their disputes over how policy should be made, as when Congress resolved a crisis over presidential impoundment of funds by setting out procedures to be followed when the President seeks to avoid spending appropriated funds. Courts mediate or adjudicate some of these disputes in their role as constitutional interpreters, as when courts set rare limits on delegation of powers.

Third, the administration of distributive policies raises a different set of process issues. At this stage in the policymaking process, we want procedures that will, at a minimum, provide the people involved with certain protections against dismissal or punishment, allow the allocation of benefits and burdens to occur in an orderly way, and protect those who receive benefits from arbitrary termination. The courts have wrestled with such concerns frequently in recent years, sometimes finding in the constitutional guarantee of due process the basis for their decision.

Our particular illustration of educators trying to keep order demands more detailed examination of this third set of process values. The two cases that follow explore the process issues raised by the termination of a benefit of public education.

GOSS v. LOPEZ

Supreme Court of the United States, 1975
419 U.S. 565, 95 S. Ct. 729

Mr. Justice White delivered the opinion of the Court.

[Various students brought a federal civil rights action against the Columbus Board of Education and various administrators of the Columbus, Ohio, Public School System (CPSS), alleging that they had been suspended from public high school in Columbus for up to 10 days without a hearing either prior to suspension or within a reasonable time thereafter. The lower court decided that such suspensions denied them due process of law contrary to the command of the Fourteenth Amendment. The defendants appealed.]

I

Ohio law, Rev. Code Ann. §3313.64 (1972), provides for free education to all children between the ages of five and 21. Section 3313.66 of the Code empowers the principal of an Ohio public school to suspend a pupil for misconduct for up to 10 days or to expel him. In either case, he must notify the student's parents within 24 hours and state the reasons for his action. A pupil who is expelled, or his parents, may appeal the decision to the Board of Education and in connection therewith shall be permitted to be heard at the board meeting. The Board may reinstate the pupil following the hearing. No similar procedure is provided in §3313.66 or any other provision of state law for a suspended student. Aside from a regulation tracking the statute, at the time of the imposition of the suspensions in this case the CPSS itself had not issued any written procedure applicable to suspensions. Nor, so far as the record reflects, had any of the individual high schools involved in this case. Each, however, had formally or informally described the conduct for which suspension could be imposed.

... The complaint sought a declaration that §3313.66 was unconstitutional in that it permitted public school administrators to deprive plaintiffs of their rights to an education without a hearing of any kind, in violation of the procedural due process component of the Fourteenth Amendment. It also sought to enjoin the public school officials from issuing future suspensions pursuant to §3313.66 and to require them to remove references to the past suspensions from the records of the students in question.

The proof below established that the suspensions arose out of a period of widespread student unrest in the CPSS during February and March 1971. Six of the named plaintiffs, Rudolph Sutton, Tyrone Washington, Susan Cooper, Deborah Fox, Clarence Byars, and Bruce Harris, were students at the Marion-Franklin High School and were each suspended for 10 days on account of disruptive or disobedient conduct committed in the presence of the school administrator who ordered the suspension. One of these, Tyrone Washington, was among a group of students demonstrating in the school auditorium while a class was being conducted there. He was ordered by the school principal to leave, refused to do so, and was suspended. Rudolph Sutton, in the presence of the principal, physically attacked a police officer who was attempting to remove Tyrone Washington from the auditorium. He was immediately suspended. The other four Marion-Franklin students were suspended for similar conduct. None was given a hearing to determine the operative facts underlying the suspension, but each, together with his or her parents, was offered the opportunity to attend a conference, subsequent to the effective date of the suspension, to discuss the student's future.

... Dwight Lopez [was another plaintiff and a student] at the Central High School [and] was suspended in connection with a disturbance in the lunchroom which involved some physical damage to school property. Lopez testified that at least 75 other students were suspended from his school on the same day. He also testified below that he was not a party to the destructive conduct but was instead an innocent bystander. Because no one from the school testified with regard to this incident, there is no evidence in the record indicating the official basis for concluding otherwise. Lopez never had a hearing. ...

II

At the outset, appellants contend that because there is no constitutional right to an education at public expense, the Due Process Clause does not protect against expulsions from the public school system. This position misconceives the nature of the issue and is refuted by prior decisions. The Fourteenth Amendment forbids the State to deprive any person of life, liberty, or property without due process of law. Protected interests in property are normally "not created by the Constitution. Rather, they are created and their dimensions are defined" by an independent source such as state statutes or rules entitling the citizen to certain benefits. Board of Regents v. Roth, 408 U.S. 564, 577, 92 S. Ct. 2701, 2709 (1972)....

Here, on the basis of state law, appellees plainly had legitimate claims of entitlement to a public education. Ohio Rev. Code Ann. §§3313.48 and 3313.64 direct local authorities to provide a free education to all residents between five and 21 years of age, and a compulsory-attendance law requires attendance for a school year of not less than 32 weeks. Ohio Rev. Code Ann. §3321.04. It is true that §3313.66 of the Code permits school principals to suspend students for up to 10 days; but suspensions may not be imposed without any grounds whatsoever. All of the schools had their own rules specifying the grounds for expulsion or suspension. Having chosen to extend the right to an education to people of appellees' class generally, Ohio may not withdraw that right on grounds of misconduct, absent fundamentally fair procedures to determine whether the misconduct has occurred.

Although Ohio may not be constitutionally obligated to establish and maintain a public school system, it has nevertheless done so and has required its children to attend. Those young people do not "shed their constitutional rights" at the schoolhouse door. Tinker v. Des Moines Independent Community School Dist., 393 U.S. 503, 506, 89 S. Ct. 733, 736 (1969).... Among other things, the State is constrained to recognize a student's legitimate entitlement to a public education as a property interest which is protected by the Due Process Clause and which may not be taken away for misconduct without adherence to the minimum procedures required by that Clause....

Appellants proceed to argue that even if there is a right to a public education protected by the Due Process Clause generally, the Clause comes into play only when the State subjects a student to a "severe detriment or grievous loss." The loss of 10 days, it is said, is neither severe nor grievous and the Due Process Clause is therefore of no relevance....

A short suspension is, of course, a far milder deprivation than expulsion. But, "education is perhaps the most important function of state and local governments," Brown v. Board of Education, 347 U.S. 483, 493, 74 S. Ct. 686, 691 (1954), and the total exclusion from the educational process for more than a trivial period, and certainly if the suspension is for 10 days, is a serious event in the life of the suspended child. [It is not] so insubstantial that suspensions may constitutionally be imposed by any procedure the school chooses, no matter how arbitrary.

III

"Once it is determined that due process applies, the question remains what process is due." Morrissey v. Brewer, 408 U.S. [471, 481, 92 S. Ct. 2593, 2600 (1972)]. We turn to that question, fully realizing as our cases regularly do that the interpretation and application of the Due Process Clause are intensely practical matters and that "[t]he very nature of due process negates any concept of inflexible procedures universally applicable to every imaginable situation." Cafeteria Workers v. McElroy, 367 U.S. 886, 895, 81 S. Ct. 1743, 1748 (1961)....

There are certain bench marks to guide us, however. Mullane v. Central Hanover Trust Co., 339 U.S. 306, 70 S. Ct. 652 (1950), a case often invoked by later opinions, said that "[m]any controversies have raged about the cryptic and abstract words of the Due Process Clause but there can be no doubt that at a minimum they require that deprivation of life, liberty or property by adjudication be preceded by notice and opportunity for hearing appropriate to the nature of the case."....At the very minimum, therefore, students facing suspension and the consequent interference with a protected property interest must be given *some* kind of notice and afforded *some* kind of hearing. "Parties whose rights are to be affected are entitled to be heard; and in order that they may enjoy that right they must first be notified." Baldwin v. Hale, 1 Wall. 223, 233 (1864).

It also appears from our cases that the timing and content of the notice and the nature of the hearing will depend on appropriate accommodation of the competing interests involved. . . .

The difficulty is that our schools are vast and complex. Some modicum of discipline and order is essential if the educational function is to be performed. Events calling for discipline are frequent occurrences and sometimes require immediate, effective action. Suspension is considered not only to be a necessary tool to maintain order but a valuable educational device. The prospect of imposing elaborate hearing requirements in every suspension case is viewed with great concern, and many school authorities may well prefer the untrammeled power to act unilaterally, unhampered by rules about notice and hearing. But it would be a strange disciplinary system in an educational institution if no communication was sought by the disciplinarian with the student in an effort to inform him of his dereliction and to let him tell his side of the story in order to make sure that an injustice is not done. . . .

We do not believe that school authorities must be totally free from notice and hearing requirements if their schools are to operate with acceptable efficiency. Students facing temporary suspension have interests qualifying for protection of the Due Process Clause, and due process requires, in connection with a suspension of 10 days or less, that the student be given oral or written notice of the charges against him and, if he denies them, an explanation of the evidence the authorities have and an opportunity to present his side of the story. The Clause requires at least these rudimentary precautions against unfair or mistaken findings of misconduct and arbitrary exclusion from school.

There need be no delay between the time "notice" is given and the time of the hearing. In the great majority of cases the disciplinarian may informally discuss the alleged misconduct with the student minutes after it has occurred. We hold only that, in being given an opportunity to explain his version of the facts at this discussion, the student first be told what he is accused of doing and what the basis of the accusation is. . . . Since the hearing may occur almost immediately following the misconduct, it follows that as a general rule notice and hearing should precede removal of the student from school. We agree with the District Court, however, that there are recurring situations in which prior notice and hearing cannot be insisted upon. Students whose presence poses a continuing danger to persons or property or an ongoing threat of disrupting the academic process may be immediately removed from school. In such cases, the necessary notice and rudimentary hearing should follow as soon as practicable, as the District Court indicated.

In holding as we do, we do not believe that we have imposed procedures on school disciplinarians which are inappropriate in a classroom setting. Instead we have imposed requirements which are, if anything, less than a fair-minded school principal would impose upon himself in order to avoid unfair suspensions. . . .

We stop short of construing the Due Process Clause to require, countrywide, that hearings in connection with short suspensions must afford the student the opportunity to secure counsel, to confront and cross-examine witnesses supporting the charge, or to call his own witnesses to verify his version of the incident. Brief disciplinary suspensions are almost countless. To impose in each such case even truncated trial-type procedures might well overwhelm administrative facilities in many places and, by diverting resources, cost more than it would save in educational effectiveness. Moreover, further formalizing the suspension process and escalating its formality and adversary nature may not only make it too costly as a regular disciplinary tool but also destroy its effectiveness as part of the teaching process. . . .

We should also make it clear that we have addressed ourselves solely to the short suspension, not exceeding 10 days. Longer suspensions or expulsions for the remainder of the school term, or permanently, may require more formal procedures. Nor do we put aside the possibility that in unusual situations, although involving only a short suspension, something more than the rudimentary procedures will be required. . . .

Affirmed.

MR. JUSTICE POWELL, with whom THE CHIEF JUSTICE [BURGER], MR. JUSTICE BLACKMUN, and MR. JUSTICE REHNQUIST join, dissenting.

The Court today invalidates an Ohio statute that permits student suspensions from school without a hearing "for not more than ten days." The decision unnecessarily opens avenues for judicial intervention in the operation of our public schools that may affect adversely the quality of education. The Court holds for the first time that the federal courts, rather than educational officials and state legislatures, have the authority to determine the rules applicable to routine classroom discipline of children and teenagers in the public schools. It justifies this unprecedented intrusion into the process of elementary and secondary education by identifying a new constitutional right: the right of a student not to be suspended for as much as a single day without notice and a due process hearing either before or promptly following the suspension. . . .

In prior decisions, this Court has explicitly recognized that school authorities must have broad discretionary authority in the daily operation of public schools. This includes wide latitude with respect to maintaining discipline and good order. . . .

The Court today turns its back on these precedents. . . .

Moreover, the Court ignores the experience of mankind, as well as the long history of our law, recognizing that there *are* differences which must be accommodated in determining the rights and duties of children as compared with those of adults. Examples of this distinction abound in our law: in contracts, in torts, in criminal law and procedure, in criminal sanctions and rehabilitation, and in the right to vote and to hold office. Until today, and except in the special context of the First Amendment issue in *Tinker*, the educational rights of children and teenagers in the elementary and secondary schools have not been analogized to the rights of adults or to those accorded college students. Even with respect to the First Amendment, the rights of children have not been regarded as "co-extensive with those of adults." *Tinker*, supra, 393 U.S., at 515, 89 S. Ct., at 741 (Stewart, J., concurring). . . .

The State's interest, broadly put, is in the proper functioning of its public school system for the benefit of *all* pupils and the public generally. Few rulings would interfere more extensively in the daily functioning of schools than subjecting routine discipline to the formalities and judicial oversight of due process. Suspensions are one of the traditional means—ranging from keeping a student after class to permanent expulsion—used to maintain discipline in the schools. It is common knowledge that maintaining order and reasonable decorum in school buildings and classrooms is a major educational problem, and one which has increased significantly in magnitude in recent years. Often the teacher, in protecting the rights of other children to an education (if not his or their safety), is compelled to rely on the power to suspend. . . .

The State's generalized interest in maintaining an orderly school system is not incompatible with the individual interest of the student. Education in any meaningful sense includes the inculcation of an understanding in each pupil of the necessity of rules and obedience thereto. This understanding is no less important than learning to read and write. One who does not comprehend the meaning and necessity of discipline is handicapped not merely in his education but throughout his subsequent life. In an age when the home and church play a diminishing role in shaping the character and value judgments of the young, a heavier responsibility falls upon the schools. When an immature student merits censure for his conduct, he is rendered a disservice if appropriate sanctions are not applied or if procedures for their application are so formalized as to invite a challenge to the teacher's authority—an invitation which rebellious or even merely spirited teenagers are likely to accept. . . .

One of the more disturbing aspects of today's decision is its indiscriminate reliance upon the judiciary, and the adversary process, as the means of resolving many of the most routine problems arising in the classroom. In mandating due process procedures the Court misapprehends the reality of the normal teacher-pupil relationship. There is an ongoing relationship, one in which the teacher must occupy many roles—educator, adviser, friend, and, at times, parent-substitute. It is rarely adversary in nature except with respect to the chronically disruptive or insubordinate pupil whom the teacher must be free to discipline without frustrating formalities.

The Ohio statute, providing as it does for due notice both to parents and the Board, is compatible with the teacher-pupil relationship and the informal resolution of mistaken disciplinary action. . . .

In my view, the constitutionalizing of routine classroom decisions not only represents a significant and unwise extension of the Due Process Clause, but it also was quite unnecessary in view of the safeguards prescribed by the Ohio statute. This is demonstrable from a comparison of what the Court mandates as required by due process with the protective procedures it finds constitutionally insufficient.

The Ohio statute, limiting suspensions to not more than eight school days, requires *written* notice including the "reasons therefor" to the student's parents and to the Board of Education within 24 hours of any suspension. The Court only requires oral *or* written notice to the pupil, with no notice being required to the parents or the Board of Education. The mere fact of the statutory requirement is a deterrent against arbitrary action by the principal. The Board, usually elected by the people and sensitive to constituent relations, may be expected to identify a principal whose record of suspensions merits inquiry. In any event, parents placed on written notice may exercise their rights as constituents by going directly to the Board or a member thereof if dissatisfied with the principal's decision. . . .

ROSE v. NASHUA BOARD OF EDUCATION
United States Court of Appeals, First Circuit, 1982
679 F.2d 279

Before Campbell, Bownes and Breyer, Circuit Judges.

Breyer, Circuit Judge.

This case raises the question of the extent to which the Fourteenth Amendment imposes "due process" obligations upon a school board seeking to suspend school bus trips briefly for disciplinary purposes. After examining the facts of this case, we have concluded that the school authorities complied with whatever obligations the Constitution might impose.

The law of the State of New Hampshire requires school districts to provide free school bus transportation to most pupils under the age of 14. N.H. Rev. Stat. Ann. §§189:6-8. Several years ago, bus drivers began to complain about vandalism and disruptive conduct on certain bus routes in Nashua. Students were apparently throwing things about inside the buses and at passing cars; they were slashing seats; they were excessively noisy and disrespectful to the drivers. Because the drivers had to watch the road, they could not tell which specific students were responsible. The private company supplying the bus service complained to the Nashua Board of Education. After hearings and consideration of alternatives, the Board adopted a suspension policy.

The policy applied to instances of serious disruption, significant vandalism, or danger. In such cases, when other methods of dealing with the disciplinary problem failed, a school official would board the bus and tell the students that the route would be suspended if the guilty students did not come forward. If this did not work, the Board's "transportation director" would write to the parents telling them that the bus route would be suspended unless the troublemakers were identified. As a last resort, the Board could suspend the route for up to five days.

Basics of Due Process

In the Constitution, due process of law is guaranteed by the Fifth Amendment, applicable to the federal government, and by the Fourteenth Amendment, applicable to state governments. These guarantees say that the federal and state governments cannot deprive any person "of life, liberty, or property, without due process of law."

The bare Due Process Clauses have been interpreted to contain substantive as well as procedural components. Substantive due process protects fundamental rights that are "implicit in ordered liberty," such as privacy. Procedural due process relies on the notion of "fundamental fairness." The former limits what the government can do; the latter establishes a floor for how it must proceed.

Procedural due process aims to assure a basically fair procedure when the government seeks to impose a significant burden on a person's life, liberty, or property. For example, it normally requires adequate notification of proceedings and the opportunity to be heard at those proceedings before governmental action unduly impairs the person's protected interest. Thus, in *Goss*, the plaintiffs successfully argued that (1) they had a property interest in public education, and temporary suspension was a significant deprivation of that interest and, therefore, (2) due process entitled them to some sort of notice and hearing.

The Supreme Court, in defining exactly what kind of notice and hearing the Constitution requires, has come to use a cost-benefit analysis that accommodates the competing concerns. The Court mandates consideration of the value, or importance, of the interest at stake; the probability of an erroneous deprivation if the procedural safeguard in question is not provided; and the cost of, or the burden imposed by, that safeguard. Upon combining and balancing those three concerns, due process will require the safeguard whenever the risk of harm without the safeguard substantially exceeds the safeguard's cost.

An economist would rephrase the Court's approach by comparing the expected error cost (the product of the probability of error without the safeguard times the cost of error if it occurs) with the direct cost of the government's providing the safeguard. Presumably, the expected error cost would have to considerably exceed the direct cost before amounting to a constitutional violation, rather than merely bad policy. That is, due process requires the safeguard if and only if:

$$P_e \, C_e \gg C_d$$

This economic approach is less opaque and more rigorous than the Court's, but both are controversial. Among other drawbacks, any cost-minimization framework tends to distort analysis by ignoring or devaluing certain values, such as the right to participate and other process values that are hard to quantify, while injecting or at least exaggerating others, such as efficiency as opposed to other outcome values. These real drawbacks (rather than such common and simplistic attacks as pointing out the obvious difficulty of putting a dollar amount on certain factors) place in dispute the framework's utility and propriety.

When several parents objected to this policy, the Board held hearings. It considered several alternatives, such as seat assignments, ID cards, even special police ("monitors") to ride the bus. But, believing that these alternatives were either too expensive, or not always effective, it retained its rule allowing temporary (five day) suspensions after advance notice to affected students and parents.

According to the Board, the policy has been successful. During the first year of the policy's operation there were only 12 suspensions. Since there are 150 school bus routes and each bus makes two trips per day for 180 school days, the total number of bus trips lost could not have amounted to more than 120 out of 54,000. And, judging from the fact that the Board wishes to keep the policy, it believes that the threat of suspension has a salutary effect on discipline. Its belief is supported by the fact that only 3 or 4 routes were suspended in the policy's second year of operation.

The objecting parents, however, claim that their children are not the ones who cause the trouble. They attack the policy as unfair, for it makes their children suffer for the sins of others, and they claim it violates both state and federal law. The district court, 506 F. Supp. 1366, rejected their legal claims, as do we....

Appellants' main argument is that New Hampshire law, as so interpreted, is unconstitutional. They claim that the Fourteenth Amendment, in forbidding deprivation of "property ... without due process of law," requires a prior hearing to determine likely guilt or innocence before the Board can deprive a pupil of bus transportation—even for five days. We do not agree.

As an initial matter, we have serious doubts about whether the pupils or their parents have asserted a property interest sufficiently weighty for the Due Process Clause to apply. No one here complains about any deprivation of education, or educational opportunity. Compare Goss v. Lopez, 419 U.S. 565, 576, 95 S. Ct. 729, 737 (1975)....

The fact that New Hampshire law guarantees free bus transportation does not seem sufficient to create a constitutionally protected interest in the *suspension-free* service that appellants seek. In deciding whether an interest in a government benefit rises to the level of protected property, the Supreme Court has us look to the reasonable expectations of those who receive the benefit....

Even if there were constitutionally protected "property" at stake, however, the appellants received the "process" they are "due." In determining whether "due process" requires a particular procedural safeguard (say, a hearing prior to deprivation), we are to take at least three factors into account: 1) the value or importance of the property interest at stake; 2) the probability of an erroneous deprivation if the safeguard is not provided; and 3) the cost of, or the burden imposed by, the safeguard.

In this case, as already pointed out, the importance of the property interest is small. The likelihood of an erroneous deprivation without a prior hearing, however, is significant. The Board's policy deprives students of bus transportation who took no part in any trouble-making activities. A prior hearing might prevent this, but at substantial cost—namely, the cost of abandoning the suspension program altogether. The program was instituted because the Board could not identify the trouble-makers in advance. To require an individual hearing is to require identification before suspension—the very thing the Board is unable to do.

The issue then comes down to the reasonableness of the suspension program itself. Appellants, citing Thompson v. Louisville, 362 U.S. 199, 80 S. Ct. 624 (1960), claim that the program is inherently unreasonable, for it punishes the "innocent" along with the "guilty." We are not dealing here, however, with criminal punishments or with sending someone to prison without evidence. At issue is discipline on school buses, quite another matter, and one where the lessons drawn from criminal trials may not be totally appropriate. On the one hand, the notion of penalizing a whole class (by, say, keeping them after school or canceling "recess") because of trouble caused by a few is (or at least used to be) fairly common in the world of school discipline. The serious risks and dangers associated with throwing objects in and outside of moving buses, on the other hand, are obvious, and warrant serious measures aimed at avoiding them. Moreover, the Board here has held full hearings on its policy, it has considered alternatives, and it has decided that its policy offers the most promising avenue to avoid vandalism, disruption, and driving hazards on school buses. We cannot find that judgment unreasonable, particularly when the Supreme Court "has repeatedly emphasized the need for affirming the comprehensive authority of the States and . . . school officials, consistent with fundamental constitutional safeguards, to prescribe control of conduct in the schools." Tinker v. Des Moines School District, 393 U.S. 503, 507, 89 S. Ct. 733, 736 (1969).

From a constitutional perspective, then, we find no interests here at stake either sufficiently great in amount or fundamental in nature to require greater procedural protection than the Board has offered—particularly when increased protection would merely prevent the implementation of a reasonable disciplinary policy aimed at securing the safety of the children riding school buses.

For these reasons, the decision of the district court is

Affirmed.

NOTES

1. What competing values are at stake in these two cases? Can you state the position of the first case's dissent in terms of process values?

2. Justice White and the Supreme Court leave it to the lower courts to apply the *Goss* pronouncement. Justice Powell and his fellow dissenters at one point claimed that "[n]o one can foresee the ultimate frontiers of the new 'thicket' the Court now enters." They were concerned that bad grades, failure to be promoted to the next grade, exclusion from interscholastic athletics or other extracurricular activities, transfers to new schools, and tracking decisions would be challenged in the courts. Does the Constitution require the schools to provide notice, a hearing, and other protections before they take such actions? Are you satisfied that the court of appeals in *Rose* got the balance right?

3. Can you deduce from these two cases what process the Constitution demands for the welfare recipient threatened with a cutoff of support? the contractor who loses a bid to build a new submarine? the loser of a government lottery?

Section Five
ROLES OF PRIVATE CITIZENS AND THEIR LAWYERS

A. Program Development

Private citizens and their lawyers play important and varied roles in public-benefit conferral. Citizens elect the legislators who debate and pass upon taxation and spending bills; the electorate also elects the chief executives who bear final responsibility for the implementation of public-benefit legislation. Political campaigns to which citizens devote their time or money are part of the processes we have devised for selecting candidates and choosing among them. Campaigns and elections are characteristic of every level of government, from local school boards to the national presidency, serving as they do to legitimate and limit the exercise of governmental power. So much is obvious to anyone schooled in the basics of American government.

Most of us are aware, too, of the citizens' power to contact legislators and other policymakers to press for new programs or for new benefits under existing programs. Some citizens make these contacts directly, and a few even stay in regular communication. Or individuals may join or create a group of like-minded people and try to influence lawmakers that way. Their communication may be through direct political action such as street demonstrations, or through more orderly processes involving letter writing, paid lobbying, and the like. These groups, particularly those organized to provide long-term benefits to their members, are so common and so important to our form of government that some theorists see in pressure-group politics the essence of the American political system.

The kind of politicking—electoral or pressure—that occurs between legislators and citizens seems to depend on the policy in question. The key variables, according to political scientists James Q. Wilson & John J. DiIulio, Jr., American Government 475–79 (10th ed. 2006), lie in the perceived distribution of benefits and burdens embedded in the policy. The accompanying diagram illustrates the overall pattern.

First, where both the benefits and the burdens to support the policy are widely distributed, as in social security or national defense, the attitudes of popular majorities play an important role in determining what legislators will do. Debate tends to be broad-based and open.

Second, when benefits are concentrated on a few, but burdens are widely shared and therefore not particularly onerous for any given individual, so-called client politics is the rule, and ordinary citizens seldom play an active role. Examples are price supports for farmers and public-works projects.

Third, much the same is true when both benefits and burdens are concentrated, as when Congress enacts a tariff that hurts one industry but benefits another. In such situations, the directly affected and well-organized interest groups attempt to influence policy.

Fourth, when benefits are distributed broadly, but burdens are concentrated on a few, one might anticipate that legislators would not act at all. Those who stand to benefit from the distributive policy do not benefit enough individually to induce them to act, and those who would be burdened have good reason to fight any imposition. Yet, government does selectively impose substantial burdens, even on powerful corporations, in part because policy "entrepreneurs" like Ralph Nader and organizations that claim to represent the public interest can mobilize pressure in favor of such legislation.

	If perceived burdens are:	
	Distributed	Concentrated
Distributed	Majoritarian politics	Entrepreneurial politics
If perceived benefits are:		
Concentrated	Client politics	Interest-group politics

Discussion so far has emphasized the role of citizens in directly influencing the political process. The indirect influence of the citizenry is broader, however. Public opinion helps set the policy agenda, and thus defines the needs to which governmental bodies respond and also decides the means appropriate to the task. Consider, for example, contemporary interest in environmental protection, gender equality, and product safety—concerns that might have been, but were not, salient to earlier generations. Just how societies arrive at their policy agendas and how they reach consensus on the tools of government appropriate to the task are not always obvious.

Lawyers, of course, are active throughout program development. They act as advisers and negotiators for their clients. They even act as lobbyists. They may act as litigators before, during, and after program development.

B. Program Administration

We know more about how citizens and their lawyers influence the carrying out of programs already adopted. An important point to remember in considering their role at this stage in the policy process is that distributive policies are not self-actualizing. Frances Kahn Zemans, Legal Mobilization: The Neglected Role of the Law in the Political System, 77 Am. Pol. Sci. Rev. 690, 694 (1983), stressed this point: "Although what one gets is most certainly *related* to governmental allocative decisions, to a substantial degree what citizens *receive* from the government is dependent upon the demands they make for their entitlements and upon participation in the policy-implementation as well as the policy-making process. In particular, what the populace actually receives from government is to a large extent dependent upon their willingness and ability to assert and use the law on their own behalf."

Sometimes citizen participation is mandated by law. Most federal grant programs have citizen participation requirements, although they vary in the means they employ to solicit citizen opinion. The Economic Opportunity Act of 1964, for example, mandated "maximum feasible participation" from the poor, a provision that proved highly controversial among the local officials whose authority this requirement displaced. More common requirements that administrators hold public hearings and take views expressed there into account are less controversial and apparently less effective. Most often, however, citizen participation in program administration involves a good deal of self-starting initiative.

How do citizens and their lawyers get involved? Strategies and tactics depend on the stage at which the citizen or lawyer intervenes. For example, the following excerpt beautifully makes the point that one addresses an avowed policy-maker differently from how one addresses a supposed law-applier.

JULIUS COHEN, SOME OBSERVATIONS ON ADVOCACY: JUDICIAL AND LEGISLATIVE
41 A.B.A. J. 656, 656–59 (1955)*

Take the case of the judicial advocate who seeks to persuade a court that a statute ought to be invalidated because it denies substantive due process; assume, too, that it is a case of first impression. If substantive due process and reasonableness are to be equated, the advocate's job primarily would be to demonstrate to the court that the statute is an unreasonable exercise of legislative power. Although he may, by the use of legal symbols, endeavor to create the impression that it is the court's duty in the case to *discover* the law applicable to it, actually, he knows that the court's function in the case is really *creative*: it legislates. The case being of first impression, the court's choice between competing legal formulations and analogies must in the end be based on policy considerations—not on what the law *is*, but what it *ought* to be.

Now, consider the case of the legislative advocate who seeks to persuade a legislative committee that a bill ought not to be recommended for passage because, if enacted, it would be an unreasonable exercise of legislative power. Here, the advocate does not even try to disguise the fact that what is involved is a legislative matter and that the issue is the reasonableness or unreasonableness of the proposal. Here, the policy considerations that are involved are given a better chance to be laid bare; there is no need to insulate them with legal symbolism....

The judicial advocate would not expect a judge to have made up his mind on the issue of due process prior to the arguments on the merits—that is, without disqualifying himself. The legislative advocate, on the other hand, would not think it unusual for a committee member to sit in judgment on a bill even though he has made private or public commitments concerning it prior to the hearing—this despite the aura of judiciousness that usually permeates the legislative hearing. On the judicial level, a distinction is maintained between the function of the adversary and the function of the judge; on the legislative level it is not uncommon at a hearing for a committee member—even the chairman—to participate in the judging of a bill that he himself has sponsored....

Counsel arguing the invalidity of a statute would never think of approaching the judge privately in order to prepare the groundwork for a favorable disposition of the case in court; nor would he venture forth privately to add to or embellish an argument after the hearing is closed. Such procedure, however, is not surprising to the legislative advocate. Pre-hearing and post-hearing access to committee members who later sit in judgment on a legislative proposal is quite normal. It is an accepted technique for cultivating favorable predispositions and for obtaining as many prior commitments as are possible before the actual hearing on the merits of the measure.

Despite the inadequacy of the judicial machinery to evaluate the complex data that are often involved in due process cases, the judicial advocate nevertheless expects the decision of the court to be made impartially after due consideration and deliberation of the arguments presented. The expectations are not as high for the legislative

---

advocate, for there are many other factors that might be controlling: previous political commitments by committee members concerning the measure, predispositions, pre-hearing and post-hearing access, a private call from the chairman or a party functionary urging a committee member to "go along," promises or threats of reprisals from fellow legislators, or pressure from constituents or groups who might be helpful to political fortunes....

In the hypothetical due process case, and in the case involving [a] ... legislative proposal, the ends sought by the legislative and judicial advocate are essentially the same. The difference is primarily in the locus of the battlegrounds and in the methods and weapons of combat. Many who see action on the legislative front yearn for the application of judicial standards of impartiality to legislative policy-making. Many who battle on the judicial front wish that more legislative forthrightness would be applied, and that some of the legislative investigative resources would be made available to the task of judicial policy-making. There is much, apparently, that one forum can learn—and unlearn—from the other.

C. Illustration of Private Involvement: Public Education

INSTRUCTIONAL CONTENT

Think for a moment about the range of decisions necessary to make a school system operate. The problems of structure and staffing are fundamental, but they are by no means the only important issues that must be confronted if the public schools are to operate. Somehow decisions must be reached about what courses will be offered and what they will cover; how large classes will be, and where and when they will meet; what support services will be available and for whom; what lab equipment, library books, and computers will be purchased; what after-school activities will be sponsored or allowed space for meetings; how to handle discipline; and so on.

A variety of lawmakers collaborate to deal with these concerns. Take curriculum and other such instructional matters as the first of our three brief illustrations of participation by citizens and their lawyers in program administration.

The legislatures have ultimate power over the curriculum and many other matters relating to the delivery of educational content but infrequently exercise it. When a legislature does involve itself, the only limits upon its discretion are the federal and state constitutions that restrict all its legislative action, which means that the legislature has a fairly free hand—although sometimes constitutional guarantees impose real limits on the power of legislators and other authorized lawmakers to mold course content, as, say, were they to require equal time in biology class for the biblical theory of creation. And the federal legislature, acting within its constitutional bounds, could in theory limit the state legislatures, although it is very far from active as to course content.

Usually, the legislatures delegate their authority over educational content. A typical state legislature delegates some authority over curricular innovation to central agencies and the state education commissioner. Besides advising

the state legislature and local boards on education-related issues, these officials make curricular law by laying down regulations on matters such as
required courses of study, and they also adjudicate disputes about course
content pursued by parents and others. For a typical example of the regulations, New York's very detailed provisions begin like this for pre-kindergarten,
in 8 NYCRR 100.3(a):

(1) Each such school operating a prekindergarten or kindergarten program
shall establish and provide an educational program based on and adapted to the
ages, interests and needs of the children. Learning activities in such programs
shall include:

(i) development of communication skills and exposure to literature;

(ii) dramatic play, creative art and music activities;

(iii) participation in group projects, discussion and games;

(iv) science and mathematical experiences;

(v) large muscle activities in prekindergarten and instruction in
physical education in kindergarten pursuant to section 135.4(c)(2)(i) of
this Title; and

(vi) instruction in health education for students in kindergarten pursuant to section 135.3(b) of this Title.

(2) Each such school operating a prekindergarten and/or kindergarten
program shall establish and provide an early literacy program based on and
adapted to the needs, ages and interests of the students. Elements of early literacy
programs shall include, but not be limited to:

(i) use of reading to obtain meaning from print;

(ii) frequent and intensive opportunities to read for learning and for
pleasure;

(iii) activities that teach regular spelling-sound relationships;

(iv) learning about the nature of the alphabetic writing system; and

(v) understanding the structure of spoken words.

(3) Each such school operating a prekindergarten or kindergarten program
shall develop procedures to actively involve each child's parents or guardians in
such programs.

A totally typical example of the internal judicial powers is In re Appeal of
Percosky, 6 N.Y. Educ. Dep't Rep. 46 (1966):

ALLEN, JR., COMMISSIONER.—The appellants complain that the "Initial Teaching
Alphabet Program" is being given in only one of three first grade classes and
should be given in at least two. The voters of the district do not have the legal
power to establish the courses of study in the schools of the district. This is a
matter which is vested by law in the board of education subject to the curriculum
requirements and general supervisory powers established by the statute and by
the State Education Department. There is nothing in the record before me to
indicate that the respondent has acted illegally or in an arbitrary or capricious
manner.

The appeal is dismissed.

Nevertheless, it is the local school boards, administrators, and teachers who dominate specific curricular decisions, although of course they must stay within the limits of their state-delegated authority. In most states, the school boards have some power (granted by the legislature) to veto or pass upon changes in courses offered. Superintendents and other supervisory personnel are principal players. Teachers and teachers' organizations are the source of many ideas about curriculum, but they seldom act alone.

Thus, parents or other local residents of a school district do not generally have any direct power over curriculum. The laws make no express provision for citizen participation. After all, the "people" are not professionally qualified, and they usually lack adequate opportunities for collective deliberation. Of course, voters can exert some indirect influence by voting out the local board (or rejecting the proposed district budget, if submitted to a vote), but this is a blunt tool for shaping local school policy. Voters can expect to have even less influence over curricular policies set by central officials. And as we have said, the state legislature, potentially a more responsive body of government, does not usually concern itself with course offerings.

Still, the success of some persons in enlisting the power of courts to patrol the curriculum is a reminder that citizens, without being invited to participate, can still influence the administration of public policy. Even when those who legally challenge distributive policies do not ultimately prevail, they can have an impact on policy administration, because administrators often respond to pressures generated by the publicity associated with litigation. Indeed, the mere threat of litigation, or even of adverse publicity, can also change policy administration. Consider, for example, the probable impact of citizen complaints about questionable books in the school library on the acquisition and removal policies of the school library staff.

In fact, these citizen pressures may be so successful that they instigate reactive litigation by other citizens pushing the other way. In the *Pico* case that follows, we see a famous example of such reactive litigation.

Recall the general context here is that local school officials have a lot of control over the curriculum and other instructional matters. Courts will step in to enforce state-imposed restrictions. But courts incline to defer to school officials' professional expertise and judgment. The judges' operational method, moreover, is limited: they can veto decisions about instructional matters under some circumstances, but they are not ordinarily policy innovators.

A court will also step in if students or teachers can establish a fairly serious infringement of their constitutional interests, especially if the direction of the school officials' action was restrictive on the flow of ideas. In *Pico*, the plurality and the dissenters differ in the scope they would give judges to veto school-board decisions about educational policy—in this instance, the removal of books from a school library on Long Island.

BOARD OF EDUCATION, ISLAND TREES UNION FREE SCHOOL DISTRICT NO. 26 v. PICO

Supreme Court of the United States, 1982
457 U.S. 853, 102 S. Ct. 2799

JUSTICE BRENNAN:

[Prompted by a politically conservative organization of parents, the school board removed these nine books from the high school and junior high school libraries, apparently because of the moral danger they posed:]

- *Soul on Ice* by Eldridge Cleaver;
- *A Hero Ain't Nothing But a Sandwich* by Alice Childress;
- *The Fixer* by Bernard Malamud;
- *Go Ask Alice* by Anonymous;
- *Slaughterhouse Five* by Kurt Vonnegut, Jr.;
- *The Best Short Stories by Negro Writers* ed. by Langston Hughes;
- *The Naked Ape* by Desmond Morris;
- *Reader for Writers* ed. by Jerome Archer; and
- *Down These Mean Streets* by Piri Thomas.

Students then brought this federal civil rights action against the school board and its members, claiming a violation of the First Amendment. The district court granted the defendants summary judgment. The court of appeals reversed.]

...Petitioners [the defendants] rightly possess significant discretion to determine the content of their school libraries. But that discretion may not be exercised in a narrowly partisan or political manner. If a Democratic school board, motivated by party affiliation, ordered the removal of all books written by or in favor of Republicans, few would doubt that the order violated the constitutional rights of the students denied access to those books. The same conclusion would surely apply if an all-white school board, motivated by racial animus, decided to remove all books authored by blacks or advocating racial equality and integration. Our Constitution does not permit the official suppression of *ideas*. Thus whether petitioners' removal of books from their school libraries denied respondents their First Amendment rights depends upon the motivation behind petitioners' actions. If petitioners *intended* by their removal decision to deny respondents access to ideas with which petitioners disagreed, and if this intent was the decisive factor in petitioners' decision, then petitioners have exercised their discretion in violation of the Constitution. To permit such intentions to control official actions would be to encourage the precise sort of officially prescribed orthodoxy unequivocally condemned in [West Virginia Board of Education v. Barnette, 319 U.S. 624, 63 S. Ct. 1178 (1943) (striking down compulsory flag salute and pledge)]. On the other hand, respondents implicitly concede that an unconstitutional motivation would *not* be demonstrated if it were shown that petitioners had decided to remove the books at issue because those books were pervasively vulgar. Tr. of Oral Arg. 36. And again, respondents concede that if it were demonstrated that the removal decision was based solely upon the "educational suitability" of the books in question, then their removal would be "perfectly permissible." Id., at 53. In other words, in respondents' view such motivations, if decisive of petitioners' actions, would not carry the danger of an official suppression of ideas, and thus would not violate respondents' First Amendment rights.

...In brief, we hold that local school boards may not remove books from school library shelves simply because they dislike the ideas contained in those books and seek by their removal to [in *Barnette*'s words] "prescribe what shall be orthodox in politics, nationalism, religion, or other matters of opinion."...

[Justices Marshall, Blackmun, and Stevens agreed, sending the case back down for trial. Justice White concurred in the affirmance on the sole ground that an unresolved factual issue—the reasons underlying the board's removal of the books—precluded summary judgment and so required trial; his refusal to reach the First Amendment issue meant that there was no Supreme Court majority position on that point.

[Chief Justice Burger and Justices Powell, Rehnquist, and O'Connor dissented. They wished to keep the federal courts out of running school libraries. They added, in an opinion by the Chief Justice:]

We can all agree that as a matter of *educational policy* students should have wide access to information and ideas. But the people elect school boards, who in turn select administrators, who select the teachers, and these are the individuals best able to determine the substance of that policy. The plurality fails to recognize the fact that local control of education involves democracy in a microcosm. In most public schools in the United States the *parents* have a large voice in running the school. Through participation in the election of school board members, the parents influence, if not control, the direction of their children's

education. A school board is not a giant bureaucracy far removed from accountability for its actions; it is truly "of the people and by the people." A school board reflects its constituency in a very real sense and thus could not long exercise unchecked discretion in its choice to acquire or remove books. If the parents disagree with the educational decisions of the school board, they can take steps to remove the board members from office. Finally, even if parents and students cannot convince the school board that book removal is inappropriate, they have alternative sources to the same end. Books may be acquired from bookstores, public libraries, or other alternative sources unconnected with the unique environment of the local public schools.

NOTES

1. You should note what an incredibly narrow issue the Court addressed. This case involved a school library removing books, by an irregular procedure and for questionable reasons. Even in other situations quite close on the facts, doubts predominate. See, e.g., United States v. Am. Library Ass'n, 539 U.S. 194 (2003) (holding constitutional a federal law requiring federally funded public libraries to use internet filters); Mark S. Nadel, The First Amendment's Limitations on the Use of Internet Filtering in Public and School Libraries: What Content Can Librarians Exclude?, 78 Tex. L. Rev. 1117 (2000).

2. Even supposing that Justice Brennan's test, which looks for official motivation to suppress disliked ideas, is workable in its context, it becomes less useful as one moves further from *Pico*'s facts: removal of books from a school library for more "socially acceptable" reasons, such as the removal of *Adventures of Huckleberry Finn* for being racist; setting the library's policy for acquiring books, as distinguished from removing them as in *Pico*; and, of course, any of the countless curricular decisions made outside the library and in the classroom. See Anne Proffitt Dupre, Speaking Up: The Unintended Costs of Free Speech in Public Schools 107–37 (2009). Generally, as one moves away from *Pico*'s facts and toward such issues, the school officials' range of discretion grows.

SPECIAL EDUCATION

In the old days, public education seriously slighted or even excluded mentally or physically disabled children. Although some states adopted remedial policies, real progress came only in the early 1970s, when a couple of lower federal courts held that their total exclusion from public education violated the Equal Protection Clause and that the absence of procedures violated the Due Process Clause.

Then in 1975, Congress passed the statute that would become the Individuals with Disabilities Education Act (IDEA), 20 U.S.C. §§1400–1482.

IDEA provides federal funds to assist state and local agencies in educating disabled children, but it conditions that funding upon compliance with extensive procedures and goals. The Act's basic policy goal is a "free appropriate public education that emphasizes special education and related services," tailored to the unique needs of the child by means of a written Individualized Education Program (IEP). That education must come in the "least restrictive environment" appropriate to needs, preferably by mainstreaming the student in regular classes. The IEP is formulated by a group including the school officials and the child's teachers and parents, and it is annually reviewed. IDEA specifies lots of processes for the school to follow.

So, IDEA takes a route toward ensuring that those affected by a benefit program will have a voice in running it. The statute gives parents important rights to consult and to challenge school administrators as they arrive at an IEP in pursuit of a "free appropriate public education."

Just what that last-quoted phrase means, however, Congress did not say. In *Board of Education v. Rowley*, a critical case but one representative of a plethora of consequent litigation, the Supreme Court had to grapple with the question of what standard to apply when statutory procedures fail to produce consensus between parents and educators on how to educate a disabled child.

BOARD OF EDUCATION v. ROWLEY
Supreme Court of the United States, 1982
458 U.S. 176, 102 S. Ct. 3034

JUSTICE REHNQUIST delivered the opinion of the Court:

[Amy Rowley was a mainstreamed first-grade student in Peekskill, New York, who had considerable loss of hearing but was an excellent lipreader. The school made accommodations that included an FM hearing aid and special instruction but rejected as unnecessary the parents' demands for a full-time sign-language interpreter. So, the parents pursued the extensive administrative review available and then sought judicial review in federal court. The lower courts decided for the plaintiffs, on a ruling that the predecessor statute to IDEA entitled Amy to an *equal* opportunity to achieve her full potential and on a finding that, although she was performing above average, she was not doing as well as she could if she could hear. By the following opinion, the Supreme Court reversed, saying that the outcome turned on statutory interpretation.]

According to the definitions contained in the Act, a "free appropriate public education" consists of educational instruction specially designed to meet the unique needs of the handicapped child, supported by such services as are necessary to permit the child "to benefit" from the instruction. Almost as a checklist for adequacy under the Act, the definition also requires that such instruction and services be provided at public expense and under public supervision, meet the State's educational standards, approximate the grade levels used in the State's regular education, and comport with the child's IEP. Thus, if personalized instruction is being provided with sufficient supportive services to permit the child to benefit from the instruction, and the other items on the definitional checklist are satisfied, the child is receiving a "free appropriate public education" as defined by the Act....

... By passing the Act, Congress sought primarily to make public education available to handicapped children. But in seeking to provide such access to public education, Congress did not impose upon the States any greater substantive educational standard than would be necessary to make such access meaningful....

The educational opportunities provided by our public school systems undoubtedly differ from student to student, depending upon a myriad of factors that might affect a particular student's ability to assimilate information presented in the classroom. The requirement that States provide "equal" educational opportunities would thus seem to present an entirely unworkable standard requiring impossible measurements and comparisons. Similarly, furnishing handicapped children with only such services as are available to nonhandicapped children would in all probability fall short of the statutory requirement of "free appropriate public education"; to require, on the other hand, the furnishing of every special service necessary to maximize each handicapped child's potential is, we think, further than Congress intended to go. Thus to speak in terms of "equal" services in one instance gives less than what is required by the Act and in another instance more. The theme of the Act is "free appropriate public education," a phrase which is too complex to be captured by the word "equal" whether one is speaking of opportunities or services....

...We therefore conclude that the "basic floor of opportunity" provided by the Act consists of access to specialized instruction and related services which are individually designed to provide educational benefit to the handicapped child....

When the language of the Act and its legislative history are considered together, the requirements imposed by Congress become tolerably clear.... In addition, the IEP, and therefore the personalized instruction, should be formulated in accordance with the requirements of the Act and, if the child is being educated in the regular classrooms of the public education system, should be reasonably calculated to enable the child to achieve passing marks and advance from grade to grade.

...[A] court's inquiry...is twofold. First, has the State complied with the procedures set forth in the Act? And second, is the individualized educational program developed through the Act's procedures reasonably calculated to enable the child to receive educational benefits? If these requirements are met, the State has complied with the obligations imposed by Congress and the courts can require no more.

In assuring that the requirements of the Act have been met, courts must be careful to avoid imposing their view of preferable educational methods upon the States. The primary responsibility for formulating the education to be accorded a handicapped child, and for choosing the educational method most suitable to the child's needs, was left by the Act to state and local educational agencies in cooperation with the parents or guardian of the child....

Justice Blackmun, concurring in the judgment:
...Rather, the question is whether Amy's program, *viewed as a whole*, offered her an opportunity to understand and participate in the classroom that was substantially equal to that given her nonhandicapped classmates....

Justice White, with whom Justice Brennan and Justice Marshall join, dissenting:
...It would apparently satisfy the Court's standard of "access to specialized instruction and related services which are individually designed to provide educational benefit to the handicapped child" for a deaf child such as Amy to be given a teacher with a loud voice, for she would benefit from that service. The Act requires more.... The basic floor of opportunity is instead, as the courts below recognized, intended to eliminate the effects of the handicap, at least to the extent that the child will be given an equal opportunity to learn if that is reasonably possible....

...Because the standard of the courts below seems to me to reflect the congressional purpose and because their factual findings are not clearly erroneous, I respectfully dissent.

NOTES

1. A professor and lawyer with expertise in the field of special education accuses the majority of "blatant disregard of Congressional intent" in the *Rowley* case, induced by "its unspoken fear that a contrary result would have opened the floodgates by allowing every seriously handicapped child in the nation to receive full-time individualized educational assistance where needed." Bonnie Poitras Tucker, *Board of Education of the Hendrick Hudson Central School District v. Rowley: Utter Chaos,* 12 J.L. & Educ. 235, 235 (1983). Would all restrictions have come off if the Court had adopted the dissent's interpretation of the statute?

2. If the child is so disabled that he or she cannot benefit from education, IDEA still gives a right to education. It embodies a " 'zero-reject' policy. . . . Public education is to be provided to all handicapped children, unconditionally and without exception." Timothy W. v. Rochester, N.H., School District, 875 F.2d 954, 960, 966 (1st Cir. 1989).

HOME SCHOOLING

When citizens mobilize to challenge distributive programs, it is usually to overturn legal requirements or administrative practices that cut them out of policy benefits, or to avoid the imposition of taxes or other burdens. On occasion, though, citizens want to exit a public-benefit program. Sometimes, exiting from a program can prove surprisingly difficult. The government has some right to prevent citizens from doing without, or even from trying to provide certain benefits for themselves without government assistance or oversight.

We have not earlier stressed that the states, in providing a free and universal public education, have now also made it a compulsory education through a certain age. Compulsory schooling was a later development, as Americans did not generally accept it until the end of the nineteenth century. According to Mark G. Yudof, David L. Kirp, Betsy Levin & Rachel F. Moran, Educational Policy and the Law 13 (4th ed. 2002):

> Massachusetts passed the first compulsory education law in 1852, requiring that all children between the ages of eight and fourteen attend school for at least twelve weeks a year; twenty-eight states passed similar legislation in the years following the Civil War. But compulsory education, although legally required, did not immediately become social fact. The resistance of some educators affords one explanation of this phenomenon. In Auburn, New York, School Superintendent B.B. Snow voiced a common sentiment: "The compulsory attendance of the element attempted to be reached by law would be detrimental to the well-being of any respectable school." In many school systems, there was insufficient space to accommodate this class of youngsters: in Illinois, for instance, school buildings could house only one-third of all eligible schoolchildren, while in New York City the average elementary school class enrolled seventy-five pupils. The insatiable demand for cheap labor continued to be satisfied by the hiring of school-age youngsters, and officials—many of whom believed that the education of workers'

children was a waste of time—often ignored these violations of the law. An 1884 report drafted by Charles Peck, New York commissioner of statistics of labor, pronounced the compulsory education statute a "dead letter." In the South, compulsory attendance laws were not enforced until well into the twentieth century, and the educational needs of black children were given lowest priority.

Compulsory schooling obviously intrudes on individual autonomy and on the parental rights to rear and control their own children. Still, the states have this power to act for the well-being of children, because sometimes parents are not up to the task of education. See Prince v. Mass., 321 U.S. 158, 64 S. Ct. 438 (1944) (overriding a parent who was making child work).

The state's power is not unlimited, however. The state cannot require attendance at a public school. The parents can insist on their children attending private school, although private schools are subject to reasonable state regulation. See Pierce v. Soc'y of Sisters of Holy Names, 268 U.S. 510, 45 S. Ct. 571 (1925); cf. Wisc. v. Yoder, 406 U.S. 205, 92 S. Ct. 1526 (1972) (exempting Amish from required secondary education).

Still, under the so-called *Pierce* compromise, the state can make children go to a *school*. There is no right to home schooling. The state has a stronger interest than the parents, not only in the quality of the education but also in the socialization of the student.

Nonetheless, as a matter of legislative grace, the state can grant relief from its requirement of compulsory education. In fact, all states do allow home schooling, but usually only subject to strict terms and conditions. Prominent examples of the prevailing restrictions are teacher certification and student testing requirements. The next case tests the limits of legislative prerogative.

SWANSON ex rel. SWANSON v. GUTHRIE INDEPENDENT SCHOOL DISTRICT NO. I-L
United States Court of Appeals for the Tenth Circuit, 1998
135 F.3d 694

Before BRORBY and McWILLIAMS, CIRCUIT JUDGES, and BLACK, DISTRICT JUDGE [sitting by designation].

BLACK, DISTRICT JUDGE:
[Annie Swanson was a home-schooled eighth-grader in Guthrie, Oklahoma, who wished to attend public school on a part-time basis to study foreign language, music, and some science. The reason for her home schooling was religious, in that her parents wished to teach her Christian principles that the public-school curriculum excluded. The school board refused permission by adopting a policy "that all students enrolling in Guthrie Public Schools must do so on a full-time basis. Full-time basis shall be defined as attending classes for the full instructional day within the public school system or in conjunction with another state accredited institution such as vocational-technical school or a college or university for concurrent enrollment. The only exceptions to this policy shall be for fifth-year seniors and special education students whose IEP's require variations of student schedules." The reason for its policy was that part-time students did not count for state-aid purposes. Annie and her parents sued in a federal district court, which granted the defendants summary judgment.]

The question at issue in this case is the validity of the rule or regulation enacted by the school board, as it impacts on Plaintiffs' right to the free exercise of their religion. Plaintiffs maintain that the part-time-attendance policy is a burden, albeit indirect, on the full and free exercise of their religious beliefs concerning the way in which children should be raised and educated....

As a general proposition, a law (or policy) that is neutral and of general applicability need not be justified by a compelling governmental interest even if that law incidentally burdens a particular religious practice or belief....

...Plaintiffs do not attempt to argue that the policy directly burdens their right to free expression, nor could they. The policy does not prohibit them from home-schooling Annie in accordance with their religious beliefs, and does not force them to do anything that is contrary to those beliefs....The board's policy therefore does not violate traditional free-exercise principles....

We have no quarrel with Plaintiffs' assertion that Annie's parents have a constitutional right to direct her education, up to a point. For example, they have a right to send her to a private school, whether that school is religious or secular. See Pierce v. Society of Sisters, 268 U.S. 510, 45 S. Ct. 571 (1925). Numerous cases, however, have made it clear that this constitutional right is limited in scope. Federal courts addressing the issue have held that parents have no right to exempt their children from certain reading programs the parents found objectionable, or from a school's community-service requirement, or from an assembly program that included sexually explicit topics.... Other courts have determined that home-schooled children may be subjected to standardized testing to assess the quality of education the children are receiving, even over the parents' objections. Murphy v. State of Arkansas, 852 F.2d 1039 (8th Cir. 1988). In addition, states may constitutionally require that teachers at religiously-oriented private schools be certified by the state. Fellowship Baptist Church v. Benton, 815 F.2d 485 (8th Cir. 1987). The case law in this area establishes that parents simply do not have a constitutional right to control each and every aspect of their children's education and oust the state's authority over that subject....

The claimed constitutional right Plaintiffs wish to establish in this case is the right of parents to send their children to public school on a part-time basis, and to pick and choose which courses their children will take from the public school. Plaintiffs would have this right override the local school board's explicit decision to disallow such part-time attendance (except where the school would receive state funding for the part-time attendee). However, decisions as to how to allocate scarce resources, as well as what curriculum to offer or require, are uniquely committed to the discretion of local school authorities, as the cases cited above demonstrate....

...Plaintiffs argue (as they explicitly acknowledged at oral argument) that if anyone is allowed to attend the public school part-time, Annie must be allowed to do so also, because her motivation for wanting to do so is religious. According to Plaintiffs' argument, if a governmental entity offers a benefit such as part-time attendance under limited qualifying conditions, and a claimant's religious beliefs or practices prevent him or her from meeting those conditions, the benefit must be awarded to the claimant despite the failure to meet the conditions.

...Despite Plaintiffs' arguments to the contrary, what they seek in this case is special treatment not accorded other home-schooled or private-schooled students. They seek an added exception to the part-time attendance policy, that would accommodate people who home-school for religious reasons. Nothing in the Free Exercise Clause requires that such special treatment be provided.[7]...

---

7. In fact, there is a real possibility that creating an exception for religious purposes but not for secular purposes would run afoul of the Establishment Clause, which complements the Free Exercise Clause by prohibiting discrimination in favor of, rather than against, a certain religion or religions. See, e.g., Board of Educ. of Kiryas Joel Village School Dist. v. Grumet, 512 U.S. 687, 696, 706, 114 S. Ct. 2481, 2487–88, 2492–93 (1994) (proper respect for both Free Exercise Clause and Establishment Clause requires neutrality toward religion, favoring neither one religion over others nor religious adherents over nonadherents; statute that singled out a particular religious sect for special treatment in school context violated First Amendment) ....

Basics of the Religion Clauses

About 3 percent of U.S. children are receiving a home schooling, and the number is growing fast. Still, numerically much more important, at 13 percent, are private schools. But any discussion of private schools inevitably leads much more deeply into the thicket of law on religious freedom, because almost 80 percent of students in private schools are attending religious schools. Of course, that thicket infiltrates all of education law, because religion so closely links with the teaching function: all religions engage in teaching, and all public education at least impinges on any religion.

The First Amendment, applicable to the states through the Fourteenth Amendment, invalidates "law respecting an establishment of religion, or prohibiting the free exercise thereof." Thus, it has two religion clauses that prohibit the establishment of religion *and* guarantee the free exercise of religion. Together the two clauses seem to erect a wall of separation between church and state, by trying to render the state neutral in matters of religion. But the two clauses can conflict, just as *Swanson* suggests in its footnote 7. As the state bends backward to satisfy one clause, it very well may fall into violation of the other clause.

The Establishment Clause prohibits governmental actions that have a purpose to aid or hurt any religion or have a primary effect that advances or inhibits any religion. Many education cases have arisen under this vague test, most often challenging official injection of religion into public schools or public support of parochial schools. For some examples, the holdings make school prayer unconstitutional, while silent meditation may not be; over recent years, the Supreme Court has converted from widely rejecting public funding of religious schools to approving all sorts of schemes just short of direct general aid to religious schools.

The Free Exercise Clause allows the individual to pursue his or her religion. It keeps the government out of the individual's beliefs, but it does not prohibit all regulation of the individual's conduct. As already observed, the state cannot require attendance at a public rather than a parochial school, but the state can subject all schools to reasonable state regulation. For example, in the public schools, the school officials can dictate the curriculum, including a course on sex education that some religious people might find offensive, but they cannot deny religious student groups access to school facilities that is equal to the access enjoyed by other groups.

Plaintiffs have attempted to portray this case as one involving religious discrimination against Christian home-schoolers. The record provided to the district court and this court, however, indicates that it involves only financial distinctions between certain part-time students and all home-schoolers, secular or religious, as well as private-school students. Since this case involved only a neutral rule of general applicability, it was sufficient for Defendants to prove a reasonable relationship between the part-time-attendance policy and a legitimate purpose of the school board. Plaintiffs have not argued that Defendants failed to meet this low threshold, and it is clear that Defendants have satisfied it. Therefore, the district court's decision dismissing all of Plaintiffs' claims is AFFIRMED.

Section Six
IMPROVING THE PUBLIC-BENEFIT INSTRUMENT

A. Improvements at the Top

Public-benefit conferral, as we have seen, depends heavily on legislative initiative, executive leadership, and administrative processing. There is no shortage of ideas on how any of these could be improved. Every election year, for example, political analysts speculate about the defects in our electoral system, and some of these speculations have led to reform legislation. Occasionally the courts even become involved in the reform process, as in Baker v. Carr, 369 U.S. 186, 82 S. Ct. 691 (1962), the historic Supreme Court decision mandating the rule of one person–one vote. Likewise, governmental processes, such as the legislative process with its delays, frustrations, and vulnerability to the pressure of special interests, are the objects of constant critical attention from scholars, journalists, and others. On this front, too, reforms are often suggested and occasionally adopted.

Rather than pursuing such imposing topics, we shall here continue our consideration of the difficult problem of maintaining some measure of popular control over the bureaucracy that distributes public benefits. The next two excerpts differ in their analysis of a possible route to improving public-benefit conferral by increasing control at the top. They usefully represent the contrasting sides of an essential but eternal debate. The first wants the branches of government to renew their policing of overbroad delegation of powers. The second contends that this approach is not only unrealistic but also undesirable. Yet, each of the excerpts presents itself as charting a middle way. Does either succeed? What is the middle way?

THEODORE J. LOWI, THE END OF LIBERALISM
300–03, 305, 307 (2d ed. 1979)

[Professor Lowi calls on the Supreme Court to declare "unconstitutional any delegation of power to an administrative agency or to the president that is not accompanied by clear standards of implementation." He admits that doing so will make it harder to frame and enact programs. But he suggests two ways to compensate, the first being:]

Administrative formality would simply be a requirement for early and frequent administrative rule-making. When an agency formulates a general rule it is without any question committing a legislative act. But in so doing, the agency is simply carrying out the responsibility delegated to it by Congress in the enabling statute for that agency, and is also carrying out the general intent of Congress as spelled out in the Administrative Procedure Act. This power to promulgate general rules has been validated by the Supreme Court. But the trouble is, few agencies do this, and even fewer like to do it. Most of the administrative rhetoric in recent years espouses the interest-group ideal of administration by favoring the norms of flexibility and decision by bargaining. Pluralism applied to administration usually takes the practical form of an attempt to deal with each case on its merits. But the ideal of case-by-case administration is in most instances a myth. Few persons affected by a decision have an opportunity to be heard. And each agency, regulatory or not, disposes of the largest proportion of its cases without any procedure at all, least of all by formal adversary processes. In practice, agencies end up with the worst of case-by-case adjudication *and* of rule-making. They try to work without rules in order to live with the loose legislative mandate, and then they try to treat their cases and practices as though they were operating under a rule....

The second approach to the problem of Congress's inherent inability to live by the juridical principle, codification, is highly consistent with and complementary to the first. Even if Congress is unable to provide good legislative guidelines at the time of the passage of the original organic act, there is no reason why Congress has to remain permanently incapable. [With the thought "that Congress ought to be able to learn from its own experience," he specifies codification as "nothing more than the effort to systematize, digest, and simplify all of the provisions of law relating to a particular subject."] Everyone would be aware of the fact that the first enactment is only the beginning. Every administrator would be making decisions with an eye toward review for consistency, and every agency would have incentive to influence this process by promulgation of the early rules.... Every regulated corporation and individual would be pushing the regulatory agency toward general rulings and away from individual decisions because of the knowledge that these are likely to become legislation eventually. Finally, when these rulings are brought back to Congress and put through the regular legislative mill, they will not only be elevated in stature as law but very probably would go through further change and further clarification on their way back to the administrative agency. The regulator would then be participating in the legislative process in a way that is consonant with the Constitution....

JEFFREY L. PRESSMAN & AARON WILDAVSKY, IMPLEMENTATION
168–70, 172, 175–76 (3d ed. 1984)*

We begin by observing that the essential constituents of any policy are objectives and resources. In most policies of interest, objectives are characteristically multiple (because we want many things, not just one), conflicting (because we want different things), and vague (because that is how we can agree to proceed without having to agree also on exactly what to do). So if the objectives are not uniquely determined, neither are the modes of implementation for them.

Because of cognitive limitations and the dynamic quality of our environment, moreover, there is no way for us to understand at first all the relevant constraints on resources. We can discover and then incorporate them into our plans only as the implementation process unfolds....

Policies are continuously transformed by implementing actions that simultaneously alter resources and objectives. Varying the amount of resources need not require doing more or less of the same thing: one might do quite different things with $1 million than if one had $10 million. Altering objectives may change the significance of behaviors that are seemingly the same. Suppose the actual purpose of a system of effluent charges gradually shifts from pollution control to raising general revenue. The fiscal and administrative mechanisms may remain the same, but the policy would change significantly....

How well policies respond to opportunities, how well they facilitate adaptation and error correction, are qualities insufficiently discussed. For our purposes, however, it is more important to observe that keeping things going rather than getting things started is the ordinary condition of administration. It is not policy design but redesign that occurs most of the time.... Indeed, old patterns of behavior are often retrospectively

---

rationalized to fit new notions about appropriate objectives. We do not always decide what to do and succeed or fail at it; rather, we observe what we have done and try to make it consistent in retrospect. If Head Start finds it difficult to demonstrate lasting improvement in children's reading abilities, it may stress its clear capacity for increasing parents' involvement, which in turn may lead to educational improvement in their children. We choose after the act as well as before....

Since administrative discretion can be used as a cover for arbitrary behavior that is unrelated to policy intentions, some authors feel that the problem of administration is, purely and simply, one of controlling discretion. Controlling it how? Unless one is willing to assume that policies spring fully armed from the forehead of an omniscient policymaker, discretion is both inevitable and necessary. Unless administration is programmed—a robot comes to mind—discretion can be controlled only by indirect means. Again, we must rely on learning and invention rather than on instruction and command. In punishing his generals for failing to execute his orders faithfully even when their disobedience brought him victory, Frederick the Great of Prussia was at least consistent. We require the impossible when we expect our bureaucrats to be at the same time literal executors and successful implementers of policy mandates. Something has to be left to chance. In a world of uncertainty, success is only loosely correlated with effort, and chance can never be ruled out as the main cause of either success or failure. To the extent that success *is* related to effort, it depends more on "knowing how" than on "knowing that," on the ability to select appropriate types of behavior and rules of conduct, more than on abstract knowledge of decision rules or on blind obedience to directives....

How effectively can implementation bring out one rather than another range of results? The more general an idea and the more adaptable it is to a range of circumstances, the more likely it is to be realized in some form, but the less likely it is to emerge as intended in practice. The more restricted the idea, and the more it is constrained, the more likely it is to emerge as predicted, but the less likely it is to have a significant impact. At one extreme we have the ideal type of the perfectly preformed policy idea; it only requires execution, and the only problems it raises are those of control. At the other extreme, the policy idea is only an expression of basic principles and aspirations, a matter for philosophical reflection and political debate. In between, where we live, is a set of more or less developed potentialities embedded in pieces of legislation, court decisions, and bureaucratic plans.

B. Improvements at the Bottom

We now introduce the debate over ways to increase popular control at the bottom of the power hierarchy. And for this we return to the illustration of public education. But the aim of this specific illustration is to raise the most general of all issues concerning the public-benefit instrument, one that will arise in connection with every public-benefit program: the proper balance between public and private.

Education has always posed this most general issue. But it was not until the mid-1960s that the basic structure of American education become controversial. Criticism then began to focus on tendencies toward coercion and conformity allegedly fostered by government's strong role in primary and secondary education. Some critics suggested dismantling the school system in the United States. A leading voice was that of Ivan Illich, the anarchist social critic. In his book, Deschooling Society (1971), he argued against the institutionalization of education and in favor of self-directed education and peer-matching networks called learning webs. He even proposed a new article in the Bill of Rights that would read: "The State shall make no law with respect to the establishment of education."

More recently, others have attacked the monopolistic tendencies of the current system. Those in the disestablishment movement want to get the government out of education, putting parents back in charge to make private arrangements, while "freeing American education from government control and pompous academic collusion." Kerry L. Morgan, Real Choice Real Freedom in American Education, at xvi (1997).

Others more realistically have sought to break the government's virtual monopoly. They lament the current system of limited choice, without going so far as to suggest abolition or total disestablishment. These writers stress that it is only the poor who must send their children to public school. They also criticize the requirement that families who seek alternatives to the public schools must pay both school taxes and the cost of private schooling, with no tax breaks to ease this double burden. This means of ordering the distribution of educational benefits, critics argue, ensures that those who cannot readily afford the extra cost of private education have no freedom of choice. Roger A. Freeman, Educational Tax Credits, in The Public School Monopoly 471, 487 (Robert B. Everhart ed., 1982), put it this way:

> Is it proper for government to force parents to send their children to a school which they would not choose if they had an option? Why should an option be available only to affluent parents? Is it good public policy and is it educationally productive to make alternative schools—whose spirit is more conducive to learning—inaccessible to most children? If millions of parents prefer the discipline enforced in nonpublic schools, why should they not have an opportunity to send their children there even if their economic circumstances do not allow them to pay high tuition charges?

"VOUCHERS"

All that sounds sort of vague. How does one translate this discontent into a specific proposal? An important step was taken by John E. Coons & Stephen D. Sugarman, Education by Choice 10, 12–14, 47 (1978),* in which the two law professors expanded on the idea thus:

> There is no easy way to tell if the needs and wants of most families are served by the local public school. The widespread criticism of American education in the 1960s and 1970s suggests they are not. Rather it seems likely that the preferences and phobias of many go undiscovered and unsatisfied. In place of compulsory assignment, many children and their families might prefer programs emphasizing science, the classics, McGuffey's reader, music, the Baltimore Catechism, or the sayings of Chairman Mao. Some might want an outdoor school, a school in a

---

* Copyright © 1978 by University of California Press. Reprinted by permission of authors.

living room, a school that starts at 7:00 and ends at noon, a school with the long vacation in the fall, or a school whose teachers are artisans or otherwise employed part-time outside the school. Likewise, many teachers might wish they were free to enlist children in the enterprise of learning by offering the bait of their special abilities in dance, botany, French, Chinese culture, or the teachings of Muhammed. What we do know is that—even given a harmony of objectives among school, teacher, parent, and student—many families find it extremely difficult today to get the child and the preferred experience together except by happy accident....

...Instead of government potatoes, poor families today are usually given money for the purchase of soup, soap, or stockings. In general this seems wise; not everybody likes potatoes or is nourished by them. Of course, some will decide to nourish themselves on booze, and this is a problem, especially where children suffer as a consequence. Thus the government sometimes earmarks the transfers to narrow the range of choice; for example, under the food stamp and Medicaid programs the government provides stamps or cards that can be used only to satisfy needs for food or for health care. Even with their restrictions, such programs are very different from those that simply give the recipients government soup and government doctors. Stamps and cards allow their holders to choose among foods and physicians.

Why not distribute school dollars in this way and permit the family to choose among educators? Just as some children may be allergic to the government's potato, some may be allergic to its schools or teachers. Yet the state has chosen not only to operate its own schools but, in practical economic effect, has required most children to attend them. The decision to leave the average family powerless regarding education, while permitting its choice of material goods, seems eccentric. Many families might be content with a relatively uniform and choiceless style of health maintenance or even an imposed diet, if it were adequate. Concerning the training of minds, a wider variety of opinions seems to obtain. One would suppose choice to be more, rather than less, significant to the family with respect to education than other human needs.

Of course, the stronger interest in choice might be seen as the very problem. Defenders of the status quo remind us that a certain level of education is essential in a democratic society, and that if families were given money to purchase education where they pleased, some would select the scholastic equivalent of booze. This fear is justified if the only alternative to herding the nonrich into public schools is outright parentocracy. But such a policy dilemma is hard to credit, at least on its face. The public and private schools created under any politically viable system of family choice would be required by law to meet a fair minimum standard. The child of the wayward parent would not face the dubious exchange of one educational autocrat (the state) for another (the parent); instead, he would be party to a balanced regime. The state would mandate that all children receive whatever elements of education command a public consensus. This could probably assure no more than exposure to the agreed minimum, but note that this is equally true of the existing scheme. Indeed, one argument for more voluntarism is that it will increase the rate at which children actually achieve the minimum. And beyond those politically determined essentials, families would be assured the economic capacity to pursue their educational preferences....

Viewed as a system of decision location, the present educational structure can be described largely as a regime of local government employees and elected officials who have been empowered to decide what form of education is in the best interest of the children resident within their district. These agents—school board members, administrators, and teachers—are moderately constrained by higher government authorities and by the attitudes of local residents, which together set political limits on the range of tolerable educational practices. Children themselves rarely have anything to say about their school assignment except as it may influence the location of family residence. Once residence is decided, individual public school families have little formal voice in determining the education their child receives, though the sophisticated parent with spare time may employ harassment and persuasion to secure a preferred assignment.

If we were to attribute to this present "decentralized" scheme a primary concern for the best interest of individual children, its rationale would have to be that—apart from those families able to pay for private schools or a change of residence—local government agents make better school assignments for individual children they have never met than would the family, even were the family to be supported by professional counseling. The underlying argument would be that, by imposing on individual children the decisions made for them by professional and elected local decision makers, the public system gives them advantages unattainable by any other form of assignment. He receives the benefits of educational expertise while eluding the risks of mistakes, negligence, and exploitation by those amateurs who are his family. Power is placed in the hands of disinterested elders and experts who are outside the family yet are subject to public scrutiny.

More precisely, vouchers would be portable scholarships provided by the government from tax funds and cashable by parents or students at any school, public or private. It was indeed the contrast between public and private schools that had generated the voucher idea as a reform proposal.

Reformers had looked at the public schools and found them remarkably and discouragingly uniform, despite their supposed local control. In fact, politics and bureaucracy have the effect of undermining local control and, instead, fostering top-down control and resistance to any change. By virtue of their being free to the parents, public schools could attract students without being particularly good at education.

In contrast, private schools are market-driven. They cannot just assume students will attend, because the parents have a real exit option. This fact guarantees that the local parents and even the children will enjoy a loud voice in the schools' running. If society were to shift from public to private schools, society would see a major shift in lawmaking and law-applying power from government officials to private persons. The schools would be much more varied as a result.

Under a voucher scheme, the theory goes, all schools would have to fight for the funds. The schools would have to listen and please their consumers. The free competition would then produce diverse forms of quality education. To put it another way, the motivation for vouchers was the feeling that, with respect to education, what is wrong with public-benefit conferral is the public part: we need to move toward privatization in order to reassert popular control.

In the 1980s, which was an era of deregulation, support for the privatizing voucher idea found receptive ears. The debate consequently escalated. But what was the debate? Assuming that proponents had their facts right, which is admittedly questionable, vouchers sounded like such a good idea—at least until one stepped back and reconsidered the goals of public education. Henry M. Levin, Educational Vouchers and Social Policy, in Care and Education of Young Children in America 106, 116–20 (Ron Haskins & James J. Gallagher eds., 1980),* did so at the time:

> Perhaps the greatest social dilemma raised by vouchers is the potential divergence between private choices and the social benefits of education. Presumably, so many of our social resources are devoted to education because the reproduction of our social, economic, and political systems depends heavily on preparing the young to understand and participate in these systems....
>
> This concern has at least two major dimensions: First, the schools are expected to provide students with an understanding of the role and functioning of our democratic system of government as well as to prepare them for participating in such a system. Second, the schools are expected to create and sustain a system of social mobility in which a child's eventual income and occupational status are not linked inextricably to those of his parents....
>
> A major function of the public schools is the transmission of a common language, heritage, set of values, and knowledge necessary for appropriate political functioning in our democratic society. To a large degree, the schools attempt to reproduce these traits through a common curriculum and heterogeneous enrollments. That is, we presume that exposure to a variety of students from different backgrounds and to a common curriculum of social studies and civic content will prepare students adequately to participate in democratic institutions.
>
> In almost every respect, the voucher approach would violate these premises by encouraging separation and stratification of students according to parental commitments and orientations and by tailoring curricula to appeal to and reinforce these parental concerns....
>
> ... Even though there will be differences from plan to plan, vouchers will tend to create greater transmission of inequalities from generation to generation than the present public schools. This problem tends to assert itself because parents seem to pursue child-rearing patterns that are consistent and reinforce their own values and class position in the society. This can best be understood by considering what these values are and how they might affect the choice of school.
>
> Let us assume parents wish to select that school which they believe will have the most chance of making their child a success in life. Clearly, the rules for success differ according to where parents are situated in the productive and occupational hierarchy. Kohn has shown that working-class families seem to emphasize conformity in their children (obedience to rules), whereas parents in relatively higher occupational positions stress independence and ability to choose among available alternatives. The research of Hess and Shipman on

---

* Copyright © 1979 by Ablex Publishing Company. Reprinted by permission.

maternal-child interactions also tends to substantiate these differences, with lower-class mothers stressing a "do as I tell you" approach in teaching their children and middle-class mothers seemingly using a more heuristic approach. . . .

If parents choose those school environments they believe will maximize the probability of success as defined within the context of their experience, the working-class child will get schooling that reinforces working-class orientations, and upper-class children will attend schools that orient them toward the upper echelons of the occupational hierarchy. . . .

Further, to the degree that social class stratification increased, it would become easier to identify individuals for particular positions in the social class hierarchy by the schools they attend. Each school would connote a different breeding or charter that would have a certification value in preparing individuals for further educational opportunities or positions in the labor market. Even without identifying the actual proficiencies of students as individuals, the information connoted by the class orientation of schooling would tend to serve a stratification role.

The voucher approach to education represents a paradox. It seems reasonable to believe that greater choice among consumers and increased institutional responsiveness will enhance the welfare of society. At a rhetorical level, we would be improving the ability of families to obtain the education they want for their children. But as I have demonstrated, the expansion of choices and market responsiveness will be much greater for upper-income groups than for lower-income and minority citizens, and the element of choice will lead insidiously to an even greater degree of class stratification and socialization than exists now. That these latter effects will be based upon individual "choices" and "preferences" means that the exacerbation of social-class differences in the fortunes of children will be considered the responsibility of parents who chose the schools rather than the responsibility of the class-oriented society that predetermined the parents' values leading to the choices.

The federal government and a number of cities, such as Milwaukee and Cleveland, started limited experiments with vouchers in the 1990s. If this challenge to the favored treatment of the public schools were to result in widespread federal or state legislation, as embodied in a voucher plan or at least some tuition tax deduction scheme—and were this legislation to be held valid under the U.S. Constitution, as it was in Zelman v. Simmons-Harris, 536 U.S. 639, 122 S. Ct. 2460 (2002) (holding that vouchers could go to religious schools in Ohio), and Mueller v. Allen, 463 U.S. 388, 103 S. Ct. 3062 (1983) (approving tax credits)—the shape of public education as we now know it would change significantly. The proportion of children enrolled in public schools, currently about 85 percent of the total school-age population, would certainly drop, although the size of the decline would depend on how much the new government subsidies cut into the costs of sending children to private schools.

Widespread adoption of voucher plans and a consequent decline in the reach of public schools did not occur, but the debate remained a live one in every state legislature. And courts began to reenter the controversy, as some struck down voucher plans on state constitutional grounds. Compare, e.g., Holmes v. Bush, 919 So. 2d 398 (Fla. 2006) (holding that vouchers violate the state constitution's "uniformity" clause, which requires "a uniform, efficient, safe, secure, and high quality system of free public schools"), with, e.g., Jackson v. Benson, 218 Wis. 2d 835, 578 N.W.2d 602 (1998) (holding that vouchers do not violate the state constitution's uniformity clause or any other constitutional provision). Perhaps, however, the moment for vouchers has passed, as political support is ebbing.

In sum, this is another education-law dispute that is highly instructive in how it has played out over time. See generally James G. Dwyer, Vouchers Within Reason (2002).

"STANDARDS"

Educational reformers have begun to push their next panacea: standards-based education. The following excerpt describes this shift from voucher plans to schools' accountability, with sanctions under set standards, as a movement from market-based reform back to a more government-controlled system. Let the next debate begin!

AARON J. SAIGER, LEGISLATING ACCOUNTABILITY: STANDARDS, SANCTIONS, AND SCHOOL DISTRICT REFORM

46 Wm. & Mary L. Rev. 1655, 1656–59 (2005)*

"Hold the public schools accountable!" This clarion cry, first heard in state capitals in the late 1980s, has since been repeated and amplified by many states, by the courts, and most recently, by the federal government [in the No Child Left Behind Act of 2001, 20 U.S.C. §§6301 et seq.]. Only where school districts and schools are held to "account," the theory goes, ought one expect any program of school reform to be truly effective. Because unaccountable school districts lack incentives to succeed, waves of school reform have

---

* Copyright 2005 by the William and Mary Law Review.

been able to wash over the nation's most troubled school districts for decades without substantially ameliorating their dismal and disgraceful performance.

There can be no doubt that the programs grouped under the general rubric of the "New Accountability" mark an important shift in efforts to reform these troubled districts. Accountability reforms operate in the public sphere, implicitly denying the claim that only markets can solve the problems of failing schools. They rely upon legislative and executive action, rather than locating the power to reform troubled schools in judges, who have limited control over schools' activities, no ongoing experience with education, and a constrained repertoire of remedies. And instead of regulating top-down, accountability reforms encourage flexibility at the local level where educational programs are implemented; they impose demands regarding outcomes and information sharing but leave local officials to find the best ways to reach the standards the programs impose.

. . . Public debate has focused on the wisdom and validity of testing students to measure their performance, the risks of regimenting education across a diversity of schools and modes of inquiry, the proper measurement of educational improvement, and the educational legitimacy of setting standards for schools in the first place. The debate has come—implicitly in many cases and explicitly in some—largely to identify the New Accountability entirely with the practices of standard-setting, testing, and the dissemination of information about results.

To make such an identification is to miss the reason that policymakers adopted a banner of "accountability" rather than simply one of "standards": American schools and school districts are peculiarly unaccountable institutions. They are insulated from the consequences of malfeasance by their natural monopoly over policy implementation, which ultimately must occur in classrooms widely dispersed and difficult to monitor; they are even more insulated by the peculiar intergovernmental structure of American education, which distributes responsibility for schools across two types of governments—states and school districts. Although the state is the locus of constitutional authority over school policy, school districts enjoy virtually total power over policy implementation. This gives districts unusual freedom to pursue their own self-interest, which often diverges from the state's educational agenda. District resistance to externally motivated policy change is the shoal upon which many previous education reform efforts have foundered. The fundamental task of accountability is to undermine district power to resist reform—not so much to define standards as to discover how to hold schools and school districts to whatever standards are established.

To do this requires attention above all not to standards but to sanctions. At the intuitive heart of the term "accountability" is that failure should compel consequences. The new accountability programs the states have adopted do not merely set standards for districts and schools to meet—they impose punishments for failure. In order to confront local leaders with genuine incentives to reform, moreover, these punishments are of a particular kind. Accountability sanctions are designed to curtail or eliminate local power. The ultimate sanction is "disestablishment": the school board and superintendent in a district failing persistently are unseated, and authority over all school matters reverts to the state. Unlike judicial reform decrees or hierarchical diktats from state education departments, for which less-than-faithful implementation by a district carries few consequences, or market reforms, where the consequences of poor performance are attenuated, a disestablishment threat is vivid. Local officials at risk of losing their authority to manage district affairs have every reason to align their activities to an extent with state preferences.

Section Seven
LIMITATIONS OF LAW AS A PUBLIC-BENEFIT INSTRUMENT

A. The Big Picture

The aims of public-benefit programs tend to be expansive (and expensive). Consider, for example, the myriad of statutes and regulations addressed to providing adequate medical care, efficient transportation, and national defense. And the long-term trend is toward a broader role for government in providing security and other benefits to individuals and organizations, despite recurrent moods favoring some dismantling of government intervention.

The tendency toward an ever-expanding governmental role is obvious when one considers just how recent much important social-welfare legislation is. Old-age assistance, aid to dependent children, disaster relief, government-subsidized mass transit, the space shuttle, tuition benefits for college students, company bailouts—all of these government activities are less than a century old, and many are much younger.

Considering the range of problems that government tackles with the public-benefit instrument, it should come as no surprise that the instrument's effectiveness is limited. For a suggestion of such a limitation, the government can more effectively bestow tangible benefits, such as mail delivery, than intangible benefits, such as instilling a communitarian spirit in its citizens. For another example, there are varied limits on the burdens imposable by government. On the one hand, the laity and some politicians seem to ignore the limitations of law, and they are consequently all too willing to throw money at any social problem. On the other hand, the constraints within which every public-benefit program must proceed have often provoked calls for reducing or even eliminating certain distributive programs. This sharp difference of opinion makes it all the more important to study limitations on this legal instrument.

The argument that government cannot do all that is asked of it is not new. It predates even the dramatic expansion of social-welfare activities. Note that the author of the following remarks was a prominent nineteenth-century social theorist. Evaluate the generic limitations on the public-benefit instrument that he says exist.

HERBERT SPENCER, OVER–LEGISLATION
in 3 Essays: Scientific, Political, and Speculative 229, 232–33, 235, 271 (1891)

Thus, while every day chronicles a failure, there every day reappears the belief that it needs but an Act of Parliament and a staff of officers, to effect any end desired. Nowhere is the perennial faith of mankind better seen. Ever since society existed Disappointment has been preaching—"Put not your trust in legislation"; and yet the trust in legislation seems scarcely diminished.

Did the State fulfil efficiently its unquestionable duties, there would be some excuse for this eagerness to assign it further duties.... [H]ad we, in short, proved its efficiency as judge and defender, instead of having found it treacherous, cruel, and anxiously to be shunned, there would be some encouragement to hope other benefits at its hands. . . .

. . . [T]he new work is not of the same order as the old, but of a more difficult order. Ill as government discharges its true duties, any other duties committed to it are likely to be still worse discharged. To guard its subjects against aggression, either individual or national, is a straightforward and tolerably simple matter; to regulate, directly or indirectly, the personal actions of those subjects is an infinitely complicated matter. It is one thing to secure to each man the unhindered power to pursue his own good; it is a widely different thing to pursue the good for him. To do the first efficiently, the State has merely to look on while its citizens act; to forbid unfairness; to adjudicate when called on; and to enforce restitution for injuries. To do the last efficiently, it must become an ubiquitous worker—must know each man's needs better than he knows them himself—must, in short, possess superhuman power and intelligence. . . .

. . . And if an institution undertakes, not two functions but a score—if a government, whose office it is to defend citizens against aggressors, foreign and domestic, engages also to disseminate Christianity, to administer charity, to teach children their lessons, to adjust prices of food, to inspect coal-mines, to regulate railways, to superintend house-building, to arrange cab-fares, to look into people's stink-traps, to vaccinate their children, to send out emigrants, to prescribe hours of labour, to examine lodging-houses, to test the knowledge of mercantile captains, to provide public libraries, to read and authorize dramas, to inspect passenger-ships, to see that small dwellings are supplied with water, to regulate endless things from a banker's issues down to the boat-fares on the Serpentine—is it not manifest that its primary duty must be ill discharged in proportion to the multiplicity of affairs it busies itself with? Must not its time and energies be frittered away in schemes, and inquiries, and amendments, in discussions, and divisions, to the neglect of its essential business?

B. A Final Illustration of Conferral Program: Public Education, Yet Again

Formulating generic limitations on the public-benefit instrument is a tough task. Instead, we need to consider an illustration, because thinking about the limits of the public-benefit instrument can really be done only in specific terms. And once again we turn to the illustration of public education. But, once again our aim in using a specific illustration is to raise in your mind similar issues concerning other public-benefit programs.

Public educational policy is a particularly telling case in point on limits of the public-benefit instrument, perhaps because public education is, at least relatively speaking, a successful policy. Still, contradictions abound in its goals and accomplishments. Real and severe limits exist on what public education can and should do.

POSSIBLE GOALS

The primary aim of our policy of providing free and universal schooling through high school is, obviously, to educate the young. So, we make primary and secondary education compulsory. Yet that is hardly an ideal approach. An education is not a thing one receives—it is a process in which one participates. "Compulsory education," in a real sense, is a contradiction in terms. Not everyone can or will participate even if present.

Public educational goals and accomplishments are limited, too, by financial considerations: by political pressures, whether coming from majoritarian politics or from special-interest groups; by lack of knowledge among the education experts or in the community leaders who set some educational policies, as well as in those who administer educational programs; and by the capacities of administrative and teaching personnel—teachers can simply become exhausted by the strain of dealing face-to-face with a demanding and sometimes unruly clientele.

As we developed in the discussion of vouchers, another important aim of public education is to redress inequalities of opportunity. But how far can education go to equalize the opportunities of racially diverse children, of rich and poor children, and of children who differ in capabilities and motivation? Would we even want to equalize opportunities across the range of talents and personalities? Moreover, some such educational aims conflict with others, such as promoting racial integration while also maintaining a neighborhood focus for schools.

Other aims, such as fostering citizenship and democratic values in young people, raise questions of both desirability and achievability. New York's Education Law §801 treats "courses of instruction in patriotism and citizenship and in certain historic documents" and begins this way:

> In order to promote a spirit of patriotic and civic service and obligation and to foster in the children of the state moral and intellectual qualities which are essential in preparing to meet the obligations of citizenship in peace or in war, the regents of The University of the State of New York shall prescribe courses of instruction in patriotism, citizenship, and human rights issues, with particular attention to the study of the inhumanity of genocide, slavery (including the freedom trail and underground railroad), the Holocaust, and the mass starvation in Ireland from 1845 to 1850, to be maintained and followed in all the schools of the state. The boards of education and trustees of the several cities and school districts of the state shall require instruction to be given in such courses, by the teachers employed in the schools therein. All pupils attending such schools, over the age of eight years, shall attend upon such instruction. Similar courses of instruction shall be prescribed and maintained in private schools in the state, and all pupils in such schools over eight years of age shall attend upon such courses.

Then §801-a, which treats "instruction in civility, citizenship and character education," continues:

> The regents shall ensure that the course of instruction in grades kindergarten through twelve includes a component on civility, citizenship and character education. Such component shall instruct students on the principles of honesty,

tolerance, personal responsibility, respect for others, observance of laws and rules, courtesy, dignity and other traits which will enhance the quality of their experiences in, and contributions to, the community. The regents shall determine how to incorporate such component in existing curricula and the commissioner shall promulgate any regulations needed to carry out such determination of the regents.

SKIPWORTH v. BOARD OF EDUCATION
Colorado Court of Appeals, 1994
874 P.2d 487

JUDGE ROTHENBERG:

Plaintiffs, David and Kathryn Skipworth, Virgil and Linda Pineda, and Dale L. Thomas, appeal the dismissal of their claims against the Board of Education of Woodland Park School District....

Plaintiffs are the parents of high school students in the Woodland Park district. They sued the board of education... in a dispute about a world literature class....

Plaintiffs' complaint and amended complaint sought declaratory relief and damages for the defendants' alleged breach of a statutory or constitutional duty to teach morality in the public schools.

The defendants filed motions to dismiss which were granted when the trial court concluded that plaintiffs had failed to state a claim upon which relief could be granted....

...Nevertheless, plaintiffs maintain that: (1) "Certain studies plainly essential to good citizenship must be taught in the public schools"; and (2) "Morality is essential to good citizenship and must be taught in the public schools."...

...In arguing for the existence of a duty here, plaintiffs first claim they have a fundamental right to a thorough education for their children by virtue of Colo. Const. art. IX, §2, and that such a thorough education includes the teaching of morality. We are unpersuaded....

Finally, plaintiffs claim the board of education is statutorily mandated to teach morality. Again, we disagree.

The board of education has been given statutory authority to "determine the educational programs to be carried on in the schools of the district." Section 22-32-109(1)(t), C.R.S. (1988 Repl. Vol. 9). However, the board's discretion is not unlimited, and the General Assembly has specified certain subjects that must be taught. These subjects are: the history, culture, and civil government of Colorado and the United States, including the history, culture, and contributions of minorities, see §22-1-104; honor and use of the flag, see §22-1-106; the federal constitution, see §22-1-108; and the effect of alcohol and controlled substances. See §22-1-110. The method in which these subjects are to be taught and the emphasis to be placed upon standards of conduct, discipline, and values in general is within the province of the board of education and not this court. See generally Moskowitz, The Making of the Moral Child: Legal Implications of Values Education, 6 Pepp. L. Rev. 105 (1978)....

In summary, the General Assembly has given the board of education authority to choose which non-mandatory subjects are taught in the public schools. And, absent a constitutional or statutory violation, which has not been shown here, this court lacks the authority to interfere with the exercise of that discretion. As Justice Blackmun noted in a concurring opinion in Board of Education v. Pico, 457 U.S. 853, 880, 102 S. Ct. 2799, 2815 (1982): "School officials must be able to choose one book over another, without outside interference, when the first book is deemed more relevant to the curriculum, or better written, or when one of a host of other politically neutral reasons is present."...

The judgment is affirmed, and the cause is remanded for further proceedings in accordance with this opinion [to award attorney's fees for bringing a frivolous suit and appeal].

PLANK and MARQUEZ, JJ., concur.

MICHAEL B. KATZ, THE PRESENT MOMENT IN EDUCATIONAL REFORM
41 Harv. Educ. Rev. 342, 355–57 (1971)*

It must be emphasized that, opinion to the contrary notwithstanding, people ask no more of schools today than they did a hundred and twenty-five years ago. Even then the schools were asked to do the impossible. As we have seen, the purpose of the school people has been more the development of attitudes than of intellect, and this continues to be the case. It is true, and this point must be stressed, of radical reformers as well as of advocates of law and order. The latter want the schools to stop crime and check immorality by teaching obedience to authority, respect for the law, and conformity to conventional standards. The former want the schools to reform society by creating a new sense of community through turning out warm, loving, noncompetitive people.

The human qualities that radical reformers seek in and through the schools are very beautiful ones; if achieved, they would give us a worthier and lovelier society. But it is no more realistic to charge the schools with the creation of such qualities than it is to expect them to fulfill traditional moralistic aims. Whatever values one attaches to the counter-culture, whatever interpretation one gives to social conflict and crime, it is clear that the powers of schooling have been vastly overrated. Despite substantial financing and a captive audience, the schools have not been able to attain the goals set for them, with remarkably little change, for the last century and a quarter. They have been unable to do so because those goals have been impossible to fulfill. They require fundamental social reform, not the sort of tinkering that educational change has represented. If, by some miracle, the radical reformers were to capture the schools, and only the schools, for the next century, they would have no more success than educational reformers of the past.

The moral should be clear. Educational reformers should begin to distinguish between what formal schooling can and cannot do. They must separate the teaching of skills from the teaching of attitudes, and concentrate on the former. In actual fact, it is of course impossible to separate the two; attitudes adhere in any form of practice. But there is a vast difference between leaving the formation of attitudes untended and making them the object of education.

This is a radical position, despite the ordinary presumption to the contrary. In the popular version, schools once upon a time concentrated on the three R's. With no nonsense and remarkable success, they taught children to read, write, cipher, and spell. Then along came progressivism, which turned the schools into a combination social-service and life-adjustment bureau, forgetting, in the process, all about training in skills and the importance of the intellect. That history is simply false. The denigration of intellect and the neglect of skills have been continuing features of the history of public education; early school promoters believed quite as much as progressives that they were creating institutions to alleviate and prevent social problems.

There is a lot of talk about the foisting of middle-class values onto working-class children through the schools. In fact that happens to be an oversimplification....The values taught by the schools are not the historically tough, ascetic values of the bourgeois. Be that as it may, although schools do confront children with values that may be different from their own or from those of their parents, attempting to reverse the case may not prove desirable either. The way out of this problem, it seems to me, is once again to take the schools out of the business of shaping attitudes. Have them attend to skills, especially, in the beginning, reading, and the question of whose values control the schools becomes largely irrelevant. For it is my premise that the desire that children become functionally literate and able to understand mathematics is nearly universal; it is as important to poor as to affluent parents.

To talk of cultural deprivation is to patronize the poor; it also is to deflect effort away from the education that they need. Beyond this, people have a right to hold whatever beliefs and whatever attitudes they please; that is the only consistent position for a civil libertarian. It follows that the

---

* Copyright Michael B. Katz. Reprinted by permission.

attempt in schools to define one set of attitudes as superior to another, the attempt to teach patriotism, conventional morality, or even their opposite in a compulsory public institution represents a gross violation of civil rights.

My point is that educational theory should define strictly educational tasks and that schools should concentrate on those. Any such definition must include, at one end of the spectrum, fundamental skills; at the other, it must exclude the conscious attempt to formulate social attitudes. I am not arguing for what has been traditional in much educational practice; mental gymnastics for their own sake or the forced study of useless disciplines is indefensible. So is the rigid, authoritarian atmosphere of most schools. Schools should be made open, humane places for the simple reason that children have every right to be happy and to be treated with dignity and respect.

APPROPRIATE GOALS

As those New York statutes and the *Skipworth* case suggest, state government has a relatively free hand in deciding how to socialize the children and in choosing both what to teach and what not to teach in that connection. But, as a policy matter and as Professor Katz timelessly asks, what should its decision be?

Our society needs or at least wants its citizens to be autonomous individuals. But any society needs children to acquire community culture as well as civic values. We would consider public education a failure if all it turned out were unconstrained and alienated individuals, even if very well-informed ones. We probably want children to learn something of citizenship, loyalty, democratic values, love of country, and so on. Of course, public education here and abroad is sometimes the vehicle of indoctrination.

To some degree autonomy and acculturation are mutually reinforcing, but to another degree they are at odds. Our schools must seek a balance. See Mark G. Yudof, Library Book Selection and the Public Schools: The Quest for the Archimedean Point, 59 Ind. L.J. 527 (1984). Our approach of putting the government in charge of the search for this balance is obviously dangerous. Government officials, for one thing, are apt to cultivate a fairly uncritical acceptance of the status quo among the student body.

Our approach of putting the government in charge is also a little surprising, in that we have traditionally worried so much about the government *suppressing* its citizens' thoughts, but here we seem to worry much less about its role in *formulating* citizens' thoughts. For example, we more closely constrain a school library's removal of a book than its decision not to buy it in the first place. Nonetheless, we have to recognize that the very concept of public education necessitates that the educators have the authority to decide what to teach and what not to teach. There will be some outer limit on that authority, but—given the uncertainty about who is to formulate this outer limit and even whether any such limit can exist in comprehensible and enforceable form—the outer limit will not overly restrict the educators' decisions.

A comforting—or disturbing—insight here is that "values education" can never be fully realized in a school setting. Again, limitations do exist on what education can accomplish. Extracurricular influences, including parents, churches, and peers, play a bigger role in socialization. At best, schools have the role of reinforcer or corrector, or perhaps of insurer that at least some socialization occurs for all children. More importantly, values education often has no good effect at all. Some children will be turned off by efforts to teach them patriotism and civic values. Even receptive children will not fully internalize the social norms their schools promote. The fact is there are limitations on the public-benefit instrument.

Section Eight
SUMMARY

When a person thinks about law, ideas of civil and criminal law, and even administrative law, come easily. By contrast, the public-benefit instrument, although familiar to all in operation, does not fit into most people's ideas of law but rather brings politics to mind. Thus, the beginning of this chapter expended some effort in justifying the inclusion of public-benefit conferral as an instrument of law. The bottom line was that legal ordering plays an important and indeed necessary role in program development and administration. For additional reading, see David H. Rosenbloom & Rosemary O'Leary, Public Administration and Law (2d ed. 1996).

This commonality with other legal instruments does not mean that the public-benefit instrument lacks distinctiveness. Its peculiar nature required us to develop a framework for considering the myriad sorts of public benefits. Of course, benefits implicate burdens, and so we had to give sustained attention to the system of taxation in our treatment of this instrument's methodology.

Public-benefit lawmaking is somewhat distinctive too. Beyond state and federal legislatures, administrators, and courts, we broadened the focus to include the street-level bureaucrats who actually run the programs. This section of the chapter exposed the lawmakers' work in program development by means of its recurrent illustration of public education, considering both the obvious benefits of that program and also the less obvious burdens of the associated taxation. In particular, our focus fell on the lawmakers' efforts to ensure ever-elusive equality, or at least the minimum of "equal protection of the laws," in prescribing public education's benefits and burdens. For additional sources on the law of education, see Kern Alexander & M. David Alexander, The Law of Schools, Students and Teachers in a Nutshell (3d ed. 2003); James A. Rapp, Education Law (2007); Richard S. Vacca & William C. Bosher, Jr., Law and Education (7th ed. 2008).

Applying public-benefit law is likewise distinctive, because that law is implemental in nature, aiming mainly at getting organized and then at overseeing routine operation. Again, the illustration of public education provided a concrete context for exposing program administration. In particular, our focus fell on governmental efforts to ensure fairness, or at least the minimum of "due process of law," in terminating a benefit of public education. For additional reading, see Kenneth Culp Davis, Discretionary Justice (1969); Jerry L. Mashaw, Bureaucratic Justice (1983).

As usual, private citizens and their lawyers are busy in program development and especially in program administration. For additional reading, see V.O. Key, Jr., The Responsible Electorate (1966); Peter H. Schuck, Suing Government: Citizen Remedies for Official Wrongs (1983). Instructional content, special education, and home schooling provided the illuminating examples in this section.

Consideration of possible improvements of the public-benefit instrument continued the theme of private persons' involvement. Reform of the political apparatus could yield better popular control. For additional reading, see Samuel Krislov & David H. Rosenbloom, Representative Bureaucracy and the American Political System (1981). More likely, popular control could reassert itself at a lower level. For example, the institution of school vouchers is a way, albeit a problematic one, toward enhancing freedom of choice in the provision of public education.

Finally, limitations exist on what the public-benefit instrument, even if reformed, could achieve. Some benefits remain unattainable, while some burdens are just too heavy. Some of the limitations of law here are obvious, some less so. For additional reading, see Daniel A. Mazmanian & Paul A. Sabatier, Implementation and Public Policy (1983). And for a final example, even assuming the law decides that teaching morality should be part of the public education function, one would have to concede that such a goal lies in large part beyond the limits on what law can do.

Chapter 5

LAW AS AN INSTRUMENT FOR

FACILITATING

PRIVATE ARRANGEMENTS

Legal rules defining the ways in which valid contracts or wills or marriages are made ... provide individuals with facilities for realizing their wishes ... within the coercive framework of the law. The power thus conferred ... is one of the great contributions of law to social life ....

H.L.A. HART

Section One
INTRODUCTION TO THE PRIVATE-ARRANGEMENT INSTRUMENT

Materials Drawn Mainly from Contract Law

In our and many other societies, people achieve their goals by making arrangements with others—without the intrusion of the government. For example, when you agree to mow your neighbor's lawn for $15 per week, when you incorporate your burgeoning gardening business, when you marry a gardening customer, when you join a private gardening club, or when you write a will leaving your gardening fortune to your child, you exercise individual choice, determination, and judgment in ordering your own affairs. Private arrangements of this nature also stimulate the economy by helping to ensure the efficient distribution of goods and services. You mow lawns because you value the money you are paid more than the costs of mowing, and your customers hire you because they value your services more than the money they must pay. Can you imagine instead a government attempting to provide all of the gardening services demanded by the population? Because of these and other benefits of the private arrangements focused on in this chapter, you should not be surprised that many societies utilize law as an instrument to facilitate private arrangements.

Some arrangements are inherently private in Western culture, such as marriage and parenthood. Other arrangements are too cumbersome or costly in the hands of government administrators. Consider the array of bureaucrats that would be required to administer the food and clothing needs of the population. Still other activities could be either private or public. For example, the basic means of production are in part owned publicly in Britain, but they are in private hands in the United States. Societies spend lots of time trying to achieve the appropriate balance of public and private.

The private-arrangement instrument is distinct from the other instruments studied in Chapters 1 through 4. Unlike the other instruments, the primary thrust of the private-arrangement instrument is to enable private citizens to achieve their goals by themselves. The instrument does not give things to people (public-benefit conferral); its primary goal is not to regulate nor to prohibit conduct (administrative and penal instruments, respectively), nor is its primary goal to remedy peoples' grievances for wrongs done by others (remedial instrument).

Private parties determine the content of their arrangements, acting as private legislators. Your contract with your neighbor for lawn-mowing services is your and your neighbor's own private law, every bit as enforceable as the most official legislative enactment. Substituting official for private judgment would destroy the essence of the private-arrangement instrument. If officials decided the proper fee for mowing your neighbor's lawn, for example, the resulting arrangement would not be essentially private. Private parties also generally administer their arrangements, in contrast to the other instruments in which officials typically perform substantial roles. Of course, officials, mainly in the form of judges or arbitrators, step in when something goes awry and enforcement mechanisms are necessary.

The law facilitates private arrangements in three primary ways. First, the law grants private persons the legal power to create various private arrangements (e.g., you have the power to create an enforceable contract with your neighbor to mow her lawn for remuneration). Second, the law specifies the steps you must take to create a legally recognized arrangement, such as the steps necessary to contract with your customer or to incorporate your gardening business. Third, the law specifies the legal consequences of the resulting arrangement, such as your right to enforce your contract with your neighbor through legal remedies.

We shall examine each of these methods of facilitation in detail in this chapter. But this study of how the law facilitates private arrangements also focuses on many additional topics, once you get a feel for the nature of private-arrangement law. The chapter presents materials on how culture, psychology, and other forces influence and are influenced by private-arrangement law. Other topics include the legislative and judicial methods of creating and administering private-arrangement law, alternative dispute resolution techniques, the various roles of lawyers and private citizens in structuring private arrangements, and the shortcomings and limitations of private-arrangement law. As do the other chapters in Part One, Chapter 5 includes the following sections:

- Section Two, Private-Arrangement Methods, introduces various private arrangements recognized and facilitated by law, examines "rules of validation," which enumerate the steps necessary to create legally enforceable private arrangements, and investigates the legal consequences of entering a private arrangement.

- Section Three, Making Private-Arrangement Law, studies how private persons, legislatures, and courts create private-arrangement law.
- Section Four, Applying Private-Arrangement Law, surveys some forums for applying private-arrangement law, such as courts and arbitration proceedings.
- Section Five, Roles of Private Citizens and Their Lawyers, follows private parties as they create a private arrangement and resolve a dispute. The section also studies the role of lawyers at the various stages of creation, performance, and dispute resolution.
- Section Six, Improving the Private-Arrangement Instrument, identifies and discusses some of the ways the law could better facilitate private arrangements.
- Section Seven, Limitations of Law as a Private-Arrangement Instrument, focuses on inherent limitations in the law's facilitation of private arrangement, such as the inability of lawmakers to predict human behavior accurately and to understand fully people's motives and goals.

Section Two
PRIVATE-ARRANGEMENT METHODS

In this section, we look more closely at the three primary methods the law uses to facilitate private arrangements. First, we introduce many of the kinds of private arrangements recognized and enforced by the law. Second, we offer some examples of rules of validation—rules that specify the steps to be taken to create a private arrangement. Third, we investigate some of the legal consequences of private arrangements.

A. Types of Private Arrangements

The law recognizes and enforces many types of private arrangements. Here we introduce some of these. The last arrangement introduced, contract, will be our focus in the subsequent sections of the chapter to illustrate how the law facilitates private arrangements.

PRIVATE ASSOCIATIONS

Private associations come in all shapes, sizes, and subject matters, including large and small recreational, religious, political, educational, and charitable organizations. People form these organizations when they learn of common interests and goals that are facilitated by group rather than individual action.

De Tocqueville interestingly compared "aristocratic" and "democratic" societies in this regard in 2 Alexis de Tocqueville, Democracy in America 128–30 (1961) (1st Eng. ed., London 1840):

> Aristocratic communities always contain, amongst a multitude of persons who by themselves are powerless, a small number of powerful and wealthy citizens, each of whom can achieve great undertakings single-handed. In aristocratic societies men do not need to combine in order to act, because they are strongly held together. Every wealthy and powerful citizen constitutes the head of a permanent and compulsory association, composed of all those who are dependent upon him, or whom he makes subservient to the execution of his designs.
>
> Amongst democratic nations, on the contrary, all the citizens are independent and feeble; they can do hardly anything by themselves, and none of them can oblige his fellowmen to lend him their assistance. They all, therefore, fall into a state of incapacity, if they do not learn voluntarily to help each other. If men living in democratic countries had no right and no inclination to associate for political purposes, their independence would be in great jeopardy....

Private associations not only allow people better to pursue interests and achieve goals, but also offer social support. As to the latter, "voluntary associations relieve the feeling of isolation which tends to plague modern society. They provide opportunity for creativity and responsibility. Because of their presence a person is not forced to choose between conformity with the majority and complete isolation: he has numerous choices and can indulge his idiosyncrasies with others of similar inclination." Developments in the Law—Judicial Control of Actions of Private Associations, 76 Harv. L. Rev. 983, 988 (1963).

The availability of private associations also leads to political stability. People typically belong to many associations, some of which have conflicting interests. This decreases the possibility that members of any particular association will feel completely estranged from society as a whole:

> The more numerous and diversified organized groups become, the more individuals will tend to develop loyalties to associations which have conflicting interests. Such overlapping loyalties decrease the danger that any particular group of individuals will find all its basic interests opposed to those of the rest of society and react by rejecting the norms which underpin the political system, thus frustrating the possibility of resolving conflict by compromise. One reason why the American labor movement developed with less violence, less fragmentation of society and less appeal to radical doctrine than did its European counterparts was the fact that unionists had loyalties to church, ethnic communities and other associations not organized along economic class lines.

Id. at 989.

CORPORATIONS

The law recognizes a corporation as a legal entity separate and distinct from its shareholders. Accordingly, a corporation holds property apart from its members.

A creditor usually cannot look to an individual shareholder's assets to satisfy a debt of the corporation. Similarly, a creditor usually cannot look to the corporation's assets to satisfy a debtor-shareholder's debts. In addition, a corporation, as a legal entity, continues in existence notwithstanding changes to its membership. Further, a corporation can sue others or can be sued.

There are many types of corporations, including business, public, and charitable corporations. All share the characteristics mentioned above.

WILLS

A will is a legal instrument that directs how a person wishes to dispose of her property upon her death. The will is completely inoperative until the testator's death. The party who makes the will, called the "testator," can change her mind as to the dispositions in the will and revoke the will or write a new will to replace the old.

For the most part, the testator can leave her property in any way she desires, meaning there is "freedom of testation." An exception is in favor of the surviving spouse. One writer has remarked, "The power of disposition [of property in a will] is felt psychologically to constitute an essential element of power over property." Lawrence M. Friedman, The Law of the Living, The Law of the Dead: Property, Succession, and Society, 1966 Wis. L. Rev. 340, 355. Other writers set forth additional reasons for "the power of testation":

> It has been said to be a necessary complement of the immortality of the soul, a stimulus to increased productive or acquisitive activity, a means of maintaining family discipline, and a postulate necessarily flowing from the democratic principle of freedom. Freedom of testation, as an alternative to the fixed, unbending rules of intestacy [dying without a will], permits a property owner flexibility in considering and weighing the individual needs and deserts of the various members of his family as well as of other persons and institutions that may be dependent upon him.

Max M. Rheinstein & Mary Ann Glendon, The Law of Decedents' Estates 8 (1971).

CONTRACTS

A contract is a legally enforceable agreement. An agreement consists of promises made by parties to each other in the form of "I promise to do X, if you promise to do Y." Enforceable agreements (contracts) can be simple, such as your agreement to mow your neighbor's lawn for $25, or complex, such as an agreement between corporate titans to exchange millions of dollars of property. Agreements between parties create expectations that the other party will perform.

Not all agreements are legally enforceable. For example, the parties must intend to be legally bound. So if you promise your mother to wash the dishes in exchange for more dessert, you may have an agreement, but it is not likely that either of you intends to be legally bound.

Contract law deals with the important issue of which agreements society should enforce and why it should enforce them. The role of contract law

> has as its ultimate purpose the security of those reasonable expectations that arise from agreement between seller and buyer, borrower and depositor, stockholder and corporation, employer and organized employees. This is essentially Bentham's analysis and it has never been improved on. . . . In "progressive" societies, . . . one's legal rights and duties depend far less on caste or fixed social condition and far more on expectations created and obligations assumed by his own contracts.

Harry W. Jones, The Jurisprudence of Contracts, 44 U. Cin. L. Rev. 43, 48 (1975).

THE IMPORTANCE OF PRIVATE ARRANGEMENTS

The purpose of the above partial inventory of private arrangements is to illustrate very briefly their importance to society. It should be no surprise that the law supports these arrangements in part by giving people the power to make them. Each arrangement contributes to the well-being of society by helping people to achieve their purposes, whether it be to organize an association to pursue common purposes, to create a corporation that insulates its members from liability, to leave property upon death, or to reach an agreement to exchange property or services. These are only a few examples of private arrangements facilitated by law.

Some people think that some arrangements are too heavily regulated by the state and should be more private. For example, some scholars interested in marriage believe that most mandatory laws regarding marriages (including the prohibition against same-sex marriages) are out of date because of the loosening of social norms. In fact, some writers believe that the law should treat marriages more like everyday contracts, so that parties can create terms that work for them. Under this model, the parties could choose, for example, the duration of their marriage, the amount of support, and how to resolve disputes. Supporters of this model suppose that partners would be better off with more freedom in marriage terms than under existing rigid marriage regulations. Opponents believe, among other things, that couples who are in love and trust each other do not usually want to plan and bargain over marriage terms. The next excerpt elaborates on these themes.

ELIZABETH S. SCOTT & ROBERT E. SCOTT, MARRIAGE AS RELATIONAL CONTRACT
84 Va. L. Rev. 1225, 1238–41 (1998)

[S]cholars, and others who believe that the conception of marriage as contract distorts and undermines the meaning of this unique relationship, regret family law's trend toward private ordering. If the contractual theory of marriage prevails, these scholars warn, marriage will no longer be understood as a cooperative, altruistic relationship characterized by long-term commitment; instead, it will be transformed into a relationship of two self-interested persons (usually described as atomistic) who enter into a limited agreement in which each seeks to advance selfish goals and under which both are likely to behave opportunistically. When such a marriage no longer serves the individual self-interest of either party, the relationship is discarded in favor of a more desirable alternative, at great cost to the discarded spouse and children. According to communitarian critics, a contractual model of marriage contrasts starkly with one in which marriage was a permanent and stable commitment, inviting the couple instead to "unite temporarily for their mutual convenience."

The law's embrace of private ordering in marriage is part of a broader policy of maximizing the freedom of individuals to pursue personal ends in intimate relationships. Those who dislike the individualistic norm tend to view its various expressions in divorce law as all of a piece. Thus, on the view of many communitarian critics, an understanding of the marriage relationship in contractual terms is inevitably linked to limited commitment motivated by selfish interest, to a unilateral right of termination, and to policies promoting a clean break without regret when marriage ends. . . .

The law's ability to regulate the marriage relationship is more limited under a contractual regime than under traditional law. From the perspective both of those who regret the modern stance of moral neutrality toward marriage and those who endorse it as a core value in liberal society, the limited function of law is seen as an integral component of a contractual regime. The law's principal role in such a regime is to provide the background rules for enforcing marital contracts, a function that, it is often assumed, requires formal passivity about the substance of the agreements that couples make. A further implication of taking private ordering seriously, on this view, is that the law becomes indifferent to choices about intimate arrangements and neutral as between cohabitation and marriage. The upshot is that a contractual model of marriage negates the ability of the state to promote marital stability, a key focus of traditional law.

Many critics of modern divorce law target the abolition of fault grounds for divorce as exemplifying the deficiencies of the new legal regime. This criticism, however, takes very different forms.

Communitarian scholars view fault grounds for divorce as expressing a societal consensus about the moral obligations spouses owe to one another. A breach that constitutes a fault ground is a serious moral violation, one that causes an injury to the innocent spouse and society, and should be punished. It follows that the abolition of fault is emblematic of an amoral stance toward marital obligation and an endorsement of the parties' authority over the terms of the relationship. The no-fault "reform" is thus seen as inextricably linked to the modern conception of marriage as contract. With the removal of fault, marriage is more like a commercial venture. The couple is free to set the terms that serve their interests and to terminate the relationship when it is no longer useful to them. Under the no-fault regime, the notion of condemning a moral wrong is as out of place as it would be in a commercial contract.

Law and economics critics also regret the removal of fault, but on contractual rather than moral grounds. They treat the marriage vows as essential terms of the marital contract. A spouse who is guilty of a fault ground commits a breach of the marriage contract and should be liable for damages. The removal of fault grounds and the ability of spouses unilaterally to abandon the marriage under modern divorce law eliminates any remedy for breach and makes the contract illusory and unenforceable. This, in turn, encourages opportunistic behavior because no effective sanction deters defection from a norm of mutual cooperation. In such a regime, traditional wives, whose most valuable performance occurs in the early years of the marriage (childbearing and rearing years) are vulnerable to strategic behavior by their husbands, whose performance increases in value over the years of the marriage as their earning power increases. Husbands are motivated to appropriate the benefits of their wives' performance and thereafter either leave the marriage or defect from the relationship. For this reason, wives are deterred from undertaking optimal marriage-specific investments. These critics argue that by resurrecting fault as a criterion for property settlement and support determinations, breach of performance of the marriage vows could (and would) be recognized as the basis for a remedy upon divorce. With the abolition of fault, the current scheme of legal regulation has contributed to the instability of marriage and undermined the welfare of wives and children.

B. Rules of Validation

The law facilitates private arrangements, not only by recognizing them and allowing people to make them, but also by creating legal instructions for creating such arrangements. Such rules we call rules of validation. They can be court-made or statutory. Here we narrow the focus to rules of validation in the areas of contracts, which are predominantly court-made rules, and corporations, which are predominantly rules enacted by legislatures. Most people think of contracts and corporations as two of the most important private arrangements facilitated by law.

We offer these rules so that you can better understand not only the nature of private-arrangement law and what it does, but also its shortcomings and limitations in achieving its purposes. As such, the rules offered in this subsection serve as a backdrop and basis for evaluation of the materials in the rest of this chapter.

CONTRACTS

We next set out the two most important requirements for enforceable contracts. There must be an agreement, and the agreement must constitute a "bargained-for exchange."

Rule # 1: An Enforceable Contract Requires an Agreement. The rules defining an agreement enable us to distinguish between mere talk, negotiations, preliminary drafts, and the like, on the one hand, and legally enforceable contracts, on the other hand. If you tell your friend, Ira, that you are thinking of selling your car to him for $400, he cannot bind you to anything even if he tells you that he agrees to purchase the car. You and Ira did not reach an agreement.

Conversely, if you say to Ira something like, "I offer my 1972 Datsun 510 to you for $400, as is," and he accepts your offer, you are bound, even if inwardly you were joking or otherwise had no intention to sell the car. In other words, contract law enforces agreements based on apparent, not actual, intentions. Although the next case, *Lucy v. Zehmer*, involves amusing facts, it is rather famous among people who know contract law for illustrating this point. As you read the case, think about the possible reasons for this approach.

[handwritten in margin: When do you need a notary? ←]

LUCY v. ZEHMER
Supreme Court of Appeals of Virginia, 1954
196 Va. 493, 84 S.E.2d 516

BUCHANAN, JUSTICE:
This suit was instituted by W.O. Lucy and J.C. Lucy, complainants [and brothers], against A.H. Zehmer and Ida S. Zehmer, his wife, defendants, to have specific performance of a contract by which it was alleged the Zehmers had sold to W.O. Lucy a tract of land owned by A.H. Zehmer in Dinwiddie county containing 471.6 acres, more or less, known as the Ferguson farm, for $50,000. J.C. Lucy, the other complainant, is a brother of W.O. Lucy, to whom W.O. Lucy transferred a half interest in his alleged purchase.

The instrument sought to be enforced was written by A.H. Zehmer on December 20, 1952, in these words: "We hereby agree to sell to W.O. Lucy the Ferguson Farm complete for $50,000.00, title satisfactory to buyer," and signed by the defendants, A.H. Zehmer and Ida S. Zehmer.

The answer of A.H. Zehmer admitted that at the time mentioned W.O. Lucy offered him $50,000 cash for the farm, but that he, Zehmer, considered that the offer was made in jest; that so thinking, and both he and Lucy having had several drinks, he wrote out "the memorandum" quoted above and induced his wife to sign it; that he did not deliver the memorandum to Lucy, but that Lucy picked it up, read it, put it in his pocket, attempted to offer Zehmer $5 to bind the bargain, which Zehmer refused to accept, and realizing for the first time that Lucy was serious, Zehmer assured him that he had no intention of selling the farm and that the whole matter was a joke. Lucy left the premises insisting that he had purchased the farm.

Depositions were taken and the decree appealed from was entered holding that the complainants had failed to establish their right to specific performance, and dismissing their bill. The assignment of error is to this action of the court.

W.O. Lucy, a lumberman and farmer, thus testified in substance: He had known Zehmer for fifteen or twenty years and had been familiar with the Ferguson farm for ten years. Seven or eight years ago he had offered Zehmer $20,000 for the farm which Zehmer had accepted, but the agreement was verbal and Zehmer backed out. On the night of December 20, 1952, around eight o'clock, he took an employee to McKenney, where Zehmer lived and operated a restaurant, filling station and motor court. While there he decided to see Zehmer and again try to buy the Ferguson farm. He entered the restaurant and talked to Mrs. Zehmer until Zehmer came in. He asked Zehmer if he had sold the Ferguson farm. Zehmer replied that he had not. Lucy said, "I bet you wouldn't take $50,000.00 for that place." Zehmer replied, "Yes, I would too; you wouldn't give fifty." Lucy said he would and told Zehmer to write up an agreement to that effect. Zehmer took a restaurant check and wrote on the back of it, "I do hereby agree to sell to W.O. Lucy the Ferguson Farm for $50,000 complete." Lucy told him he had better change it to "We" because

Mrs. Zehmer would have to sign it too. Zehmer then tore up what he had written, wrote the agreement quoted above and asked Mrs. Zehmer, who was at the other end of the counter ten or twelve feet away, to sign it. Mrs. Zehmer said she would for $50,000 and signed it. Zehmer brought it back and gave it to Lucy, who offered him $5 which Zehmer refused, saying, "You don't need to give me any money, you got the agreement there signed by both of us."

The discussion leading to the signing of the agreement, said Lucy, lasted thirty or forty minutes, during which Zehmer seemed to doubt that Lucy could raise $50,000. Lucy suggested the provision for having the title examined and Zehmer made the suggestion that he would sell it "complete, everything there," and stated that all he had on the farm was three heifers.

Lucy took a partly filled bottle of whiskey into the restaurant with him for the purpose of giving Zehmer a drink if he wanted it. Zehmer did, and he and Lucy had one or two drinks together. Lucy said that while he felt the drinks he took he was not intoxicated, and from the way Zehmer handled the transaction he did not think he was either. ✱

December 20 was on Saturday. Next day Lucy telephoned to J.C. Lucy and arranged with the latter to take a half interest in the purchase and pay half of the consideration. On Monday he engaged an attorney to examine the title. The attorney reported favorably on December 31 and on January 2 Lucy wrote Zehmer stating that the title was satisfactory, that he was ready to pay the purchase price in cash and asking when Zehmer would be ready to close the deal. Zehmer replied by letter, mailed on January 13, asserting that he had never agreed or intended to sell.

Mr. and Mrs. Zehmer were called by the complainants as adverse witnesses. Zehmer testified in substance as follows:

He bought this farm more than ten years ago for $11,000. He had had twenty-five offers, more or less, to buy it, including several from Lucy, who had never offered any specific sum of money. He had given them all the same answer, that he was not interested in selling it. On this Saturday night before Christmas it looked like everybody and his brother came by there to have a drink. He took a good many drinks during the afternoon and had a pint of his own. When he entered the restaurant around eight-thirty Lucy was there and he could see that he was "pretty high." He said to Lucy, "Boy, you got some good liquor, drinking, ain't you?" Lucy then offered him a drink. "I was already high as a Georgia pine, and didn't have any more better sense than to pour another great big slug out and gulp it down, and he took one too."

After they had talked a while Lucy asked whether he still had the Ferguson farm. He replied that he had not sold it and Lucy said, "I bet you wouldn't take $50,000.00 for it." Zehmer asked him if he would give $50,000 and Lucy said yes. Zehmer replied, "You haven't got $50,000.00 in cash." Lucy said he did and Zehmer replied that he did not believe it. They argued "pro and con for a long time," mainly about "whether he had $50,000 in cash that he could put up right then and buy that farm."

Finally, said Zehmer, Lucy told him if he didn't believe he had $50,000, "you sign that piece of paper here and say you will take $50,000.00 for the farm." He, Zehmer, "just grabbed the back off of a guest check there" and wrote on the back of it. At that point in his testimony Zehmer asked to see what he had written to "see if I recognize my own handwriting." He examined the paper and exclaimed, "Great balls of fire, I got 'Firgerson' for Ferguson. I have got satisfactory spelled wrong. I don't recognize that writing if I would see it, wouldn't know it was mine."

After Zehmer had, as he described it, "scribbled this thing off," Lucy said, "Get your wife to sign it." Zehmer walked over to where she was and she at first refused to sign but did so after he told her that he "was just needling him [Lucy], and didn't mean a thing in the world, that I was not selling the farm." Zehmer then "took it back over there . . . and I was still looking at the dern thing. I had the drink right there by my hand, and I reached over to get a drink, and he said, 'Let me see it.' He reached and picked it up, and when I looked back again he had it in his pocket and he dropped a five dollar bill over there, and he said, 'Here is five dollars payment on it.' . . . I said, 'Hell no, that is beer and liquor

talking. I am not going to sell you the farm. I have told you that too many times before.' " . . .

On examination by her own counsel [Mrs. Zehmer testified] that her husband laid this piece of paper down after it was signed; that Lucy said to let him see it, took it, folded it and put it in his wallet, then said to Zehmer, "Let me give you $5.00," but Zehmer said, "No, this is liquor talking. I don't want to sell the farm, I have told you that I want my son to have it. This is all a joke." Lucy then said at least twice, "Zehmer, you have sold your farm," wheeled around and started for the door. He paused at the door and said, "I will bring you $50,000.00 tomorrow. . . . No, tomorrow is Sunday. I will bring it to you Monday." She said you could tell definitely that he was drinking and she said to her husband, "You should have taken him home," but he said, "Well, I am just about as bad off as he is." . . .

The defendants insist that the evidence was ample to support their contention that the writing sought to be enforced was prepared as a bluff or dare to force Lucy to admit that he did not have $50,000; that the whole matter was a joke; that the writing was not delivered to Lucy and no binding contract was ever made between the parties.

It is an unusual, if not bizarre, defense. When made to the writing admittedly prepared by one of the defendants and signed by both, clear evidence is required to sustain it.

In his testimony Zehmer claimed that he "was high as a Georgia pine," and that the transaction "was just a bunch of two doggoned drunks bluffing to see who could talk the biggest and say the most." That claim is inconsistent with his attempt to testify in great detail as to what was said and what was done. It is contradicted by other evidence as to the condition of both parties, and rendered of no weight by the testimony of his wife that when Lucy left the restaurant she suggested that Zehmer drive him home. The record is convincing that Zehmer was not intoxicated to the extent of being unable to comprehend the nature and consequences of the instrument he executed, and hence that instrument is not to be invalidated on that ground. It was in fact conceded by defendants' counsel in oral argument that under the evidence Zehmer was not too drunk to make a valid contract.

The evidence is convincing also that Zehmer wrote two agreements, the first one beginning "I hereby agree to sell." Zehmer first said he could not remember about that, then that "I don't think I wrote but one out." Mrs. Zehmer said that what he wrote was "I hereby agree," but that the "I" was changed to "We" after that night. The agreement that was written and signed is in the record and indicates no such change. Neither are the mistakes in spelling that Zehmer sought to point out readily apparent.

The appearance of the contract, the fact that it was under discussion for forty minutes or more before it was signed; Lucy's objection to the first draft because it was written in the singular, and he wanted Mrs. Zehmer to sign it also; the rewriting to meet that objection and the signing by Mrs. Zehmer; the discussion of what was to be included in the sale, the provision for the examination of the title, the completeness of the instrument that was executed, the taking possession of it by Lucy with no request or suggestion by either of the defendants that he give it back, are facts which furnish persuasive evidence that the execution of the contract was a serious business transaction rather than a casual, jesting matter as defendants now contend. . . .

If it be assumed, contrary to what we think the evidence shows, that Zehmer was jesting about selling his farm to Lucy and that the transaction was intended by him to be a joke, nevertheless the evidence shows that Lucy did not so understand it but considered it to be a serious business transaction and the contract to be binding on the Zehmers as well as on himself. The very next day he arranged with his brother to put up half the money and take a half interest in the land. The day after that he employed an attorney to examine the title. The next night, Tuesday, he was back at Zehmer's place and there Zehmer told him for the first time, Lucy said, that he wasn't going to sell and he told Zehmer, "You know you sold that place fair and square." After receiving the report from his attorney that the title was good he wrote to Zehmer that he was ready to close the deal.

Not only did Lucy actually believe, but the evidence shows he was warranted in believing, that the contract represented a serious business transaction and a good faith sale and purchase of the farm.

In the field of contracts, as generally elsewhere, "We must look to the outward expression of a person as manifesting his intention rather than to his secret and unexpressed intention. 'The law imputes to a person an intention corresponding to the reasonable meaning of his words and acts.'" First Nat. Exchange Bank of Roanoke v. Roanoke Oil Co., 169 Va. 99, 114, 192 S.E. 764, 770.

At no time prior to the execution of the contract had Zehmer indicated to Lucy by word or act that he was not in earnest about selling the farm. They had argued about it and discussed its terms, as Zehmer admitted, for a long time. Lucy testified that if there was any jesting it was about paying $50,000 that night. The contract and the evidence show that he was not expected to pay the money that night. Zehmer said that after the writing was signed he laid it down on the counter in front of Lucy. Lucy said Zehmer handed it to him. In any event there had been what appeared to be a good faith offer and a good faith acceptance, followed by the execution and apparent delivery of a written contract. Both said that Lucy put the writing in his pocket and then offered Zehmer $5 to seal the bargain. Not until then, even under the defendants' evidence, was anything said or done to indicate that the matter was a joke. Both of the Zehmers testified that when Zehmer asked his wife to sign he whispered that it was a joke so Lucy wouldn't hear and that it was not intended that he should hear.

The mental assent of the parties is not requisite for the formation of a contract. If the words or other acts of one of the parties have but one reasonable meaning, his undisclosed intention is immaterial except when an unreasonable meaning which he attaches to his manifestations is known to the other party. Restatement of the Law of Contracts, Vol. I, §71, p. 74. . . .

An agreement or mutual assent is of course essential to a valid contract but the law imputes to a person an intention corresponding to the reasonable meaning of his words and acts. If his words and acts, judged by a reasonable standard, manifest an intention to agree, it is immaterial what may be the real but unexpressed state of his mind. 17 C.J.S., Contracts, §32, p. 361; 12 Am. Jur., Contracts, §19, p. 515.

So a person cannot set up that he was merely jesting when his conduct and words would warrant a reasonable person in believing that he intended a real agreement.

Whether the writing signed by the defendants and now sought to be enforced by the complainants was the result of a serious offer by Lucy and a serious acceptance by the defendants, or was a serious offer by Lucy and an acceptance in secret jest by the defendants, in either event it constituted a binding contract of sale between the parties. . . .

The complainants are entitled to have specific performance of the contract sued on. The decree appealed from is therefore reversed and the cause is remanded for the entry of a proper decree requiring the defendants to perform the contract in accordance with the prayer of the bill.

Reversed and remanded.

[handwritten margin notes: Holding — Lucy wins, Contract is Valid.]

NOTES

1. *Lucy v. Zehmer* may be wrongly decided. Plentiful evidence suggested that Zehmer was joking. Consider, for example, where and when the "negotiations" took place, the drinking, and Zehmer's previous refusals to sell the farm. Further, the "agreement," although written, was almost hopelessly incomplete. Contracts for the sale of land usually consist of three or four pages of printed form contract, including a detailed description of the property and terms governing title, mortgage commitments, and time and place for completing the transaction. Compare Lucy and Zehmer's "contract."

2. Even if the court's decision on the facts is incorrect, much more important is the law that the court applied in the case. The court ruled that it " 'must look to the outward expression of a person as manifesting his intention rather than to his secret and unexpressed intention.'" Another judge made the same point in more flowery prose: "A contract has, strictly speaking, nothing to do with the personal, or individual, intent of the parties. . . . If . . . it were proved by twenty bishops that either party, when he used the words, intended something else than the usual meaning which the law imposes upon them, he would still be held, unless there were some mutual mistake, or something else of the sort." Hotchkiss v. Nat'l City Bank of New York, 200 F. 287, 293 (S.D.N.Y. 1911), aff'd, 201 F. 664 (2d Cir. 1912), aff'd, 231 U.S. 50, 34 S. Ct. 20 (1913). The court in *Lucy v. Zehmer* therefore held that the parties entered an enforceable contract even if Zehmer was not serious, because Lucy reasonably believed Zehmer was serious: "[T]he evidence shows he was warranted in believing . . . that the contract represented a serious business transaction." The requirement that Lucy's belief be reasonable is known as the objective test of assent.

3. The court suggests that Lucy's belief about Zehmer's intentions must not only be reasonable, but honest as well: "[T]he evidence shows that Lucy . . . considered it to be a serious business transaction." The requirement that Lucy's belief be honestly held is a subjective test of what Lucy was actually thinking. Keep in mind, though, that Zehmer's subjective intent is irrelevant.

Chitchat Among Friends May Not Create a Contract

The Associated Press reported that Jay Arsenault caught Barry Bonds' 600th home run. A friend gave Jay his ticket to the game after Jay promised to split any proceeds if he caught Bonds' home-run ball. Putting aside the question of the value of the ball after all of the revelations about Bonds' steroid use, must Jay live up to his promise? Perhaps not. Under the objective test of intent to contract that you saw applied in *Lucy v. Zehmer*, a reasonable interpretation of the "agreement" here may be that Jay and his friend had no intention of entering a binding agreement, but were simply engaging in "chitchat," especially since the odds were so low that Jay would actually catch Bonds' 600th home run ball.

In *Lucy v. Zehmer*, Zehmer is bound if a reasonable person would believe (the objective test of assent) and Lucy honestly believed (the subjective test of assent) that Zehmer intended to contract. You can see from *Lucy v. Zehmer* that courts resolve the objective test of assent by examining the circumstances, including the language and length of the supposed agreement, the length, quality, and setting of the negotiations, the subject matter of the contract, the previous conduct of the parties, and anything else that may be relevant in the particular circumstances.

Why does contract law utilize the objective test of a party's assent? In this way, contract law protects people like Lucy who rely on their contracts. Further, the approach encourages such reliance. You can rely on your contract for the sale of your car because your buyer cannot avoid it simply by claiming that she was joking. Nevertheless, some people such as Zehmer (if he really was joking) will be bound to a contract when they did not intend to contract. Thus, to this extent, contract law does not support Zehmer's autonomy. Quite the opposite.

In the *Lefkowitz* case that follows, also a famous case, we see that courts apply the objective test of assent to other related issues of contract formation.

LEFKOWITZ v. GREAT MINNEAPOLIS SURPLUS STORE, INC.
Supreme Court of Minnesota, 1957
251 Minn. 188, 86 N.W.2d 689

Murphy, Justice:

This is an appeal from an order of the Municipal Court of Minneapolis denying the motion of the defendant for amended findings of fact, or, in the alternative, for a new trial.

The order for judgment awarded the plaintiff the sum of $138.50 as damages for breach of contract.

This case grows out of the alleged refusal of the defendant to sell to the plaintiff a certain fur piece which it had offered for sale in a newspaper advertisement. It appears from the record that on April 6, 1956, the defendant published the following advertisement in a Minneapolis newspaper:

Saturday 9 A.M. Sharp
3 Brand New
Fur Coats
Worth to $100.00
First Come
First Served

$1

Each

On April 13, the defendant again published an advertisement in the same newspaper as follows:

Saturday 9 A.M.
2 Brand New Pastel
Mink 3–Skin Scarfs
Selling for $89.50
Out they go
Saturday, Each. . . . $1.00
1 Black Lapin Stole
Beautiful,
worth $139.50. . . . $1.00
First Come
First Served

The record supports the findings of the court that on each of the Saturdays following the publication of the above-described ads the plaintiff was the first to present himself at the appropriate counter in the defendant's store and on each occasion demanded the coat and the stole so advertised and indicated his readiness to pay the sale price of $1. On both occasions, the defendant refused to sell the merchandise to the plaintiff, stating on the first occasion that by a "house rule" the offer was intended for women only and sales would not be made to men, and on the second visit that plaintiff knew defendant's house rules.

The trial court properly disallowed plaintiff's claim for the value of the fur coats since the value of these articles was speculative and uncertain. The only evidence of value was the advertisement itself to the effect that the coats were "Worth to $100.00," how much less being speculative especially in view of the price for which they were offered for sale. With reference to the offer of the defendant on April 13, 1956, to sell the "1 Black Lapin Stole . . . worth $139.50 . . ." the trial court held that the value of this article was established and granted judgment in favor of the plaintiff for that amount less the $1 quoted purchase price.

. . . [The defendant] relies upon authorities which hold that, where an advertiser publishes in a newspaper that he has a certain quantity or quality of goods which he wants to dispose of at certain prices and on certain terms, such advertisements are not offers which become contracts

as soon as any person to whose notice they may come signifies his acceptance by notifying the other that he will take a certain quantity of them. Such advertisements have been construed as an invitation for an offer of sale on the terms stated, which offer, when received, may be accepted or rejected and which therefore does not become a contract of sale until accepted by the seller; and until a contract has been so made, the seller may modify or revoke such prices or terms.

. . . On the facts before us we are concerned with whether the advertisement constituted an offer, and, if so, whether the plaintiff's conduct constituted an acceptance.

There are numerous authorities which hold that a particular advertisement in a newspaper or circular letter relating to a sale of articles may be construed by the court as constituting an offer, acceptance of which would complete a contract.

The test of whether a binding obligation may originate in advertisements addressed to the general public is "whether the facts show that some performance was promised in positive terms in return for something requested." 1 Williston, Contracts (Rev. ed.) §27.

The authorities above cited emphasize that, where the offer is clear, definite, and explicit, and leaves nothing open for negotiation, it constitutes an offer, acceptance of which will complete the contract. The most recent case on the subject is Johnson v. Capital City Ford Co., La. App., 85 So. 2d 75, in which the court pointed out that a newspaper advertisement relating to the purchase and sale of automobiles may constitute an offer, acceptance of which will consummate a contract and create an obligation in the offeror to perform according to the terms of the published offer.

Whether in any individual instance a newspaper advertisement is an offer rather than an invitation to make an offer depends on the legal intention of the parties and the surrounding circumstances. We are of the view on the facts before us that the offer by the defendant of the sale of the Lapin fur was clear, definite, and explicit, and left nothing open for negotiation. The plaintiff having successfully managed to be the first one to appear at the seller's place of business to be served, as requested by the advertisement, and having offered the stated purchase price of the article, he was entitled to performance on the part of the defendant. We think the trial court was correct in holding that there was in the conduct of the parties a sufficient mutuality of obligation to constitute a contract of sale.

The defendant contends that the offer was modified by a "house rule" to the effect that only women were qualified to receive the bargains advertised. The advertisement contained no such restriction. This objection may be disposed of briefly by stating that, while an advertiser has the right at any time before acceptance to modify his offer, he does not have the right, after acceptance, to impose new or arbitrary conditions not contained in the published offer.

Affirmed.

NOTES

1. The store was not liable for the first advertisement on April 6, according to the court, because the value of the articles was "speculative and uncertain." Two defenses arise from this observation. First, a reasonable person might not believe the advertisement was an offer because the lack of sufficient information suggests the store did not intend to make a specific offer. Second, contract law does not enforce contracts if the remedy is too speculative. Here, the court could not fashion an appropriate remedy when the value of the articles is unknown.

2. Arguably, the store should not have been liable based on the April 13 advertisement either because Lefkowitz actually knew the house rule that only women could purchase. After all, the facts show that the store told him the house rule on April 6.

3. *Lefkowitz v. Great Minneapolis Surplus Store* utilizes the objective test of assent and applies it to newspaper advertisements. The issue is whether a reasonable person would believe the store intended to be bound upon an acceptance by a member of the reading public. In situations where the answer to that question is "yes," contract law calls the advertisement an offer.

The same test of an offer applies whether the communication is in a newspaper or made in some other manner. The court in Leonard v. Pepsico, Inc., 210 F.3d 88, 89 (2d Cir. 2000), considered a television promotion:

> In 1995, defendant-appellee Pepsico, Inc. conducted a promotion in which it offered merchandise in exchange for "points" earned by purchasing Pepsi Cola. A television commercial aired by Pepsico depicted a teenager gloating over various items of merchandise earned by Pepsi points, and culminated in the teenager arriving at high school in a Harrier Jet, a fighter aircraft of the United States Marine Corps. For each item of merchandise sported by the teenager (a T shirt, a jacket, sunglasses), the ad noted the number of Pepsi points needed to get it. When the teenager is shown in the jet, the ad prices it as 7 million points.
>
> Plaintiff-appellant John D.R. Leonard alleges that the ad was an offer, that he accepted the offer by tendering the equivalent of 7 million points, and that Pepsico has breached its contract to deliver the Harrier jet. Pepsico characterizes the use of the Harrier jet in the ad as a hyperbolic joke ("zany humor"), cites the ad's

reference to offering details contained in the promotional catalog (which contains no Harrier fighter plane), and argues that no objective person would construe the ad as an offer for the Harrier jet.

The United States District Court for the Southern District of New York (Wood, J.) agreed with Pepsico and granted its motion for summary judgment on the grounds (1) that the commercial did not amount to an offer of goods; (2) that no objective person could reasonably have concluded that the commercial actually offered consumers a Harrier Jet; and (3) that the alleged contract could not satisfy the New York statute of frauds.

We affirm for substantially the reasons stated in Judge Wood's opinion. See 88 F. Supp. 2d 116 (S.D.N.Y. 1999).

Based on *Lefkowitz* and *Leonard*, do you think a reasonable person would believe that radio disk jockey Ben Stone made an offer when he announced that anyone who got a permanent "93 Rock" tattoo on his or her forehead would receive $30,000 per year for five years? A couple of people did so. Assume Taylor Plantations, a sophomore at a local college, was one of them. Is Taylor entitled to the money? What would a reasonable person believe about the announcement?

Rule # 2: An Enforceable Contract Requires a Bargained-For Exchange. Contract law does not enforce all promises. For example, if Alvin makes you a simple *gift promise*, "I promise to give you $100," the promise is normally not enforceable even if Alvin intends to perform when he makes the promise. By contrast, if Alvin asks for something in exchange for the $100—for example, he asks you to mow his lawn—and if you agree, the agreement is enforceable. An agreement in which each party extracts something from the other (a promise of $100 in exchange for a promise of the lawn-mowing service) is called a *bargained-for exchange*. The price you must pay for Alvin's promise is your promise to mow his lawn, and contract law calls this promise consideration. Contract law says Alvin's promise is "supported by consideration" and therefore enforceable.

Sometimes it is difficult to distinguish gift promises from bargained-for exchanges. One of your editors illustrated the point in Robert A. Hillman, Principles of Contract Law 16 (2d ed. 2009):

> Suppose a "benevolent" person, Ron D. Jockefeller, promises to buy clothes for a homeless person if the homeless person walks to a clothing store a few blocks away. If the homeless person walks to the store, is Jockefeller's promise of the clothes enforceable? Only if Jockefeller "bargained for" the homeless person to walk to the store, which in turn depends on whether Jockefeller's motive was to extract the walk as the price of the promise of clothes. But in order to understand Jockefeller's motive, we need more facts. Suppose Jockefeller owned a restaurant and the homeless person had camped out in front of the restaurant. These facts support a finding that Jockefeller's motive for his promise was to remove the homeless person from the vicinity of the restaurant and we can therefore say that Jockefeller "bargained for" the homeless person's walk to the clothing store. But if Jockefeller did not own a restaurant and made the promise, not because he would get something in return, but simply because he is a

wonderful person, the promise would constitute a gift promise and be unenforceable. The homeless person still must walk to the store to pick up the gift. But those in the know say that the trip to the store is a condition necessary to pick up a gift, not consideration to support Jockefeller's promise.

A promisor's gratitude for someone's past good conduct or services does not constitute consideration because the promisor does not extract anything from the other party. That other party does not supply anything *as the price* of the promise, as we see in the following case from New York's highest court.

DOUGHERTY v. SALT

New York Court of Appeals, 1919
227 N.Y. 200, 125 N.E. 94

Action by Charles Napoleon Dougherty, an infant, by Susan M. Teves, his guardian, against Emma L. Salt, as executrix of the last will and testament of Helena M. Dougherty, deceased. From a judgment of the second department of the Appellate Division of the Supreme Court (184 App. Div. 910, 170 N.Y. Supp. 1076), reversing a judgment of the Trial Term, which set aside a verdict of the jury in favor of plaintiff and dismissed the complaint, and reinstating the verdict and directing judgment thereon, the defendant appeals. . . .

CARDOZO, J:

The plaintiff, a boy of eight years, received from his aunt, the defendant's testatrix, a promissory note for $3,000, payable at her death or before. Use was made of a printed form, which contains the words "value received." How the note came to be given was explained by the boy's guardian, who was a witness for his ward. The aunt was visiting her nephew.

When she saw Charley coming in, she said, "Isn't he a nice boy?" I answered her, "Yes; that he is getting along very nice, and getting along nice in school"; and I showed where he had progressed in school, having good reports, and so forth, and she told me that she was going to take care of that child; that she loved him very much. I said, "I know you do, Tillie, but your taking care of the child will be done probably like your brother and sister done, take it out in talk." She said, "I don't intend to take it out in talk; I would like to take care of him

now." I said, "Well, that is up to you." She said, "Why can't I make out a note to him?" I said, "You can, if you wish to." She said, "Would that be right?" And I said, "I do not know, but I guess it would; I do not know why it would not." And she said, "Well, will you make out a note for me?" I said, "Yes, if you wish me to," and she said, "Well, I wish you would."

A blank was then produced, filled out, and signed. The aunt handed the note to her nephew, with these words:

You have always done for me, and I have signed this note for you. Now, do not lose it. Some day it will be valuable.

The trial judge submitted to the jury the question whether there was any consideration for the promised payment. Afterwards, he set aside the verdict in favor of the plaintiff, and dismissed the complaint. The Appellate Division, by a divided court, reversed the judgment of dismissal, and reinstated the verdict on the ground that the note was sufficient evidence of consideration.

We reach a different conclusion. The inference of consideration to be drawn from the form of the note has been so overcome and rebutted as to leave no question for a jury. This is not a case where witnesses, summoned by the defendant and friendly to the defendant's cause, supply the testimony in disproof of value. Strickland v. Henry, 175 N.Y. 372, 67 N.E. 611. This is a case where the testimony in disproof of value comes from the plaintiff's own witness, speaking at the plaintiff's instance. The transaction thus revealed admits of one interpretation, and one only. The note was the voluntary and unenforcible promise of an executory gift. Harris v. Clark, 3 N.Y. 93; Holmes v. Roper, 141 N.Y. 64, 66, 36 N.E. 180. This child of eight was not a creditor, nor dealt with as one. The aunt was not paying a debt. She was conferring a bounty. Fink v. Cox, 18 Johns 145. The promise was neither offered nor accepted with any other purpose. "Nothing is consideration that is not regarded as such by both parties." Philpot v. Gruninger, 14 Wall. 570, 577 . . . .

A note so given is not made for "value received," however its maker may have labeled it. The formula of the printed blank becomes, in the light of the conceded facts, a mere erroneous conclusion, which cannot overcome the inconsistent conclusion of the law. . . . The plaintiff through his own witness, has explained the genesis of the promise, and consideration has been disproved. Neg. Instr. Law, §54 (Consol. Laws, c. 38).

We hold, therefore, that the verdict of the jury was contrary to law, and that the trial judge was right in setting it aside. [The court next ordered a new trial based on an issue unrelated to the contract-law issues.]

Contract law generally does not enforce gift promises such as Aunt Helena's for several reasons. For one thing, Charley's guardian seems to have goaded Helena into making the promise, and contract law should enforce promises only when a promisor truly wants to contract. For another, society may not want to devote the resources necessary to enforce gift promises between family members because such promises are numerous and often not very important.

Even if gift promises are important, for example, because they distribute wealth from richer to poorer people, *legal* enforcement of gift promises ironically might make people wary of making such promises in the first place. Would you want to make a gift promise if you knew you could not change your mind? Further, the recipient of your largesse might devalue your promise, believing that your motive for following through on your promise was not friendship or gratitude, but legal coercion. See Melvin Aron Eisenberg, The World of Contract and the World of Gift, 85 Cal. L. Rev. 821 (1997).

An Exception to the Requirement of Consideration: Promissory Estoppel. A promise that induces reasonable reliance is enforceable even without consideration. The law formulated this approach, called promissory estoppel, to protect people from the harm they would suffer if they reasonably relied on a promise that was later declared unenforceable for lack of consideration. A famous judge, Learned Hand (what a great name for a judge), made the point as follows in James Baird Co. v. Gimbel Bros., 64 F.2d 344, 346 (2d Cir. 1933):

> Offers are ordinarily made in exchange for a consideration, either a counter-promise or some other act which the promisor wishes to secure. In such cases they propose bargains; they presuppose that each promise or performance is an inducement to the other. But a man may make a promise without expecting an equivalent; a donative promise, conditional or absolute. . . . The doctrine of "promissory estoppel" is to avoid the harsh results of allowing the promisor in such a case to repudiate, when the promisee has acted in reliance upon the promise.

The next case, *Elvin Associates v. Franklin*, illustrates the use of promissory estoppel.

ELVIN ASSOCIATES v. FRANKLIN

United States District Court, Southern District of New York, 1990
735 F. Supp. 1177

WHITMAN KNAPP, DISTRICT JUDGE:

[Springer, a producer of Broadway musicals, contacted Aretha Franklin about playing the title role in a musical about Mahalia Jackson. After Franklin expressed her strong interest, the parties negotiated for several months and worked out most of the details. During negotiations, Franklin assured Springer that the producer's final proposal was acceptable and that she would perform. In reliance, Springer incurred substantial expenses making arrangements for the production, even though the parties never signed a final agreement and Springer learned that Franklin had canceled several obligations because of a newly developed fear of flying. Franklin never appeared for rehearsals, and Springer sued.]

The central issue pertaining to plaintiff's claim for breach of contract is whether or not the parties to that proposed contract... evinced an intent not to be formally bound before execution of a written, integrated contract. Language inserted in a draft of the agreement referring to its validity upon execution has generally been found to be strong (though not conclusive) evidence of intent *not* to be bound prior to execution.... Although we based our tentative findings largely on the fact that all of the incidental terms had been worked out by the final draft, and that the understanding was that Franklin would sign the agreement when she came to New York, there remains the obstacle of the preamble that Kramer, [Springer's lawyer], drafted and that remained in every draft, namely: "This letter, when countersigned by you, shall constitute our understanding until a more formal agreement is prepared." After reviewing the above cited authorities and the post-trial submissions, we are constrained to find that such language indicates that [Franklin] was not to be contractually bound to Springer until the draft agreement was executed.... The cause of action for breach of contract must therefore be dismissed....

That, however, does not end the case. As above noted, plaintiff has asserted, in the alternative, a right to recover on a theory of promissory estoppel....

It is difficult to imagine a more fitting case for applying the doctrine.... [W]e find that [Franklin] had unequivocally and intentionally committed herself to appear in the production long before the day on which it was intended that the finalized agreement with her corporation would be signed.

First, it is clear from the testimony of all of the witnesses that Franklin was enthusiastic about appearing in the production and that at all times during the relevant period gave it the highest professional priority. She early on stated to Springer: "This is what I am doing." Combined with her oral agreement, through her agents, to the basic financial terms of her engagement, her continued expression of this enthusiasm to Springer more than amply afforded Springer a reasonable basis for beginning to make the various arrangements and expenditures necessary to bring the production to fruition.

Second, Franklin could not possibly have assumed that Springer could have performed his obligations to her—which, among other things, included arranging a complicated schedule of performances to commence shortly after her arrival in New York—without committing himself to and actually spending considerable sums prior to her affixing her signature to the contract on the date of such arrival. Throughout the time that he was making those commitments and advancing the necessary sums, she accepted his performance without any disclaimer of her prior promises to him. Indeed, she actively participated in many aspects of the necessary arrangements.

Third, Franklin's expression to Springer of her fear of flying did not, as she has contended, make her promise conditional or coat it with a patina of ambiguity that should have alerted Springer to suspend his efforts to mount the production. Although Franklin rejected Springer's offer to make alternative ground transportation arrangements, her primary reason for doing so was that she was determined to overcome her fear of flying, and it was reasonable for Springer to rely on her reassurances that she would be able to fly. Moreover, it was also entirely reasonable for him to assume that if she could not overcome her fear she would travel to New York by other means, even if it meant spreading the trip over several days. In short, Franklin's fear of flying provides no basis whatsoever for avoiding liability for failing to fulfill her promise, reiterated on several occasions, to appear in "Mahalia." If she could not bring herself to fly, she should have traveled by way of ground transportation. It has not been established that she was otherwise unable to come to New York to meet her obligations.

We conclude that under the circumstances as we have outlined them it would be unconscionable not to compensate Springer for the losses he incurred through his entirely justified reliance on Franklin's oral promises. A determination of the exact amount to be awarded has been reserved for a later trial on damages. . . .

Springer won the case.

NOTES

1. Why did the court fail to give Franklin any respect?
2. The following two statements of the court seem inconsistent: (a) "[Franklin] was not to be contractually bound to Springer until the draft agreement was executed"; (b) "[W]e find that she had unequivocally and intentionally committed herself to appear in the production long before the day on which it was intended that the finalized agreement with her corporation would be signed." The only way Franklin could *contractually* commit herself to Springer's project was to sign the contract. The court nevertheless found that she could *legally* commit herself by promising to perform if the promise induced Springer to rely on her promise. The latter result is not really based on facilitating private arrangements but on remedying people's grievances, a subject studied in Chapter 1.

CORPORATIONS

We now briefly take up another kind of private arrangement so that you can compare and contrast rules of validation created by courts (contracts) and those created by legislatures (corporations). Recall that an important reason for forming corporations is to allow people to shelter their own wealth from that of their business creation: "Corporate law holds as one of its central principles that courts must treat a corporation as a 'legal entity' . . . a body formally removed from its individual shareholders. Once a shareholder is legally separated from his corporation, he is only liable for the amount he invested in the business venture." Handel C.H. Lee & David M. Blumenthal, Parent Company and Shareholder Liability: "Piercing the Veil" of Chinese Corporate Subsidiaries, 5 Bus. L. Int'l 221, 222 (2004). So, limited liability creates incentives for people to form and invest in corporations in the first place.

The following statutory rules taken from Oregon illustrate how people can form this private arrangement.

Oregon Revised Statutes

65.044 Incorporators.

One or more individuals 18 years of age or older, a domestic or foreign corporation, a partnership or an association may act as incorporators of a corporation by delivering articles of incorporation to the Secretary of State for filing.

65.047 Articles of incorporation.

(1) The articles of incorporation formed pursuant to this chapter subsequent to October 3, 1989, shall set forth:

(a) A corporate name for the corporation that satisfies the requirements of ORS 65.094;

(b) One of the following statements or words of similar import:

(A) This corporation is a public benefit corporation;

(B) This corporation is a mutual benefit corporation; or

(C) This corporation is a religious corporation;

(c) The address, including street and number, of the corporation's initial registered office and the name of its initial registered agent at that location;

(d) The name and address of each incorporator;

(e) An alternate corporate mailing address which shall be that of the principal office, as defined in ORS 65.001, to which notices, as required by this chapter, may be mailed until the principal office of the corporation has been designated by the corporation in its annual report;

(f) Whether or not the corporation will have members as that term is defined in this chapter; and

(g) Provisions regarding the distribution of assets on dissolution.

(2) The articles of incorporation may set forth:

(a) The names and addresses of the initial directors;

(b) Provisions regarding:

(A) The purpose or purposes for which the corporation is organized;

(B) Managing and regulating the affairs of the corporation;

(C) Defining, limiting and regulating the powers of the corporation, its board of directors, and members or any class of members; . . . .

(3) The incorporator or incorporators must sign the articles and before including the name of any individual as a director shall state that they have obtained the consent of each director named to serve.

(4) The articles of incorporation need not set forth any of the corporate powers enumerated in this chapter but may restrict them in order to meet federal tax code requirements or other purposes.

65.051 Incorporation.

(1) Unless a delayed effective date is specified, the corporate existence begins when the articles of incorporation are reviewed, accepted and filed by the Secretary of State.

(2) The Secretary of State's filing of the articles of incorporation is conclusive proof that the incorporators satisfied all conditions precedent to incorporation applicable at the time of incorporation . . . .

You can see the stark difference in the methods for forming enforceable contracts and viable corporations. Generally, people can form contracts informally, simply by making mutual promises. Corporation formation requires satisfying lots of ministerial tasks (for example, drafting articles of incorporation with all of the details listed in the Oregon statute).

One possible reason for the difference is that to ensure maximum freedom of contract few hurdles should be placed in front of parties seeking to contract. Another possible reason is that corporate existence has a great potential to affect third parties, such as creditors of the corporation, so the law responsibly draws up a series of bright-line requirements before an organization can claim that status. But analysts point out that filing the appropriate papers to create a corporation is not very onerous either.

ADDITIONAL PERSPECTIVES ON WHY THE LAW FACILITATES PRIVATE ARRANGEMENTS

Thus far, we have focused on personal freedom as a principal explanation for why society utilizes law to facilitate private arrangements. This is not the only perspective. For example, Professor Eric Posner enumerates and evaluates some of the theories that purport to explain why society enforces contracts:

> Fried argues that contracts should be enforced because individuals have a moral obligation to keep their promises. Fried's theory has the virtue of simplicity but cannot explain the many ways that contract law refuses to enforce promises. Unreciprocated offers, promises that lack consideration, promises that violate the Statute of Frauds, promises that lack specific terms—all of these promises are, in ordinary cases, not enforced. . . .
>
> Fuller and Perdue argue that contracts should be enforced in order to prevent one party, the promisor, from benefitting at the expense of the other party. Corrective justice demands that the breaching promisor make the promisee whole. . . .
>
> Historical explanations of contract law once held promise, but early enthusiasm has given way to skepticism. Consider the attempt to link trends in contract-law doctrine to the rise of the welfare state. Scholars claimed that the increasing informality of contract law over the last century, and especially the rise of promissory estoppel, showed courts moving away from laissez faire and toward statism and the enforcement of community standards. The convenient link to other trends in political economy, and specifically the rise of the welfare state, obscured the poor fit between the theory and doctrinal trends. The rise of promissory estoppel, for example, could be interpreted as reflecting judicial impatience with a formality—the consideration doctrine—that interfered with, rather than promoted, private contracting. Contract doctrine can coexist with many different political systems, and broad trends, such as the decline of formalism, do not necessarily reflect changes in politics or morality.

Eric A. Posner, Economic Analysis of Contract Law After Three Decades: Success or Failure?, 112 Yale L.J. 829, 870-74 (2003).

An additional theory for enforcing agreements comes from economic analysis of law. A prominent school of economic analysts observes that through the process of exchange, people allocate society's scarce resources. Exchange is socially valuable because it moves resources to "higher-valued uses" and therefore increases "allocative efficiency." By this analysts mean that (1) people exchange goods and services because they value what they get more than what they give up; (2) an exchange therefore increases the wealth of each of the parties and therefore society's overall wealth; and (3) people thus promote society's interests by pursuing their own self-interest. Critics of this approach assert, however, that economic analysis assumes simplistically that people's motivation is based rationally on the desire to maximize their welfare as measured by an increase in wealth. Such an assumption ignores the complexities and contradictions of human behavior. Critics believe economic analysts ignore altruism, fairness, and reciprocity, to name a few of people's noneconomic motivations.

Finally, certain critics of contract law, most prominently in the latter part of the twentieth century, claim that contract rules are relatively "indeterminate," meaning that courts applying rules can reach virtually any decision they please because of the vagueness of the legal rules. Because courts are ideologically aligned with commercial interests, these critics maintain, the purpose of contract law is to achieve results that support these interests at the expense of the poor. Contract law thus helps maintain society's status quo. Opponents of this set of views contest contract law's indeterminacy and reject the idea that contract decisions play any ideological role. They point to contract rules that often protect the underdog, such as promissory estoppel.

C. Legal Remedies

Recall that the law facilitates private arrangements primarily in three ways:

- it gives people the power to create private arrangements;
- it creates rules of validation so that people know how to create (or avoid) an enforceable private arrangement; and
- it specifies the legal consequences of a private arrangement by creating legal remedies.

We again focus on contracts and corporations in studying the legal consequences of private arrangements. Again, our goal is not to teach all of remedial law or to make you into lawyers. Instead, we sample remedial law so that you can evaluate how well private-arrangement law realizes its goals.

By way of introduction, however, let us consider generally the range of legal consequences that may flow from a private arrangement. Some private arrangements are legally enforceable when made, others are not. For example, a contract becomes immediately binding on both parties, but people who write wills can revoke them. Some private arrangements impose quasi-official duties on others, such as the appointment of an executor of a will. A private arrangement may confer a particular status on the participants, such as marriage or membership in an organization. Such status affords the participants certain privileges, such as a marital partner's right to support and a union member's procedural rights in disciplinary proceedings.

Also, a private arrangement may provide various remedies for its breach, such as claims for money damages for contract breach. But certainly not all disputes involving private arrangements ultimately lead to legal intervention.

CONTRACTS

Contract remedies generally consist either of money damages or of specific performance, which is a court decree ordering a party to perform the contract.
(Recall the remedy in *Lucy v. Zehmer*, where the court ordered the Zehmers
to convey the land to Lucy.) We now look more closely at each kind of remedy.

Money Damages.   The goal of contract damages is to put the aggrieved party
in as good a position as if the contract had not been broken. Contract law calls
these damages expectation damages because they give the aggrieved party what
she expected under the contract. Such damages facilitate private arrangements
because they assure a contracting party that she can rely on the contract knowing
that she will receive either the promised performance or the equivalent in money
damages. People will thus be encouraged to enter contracts in the first place.

Expectation damages consist of "general damages" and "consequential
damages." The former are damages that arise naturally from the breach in the
sense that every aggrieved party would suffer them upon breach. Consequential
damages, or special damages, are damages peculiar to the circumstances of the
injured party. So, if you agree to purchase a lawn mower for your gardening
business, but the seller never delivers the mower (and you do not pay), you
suffer damages measured by the difference between the market value of the
mower (say, $300) and the contract price (say, $200), which produces $100
in general damages. Every purchaser of goods who agrees to pay $200 for
goods worth $300 suffers $100 in damages. But not every purchaser of a
lawnmower is in the gardening business and loses profits because the business
cannot mow lawns as, we shall assume, you do. So you can also make a claim for
lost profits, a form of consequential damages. The two kinds of damages together
will give you your lost expectancy.

The following two cases illustrate the concepts of general and consequential
damages, respectively. *Cooper v. Clute* shows a court applying the market-
contract differential measure of general damages, but in a situation where the
buyer experienced no damages. *Hadley v. Baxendale*, a famous case in contract
law decided in England in the nineteenth century but still followed by U.S. courts
today, illustrates that contract law does not always award consequential
damages because of countervailing policy concerns.

COOPER v. CLUTE
Supreme Court of North Carolina, 1917
174 N.C. 366, 93 S.E. 915

BROWN, J.:

[The plaintiff appealed an adverse judgment.]
...The findings of the jury establish that the
defendant entered into a contract with plaintiff
to deliver to him at the Hilton compress, near
Wilmington, 1,430 bales of cotton not compressed
at the price of 10⅞ cents per pound, delivery to be
made on February 26, 1916; that plaintiff
was ready, able, and willing to take and pay for
the cotton according to contract; that defendant
failed to deliver the cotton; and that its market
value at time and place of delivery was 10⅞ cents
per pound.

The measure of damage to be recovered for
breach of an executory contract of this character is
well settled to be the difference between the contract
price and the actual or market value of the property at

the time and place of the breach of the contract. Under this rule, if the market value is the same as the contract price when the contract is breached, [no general] damages can be recovered. . . .

Plaintiff contends that the court should have rendered judgment for plaintiff for the difference between 10⅞ cents, the contract price, and 11.03 cents, which plaintiff claims the defendant received from Sprunt for the cotton. The plaintiff tendered no such issue, and there is no finding of fact that defendant received 11.03 for the cotton.

But that is immaterial. The written contract shows that the defendant did not sell to plaintiff an particular cotton. Defendant could have performed the contract by purchasing similar cotton on the market and making the delivery.

. . . The evidence is conflicting as to the value of similar cotton at place of delivery on February 26, 1916, but the jury have fixed it at 10⅞, which is the contract price. It therefore follows that the plaintiff has sustained no actual damage.

No error.

NOTES

1. Cooper did not recover general damages because the market value and contract price were the same. But what about damages based on Clute's apparent sale to Sprunt? The court easily handles this issue too, because of the absence of a finding that the sale ever took place and because Clute, if he did sell to Sprunt, did not sell cotton that was identified as Cooper's cotton.

2. Suppose Clute did sell cotton to Sprunt that was earmarked for Cooper. The better view in contract law is that Cooper still cannot recover Clute's gain from breaching the contract. Cooper is not injured by Clute's breach because the contract price and market price are the same, so Cooper's theory for recovery cannot be based on expectation damages. Cooper might argue that Clute was unjustly enriched by his breach, but the cotton, although earmarked for Cooper, was not yet his property. All Cooper had was a contract expectancy, which Cooper could have satisfied by going out on the market and purchasing substitute identical cotton at the same price.

3. The next case, *Hadley v. Baxendale*, is important for prominently introducing the concept of consequential damages into Anglo-American law. In fact, it is so important, here's how one of your editors introduced the case: "*Hadley v. Baxendale* may be the most famous contracts case. Perhaps it is one of the most famous cases in any field of Anglo-American jurisprudence. Maybe it is the most important piece of writing in the English language. Well, I may be getting carried away. . . ." Robert A. Hillman, Principles of Contract Law 159 (2d ed. 2009).

HADLEY v. BAXENDALE

Exchequer, 1854
156 Eng. Rep. 145

At the trial before Crompton, J., at the last Gloucester Assizes, it appeared that the plaintiffs carried on an extensive business as millers at Gloucester; and that, on the 11th of May, their mill was stopped by a breakage of the crank shaft by which the mill was worked. The steam-engine was manufactured by Messrs. Joyce & Co., the engineers, at Greenwich, and it became necessary to send the shaft as a pattern for a new one to Greenwich. The fracture was discovered on the 12th, and on the 13th the plaintiffs sent one of their servants to the office of the defendants, who are the well-known carriers trading under the name of Pickford & Co., for the purpose of having the shaft carried to Greenwich. The plaintiffs' servant told the clerk that the mill was stopped, and that the shaft must be sent immediately; and in answer to the inquiry when the shaft would be taken, the answer was, that if it was sent up by twelve o'clock any day, it would be delivered at Greenwich on the following day. On the following day the shaft was taken by the defendants before noon, for the purpose of being conveyed to Greenwich, and the sum of £2, 4s. was paid for its carriage for the whole distance; at the same time the defendants' clerk was told that a special entry, if required, should be made to hasten its delivery. The delivery of the shaft at Greenwich was delayed by some neglect; and the consequence was, that the plaintiffs did not receive the new shaft for several days after they would otherwise have done, and the working of their mill was thereby delayed, and they thereby lost the profits they would otherwise have received.

On the part of the defendants, it was objected that these damages were too remote, and that the defendants were not liable with respect to them. The learned Judge left the case generally to the jury, who found a verdict with [£50] damages. . . .

[The defendants moved] for a new trial, on the ground of misdirection. . . .

The judgment of the Court was now delivered by Alderson, B.:

We think that there ought to be a new trial in this case; but, in so doing, we deem it to be expedient and necessary to state explicitly the rule which the Judge, at the next trial, ought, in our opinion, to direct the jury to be governed by when they estimate the damages. . . .

"There are certain established rules," this Court says, in Alder v. Keighley, 15 M. & W. 117, "according to which the jury ought to find." And the Court, in that case, adds: "and here there is a clear rule, that the amount which would have been received if the contract had been kept, is the measure of damages if the contract is broken."

Now we think the proper rule in such a case as the present is this:—Where two parties have made a contract which one of them has broken, the damages which the other party ought to receive in respect of such breach of contract should be such as may fairly and reasonably be considered either arising naturally, i.e., according to the usual course of things, from such breach of contract itself, or such as may reasonably be supposed to have been in the contemplation of both parties, at the time they made the contract, as the probable result of the breach of it. Now, if the special circumstances under which the contract was actually made were communicated by the plaintiffs to the defendants, and thus known to both parties, the damages resulting from the breach of such a contract, which they would reasonably contemplate, would be the amount of injury which would ordinarily follow from a breach of contract under these special circumstances so known and communicated. But, on the other hand, if these special circumstances were wholly unknown to the party breaking the contract, he, at the most, could only be supposed to have had in his contemplation the amount of injury which would arise generally, and in the great multitude of cases not affected by any special circumstances, from such a breach of contract. For, had the special circumstances been known, the parties might have specially provided for the breach of contract by special terms as to the damages in that case; and of this advantage it would be very unjust to deprive them. . . . Now, in the present case, if we are to apply the principles above laid down, we find that the only circumstances here communicated by the plaintiffs to the defendants at the time the contract was made, were, that the article to be carried was the broken shaft of a mill, and that the plaintiffs were the millers of that mill. But how do these circumstances shew reasonably that the profits of the mill must be stopped by an unreasonable delay in the delivery of the broken shaft by the carrier to the third person? Suppose the plaintiffs had another shaft in their possession put up or putting up at the time, and that they only wished to send back the broken shaft to the engineer who made it; it is clear that this would be quite consistent with the above circumstances, and yet the unreasonable delay in the delivery would have no effect upon the intermediate profits of the mill. Or, again, suppose that, at the time of delivery to the carrier, the machinery of the mill had been in other respects defective, then, also, the same results would follow. Here it is true that the shaft was actually sent back to serve as a model for a new one, and that the want of a new one was the only cause of the stoppage of the mill, and that the loss of profits really arose from not sending down the new shaft in proper time, and that this arose from the delay in delivering the broken one to serve as a model. But it is obvious that, in the great multitude of cases of millers sending off broken shafts to third persons by a carrier under ordinary circumstances, such consequences would not, in all probability, have occurred; and these special circumstances were here never communicated by the plaintiffs to the defendants. It follows, therefore, that the loss of profits here cannot reasonably be considered such a consequence of the breach of contract as could have been fairly and reasonably contemplated by both the parties when they made this contract. For such loss would neither have flowed naturally from the breach of this contract in the great multitude of such cases occurring under ordinary circumstances, nor were the special circumstances, which, perhaps, would have made it a reasonable and natural consequence of such breach of contract, communicated to or known by the defendants. The Judge ought, therefore, to have told the jury, that, upon the facts then before them, they ought not to take the loss of profits into consideration at all in estimating the damages. There must therefore be a new trial in this case.

Hadley v. Baxendale establishes that an aggrieved party can recover consequential damages only if they are reasonably foreseeable to the breaching party at the time of contracting (damages "such as may reasonably be supposed to have been in the contemplation of both parties, at the time they made the contract, as the probable result of the breach of it"). The miller's lost profits are not recoverable consequential damages. Not every miller would lose profits because of the carrier's delay. The court points out, for example, that a miller might have a substitute crank shaft or the mill might have been stopped for another reason.

The *Hadley* test depends on what a breaching party should reasonably know, not what it actually knows. It does not require the aggrieved party to explain the consequences of breach to the breaching party in every case. If the carrier had already transported the miller's crank shaft many times and knew that the miller shut down the mill each time, the carrier reasonably should have known the consequences of delay. Or suppose the carrier delivered only crank shafts; again, the carrier reasonably should know about the consequences of delay.

The case recites two different views of the facts: (a) the defendants' clerk "was told that the mill was stopped, that the shaft must be delivered immediately . . . and that a special entry, if required, should be made to hasten its delivery"; and (b) "we find that the only circumstances here communicated by the plaintiffs to the defendants at the time the contract was made, were, that the article to be carried was the broken shaft of a mill, and that the plaintiffs were the millers of that mill." Later decisions explain that the first recitation was from the court reporter, which the court rejected in the body of the opinion by Baron Alderson. If the court had accepted the court reporter's version, the carrier would have been liable for the miller's consequential damages because the damages would have been foreseeable.

American courts have almost unanimously accepted the *Hadley* rule of awarding only foreseeable consequential damages. What are the policies supporting the rule? For one thing, it would not be fair to hold the carrier liable if it did not know and should not have foreseen the consequences of delay. Surely, the carrier would have charged more, refused to contract, or taken extra precautions if it had known of the consequences of delay. In addition, the decision creates incentives for contracting parties to disclose their special circumstances. Millers will disclose to carriers the consequences of delay, for example, so that they can recover their lost profits should the carrier still breach. Without the *Hadley* rule, the miller would not disclose because revealing the information would probably cause the carrier to raise its price to cover the extra risk. See Ian Ayres & Robert Gertner, Filling Gaps in Incomplete Contracts: An Economic Theory of Default Rules, 99 Yale L.J. 87 (1989).

Specific Performance.   Recall again the case of *Lucy v. Zehmer*, set forth previously. There the court remanded the case for the entry of a decree ordering the Zehmers to perform the contract. This remedy is different from the money-damages remedy studied in *Cooper v. Clute* and *Hadley v. Baxendale*.

In the middle ages, English courts consisted of courts of equity and courts of law. These courts differed in many ways, including the substance of their rules and the remedies they administered. Courts of law applied the common law, which included some rather rigid substantive rules. Courts of equity developed more flexible equitable principles they could use to avoid the harsh results of the common law.

Courts of equity also developed remedial principles, including specific performance. An aggrieved purchaser of land, for example, could obtain a court decree ordering the seller to convey the land, which could be enforced by the use of the court's contempt power. The contempt power meant that a court could throw the seller in jail if the seller did not abide by the court order. Compare this specific performance order with the enforcement procedure in a law court after a judgment. A party could enforce the law judgment only by arranging for an official to seize the seller's property to pay the judgment. But equity courts did not want to usurp the role of law courts and thus only selectively granted specific performance. In fact, the equity court consistently declined when the legal remedy of damages was adequate to compensate the aggrieved party.

Today, for the most part, the law and equity courts have merged into one court system of general jurisdiction. Still, some substantive rules and remedial principles reflect the historical distinctions between the courts.

Courts continue to grant specific performance only when money damages are inadequate as a remedy, meaning that money cannot adequately compensate the aggrieved party for the breach of contract. For example, courts decline to grant specific performance in sale-of-goods cases if money damages are adequate. Nevertheless, if the subject matter of the contract is unique, such as a contract for the sale of an original Rembrandt painting, courts do not hesitate to order performance. On the one hand, contract law assumes that land is unique so that the only way to compensate the injured purchaser for the breach is to give the purchaser the land. Courts therefore routinely grant specific performance to aggrieved purchasers of land. On the other hand, courts rarely grant specific performance to employers because the Thirteenth Amendment of the Constitution prohibits involuntary servitude. But courts often do order an employee not to work for another employer, which effectively works like a specific performance decree. For example, if you were a professional singer under contract to the producers of *Les Misérables*, what would you do if a court ordered you not to perform in any other musical? You would perform in *Les Misérables* (or go hungry!).

In many parts of the world, specific performance is the preferred remedy. Why are Anglo-American courts reluctant to grant specific performance? Part of the reason may be historical—that is the way courts of equity used to operate. In addition, courts are wary of specific performance in part because of concerns about retaining jurisdiction to ensure that the defendant performs—courts are better equipped to dispose of cases, not to supervise performance—and in part because of reluctance to use their contempt power, which often requires courts to put people in jail or to make them pay large fines. The next case illustrates a court's use of the contempt power.

WILSON v. SANDSTROM

Supreme Court of Florida, 1975
317 So. 2d 732

ADKINS, CHIEF JUSTICE:

This is an original proceeding in habeas corpus wherein 18 owners of racing greyhounds seek relief from incarceration resulting from violation of an injunctive order of the circuit court entered July 8, 1975. A return to the petition has been filed....

For clarity, West Flagler Associates, Ltd., the owner and operator of the race track is hereinafter referred to as Flagler; the owners of the greyhounds used at the race track are referred to as the kennel owners.

Flagler instituted suit against the kennel owners and a kennel owners' association seeking a temporary and permanent mandatory injunction requiring the defendants to comply with contracts for furnishing greyhounds to the race track commencing July 3, 1975. The State of Florida and Metropolitan Dade County were allowed to intervene as parties-plaintiff.

Flagler alleged that under the contract it granted exclusive right to the named kennel owners to race their dogs and agreed to furnish purses, and that Flagler has complied with the contract....

Under the contracts the kennel owners agreed not to take any action which would be detrimental to the race track and greyhound racing. It was specifically provided that the kennel owners would not do any act which would bring about a temporary or permanent cessation or suspension of racing during the period of time covered by the contract.

It was alleged that under the rules of the Department of Business Regulation the kennel owners were required to present their dogs for schooling in June for the race meet commencing July 3, 1975. On June 10, 1975, the kennel owners [notified Flagler that they desired to renegotiate provisions of their agreement with Flagler and implicitly threatened not to furnish any greyhounds without a new agreement]. As a result, Flagler alleges it would be unable to conduct its race meet; that the kennel owners are required to supply "chattel of unusual and unique character; namely racing greyhounds which are not readily obtainable in the ready market". Flagler alleges that it will not be able to get the owners to supply greyhounds and suffers irreparable damage for each day it is not open. . . .

. . . [The state court entered an order on July 3, 1975, granting a] temporary mandatory injunction. This order recited that the State of Florida was suffering a loss of tax revenue of $64,000 per day, and that Flagler was suffering irreparable damage because of the kennel owners' refusal to supply dogs. The court ordered immediate compliance with the contracts by the filing of entries not later than July 4, 1975, at 10:00 a.m.; that upon refusal of the kennel owners to file entries that Perrine Palmer take custody and control of the dogs for the purpose of running them.

The kennel owners refused to submit their entry and Palmer attempted to take control of the dogs. Because of the number of dogs and inability to get adequate help, a hearing was held at the request of the receiver [Palmer] on July 5, 1975. Custody of the dogs was thereupon returned to the kennel owners, who were informed that a contempt hearing would be held on Monday, July 7, 1975. . . .

At the hearing on July 7, 1975, each kennel owner was called to the stand and interrogated concerning his knowledge of the order and whether he had willfully and deliberately refused to comply with the order of July 3, 1975. On July 8, 1975, the kennel owners were adjudged guilty of contempt and 18 of them were incarcerated in the Dade County penal facilities. These are the petitioners in the habeas corpus proceeding. . . .

A mandatory temporary injunction may be issued requiring specific performance of a contract. Bowling v. National Convoy and Trucking Co., 101 Fla. 634, 135 So. 541 (1931). . . .

The record clearly demonstrates that the kennel owners willfully and deliberately violated the injunctive order of the court. The courts and judges have inherent power by due course of law to punish by appropriate fine or imprisonment or otherwise any conduct that in law constitutes an offense against the authority and dignity of a court or a judicial officer in the performance of judicial functions. State ex rel. Buckner v. Culbreath, 147 Fla. 560, 3 So. 2d 380 (1941). The sole reason for the incarceration of the kennel owners was their willful failure to comply with the temporary injunctive order of the court. Just as in any other [civil] contempt proceedings, the kennel owners carry the keys of their prison in their own pocket. Demetree v. State, 89 So. 2d 498 (Fla. 1956).

. . . Misunderstandings among parties should be adjusted where possible without litigation, for a fair settlement is preferable to a good law suit. On the other hand, the judicial process is always available in the event the fair settlement is not reached. When the judicial process is involved, all parties are bound by the orders and judgments of the court having jurisdiction until such orders or judgments are reversed or modified by an appellate court. Although the kennel owners may feel justified in their complaints, their course of action in depriving the State and the counties of needed revenue certainly warrants the actions of the trial court. Their business is profitable only by virtue of a State statutory permission to operate dog tracks guided by regulatory measures adopted by the State. It might be said they are "biting the hand that feeds them".

In summary, we hold that . . . the orders entered by the trial court were proper under the circumstances and without error. The writ of habeas corpus is discharged and the petitioners therein are remanded to the custody of respondent, such incarceration to begin on Tuesday, July 22, 1975, at 5:00 p.m. . . .

It is so ordered.

ROBERTS, OVERTON and ENGLAND, JJ., concur.

BOYD, J., concurs in part and dissents in part with opinion. . . .

When a party disregards a court order she may be held in contempt. A widely held view is that "the major purpose of the law of contempt is to maintain and preserve the dignity of the judiciary and the orderly administration of justice."

Forbes v. State, 933 So. 2d 706 (Fla. App. 2006). For example, would you have much respect for courts if parties frequently disregarded their orders?

The purpose of the use of the contempt power to incarcerate the kennel owners in *Wilson v. Sandstrom* is to encourage them to comply with the order, not to punish them. This idea is the genesis of another often repeated phrase, that the kennel owners "carry the keys of their prison in their own pocket." This means that the kennel owners can get out of jail whenever they want, simply by agreeing to furnish the dogs.

CORPORATIONS

Perhaps the most important legal consequence of setting up a corporation is the limited liability of shareholders of the corporation, meaning that creditors of the corporation can rarely look to the individual assets of the shareholders to satisfy a claim against the corporation. The following case and excerpt illustrate the point. You will see that even if incorporators fail to strictly comply with the rules for setting up a corporation, limited liability may still apply.

CRANSON v. IBM
Court of Appeals of Maryland, 1964
234 Md. 477, 200 A.2d 33

HORNEY, JUDGE:

On the theory that the Real Estate Service Bureau was neither a de jure nor a de facto corporation and that Albion C. Cranson, Jr., was a partner in the business conducted by the Bureau and as such was personally liable for debts, the International Business Machines Corporation brought this action against Cranson for the balance due on electric typewriters purchased by the Bureau. At the same time it moved for summary judgment and supported the motion by affidavit. In due course, Cranson filed a general issue plea and an affidavit in opposition to summary judgment in which he asserted in effect that the Bureau was a de facto corporation and that he was not personally liable for its debts.

The agreed statement of facts shows that in April 1961, Cranson was asked to invest in a new business corporation which was about to be created. Towards this purpose he met with other interested individuals and an attorney and agreed to purchase stock and become an officer and director. Thereafter, upon being advised by the attorney that the corporation had been formed under the laws of Maryland, he paid for and received a stock certificate evidencing ownership of shares in the corporation, and was shown the corporate seal and minute book. The business of the new venture was conducted as if it were a corporation, through corporate bank accounts, with auditors maintaining corporate books and records, and under a lease entered into by the corporation for the office from which it operated its business. Cranson was elected president and all transactions conducted by him for the corporation, including the dealings with I.B.M., were made as an officer of the corporation. At no time did he assume any personal obligation or pledge his individual credit to I.B.M. Due to an oversight on the part of the attorney, of which Cranson was not aware, the certificate of incorporation, which had been signed and acknowledged prior to May 1, 1961, was not filed until November 24, 1961. Between May 17 and November 8, the Bureau purchased eight typewriters from I.B.M., on account of which partial payments were made, leaving a balance due of $4,333.40, for which this suit was brought.

Although a question is raised as to the propriety of making use of a motion for summary judgment as the means of determining the issues presented by the pleadings, we think the motion was appropriate. Since there was no genuine dispute as to the material facts, the only question was whether I.B.M. was entitled to judgment as a matter of law. The trial court found that it was, but we disagree.

The fundamental question presented by the appeal is whether an officer of a defectively incorporated association may be subjected to personal liability under the circumstances of this case. We think not.

Traditionally, two doctrines have been used by the courts to clothe an officer of a defectively incorporated association with the corporate attribute of limited liability. The first, often referred to as the doctrine of de facto corporations, has been applied in those cases where there are elements showing: (1) the existence of law authorizing incorporation; (2) an effort in good faith to incorporate under the existing law; and (3) actual use or exercise of corporate powers. Ballantine, Private Corporations, §23; 8 Fletcher, Cyclopedia of the Law of Private Corporations, §3777; 13 Am. Jur., Corporations, §§49–56; 18 C.J.S. Corporations §99. The second, the doctrine of estoppel to deny the corporate existence, is generally employed where the person seeking to hold the officer personally liable has contracted or otherwise dealt with the association in such a manner as to recognize and in effect admit its existence as a corporate body. Ballantine, op. cit., §29; Machen, Modern Law of Corporations, §§278–282; 18 C.J.S. op. cit. §109.

It is not at all clear what Maryland has done with respect to the two doctrines. There have been no recent cases in this State on the subject and some of the seemingly irreconcilable earlier cases offer little to clarify the problem. . . .

. . . There is, as we see it, a wide difference between creating a corporation by means of the de facto doctrine and estopping a party, due to his conduct in a particular case, from setting up the claim of no incorporation. Although some cases tend to assimilate the doctrines of incorporation de facto and by estoppel each is a distinct theory and they are not dependent on one another in their application. See 8 Fletcher, op. cit., §3763; France on Corporations (2nd ed.), §29; 18 C.J.S. op. cit. §111h. Where there is a concurrence of the three elements necessary for the application of the de facto corporation doctrine, there exists an entity which is a corporation de jure against all persons but the state. On the other hand, the estoppel theory is applied only to the facts of each particular case and may be invoked even where there is no corporation de facto. Accordingly, even though one or more of the requisites of a de facto corporation are absent, we think that this factor does not preclude the application of the estoppel doctrine in a proper case, such as the one at bar.

I.B.M. contends that the failure of the Bureau to file its certificate of incorporation debarred *all* corporate existence. But, in spite of the fact that the omission might have prevented the Bureau from being either a corporation de jure or de facto, we think that I.B.M. having dealt with the Bureau as if it were a corporation and relied on its credit rather than that of Cranson, is estopped to assert that the Bureau was not incorporated at the time the typewriters were purchased. In 1 Clark and Marshall, Private Corporations, §89, it is stated:

> The doctrine in relation to estoppel is based upon the ground that it would generally be inequitable to permit the corporate existence of an association to be denied by persons who have represented it to be a corporation, or held it out as a corporation, or by any persons who have recognized it as a corporation by dealing with it as such; and by the overwhelming weight of authority, therefore, a person may be estopped to deny the legal incorporation of an association which is not even a corporation de facto.

In cases similar to the one at bar, involving a failure to file articles of incorporation, the courts of other jurisdictions have held that where one has recognized the corporate existence of an association, he is estopped to assert the contrary with respect to a claim arising out of such dealings.

Since I.B.M. is estopped to deny the corporate existence of the Bureau, we hold that Cranson was not liable for the balance due on account of the typewriters.

Judgment reversed; the appellee to pay the costs.

FRANK H. EASTERBROOK & DANIEL R. FISCHEL, THE ECONOMIC STRUCTURE OF CORPORATE LAW
40-41 (1991)

Limited liability is a distinguishing feature of corporate law—perhaps *the* distinguishing feature. Although partners are personally liable for the debts of a partnership, shareholders are not liable for the debts of a corporation.... [L]imited liability seems to be the antithesis of contract, a privilege bestowed on investors. In exchange for this boon, many argue, corporations should be required to submit to regulation, or do favors for customers and workers and neighbors.

Not so fast. Limited liability may be depicted as anticontractual only if it is inaccurately described. *Corporations* do not have "limited liability"; they must pay all their debts, just as anyone else must (unless, in either event, they receive absolution in bankruptcy). To say that liability is "limited" means that the investors in the corporation are not liable for more than the amount they chip in. A person who pays $100 for stock risks that $100, but no more. A person who buys a bond for $100 or sells goods to a firm for $100 on credit risks $100, but no more. Managers and other workers are not vicariously liable for a firm's deeds. No one risks more than he invests.

. . . .

The distinctive aspects of the publicly held corporation—delegation of management to a diverse group of agents and risk bearing by those who contribute capital—depend on an institution like limited liability. If limited liability were not the starting point in corporate law, firms would create it by contract—which is not hard to do.... A legal rule enables firms to obtain the benefits of limited liability at lower cost.

D. Secondary Methods for Facilitating Private Arrangements

The preceding materials in this section examined the primary methods of law as an instrument of private arrangements. The law also facilitates private arrangements in less direct or in secondary ways. For example, the law assists private parties in obtaining information necessary to enter private arrangements. Governmental market and weather reports, requirements of full disclosure in certain dealings, and land registries are illustrative. Laws that provide for and protect a uniform monetary system or a system of weights and measures are additional examples of secondary facilitation.

Private arrangements also depend on the other legal instrumentalities studied in this book for secondary support. Public-benefit conferral, such as the creation of highway, communication, and educational systems, obviously facilitates private arrangements. Administrative rules such as those regulating interstate commerce and anticompetitive behavior are facilitative also. In addition, the remedial and penal instruments ensure that people can be secure in person and property.

Section Three
MAKING PRIVATE-ARRANGEMENT LAW

Private citizens, legislatures, and courts all play a role in making private-arrangement law. People make private arrangements, such as entering agreements, drafting wills, or forming corporations, that constitute law in the sense that they create legal obligations that courts can enforce. Legislatures enact laws that specify how to enter private arrangements, such as corporations, and set forth remedies for breaking private arrangements. Courts promulgate rules of validation and rules denominating the legal consequences of a private arrangement. We now consider each of these lawmakers—private citizens, legislatures, and courts in turn.

A. Private Citizens

Most private arrangements are made by individuals, either with the aid of lawyers or without them, and are completed without the intervention of courts or others. For example, if you agree to mow your neighbor's lawn each Thursday during July and August for $15 per week, chances are that you and your neighbor will carry out your agreement without dispute. Even when a dispute does arise, you and your neighbor may refer to your agreement as support for your respective positions ("we agreed on Thursdays, not Wednesdays") and most likely settle the dispute voluntarily without resort to a court. If a dispute cannot be resolved by the parties, a court may enforce the arrangement. The "law" of your private arrangement is thus found in your agreement (or, if you are engaging in a different kind of private arrangement, in your will, articles of incorporation, club bylaws, etc.). For this reason, we say that people usually make their own private-arrangement law.

The following illustrative episode is based on actual facts. The Whites wished to buy residential property next to the Benkowskis, but the Benkowskis' well provided the only water for the property. The Whites asked the Benkowskis to agree to a water-supply agreement. The parties signed the following agreement, drafted by a real estate agent. (We shall see in Section Five that they would have been better off consulting a lawyer!)

AGREEMENT AS TO SUPPLY OF WATER

This agreement, made this 28 day of November, 1962, between Paul Benkowski Jr., and Ruth Benkowski, his wife (first parties), and Virgil A. White and Gwynneth A. White, his wife (second parties),

WITNESSETH

WHEREAS, first parties are the owners of the following described real estate situated in the City of Oak Creek, Milwaukee County, Wisconsin, to-wit:

[The legal description of real estate is omitted.]

AND, WHEREAS, second parties are the owners of the following described real estate situated in the City of Oak Creek, Milwaukee County, Wisconsin, to-wit:

[The legal description of real estate is omitted.]

* This agreement shall become null and void whenever water is supplied by any municipal system or if the existing well should go dry or become inadequate to supply said 2 homes or if second parties would drill their own well.

AND, WHEREAS, there is now situated on the above real estate of first parties, one certain water well operated by an electric submersible system motor,

AND, WHEREAS, the parties hereto desire that the source of water from the well upon parties of the first part's property be supplied unto the parties of the second part's home through the system of piping now there existing, it is hereby mutually agreed:

1. That first parties will furnish water for the use of the occupants of the house located on the lands of the second parties for a period of ten (10) years from _____ November, 1962.

2. That the second parties will pay for said water supply service the sum of Three ($3.00) Dollars per month, commencing with 1 December, 1962, payable on the first day of each and every month, in advance, and that in addition, second parties shall contribute to first parties, one-half (½) of the cost of any repairs or maintenance expense to said water system; also including replacements of motor, tank or accessories; (* above)

3. It is further hereby agreed between the parties hereto that at the end of the ten year period referred to in Paragraph One above, parties of the second part shall have the option to renew this agreement.

This agreement shall be binding upon and shall extend unto the respective grantees, successors, heirs, executors, administrators and assigns of each of the respective parties hereto.

IN WITNESS WHEREOF, the parties hereto have hereunto set their hands and seals of the day and year first above written.

WITNESSES TO FOUR SIGNATURES:

_____ Paul Benkowski Jr.

_____ Ruth Benkowski

_____ Virgil A. White

_____ Gwynneth A. White

The above document signed by the Whites and Benkowskis satisfies the contract rules of validation that we already have encountered. It evidences an agreement between the parties that is supported by consideration. Does this make the agreement law? Legal theorists called positivists would say no because for them law is essentially rules promulgated by officials in power. See, e.g., 1 John Austin, Lectures on Jurisprudence 180–85, 225–26 (Robert Campbell ed., 4th ed., London 1873) ("general commands of a sovereign legislature backed by sanctions"). On the other hand, the agreement between the Whites and Benkowskis creates legal duties enforced, if necessary, by the courts. This is a form of law too.

Legal recognition of such private agreements benefits society. We have already discussed the importance of the principle of private autonomy in the introduction to this chapter. In addition, the Whites valued the water more than the $3 per month, and the Benkowskis valued the $3 per month more than the water. The exchange thus is efficient in the sense that performance makes both parties better off and no one worse off.

B. Legislatures

North Dakota Century Code

10–19.1–12 Effective date of incorporation.

The corporate existence begins upon the issuance of the certificate of incorporation or at a later date as specified in the articles of incorporation. The certificate of incorporation is conclusive evidence that all conditions precedent and required to be performed by the incorporators have been performed and that the corporation has been incorporated under this chapter, except as against this state in a proceeding to cancel or revoke the certificate of incorporation or for involuntary dissolution of the corporation.

The North Dakota state legislature enacted the statute above, which the governor of the state signed into law. In Weiss v. Anderson, 341 N.W.2d 367, 371 (N.D. 1983), the Supreme Court of North Dakota said: "A corporation cannot exist without the consent or grant of the sovereign. Under North Dakota statutory law, the corporate existence begins upon the issuance of the certificate of incorporation by the Secretary of State, and the certificate of incorporation is conclusive evidence that all conditions precedent have been performed." The North Dakota statute is representative of other states' statutes on incorporation.

Legislatures also specify remedies for breaches of private arrangements and adopt rules prohibiting certain kinds of agreements. Uniform Commercial Code §2–716, a standard state statute authorizing specific performance in certain circumstances involving the sale of goods, is an example of the former, and the Sherman Antitrust Act, 15 U.S.C. §§1–7, an important federal law prohibiting certain contracts in restraint of trade, is an example of the latter. Legislatures may also enact rules of disclosure, such as consumer protection legislation requiring disclosure of rates of interest, and rules attaching certain legal consequences to an arrangement, such as the support duties of a spouse.

Legislatures influence private-arrangement law in less direct ways as well, as suggested by Jerry L. Mashaw & Richard A. Merrill, An Introduction to the American Public Law System 936 (1975):

> [W]ith the proliferation of public regulatory legislation in this century it would be surprising if judges had not increasingly looked to statutes, and to the legal principles they were perceived as embodying, in the course of resolving essentially private disputes. The introduction of public regulation is, after all, premised on the notion that private transactions, and the supportive structure of tort, contract, and property law that makes them possible, are inadequate to accomplish desired social goals. A regulatory statute may therefore be viewed by courts as altering the social presuppositions upon which the private law has developed, although the statute makes no explicit change in the private legal order or that part of it directly relevant to decision of a particular case.

C. Courts

Through case decisions, the judiciary promulgates rules of validation and rules specifying the legal consequences of private arrangements. We have seen, for example, that judges make the rules defining agreement, consideration, and general and consequential damages. Courts also interpret legislation governing private arrangements and the language of parties' private arrangements. The next two cases illustrate these latter two judicial roles, respectively. The first case, the venerable *Riggs v. Palmer*, is still today the most famous case on the subject of the right of a wrongdoer to inherit under a will. It raises interesting questions on the relationship of legislatures and courts in a very colorful setting. The second case, *Ermolieff v. RKO Radio Pictures, Inc.*, also a leading case, examines how courts interpret, not legislative enactments, but parties' private agreements.

RIGGS v. PALMER

Court of Appeals of New York, 1889
115 N.Y. 506, 22 N.E. 188

EARL, J.:

On the 13th day of August, 1880, Francis B. Palmer made his last will and testament, in which he gave small legacies to his two daughters, Mrs. Riggs and Mrs. Preston, the plaintiffs in this action, and the remainder of his estate to his grandson, the defendant Elmer E. Palmer, subject to the support of Susan Palmer, his mother, with a gift over to the two daughters, subject to the support of Mrs. Palmer, in case Elmer should

survive him and die under age, unmarried, and without any issue. The testator, at the date of his will, owned a farm, and considerable personal property. He was a widower, and thereafter, in March, 1882, he was married to Mrs. Bresee, with whom, before his marriage, he entered into an antenuptial contract, in which it was agreed that in lieu of dower and all other claims upon his estate in case she survived him she should have her support upon his farm during her life, and such support was expressly charged upon the farm. At the date of the will, and subsequently to the death of the testator, Elmer lived with him as a member of his family, and at his death was 16 years old. He knew of the provisions made in his favor in the will, and, that he might prevent his grandfather from revoking such provisions, which he had manifested some intention to do, and to obtain the speedy enjoyment and immediate possession of his property, he willfully murdered him by poisoning him. He now claims the property, and the sole question for our determination is, can he have it? . . .

What could be more unreasonable than to suppose that it was the legislative intention in the general laws passed for the orderly, peaceable, and just devolution of property that they should have operation in favor of one who murdered his ancestor that he might speedily come into the possession of his estate? Such an intention is inconceivable. We need not, therefore, be much troubled by the general language contained in the laws. Besides, all laws, as well as all contracts, may be controlled in their operation and effect by general, fundamental maxims of the common law. No one shall be permitted to profit by his own fraud, or to take advantage of his own wrong, or to found any claim upon his own iniquity, or to acquire property by his own crime. These maxims are dictated by public policy, have their foundation in universal law administered in all civilized countries, and have nowhere been superseded by statutes. . . .

. . . It was evidently supposed that the maxims of the common law were sufficient to regulate such a case, and that a specific enactment for the purpose was not needed. For the same reasons the defendant Palmer cannot take any of this property as heir. Just before the murder he was not an heir, and it was not certain that he ever would be. He might have died before his grandfather, or might have been disinherited by him. He made himself an heir by the murder, and he seeks to take property as the fruit of his crime. What has before been said as to him as legatee applies to him with equal force as an heir. He cannot vest himself with title by crime. My view of this case does not inflict upon Elmer any greater or other punishment for his crime than the law specifies. It takes from him no property, but simply holds that he shall not acquire property by his crime, and thus be rewarded for its commission.

[Elmer Palmer was enjoined from using any of the property left by Francis Palmer to him, the will was declared ineffective to pass title to him, and he was deprived of any interest in the estate.]

GRAY, J., (dissenting). . . . [I]f I believed that the decision of the question could be affected by considerations of an equitable nature, I should not hesitate to assent to views which commend themselves to the conscience. But the matter does not lie within the domain of conscience. We are bound by the rigid rules of law, which have been established by the legislature, and within the limits of which the determination of this question is confined. The question we are dealing with is whether a testamentary disposition can be altered, or a will revoked, after the testator's death, through an appeal to the courts, when the legislature has by its enactments prescribed exactly when and how wills may be made, altered, and revoked, and apparently, as it seems to me, when they have been fully complied with, has left no room for the exercise of an equitable jurisdiction by courts over such matters. . . .

The statutes of this state have prescribed various ways in which a will may be altered or revoked; but the very provision defining the modes of alteration and revocation implies a prohibition of alteration or revocation in any other way. The words of the section of the statute are: "No will in writing, except in the cases hereinafter mentioned, nor any part thereof, shall be revoked or altered otherwise," etc. Where, therefore, none of the cases mentioned are met by the facts, and the revocation is not in the way described in the section, the will of the testator is unalterable. . . .

I cannot find any support for the argument that [Elmer's] succession to the property should be avoided because of his criminal act, when the laws are silent. Public policy does not demand it; for the demands of public policy are satisfied by the proper execution of the laws and the punishment of the crime. . . . The appellants' argument practically amounts to this: that, as the legatee has been guilty of a crime, by the commission of which he is placed in a position to sooner receive the benefits of the testamentary provision, his rights to the property should be forfeited, and he should be divested of his estate. To allow their argument to prevail would involve the diversion by the court of the testator's estate into the hands of persons whom, possibly enough, for all we know, the testator might not have chosen or desired as its recipients. Practically the court is asked to make another will for the testator....

DANFORTH, J., concurs [in dissent].

NOTES

1. If the majority followed Francis's will, Elmer, his grandson, would have received his inheritance. Instead, the court relied on "fundamental maxims of the common law," "public policy," and "universal law" to deny Elmer.

2. According to the dissent, however, the governing statute lists the various ways in which wills can be "altered or revoked," none of which included murdering Francis. The dissent believed that courts are supposed to interpret the law, not make it. You should not be outraged by the dissent's position. After all, Elmer is unlikely to enjoy his inheritance behind bars. Further, a decision against him implies that courts can invoke "fundamental maxims," etc. in other situations. A good argument can be made that we do not want courts to have such power to override statutes.

Riggs Today

A century after *Riggs v. Palmer*, a husband shot and killed his wife and, from prison, claimed $25,000 from his wife's estate and life insurance policy. The husband had been convicted of second-degree manslaughter. The New York Times, Apr. 29, 1984, §1, at 42, reported that the surrogate "ruled that the policy set in the *Palmer* case was still applicable. Even though second-degree manslaughter is a lesser offence [involving recklessness rather than intent], it is still punishable by 15 years in prison—and, therefore, it is 'within the category of such iniquity that its perpetrator should be precluded from profiting from his course of conduct.'"

At this writing, another murderer is holding up the distribution of proceeds of his wife's life insurance policy under a Minnesota law that prohibits anyone who "feloniously and intentionally" kills someone from benefitting from the victim-insured's life insurance policy. The problem is that the law requires a "final judgment of conviction" before the insurance company can distribute the proceeds to other beneficiaries. Although the Minnesota Supreme Court affirmed the conviction, the murderer has filed a federal habeas corpus petition in which the murderer claims Minnesota violated his constitutional rights, and such proceedings can drag on for many years. See Minneapolis Star Trib., Apr. 1, 2007, available at http://www.startribune.com/462/story/1094142.html.

ERMOLIEFF v. RKO RADIO PICTURES, INC.

Supreme Court of California, 1942

19 Cal. 2d 543, 122 P.2d 3

CARTER, JUSTICE:

Plaintiff and defendant are producers and distributors in the motion picture industry. Plaintiff was the owner and producer of a foreign language motion picture entitled "Michael Strogoff," based on a novel by Jules Verne, which prior to July 6, 1936, he had produced in the German and French languages. On that date the parties entered into a contract in which plaintiff granted to defendant the exclusive right to produce and distribute an English version of that picture in only those "countries or territories of the world" listed on an exhibit annexed to the contract. On the exhibit is listed among other places "The United Kingdom." Plaintiff reserved the rights in the picture in both foreign and English languages in all countries or territories not listed in the exhibit. The contract was modified in December, 1936, and September, 1937, to add other countries or territories to the list. Plaintiff commenced the instant action on May 8, 1940, pleading the contract and its modifications and alleging that defendant had produced an English version of the picture under the title "Soldier and a Lady" in the United States and elsewhere; and that a controversy had arisen between the parties as to the countries and territories granted to defendant and those reserved by plaintiff under the contract and its modifications. Those allegations were admitted by defendant and it alleges that the only controversy between the parties is with respect to the area referred to as "The United Kingdom"; that the only dispute is whether "The United Kingdom," in which the contract grants rights to defendant, includes Eire or the Irish Free State; and that there is a custom and usage in the motion picture industry that that term does include Eire and that such usage is a part of the contract. Both the complaint and the answer pray for declaratory relief, namely, a declaration of their rights with respect to those areas embraced in the contract which are in dispute.

It was stipulated that the sole issue with respect to the territory embraced in the contract was whether defendant or plaintiff held the rights in the picture in Eire, which in turn depended upon whether The United Kingdom included Eire; that defendant did distribute the picture in Eire, and that The United Kingdom, from a political and legal viewpoint, did not include Eire, the latter being independent from it. . . .

Defendant asserts, however, that the judgment must be reversed because of the granting of plaintiff's motion to strike defendant's evidence that according to the custom and usage of the moving picture industry Eire is included in The United Kingdom. With that contention we agree. Both plaintiff and defendant are engaged in the business of producing and distributing moving pictures and rights in connection therewith. Defendant's evidence consisted of the testimony of several witnesses familiar with the distribution of motion pictures to the effect that in contracts covering the rights to produce pictures the general custom and usage was that the term "The United Kingdom" included Eire, the Irish Free State. Plaintiff's motion to strike out all of that evidence on the ground that it was incompetent, irrelevant and immaterial was granted. Plaintiff, reserving his objection to defendant's evidence, offered contrary evidence concerning such custom and usage.

The correct rule with reference to the admissibility of evidence as to trade usage under the circumstances here presented is that while words in a contract are ordinarily to be construed according to their plain, ordinary, popular or legal meaning, as the case may be, yet if in reference to the subject matter of the contract, particular expressions have by trade usage acquired a different meaning, and both parties are engaged in that trade, the parties to the contract are deemed to have used them according to their different and peculiar sense as shown by such trade usage. Parol evidence is admissible to establish the trade usage, and that is true even though the words are in their ordinary or legal meaning entirely unambiguous, inasmuch as by reason of the usage the words are used by the parties in a different sense. The basis of this rule is that to accomplish a purpose of paramount importance in interpretation of documents, namely, to ascertain the true intent of the parties, it may well be said that the usage evidence does not alter the contract of the parties, but on the contrary gives the effect to the words there used as intended by the parties. The usage becomes a part of the contract in aid of its correct interpretation....

The judgment is reversed [for retrial].

SIMILARITIES AND DIFFERENCES IN INTERPRETING STATUTES AND AGREEMENTS

In *Ermolieff v. RKO Radio Pictures*, the source of law is the parties' written agreement, not a statute, but similarities in the interpretation process are obvious. As with the statute in *Riggs v. Palmer*, the court must supplement the language of the agreement, here with evidence of the trade custom that the United Kingdom includes Eire. In both cases, the court enforces the presumed intention of the drafter, either the legislature or the parties.

There are, of course, also many differences between interpreting statutes and private agreements. Some of these are enumerated in Harry W. Jones, E. Allan Farnsworth & William F. Young, Cases and Materials on Contracts 260 (1965):

> To what extent are the rules and techniques for the interpretation of other kinds of legal writings applicable to contracts? Consider contracts, statutes and wills. In each case an "intention" is sought—that of the parties in the case of a contract, that of the legislature in the case of a statute, and that of the testator in the case of a will. Is it significant that there are two contracting parties but only one legislature and only one testator? Does the existence of a bicameral legislature pose the same kinds of problems as to intention that the existence of two contracting parties poses? Is it significant that when a dispute over interpretation arises parties to the contract are usually available to testify as to their intention, whereas testators are not? Is there a difference in the care ordinarily used in the drafting of contracts, statutes and wills? If so, should this affect their interpretation? Compare an oral contract with the Uniform Commercial Code; compare an oil concession agreement between a large American company and a foreign government with a state statute for the protection of fur-bearing animals. Are there important differences in the numbers of people affected by interpretation? Compare a contract for the sale of a private home with the Internal Revenue Code; compare a standard insurance policy with a private bill to compensate an injured person for damages caused by a state employee. How probable is it that an interpretation in one case will be followed in like future cases involving the same language contained in a contract? a statute? a will? If the court's interpretation did not, in fact, accord with the appropriate intention, how easy a matter is it to make appropriate changes to govern future disputes in the case of contracts? statutes? wills?

Section Four
APPLYING PRIVATE-ARRANGEMENT LAW

Private-arrangement law applies when people enter arrangements or when they determine their rights under arrangements. If a person asks a lawyer how to make a will or how to enter a contract, or whether to change a will in light of a divorce or whether to perform at a particular time under a contract, lawyers must interpret and apply private-arrangement law to answer the question. All of these functions can occur, of course, in the absence of any dispute.

If the parties do begin to quarrel, they usually settle their dispute without the need for a formal proceeding. When this is impossible and they seek a formal resolution, the forum may be a court or a less traditional forum such as an arbitration proceeding or mediation. The following excerpt briefly explains these latter two avenues of dispute resolution.

JACK M. SABATINO, ADR AS "LITIGATION LITE": PROCEDURAL AND EVIDENTIARY NORMS EMBEDDED WITHIN ALTERNATIVE DISPUTE RESOLUTION
47 Emory L.J. 1289, 1290, 1296–98 (1998)

The phenomenon of "lite" ice cream, and other "lite" products, parallels the increasingly common diversion of conflicts in this country from traditional courtroom trials to "alternative" dispute resolution mechanisms ("ADR"), sometimes also referred to as "complementary" dispute resolution ("CDR"). Disputants are often unable or unwilling to bear the excesses of our elaborate civil justice system: expensive and time-consuming modes of discovery; formalistic motion practice; complicated filing requirements; unpredictable and oft-delayed trial dates; and cumbersome evidentiary rules that govern activities in the courtroom. Daunted by such burdensome features, many parties have turned away (or, in some court-annexed programs, have been diverted away) from the "real thing" and are attempting to secure justice in different fora. So we now are in an era in which arbitrations, mediations, "summary jury trials," "early neutral evaluations," "mini-trials," "med-arbs," and other forms of ADR are rivaling traditional adjudication....

Alternative dispute resolution in the United States currently takes a variety of forms. The principal ones are arbitration and mediation, but each of these has variations, and other ADR methods such as early neutral evaluation, mini-trials, med-arbs, and summary jury trials are widely practiced.

Arbitration characteristically refers to an adjudicative process in which a designated neutral person (or a panel of neutrals) conducts hearings and considers evidence. The arbitrator then issues an award, based on the arbitrator's views of the merits of the disputants' contentions, deciding or proposing to resolve, the underlying dispute. Arbitration may be binding, and thereafter subject only to very restricted judicial review, or non-binding. It may be invoked on a mandatory basis, usually pursuant to a contractual agreement to arbitrate, or voluntarily pursued by the disputants. At times courts may require or suggest that parties in pending lawsuits arbitrate their claims through a program of "court-annexed" arbitration.

Commercial arbitration has been practiced for centuries and statutorily authorized for decades. In 1925, Congress passed the Federal Arbitration Act ("FAA"), which currently declares:

A written provision in any...contract evidencing a transaction involving commerce to settle by arbitration a controversy thereafter arising out of such contract or transaction...shall be valid, irrevocable, and enforceable, save upon such grounds as exist at law or in equity for the revocation of any contract.

Additionally, thirty-three states and the District of Columbia have adopted the Uniform Arbitration Act ("UAA"), which was issued in 1955 by the National Conference of Commissioners on Uniform State Laws. The UAA likewise proclaims the general enforceability of arbitration agreements, and also codifies various procedures for such arbitrations. A variety of local court rules and statutes also establish assorted processes for arbitration.

Mediation, by comparison, is a process in which a neutral person meets with disputants and attempts to assist them in reaching an agreement that either resolves their differences or satisfactorily accommodates their respective interests in spite of those differences. Mediation can be "facilitative," "evaluative," or both. In facilitative mediation, the neutral attempts to forge consensus by helping the parties communicate their views and proposals to one another, and to sort out their individual interests and priorities in the bargaining process. A facilitative mediator generally will approach those tasks in a non-judgmental way. In evaluative mediation, the mediator expresses reactions to what he or she perceives to be the merits of the disputants' respective positions. Evaluative mediation seeks to get each disputant to appreciate more realistically the weaknesses of his or her position, and the downside risks of failing to achieve a compromise. Frequently a mediator will intermittently deploy both facilitative and evaluative strategies within the same mediation. Because mediation is a consensual process, it may conclude without the attainment of a resolution. Mediation of business disputes may be conducted through court-annexed programs or through private-sector services.

How does a private-arrangement dispute end up in a less traditional forum such as an arbitration proceeding? An agreement may provide for this manner of dispute resolution. For example, an agreement between a professional athlete and his or her team owner typically includes a provision calling for arbitration of disputes. Collective bargaining agreements between unions and employers generally provide internal grievance procedures. Trade associations also frequently provide for arbitration of disputes between members. Simple commercial contracts may also call for arbitration, as in the following sample provision:

ARBITRATION

A. All questions subject to arbitration under this Contract shall be submitted to arbitration at the choice of either party to the dispute.

B. The parties may agree upon one arbitrator. In all other cases there shall be three arbitrators. One arbitrator shall be named by each party to this Contract; each party shall notify the other party and the Engineer of such choice in writing. The third arbitrator shall be chosen by the two arbitrators named by the parties. If the two arbitrators fail to select a third within fifteen days, the third arbitrator shall be chosen by the presiding officer of the bar association nearest to the location of the work. Should the party demanding arbitration fail to name an arbitrator within ten days of his demand, his right to arbitration shall lapse. Should the other party fail to choose an arbitrator within the said ten days, the presiding officer of the bar association nearest to the location of work shall appoint such arbitrator. Should either party refuse or neglect to supply the arbitrators with any papers or information demanded in writing, the arbitrators are empowered by both parties to proceed ex parte.

> C. If there be one arbitrator, his decision shall be binding; if there are three, the decision of any two shall be binding. Such decision shall be a condition precedent to any right of legal action, and wherever permitted by law it may be judicially enforced.

A dispute also may be resolved by arbitration or some other form of dispute settlement because the parties agree to that approach after a dispute has arisen.

Why would parties seek dispute resolution other than in courts? Arbitration, for example, is often less expensive and time-consuming than litigation. Arbitrators often ignore formalities of proof, such as the hearsay rule (testimony about what another person told the witness is not generally admissible in court, but is in arbitration). In addition, the parties are often entitled to select their own arbitrators. But there is a dark side to arbitration, at least in the consumer context, as revealed in the following excerpt.

KATHERINE VAN WEZEL STONE, RUSTIC JUSTICE: COMMUNITY AND COERCION UNDER THE FEDERAL ARBITRATION ACT
77 N.C. L. Rev. 931, 933–36 (1999)

A Gateway 2000 computer arrives in a box together with numerous advertising brochures, instruction manuals, and forms setting out product descriptions, warranties, and other technical information concerning the purchase. One of these forms, entitled "Standard Terms and Conditions," states, "[a]ny dispute or controversy arising out of or relating to this Agreement or its interpretation shall be settled exclusively and finally by arbitration." Arbitration clauses such as this one are often buried in fine print and obscure language so that they are, for all practical purposes, invisible to the average consumer. Even if visible, however, the average consumer has no reason to suspect that the clause is anything but innocuous.

Arbitration is an increasingly common feature of modern life. Once confined to the specialized provinces of international commercial transactions and labor-management relations, arbitration clauses now appear in many day-to-day consumer transactions. Banks frequently include arbitration clauses in their terms for maintaining bank accounts; health maintenance organizations ("HMOs") routinely have provisions requiring that all disputes between the health consumer

and the HMO be arbitrated; employment handbooks often state that employees must utilize arbitration to resolve employment-related disputes; many standard residential and commercial lease forms say that all disputes between the tenant and the landlord must be submitted to arbitration; homeowner associations and residential condominiums frequently include arbitration clauses in their charter documents. Before long, routine consumer products, like Gateway Computers, will come with product and warranty information that includes a mandatory arbitration clause....

In tandem with the expanded use of arbitration in consumer transactions has been an expansion in the scope of arbitration within the legal order. In recent years, the Supreme Court has reinterpreted the Federal Arbitration Act ("FAA"), the statute that defines the boundary between the public legal system and arbitration. The FAA provides that agreements to arbitrate are "valid, irrevocable, and enforceable." Before the 1980s, the FAA was interpreted as applying only to federal question cases or diversity cases involving commerce that were in federal court. Further, the FAA applied only to cases that were in federal court on an independent federal question basis. In the past fifteen years, however, the Supreme Court has expanded the reach of the FAA and has adopted a national policy of promoting the use of arbitration in all relationships that have a contractual element.

This Article describes the expanding scope of arbitration under the FAA and explains the trend in light of the history of the statute. It concludes that the Supreme Court's expansive doctrines, when applied to consumer transactions, contravene the statute's intent and undermine many important due process and substantive rights. In brief, the argument is as follows: The FAA, which made agreements to arbitrate judicially enforceable, was designed to facilitate arbitration between members of trade associations. It was enacted to further a vision of voluntarism, delegation, and self-regulation within the business and commercial communities. Recently, courts have applied the FAA in contexts such as consumer transactions and employment relations that often go far beyond the original understanding of the legislation. By such interpretations of the FAA, courts condone and encourage the use of arbitration to resolve disputes between individuals and entities who, far from sharing in a common normative community, occupy vastly different positions of power vis-à-vis each other. These expansive interpretations of the FAA facilitate the exercise of invisible private coercion in many facets of contemporary life.

If the parties utilize alternative dispute resolution but one of the parties is dissatisfied with the outcome, she may look to the courts for relief. However, often she will come away disappointed. Fudickar v. Guardian Mutual Life Insurance Co., 62 N.Y. 392, 399–400 (1875), stated the traditional approach of courts to arbitration decisions, which is still prevalent today:

> The arbitrator is a judge appointed by the parties; he is by their consent invested with judicial functions in the particular case; he is to determine the right as between the parties in respect to the matter submitted, and all questions of fact or law upon which the right depends are, under a general submission, deemed to be referred to him for decision. The court possesses no general supervisory power over awards, and if arbitrators keep within their jurisdiction their award will not be set aside because they have erred in judgment either upon the facts or the law. If courts should assume to rejudge the decision of arbitrators upon the merits, the value of this method of settling controversies would be destroyed, and an award instead of being a final determination of a controversy would become but one of the steps in its progress. The courts in this State have adhered with great steadiness to the general rule that awards will not be opened for errors of law or fact on the part of the arbitrator.

Section Five
ROLES OF PRIVATE CITIZENS AND THEIR LAWYERS*

Private citizens, often working with their lawyers, create their private arrangement and define its content. They also determine whether to contest any performance or nonperformance of the other party. To illustrate, let us return to the

---

* This section is based on Robert S. Summers & Robert A. Hillman, Contract and Related Obligation 5–26 (5th ed. 2006).

White and Benkowski arrangement for the supply of water, introduced in Section Three. Recall that the Benkowskis agreed to supply water from their well to the Whites in an agreement drafted by a real estate agent. We continue the story after the Whites moved into their new home.

The Whites and Benkowskis enjoyed a harmonious relationship until the fall of 1963, when, according to Mrs. White, Mrs. Benkowski called the Whites' daughter an "S.O.B." because she picked an apple in the Benkowskis' yard. Later, when Mrs. White came to the defense of her daughter, Mrs. Benkowski called Mrs. White "a redheaded bitch." The dispute escalated further when Mr. White, a police officer, claimed that Mr. Benkowski told Mr. White's superior officer that White attempted to run over the Benkowskis' child and threw wild parties. Both accusations were false.

The Benkowskis then claimed that the Whites used too much water. The Benkowskis proceeded on several occasions in early 1964 to cut off the Whites' water supply. Because the parties could not resolve their differences, the Whites brought a lawsuit against the Benkowskis. We now present the final resolution of the case—before considering how the parties might have utilized lawyers to reach a better agreement.

WHITE v. BENKOWSKI

Supreme Court of Wisconsin, 1967
37 Wis. 2d 285, 155 N.W.2d 74

This case involves a neighborhood squabble between two adjacent property owners.

Prior to November 28, 1962, Virgil and Gwynneth White, the plaintiffs, were desirous of purchasing a home in Oak Creek. Unfortunately, the particular home that the Whites were interested in was without a water supply. Despite this fact, the Whites purchased the home.

The adjacent home was owned and occupied by Paul and Ruth Benkowski, the defendants. The Benkowskis had a well in their yard which had piping that connected with the Whites' home.

On November 28, 1962, the Whites and Benkowskis entered into a written agreement wherein the Benkowskis promised to supply water to the White home for ten years or until an earlier date when either water was supplied by the municipality, the well became inadequate, or the Whites drilled their own well. The Whites promised to pay $3 a month for the water and one-half the cost of any future repairs or maintenance that the Benkowskis well might require. As part of the transaction, but not included in the written

agreement, the Whites gave the Benkowskis $400 which was used to purchase and install a new pump and an additional tank that would increase the capacity of the well.

Initially, the relationship between the new neighbors was friendly. With the passing of time, however, their relationship deteriorated and the neighbors actually became hostile. In 1964, the water supply, which was controlled by the Benkowskis, was intermittently shut off. Mrs. White kept a record of the dates and durations that her water supply was not operative. Her record showed that the water was shut off on the following occasions:

> March 5, 1964, from 7:10 p.m. to 7:25 p.m.
> March 9, 1964, from 3:40 p.m. to 4:00 p.m.
> March 11, 1964, from 6:00 p.m. to 6:15 p.m.
> June 10, 1964, from 6:20 p.m. to 7:03 p.m.

The record also discloses that the water was shut off completely or partially for varying lengths of time on July 1, 6, 7, and 17, 1964, and on November 25, 1964.

Mr. Benkowski claimed that the water was shut off either to allow accumulated sand in the pipes to settle or to remind the Whites that their use of the water was excessive. Mr. White claimed that the Benkowskis breached their contract by shutting off the water.

Following the date which the water was last shut off (November 25, 1964), the Whites commenced an action to recover compensatory and punitive damages for an alleged violation of the agreement to supply water. A jury trial was held. Apparently it was agreed by counsel that for purposes of the trial "plaintiffs' case was based upon an alleged deliberate violation of the contract consisting of turning off the water at the times specified in the plaintiffs' complaint." [The reporter then set forth the special verdict submitted to the jury.]

Before the case was submitted to the jury, the defendants moved to strike the verdict's punitive-damage question. The court reserved its ruling on the motion. The jury returned a verdict which found the Benkowskis maliciously shut off the Whites' water supply for harassment purposes. Compensatory damages were set at $10 and punitive damages at $2,000. On motions after verdict, the court reduced the compensatory award to $1 and granted defendants' motion to strike the punitive-damage question and answer.

Judgment for plaintiffs of $1 was entered and they appeal.

WILKIE, J.:

Two issues are raised on this appeal.

1. Was the trial court correct in reducing the award of compensatory damages from $10 to $1?

2. Are punitive damages available in actions for breach of contract?

Reduction of Jury Award

The evidence of damage adduced during the trial here was that the water supply had been shut off during several short periods. Three incidents of inconvenience resulting from these shut-offs were detailed by the plaintiffs. Mrs. White testified that the lack of water in the bathroom on one occasion caused an odor and that on two other occasions she was forced to take her children to a neighbor's home to bathe them. Based on this evidence, the court instructed the jury that: [the court here set forth the portion of the jury charge indicating that the Whites could recover only nominal damages for their harm suffered from the breach].

Plaintiffs did not object to this instruction. In the trial court's decisions on motions after verdict it states that the court so instructed the jury because, based on the fact that the plaintiffs paid for services they did not receive, their loss in proportion to the contract rate was approximately 25 cents. This rationale indicates that the court disregarded or overlooked Mrs. White's testimony of inconvenience. In viewing the evidence most favorable to the plaintiffs, there was some injury. The plaintiffs are not required to ascertain their damages with mathematical precision, but rather the trier of fact must set damages at a reasonable amount. Notwithstanding this instruction, the jury set the plaintiffs' damages at $10. The court was in error in reducing that amount to $1.

The jury finding of $10 in actual damages, though small, takes it out of the mere nominal status. The award is predicated on an actual injury. This was not the situation present in Sunderman v. Warnken.[2] *Sunderman* was a wrongful-entry action by a tenant against his landlord. No actual injury could be shown by the mere fact that the landlord entered the tenant's apartment, therefore damages were nominal and no punitory award could be made. Here there was credible evidence which showed inconvenience and thus actual injury, and the jury's finding as to compensatory damages should be reinstated.

Punitive Damages

If a man shall steal an ox, or a sheep, and kill it, or sell it; he shall restore five oxen for an ox, and four sheep for a sheep.[3]

Over one hundred years ago this court held that, under proper circumstances, a plaintiff was entitled to recover exemplary or punitive damages.[4]

Kink v. Combs[5] is the most recent case in this state which deals with the practice of permitting

---

2. (1947), 251 Wis. 471, 29 N.W.2d 496.
3. Exodus 22:1.
4. McWilliams v. Bragg (1854), 3 Wis. 377.
5. (1965), 28 Wis. 2d 65, 135 N.W.2d 789.

punitive damages. In *Kink* the court relied on Fuchs v. Kupper[6] and reaffirmed its adherence to the rule of punitive damages.

In Wisconsin compensatory damages are given to make whole the damage or injury suffered by the injured party. On the other hand, punitive damages are given

> on the basis of punishment to the injured party not because he has been injured, which injury has been compensated with compensatory damages, but to punish the wrongdoer for this malice and to deter others from like conduct.[8]

Thus we reach the question of whether the plaintiffs are entitled to punitive damages for a breach of the water agreement.

The overwhelming weight of the authority supports the proposition that punitive damages are not recoverable in actions for breach of contract. In Chitty on Contracts, the author states that the right to receive punitive damages for breach of contract is now confined to the single case of damages for breach of a promise to marry.

Simpson states:

> Although damages in excess of compensation for loss are in some instances permitted in tort actions by way of

punishment . . . in contract actions the damages recoverable are limited to compensation for pecuniary loss sustained by the breach.[11]

Corbin states that as a general rule punitive damages are not recoverable for breach of contract.[12] . . .

Persuasive authority from other jurisdictions supports the proposition (without exception) that punitive damages are not available in breach of contract actions. This is true even if the breach, as in the instant case, is wilful.

Although it is well recognized that breach of a contractual duty may be a tort, in such situations the contract creates the relation out of which grows the duty to use care in the performance of a responsibility prescribed by the contract. Not so here. No tort was pleaded or proved.

Reversed in part by reinstating the jury verdict relating to compensatory damages and otherwise affirmed. Costs to appellants.

---

6. (1963), 22 Wis. 2d 107, 125 N.W.2d 360.
8. Malco, Inc. v. Midwest Aluminum Sales (1961), 14 Wis. 2d 57, 66, 109 N.W.2d 516, 521.
11. Simpson, Contracts, (2d ed. hornbook series), p. 394, sec. 195.
12. 5 Corbin, Contracts, p. 438, sec. 1077.

Now consider what might have occurred had the Whites consulted a lawyer before making the agreement with the Benkowskis. Generally, the lawyer's roles would have included the following:

Planning the basic agreement. To assist the client in making an agreement that will avoid disputes and unexpected consequences, the lawyer must understand the client's goals and motives. Often helpful is asking directly, "What do you wish to achieve by making this agreement?" The lawyer must plan a flexible agreement because the client's needs may change over time. For example, a buyer of goods from a particular seller may need different quantities over time, so the lawyer should not draft a fixed quantity contract for this client. Instead, the lawyer should draft a "requirements contract," in which the seller agrees to supply all of the buyer's needs and the buyer agrees to buy only from the seller.

Planning for compliance with the law. The lawyer must make sure the agreement complies with the law. For example, sale-of-goods law includes a rule that a requirements buyer cannot demand a quantity that is "unreasonably dispro-portionate" to any prior estimate of the buyer's needs.

Planning for risks. The lawyer must also plan for the possibility that things will go wrong. For example, is the buyer in our requirements contract entitled to performance if the seller experiences a shortage of raw materials? What if the buyer's need for the goods evaporates because of a fire that destroys the buyer's business? Lawyers often include a "force majeure clause" to allocate such risks, as in the following example:

a. The term "Force Majeure" as used herein shall mean and include: . . . lack of labor or means of transportation of labor or material; Acts of God; insurrection; flood; strike.

b. If by reason of Force Majeure as herein defined, lessee is prevented from or delayed in drilling, completing or producing any wells for oil, gas or other mineral on the leased premises, then while so prevented or during the period of such delay lessee shall be relieved from all obligations, whether express or implied, imposed on lessee under this lease, to drill, complete or produce such well or wells on the leased premises, and lessee shall not be liable in damages and this lease shall not be subject to can-cellation for failure of lessee to drill, complete or produce such well or wells during the time lessee is relieved from all obligations to do so.

Negotiating the terms. Parties do not always agree on the terms of a prospective arrangement. The lawyer may be called on to negotiate with the other side over various terms. Negotiation is, of course, not limited to this stage of a transaction. A lawyer may negotiate the terms of a settlement if an agreement breaks down, as discussed in the next excerpt.

HARRY T. EDWARDS & JAMES J. WHITE, *THE LAWYER AS A NEGOTIATOR*
112–13 (1977)*

[I]t is perhaps useful to state three propositions, truisms really, that hold true for almost every negotiation and that define the negotiator's role to a considerable degree. In every negotiation a principal responsibility of the negotiator is to find his opponent's settling point. In almost every negotiation in which there is at least a mod-erately well-defined controversy the opponent will have or will develop some point at which he will settle. With a union in a bargaining session this may be the number of cents per hour it must have in order not to strike; for the plaintiff's law-yer, the number of dollars he must receive in set-tlement in order not to go to trial; for the landlord

this is the minimum number of dollars and cents per square foot at which he will lease.

In any negotiation, and particularly in lawsuit settlement negotiation, the opposing negotiators may have widely different views of the same case. Commonly, one will assign a lower value to an opponent's case than the opponent will assign to it. Because of that fact and because one assumes that the opponent regards his case as stronger than it looks from across the table, nego-tiators frequently assume the opponent's settling point is higher than it really is. One should always keep the possibility in mind—notwithstanding the statements of the opposing negotiator—that his opponent has evaluated his own case as weaker than you evaluate it. If somehow one can determine that settling point, he can settle the case for that amount not for some higher amount which he has placed on the case himself.

The logical corollary to the foregoing principle is that one should not reveal his own settling point. Much of the material that follows on nonverbal communication is designed to assist the negotiator in reading his opponent. Conversely the negotiator should be aware that he is transmitting not only verbal but also nonverbal signals. Particularly if his settling point is some distance from the point at which he is bargaining, one should use care not to reveal that settling point. Presumably in the optimal negotiation, one will determine his opponent's settling point without revealing his own. Doubtless such absolute knowledge on one side coupled with absolute ignorance on the other seldom occurs in practice.

The third truism with respect to most negotiations deals with the negotiator's responsibility to change his opponent's position. In some cases it will be enough simply to know the opponent's settling point and to agree to settle at that point. More commonly it will be the job of the negotiator not only to determine the settling point but also to convince the opponent that his case has a lower value than he has put upon it.

If lawyers for each side of a negotiation follow Edwards and White's advice that "one should not reveal his own settling point," will the negotiation ever lead to agreement? Lawyers for each side frequently communicate, trying to convince the other of the strength of their own case. The lawyer who becomes convinced of the weakness of her case usually makes the first offer of settlement to avoid a larger judgment against the client.

Consider again the plight of the Whites and the Benkowskis. If the Whites had consulted a lawyer, a letter like the one that follows might have been prepared. Evaluate the letter in terms of the lawyer's roles.

Virgil & Gwynneth White
3837 East Garden Place
Oak Creek, Wisconsin

Dear Mr. & Mrs. White:

You have asked me to draft an agreement with Paul and Ruth Benkowski to supply you with water from their well through existing pipes connected to your new home. You have told me that you have already agreed to a monthly service charge of $3.00 to be paid in advance on the first day of each month, that you have agreed to pay $400 for a new pump and an additional tank, and that you have agreed to pay one-half of the cost of additional repairs, maintenance or replacement expenses. The agreement is to last for ten years with an option to renew, but will terminate when water is supplied by a municipal system or the Benkowskis' well goes dry or is inadequate to supply the two homes, or if you drill your own well.

Before I draft the agreement there are certain additional issues that we should clear up with the Benkowskis. Concerning the duration of the

---

agreement, if you exercise the renewal option is the renewal period for ten years? May you renew the agreement more than once? You certainly should have that right since you do not want to be without a water supply after one renewal period. Are you *required* to be connected to the municipal system if it becomes available or may you continue to receive water from the Benkowskis' well (it may be cheaper from the Benkowskis)? When does the Benkowskis' well "become inadequate" to supply both homes? For example, will merely one or a few periods of low water pressure be sufficient? We need to discuss this further with the Benkowskis and see if we can nail down some agreement on precisely when the well "becomes inadequate."

Concerning the price to you of the water service, does the $3.00-per-month charge continue under all circumstances during the period of the agreement? For example, suppose the value of water increases dramatically because of a drought or pollution or the like? We need to include a provision specifically indicating that such events do not trigger a right of the Benkowskis to raise the price (or to get out of the agreement). In addition, you agree to pay one-half of repairs, maintenance and replacement costs to the system. We should make it clear that only such repairs, maintenance and replacement costs that are necessary to continue the supply of water to both homes are included, not repairs, etc., that are solely beneficial to the Benkowskis.

Payment is to be on the first day of each month. We should include a provision enabling you to pay "on or about" the first day of each month in case you are slightly late in a particular month.

Are there to be any limits on your usage of water? I assume that the Benkowskis' attorney (if they retain one) will raise this issue. If the issue is not raised, we need to decide whether to raise it ourselves by seeking a provision specifically ensuring that you can use all of the water you desire. Offering such a provision may prod the Benkowskis into seeking a price scheme based on the amount of water-usage. I assume that we can agree on a mutually agreeable scale. If we remain silent on this issue, I can foresee disagreements about water usage later on, so perhaps we should consider the issue now.

We also need to consider whether there should be any adjustment of the $3.00-per-month fee in case of an inadvertent interruption of the water supply, for example, because of equipment failure. In addition, are the Benkowskis going to warrant the quality of the water? We should include such a promise if possible. We could require that the water meet the potability standards of the local department of health.

Finally, while I know you people are on good terms now, unfortunately we lawyers have seen too many deals go sour. So it is appropriate to think of remedies that you desire if the Benkowskis breach their agreement; for example, by turning off the water on you. We should try to get an agreement as to how much the Benkowskis will have to pay you for each hour that the water is purposefully turned off to discourage such behavior, should your relationship with the Benkowskis not remain cordial. Such an amount must necessarily reflect the damages to you or it will not be legally enforceable.

> We need to have a meeting first on these matters, and then later with the Benkowskis. Of course we will need to compromise on many of them, but the important thing is to have your agreement clearly deal with these issues so as to avoid trouble in the future.
>
> > Sincerely yours,
> > Jean L. Smith

Based on Jean L. Smith's letter, did she do a good job of planning? Think of all of the issues and contingencies she raises that the real estate agent ignored, including the length of the renewal option, the meaning of "become inadequate," bases for raising the $3 charge, if any, limits on water usage, and the quality of the water.

MORE ON THE ROLE OF PRIVATE-ARRANGEMENT LAWYERS IN SOCIETY

Lawyers do not look kindly on agreements drafted by real estate agents. But not everyone can afford a lawyer. Further, in some cases, lawyers may be counterproductive by raising issues that push the parties apart. For example, Rollie Massimino, head coach of Villanova's basketball team in the mid-1980s, explained why he did not accept the head coaching job with the New Jersey Nets: "The Nets were very professional in all their dealings with me. We had some 20 telephone conversations and about five face-to-face meetings. Everything was agreed on verbally and then the lawyers took over with their legalese and there were snags." Ithaca Journal, June 26, 1985, at 16.

We can learn more about the role of lawyers by studying actual contracts drafted by lawyers, which can be thought of as "social artifacts," meaning discrete objects "consciously produced or transformed by human activity, under the influence of the physical and/or cultural environment." Mark Suchman, The Contract as Social Artifact, 37 Law & Soc'y Rev. 91, 98 (2003). Just as sociologists study conventional artifacts such as "fire extinguishers, parachutes, or cardiac defibrillators" along various dimensions, such as their technical and symbolic properties and on a micro or macro level, researchers can apply these social scientific methods to the study of contract texts. In short, Suchman explains:

> Like most artifacts, contracts often emerge from the labors of specific artisans; but also like most artifacts, contracts necessarily bear the markings of broader social contexts. Like most artifacts, contracts have material uses, and contract provisions often act as practical technologies; but again like most artifacts, contracts also have cultural meanings, and contract provisions sometimes act not as technologies but as symbols.

What would such an approach yield? Suchman asserts that the study of actual contracts illuminates the role of contract in society, such as shedding light on how innovation in drafting contracts can change industry practices and on how path dependence, following the acceptance of a particular contract approach, can lead to inferior contract designs. In addition, the study of contract texts may help explain how lawyers contribute to a community's norms and practices. In fact, another Suchman study entitled "The Contracting Universe" looks at the role of local law firms in the development of Silicon Valley venture capital financing contracts. The data consist of over 100 venture capital financing contracts drafted by lawyers over a 15-year period and reveal the significant role of lawyers in contributing to that community's norms and practices. Suchman's conclusion is in part a refutation of the negative perspective that lawyers simply "drain...the productive economy." Instead, he writes that in Silicon Valley, "lawyers do not just engineer technical 'devices' that allow specific clients to capture excess economic value in specific transactions; Silicon valley lawyers also play a key intermediary role in institutionalizing the characteristic beliefs, rituals and practices of an entire organizational community."

In contrast to Suchman's conclusion, consider the view of other analysts who have collected empirical evidence that business people often plan and draft their agreements informally and without the aid of lawyers. Because business people often are quite comfortable with their contracting partners, keen on doing additional business with them in the future, and desirous of establishing good reputations, they act flexibly and cooperatively in a contract relation. Business people believe that law and lawyers just get in the way and symbolize distrust and selfishness. Instead of law, business people rely on nonlegal cultures and customs to govern their relations. The next two excerpts amplify these views. The first focuses on why business people sometimes avoid lawyers, and the second explains how nonlegal sanctions are the glue that hold deals together.

STEWART MACAULAY, THE USE AND NON–USE OF CONTRACT IN THE MANUFACTURING INDUSTRY
Prac. Law., Nov. 1963, at 14, 17–18

Most businessmen I have talked to have an attitude toward contracts that can be best described as indifferent or even hostile to the whole idea. They remark, "Contracts are a waste of time. We've never had any trouble, because we know our customers and our suppliers. If we needed a contract with a man, we wouldn't deal with him." "Lawyers are overprotective and just get in the way of buying or selling. If business had to be done by lawyers as buyers and sellers, the

economy would stop. No one would buy or sell anything; they'd just negotiate forever."

Yet, some businessmen look at things differently: "We've been sued (or our competitor has been sued), and one ought to be careful. There is no need to skate on thin ice legally. We've learned the hard way." "If you get the intent spelled out, you won't have any trouble. People perform commitments they understand. It's worth a little extra time to make sure everyone is talking about the same thing."...

When disputes occur, there is a hesitancy to use legal sanctions or even to refer to the contract. Businessmen try to "work things out without bringing lawyers into it." Contract lawsuits and appellate cases concerning contract problems are relatively rare.

Businessmen can deal without contract for obvious reasons. They have little, if any, trouble, even if they run risks of trouble. It is in the interest of everyone to perform agreements. There are personal relationships between buyers and sellers on all levels of the two corporations. Purchasing agents know salesmen, corporate presidents know corporate presidents, and so forth. This creates an incentive to get along in a continuing relationship. Most importantly, the two businesses want to do business in the future. You don't get repeat orders from unsatisfied customers, and one's reputation can influence future business if word gets around. And word does get around.

Using contract, of course, can have a number of disadvantages. If, in planning a business transaction, one is going to mention all the horrible things that can happen, he may scare off the other side so that the deal is lost. If one does set up a contractual relationship, there is some risk that one will get only performance to the letter of the contract most narrowly construed. Conversely, there is also a risk that one will be held to the letter of the contract and lose "flexibility." Using legal sanctions for breach of contract to settle disputes is costly. Usually it ends the business relationship between the parties. Furthermore, I need not tell you that lawsuits and lawyers cost money.

Of course, there is some use of legal sanctions. Typically, this occurs when someone with power thinks the gains from proceeding this way outweigh the costs. Often this is the lawyer's view, but lawyers do not always get to run their clients' affairs in the way lawyers might wish to run them.

DAVID CHARNY, NONLEGAL SANCTIONS IN COMMERCIAL RELATIONSHIPS
104 Harv. L. Rev. 375, 392–95 (1990)

The nonlegal sanction for breach of a commitment is the sacrifice of something valuable to the breaching party—a value often called the "bond" posted by that party. Three types of bonds are common in commercial transactions. The simplest type of nonlegal sanction is the sacrifice of *a relationship-specific prospective advantage.* The committing party places a particular asset under the control of another party; that party will confiscate or destroy the asset if the promisor breaches. The posting of collateral for a loan provides a familiar, albeit imperfect, example. Other examples include a franchisor's rendering the franchisee's investment worthless by revoking the right to use a trademark and a bank's destroying a small business by cutting off a line of credit or calling a note payable on demand. A particularly important and common form of relationship-specific prospective advantage is the opportunity to deal again with the same transactor—the "repeat deal." The asset posted is the value of future dealings; if one party breaches, the other party will terminate the relationship and refuse to deal with the breacher again, destroying the asset.

A second type of nonlegal sanction is loss of *reputation* among market participants. The promisor develops a reputation for reliability among market participants who are potential transactors. If the promisor improperly breaches his commitments, he damages his reputation and thereby loses valuable opportunities for future trade. Familiar examples of reputational bonds include trademarks in consumer markets and credit ratings for individual and corporate borrowers.

A third type of nonlegal sanction is the sacrifice of *psychic and social goods.* The breaching promisor may suffer loss of opportunities for important or pleasurable associations with others, loss of self-esteem, feelings of guilt, or an unfulfilled desire to think of himself as trustworthy and competent. An unsavory businessperson may be snubbed at the local club or suffer pangs of guilt during the Sunday sermon. Encouraging trust among workers or long-term customers is one function of the "corporate culture" of firms and of the feeling of responsibility to clientele that may develop at schools, banks, or other "quasi-public" institutions.

These three types of nonlegal sanctions operate side-by-side with legal sanctions. . . .

Indeed, contracts that formally provide for legal sanctions depend upon nonlegal sanctions for their effectiveness whenever the legal sanctions are ineffective in inducing the promisor to perform.

Section Six
IMPROVING THE PRIVATE-ARRANGEMENT INSTRUMENT

To a large extent, the preceding materials in this chapter have focused on the importance to society of enforcing private arrangements. Admittedly, excusing parties from their obligations undermines people's confidence in their contracts if too easily granted. But in some situations enforcement may be counterproductive, for a number of reasons.

For example, a party may have a legitimate reason for failing to perform a contract, such as unanticipated circumstances that make performance unfairly onerous. Courts sometimes have excused promisors from contract obligations for this reason, a specific example being when a seller promises to deliver goods at a set price, but a disruption in the market makes the goods prohibitively expensive and difficult for the seller to procure. Regrettably, the grounds for determining whether to excuse such a promisor are imprecise: generally performance must be "impracticable," a highly context-dependent standard. Creating more definitive standards for excusing parties would therefore improve contract law.

Enforcement of private arrangements also may be counterproductive if a party had not freely assented to the arrangement. For example, freedom of contract is rather hollow if one party can dictate unfair and unreasonable terms. Friedrich Kessler, a noted contract analyst of the twentieth century, focusing on the problem of the use of standard forms by big business, put it this way:

> With the decline of the free enterprise system due to the innate trend of competitive capitalism towards monopoly, the meaning of contract has changed radically. Society, when granting freedom of contract, does not guarantee that all members of the community will be able to make use of it to the same extent. On the contrary, the law, by protecting the unequal distribution of property, does nothing to prevent freedom of contract from becoming a one-sided privilege. Society, by proclaiming freedom of contract, guarantees that it will not interfere with the exercise of power by contract. Freedom of contract enables enterprises to legislate by contract and, what is even more important, to legislate in a substantially authoritarian manner without using the appearance of authoritarian forms. Standard contracts in particular could thus become effective instruments in the

hands of powerful industrial and commercial overlords enabling them to impose a new feudal order of their own making upon a vast host of vassals.

Friedrich Kessler, Contracts of Adhesion—Some Thoughts About Freedom of Contract, 43 Colum. L. Rev. 629, 640–41 (1943). Contract law employs the doctrine of unconscionability to try to distinguish contracts that should be enforced based on the principle of freedom of contract from those that are problematic because of the lack of fairness in the formation process or the resulting terms, or both. Sadly, most renditions of the doctrine do not bother to define what is and what is not unconscionable, leaving it to the courts to try to figure it out case by case. Look at the Uniform Commercial Code provision below, a representative unconscionability provision. Then, to get a feel for how courts administer the doctrine of unconscionability, consider the *Williams* case that follows.

Uniform Commercial Code

§2–302. Unconscionable Contract or Clause.

(1) If the court as a matter of law finds the contract or any clause of the contract to have been unconscionable at the time it was made the court may refuse to enforce the contract, or it may enforce the remainder of the contract without the unconscionable clause, or it may so limit the application of any unconscionable clause as to avoid any unconscionable result.

(2) When it is claimed or appears to the court that the contract or any clause thereof may be unconscionable the parties shall be afforded a reasonable opportunity to present evidence as to its commercial setting, purpose and effect to aid the court in making the determination.

WILLIAMS v. WALKER–THOMAS FURNITURE CO.

United States Court of Appeals, District of Columbia Circuit, 1965
350 F.2d 445

Before Bazelon, Chief Judge, and Danaher and Wright, Circuit Judges.

J. Skelly Wright, Circuit Judge:

Appellee, Walker-Thomas Furniture Company, operates a retail furniture store in the District of Columbia. During the period from 1957 to 1962 each appellant in these cases purchased a number of household items from Walker-Thomas, for which payment was to be made in installments. The terms of each purchase were contained in a printed form contract which set forth the value of the purchased item and purported to lease the item to appellant for a stipulated monthly rent payment.

The contract then provided, in substance, that title would remain in Walker-Thomas until the total of all the monthly payments made equaled the stated value of the item, at which time appellants could take title. In the event of a default in the payment of any monthly installment, Walker-Thomas could repossess the item.

The contract further provided that "the amount of each periodical installment payment to be made by [purchaser] to the Company under this present lease shall be inclusive of and not in addition to the amount of each installment payment to be made by [purchaser] under such prior leases, bills or accounts; *and all payments now and hereafter made by [purchaser] shall be credited pro rata on all outstanding leases, bills and accounts* due the Company by [purchaser] at the time each such payment is made."

(Emphasis added.) The effect of this rather obscure provision was to keep a balance due on every item purchased until the balance due on all items, whenever purchased, was liquidated. As a result, the debt incurred at the time of purchase of each item was secured by the right to repossess all the items previously purchased by the same purchaser, and each new item purchased automatically became subject to a security interest arising out of the previous dealings.

On May 12, 1962, appellant Thorne purchased an item described as a Daveno, three tables, and two lamps, having total stated value of $391.10. Shortly thereafter, he defaulted on his monthly payments and appellee sought to [take back] all the items purchased since the first transaction in 1958. Similarly, on April 17, 1962, appellant Williams bought a stereo set of stated value of $514.95. She too defaulted shortly thereafter, and appellee sought to [take back] all the items purchased since December, 1957. The Court of General Sessions granted judgment for appellee. The District of Columbia Court of Appeals affirmed, and we granted appellants' motion for leave to appeal to this court.

Appellants' principal contention, rejected by both the trial and the appellate courts below, is that these contracts, or at least some of them, are unconscionable and, hence, not enforceable. In its opinion in Williams v. Walker-Thomas Furniture Company, 198 A.2d 914, 916 (1964), the District of Columbia Court of Appeals explained its rejection of this contention as follows:

> Appellant's second argument presents a more serious question. The record reveals that prior to the last purchase appellant had reduced the balance in her account to $164. The last purchase, a stereo set, raised the balance due to $678. Significantly, at the time of this and the preceding purchases, appellee was aware of appellant's financial position. The reverse side of the stereo contract listed the name of appellant's social worker and her $218 monthly stipend from the government. Nevertheless, with full knowledge that appellant had to feed, clothe and support both herself and seven children on this amount, appellee sold her a $514 stereo set.

We cannot condemn too strongly appellee's conduct. It raises serious questions of sharp practice and irresponsible business dealings. A review of the legislation in the District of Columbia affecting retail sales and the pertinent decisions of the highest court in this jurisdiction disclose, however, no ground upon which this court can declare the contracts in question contrary to public policy. We note that were the Maryland Retail Installment Sales Act, Art. 83 §§128–153, or its equivalent, in force in the District of Columbia, we could grant appellant appropriate relief. We think Congress should consider corrective legislation to protect the public from such exploitive contracts as were utilized in the case at bar.

We do not agree that the court lacked the power to refuse enforcement to contracts found to be unconscionable. In other jurisdictions, it has been held as a matter of common law that unconscionable contracts are not enforceable. While no decision of this court so holding has been found, the notion that an unconscionable bargain should not be given full enforcement is by no means novel. In Scott v. United States, 79 U.S. (12 Wall.) 443, 445 (1870), the Supreme Court stated:

> ...If a contract be unreasonable and unconscionable, but not void for fraud, a court of law will give to the party who sues for its breach damages, not according to its letter, but only such as he is equitably entitled to....

Since we have never adopted or rejected such a rule, the question here presented is actually one of first impression.

Congress has recently enacted [for application in the District of Columbia] the Uniform Commercial Code, which specifically provides that the court may refuse to enforce a contract which it finds to be unconscionable at the time it was made. 28 D.C. Code §2–302 (Supp. IV 1965). The enactment of this section, which occurred subsequent to the contracts here in suit, does not mean that the common law of the District of Columbia was otherwise at the time of enactment, nor does it preclude the court from adopting a similar rule in the exercise of its powers to develop the common law for the District of Columbia. In fact, in view of the absence of prior authority on the point, we consider the congressional adoption of §2–302 persuasive authority for following the rationale of the cases from which the section is explicitly derived. Accordingly, we hold that where the element of unconscionability is present at the time a contract is made, the contract should not be enforced.

Unconscionability has generally been recognized to include an absence of meaningful choice on the part of one of the parties together with contract terms which are unreasonably favorable to the other party. Whether a meaningful choice is present in a particular case can only be determined by consideration of all the circumstances surrounding the transaction. In many cases the meaningfulness of the choice is negated by a gross inequality of bargaining power. The manner in which the contract was entered is also relevant to this consideration. Did each party to the contract, considering his obvious education or lack of it, have a reasonable opportunity to understand the terms of the contract, or were the important terms hidden in a maze of fine print and minimized by deceptive sales practices? Ordinarily, one who signs an agreement without full knowledge of its terms might be held to assume the risk that he has entered a one-sided bargain. But when a party of little bargaining power, and hence little real choice, signs a commercially unreasonable contract with little or no knowledge of its terms, it is hardly likely that his consent, or even an objective manifestation of his consent, was ever given to all the terms. In such a case the usual rule that the terms of the agreement are not to be questioned should be abandoned and the court should consider whether the terms of the contract are so unfair that enforcement should be withheld.

In determining reasonableness or fairness, the primary concern must be with the terms of the contract considered in light of the circumstances existing when the contract was made. The test is not simple, nor can it be mechanically applied.

The terms are to be considered "in the light of the general commercial background and the commercial needs of the particular trade or case." Corbin suggests the test as being whether the terms are "so extreme as to appear unconscionable according to the mores and business practices of the time and place." 1 Corbin, [Contracts §128 (1963)]. We think this formulation correctly states the test to be applied in those cases where no meaningful choice was exercised upon entering the contract.

Because the trial court and the appellate court did not feel that enforcement could be refused, no findings were made on the possible unconscionability of the contracts in these cases. Since the record is not sufficient for our deciding the issue as a matter of law, the cases must be remanded to the trial court for further proceedings.

So ordered.

DANAHER, CIRCUIT JUDGE (dissenting):

The District of Columbia Court of Appeals obviously was as unhappy about the situation here presented as any of us can possibly be. Its opinion in the *Williams* case, quoted in the majority text, concludes: "We think Congress should consider corrective legislation to protect the public from such exploitive contracts as were utilized in the case at bar."

My view is thus summed up by an able court which made no finding that there had actually been sharp practice. Rather the appellant seems to have known precisely where she stood.

There are many aspects of public policy here involved. What is a luxury to some may seem an outright necessity to others. Is public oversight to be required of the expenditures of relief funds? A washing machine, e.g., in the hands of a relief client might become a fruitful source of income. Many relief clients may well need credit, and certain business establishments will take long chances on the sale of items, expecting their pricing policies will afford a degree of protection commensurate with the risk. Perhaps a remedy when necessary will be found within the provisions of the "Loan Shark" law, D.C. Code §§26–601 et seq. (1961).

I mention such matters only to emphasize the desirability of a cautious approach to any such problem, particularly since the law for so long has allowed parties such great latitude in making their own contracts. I dare say there must annually be thousands upon thousands of installment credit transactions in this jurisdiction, and one can only speculate as to the effect the decisions these cases will have. I join the District of Columbia Court of Appeals in its disposition of the issues.

"There's no justice in the world, Kirkby, but I'm not convinced that this is an entirely bad thing."

NOTES

1. The effect of the "cross-collateral clause" described in the case is that Walker-Thomas could repossess *every* item that Mrs. Williams had purchased, upon her default on *any one* of them, because Walker-Thomas retained a balance due on all of them until Williams paid off her entire debt. This surely bothered the court, along with the disparity between price and value.

2. The dissent in *Walker-Thomas* worries in part that the effect of a finding of unconscionability in cases such as *Walker-Thomas* will be that Mrs. Williams will no longer be able to purchase items, such as stereo sets, because the credit risk will prompt merchants to decline to sell to poor people. Economic analysts of law support this position. As another writer has pointed out:

[E]conomists typically argue that courts should not avoid contracts because of the unequal bargaining power of the parties. When contracts appear to have very high price terms, a court could determine only with great difficulty whether the high price is due to market power or fluctuations in the costs of inputs. A high interest rate, for example, could result from the creditor's judgment about the risk of default posed by a particular debtor, and generally courts should defer to such judgments. A determination that the creditor has market power requires an evaluation of the structure of the market, a notoriously difficult enterprise usually reserved for antitrust litigation. A seller or creditor with temporary market power as a result of a patent, or some innovation that other market participants have not had a chance to imitate, should (arguably) be permitted to reap above-market returns, for that is how innovation is encouraged in a market economy.

When contracts appear to have harsh nonprice terms, there is another reason for thinking that these terms are unobjectionable. Even if the seller or creditor has market power, it has the right incentive to supply the terms that parties desire. For example, a debtor might be willing to consent to a harsh remedial term in return for a low interest rate. And a supplier might be willing to give the buyer the power to terminate the contract with little notice, if that is the only way to get the buyer's business. The party with market power will supply terms if the other parties want them and will charge them a fee, but will not force terms on parties that do not want them, for generally the most efficient way to exploit market power is through the price term. Although there are models in which a combination of market power and asymmetric information can result in inefficient terms, they justify nonenforcement only under complex and hard-to-identify conditions.

Eric A. Posner, Economic Analysis of Contract Law After Three Decades: Success or Failure?, 112 Yale L.J. 829, 843 (2003).

3. The court in *Walker-Thomas* neglected to mention that the plaintiff was African-American and on assistance. Should the court have mentioned this explicitly? One writer observed:

The consequences of such an oversight should not be lightly dismissed. As an initial matter, the omission creates an inaccurate account of what transpires at the metaphorical bargaining table, potentially undermining the intended effect of any legal remedy aiming to uphold the economic rights of the relatively "weaker" bargaining party. At a deeper level, the oversight reinforces the detachment or disengagement between contract law and race, removing from the contractual picture a highly sensitive, complicated social matter. But the removal of race from contract discussion does not innocuously simplify the issues. Rather, it implies that race has no relevance to discussions of fairness or burden within the bargaining transaction at all. It effectively extinguishes the relevance of race, with the associated influences of racial perceptions and racist intents, from contract-law discourse. At the same time, by misrepresenting the actual interactions between race and law in market transactions, and by ignoring the real social pressures that may unfairly manipulate the bargaining process, contract law's avoidance of discussions of race ultimately risks occluding the potential in contract law affirmatively to uphold the economic rights of racial minorities. The danger is . . . that those whose economic rights are most challenged will not be able to access the laws and rules that purport to uphold everyone's economic rights.

Julian S. Lim, Tongue-Tied in the Market: The Relevance of Contract Law to Racial-Language Minorities, 91 Cal. L. Rev. 579, 593-94 (2003). For an even broader perspective, consider the following:

Unconscionability cases invariably involve two differing cultures or at least subcultures. . . . Cultural considerations are often unavoidable, and may entail attention to race, ethnicity, class, gender, national origin, sexual orientation, age, and other considerations which should be *explicitly* analyzed to uncover how and whether those traits and circumstances affected a party's culture and how and whether this culture affected an allegedly unconscionable transaction.

Augusto C. Lima, When Harry Met Kreutziger: A Look Into Unconscionability Through the Lenses of Culture (2008) (unpublished manuscript), available at http://ssrn.com/abstract=1124922.

Unconscionability Issues Arise in Disparate Settings

Unconscionability claims arise in many different settings, not just in sale-of-goods cases such as *Walker-Thomas*. For example, consider the unusual case of Knudsen v. Lax, 17 Misc. 3d 350, 842 N.Y.S.2d 341 (County Ct. 2007). The court considered whether a tenant with three young daughters can terminate a lease without liability because the landlord rented an adjacent apartment to a convicted sex offender. The lease contained an acceleration clause that made the tenant liable for all of the remaining rent if the

tenant abandoned the lease for any reason. The court first discussed criminal law's sex offender notification requirements that help keep "a sex offender away from the vicinity of children." Next, the court noted that the landlord was able to "impose" the lease on the tenant because of a "disparity of bargaining power" between the parties and because the lease was a standard form. The court therefore found the acceleration clause unconscionable.

MORE ON THE ROLE OF COURTS AND LEGISLATURES

The dissent in *Walker-Thomas* believed any regulation of standard-form contracts should come from the legislature, not the courts. In this regard, consider again the material presented in Section Three of this chapter concerning the roles of legislatures and courts, and the following excerpt that highlights the inconclusiveness of this debate.

ROBERT A. HILLMAN, DEBUNKING SOME MYTHS ABOUT UNCONSCIONABILITY: A NEW FRAMEWORK FOR U.C.C. SECTION 2-302
67 Cornell L. Rev. 1, 27-29 (1982)*

Broad legislative standards that delegate to courts the responsibility of "legislating" are often criticized on the theory that courts are ill-equipped to evaluate social policy issues. Judges, it is said, do not have sufficient resources or time to evaluate the effects of their decisions on society, while vast resources are available to legislators to investigate such matters. At best, courts can compare the conduct of similar commercial parties

to determine whether particular behavior fits a community standard; but this approach to fairness questions ensures adherence to the "predominant morals of the marketplace" and precludes serious consideration of more desirable alternatives.

Even if the judiciary is equipped to explore issues of social policy and the effects of alternative approaches on society, the argument goes, the common law process may be an inferior method of achieving the social policy goals that are ultimately identified. For example, Professor Leff contended that after cases such as *Williams v.*

Walker-Thomas Furniture Co., sellers affected by unconscionability findings simply will alter their forms slightly to avoid repetition of the findings and that these alterations will not cure the fundamental ills of the sellers' practices. Nor will the decisions curb similar abuses that are not addressed specifically by the cases. Leff maintained that common law development is costly, time-consuming, and possibly ineffective: "One cannot think of a more expensive and frustrating course than to seek to regulate goods or 'contract' quality through repeated lawsuits against inventive 'wrongdoers.'"

These arguments in favor of legislative control over social policy issues have been challenged. For example, Professor [Richard] Posner has suggested that judge-created rules are more "efficiency-promoting" than legislative rules. Appellate judges, he asserts, view the parties as representing activities and make their decisions based on which activity is more valuable economically. Legislators, on the other hand, are subject to interest group pressure and depend on the electoral process; therefore, they "sell" legislation to those parties that can enhance their prospects of reelection. One may question Posner's premise that judges adhere to a model of economic efficiency and that efficiency is the appropriate basis upon which to make policy. Nevertheless, his theory does point out that, at least to the extent that judges are insulated from lobbying groups and politics, judicial decisions can be more objective than decisions made by their legislative counterparts.

The argument that the common law process is an inferior method of achieving favorable reform may also be overdrawn. The general threat of an unconscionability finding may have an in terrorem effect that alone deters sellers from including suspect terms in commercial agreements. In addition, legislators cannot successfully draft legislation to encompass unforeseen circumstances. New approaches are needed to deal with unforeseen problems constantly disclosed through litigation; many of these problems occur with sufficient frequency so that it would be unfair and inefficient to await legislative enactment. For this reason, legislative regulation of contract terms generally has been confined to distinct segments of business such as the insurance industry, where issues are already well-defined and narrowed.

The availability of judicial intervention ensures that fairness in particular controversies is achieved. As suggested earlier, some consumers are entitled to protection from egregious contract terms because, despite the clarity of disclosure of the offending terms, they are incapable of comprehending the significance of the agreement. Courts can evaluate the facts of a particular case to determine whether the consumer was capable of understanding the subject of disclosure. Legislatures, on the other hand, can only establish broad classifications of those consumers who should not be presumed to have assented.

Unfair Terms

One suggestion for improving contract law's rather amorphous approach to sorting out agreements or terms in standard forms that should not be enforced is for the lawmaker to compile a list of terms that should not be enforceable under any circumstances. For example, the cross-collateral clause in *Williams v. Walker-Thomas* may be a candidate for nonenforcement. The European Union in its 1993 Directive on Unfair Contract Terms sets forth a nonexclusive list of unfair clauses in non-negotiated agreements. These include clauses such as:

(a) excluding or limiting the legal liability of a seller or supplier in the event of the death of a consumer or personal injury to the latter resulting from an act or omission of that seller or supplier;

(b) inappropriately excluding or limiting the legal rights of the consumer vis-à-vis the seller or supplier or another party in the event of total or partial non-performance or inadequate performance by the seller or supplier of any of the contractual obligations . . . ;

(d) permitting the seller or supplier to retain sums paid by the consumer where the latter decides not to conclude or perform the contract, without providing for the consumer to receive compensation of an equivalent amount from the seller or supplier where the latter is the party cancelling the contract;

(e) requiring any consumer who fails to fulfil his obligation to pay a disproportionately high sum in compensation; . . .

(j) enabling the seller or supplier to alter the terms of the contract unilaterally without a valid reason which is specified in the contract;

(k) enabling the seller or supplier to alter unilaterally without a valid reason any characteristics of the product or service to be provided . . . .

For a recent set of examples that could appear on anyone's list of unenforceable terms, think about the following clauses that in one form or another regularly appear in electronic standard forms when you download software from the Internet:

"You may not criticize this product publicly."

"Using this product means you will be monitored."

"By signing this contract, you also agree to every change in future versions of it; end user license agreements are subject to change without notice."

"We are not responsible if this product messes up your computer."

See Dangerous Terms: A User's Guide to EULA, Electronic Frontier Foundation, http://www.eff.org/wp/eula.php.

One problem with creating lists of unfair clauses is that lawmakers may select an over- or under-inclusive set of clauses for exclusion. Another is that some clauses on the list may be perfectly reasonable in some circumstances; for example, a seller may even be able to justify a cross-collateral clause if its clientele's credit risk is exceptionally high.

A different approach to the standard-form problem on the Internet is to require a "cooling-off period" in which a contracting party could change her mind and avoid the contract. However, contracting could become very expensive for e-businesses if a party could reverse course after contracting. A more modest idea for improving contract law's protection against unfair clauses is just to make sure that people have notice of the clauses and the opportunity to read them before contracting.

STANDARD-FORM CONTRACTING IN THE ELECTRONIC AGE

Private citizens and businesses encounter standard forms when they make contracts on the Internet. The *Caspi* case and the materials that follow illustrate the role of contract law in this context.

CASPI v. MICROSOFT NETWORK
Superior Court of New Jersey, 1999
323 N.J. Super. 118, 732 A.2d 528, cert. denied,
162 N.J. 199, 743 A.2d 851 (1999)

KESTIN, J.A.D.:

We are here called upon to determine the validity and enforceability of a forum selection clause contained in an on-line subscriber agreement of the Microsoft Network (MSN), an on-line computer service. The trial court granted defendants' motion to dismiss the complaint on the ground that the forum selection clause in the parties' contracts called for plaintiffs' claims to be litigated in the State of Washington. Plaintiffs appeal. We affirm.

The amended class action complaint in eighteen counts sought diverse relief against two related corporate entities, The Microsoft Network, L.L.C. and Microsoft Corporation (collectively, Microsoft). Plaintiffs asserted various theories including breach of contract, common law fraud, and consumer fraud in the way Microsoft had "rolled over" MSN membership into more expensive plans. Among the claims was an accusation that Microsoft had engaged in "unilateral negative option billing," a practice condemned by the attorneys general of twenty-one states, including New Jersey's, with regard to a Microsoft competitor, America Online, Inc. Under the practice as alleged, Microsoft, without notice to or permission from MSN members, unilaterally charged them increased membership fees attributable to a change in service plans.

The four named plaintiffs are members of MSN. Two reside in New Jersey; the others in Ohio and New York. Purporting to represent a nationwide class of 1.5 million similarly aggrieved MSN members, plaintiffs, in May 1997, moved for multi-state class action certification. See R. 4:32.

Shortly thereafter, defendants moved to dismiss the amended complaint for lack of jurisdiction and improper venue by reason of the forum selection clause which, defendants contended, was in every MSN membership agreement and bound all the named plaintiffs and all members of the class they purported to represent. That clause, paragraph 15.1 of the MSN membership agreement, provided:

> This agreement is governed by the laws of the State of Washington, USA, and you consent to the exclusive jurisdiction and venue of courts in King County, Washington in all disputes arising out of or relating to your use of MSN or your MSN membership. . . .

On November 13, 1997, Judge Fitzpatrick, in a written opinion, expressed his reasons for dismissing the complaint based upon the forum selection clause. Given that conclusion . . . plaintiffs' motion to certify the class was denied as moot. Conforming orders were entered on the same date. . . .

The background of the matter was depicted in the . . . opinion:

Before becoming an MSN member, a prospective subscriber is prompted by MSN software to view multiple computer screens of information, including a membership agreement which contains the above clause. MSN's membership agreement appears on the computer screen in a scrollable window next to blocks providing the choices "I Agree" and "I Don't Agree." Prospective members assent to the terms of the agreement by clicking on "I Agree" using a computer mouse. Prospective members have the option to click "I Agree" or "I Don't Agree" at any point while scrolling through the agreement. Registration may proceed only after the potential subscriber has had the opportunity to view and has assented to the membership agreement, including MSN's forum selection clause. No charges are incurred until after the membership agreement review is completed and a subscriber has clicked on "I Agree." . . .

Judge Fitzpatrick correctly discerned that New Jersey follows the logic of the United States

Supreme Court decision in Carnival Cruise Lines v. Shute, 499 U.S. 585, 111 S. Ct. 1522 (1991).... In *Carnival*, cruise ship passengers were held to a forum selection clause which appeared in their travel contract. The clause enforced in *Carnival* was very similar in nature to the clause in question here, the primary difference being that the *Carnival* clause was placed in small print in a travel contract while the clause in the case sub judice was placed on-line on scrolled computer screens....

[Judge Fitzpatrick held that] plaintiffs and the class which they purport to represent were given ample opportunity to affirmatively assent to the forum selection clause. Like *Carnival*, plaintiffs here "retained the option of rejecting the contract with impunity." 499 U.S. 585, 111 S. Ct. 1522....

After reviewing the record in the light of the arguments advanced by the parties, we are in substantial agreement with the reasons for decision articulated by Judge Fitzpatrick.... New Jersey's interest in assuring consumer fraud protection will not be frustrated by requiring plaintiffs to proceed with a lawsuit in Washington as prescribed by the plain language of the forum selection clause.... If a forum selection clause is clear in its purport and has been presented to the party to be bound in a fair and forthright fashion, no consumer fraud policies or principles have been violated....

The only viable issues that remain bear upon the argument that plaintiffs did not receive adequate notice of the forum selection clause, and therefore that the clause never became part of the membership contract which bound them. A related, alternative argument is that the question of notice is a factual matter that should be submitted to a jury. Defendants respond by arguing that 1) in the absence of fraud, a contracting party is bound by the provisions of a form contract even if he or she never reads them; 2) this clause met all reasonable standards of conspicuousness; and 3) the sign-up process gave plaintiffs ample opportunity to review and reject the agreement. Defendants also contend that notice is a question of law, decidable by a court, not a jury.

The holding in Carnival Cruise Lines v. Shute, 499 U.S. 585, 111 S. Ct. 1522 (1991), does not dispose of the notice question because the plaintiffs there had "essentially . . . conceded that they had notice of the forum-selection provision[,]" by

stating that they "'[did] not contest . . . that the forum selection clause was reasonably communicated to [them], as much as three pages of fine print can be communicated.'" Id. at 590, 111 S. Ct. at 1525. The dissenting justices described the format in which the forum selection clause had been presented as "in the fine print on the back of the [cruise] ticket." Id. at 597, 111 S. Ct. at 1529 (Stevens, J., dissenting).

The scenario presented here is different because of the medium used, electronic versus printed; but, in any sense that matters, there is no significant distinction. The plaintiffs in *Carnival* could have perused all the fine-print provisions of their travel contract if they wished before accepting the terms by purchasing their cruise ticket. The plaintiffs in this case were free to scroll through the various computer screens that presented the terms of their contracts before clicking their agreement.

Also, it seems clear that there was nothing extraordinary about the size or placement of the forum selection clause text. By every indication we have, the clause was presented in exactly the same format as most other provisions of the contract. It was the first item in the last paragraph of the electronic document. We note that a few paragraphs in the contract were presented in upper case typeface, presumably for emphasis, but most provisions, including the forum selection clause, were presented in lower case typeface. We discern nothing about the style or mode of presentation, or the placement of the provision, that can be taken as a basis for concluding that the forum selection clause was proffered unfairly, or with a design to conceal or de-emphasize its provisions. To conclude that plaintiffs are not bound by that clause would be equivalent to holding that they were bound by no other clause either, since all provisions were identically presented. Plaintiffs must be taken to have known that they were entering into a contract; and no good purpose, consonant with the dictates of reasonable reliability in commerce, would be served by permitting them to disavow particular provisions or the contracts as a whole. See Rudbart v. North Jersey Dist. Water Supply Comm'n, 127 N.J. 344, 351–53, 605 A.2d 681 (referring to the principle that a contracting party may be bound by the terms of a form contract even if he or she has never read them), cert. denied, 506 U.S. 871, 113 S. Ct. 203 (1992).

The issue of reasonable notice regarding a forum selection clause is a question of law for the court to determine.... We agree with the trial court that, in the absence of a better showing than has been made, plaintiffs must be seen to have had adequate notice of the forum selection clause. The resolution of this notice issue, at this stage of the litigation between plaintiffs and defendants must, of course, be seen to be without prejudice to any showing either party may have the opportunity to make in another jurisdiction in a plenary proceeding on the contract regarding issues apart from the validity and enforceability of the forum selection clause.

Affirmed.

NOTES

1. A forum selection clause designates where a lawsuit may or must be brought. Here, the clause designated King County, Washington. That certainly is expedient for MSN, but obviously very inconvenient for members of the MSN Network from distant states. Nevertheless, the court concludes that MSN adequately presented the term and enforces it. Courts and commentators have come to call the MSN process of contracting "clickwrap" in that it requires a party to click "I agree" to terms presented on the screen before the party can complete the download.

2. Most Internet users have more time to peruse a form than people who sign paper forms. Nevertheless, Internet users, thrilled with the speed and convenience of internet shopping, often are impatient, even "click happy." Perhaps the court in *Caspi* should have taken this into account.

Some internet sites do not make their forms as available as MSN, but instead employ "browsewrap." For example, at the time of this writing, one popular site hides a link that leads to the standard form at the bottom of its home page. The form's "terms and conditions" proclaim that use of the site, without clicking any agreement button, constitutes agreement to the terms and conditions. The *Caspi* court presumably would not have approved of this process. Nevertheless, some businesses continue to use browsewrap strategies because some courts still enforce them:

> The conclusion of the terms paragraph states "[b]y submitting this query, you agree to abide by these terms."... Verio does not argue that it was unaware of these terms, only that it was not asked to click on an icon indicating that it accepted the terms. However, in light of this sentence at the end of Register.com's terms of use, there can be no question that by proceeding to submit a WHO IS query, Verio manifested its assent to be bound by Register.com's terms of use, and a contract was formed and subsequently breached.

Register.com, Inc. v. Verio, Inc., 126 F. Supp. 2d 238, 248 (S.D.N.Y. 2000), aff'd, 356 F.3d 393 (2d Cir. 2004).

Caspi focuses on the notice and opportunity to read terms. But if people do not read the standard forms, even if made aware of them and even if they have easy access to them, then disclosure of terms is irrelevant. In fact, there may be little the law can do to make people read their forms. We elaborate on this limit of the law in the next section.

MORE IMPROVEMENTS TO THE PRIVATE-ARRANGEMENT INSTRUMENT

As a general matter, rules of validation must be sufficiently clear and simple to encourage, or at least not discourage, the exercise of private powers. For example, rules of validation, such as offer and acceptance, should facilitate the formation of arrangements, not impede them.

Private-arrangement law should also offer clear, logical, consistent, and fair remedies for breach. At the same time, the law should support private dispute resolution so that parties can avoid the time and expense of litigation; dispute-resolution processes that avoid the adversarial process altogether, such as those suggested earlier in this chapter for family disputes, should be available when such processes best facilitate and handle dispute resolution. Government should also provide, through courts and other bodies, administrative supervision when needed, such as for the administration of wills.

Individuals trained in the law should be accessible to people who require advice and aid either in setting up a private arrangement or in administering it. The problems of the White and Benkowski agreement drafted by a real estate agent was not merely propaganda for the legal industry! Of course, the costs involved in retaining a lawyer for a simple transaction sometimes outweigh the benefits of the services. Private-arrangement law must therefore facilitate agreements made without lawyers, for example, by promoting the use of plain language and avoiding technical interpretations of language.

Most legal systems strive for all of the foregoing elements. Many, if not all, of them fall short in various ways. There is always room for improvement—more in some legal systems than in others. In Anglo-American legal systems, relevant proposals for reform are common.

Section Seven
LIMITATIONS OF LAW AS A PRIVATE-ARRANGEMENT INSTRUMENT

What are the law's limits in facilitating private arrangements? We just suggested the need for finding the proper balance between conflicting policies of private-arrangement law. For example, the law must deny those with powerful bargaining advantages the right to dictate unconscionable terms, but at the same time the law must not usurp the parties' power to make their own deals. Can the law successfully draw such a line? Consider the guidance offered by the official comment to Uniform Commercial Code §2–302: "The principle is one of the prevention of oppression and unfair surprise . . . and not of disturbance of allocation of risks because of superior bargaining power." This is not much guidance at all. But one *limitation* of the law may be that greater certainty is impossible.

Another limitation of private-arrangement law is that it cannot guarantee that the parties will achieve their goals. This is so largely because of the varied and personal nature of these aims. Through marriage, parties seek love and happiness. A person writing a will may hope a beneficiary will become financially independent. Contracting parties may want financial satisfaction. The goals of people in setting up corporations, joining churches, and becoming members of social clubs or other organizations are also numerous and varied.

Private-arrangement law cannot guarantee success of an arrangement for additional reasons. First, people's goals may be unclear in their own minds or they may change their minds. For an example of the latter, consider the high divorce rate in this country. Second, even if individuals know what they want, they may choose an inappropriate arrangement to secure their goal. For example, a prenuptial agreement that determines the financial repercussions if the marriage breaks up may cause divisions between a couple and do more harm than good. Third, private-arrangement law cannot ensure that the parties will perform adequately. For example, if an opera star, a painter, or a musician were to perform a contract only because of a court order of specific performance, he would likely do a very poor job.

The rest of this section focuses on still another limitation of private-arrangement law. In general, a law will achieve its goals only if lawmakers understand and accurately predict human behavior. Otherwise, a law may produce surprising results. For an example pertinent to private-arrangement law, we know that consumers may decline to read their contracts regardless of the "duty to read" rule of contract law, which binds people to the terms of their signed contracts even if they are unaware of the terms. Consumers figure that the returns from reading a form do not outweigh the costs in time and effort, in part because they will not understand what they read and have no bargaining power to change terms. In addition, consumers are generally too optimistic that nothing will go wrong, and so do not worry about the contents of their contracts. Can the law create better incentives for consumers to read their contracts? Suppose you want to download virus-protection software from the Internet. Before you can proceed, you must click "I agree" on a long standard form that appears in a box on your screen. Admit it. The last thing you want to do is stop and study the typically lengthy and obscure standard form. Instead, you find the place to click "I agree," and click away! On the assumption that disclosure is important to deter business overreaching, is there anything that the law can do to encourage you to read the e-form, beyond binding you to the terms once you click "I agree"?

One possibility is to require still more disclosure. The law could require merchants conducting business on the Internet to disclose their e standard terms on their homepage, so that consumers can read and compare terms prior to any particular transaction. Such disclosure should not be very costly to business, because most businesses already have websites and because posting additional items is inexpensive. But the success of mandatory website disclosure depends on whether it will increase reading.

Unfortunately, creating a better opportunity to read simply may not work. Many of the reasons consumers do not read standard forms—time investment, difficulty of understanding, lack of bargaining power, and over-optimism—exist before a particular transaction, perhaps even to an exaggerated degree. In addition, e-consumers, attracted to the speed and fun of the Internet, are unlikely to take the time to compare terms. Consider, for example, the following description of the mindset of Internet shoppers:

> Analysis of [Internet] shopping is still relatively novel . . . . One study identifies two major types of shoppers on the Internet.[79] One type, the "convenience" shopper has a particular purchase in mind and rationally uses the Internet to reduce search costs, such as by using a search engine to gather information on and to compare prices and by reading product reviews online. The "recreational" shopper, on the other hand, shops for the sheer enjoyment of the experience and, stimulated by the interactive nature of the Internet, often purchases impulsively. Recreational shoppers "may be driven by need to purchase rather than need for a product." Analysts report that recreation may be "more important than convenience for online shoppers." Even shoppers who begin their shopping experience rationally to reduce the costs of their transaction may ultimately engage in impulse buying. The Internet environment apparently contributes to impulse purchasing because of its anonymity (people purchasing impulsively prefer privacy), availability 24 hours a day, and other "recreational shopping features," such as "email alerts of new products and special offers." In short, the online environment may contribute to impulsivity and even addictive purchasing among consumers. For consumers who succumb, Internet shopping may consist in large part of "consumers who utilize interactive features [to] enter a seamless sequence of responses, a 'flow' state in which their sense of time and reality becomes distorted and their self-control is diminished."
>
> On the other hand, some characteristics of online shopping may contribute to shopping rationality. Convenient access to prices, search engines that easily take consumers to competitors' sites, shopping carts, product reviews, and the absence of a hands-on bonding experience with a product moderate consumer impulsivity.

Robert A. Hillman, Online Boilerplate: Would Mandatory Website Disclosure of e-Standard Terms Backfire?, 104 Mich. L. Rev. 837, 851 (2006).

Some commentators posit that the presence of internet "watchdog" groups, which might spread the word over the internet about unreasonable contractual practices, create incentives for e-businesses to write fair terms. For example, we have noted that the Electronic Frontier Foundation compiles a list of "dangerous terms" on its website. But watchdog groups will fail in their purpose if people do not take the time to read the material on such sites.

Not only may law be ineffectual to achieve certain purposes, but lawmaking efforts may actually backfire, producing a result opposite from what was intended. Consider in this regard another excerpt from the above-cited article.

---

79. Junghyun Kim & Robert LaRose, Interactive E-Commerce: Promoting Consumer Efficiency or Impulsivity?, 10 J. of Computer-Mediated Comm. (Nov. 2004), available at http://jcmc.indiana.edu/vol10/issue1/kim_larose.html (last accessed on Mar. 4, 2005).

ROBERT A. HILLMAN, ONLINE BOILERPLATE: WOULD MANDATORY WEBSITE DISCLOSURE OF E–STANDARD TERMS BACKFIRE?

104 Mich. L. Rev. 837, 837–40, 854–56 (2006)*

A law backfires when it produces results opposite from those its drafters intended. Lots of laws may have backfired. For example, people opposed to hate crimes legislation think that the laws "inflame prejudice rather than eradicate it." The Endangered Species Act, according to some analysts, has helped destroy rather than preserve the creatures listed by the Act. Even consumer protection laws, some believe, increase prices and confuse consumers instead of protecting them.

This Article analyzes whether mandatory website disclosure of e-standard terms, advocated by some as a potential solution to market failures when consumers contract over the Internet, is another potential legal backfire. By mandatory website disclosure, I do not mean a "clickwrap" presentation of terms, in which a consumer must click "I agree" or the like on a screen presenting the terms prior to the completion of a transaction in progress. Mandatory website disclosure would require a business to maintain an Internet presence and to post its terms prior to any particular transaction so that a consumer could read and compare terms without making a purchase at all.

The problem is not that mandatory website disclosure would increase the cost of doing business, which would be passed on to consumers in the form of higher prices. Businesses have been unable to demonstrate that displaying their terms on their websites would be costly. Nor should drafting rules that implement the law be too difficult. Businesses could be required to display their terms on their homepage or on another page reachable directly through a clearly identified hyperlink. Further, businesses could be required to prove the availability of their terms by furnishing relatively inexpensive archival records of their websites. Mandatory website disclosure may backfire, however, because it may not increase reading or shopping for terms or motivate businesses to draft reasonable ones, but instead, may make heretofore suspect terms more likely enforceable....

...My preliminary empirical work on e-consumer reading of standard forms, as well as studies of e-shopping behavior, suggests that advance disclosure of terms likely will fail to increase reading or shopping for terms. This should be no surprise. Despite the opportunity to read, most e-consumers may still have ample rational reasons for not reading and cognitive processes that deter reading and processing terms. In addition, e-consumers, drawn to the speed and novelty of the Internet, are unlikely to have the patience or discipline to compare terms regardless of when the terms become available. Further, watchdog groups may not positively motivate businesses because they may lack influence and because businesses may conclude that the benefits of particular terms outweigh any potential costs in adverse publicity.

In light of the potential failure of mandatory website disclosure to increase reading and to discipline businesses, the only effects of the proposal may be to insulate businesses from claims of procedural unconscionability and to create a safe harbor for businesses to draft suspect terms. My goal is not to claim that mandatory website disclosure will certainly backfire so that the proposal should be taken off the table. In fact, I conclude that mandatory website disclosure ultimately may be the most viable alternative. I simply want to elaborate on the reasons that the possibility of backfire should be taken seriously before moving in the direction of mandatory website disclosure....

If courts rarely strike a contract or term based solely on one or the other kind of unconscionability, but use a sliding scale of procedural and substantive unconscionability, what will be the outcome of mandatory website disclosure? Perhaps marginal terms, insufficiently outlandish to motivate a court to strike them on substantive unconscionability grounds alone, will be enforceable because of their early disclosure on the website. For example, consider the term . . . allowing a software vendor to "collect[] certain non-personally identifiable information about [a consumer's] Web surfing and computer usage." If such authorization to "follow around" the consumer is fully disclosed on the vendor's webpage, I doubt that a court would strike it on substantive unconscionability grounds alone.

The result of mandatory website disclosure would constitute a legal backfire. . . .

Despite all that has been said, mandatory website disclosure may still be the best strategy for dealing with the problem of e-standard forms. As mentioned, other solutions present significant problems of their own. Further, mandatory website disclosure is cheap, substantiates the claim of consumer assent, and constitutes a symbolic victory for those advocating greater fairness in e-standard-form contracting.

Of course, mandatory website disclosure is attractive for these reasons only if my fear of a legal backfire proves exaggerated because the benefits of disclosure outweigh the costs of the enforcement of some questionable terms. And perhaps I am being unduly pessimistic about the possibility that disclosure will backfire. After all, if disclosure were a good strategy for businesses to avoid unconscionability claims and of little concern because consumers do not read their standard forms, one would expect to see lots of precontract disclosure of e-standard forms already. Businesses tempted to draft unfair terms must therefore believe that disclosure benefits consumers. But I am not convinced by this argument. Business decisionmakers may themselves fail to make rational decisions for much the same reasons as consumers. For example, businesses may be unduly risk averse concerning the outcome of disclosure and therefore prefer to hide their marginal terms, even though disclosing them actually would work to their advantage.

Ultimately, optimism about disclosure may depend on one's time frame for measuring the law's effects. Even if disclosure backfires in the short term, perhaps eventually the word will get out about a business's unsavory terms. Consider the experience of cigarette manufacturers who, in response to legislation, put warning labels on their packages. For a considerable period of time, these labels helped manufacturers " 'fend[] off smokers' suits'" based on smokers' assumption of the risk. As a result, "[w]hat was intended as a burden on tobacco became a shield instead." In the long run, however, the package warnings, along with the many revelations about cigarette manufacturers' attempts to hide other adverse facts about their products, led to a massive change in public opinion and, ultimately, to serious legal sanctions against the cigarette companies. Perhaps mandatory website disclosure will also have a long-term beneficial effect.

NOTES

1. If the law cannot increase reading of standard forms, what can it do to protect people from unfair contract terms? Section Six of this chapter briefly mentioned other possible solutions such as compiling a list of unlawful clauses or prescribing a cooling-off period. But recall that these approaches may not work either. Lawmakers may compile an unwise set of clauses for exclusion. And a cooling-off period raises serious questions about the costs to businesses—and the unlikelihood that people will read the terms during the cooling-off period.

2. Mandatory website disclosure may have a long-term beneficial effect analogous to the experience under the warning-label legislation for cigarettes. But many other forces may have been at work in the latter case, leading to legal sanctions against the companies.

Another Kind of e-Commerce Problem

The failure of consumers to read their standard forms is not the only problem exacerbated by e-commerce. For example, recently Target.com offered a top-of-the-line car seat, usually sold at $279.99, for $42.99. Within hours, the car seats were sold out. But those seemingly lucky purchasers were not so fortunate after all. Before delivery, they received an e-mail from Target stating that "[D]ue to an unexpected error," the car seat was "incorrect[ly] priced." The message went on to state that "[d]espite our best efforts, a small number of items on our site are occasionally mis-priced.... This e-mail was sent from a notification-only address that cannot accept incoming e-mail. Please do not reply to this message. If you have further questions please visit our online Help department."

E-commerce makes it easier for vendors and consumers to buy and sell, but it also magnifies potential problems such as Target's mistake. For example, Target's error is potentially much more serious because of the reach of sellers' advertisements over the Internet. Contract law in the paper world would support Target's right to rescind the sales, so long as customers had not detrimentally relied on the deal, such as by foregoing some other advantageous sale of car seats, and so long as Target could prove its error was not simply bad judgment. But the question remains whether contract law's approach to such mistakes should change in the electronic world.

Section Eight
SUMMARY

The law's private-arrangement instrument facilitates people achieving their goals by giving them the power to make their own arrangements, by creating "rules of validation," which consist of the legal instructions for making private arrangements, and by specifying the legal consequences of an arrangement once made. We have reviewed some of the many types of private arrangements recognized by the law, including private associations, corporations, wills, and, the focus in this chapter, contracts. We have spent some time elaborating on rules of validation and remedies in the contracts field to clarify how the law facilitates private arrangements. For example, we learned that parties must make an agreement supported by "consideration," which is something bargained for and given in exchange for the other party's promise. By observing this rule of validation, parties can create enforceable contract obligations or, for that matter, understand how to avoid them. We have also seen that if a party breaks a contract, the injured party can receive "expectation damages," designed to put the injured party in as good a position as if there had been no breach. Such a remedy, allows a contracting party to rely on a contract secure in the knowledge that the party will receive performance or its equivalent in damages.

We have also discussed the role of legislatures, courts, and private citizens in making private-arrangement law. We have seen that legislatures sometimes enact rules of validation, such as the rules to establish a corporation, while courts created the rules for enforcement of contracts. We have seen that courts also interpret legislative enactments, such as the rules concerning enforcement of wills and trusts. But essentially the private-arrangement instrument is private in the sense that people make their own law (sometimes with the aid of lawyers) by making and performing their own arrangements. We have also spent some time evaluating whether these institutions and parties play appropriate roles in lawmaking and application.

We have also reviewed the role of lawyers in making and enforcing private arrangements. In the field of contract law, lawyers help their clients plan, negotiate, and draft agreements. We have seen that a challenge for lawyers is to foresee potential stumbling blocks to the performance of agreements and to provide for their resolution in the agreement. However, lawyers must avoid "overdrafting" the agreement so that the parties will not want to commit to it in the first place. For example, would the Whites and Benkowskis have completed an agreement if their lawyers presented them with a long, complex draft full of legalese? Probably not. Of course, in light of what happened, that may have been a good thing in their case. In fact, in some contexts, the role of lawyers and contract law is diminished because the parties prefer to rely on trust and flexibility to govern their relation. Such parties also rely on nonlegal sanctions such as the potential for a diminished reputation if a party breaks a promise.

Private-arrangement law faces the challenge of finding the right balance between affording the parties the freedom to make their own agreements without the interference of government and policing agreements to deter unfair advantage-taking by one party. For example, we have seen that bargaining power disparities can lead to unconscionable terms and contracts, but the line between effective bargaining and coercion is hardly bright. In addition, we have seen how modern technology exacerbates problems of assent to contracts, such as in the context of standard-form contracts offered over the Internet. A clear limitation of private-arrangement law in this context is that there is little that the law can do to convince people to read the small-print boilerplate of standard forms before clicking on the "I agree" icon.

Private agreement law has limitations that go beyond such challenges. For example, the economic downturn of 2008 and 2009 was the product, in large part, of banks and borrowers making foolish loan agreements that would likely fail. A large reason for these unwise loans was greed on the part of the banks that, in the short term, made large profits off these loans, and the lack of caution on the part of the borrowers who agreed to unrealistic debt. Private-arrangement law cannot create incentives for people to be benevolent and wise.

For those interested in reading further about private-arrangement law, excellent general treatments include Henry M. Hart, Jr. & Albert M. Sacks, The Legal Process ch. 2 (William N. Eskridge, Jr. & Philip P. Frickey eds., 1994), and Alan B. Morrison, Fundamentals of American Law (2005). Ian Ayres & Gregory Klass, Insincere Promises: The Law of Misrepresented Intent (2005), is an interesting take on promise enforcement in contract law. Charles B.

Craver, Effective Legal Negotiation and Settlement (3d ed. 1997), is, as the title suggests, a good primer on negotiation and settlement of disputes. The best treatments of bargaining power problems are older classics, such as Robert L. Hale, Force and the State: A Comparison of "Political" and "Economic" Compulsion, 35 Colum. L. Rev. 149 (1935), Friedrich Kessler & Edith Fine, Culpa in Contrahendo, Bargaining in Good Faith, and Freedom of Contract: A Comparative Study, 77 Harv. L. Rev. 401 (1964), and Anthony T. Kronman, Contract Law and Distributive Justice, 89 Yale L.J. 472 (1980).

THE

ENDS

OF LAW

Chapter 6

Law Can Help Promote Safety

Chapter 7

Law Can Help Promote Equality

Each of the foregoing chapters contains an introduction, then five sections that respectively apply the five legal instruments to the social end, and finally a summary.

INTRODUCTORY NOTE TO PART TWO

In Part One we treated the nature of law principally by considering the range and limits of law's methodology. The central question was *how* law does what it does. Chapters 1 through 5 compared and differentiated the five basic instruments of law, which constitute the means at law's disposal.

Thus far, however, we have slighted part of law's nature: we have not considered many of the social tasks to which people commonly assign law. Part Two, then, elaborates on *what* law does. What can law do and not do? That is, what are the range and limits of the functions of law? As to efficacy on the ends of law, four themes predominate.

First, modern societies assign a variety of tasks to law. The variety is wide, the end uses may be good or bad, and different societies discharge different functions in different degrees by different methods. We employ illustration to suggest this variety. In this part, we look at how law can help promote safety and equality in U.S. society. Chapter 6 considers safety, an old and tangible concern rooted in tort and private law. Chapter 7 considers equality, a newer and more intangible effort emerging from constitutional and public law. Comparisons and contrasts between these two chapters should lead you to a deeper understanding of the ends of law.

Second, observe that the foregoing formulation of the illustrative tasks contains the words "can help promote." This formulation acknowledges that law does not always achieve society's aims. But those words express more than that. A common, as well as a professional, fallacy about law is that what law does achieve, it achieves all alone. Morality, however, assists the penal instrument, does it not? For another example, self-interest makes the job of safety regulation vastly easier. Thus, law receives large assists from nonlegal means—a second theme we develop through Part Two.

Third, law typically does not rely on just one of its basic instruments to address a given social problem. It may apply a variant of a basic instrument. It may invent a combination mode that draws ideas from several of the basic instruments. Or, most likely, law brings a number of the five instruments to bear simultaneously, and in their characteristically different ways, on the social task. Consider again the example of slaughter on the highways. Here, remedies are available that allow the injured or bereaved to exact monetary compensation (the remedial instrument); punishment is imposed for reckless or drunken driving (the penal instrument); licenses are required of drivers (the administrative instrument); safe highways can be constructed and maintained (the public-benefit instrument); and insurers protect the injured against crippling losses (the private-arrangement instrument). In this part, each of the two chapters centers on five sections that explore how the five basic instruments can all contribute to promoting safety or equality.

Fourth, Part Two develops the theme that one may fruitfully view law from the vantage point of an imaginary social engineer or manager who has power over the law's resources and has responsibility for their rational allocation to given tasks. Total rationality is admittedly impossible, because the manager does not know enough and cannot anticipate all consequences of action. And many social phenomena are not readily subject to conscious alteration, but instead change through some poorly understood and evolutionary process. Nevertheless, the managerial viewpoint, when combined with the conception of law as five distinct instruments, has value as a critical apparatus in several ways.

Along a first dimension, we may criticize the appropriateness of the selection among the legal instruments. The manager might choose an *inapt* instrument for the job. For example, if the end were to ensure a minimal living standard for all members of the society, we would then expect less reliance on remedial methods and more on public-benefit conferral. Or the manager's choice of an instrument might be otherwise *unwise*, being impractical or somehow detrimental. For example, use of the private-arrangement instrument to achieve a minimal living standard for everyone may be unwise. Or the manager's resort to a particular instrument might under the circumstances be *unnecessary*, and hence wasteful or even counterproductive. For example, given that drug manufacturers are already subject to civil remedies for most injuries they inflict, and given that the administrative instrument already supervises the manufacturing process, invoking the penal instrument by imposing criminal liability for producing unsafe drugs may be unnecessary. Or the manager might employ an *insufficient* number of instruments. For example, we have already indicated how all five basic instruments prove useful in combating the problem of slaughter on the highways.

A second dimension of criticism looks not at the selection among instruments but at the effectiveness of their use. Even if a particular instrument is appropriate for a given task, the manager might not be using it in its most effective form. The manager may have framed an ineffective remedy for the grievance, an unduly stringent penalty for the crime, an unrealistic regulatory standard to meet, and so on.

A third dimension of criticism then opens up. In Part One we examined the distinctive conditions for maximal effectiveness of each of the law's instruments. This led us to consider their correlative limitations. When this kind of critical evaluation is applied to all five instruments in relation to a given social problem, we can ascertain whether law as a whole is likely to be less effective in dealing with this problem than in dealing with others, or whether law stands much of a chance of success at all especially in comparison to society's nonlegal means. That is, Part Two not only will refine your idea of the nature of law by stressing its functions but also will heighten your consciousness of the limits of law as a whole.

Chapter 6

LAW CAN HELP

PROMOTE SAFETY

[I]t is the right of the people ... to institute new government, laying its foundation on such principles, and organizing its powers in such form, as to them shall seem most likely to effect their safety and happiness.

DECLARATION OF INDEPENDENCE

Section One
INTRODUCTION

This chapter focuses on the problem of product safety and on the law that responds to this problem. Our goal, however, is not to teach the ins and outs of product safety law, but to illustrate how each of the law's five basic instruments that you studied in the first five chapters of this book can help achieve an important social goal. Here the goal is safety and, specifically, product safety.

No one should be surprised that law deals with the problem of product safety. Today, people can choose from many thousands of products, many of which are complex and dangerous, leading to more and more injuries and deaths. Injuries and death may result from product design defects, defects in manufacturing, or failure to warn about proper usage. Consider the power lawn mower. In the late 1940s, injuries caused by such mowers were unusual, but as technology increased their power and sophistication and as consumers increasingly used such mowers, injuries increased exponentially. See 1 Louis R. Frumer & Melvin I. Friedman, Products Liability §1, at 4–5 (1984) (reporting that a 24-inch blade of a power lawn mower can pick up an object and hurl it at a speed of 225–240 mph).

Although injuries from defective products are increasing and although the public may clamor for legal relief, it is not self-evident what form relief should take or even whether in some circumstances there should be any relief. As you consider the materials in this chapter, remember that the most fundamental question is whether the law should step in at all. The two excerpts that close this introduction deal with this question.

Assuming that society should use law to increase product safety, you should also evaluate the appropriateness of the use of each legal instrument in achieving this goal. For example, should criminal liability be imposed on companies that produce unreasonably dangerous products? To answer this question, one must focus on the particular characteristics of the penal instrument, but the problem is also a comparative one. Are other instruments better suited to achieve the goal of protecting people from dangerous products? If manufacturers are civilly, not criminally, liable for negligent manufacture and for breach of contract, for example, are criminal sanctions or, for that matter, administrative regulations necessary? One may conclude that a combination of instruments best serves the particular goal. Or one may conclude that none of the law's instruments alone or in concert with others can achieve the goal. This chapter is about the law's limits as well as its functions.

Even assuming the appropriateness of a particular legal instrument, another issue is whether society utilizes the instrument effectively. For example, some argue that punitive damages should not be recoverable for injuries resulting from product defects because, among other reasons, companies will simply raise the prices of their products to finance their punitive liability. Even if this criticism is correct, however, other forms of civil relief may be effective to compel companies to manufacture safer products, and lawmakers must consider such alternatives. As you read this chapter, consider whether any appropriate instrument of the law is misused and what changes in application you would propose.

But first, should society utilize law to help solve the problem of product safety? If so, what should that law look like? Jim Chen and Daniel J. Gifford point out that "American law . . . has sampled numerous approaches to the product safety problem," including relying on "market mechanisms," government regulation, and cost-benefit analysis. Jim Chen & Daniel J. Gifford, Law As Industrial Policy: Economic Analysis of Law in a New Key, 25 U. Mem. L. Rev. 1315, 1335-36 (1995). Consider the following views of two important product-safety analysts of the late twentieth century.

RICHARD A. EPSTEIN, MODERN PRODUCTS LIABILITY LAW
5-7 (1980)*

It is useful to trace products liability law through three main stages in its development. The first stage, from *Winterbottom v. Wright*[4] in 1842 until *MacPherson v. Buick Motor Co.*[5] in 1916, had as its major premise the belief that the grave administrative complications and adverse social consequences of products liability suits were so manifest that strenuous efforts were needed to fashion "fixed and definite" rules to prevent the economic ruin of product suppliers. In most cases, but not all, the result of this attitude was to place upon product users and consumers the burden of ferreting out and correcting all manner of product

weaknesses and deficiencies. The privity rule— riddled with exceptions before it toppled—was a major tool, but by no means the only one, used to achieve that end. The need to prove the defendant's negligence helped insulate manufacturers from liability for defective products they placed upon the marketplace. The narrow conception of causal connection spared them liability whenever the negligence of other parties farther down the chain of distribution and use substantially contributed to the occurrence of injury. Strong affirmative

---

4. 10 M. & W. 109, 152 Eng. Rep. 402 (Exch. 1842).
5. 217 N.Y. 382, 111 N.E. 1050 (1916).

defenses, whether of contributory negligence or assumption of risk, placed still further obstacles in the way of recovery, and rigorous requirements of proof everywhere blocked the plaintiff. The law was altogether too restrictive, as many of the barriers to recovery could not be justified either as a matter of substantive principle or administrative necessity.

The second stage of the development began with the epic decision in *MacPherson v. Buick* and continued until, roughly speaking, shortly after the publication in 1965 of the Restatement (Second) of Torts. In this period products liability law achieved what in retrospect appears to be the best balance between the dual constraints of substantive justice and administrative need. The manufacturer was required to supply the individual consumer with the product that had been promised or take the consequences if that product proved dangerous because it deviated from the manufacturer's own formula, design, or performance standards. The individual consumer or user was bound, as a condition of recovery, to treat that product with the respect that it deserved, to use it in the proper way and for its appropriate ends. The legal rules functioned like an elaborate set of implied contracts that carefully distributed losses from product-related accidents in accordance with the shared expectations of manufacturer and user. The privity limitation upon recovery was everywhere rejected; the negligence requirements were first eroded and then eliminated; the defect requirement in products liability actions was sensibly applied, if not always fully defined; and a workable set of affirmative defenses tied the fortunes of the injured party to his own conduct. While by no means perfect, the system evenly distributed the burdens of loss between manufacturers and consumers.

The third stage of development, which began sometime between 1968 and 1970, starts from totally different philosophical premises. Administrative necessities, which loomed all too large in the nineteenth century, are taken all too lightly by modern judges. In the surge toward ever greater public control, courts have radically redefined the relative obligations of manufacturers and consumers. The plaintiff must still show some defect in the defendant's product, but the defect concept has been expanded far beyond its traditional confines. No longer can a product escape legal scrutiny because it was supplied in the very condition in which the defendant represented it to be, for now in many jurisdictions a jury may treat that product as defective if it thinks that some alternative design or plan on balance is preferable. As a common law matter, the entire system cares much less for contractual models for setting liability and much more for public law models of regulation—judicial regulation to be sure, but regulation nonetheless.

The redefinition of the manufacturer's obligation has brought with it a correlative shift in the obligations of the product consumer. Whereas the consumer was once regarded as an essential and responsible link in the chain of product use, today he is often viewed more as an object of legal protection and less as a bearer of independent responsibilities. Instead of being held accountable for the consequences of his own misconduct, the consumer is all too often insulated from his own recklessness, foolishness, and neglect.

MARSHALL SHAPO, A NATION OF GUINEA PIGS
xi, xiv–xv, 90, 253–56 (1979)

The march of science has proved a boon for most, but it also has brought tragedy to a few.

The media deluge us with stories about beneficial products of scientific progress that cause or threaten harm to those in no position to make meaningful choices. The case of oral contraceptives is a benchmark in the history of medical progress. Though the Pill has freed millions from sexual constraints, it has proved, over a decade of marketing, to have serious side effects for a relatively small number of users, and the returns on its long-term consequences are not in yet. The seemingly miraculous versatility of the sex hormones used to prevent conception has been utilized in other ways to preserve it, and in the fullness of the cycle of the life they control, to promote growth. Thus, the hormone diethylstilbestrol (DES) has been employed to prevent miscarriages, and also to improve the rate of weight gain in livestock. Yet in the former instance there is evidence that it has caused cancers in the very children whose conception it fostered. And in the latter case, controversy has arisen about the possible cancer-causing properties of the tiny residues of the chemical in marketed meat. . . .

. . . [A] major thesis of this book is that over a period of about forty years a consensus has developed among the American people and their representatives about the risks that attend the benefits of scientific and technological progress. This consensus holds in effect that when concern and suspicion about these potential hazards find

their way into the public eye, Americans adopt a generally risk-averse perspective on being exposed to dangers that are cumulative, unseen, and uncertain over the long term. A large part of this concern, articulated as well as implicit in several safety-focused statutes, is based in motives of self-protection against the uncertain danger. Part of it is founded in a sense that we should make strong efforts to limit the exposure of random groups of the population to the risks of serious physical injury or even death from dangers that are unpredictable and unknowable and may strike without warning. This view may be especially strong when the traumatic connotations of dangers that "strike" cannot adequately describe a process that may take months or even years in the human body. Further, when public anxiety about such hazards finds its way into legislation, judges tend to credit this risk averse tendency, motivated interstitially by the factors described above as well as responding to the specific public concern embodied in safety statutes.

Professor Epstein describes the evolution of product safety law and concludes that by the 1970s the law became overprotective of consumers, who could recover even if they ignored their responsibilities. Even if Epstein's estimation of the law at that time was accurate, subsequently the pendulum appears to have swung back toward a greater balance between consumer protection and consumer responsibility. Today, consumer fault will reduce the chance of recovery in several ways. Further, the definition of a "defective" product seems to have narrowed. We shall look more closely at these issues in Section Three of this chapter.

At times, the popular press seems to fuel the perception that product liability law is out of control in favor of consumers. For example, newspapers invariably highlight accounts of inexplicable jury awards, often of huge sums. For example, the press was full of accounts of the award of $2.9 million to a McDonald's customer who burned herself when she spilled her hot coffee. Many accounts omitted the fact that she suffered severe burns and that the coffee was 20 degrees hotter than most vendors' coffee. Moreover, the parties settled the case for $600,000. Notwithstanding the actual facts, cases such as these have instigated attempts by lawmakers to cap product liability awards or at least punitive damages.

Professor Shapo explains why a country with a heritage of self-reliance would nonetheless produce product safety laws. He believes that even self-reliant people are wary of risk when they cannot protect themselves. As the introduction to this section suggests, people cannot protect themselves because of the flood of sophisticated and dangerous products on the market.

Law and Social Change

The discussion in Section One describes changes, not only in the law, but in people's attitudes and perceptions about product safety. There is an obvious relationships between the law and public opinion, mores, and attitudes:

> Law ... is both an independent and dependent variable in and of social change, a cause and an effect. In the United States, for example, enacted laws have given or taken away the rights of women and people of color, forced native populations off tribal lands, and granted civil rights and ownership of property to select groups at the expense of others. . . . These

examples suggest that law responds to the social environment. . . .

Sheryl J. Grana & Jane C. Ollenburger, The Social Context of Law 145 (1999). Consider the law that required cigarette manufacturers to place warning labels on their packages. At first, the labels helped manufacturers fight off lawsuits based on the theory that smokers assumed the risk of contracting diseases. In the long run, however, the package warnings, as well as revelations about cigarette manufacturers' attempts to hide the ramifications of smoking, led to a massive change in public opinion about smoking. This, in turn, led to more serious legal remedies for smokers.

Section Two

PRODUCT SAFETY AND THE PRIVATE-ARRANGEMENT INSTRUMENT

Chapter 5 focused on how private individuals arrange their affairs and how law facilitates those arrangements. Enforcing private contracts is one method of dealing with the problem of product safety. A seller may promise that its goods are free from defects in order to make a sale. A seller who makes such a promise is liable if the product proves to be defective. Such potential liability will presumably encourage sellers to exercise care in manufacturing and distributing products.

Still, private contracting may not ensure product safety. First, some sellers may be able to raise prices to cover potential liability for defects. Second, lots of issues must be settled in favor of a buyer before the seller is liable. For example, what was the content of the seller's promise (i.e., what representations concerning the product's quality—called warranties—did the seller make and did the seller disclaim any liability in the contract)? What representations and promises by the seller were inaccurate? In addition, who is entitled to sue and who can be sued for a product defect? (Can a friend of the buyer who uses a defective product bring a breach of warranty action for injuries suffered while using the product? May an injured buyer sue the remote manufacturer of a product instead of the retail store where the buyer purchased the product?)

The potential for a seller to escape liability based on any of these issues creates a disincentive for sellers to make their products safe. Other disincentives include the likelihood that buyers will not sue because of the costs of litigation, including legal fees and inconvenience.

What follows is a brief overview of product-warranty law. Although we cannot hope to resolve all of the above issues in this chapter, this overview permits you to see the strengths and weakness of this law in achieving product safety.

Much of the product-warranty law has been enacted by state legislatures. The Uniform Commercial Code (U.C.C.), drafted by practicing lawyers, judges, and law professors to govern commercial transactions and subsequently enacted, at least in part, by each of our 50 state legislatures, contains rules pertaining to warranty law in its Article 2, which deals with the sale of goods. Article 2 warranties include "express" warranties and "implied" warranties.

Express warranties include sellers' promises or representations about the quality of goods. To constitute an express warranty, a promise or representation must be more than the salesperson's opinion, sometimes called "puffing." Generally, the more specific and verifiable a promise or representation, the more likely the communication creates an express warranty. Thus, a salesperson's assertion that a television is "A-1" probably does not create an express warranty, but a statement that an LCD flat screen will last a minimum of ten years probably does create one. An affirmation or the like must also constitute the "basis of the bargain" to create a warranty. Generally, the test of "basis of the bargain" focuses on whether a reasonable purchaser would rely on the affirmation. Although express warranties seemingly provide some protection to consumers of defective products, sellers can disclaim such warranties in the contract of sale so long as the disclaimer is "consistent" with statements or writings that would otherwise be express warranties.

Implied warranties do not require a seller to make a promise or representation. They arise by "operation of law," meaning that the law (here Article 2) creates them automatically when the seller sells the goods. For example, the "implied warranty of merchantability" arises when a seller is in the business of selling goods of the kind sold, even if the seller made no promises or representations about the quality of the goods. Merchantability requires that the goods are "fit for the ordinary purpose for which such goods are used." U.C.C. §2-314(2)(c). This means roughly that they are of average quality for that kind of goods. The implied warranty of merchantability sounds protective of consumers, but sellers can exclude the warranty in the contract of sale. You have probably encountered language such as "seller disclaims the implied warranty of merchantability" when you have purchased goods. In addition, a buyer may have a hard time demonstrating that a product is not fit. For example, courts have held that cigarettes are fit for their ordinary purpose even though they may eventually kill you. The following case further investigates the meaning of merchantability.

WEBSTER v. BLUE SHIP TEA ROOM

Supreme Judicial Court of Massachusetts, 1964
347 Mass. 421, 198 N.E.2d 309

REARDON, JUSTICE:

This is a case which by its nature evokes earnest study not only of the law but also of the culinary traditions of the Commonwealth which bear so heavily upon its outcome. It is an action to recover damages for personal injuries sustained by reason of a breach of implied warranty of food served by the defendant in its restaurant. An auditor, whose findings of fact were not to be final, found for the plaintiff. On a retrial in the Superior Court before a judge and jury, in which the plaintiff testified, the jury returned a verdict for her. The defendant is here on exceptions to the refusal of the judge (1) to strike certain portions of the auditor's report, (2) to direct a verdict for the defendant, and (3) to allow the defendant's motion for the entry of a verdict in its favor under leave reserved.

The jury could have found the following facts: On Saturday, April 25, 1959, about 1 P.M., the plaintiff, accompanied by her sister and her aunt, entered the Blue Ship Tea Room operated by the defendant. The group was seated at a table and supplied with menus.

This restaurant, which the plaintiff characterized as "quaint," was located in Boston "on the third floor of an old building on T Wharf which overlooks the ocean."

The plaintiff, who had been born and brought up in New England (a fact of some consequence), ordered clam chowder and crabmeat salad. Within a few minutes she received tidings to the effect that "there was no more clam chowder," whereupon she ordered a cup of fish chowder. Presently, there was set before her "a small bowl of fish chowder." She had previously enjoyed a breakfast about 9 A.M. which had given her no difficulty. "The fish chowder contained haddock, potatoes, milk, water and seasoning. The chowder was milky in color and not clear. The haddock and potatoes were in chunks" (also a fact of consequence). "She agitated it a little with the spoon and observed that it was a fairly full bowl.... It was hot when she got it, but she did not tip it with her

spoon because it was hot... but stirred it in an up and under motion. She denied that she did this because she was looking for something, but it was rather because she wanted an even distribution of fish and potatoes." "She started to eat it, alternating between the chowder and crackers which were on the table with...[some] rolls. She ate about 3 or 4 spoonfuls then stopped. She looked at the spoonfuls as she was eating. She saw equal parts of liquid, potato and fish as she spooned it into her mouth. She did not see anything unusual about it. After 3 or 4 spoonfuls she was aware that something had lodged in her throat because she couldn't swallow and couldn't clear her throat by gulping and she could feel it." This misadventure led to two esophagoscopies at the Massachusetts General Hospital, in the second of which, on April 27, 1959, a fish bone was found and removed. The sequence of events produced injury to the plaintiff which was not insubstantial.

We must decide whether a fish bone lurking in a fish chowder, about the ingredients of which there is no other complaint, constitutes a breach of implied warranty under applicable provisions of the Uniform Commercial Code, the annotations to which are not helpful on this point. As the judge put it in his charge, "Was the fish chowder fit to be eaten and wholesome?... [N]obody is claiming that the fish itself wasn't wholesome.... But the bone of contention here—I don't mean that for a pun—but was this fish bone a foreign substance that made the fish chowder unwholesome or not fit to be eaten?"

The plaintiff has vigorously reminded us of the high standards imposed by this court where the sale of food is involved (see Flynn v. First Natl. Stores Inc., 296 Mass. 521, 523, 6 N.E.2d 814) and has made reference to cases involving stones in beans (Friend v. Childs Dining Hall Co., 231 Mass. 65, 120 N.E. 407, 5 A.L.R. 1100), trichinae in pork (Holt v. Mann, 294 Mass. 21, 22, 200 N.E. 403), and to certain other cases, here and elsewhere, serving to bolster her contention of breach of warranty.

The defendant asserts that here was a native New Englander eating fish chowder in a "quaint"

Boston dining place where she had been before; that "[f]ish chowder, as it is served and enjoyed by New Englanders, is a hearty dish, originally designed to satisfy the appetites of our seamen and fishermen"; that "[t]his court knows well that we are not talking of some insipid broth as is customarily served to convalescents." We are asked to rule in such fashion that no chef is forced "to reduce the pieces of fish in the chowder to minuscule size in an effort to ascertain if they contained any pieces of bone." "In so ruling," we are told (in the defendant's brief), "the court will not only uphold its reputation for legal knowledge and acumen, but will, as loyal sons of Massachusetts, save our world-renowned fish chowder from degenerating into an insipid broth containing the mere essence of its former stature as a culinary masterpiece." Notwithstanding these passionate entreaties we are bound to examine with detachment the nature of fish chowder and what might happen to it under varying interpretations of the Uniform Commercial Code.

Chowder is an ancient dish preexisting even "the appetites of our seamen and fishermen." It was perhaps the common ancestor of the "more refined cream soups, purees, and bisques." Berolzheimer, The American Woman's Cook Book (Publisher's Guild Inc., New York, 1941) p. 176. The word "chowder" comes from the French "chaudière," meaning a "cauldron" or "pot." "In the fishing villages of Brittany... 'faire la chaudière' means to supply a cauldron in which is cooked a mess of fish and biscuit with some savoury condiments, a hodge-podge contributed by the fishermen themselves, each of whom in return receives his share of the prepared dish. The Breton fishermen probably carried the custom to Newfoundland, long famous for its chowder, whence it has spread to Nova Scotia, New Brunswick, and New England." A New English Dictionary (MacMillan and Co., 1893) p. 386. Our literature over the years abounds in references not only to the delights of chowder but also to its manufacture. A namesake of the plaintiff, Daniel Webster, had a recipe for fish chowder which has survived into a number of modern cookbooks and in which the removal of fish bones is not mentioned at all. One old time recipe recited in the New

English Dictionary study defines chowder as "A dish made of fresh fish (esp. cod) or clams, stewed with slices of pork or bacon, onions, and biscuit. 'Cider and champagne are sometimes added.'" Hawthorne, in The House of the Seven Gables (Allyn and Bacon, Boston, 1957) p. 8, speaks of "[a] codfish of sixty pounds, caught in the bay, [which] had been dissolved into the rich liquid of a chowder." A chowder variant, cod "Muddle," was made in Plymouth in the 1890s by taking "a three or four pound codfish, head added. Season with salt and pepper and boil in just enough water to keep from burning. When cooked, add milk and piece of butter." The recitation of these ancient formulae suffices to indicate that in the construction of chowders in these parts in other years, worries about fish bones played no role whatsoever. This broad outlook on chowders has persisted in more modern cookbooks. "The chowder of today is much the same as the old chowder...." The American Woman's Cook Book, supra, p. 176. The all embracing Fannie Farmer states in a portion of her recipe, fish chowder is made with a "fish skinned, but head and tail left on. Cut off head and tail and remove fish from backbone. Cut fish in 2-inch pieces and set aside. Put head, tail, and backbone broken in pieces, in stewpan; add 2 cups cold water and bring slowly to boiling point...." The liquor thus produced from the bones is added to the balance of the chowder. Farmer, The Boston Cooking School Cook Book (Little Brown Co., 1937) p. 166.

Thus, we consider a dish which for many long years, if well made, has been made generally as outlined above. It is not too much to say that a person sitting down in New England to consume a good New England fish chowder embarks on a gustatory adventure which may entail the removal of some fish bones from his bowl as he proceeds. We are not inclined to tamper with age old recipes by any amendment reflecting the plaintiff's view of the effect of the Uniform Commercial Code upon them. We are aware of the heavy body of case law involving foreign substances in food, but we sense a strong distinction between them and those relative to unwholesomeness of the food itself, e.g., tainted mackerel (Smith v. Gerrish, 256 Mass. 183, 152 N.E. 318), and a fish bone in a fish chowder. Certain Massachusetts cooks might cavil at the ingredients contained in the chowder in this case in that it lacked the heartening lift of salt pork. In any event, we consider that the joys of life in New England include the ready availability of fresh fish chowder. We should be prepared to cope with the hazards of fish bones, the occasional presence of which in chowders is, it seems to us, to be anticipated, and which, in the light of a hallowed tradition, do not impair their fitness or merchantability. While we are bouyed up in this conclusion by Shapiro v. Hotel Statler Corp., 132 F. Supp. 891 (S.D. Cal.), in which the bone which afflicted the plaintiff appeared in "Hot Barquette of Seafood Mornay," we know that the United States District Court of Southern California, situated as are we upon a coast, might be expected to share our views. We are most impressed, however, by Allen v. Grafton, 170 Ohio St. 249, 164 N.E.2d 167, where in Ohio, the Midwest, in a case where the plaintiff was injured by a piece of oyster shell in an order of fried oysters, Mr. Justice Taft (now Chief Justice) in a majority opinion held that "the possible presence of a piece of oyster shell in or attached to an oyster is so well known to anyone who eats oysters that we can say as a matter of law that one who eats oysters can reasonably anticipate and guard against eating such a piece of shell...." (P. 259 of 170 Ohio St., p. 174 of 164 N.E.2d.)

Thus, while we sympathize with the plaintiff who has suffered a peculiarly New England injury, the order must be

Exceptions sustained.
Judgment for the defendant.

NOTES

1. The court frames the issue for us: "We must decide whether a fish bone lurking in a fish chowder, about the ingredients of which there is no other complaint, constitutes a breach of implied warranty [of merchantability]." The court holds that the warranty was not broken because people "should be prepared to cope with the hazards of fish bones, the occasional presence of which in chowders is, it seems to us, to be anticipated, and which, in the light of a hallowed tradition, do not impair their fitness or merchantability." Thus, a product can be fit for its ordinary purpose even if it is potentially dangerous. The issue is whether people should be aware of the risk, which supports Shapo's interpretation and explanation of product liability law set forth in Section One.

2. The decision has implications for other products. For example, cigarette companies can argue that their product is merchantable because the product meets its specifications, and, at least today, people should be aware that cigarettes are dangerous. As already mentioned, many courts have so held.

REMEDIES FOR BREACH OF WARRANTY

We can now discuss very briefly the remedies available to a buyer for breach of warranty. The remedies for breach of warranty include damages for "injury to person...proximately resulting from the breach." U.C.C. §2–715(2). Nevertheless, the seller can drastically narrow available remedies, for example, by limiting them to repair of defective parts (with the cost of labor sometimes allocated to the consumer!). The law's approach to remedies therefore also leaves sellers with little incentive to manufacture safe products.

Clarifying and Improving Warranty Protection

The discussion above points out that warranty law directs courts to attempt to interpret language creating and disclaiming express warranties consistently. Failing that, courts must find the seller responsible for any inconsistencies between words or conduct creating and negating warranties. This approach is confusing: can the language or conduct of warranty ever be "consistent" with language of disclaimer? The approach is better understood to mean that courts should protect buyers from surprising disclaimers. For example, if the seller advertises that a car will get 30 miles per gallon and repeats the representation in its brochures, most consumers would be surprised to learn that their written contract says that there are no express warranties and that they have no recourse if the car gets 10 miles per gallon.

In 1975, the United States Congress enacted warranty legislation known as the Magnuson-Moss Warranty–Federal Trade Commission Improvement Act, 15 U.S.C. §§2301–2312. When a buyer purchases consumer goods, Magnuson-Moss supplements the warranty law

we have discussed. A principal purpose of the Act is to require greater clarity and disclosure of consumer rights regarding defective products. The Act does not require a seller to make a written warranty, but if the seller makes one it must be clear and understandable to the buyer. Further, the seller must clearly identify the type of warranty it is making by labeling the warranty either "full" or "limited." The seller that makes a full warranty must satisfy certain requirements, including remedying defects quickly and without a labor charge. The drafters of Magnuson-Moss thought that most sellers would make full warranties because of competitive pressure (would you rather purchase a product with a full or limited warranty?), but most sellers appear to make limited warranties. If the seller makes any warranty, the seller cannot disclaim implied warranties. Further the seller must describe the product, identify to whom the warranty extends, and explain remedies for defects. If a seller violates Magnuson-Moss, the Federal Trade Commission can apply sanctions. The buyer also can sue the seller for the violation.

Buyers do have some remedial protections. Under U.C.C. §2–719, if a given remedy "fails of its essential purpose," because of, for example, repeated unsuccessful attempts to repair defective parts, or if the remedy limitation is "unconscionable," meaning roughly that the remedy "shocks the conscience," then the purchaser is free to pursue other remedies. Limitation of damages for personal injury is "prima facie unconscionable," meaning that the seller has the burden of proving that such a limitation is *not* unconscionable in the particular context. For a general discussion of the meaning of unconscionability, see Section Six of Chapter 5.

Early contract law permitted only those in "privity of contract" (i.e., those parties who signed a contract) to sue one another for breach. According to the privity requirement, then, only the buyer could sue for a product defect, not other people who were injured by the product, and the buyer could sue only her immediate seller, not others in the distributive chain. For example, the buyer of a defective Chevrolet could sue her car dealer, but not General Motors. The buyer's friend, who was injured while a passenger in the car, could not sue either the dealer or General Motors for breach of warranty. The drafters of the U.C.C., cognizant of some cases that diluted or ignored the privity requirement, presented the state legislatures considering passage of the U.C.C. with three alternative approaches to the question of who can sue for a product defect, ranging from people in the family or household and guests in the home to all people "who may reasonably be expected to . . . be affected by the goods." U.C.C. §2–318. Although the U.C.C. is silent on whether a buyer can sue a remote manufacturer, it invites courts to expand liability to include such parties through case law. Many courts have done just that.

In light of all of this, is warranty law sufficient to protect people from shoddy products? On the one hand, in light of the right of manufacturers and sellers to disclaim liability for both express and implied warranties, and to limit remedies, and the general lack of bargaining power of consumers to insist on greater protection (what would happen if you told your local car dealer that you will not purchase a car unless the dealer deletes all of the warranty disclaimers from the contract?), the private-arrangement instrument may be insufficient to protect people. On the other hand, some argue that in many settings consumers in the aggregate enjoy bargaining leverage. In a free-market system, sellers often must consider general consumer demand if they want to remain competitive.

Section Three
PRODUCT SAFETY AND THE REMEDIAL INSTRUMENT

As we learned in Chapter 1, the remedial instrument defines grievances, specifies remedies, and provides for enforcement of awards. This instrument can be employed in the field of product safety. For example, a consumer can bring a cause of action in negligence against a seller or manufacturer when a product defect causes personal injury or injury to property. Because the theory of recover is not based on sales warranties but on negligence, the injured consumer does not have to fight off warranty disclaimers, remedy limitations, or lack of privity. Nevertheless, the consumer faces the large hurdles of demonstrating a lack of reasonable care on the part of the defendant and, perhaps, the absence of contributory negligence. Because of dissatisfaction with both warranty and negligence theories to protect consumers adequately from defective goods, the theory of strict tort liability evolved. We now trace that history through a series of cases and other materials.

GREENMAN v. YUBA POWER PRODUCTS, INC.

Supreme Court of California, 1963
59 Cal. 2d 57, 377 P.2d 897, 27 Cal. Rptr. 697

Traynor, Justice:

Plaintiff brought this action for damages against the retailer and the manufacturer of a Shopsmith, a combination power tool that could be used as a saw, drill, and wood lathe. He saw a Shopsmith demonstrated by the retailer and studied a brochure prepared by the manufacturer. He decided he wanted a Shopsmith for his home workshop, and his wife bought and gave him one for Christmas in 1955. In 1957 he bought the necessary attachments to use the Shopsmith as a lathe for turning a large piece of wood he wished to make into a chalice. After he had worked on the piece of wood several times without difficulty, it suddenly flew out of the machine and struck him on the forehead, inflicting serious injuries. About ten and a half months later, he gave the retailer and the manufacturer written notice of claimed breaches of warranties and filed a complaint against them alleging such breaches and negligence.

After a trial before a jury, the court ruled that there was no evidence that the retailer was negligent or had breached any express warranty and that the manufacturer was not liable for the breach of any implied warranty. Accordingly, it submitted to the jury only the cause of action alleging breach of implied warranties against the retailer and the causes of action alleging negligence and breach of express warranties against the manufacturer. The jury returned a verdict for the retailer against plaintiff and for plaintiff against the manufacturer in the amount of $65,000. The trial court denied the manufacturer's motion for a new trial and entered judgment on the verdict. The manufacturer and plaintiff appeal. Plaintiff seeks a reversal of the part of the judgment in favor of the retailer, however, only in the event that the part of the judgment against the manufacturer is reversed.

Plaintiff introduced substantial evidence that his injuries were caused by defective design and construction of the Shopsmith. His expert witnesses testified that inadequate set screws were used to hold parts of the machine together so that normal vibration caused the tailstock of the lathe to move away from the piece of wood being turned permitting it to fly out of the lathe. They also testified that there were other more positive ways of fastening the parts of the machine together, the use of which would have prevented the accident. The jury could therefore reasonably have concluded that the manufacturer negligently constructed the Shopsmith. The jury could also reasonably have concluded that statements in the manufacturer's brochure were untrue, that they constituted express warranties,[1] and that plaintiff's injuries were caused by their breach. . . .

. . . [T]o impose strict liability on the manufacturer under the circumstances of this case, it was not necessary for plaintiff to establish an express warranty [or negligence]. . . . A manufacturer is strictly liable in tort when an article he places on the market, knowing that it is to be used without inspection for defects, proves to have a defect that causes injury to a human being. Recognized first in the case of unwholesome food products, such liability has now been extended to a variety of other products that create as great or greater hazards if defective.

Although in these cases strict liability has usually been based on the theory of an express or implied warranty running from the manufacturer to the plaintiff, the abandonment of the requirement of a contract between them, the recognition that the liability is not assumed by agreement but imposed by law, and the refusal to permit the manufacturer to define the scope of its own responsibility for defective products make clear that the liability is not one governed by the law of contract warranties but by the law of strict liability in tort.

---

1. In this respect the trial court limited the jury to a consideration of two statements in the manufacturer's brochure. (1) "WHEN SHOPSMITH IS IN HORIZONTAL POSITION—Rugged construction of frame provides rigid support from end to end. Heavy centerless-ground steel tubing insures perfect alignment of components." (2) "SHOPSMITH maintains its accuracy because every component has positive locks that hold adjustments through rough or precision work."

Accordingly, rules defining and governing warranties that were developed to meet the needs of commercial transactions cannot properly be invoked to govern the manufacturer's liability to those injured by their defective products unless those rules also serve the purposes for which such liability is imposed.

... The purpose of [strict tort] liability is to insure that the costs of injuries resulting from defective products are borne by the manufacturers that put such products on the market rather than by the injured persons who are powerless to protect themselves. Sales warranties serve this purpose fitfully at best. (See Prosser, Strict Liability to the Consumer, 69 Yale L.J. 1099, 1124–1134.) In the present case, for example, plaintiff was able to plead and prove an express warranty only because he read and relied on the representations of the Shopsmith's ruggedness contained in the manufacturer's brochure. Implicit in the machine's presence on the market, however, was a representation that it would safely do the

jobs for which it was built. Under these circumstances, it should not be controlling whether plaintiff selected the machine because of the statements in the brochure, or because of the machine's own appearance of excellence that belied the defect lurking beneath the surface, or because he merely assumed that it would safely do the jobs it was built to do. It should not be controlling whether the details of the sales from manufacturer to retailer and from retailer to plaintiff's wife were such that one or more of the implied warranties of the sales act arose. "The remedies of injured consumers ought not to be made to depend upon the intricacies of the law of sales." (Ketterer v. Armour & Co., D.C., 200 F. 322, 323.) To establish the manufacturer's liability it was sufficient that plaintiff proved that he was injured while using the Shopsmith in a way it was intended to be used as a result of a defect in design and manufacture of which plaintiff was not aware that made the Shopsmith unsafe for its intended use....

The judgment is affirmed.

THOMAS L. DALRYMPLE, BRIEF OPPOSING STRICT LIABILITY IN TORT
16 (Defense Research Institute, Inc. 1966)*

There is a moral element to a move from liability for fault to liability without fault. Liability for fault is within the realm of normal expectation of right in our society. Liability without fault is a strange creation which arouses the antagonism of a wrong.

As industrialization, mechanization and communication have progressed in this country, safety has become increasingly a matter of general concern. Substantial and expensive programs are pursued to impress the significance of safety upon the public consciousness. Improvements for safety are constantly sought. The doctrine of strict liability in tort runs counter to this significant public policy; manufacturers and sellers are no longer economically encouraged to exercise due care in order to prevent liabilities under this doctrine.

The doctrine of strict liability in tort has another aspect which deserves attention. This rule is a vehicle of subtle socialization. While the proponents of strict liability proclaim that it is but a means of imposing the economic impact upon manufacturers and sellers, who can bear this burden, rather than upon users and consumers, in truth the manufacturers and sellers are but collectors of funds from the ultimate users and consumers of products. Strict liability can only raise prices; so ultimately each consumer and user must underwrite the ability of others to impose liability without fault.

Pronouncement of the doctrine of strict liability in tort involves a sweeping change of the law in the form of a new public policy. This type of development is traditionally legislative, not judicial. In Lombardi v. California Packing Sales Co., 83 R.I. 51, 112 A.2d 701 (1955), the court denied recovery for breach of implied warranty in the absence of privity, saying at page 704:

> ... But it seems to us that ordinarily the declaration of such a public policy is a function of the legislature and not of the court.... We ought not to resort to judicial legislation, at least where no emergency or extreme conditions exist.

The same court has subsequently ascribed legislative approval to continued inaction of the legislature in the area of strict liability in Henry v. John W. Eshelman & Sons, 209 A.2d 46[, 48] (R.I. Sup. Ct., 1965), when, in denying recovery

for breach of implied warranty in the absence of privity, it said:

> ... A decade has passed since we declared in *Lombardi* that if any change in the law was to be made from consideration of public policy the legislature should make it. During that period the legislature has met in annual sessions and has not seen fit to alter in any way the policy of the law underlying that decision notwithstanding its attention was again called to the continuing criticism of such policy....
>
> Such long acquiescence in decisional law by the legislature, especially after its attention has been called to repeated litigious criticism of its underlying policy, is persuasive proof of at least implied legislative approval of the decisions....

WILLIAM L. PROSSER, THE ASSAULT UPON THE CITADEL (STRICT LIABILITY TO THE CONSUMER)
69 Yale L.J. 1099, 1122–24 (1960)*

[T]he arguments which have proved convincing to the courts which have accepted the strict liability are three:

1. The public interest in human life, health and safety demands the maximum possible protection that the law can give against dangerous defects in products which consumers must buy, and against which they are helpless to protect themselves; and it justifies the imposition, upon all suppliers of such products, of full responsibility for the harm they cause, even though the supplier has not been negligent.[149] This argument, which in the last analysis rests upon public sentiment, has had its greatest force in the cases of food, where there was once popular outcry against an evil industry, and injuries and actions have multiplied, and public feeling is most obvious. It is now being advanced as to other products for bodily use, such as cosmetics. It suggests that as to still other products, distinctions may yet be

* Reprinted by permission of The Yale Law Journal Company from THE YALE LAW JOURNAL, Vol. 69, pp. 1099, 1122–24.

149. "It is a well-known fact that articles of food are manufactured and placed in the channels of commerce, with the intention that they shall pass from hand to hand until they are finally used by some remote consumer. It is usually impracticable, if not impossible, for the ultimate consumer to analyze the food and ascertain whether or not it is suitable for human consumption. Since it has been packed and placed on the market as a food for human consumption, and marked as such, the purchaser usually eats it or causes it to be served to his family without the precaution of having it analyzed by a technician to ascertain whether or not it is suitable for human consumption. In fact, in most instances the only satisfactory examination that could be made would be only at the time and place of the processing of the food. It seems to be the rule that where food products sold for human consumption are unfit for that purpose, there is such an utter failure of the purpose for which the food is sold, and the consequences of eating unsound food are so disastrous to human health or life, that the law imposes a warranty of purity in favor of the ultimate consumer as a matter of public policy."

Jacob E. Decker & Sons v. Capps, 139 Tex. 609, 612, 164 S.W.2d 828, 829 (1942).

drawn according to the probable danger, the frequency of injury, and what the public reasonably and rightfully expects.

2. The supplier, by placing the goods upon the market, represents to the public that they are suitable and safe for use; and by packaging, advertising or otherwise, he does everything that he can to induce that belief. He intends and expects that the product will be purchased and used in reliance upon this assurance of safety; and it is in fact so purchased and used. The middleman is no more than conduit, a mere mechanical device, through whom the thing sold is to reach the ultimate user. The supplier has invited and solicited the use; and when it leads to disaster, he should not be permitted to avoid the responsibility by saying that he has made no contract with the consumer.[150]

3. It is already possible to enforce strict liability by resort to a series of actions, in which the retailer is first held liable on a warranty to his purchaser, and indemnity on a warranty is then sought successively from other suppliers, until the manufacturer finally pays the damages, with the added costs of repeated litigation. This is an expensive, time-consuming, and wasteful process, and it may be interrupted by insolvency, lack of jurisdiction, disclaimers, or the statute of limitations, anywhere along the line. What is needed is a blanket rule which makes any supplier in the chain liable directly to the ultimate user, and so short-circuits the whole unwieldy process. This is in the interest, not only of the consumer, but of the courts, and even on occasion of the suppliers themselves.

150. "A party who processes a product and gives it the appearance of being suitable for human consumption, and places it in the channels of commerce, expects some one to consume the food in reliance upon its appearance that it is suitable for human consumption. He expects the appearance of suitableness to continue with the product until some one is induced to consume it as food. But a modern manufacturer or vendor does even more than this under modern practices. He not only processes the food and dresses it up so as to make it appear appetizing, but he uses the newspapers, magazines, billboards, and the radio to build up the psychology to buy and consume his products. The invitation extended by him is not only to the house wife to buy and serve his product, but to the members of the family and guests to eat it. In fact, the manufacturer's interest in the product is not terminated when he has sold it to the wholesaler. He must get it off the wholesaler's shelves before the wholesaler will buy a new supply. The same is not only true of the retailer, but of the house wife, for the house wife will not buy more until the family has consumed that which she has in her pantry. Thus the manufacturer or other vendor intends that this appearance of suitability of the article for human consumption should continue and be effective until some one is induced thereby to consume the goods. It would be but to acknowledge a weakness in the law to say that he could thus create a demand for his products by inducing a belief that they are suitable for human consumption, when, as a matter of fact, they are not, and reap the benefits of the public confidence thus created, and then avoid liability for the injuries caused thereby merely because there was no privity of contract between him and the one whom he induced to consume the food."

Id. at 619, 164 S.W.2d at 832–33.

NOTES

1. *Greenman v. Yuba Power Products* introduces the idea of "strict tort liability." Liability is not based on contract law nor on negligence law, but simply on the act of putting a defective product on the market. No-fault liability of this nature, as stated in the case, is "to insure that the costs of injuries resulting from defective products are borne by the manufacturers that put such products on the market." This reasoning is consistent with Shapo's discussion of who should bear the risk of defects when people cannot protect themselves.

2. The Dalrymple excerpt sets forth the basic arguments against strict tort. He argues that strict tort deters manufacturers from exercising due care. Is he right? Certainly, one can argue that manufacturers will be more careful if they know they will be liable for defects. Dalrymple also argues that any reform in this area should be legislative and not judicial. Is he right? Chapters 1 through 5 each considered the appropriate lawmaking roles of courts and legislatures.

3. In contrast to Dalrymple, Prosser presents three arguments in favor of strict tort liability. The first argument focuses on people's inability to protect themselves, a theme first introduced by Shapo. The second argument amounts to an assertion that making and distributing defective products are in effect a misrepresentation by the manufacturer. The third argument is that strict tort efficiently saves the costs of multiple actions (consumer suing dealer, dealer suing distributor, distributor suing manufacturer). Under strict tort, the consumer can sue the manufacturer directly.

4. We now compare how the Restatement (Second) of Torts first addressed strict tort in 1965 with the refinement of the approach some 30 years later in the Restatement (Third) of Torts. You will see that the Restatement (Second) largely reflects Prosser's reasoning, whereas the Restatement (Third) significantly narrows potential liability. (Restatements, promulgated by the American Law Institute, a private law-reform organization, are not law, but lawmakers including courts find them highly influential.)

Restatement (Second) of Torts (1965)

§402A. Special Liability of Seller of Product for Physical Harm to User or Consumer

(1) One who sells any product in a defective condition unreasonably dangerous to the user or consumer or to his property is subject to liability for physical harm thereby caused to the ultimate user or consumer, or to his property, if

    (a) the seller is engaged in the business of selling such a product, and

    (b) it is expected to and does reach the user or consumer without substantial change in the condition in which it is sold.

(2) The rule stated in Subsection (1) applies although

    (a) the seller has exercised all possible care in the preparation and sale of his product, and

    (b) the user or consumer has not bought the product from or entered into any contractual relation with the seller.

Restatement (Third) of Torts: Products Liability (1998)

§1. Liability of Commercial Seller or Distributor for Harm Caused by Defective Products

One engaged in the business of selling or otherwise distributing products who sells or distributes a defective product is subject to liability for harm to persons or property caused by the defect.

§2. Categories of Product Defect

A product is defective when, at the time of sale or distribution, it contains a manufacturing defect, is defective in design, or is defective because of inadequate instructions or warnings. A product:

(a) contains a manufacturing defect when the product departs from its intended design even though all possible care was exercised in the preparation and marketing of the product;

(b) is defective in design when the foreseeable risks of harm posed by the product could have been reduced or avoided by the adoption of a reasonable alternative design by the seller or other distributor, or a predecessor in the commercial chain of distribution, and the omission of the alternative design renders the product not reasonably safe;

(c) is defective because of inadequate instructions or warnings when the foreseeable risks of harm posed by the product could have been reduced or avoided by the provision of reasonable instructions or warnings by the seller or other distributor, or a predecessor in the commercial chain of distribution, and the omission of the instructions or warnings renders the product not reasonably safe.

As originally envisioned, the Restatement (Second) §402A constituted "strict" liability for physical harm. The section required only that the product was "defective" and "unreasonably dangerous" and that the seller was in the business of selling such products. The plaintiff did not have to show negligence, nor that the parties were in a contractual relationship. Liability was "strict" in the sense that the seller could have acted reasonably in marketing the product but still be liable. The Restatement (Third) superseded §402A, with liability no longer "strict" in the cases of alleged design defects and inadequate instructions. See §2(b)–(c).

We now focus on the problem of design defects. The Restatement (Third) constitutes a return to a negligence-type standard by directing courts to evaluate the reasonableness of the manufacturer's conduct in marketing the product (it must be "reasonably safe") with the particular design (asking whether the foreseeable risks of harm from the product have been reduced or avoided by the use of a "reasonable alternative design"). Comment d to §2 in the Restatement (Third) explains further how reasonableness is to be determined:

> **Design defects: general considerations.** Whereas a manufacturing defect consists of a product unit's failure to meet the manufacturer's design specifications, a product asserted to have a defective design meets the manufacturer's design specifications but raises the question whether the specifications themselves create unreasonable risks. Answering that question requires reference to a standard outside the specifications. Subsection (b) adopts a reasonableness ("risk-utility balancing") test as the standard for judging the defectiveness of product designs. More specifically, the test is whether a reasonable alternative design would, at reasonable cost, have reduced the foreseeable risks of harm posed by the product and, if so, whether the omission of the alternative design by the seller or a predecessor in the distributive chain rendered the product not reasonably safe. . . . Under prevailing rules concerning allocation of burden of proof, the plaintiff must prove that such a reasonable alternative was, or reasonably could have been, available at time of sale or distribution. . . .

Assessment of a product design in most instances requires a comparison between an alternative design and the product design that caused the injury, undertaken from the viewpoint of a reasonable person. That approach is also used in administering the traditional reasonableness standard in negligence....

How the defendant's design compares with other, competing designs in actual use is relevant to the issue of whether the defendant's design is defective. Defendants often seek to defend their product designs on the ground that the designs conform to the "state of the art." The term "state of the art" has been variously defined to mean that the product design conforms to industry custom, that it reflects the safest and most advanced technology developed and in commercial use, or that it reflects technology at the cutting edge of scientific knowledge. The confusion brought about by these various definitions is unfortunate. This Section states that a design is defective if the product could have been made safer by the adoption of a reasonable alternative design. If such a design could have been practically adopted at time of sale and if the omission of such a design rendered the product not reasonably safe, the plaintiff establishes defect under Subsection (b).

Illustration 4. XYZ Co. manufactures above-ground swimming pools that are four feet deep. Warnings are embossed on the outside of the pools in large letters stating "DANGER—DO NOT DIVE—SHALLOW WATER." In disregard of the warnings, Mary, age 21, dove head first into an XYZ pool and suffered serious injury. Expert testimony establishes that when Mary's outstretched hands hit the pool's slippery vinyl bottom her hands slid apart, causing her to strike her head against the bottom of the pool. For the purposes of this Illustration it is assumed that the warnings were adequate and that the only issue is whether the above-ground pool was defectively designed because the bottom was too slippery. All the expert witnesses agree that the vinyl pool liner that XYZ utilized was the best and safest liner available and that no alternative, less slippery liner was feasible. Mary has failed to establish defective design under Subsection (b).

COMPARING STRICT TORT AND IMPLIED WARRANTY LAW

The next case from New York's highest court presents the issue of whether a product (here a car) can ever be nondefective under strict tort rules, yet still be unfit for its ordinary purpose under warranty law. The case illustrates what happens when two of the law's instruments seemingly contradict each other.

DENNY v. FORD MOTOR CO.
Court of Appeals of New York, 1995
87 N.Y.2d 248, 662 N.E.2d 730, 639 N.Y.S.2d 250

TITONE, JUDGE:

Are the elements of New York's causes of action for strict products liability and breach of implied warranty always coextensive? If not, can the latter be broader than the former? These are the core issues presented by the questions that the United States Court of Appeals for the Second Circuit has certified to us in this diversity action involving an allegedly defective vehicle. On the facts set forth by the Second Circuit, we hold that the causes of action are not identical and that, under the circumstances presented here, it is possible to be liable for breach of implied warranty even though a claim of strict products liability has not been satisfactorily established.

I.

As stated by the Second Circuit, this action arises out of a June 9, 1986 accident in which plaintiff Nancy Denny was severely injured when the Ford Bronco II that she was driving rolled over. The rollover accident occurred when Denny slammed on her brakes in an effort to avoid a deer that had walked directly into her motor vehicle's path. Denny and her spouse sued Ford Motor Co., the vehicle's manufacturer, asserting claims for negligence, strict products liability and breach of implied warranty of merchantability (*see*, UCC 2-314[2][c]; 2-318). The case went to trial in the District Court for the Northern District of New York in October of 1992.

The trial evidence centered on the particular characteristics of utility vehicles, which are generally made for off-road use on unpaved and often rugged terrain. Such use sometimes necessitates climbing over obstacles such as fallen logs and rocks. While utility vehicles are traditionally considerably larger than passenger cars, some manufacturers have created a category of down-sized "small" utility vehicles, which are designed to be lighter, to achieve better fuel economy and, presumably, to appeal to a wider consumer market. The Bronco II in which Denny was injured falls into this category.

Plaintiffs introduced evidence at trial to show that small utility vehicles in general, and the Bronco II in particular, present a significantly higher risk of rollover accidents than do ordinary passenger automobiles. Plaintiffs' evidence also showed that the Bronco II had a low stability index attributable to its high center of gravity and relatively narrow track width. The vehicle's shorter wheel base and suspension system were additional factors contributing to its instability. Ford had made minor design changes in an effort to achieve a higher stability index, but, according to plaintiffs' proof, none of the changes produced a significant improvement in the vehicle's stability.

Ford argued at trial that the design features of which plaintiffs complained were necessary to the vehicle's off-road capabilities. According to Ford, the vehicle had been intended to be used as an off-road vehicle and had not been designed to be sold as a conventional passenger automobile. Ford's own engineer stated that he would not recommend the Bronco II to someone whose primary interest was to use it as a passenger car, since the features of a four-wheel-drive utility vehicle were not helpful for that purpose and the vehicle's design made it inherently less stable.

Despite the engineer's testimony, plaintiffs introduced a Ford marketing manual which predicted that many buyers would be attracted to the Bronco II because utility vehicles were "suitable to contemporary life styles" and were "considered fashionable" in some suburban areas. According to this manual, the sales presentation of the Bronco II should take into account the vehicle's "suitab[ility] for commuting and for suburban and city driving." Additionally, the vehicle's ability to switch between two-wheel and four-wheel drive would "be particularly appealing to women who may be concerned about driving in snow and ice with their children." Plaintiffs both testified that the perceived safety benefits of its four-wheel-drive capacity were what attracted them to the Bronco II. They were not at all interested in its off-road use. At the close of the evidence, the District Court Judge submitted both the strict products liability claim and the breach of implied warranty claim, despite Ford's objection that the two causes of action were identical.

[The court next explained the trial judge's charge to the jury that for purposes of strict tort the jury must compare the risks and benefits of the SUV. By contrast, the charge on merchantability required the jury to determine only whether the SUV was "defective and not reasonably fit to be used for its intended purpose."]

Neither party objected to the content of these charges. In response to interrogatories, the jury found that the Bronco II was not "defective" and that defendant was therefore not liable under plaintiffs' strict products liability cause of action. However, the jury also found that defendant had breached its implied warranty of merchantability and that the breach was the proximate cause of Nancy Denny's injuries. Following apportionment of damages, plaintiff was awarded judgment in the amount of $1.2 million.

II.

In this proceeding, Ford's sole argument is that plaintiffs' strict products liability and breach of implied warranty causes of action were identical and that, accordingly, a defendant's verdict on the former cannot be reconciled with a plaintiff's verdict on the latter. This argument is, in turn, premised on both the intertwined history of the two doctrines and the close similarity in their elements and legal functions. Although Ford recognizes that New York has previously permitted personal injury plaintiffs to simultaneously assert different products liability theories in support of their claims (see, Victorson v. Bock Laundry Mach. Co., 37 N.Y.2d 395, 400, 373 N.Y.S.2d 39, 335 N.E.2d 275), it contends that the breach of implied warranty cause of action, which sounds in contract, has been subsumed by the more recently adopted, and more highly evolved, strict products liability theory, which sounds in tort. Ford's argument has much to commend it. However, in the final analysis, the argument is flawed because it overlooks the continued existence of a separate *statutory* predicate for the breach of warranty theory and the subtle but important distinction between the two theories that arises from their different historical and doctrinal root.

When products liability litigation was in its infancy, the courts relied upon contractual warranty theories as the only existing means of facilitating economic recovery for personal injuries arising from the use of defective goods. Citing statutory authority (UCC 2-314, 2-715[2][b]; former Personal Property Law §96[1]), the courts posited the existence of an implied warranty arising as an incident of the product's sale and premised a cause of action for consequential personal injuries based on breaches of that warranty.

Eventually, the contractually based implied warranty theory came to be perceived as inadequate in an economic universe that was dominated by mass-produced products and an impersonal marketplace. Its primary weakness was, of course, its rigid requirement of a relationship of privity between the seller and the injured consumer—a requirement that often could not be satisfied. Some courts (including ours) recognized certain narrow exceptions to the privity

requirement in an effort to avoid the doctrine's harsher effects. However, the warranty approach remained unsatisfactory, and the courts shifted their focus to the development of a new, more flexible tort cause of action: the doctrine of strict products liability.

The establishment of this tort remedy has, as this Court has recognized, significantly diminished the need to rely on the contractually based breach of implied warranty remedy as a means of compensating individuals injured because of defective products. Further, although the available defenses and applicable limitations principles may differ, there is a high degree of overlap between the substantive aspects of the two causes of action. Indeed, on an earlier occasion, this Court observed, in dictum, that "strict liability in tort and implied warranty in the absence of privity are merely different ways of describing the very same cause of action" Mendel v. Pittsburgh Plate Glass Co., supra, at 345, 305 N.Y.S.2d 490, 253 N.E.2d 207.

Nonetheless, it would not be correct to infer that the tort cause of action has completely subsumed the older breach of implied warranty cause of action or that the two doctrines are now identical in every respect. The continued vitality of the warranty approach is evidenced by its retention and expansion in New York's version of the Uniform Commercial Code (UCC 2-314[2][c]; 2-318). The existence of this statutory authority belies any argument that the breach of implied warranty remedy is a dead letter.

Although the products liability theory sounding in tort and the breach of implied warranty theory authorized by the UCC coexist and are often invoked in tandem, the core element of "defect" is subtly different in the two causes of action. Under New York law, a design defect may be actionable under a strict products liability theory if the product is not reasonably safe. Since this Court's decision in Voss v. Black & Decker Mfg. Co., 59 N.Y.2d 102, 108, 463 N.Y.S.2d 398, 450 N.E.2d 204, the New York standard for determining the existence of a design defect has required an assessment of whether "if the design defect were known at the time of manufacture, a reasonable person would conclude that the utility of the product did not outweigh the risk inherent in marketing a product designed in that manner." This standard demands an inquiry into such factors as (1) the product's utility to the public as a whole, (2) its utility to the individual user, (3) the likelihood that the product will cause injury, (4) the availability of a safer design, (5) the possibility of designing and manufacturing the product so that it is safer but remains functional and reasonably priced, (6) the degree of awareness of the product's potential danger that can reasonably be attributed to the injured user, and (7) the manufacturer's ability to spread the cost of any safety-related design changes (Voss v. Black & Decker Mfg. Co., supra, at 109, 463 N.Y.S.2d 398, 450 N.E.2d 204). The above-described analysis is rooted in a recognition that there are both risks and benefits associated with many products and that there are instances in which a product's inherent dangers cannot be eliminated without simultaneously compromising or completely nullifying its benefits. In such circumstances, a weighing of the product's benefits against its risks is an appropriate and necessary component of the liability assessment under the policy-based principles associated with tort law.

The adoption of this risk/utility balance as a component of the "defectiveness" element has brought the inquiry in design defect cases closer to that used in traditional negligence cases, where the reasonableness of an actor's conduct is considered in light of a number of situational and policy-driven factors.[3] While efforts have been made to steer away from the fault-oriented negligence principles by characterizing the design defect cause of action in terms of a product-based rather than a conduct-based analysis, the reality is that the risk/utility balancing test is a "negligence-inspired" approach, since it invites the parties to adduce proof about the manufacturer's choices and ultimately requires the fact finder to make "a judgment about [the manufacturer's] judgment." In other words, an assessment of the manufacturer's conduct is virtually inevitable, and, as one commentator observed, "[i]n general, . . . the strict liability concept of 'defective design' [is] functionally synonymous with the earlier negligence concept of unreasonable designing." Schwartz, New Products, Old Products, Evolving Law, Retroactive Law, 58 N.Y.U. L. Rev. 796, 803.

It is this negligence-like risk/benefit component of the defect element that differentiates strict products liability claims from UCC-based breach of implied warranty claims in cases involving design defects. While the strict products concept of a product that is "not reasonably safe" requires a weighing of the product's dangers against its over-all advantages, the UCC's concept of a "defective" product requires an inquiry only into whether the product in question was "fit for the ordinary purposes for which such goods are used" (UCC 2-314[2][c]). The latter inquiry focuses on the expectations for the performance of the product when used in the customary, usual and reasonably foreseeable manners. The cause of action is one involving true "strict" liability, since recovery may be had upon a showing that the product was not minimally safe for its expected purpose-without regard to the feasibility of alternative designs or the manufacturer's "reasonableness" in marketing it in that unsafe condition. . . .

As a practical matter, the distinction between the defect concepts in tort law and in implied warranty theory may have little or no effect in most cases. In this case, however, the nature of the proof and the way in which the fact issues were litigated demonstrates how the two causes of action can diverge. In the trial court, Ford took the position that the design features of which plaintiffs complain, i.e., the Bronco II's high center of gravity, narrow track width, short wheel base and specially tailored suspension system, were important to preserving the vehicle's ability to drive over the highly irregular terrain that typifies off-road travel. Ford's proof in this regard was relevant to the strict products liability risk/utility equation, which required the fact finder to determine whether the Bronco II's value as an off-road

---

3. In design defect cases, the alleged product flaw arises from an intentional decision by the manufacturer to configure the product in a particular way. In contrast, in strict products liability cases involving manufacturing defects, the harm arises from the product's failure to perform in the intended manner due to some flaw in the fabrication process. In the latter class of cases, the flaw alone is a sufficient basis to hold the manufacturer liable without regard to fault.

vehicle outweighed the risk of the rollover accidents that could occur when the vehicle was used for other driving tasks.

On the other hand, plaintiffs' proof focused, in part, on the sale of the Bronco II for suburban driving and everyday road travel. Plaintiffs also adduced proof that the Bronco II's design characteristics made it unusually susceptible to rollover accidents when used on paved roads. All of this evidence was useful in showing that routine highway and street driving was the "ordinary purpose" for which the Bronco II was sold and that it was not "fit"—or safe—for that purpose.

Thus, under the evidence in this case, a rational fact finder could have simultaneously concluded that the Bronco II's utility as an off-road vehicle outweighed the risk of injury resulting from rollover accidents *and* that the vehicle was not safe for the "ordinary purpose" of daily driving for which it was marketed and sold. Under the law of this State such a set of factual judgments would lead to the concomitant legal conclusion that plaintiffs' strict products liability cause of action was not viable but that defendant should nevertheless be held liable for breach of its implied promise that the Bronco II was "merchantable" or "fit" for its "ordinary purpose." Importantly, what makes this case distinctive is that the "ordinary purpose" for which the product was marketed and sold to the plaintiff was *not* the same as the utility against which the risk was to be weighed. It is these unusual circumstances that give practical significance to the ordinarily theoretical difference between the defect concepts in tort and statutory breach of implied warranty causes of action.

From the foregoing it is apparent that the causes of action for strict products liability and breach of implied warranty of merchantability are not identical in New York and that the latter is not necessarily subsumed by the former. It follows that, under the circumstances presented, a verdict such as the one occurring here—in which the manufacturer was found liable under an implied warranty cause of action and not liable under a strict products cause of action—is theoretically reconcilable under New York law....

SIMONS, JUDGE (dissenting):

I agree with the majority that causes of action in strict products liability and breach of implied warranty are not identical. In my view, however, the strict products liability claim is substantively broader than and encompasses the implied warranty claim and, thus, the jury's verdict of no defect in the products liability cause of action is not reconcilable with its finding of breach of implied warranty....

The court charged the jury that to recover in strict products liability the plaintiffs had to prove that the Bronco II was "defective" when it was placed on the market. A product is defective, the court said, if it is "not reasonably safe" when used for "its intended or reasonably foreseeable purpose." That charge was consistent with settled New York law which holds that a manufacturer or supplier may be strictly liable for injuries sustained when a product is used for its intended purpose or for an unintended but reasonably foreseeable purpose. The court charged the jury that to recover for breach of implied warranty the plaintiff was required to establish that the Bronco II was not "reasonably fit for the ordinary purpose for which it was intended." That instruction is consistent with language found in UCC 2-314(2)(c).

When these two definitions are compared, it is apparent that a defect for strict products liability purposes is broader than a defect for implied warranty purposes. The vehicle could not have been defective when used for its ordinary and intended purpose (warranty), but not defective and reasonably safe when used for its "intended or for an unintended but reasonably foreseeable purpose" (strict products liability). As the Court of Appeals observed, foreseeable use "certainly includes all uses that are 'ordinary' [and] perhaps some that are not 'ordinary'" (see, Denny v. Ford Motor Co., 42 F.3d 106, 112). The jury having concluded that the Bronco II was not defective for strict products liability purposes, could not logically conclude that it was defective for warranty purposes....

Accordingly, I dissent.

KAYE, C.J., and BELLACOSA, SMITH, LEVINE AND CIPARICK, JJ., concur with TITONE, J.

NOTES

1. The jury apparently considered the SUV's design satisfactory under a risk-utility test, meaning that, because of the utility of off-road driving, they decided Ford made a reasonable decision in its design despite the roll-over potential. However, the SUV was not fit for its ordinary purpose under the implied warranty of merchantability, based on Denny's reasonable expectations of its performance on the road.

2. The proposers of amendments to U.C.C. §2-314 drafted the following comment that would have made the strict tort and warranty standards compatible: "When recovery is sought for injury to person or property, whether goods are merchantable is to be determined by applicable state products liability law." In other words, the consumer's reasonable expectations would not be relevant to whether goods were merchantable under warranty law in cases of personal injury and injury to property. Instead, the merchantability test would be the risk-utility test of strict tort law. Expectations would still be relevant in economic loss cases. None of those amendments to the U.C.C., including the above comment, have been enacted by any state, so the problem of incompatibility still remains.

CLASS ACTIONS IN MASS TORT CASES

The next two excerpts concern the wisdom of allowing class action lawsuits for mass torts. Class actions are a "judicial mechanism to try similar individual actions either entirely together, or jointly on a piecemeal basis for common issues," and they involve numerous parties whose "claims share at least one common question of law or fact." Spencer Williams, Mass Tort Class Actions: Going, Going, Gone?, 22 Judges' J., Spring 1983, at 8, 10. Mass torts in the case of defective products constitute defects that injure a large number of people. Class actions, therefore, would seem an efficient method of determining liability for mass torts, in that multiple lawsuits could be avoided. But there are issues, as the next set of readings suggest.

SPENCER WILLIAMS, MASS TORT CLASS ACTIONS: GOING, GOING, GONE?
22 Judges' J., Spring 1983, at 8, 9–10*

State and federal trial judges are being inundated with mass filings of lawsuits by individual plaintiffs—an event unprecedented in legal history. Each plaintiff seeks compensation and a share of large punitive damage awards based on a single catastrophe or a defective product. These "big cases" are widely publicized. They involve asbestos, "Agent Orange," Dalkon Shield, DES, Rely tampons, PCBs, and countless others. Virtually thousands of courts in this country are ensnared in costly and repetitive litigation, threatening to last well into the next century.

These cases are but a harbinger of the judiciary's role in an increasingly complex society, where huge multinational corporations peddle

---

their mass-produced consumer goods and drugs by instantaneous satellite communication. In such a society, it is not an overly pessimistic prediction that, absent some legislative or judicial solution, our attempt to try these virtually identical lawsuits, one-by-one, will bankrupt both the state and federal court systems. In one year, between 1980 and 1981, there was a 17 percent increase in the filing of product liability cases in federal district courts alone; this represents approximately 15 new product cases per year for each federal judge.

The questions confronting the nation on mass product liability actions are many and varied, and transcend more mundane concerns of calendar management and court congestion:

- To what extent, if any, must the litigation preferences of each of the thousands of plaintiffs in a "big case" yield to a more socially optimal, cost-efficient form of representative adjudication?
- Is our traditional model, pitting one plaintiff's gladiator against one defendant's gladiator, an outmoded and overly expensive means to redress similar injuries inflicted by the same misconduct upon multiple plaintiffs?
- Must there be a dollar-by-dollar liability accumulated by society's producers until the business, or even an entire industry, is forced into bankruptcy, or is it more sensible to have a forum in which all potential ramifications upon workers, owners, and the future course of product development are aired in court?
- Must a single defendant be subjected to numerous and conflicting punitive damage awards, even when such awards threaten, as a legal or practical matter, to deprive future litigants of such recovery, or any recovery at all?
- Is it fair that a third of any recovery received in early litigation go to the early plaintiffs' attorneys, when injured later plaintiffs may

be left without any practical means of redress?
- Is it effective or efficient use of limited juridical resources to subject a judge to the tedious and frustrating task of presiding over identical lawsuits, or even to distribute these cases throughout the court system to occupy calendars in many courts?
- Is this one-by-one adjudication the fastest, most equitable way to permit all the injured to recover?

These questions are easy to pose, but solutions are more difficult to formulate. Perhaps we need a major reinterpretation of some procedural aspects of our traditional adversary system, but this would be a long-term endeavor. Perhaps legislative solutions to this problem will provide the easiest and best answers to these questions, but Congress may not address these issues. It could by enacting comprehensive federal products liability law for application in new administrative courts, or make serious adjustments to the bankruptcy and reorganization provisions as applied to manufacturers faced with numerous products liability claims. But until it does, the inequities and shortcomings of the present system require that we judges work in an innovative fashion, adapting aspects of the current system to address these challenging problems.

It is my belief that for those inevitable cases involving hundreds or thousands of persons injured in similar ways by a single occurrence, the class action device holds the most promise. It can be an effective tool to accommodate competing interests—each plaintiff clamoring for his slice of a large, but finite, damage pie; a defendant seeking a binding final determination of its liability for a product run amok; and a judicial system searching for the most equitable and efficient solution for all the interests involved.

MYRIAM GILLES, OPTING OUT OF LIABILITY: THE FORTHCOMING, NEAR-TOTAL DEMISE OF THE MODERN CLASS ACTION
104 Mich. L. Rev. 373, 382–88 (2005)*

[I]n the early 1980s, inventive federal district judges began to find ways . . . to address the mass torts of the day, including Agent Orange, asbestos, tobacco, DES, Dalkon Shield, and a host of others [through the use of the class action technique]. . . .

The courts in all of these cases applied legal rules in a plausible fashion to reach results they believed just or efficient. These decisions reflect identifiable values, including a concern with fairness to plaintiffs such as the mesothelioma victims likely to die before their cases may be heard, or the Dalkon Shield victims who, in the absence of collective litigation, would have likely found a destitute defendant by the time their individual actions were called. Driven by these values and concerns—these moral intuitions . . . [w]hat these courts did, really, was to certify classes to try issues. . . .

Their moment, however, was short-lived, as the judicial values animating these mass tort class certifications ran headlong into a different set of judicial values, epitomized by Chief Judge Richard A. Posner of the Seventh Circuit in the watershed *Rhone-Poulenc* case. Brought by a class comprising 120,000 hemophiliacs exposed to AIDS-infected blood, the case concerned the defendant's widely used blood-screening and extraction product. The district court certified a class solely to try the issue of defendant's negligence; at the end of the case, the jury would issue a special verdict on negligence and, if the plaintiffs won, individual class members would fan out to courtrooms across the country to try causation, damages, and any other individual issues.

. . . [T]he Seventh Circuit decertified the class. Writing for the panel, Judge Posner's focus was on the fairness of the procedures to the defendant who "might easily be facing $25 billion in potential liability (conceivably more), and with it bankruptcy. They may not wish to roll these dice. That is putting it mildly. They will be under intense pressure to settle." Clearly disinclined for this core reason to allow the certification to

stand, Judge Posner then offered other reasons for decertifying in this case, including: (i) the difficulty of applying numerous states' negligence laws in a single proceeding; and (ii) the observation that plaintiffs had lost a majority of the individual trials against the defendant to date, suggesting that a classwide showdown had not been earned.

Judge Posner's opinion swiftly became the model for other appellate courts in decertifying mass tort classes. Most famously, in *Castano v. American Tobacco Co.*, the Fifth Circuit decertified "the largest class action ever," consisting of current, former, and deceased smokers and their families. Again, the concern over the rights of defendants in mass tort class actions was paramount:

> In the context of mass tort class actions, certification dramatically affects the stakes for defendants. Class certification magnifies and strengthens the number of unmeritorious claims. Aggregation of claims also makes it more likely that a defendant will be found liable and results in significantly higher damage awards. In addition to skewing trial outcomes, class certification creates insurmountable pressure on defendants to settle, whereas individual trials would not. The risk of facing an all-or-nothing verdict presents too high a risk, even when the probability of an adverse judgment is low. These settlements have been referred to as judicial blackmail.

. . . Judge Posner's snowball was well on its way down the hill. The *Castano* decertification was followed, in quick succession, by the Sixth Circuit's decertification of a class involving penile implants, the Ninth Circuit's decertification of medical products liability classes, and the Third Circuit's decertification of an asbestos class. Finally, the Supreme Court got into the act, rejecting a prepackaged settlement deal in which

---

* Reprinted from Michigan Law Review, December 2005, Vol. 104, No. 3. Copyright 2005 by the Michigan Law Review Association.

plaintiffs and defendants agreed to certify an asbestos class for settlement purposes only. Once again, the refusal to certify was driven, in part, by concerns with "fairness" to the defendants, given the coercive settlement power of a certified class proceeding. And once again, the Court's action found doctrinal cover in the notion that the predominance of common issues is undercut by the purported difficulty of applying allegedly disparate state laws—a rationale that has become central in the majority of these decertification cases.

At this point, courts and commentators appear to agree: the mass tort class action is dead as a doornail.

NOTES

1. On the one hand, Judge Williams enumerates several problems presented by mass-tort litigation and suggests that class actions may resolve them. He implies that class actions may be efficient and fair.

2. On the other hand, Professor Gilles reports the demise of the class action in part because of the lack of fairness to defendants, who may be forced to settle even unmeritorious claims in order to avoid the prospect of crushing liability. Such potential liability could drive companies out of business or chill their prospect of putting new products on the market. Gilles also reports the problem of administering disparate state liability laws in one proceeding.

3. Another major defect of the present tort compensation system may be the amount of money that goes to lawyers who represent victims of the mass tort. N.Y. Times, Mar. 10, 1985, §3, at 9, reported that "[i]n 1983 the Rand Corporation estimated that 63 cents of every dollar spent on asbestos litigation went to the opposing attorneys and for legal costs."

"GREAT LITTLE PRODUCT, BUT LIABILITY COULD EAT YOU UP."

© Dave Carpenter. Reprinted with permission.

Section Four
PRODUCT SAFETY AND THE ADMINISTRATIVE INSTRUMENT

In Chapter 3, we learned that the administrative instrument of the law operates to prevent grievances before they arise. Administrators take steps to ensure that parties, engaging in primarily beneficial activity, comply with regulations designed to avoid grievances. This basic technique can be employed to promote the safety of goods. The following excerpt introduces the Consumer Product Safety Act, enacted by Congress to establish the Consumer Product Safety Commission.

JAMES A. HENDERSON, JR., JUDICIAL REVIEW OF MANUFACTURERS' CONSCIOUS DESIGN CHOICES: THE LIMITS OF ADJUDICATION
73 Colum. L. Rev. 1531, 1573–76 (1973)

[R]ecent enactment of the Federal Consumer Product Safety Act, creating a new administrative agency [the Consumer Product Safety Commission] empowered to establish safety standards for a wide range of consumer products, strongly suggests that the trend toward legislative and administrative standard-setting will continue. The report of the National Commission on Product Safety, upon whose recommendations the Product Safety Act is largely based, clearly indicates that the priorities of the new agency will correspond almost exactly to those product areas exerting the greatest pressures upon the courts. Included in the Act is a provision authorizing suits for damages to be brought in the federal courts by persons injured by reason of knowing violations of any consumer product safety rule. Since the role of applying administratively established standards is one for which the courts are very well suited, this provision will surely be given full effect in actions against manufacturers by injured plaintiffs. While the Act also provides that compliance with such product safety rules shall not relieve any person of liability at common law, the inherent limits of adjudication should prevent courts from making extensive use of this latter provision to establish independent design standards.

CONSUMER PRODUCT SAFETY ACT

Congress enacted the Consumer Product Safety Act, 15 U.S.C. §§2051–2083, mentioned in the Henderson excerpt, in 1972. The history of the act is briefly described in Wahba v. H & N Prescription Center, Inc., 539 F. Supp. 352, 354 (E.D.N.Y. 1982):

> The Consumer Product Safety Act was the fruit of years of work by the legislature and others who recognized that modern technology and merchandising methods posed increasing threats to the nation's consumers. Prior to 1972, Congress had enacted a number of laws designed to combat dangers posed by specific categories of consumer products. See, e.g., Flammable Fabrics Act of 1953, 15 U.S.C. §§1191–1204; Federal Hazardous Substances Act, 15 U.S.C. §§1261–1274; Child Protection Act of 1966 and Child Protection and Toy Safety Act of 1969, 15 U.S.C. §§1261–1265, 1273, 1274; Refrigerator Safety Act, 15 U.S.C. §§1211–1214; Poison Prevention Packaging Act of 1970, 15 U.S.C. §§1261, 1471–1476; Federal Caustic Poison Act, 15 U.S.C. §§401–411 (repealed); Radiation Control for Health and Safety Act of 1968, 42 U.S.C. §§263b–263n; National Traffic & Motor Vehicle Safety Act of 1966, 15 U.S.C. §§1391–1409, 1421–1426, 1431. This categorical approach "resulted in a patchwork pattern of laws which, in combination, extend[ed] to only a small portion of the multitude of products produced for consumers." Consumer Product Safety Act of 1972, House Commerce Committee, H.R. Rep. No. 1153, 92d Cong., 2d Sess. 22 (1972).
>
> In 1967 Congress established the National Commission on Product Safety to examine methods of protecting consumers against unreasonable risks of injury from household products and to propose remedies for existing legal inadequacies. Act of Nov. 20, 1967, Pub. L. No. 90-146, 81 Stat. 466. After more than two years

of study, the Commission submitted its final report to Congress in June, 1970. In 1972 the Act established the Consumer Products Safety Commission, an independent federal regulatory agency vested with broad authority to protect against hazardous consumer products. See generally P. Sherman, Products Liability for the General Practitioner, §§4.04–4.06 (1981).

The Consumer Product Safety Act "gives the [Consumer Products Safety] Commission specific powers to investigate and regulate consumer products. The heart of the Commission's regulatory authority is its power to issue 'consumer product safety standards' dictating performance requirements and warning or instruction requirements and its power to ban products that cannot be rendered safe through the enforcement of standards." William R. Goetz, Private Causes of Action Under the Reporting Rules of the Consumer Product Safety Act, 70 Minn. L. Rev. 955, 955 (1986). Manufacturers, distributors, and retailers all come under the Act. In addition, the Act includes elaborate enforcement provisions, including civil and criminal penalties, as well as injunctive relief.

Why the need for the Consumer Product Safety Act and other similar legislation? Why is the potential liability of manufacturers and suppliers for breach of warranty, negligence, and strict tort insufficient to compel manufacturers and suppliers to take greater precautions to ensure the safety of their products? According to one view, even all of this potential liability together does not prevent unsafe products from entering the market. Evidence of an increase in injuries each year suggests that private remedies may be insufficient. By increasing the price of goods, businesses can simply pass on to the public the increased costs of liability insurance or payment of judgments and settlements. Some manufacturers, in addition, are unable to incorporate all of the technological advances in safety design into their products. See 1 Louis R. Frumer & Melvin I. Friedman, Products Liability §1A.01, at 2–3 (1984).

As with the private-arrangement and remedial instruments, the administrative instrument is not without its shortcomings. For example, consider the power lawnmower. In Southland Mower Co. v. Consumer Product Safety Commission, 619 F.2d 499, 502 (5th Cir. 1980), the court pointed out that at that time:

> approximately 77,000 people [were] injured each year in the United States by contacting the blades of walk-behind power mowers. Of these injuries, an estimated 9,900 involve the amputation of at least one finger or toe, 11,400 involve fractures, 2,400 involve avulsions (the tearing of flesh or a body part), 2,300 involve contusions, and 51,400 involve lacerations. The annual economic cost inflicted by the 77,000 yearly blade-contact injuries has been estimated to be about $253 million. This figure does not include monetary compensation for pain and suffering or for the lost use of amputated fingers and toes.

Was the Consumer Product Safety Commission up to the task of protecting people from the hazards of these lawnmowers? It promulgated a Safety Standard for Walk-Behind Power Lawn Mowers, 16 C.F.R. pt. 1205 (1979), 44 Fed. Reg. 9990–10031 (Feb. 15, 1979), pursuant to §7 of the Consumer Product Safety Act.

However, the *Southland* case, 619 F.2d at 503 n.3, revealed that promulgation took *over eight years*:

> The gestation period for the safety standard was long and complex. The administrative process was initiated on August 15, 1973, when, pursuant to §10 of the CPSA, 15 U.S.C. §2059, the Outdoor Power Equipment Institute, Inc. (OPEI) petitioned the CPSC to begin a proceeding to develop a consumer product safety standard addressing the hazards of power lawn mowers and asked the Commission to adopt a voluntary standard, ANSI B71.1–1972, "Safety Specifications for Power Lawn Mowers, Lawn & Garden Tractors, & Lawn Tractors," approved by the American National Standards Institute, Inc. as the proposed consumer product safety standard. On November 16, 1973, the Commission, after considering information about injuries associated with power lawn mowers, granted that portion of OPEI's petition that requested a proceeding to develop the power lawn mower safety standard. The Commission denied OPEI's request to publish ANSI B71.1–1972, with amendments, as a proposed consumer product safety standard however.
>
> Instead, the Commission solicited offers to develop a standard pursuant to §7(b) of the CPSA, 15 U.S.C. §2056(b). Subsequently, the Commission selected Consumers Union of United States, Inc. (CU) to develop the safety standard. See 39 Fed. Reg. 37803 (1974). As the offeror, CU gave representatives of industry, consumers, and other interests the opportunity to participate in developing the standard. It submitted the resulting proposal to the Commission on July 17, 1975. The recommended standard comprehensively addressed all types of lawn mowers and lawn mower injuries and contained requirements relating to blade-contact and thrown-object injuries, as well as injuries resulting from lawn mowers' slipping, rolling, overturning, or failing to steer or brake, injuries caused by burns from direct contact with exposed heated surfaces of mowers or from fires ignited by lawn mower ignition fluids, and injuries caused by electric shock from electrically powered lawn mowers or electric ignition systems.
>
> After analyzing the recommended CU standard, on May 5, 1977, the Commission published a proposed comprehensive power lawn mower safety standard for public comment. 42 Fed. Reg. 23052 (1977). The proposal elicited more than 100 initial comments, and the Commission solicited and received further comments on these already submitted comments. 42 Fed. Reg. 34892 (1977). On June 7, 1978, the Commission published a notice that it would issue requirements addressing injuries from blade contact with walk-behind power mowers before issuing separate standards dealing with injuries associated with thrown objects, fuel and electrical hazards, and riding mowers. 43 Fed. Reg. 24697 (1978). In November 1978, the Commission requested additional comments on the safety and reliability of brake-clutch mechanisms. 43 Fed. Reg. 51638 (1978). On February 26, 1979, Part 1205—Safety Standard for Walk-Behind Power Lawn Mowers, applying only to blade-contact injuries from walk-behind power lawn mowers, was issued, to become effective December 31, 1981.

Based on the delay in promulgating the power-lawnmower standards, one can argue that the constraints on the Consumer Product Safety Commission were too great. But perhaps some lesser procedure would be too subject to error. At any rate, there are additional problems with the administrative approach to product safety besides delay, such as limits on the agency's size and budget.

The effectiveness of the administrative instrument also depends on good-faith action by administrators. Is such action guaranteed? In Ford Motor Co. v. Stubblefield, 171 Ga. App. 331, 319 S.E.2d 470 (1984), the parents of a 15-year-old girl, who was killed in a Ford Mustang that was engulfed in flames when hit from behind by another car, brought a wrongful-death action against Ford. They claimed that Ford had negligently designed and placed the fuel system of the car. One issue was the admissibility of a transcript of a taped conversation between then President Richard Nixon, Lee Iacocca, who was then president of Ford, and Henry Ford II. The court found that the transcript was admissible, stating during the course of its discussion:

> Nor was [the transcript] inadmissible on grounds of irrelevance or prejudice. While there was no specific discussion among the participants as to fuel system integrity, the meeting took place just one day after the decision of Ford's management to defer the adoption of protective devices for the fuel tanks until required by law, and the gist of the taped conversation concerned the necessity for the Department of Transportation to "cool it" as to safety requirements and how the government might make those standards more responsive to the auto makers' cost effectiveness.

We saw in Chapter 3 that the administrative instrument achieves its goals in part by creating opportunities for voluntary compliance after a departure from an administrative standard. The following news release illustrates this strategy in the context of product safety.

**U.S. CONSUMER PRODUCT SAFETY COMMISSION,
NEWS FROM CPSC
July 20, 2007**

Black & Decker Recalls Trimmers/Edgers Due to Laceration Hazard from Projectiles

WASHINGTON, D.C.—The U.S. Consumer Product Safety Commission, in cooperation with the firm named below, today announced a voluntary recall of the following consumer product. Consumers should stop using recalled products immediately unless otherwise instructed.

Name of Product: Black & Decker GH1000 Grasshog XP String Trimmer/Edgers

Units: About 202,000

Manufacturer: Black & Decker (U.S.) Inc., of Towson, Md.

Hazard: The trimmer/edger's spool, spool cap and pieces of trimmer string can come loose during use and become airborne projectiles, posing a laceration hazard to the user as well as bystanders. The trimmer/edgers can also overheat posing a burn hazard to consumers.

Incidents/Injuries: Black & Decker has received 707 reports of incidents, including 58 reports of injuries. Serious injuries included cuts to two consumers' legs that required medical attention. Minor injuries included bruises, lacerations, and facial injuries such as a welt and broken skin over a consumer's eye. There were also reports of property damage, including two broken windows.

Description: The Black & Decker GH1000 Grasshog XP String Trimmers/Edgers are electric-powered. Trimmer/edgers with date codes 200546 through 200645 (representing manufacture dates of November 14, 2005 through November 6, 2006) are included in this recall. The date code is located on the underside of the trimmer/edger's handle. Only trimmers with black spools caps are included in the recall. Those with orange spool caps are not included in the recall.

Sold at: Major home center and hardware stores nationwide from November 2005 through January 2007 for about $70.

Manufactured in: China

Remedy: Consumers should stop using the string trimmers/edgers immediately and contact Black & Decker for a free repair kit.

Consumer Contact: For additional information, contact Black & Decker at (888) 742-9158 between 8 a.m. and 5 p.m. ET Monday through Friday, or visit the firm's Web site at www.blackanddecker.com

FEDERAL PREEMPTION OF STATE-LAW TORT CLAIMS

Suppose that after the Consumer Product Safety Commission promulgated the power-mower safety standards described above, a product that complied with the standards still injured a power-mower user? Can the user sue the manufacturer for negligence or strict-tort liability? Not if federal law "preempts" these state common-law rules. When does federal law preempt state law? This is a most complex question and we will only scratch the surface here. Reduced to its essence, federal law preempts state law if Congress intended to bar the state law when it promulgated the federal law. Obviously, a broad preemption doctrine in the product liability field means less rights for product users.

In BIC Pen Corp. v. Carter, 251 S.W.3d 500 (Tex. 2008), for example, a five-year-old playing with a BIC lighter accidentally set fire to his six-year-old sister's dress and she was severely burned. Her guardian sued BIC alleging a design defect in the lighter. The Texas Supreme Court reversed a $3 million judgment against BIC, holding that the design-defect claim was preempted by federal law.

First, the court outlined the parameters of the preemption doctrine:

> The United States Constitution provides that the laws of the United States are "the supreme Law of the Land; ... any Thing in the Constitution or Laws of any State to the Contrary notwithstanding." U.S. Const. art. VI, cl. 2. Thus, when a state law conflicts with federal law, it is preempted and has no effect. State laws may conflict with federal laws and be preempted in three ways. First, "[a] federal law may expressly preempt state law." Id. (citing Cipollone v. Liggett Group, Inc., 505 U.S. 504, 516, 112 S. Ct. 2608 (1992)). Second, "federal law or regulations may impliedly preempt state law or regulations if the statute's scope indicates that Congress intended federal law or regulations to occupy the field exclusively." Id. (citing Freightliner Corp. v. Myrick, 514 U.S. 280, 287, 115 S. Ct. 1483 (1995)). Finally, state law is impliedly preempted if it "actually conflicts with federal law or regulations," because: "(1) it is impossible for a private party to comply with both state and federal requirements; or (2) state law obstructs accomplishing and executing Congress' full purposes and objectives." Id.

Next, the court explained the elaborate federal safety standards promulgated by the Consumer Product Safety Commission, which BIC had satisfied. Finally, the court held that the claim against BIC was preempted by federal law:

> [O]ne of the Commission's primary concerns was the selection of a standard that encouraged the manufacture of child-resistant lighters and their acceptance by adult users. See 16 C.F.R. §1210.5(c). Interpreting federal regulation in this area as a liability floor that may be enhanced by state law, however, undercuts the federal regulations and the Commission's conclusion that the eighty-five percent test "strikes a reasonable balance between improved safety for a substantial majority of young children and other potential fire victims and the potential for adverse competitive effects and manufacturing disruption." 58 Fed. Reg. 37,589. The Commission specifically rejected more stringent standards, noting the problems that such standards would create by reducing the utility and convenience of the product and increasing costs disproportionate to benefits. Id. Because the Commission weighed these competing concerns when drafting its standard, we conclude that imposing a common law rule that would impose liability above the federal standard is contrary to the Commission's plan and conflicts with federal law.

The Washington Post, Feb. 16, 2006, at D1, reported that the "Bush administration is using federal rulemaking to limit consumer rights to seek damages under state laws governing faulty products." The rationale of the administration, according to the newspaper, was that having only one standard would better ensure safety. Opponents contended, however, that federal safety standards should be "starting points," not "ceilings," and that liability under state law created significant incentives for manufacturers to produce safer products.

Section Five
PRODUCT SAFETY AND THE PENAL INSTRUMENT

On August 10, 1978, a Chevrolet van struck the back of a Ford Pinto car carrying three teenage girls. All three girls were killed when, upon impact, the Pinto went up in flames. The car had been designed to withstand a rear-end collision by a vehicle like the van traveling at 20 mph. Contending that Ford should have designed the Pinto to withstand a rear-end impact in the range of 30–40 mph and that the van hit the Pinto with an impact of less than 40 mph, the State of Indiana brought criminal charges against Ford for recklessly designing and manufacturing the car and failing to recall it. The prosecution's view was that Ford knew that some people would die in fires caused by rear-end collisions and that, despite possessing the appropriate technology, Ford failed to remedy the problem because of a decision that it would be too costly. State v. Ford Motor Co., No. 5,324 (Ind. Super. Ct. indictment Sept. 13, 1978).

Why bring a criminal charge against a corporation such as Ford? Are criminal charges necessary in light of the other instruments of the law that have been applied to achieve product safety? Will the penal instrument itself be effective? These are fundamental questions that you should consider while reading the next two excerpts.

ANDREW WEISSMANN, A NEW APPROACH TO CORPORATE CRIMINAL LIABILITY
44 Am. Crim. L. Rev. 1319-20, 1324-27 (2007)

Under current federal common law, a corporation is liable for the actions of its agents whenever such agents act within the scope of their employment and at least in part to benefit the corporation. The theory that has evolved is simple and seemingly logical: a corporation, being merely a person in law only, and not a real one, can act only through its employees for whom it should be held responsible.

But the simple application of vicarious liability principles can have far-reaching effects. Courts applying federal common law have upheld convictions based on vicarious criminal corporate liability even where the agent was acting contrary to express corporate policy and where a bona fide compliance program was found to be in effect....

As to the limitation that employees must be acting within the scope of their actual or apparent authority, this requirement has been interpreted so expansively that it is practically invisible in many contexts. Similarly, the requirement that an employee act to benefit the company has likewise been relaxed by a permissive interpretation; under the current doctrine, it "is not necessary that the employee be primarily concerned with benefitting the corporation, because courts recognize that many employees act primarily for their own personal gain." Indeed, such is the state of the modern doctrine of vicarious criminal corporate liability that under federal law, a corporation can be held liable for agents no matter what their place in the corporate hierarchy and regardless of the efforts in place on the part of corporate mangers to deter their conduct.

. . . .

None of the traditional goals of the criminal law or its basic concern for individual determinations of guilt supports the application of agency principles of vicarious liability where a corporation has taken all reasonable measures to conform its employees' conduct to the law. Criminal law, after all, is reserved for conduct that we find so repugnant as to warrant the severest sanction. The goals of the criminal law are to deter and punish such conduct. Where nothing more can be expected of a corporation than actions it has already undertaken, the goals of the criminal law are satisfied.

Deterrence traditionally is broken down into two components, specific and general. Specific deterrence refers generally to incapacitating the criminal to prevent or dissuade future conduct in that individual. For a real person, that incapacitation comes usually in the form of imprisonment. It can also include restrictions on one's liberty and even employment during a period of supervised release. Prison of course is not an option for a corporation. Specific deterrence of a company could, however, take the form of causing the dissolution of the company (the equivalent of a corporate death penalty), barring the company either permanently or for a period of time from engaging in certain businesses, or subjecting the corporation, like an individual, to a probationary period during which its conduct is restricted and monitored by a court.

General deterrence refers to the effect punishment of a specific defendant will have on other members of society who might be tempted to engage in similar conduct. Such deterrence is thought to work particularly well in connection with white-collar offenses and less well to deter crimes of passion, in which a criminal is thought likely to engage without much forethought to the punishment meted out to similarly-situated individuals. General deterrence is particularly apt with respect to corporate criminal conduct, which tends to be the antithesis of crimes of passion. Corporations—through boards, inside and outside counsel, and formal deliberative processes—generally pay particular attention to precedent in determining the risks and rewards of contemplated action.

The criminal law also serves a retributive function by punishing the offender" for transgressing society's starkest boundary between what it has determined to be "right and wrong" or "good and evil." It is perhaps this retributive attribute that is most elusive yet most significant to the public. What actions are deemed to be "criminal"

is a judgment by society as to what is out of bounds of acceptable societal behavior. The transgression of that boundary is itself a harm that society has determined warrants its harshest condemnation. The boundary is a societal construct, as is the degree of punishment that is warranted for exceeding that boundary.

The corporation that transgresses that boundary can be as subject to retribution as an individual. Nevertheless, there is a difference between corporate and individual retribution. Individual criminality involves basic precepts involving an assessment of individual intent, action, and voluntariness. For a corporation, criminality is a harder construct. When a corporation is held *criminally* responsible for the criminal actions of an employee, retribution requires us to first determine what it is that the corporation did or did not do that warrants criminal sanction. Where an employee has been encouraged to engage in the crime by the corporation the analysis is simple. But what of the company that did everything it reasonably could to prevent such conduct? What then? Should civil damages suffice, or is there some action or inaction by the company that nevertheless is deserving of criminal condemnation?

Imposition of corporate liability where a corporation has taken all reasonable steps to deter and detect the criminal conduct of its employee furthers none of the goals of the criminal law. Such a corporation does not need to be specifically deterred. Indeed, by definition the company has already instituted the programs and policies that the criminal justice system could properly seek in the event of conviction on its own. By the same token, general deterrence would not be served. If anything, the conviction would send to corporations with effective compliance programs the opposite message—that no good deed will go unpunished. In short, there is nothing to deter, generally or specifically. For much the same reasons, there is no valid retributive value in punishing a corporation in such circumstances. Where an individual corporate employee has transgressed, but done so in spite of all reasonable steps by the corporation to prevent such criminal conduct, the culpability of the corporation is non-existent.

Where, as in Enron or WorldCom, a corporation's senior management engages in crime that enables the company to generate artificial earnings to meet Wall Street expectations, or where an executive fudges the numbers in a quarter while management closes its eyes to what is occurring, the company has either actively encouraged crime or tolerated it since it redounded to the company's immediate economic benefit. In either situation, it is doubtful that the company had an effective compliance program, since the encouragement of criminality or willful blindness by senior management would be show-stoppers. In such cases, the company should be held responsible for the conduct of its employees because it has not taken the necessary steps to prevent and detect such crimes from occurring. By its corporate policies, or lack thereof, the company demonstrates that it is willing to encourage or at least condone criminal conduct that redounds to the benefit of the corporation.

Where, on the other hand, criminality within the corporation is not systemic or condoned, but actively discouraged, current law still allows criminal prosecution. Suppose, for example, in anticipation of an imminent grand jury subpoena, a lower-level executive and a few of her assistants at her direction destroy documents that the employees believe would hurt themselves and the company. Suppose also that the corporation has extensive programs and policies in place to prevent such activity, but that the employees nevertheless committed the crime and were soon found out and turned over by the company to the government. The corporation has taken all reasonable measures to prevent and detect such criminal action by its employees, and nothing beneficial is gained by allowing criminal liability to attach. From a retributive perspective, the main thing that the corporation has done wrong is hiring someone who ultimately committed a crime. But it is hard to understand why the mere employment of one who commits a crime, absent unusual facts such as a complete abdication of screening for clear risk signs, would trigger the sanctions of the *criminal* law.

MALCOLM E. WHEELER, MANUFACTURERS' CRIMINAL LIABILITY

in 1 Louis R. Frumer & Melvin I. Friedman, Products Liability §1B.02[1], at 12–14 (1984)*

The manufacturer of a particular product might be criminally prosecuted under either or both of two types of statutes for having produced and marketed a product with a design defect, a manufacturing defect, or inadequate warnings. One type is the criminal regulatory statute—one specifying design, performance, or warning requirements for a class of products that includes the manufacturer's product. Such a statute might be, for example, a law requiring automobiles to have seatbelts (design requirement), a law requiring automobiles to withstand collisions of a specified magnitude without leaking fuel (performance requirement), or a law requiring that fabrics of specified flammability contain a label stating that fact (warning requirement). The second type is the general criminal statute—one prohibiting conduct not necessarily linked to the manufacture and sale of a particular class of products, or even to the manufacture and sale of products generally. General criminal statutes include, for example, murder, assault, and fraud statutes.[1]

Criminal regulatory statutes reflect a legislature's judgment regarding the specific instances in which manufacturers of specific products

---

* Reprinted with permission of Matthew Bender & Company, Inc., a member of the LexisNexis Group. All rights reserved.
1. Of course, product manufacturers can be prosecuted under many other criminal statutes, such as those regulating anticompetitive conduct, occupational health and safety, pollution of the environment, and securities transactions. Generally, however, those statutes are not aimed at regulating product safety and therefore are not pertinent to this chapter.

should be held criminally responsible. The legislature often expresses such judgments indirectly, through regulations promulgated by an administrative agency created by the legislature and authorized to promulgate standards the violation of which is punishable as a crime. The statutes in this category can be as numerous and as varied as the number of products appearing in commerce.[2] As a general rule, a product manufacturer can readily determine whether its product violates such a statute, because the statute specifies requirements aimed at a particular type of product, articulates specific design features, performance standards, or warnings, and does not require the manufacturer to speculate as to whether a jury in a criminal prosecution is likely to find something about the product sufficiently dangerous to constitute a negligent, reckless, or knowing creation of danger rising to the level of criminality.

General criminal statutes, on the other hand, present product manufacturers with greater uncertainty. It is far from clear, for example, what product design or what product warning suffices to permit a jury to find a product manufacturer guilty of a general crime such as "recklessly endangering another person," defined as follows:

A person commits a misdemeanor if he recklessly engages in conduct which places or may place another person in danger of death or serious bodily injury.[3]

. . . [T]he prosecution of Ford Motor Company for reckless homicide in 1980 apparently is the only instance in which a product manufacturer has been prosecuted under a general criminal statute for having produced and sold a product with a manufacturing defect, a design defect, or an insufficient warning. Nevertheless, the broad language of several criminal statutes and of the judicial decisions interpreting those statutes, together with the increasing use of criminal sanctions to regulate the conduct of corporations generally,[4] suggests the likelihood of future attempts to prosecute product manufacturers, under general criminal statutes, for the production and sale of defective products.

---

2. See, e.g., Federal Food, Drug, and Cosmetic Act §301, 21 USC §333(a) (1976).
3. Model Penal Code §211.2 (1962).
4. There is little doubt that the use of criminal sanctions to regulate corporate conduct has increased in recent years. . . .

The discussion in the Weissmann excerpt above focuses on deterrence and retribution as the main purposes of applying criminal sanctions to corporations. What of other purposes of such sanctions, such as removal of criminals from society and rehabilitation? Can corporations effectively be removed from society? The answer is no. If a corporation's charter were revoked, management and shareholders simply could set up another corporation. What about rehabilitation? See Chapter 2. Most analysts focus on deterrence as the proper goal here.

Weissmann argues that a corporation should not be criminally liable if it "has taken all reasonable steps to deter and detect the criminal conduct of its employee." But how should the law determine whether a company has taken "all reasonable steps"? Two writers looking at the question from the vantage point of economics suggest corporations should use resources to police employees only if the costs of doing so are less than the gains in the form of "reduced social harm from criminal activity." See Daniel R. Fischel & Alan O. Sykes, Corporate Crime, 25 J. Leg. Stud. 319, 323-24 (1996). Such a cost-benefit analysis often will not be easy, of course.

Is the penal instrument suited at all to achieve the goal of product safety? Analysts point to the relative leniency of fines that usually accompany corporate criminal liability as an important weakness because profits related to decisions harmful to the public usually greatly outweigh these fines. Further, writers doubt that the stigma associated with having to pay a fine is strong enough to deter unlawful behavior. In addition, determining which individuals in a large corporation are responsible for criminal behavior often challenges the fact finder.

Mr. Wheeler, one of Ford's attorneys in the Ford Pinto case, also questions whether manufacturers should be prosecuted under general criminal statutes because of the lack of clarity in what conduct should be criminalized: "It is far from clear ... what product design or what product warning suffices to permit a jury to find a product manufacturer guilty of a general crime such as 'recklessly endangering another person....'"

Nevertheless, the Ford Pinto case was prosecuted under a general criminal statute, Indiana Code §35–42–1–5. That section and other pertinent sections of the Indiana Code in force at the time of the case provided:

> §35–42–1–5.... A person who recklessly kills another human being commits reckless homicide....
> §35–41–1–2.... "Person" means a human being, corporation, partnership, unincorporated association, or governmental entity.
> §35–41–2–3.... A corporation ... may be prosecuted for any offense; it may be convicted of an offense only if it is proved that the offense was committed by its agent acting within the scope of his authority....

One of the reasons for Ford's criminal prosecution may have been the lack of satisfactory civil sanctions. Because the victims were killed, the parents' recourse was a wrongful-death action. But, under the governing Indiana statute, the parents' recovery would have been meager. Indiana Code §34–1–1–2. The statute measured the recovery in terms of the value of the child's services from the time of death until the age of majority, less support and maintenance; and the victims had reached or were soon to reach 18, the age of majority. In addition, according to Indiana common law, damages for pain and suffering of the victims, mental anguish of the survivors, and punitive damages were *not* recoverable against Ford. See William J. Maakestad, *State v. Ford Motor Co.*: Constitutional, Utilitarian, and Moral Perspectives, 27 St. Louis U. L.J. 857, 870–71 (1983).

Ford was acquitted in March 1980, after a jury trial in the Indiana criminal proceeding. Various grounds for the acquittal were possible. The jury could have believed, for example, that the van that hit the Pinto was traveling at a speed over 40 mph, as was contended by Ford. One article reported that a postverdict poll of the jurors showed that most jurors thought Ford was reckless in its design and manufacture of the Pinto, but not in its failure to recall. Id. at 860 n.14. Because the judge did not issue an opinion, we have no view of the general merits of bringing criminal charges in such cases. The following excerpt is highly critical of the decision to bring the reckless homicide case against Ford. This is followed by two excerpts that take a decidedly different view.

MALCOLM E. WHEELER, MANUFAC-TURERS' CRIMINAL LIABILITY

in 1 Louis R. Frumer & Melvin I. Friedman, Products Liability
§1B.06, at 54–61, 73–76, 78–81 (1984)*

The events surrounding the reckless-homicide prosecution of Ford Motor Company by the State of Indiana in 1980 suggest one form of product-manufacturer conduct that many persons believe should be deterred: the use of cost-benefit analysis in which human safety is treated as just one of several factors to be weighed, when choosing among alternative product designs. Thus, for example, the prosecutor accused Ford of having "consciously decided to sacrifice human life for private profit." Others who supported the criminal prosecution denounced the company for having used "cost-benefit analysis . . . over the cost of human life." These statements indicate that advocates of the use of criminal sanctions to regulate product designs and warnings base their argument in large part on a deep-seated antipathy for any managerial or engineering analysis that, under any circumstances, would permit non-safety considerations to dictate the adoption of a product design that is less safe than an available alternative design. Accordingly, those advocates appear to believe that criminal sanctions are necessary and desirable to deter the use of such cost-benefit analysis.

That belief, however, is both illogical and clearly contrary to the consuming public's best interests. It rests on reasoning that is inherently self-contradictory, on erroneous factual premises, on a misunderstanding of the meaning of cost-benefit analysis, and on a misperception of the public interest.

First, as noted above, the very essence of deterrence theory *requires* that an actor weigh the costs and benefits of contemplated conduct in deciding whether to engage in that conduct. It would be self-contradictory, therefore, to assert that society should deter the use of cost-benefit analysis by relying upon a theory that necessarily recognizes and encourages cost-benefit analysis.

Second, it is literally impossible to prevent any person from using cost-benefit analysis (except by preventing the person from acting altogether) because the very act of choosing one form of conduct over other forms of conduct necessarily entails a cost-benefit analysis. The person who goes to work decides that the anticipated benefits of work outweigh the risk of injury that necessarily attends the trip to the place of employment; the person who plays golf decides that the anticipated pleasure of that exercise outweighs the risk of being hit by a ball or of pulling a muscle; the person who smokes, drinks, skis, swims, or rides a motorcycle decides that those pleasures are worth the attendant risks. Similar decisions are made where actors' conduct implicates the safety of other persons; for example, the parents who leave their baby unattended in bed for one hour have decided that the pleasure of turning their attention elsewhere justifies the risk that their unattended infant will injure itself in the next room.

The examples are infinite in number, because *some* danger inheres in every human action and omission; and *some* amount of safety is sacrificed by every action and omission. The variables in every instance are the probability of harm and the possible scope of the harm.

Product manufacturers—large or small, sole proprietor or large corporation, simplistic or mathematically sophisticated—are no different. Consider, for example, a manufacturer who makes automobiles for sale to the public. That manufacturer knows that a prospective car owner will want some combination of safety, durability, reliability, speed, acceleration, comfort, passenger space, luggage space, handling, ease of repair, low cost of repair, aesthetics, low price, low cost of operation, and other factors. The manufacturer also knows that it is literally impossible to maximize all of those desires; for example, more passenger

---

space and luggage space require larger overall size, which is inconsistent with better handling, better acceleration, better mileage and lower price.

Further, even within any of the many areas, balancing is required. A thoroughly rigid rear structure in an automobile will protect the fuel tank from being damaged by a rear impact, but that same rigidity will cause the occupants to suffer injury or death from whiplash and from being thrown against parts of the vehicle's interior during the impact. Similarly, lighter weight yields better handling and, therefore, better accident avoidance, but the same absence of structure increases the likelihood of injury if the car does crash.

To strike a balance among the numerous variables, the manufacturer must decide what balance the public would strike if given the chance to make a fully informed choice among available alternative designs. In a basically free-market system, the manufacturer whose product most closely approximates the public's desired balance will sell the most units. If the public values safety features over low price and fuel economy, manufacturers of safer, more expensive, less efficient cars will succeed, and the public's wishes will be satisfied. Ascertaining the public's hypothetical fully informed desires, however, is no mean task. The manufacturer may try to ascertain the public's desire through public opinion polls, dealer information, consumer letters, sales volumes, sales trends for available alternatives, market studies, or analyses of external factors. Such external factors may include population growth, family size, oil supplies, state of the national economy, weather trends, and air quality....

Just as cost-benefit analysis is a logical necessity, it in turn necessarily entails the use of some common measuring device to compare the values of entirely disparate factors; and the only readily available such device is dollars. Therefore, however arbitrary and crude the valuation process might be, the decision-maker must assign some dollar value to human life, injury, and suffering, as well as to comfort, convenience, aesthetics, and other factors. The valuation process can be intuitive, as it is in most of our personal, minute-by-minute decisions, or it can be a sophisticated, quantitative, computerized analysis. Thus, when a highway safety engineer for the government decides whether to put a stoplight, a stopsign, a traffic officer or no traffic-control device at an intersection, he cannot rationally decide which choice to make unless he first decides how much of the public's money should be spent to prevent one injury or one death; and he cannot make that decision without first putting some value on human life and limb.

The same problem faces a legislature trying to decide whether to impose a 65–mile-per-hour speed limit, a 55–mile-per-hour speed limit, a 25–mile-per-hour speed limit or a ban on all automobile traffic. Each more restrictive law will prevent more highway deaths, but each has a greater cost in terms of convenience, pleasure, and the delivery of goods and services, including health services. A rational decision requires using a common valuation tool: dollars.

Out of ignorance or for political purposes, one can argue that it is immoral to put a dollar value on human life. The inevitable effect of such a position, however, is that cost-benefit analyses will still be made by every decision-maker, but they will be made in a cruder, less informed, less open manner that is less susceptible to rational review by the public and by the courts....

Alternatively, ... one might contend that criminal sanctions are needed to deter manufacturers from marketing any product that could be made safer by using current technology, irrespective of the cost consumers might have to pay for the added safety. Costs of additional safety might include higher price, lower reliability, shorter useful life, reduced efficiency, higher maintenance and service costs, and many others.

This contention, however, ignores the indisputable fact that the public does not want all technologically feasible safety at any cost. Rather, individual citizens constantly choose to risk their own personal safety and the safety of others, including their loved ones, for a variety of reasons, including price, function, convenience, aesthetics, vanity and pleasure. For example, women wear high-heeled shoes despite the obvious risk of tripping or damaging their Achilles tendons; men undergo hair transplants despite the well-known risk of infection and other injury; men and women undergo face-lifts and other cosmetic surgery, smoke cigarettes, take drugs, drink liquor, drive over the speed limit, play contact sports, shoot guns and engage in innumerable other activities that risk their own safety and the safety of others.

Thus, if criminal sanctions were to be applied to product manufacturers for marketing products that are somewhat less safe, but somewhat cheaper, more reliable, more durable or better in some other respect, criminal sanctions should be applied with equal vigor to Congress for not lowering the speed limit below 55 miles-per-hour; to state and federal agencies responsible for the construction of highways that have curves, go over hills and have only two lanes (since all such highways are known to result in more highway deaths than straight, multi-lane highways); to drivers who drive at the maximum allowable speed rather than at a lower allowable speed; to parents who do not strap seatbelts onto their children in automobiles; to parents who give their children motorcycles and toys that (like all toys) can injure; to retail stores that sell liquor; to homeowners who burn leaves or use fireplaces; and so forth. Obviously, no sensible person wishes to apply criminal sanctions in that manner.

Alternatively, therefore, the criminal-sanctions proponent might contend that such sanctions are needed to deter manufacturers from marketing any product without giving the public the opportunity to exercise an informed choice—that is, without informing the public of every respect in which the product could be made safer, the costs of making each available safety modification and the extent to which safety would be increased by each such modification.

The absurdity of that contention can be seen by considering the implications for almost any product. For example, an automobile has approximately 14,000 parts, each of which can be made safer in at least one way, such as by using higher-grade materials or narrower manufacturing tolerances. To inform the public of each such available modification, of the effects on price, comfort, durability, fuel economy and other factors, and of the effect of each modification on the overall safety risk would require a multi-volume buyers' guide that would cost thousands of dollars and go unread by the public.

Alternatively, therefore, the criminal-sanctions proponent might contend that such sanctions are needed to deter manufacturers from marketing products that are less safe than the public wants them to be, all factors considered. This seems to be the proper basis on which to try to justify the application of criminal sanctions under a deterrence theory. Application of the deterrence theory on this basis would be consistent with the present application of criminal sanctions to deter recklessness in other forms of conduct. It would be consistent, for example, with imposing criminal sanctions against drivers who drive 60 miles-per-hour in a 55–mile-per-hour zone, but not against drivers who drive 55 miles-per-hour, even though both activities create a risk to the driver, his passengers, pedestrians and occupants of other vehicles. It would be consistent with imposing criminal sanctions against persons who fire their guns in urban areas, but not against persons who fire their guns on skeet ranges or in authorized hunting areas, even though each of these activities creates a risk to human safety. In short, the use of criminal sanctions based on a deterrence theory may be desirable where—because manufacturers have inadequate information, because of high transaction costs in negotiations between buyers and sellers and bystanders, because of a low probability that manufacturers will pay the social costs of marketing products that are less safe than the public wants when all factors are considered, or because of any other circumstance—a manufacturer is not sufficiently likely to calculate and to internalize accurately the full social costs of manufacturing a particular product.

GLENN A. CLARK, NOTE, CORPORATE HOMICIDE: A NEW ASSAULT ON CORPORATE DECISION-MAKING
54 Notre Dame Law. 911, 922–24 (1979)*

[I]t should be noted that *State v. Ford Motor Co.* presents issues which transcend those of existing precedents. Prior indictments of corporations for homicide resulted from acts of corporate agents performed within the scope of employment. The engineer recklessly operating the train or a repairman recklessly installing a gas pipe, are examples of the norm. The prosecution of Ford, however, occurs in a completely different setting. Ford's alleged illegal conduct is comprised of three acts: (1) defectively designing the vehicle, (2) defectively manufacturing the vehicle, and (3) allowing the vehicle to remain on the public highways.[91] Each of these acts is the product of a complex business decision. Both the design and manufacture of automobiles are subject to extensive federal regulation.[92] Rigorous testing precedes marketing. Defects discovered after sale to the public may involve recalls, either voluntary or compulsory.[93] Therefore, the Pinto which exploded on August 10, 1978, was the product of many substantial business decisions occurring at various levels of the corporate hierarchy. The deterrent effect of corporate liability for criminal homicide, therefore, must be assessed by the effect of conviction on this decision-making process.

The maximum penalty which can be imposed on a corporation convicted under the Indiana reckless homicide statute is a $10,000 fine.[94] The effectiveness of this sanction as a deterrent to a large, profitable corporation is questionable. The imposition of a $10,000 fine in itself is a nominal burden. Opponents of corporate criminal liability for homicide might contend that companies such as Ford are not likely to alter internal policies for fear of such sanctions. Thus, superficially, such indictments appear as futile attempts to impede corporate recklessness when deterrence is the standard of evaluation and "small" fines are the sanction.

The inherent flaw in this analysis is the assumption that the $10,000 fine is the only consequence of conviction. The negative publicity of a criminal conviction is the consequence most likely to deter reckless corporate conduct. A guilty verdict could threaten the fate of a corporation's entire product line by inspiring public mistrust and thereby jeopardizing future revenues. Short-term cost reductions due to relaxed concern for safety would have to be discounted by the potential impact on sales revenue. Therefore, the imposition of corporate criminal penalties should deter the instigation of corporate policies that produce incidents such as the Pinto explosion of August 10, 1978, by stimulating greater managerial scrutiny of the design and manufacture of products.

The Pinto case, regardless of its outcome, will also heighten corporate concern regarding recalls. A product designed and manufactured with proper care but subsequently found to be defective may be the basis of a homicide indictment. Thus, a new variable enters decisions concerning the recall of defective products. Simple cost analysis will no longer suffice because the company must account for potential public animosity in the event of criminal indictment. The net result is increased concern for product safety and consumer protection.

Arguably, a products liability suit might provide the necessary deterrence offered by criminal liability. The monetary concern is potentially much greater and the victim is compensated more directly. Also, the impact on corporate sales has the potential of being equally devastating. Although this argument has its merits, it fails to note that criminal liability is generally reserved for egregious deviations from the standard of care required of corporations. Furthermore, civil

---

* Copyright © 1979 by Notre Dame Law Review. Reprinted with permission.
91. State v. Ford Motor Co., No. 5324 (Indictment at 1).
92. See, e.g., National Traffic and Motor Vehicle Safety Act of 1966, 15 U.S.C. §§1381–1431 (1976).
93. See 15 U.S.C. §§1411–1420 (1976).
94. Ind. Code §35-50-2-6 (Supp. 1978).

remedies might not be available in all cases,[95] thus leaving criminal prosecution as the only sanction. The social and moral condemnation associated with a homicide conviction also provides an added variable of immense proportions that is not offered by civil litigation. Media coverage of such events generates national exposure. The result should be much stronger deterrence of reckless disregard for product safety.

Absent potential criminal responsibility for marketing a defective product, the value of human life is reduced to mere cost analysis. Probability distributions estimating potential consumer deaths and resulting civil liabilities pitted against the cost of adequate safety precautions threatens to become the standard of corporate decision-making. Thus, potential criminal liability provides a prophylactic variable likely to weigh heavily in contemporary decision-making models, thereby enhancing corporate responsibility to consumers.

---

95. This is the case in Indiana. Indiana law does not provide a civil remedy to the families of the deceased girls. State's Memorandum in Rebuttal to Motion to Dismiss (filed Dec. 20, 1978).

WILLIAM J. MAAKESTAD, STATE v. FORD MOTOR CO.: *CONSTITUTIONAL, UTILITARIAN, AND MORAL PERSPECTIVES*

27 St. Louis U. L.J. 857, 875–78 (1983)*

The Elkhart, Indiana community's immediate reaction to the fiery accident on U.S. Highway 33 was the kind of shock and profound sense of loss that can follow only a local tragedy which takes the lives of young people. Certain irregularities discovered during the state police's investigation that implicated Ford were discovered, however, and grief turned to outrage as many in the community began to tie together the information they were receiving locally with the legacy of Pinto deaths and injuries nationwide, which had received extensive publicity on television and in newspapers and magazines. As public and private debate intensified, the question that emerged most frequently was, "What legal response can, and should, be made?" Preliminary legal research revealed the severe limitations of civil remedies . . .; moreover, a civil remedy would do little to give fruition to the community's sentiments. If a meaningful legal response was to be forthcoming, it would have to take the form of a criminal prosecution against either a particular Ford executive, or executives, or the corporation itself. Elkhart County Prosecutor Michael A. Cosentino, who had carefully directed the investigation of the accident from the beginning, weighed the alternatives, realizing that taking any criminal action against Ford would mean an extensive commitment of time, effort, and money. Following informative conversations with attorneys who had successfully sued Ford in civil court and were therefore familiar with available documentary evidence relevant to the Pinto's development, a decision was made: an indictment by grand jury would be sought against Ford Motor Company, a corporation, for three counts of reckless homicide.[74]

We thus return to our original query: was the prosecution primarily concerned with utilitarian values or moral values? Although the law professors and their students who soon became an integral part of the volunteer prosecutorial staff may have viewed the case as an opportunity to establish a precedent and create a new means by

---

* Copyright © 1983 by Saint Louis University Law Journal. Reprinted by permission.

74. The choice between prosecuting the corporation or corporate officers is a dilemma frequently encountered in cases of corporate crime. Although most legal commentators agree that sanctions directed at corporate actors are more effective as a deterrent in most instances, it is extremely difficult to pinpoint individual responsibility for a policy or even a single decision in the labyrinthian structure of modern corporations.

which to fight corporate crime, the local prosecutor's initial and primary concern was to respond to the outrage which followed the local family's tragedy. What was actually being conceived in Indiana, then, was not a proposed panacea for the corporate crime problem but a new moral boundary of permissible corporate conduct. It should be recalled that prior to this case, Ford's conduct surrounding the Pinto had already triggered nearly every legal response possible other than criminal prosecution: civil cases involving compensatory damages, civil cases involving both compensatory and punitive damages, and federal administrative agency actions. . . . Although a jury chosen from a different community, following a change of venue, ultimately rendered a verdict of acquittal, the real significance of the prosecution was undiminished: local people who had considered their *moral boundaries* transgressed had risen up and expressed their outrage by requiring a corporation, like any other person, to stand judgment before a criminal jury. . . .

Clearly, the attempt to place criminal responsibility upon Ford for reckless homicide, an offense carrying a maximum penalty of only $30,000 ($10,000 per count) under Indiana law, holds much greater import as a symbolic declaration of public morality than it does as an instrument by which to combat corporate crime effectively in the future.

As one of Ford's defense attorneys observed after the trial, the prosecution of a serious offense against an individual is admittedly different than the prosecution of a corporation, where adverse publicity may affect the company's employees and their families, the company's suppliers and shareholders, and the consuming public. Nonetheless, if corporations are to be personified in terms of maintaining a separate legal identity cloaked with most of the protections afforded by The Bill of Rights, it should not be considered unrealistic to require that they occasionally abide by the same moral duties and submit to the same legal mechanisms through which all other persons in our society are judged.

NOTES

1. Wheeler defends Ford's cost-benefit analysis in producing the Pinto. He asserts that all decisionmaking involves weighing the costs and benefits. For example, lawmakers understand that setting the speed limit on a highway at 65 mph will cost more lives than if the speed limit were 55 mph. No one claims that such decisions should be punished criminally, although some disagree with the policy. Further, Wheeler claims that the public does not want state-of-the-art safety features, because they are too expensive.

2. Clark bemoans corporate cost-benefit analysis and justifies criminal sanctions in part because the "negative publicity" creates incentives for "greater managerial scrutiny of the design and manufacture of products."

3. Professor Maakestad points out that outrage in the community led to the Ford prosecution. This reaction tends to refute Wheeler concerning the amount of product safety desired by the public. On the other hand, the verdict in the Ford case may show that the public approves of Ford's cost-benefit approach.

4. What has been the aftermath of the Pinto case? The National Law Journal, Mar. 31, 1980, at 3, reported that prosecutors predicted more such prosecutions because a "psychological barrier" had been broken. But corporate executives thought that the attempt to "pound away at the corporations in court had peaked." The following excerpts take up the issue.

PRODUCT SAFETY & LIABILITY REPORTER (BNA)
No. 8, at 297–98 (Apr. 25, 1980)*

A Washington, D.C.-based consumer group asked Wisconsin authorities April 17 to bring criminal charges against Ford Motor Company for a transmission defect the group blames for the death of an 18-month-old boy.

In a letter to Wisconsin Attorney General Bronson C. LaFollette, the Center for Auto Safety requested that Ford and certain unnamed Ford executives be prosecuted "for homicide by reckless conduct" in the April 15 death of Michael Cannon of Hartland, Wisc.

According to the letter, the boy was drowned when the idling 1977 Thunderbird in which he was sitting while his mother opened the garage door, jumped, by itself, from "park" into "reverse" gear and backed into a 20-foot deep pond across the street from his home. The letter noted that the child was strapped into a child restraint seat at the time.

"The Center believes that Michael's death was caused by a defective automatic transmission that Ford has known about for at least 10 years," the group told LaFollette. Only two days before the fatality, the center told reporters at a Washington, D.C., press conference that automatic transmissions in as many as 26 million Fords can jump from "park" into "reverse" while the engine is idling, and threatened to sue the National Highway Traffic Safety Administration to force a recall of the involved vehicles (Current Report, Apr. 18, 1980, p. 286).

_____

* Reprinted by permission from PRODUCT SAFETY & LIABILITY REPORTER, copyright 1980 by The Bureau of National Affairs, Inc., Washington, D.C.

PRODUCT SAFETY & LIABILITY REPORTER (BNA)
No. 8, at 356 (May 23, 1980)*

The Wisconsin attorney general's office decided not to bring criminal charges against Ford Motor Company for the death of a 15-month-old child, following a coroner's jury determination that not enough facts were presented to establish criminal negligence.

Calls for criminal prosecution of Ford came from the Center for Auto Safety, a Washington, D.C.-based consumer group, which claimed that a defect in the transmission of a Ford car was responsible for the death of a 15-month-old Hartland, Wisc. boy....

Not Enough Evidence

A six-member jury, impanelled by the Waukesha County, Wisc. coroner, however, concluded after two days of hearings...[in their verdict:] "We do not find the negligence of Ford Motor Company to fulfill our understanding of the legal definition of criminal negligence, because that definition calls for the establishment of an existing high probability of death or serious injury to another; and we can not establish what we determine to be a high probability of incidence (sic) on the basis of evidence presented to us."

But Design Found Faulty

But the jury did determine that Ford "has been aware of an existent problem in design and function of their FMX and C6 transmissions

_____

* Reprinted by permission from PRODUCT SAFETY & LIABILITY REPORTER, copyright 1980 by The Bureau of National Affairs, Inc., Washington, D.C.

which has caused involuntary shifting from the indicated park position to reverse causing involuntary movement of the vehicle which has in some cases resulted in death, personel (sic) injury, and/or property damage."

In addition, the jury said, "It is our determination that the major perpetrating cause of the accident resulting in the death of Michael Cannon was this faulty design and function and the Ford Motor Company's omission of its correction."

DONALD J. MIESTER, JR., COMMENT, CRIMINAL LIABILITY FOR CORPORATIONS THAT KILL
64 Tul. L. Rev. 919, 929-30 (1990)

Since *Ford Motor*, three states have upheld the prosecution of corporations for negligent homicide. Even more significant have been the several cases since *Ford Motor* that have continued the trend towards holding corporations liable for reckless behavior. In 1984 a New Jersey grand jury indicted a corporation for reckless homicide. This indictment charged that the Six Flags Corporation had recklessly endangered human life by using a highly flammable foam rubber padding on the walls of its New Jersey amusement park's haunted house. Although the corporation knew the pads could easily catch fire, it did not try to fireproof them or install either smoke detectors or sprinkler systems. In 1984 an unidentified youth touched a cigarette lighter to the padding, which

burst into flame, killing eight children. After a controversial trial, the corporation was acquitted.

The first conviction of a corporate defendant for a charge greater than negligent homicide came soon after *Six Flags*. On June 14, 1985, Film Recovery Systems, Inc. and its sister company, Metallic Mining Systems, were found guilty of involuntary manslaughter for the death of Stefan Golab, an immigrant worker hired to clean vats of cyanide. The corporations were found to have concealed evidence of the cyanide's deadly effects from the workers and even had gone so far as to scrape the skull-and-crossbones warning labels off the cyanide vats. As a result of their convictions, the two corporations were fined a total of $ 48,000. In that same year, the Glendale Convalescent Center in Wisconsin pleaded no contest to reckless homicide concerning the death of a seventy-eight-year-old patient.

In the latter 1990s, the movement to criminalize corporate behavior concerning product defects lost steam. But in 2006, the U.S. Senate judiciary committee held a hearing on whether to criminalize companies that knowingly manufacture and distribute a defective product. Portions of the transcript of the hearing follow. The transcript reveals the continuing diversity of views on this subject.

DEFECTIVE PRODUCTS: WILL CRIMINAL PENALTIES ENSURE CORPORATE ACCOUNTABILITY?

Hearing Before the S. Comm. on the Judiciary, 109th Cong. (2006) available at http://www.access.gpo.gov/congress/senate/pdf/109hrg/27707.pdf.

OPENING STATEMENT OF HON. ARLEN SPECTER, A U.S. SENATOR
FROM THE STATE OF PENNSYLVANIA

The issue at hand came into very sharp focus many years ago with the Pinto case, where there were corporate documents which showed that the gas tank was placed in a dangerous position because it was cheaper to put the gas tank in that locale and to pay damages for injuries and deaths, that it would be a matter of corporate profitability.

That case made a fair size impact on me personally. I was district attorney of Philadelphia at the time. There ultimately was a prosecution in that case by a local prosecutor in Indiana, I believe, and there was an acquittal. From all indications, the case was not handled as well as it might have been, certainly not as well as a Federal prosecution would be.

. . .

The problems continue at the present time with a story just last week in the New York Times concerning the Guidant Corporation, where there was knowledge for 3 years that its heart defibrillator might short-circuit and fail after being implanted. The publication in the New York Times suggested that a number of patients might have died there, and the problem is as current as the Guidant case and we will hear some testimony on that today.

STATEMENT OF JOHN ENGLER, FORMER GOVERNOR OF MICHIGAN,
AND PRESIDENT, NATIONAL ASSOCIATION OF MANUFACTURERS,
WASHINGTON, D.C.

We are grateful for the invitation and the opportunity to testify on this very important question: Would it be wise to make the act of knowingly allowing a defective to be introduced into the stream of interstate commerce a criminal offense?

While this proposal may be well-intentioned, the NAM believes it is fraught with many unforeseen and potentially counterproductive consequences. The National Association of Manufacturers does not defend any manufacturing employee who would intentionally introduce a defective product into the marketplace. However, we are here today because of our concern about the real-world and practical difficulties of criminalizing what often are subjective judgments.

. . .

Defining "product defect" is one of the most complex and varied aspects of product liability, as evidenced by the numerous variations of product defect standards among the States. At the same time, the legal concept of what constitutes a criminal act is sort of being whittled away by the courts.

Imagine the dilemma faced by a manufacturer who keeps very precise records about products that are returned. What if one or more proved to be defective? Even if the defect rate is extremely low, would the manufacturer knowingly be placing a defective product into the stream of interstate commerce simply because the product line is not one hundred percent defect-free? Are we seeking to hold a manufacturer criminally liable for the one-in-a-million problem? By the same token, would criminal intent be established if there was a warning label and that warning label was not clear enough for every single consumer user of the product to understand?

Every product can cause injury under some circumstances. Justice Breyer wrote, "Using this vivid example, over the next 13 years we could expect more than a dozen deaths from ingested toothpicks." If product liability violations were criminalized, actual victims also might find themselves forced to wait out the criminal justice system.

. . .

Poorly conceived legislation could end up forestalling fact-finding, including how and why the problem occurred. It could also worsen the U.S.'s comparative advantage, or in this case disadvantage, in legal costs which, expressed in GDP terms, are twice as high as in other industrial nations that we compete everyday with.

As you consider this matter, I hope that this Committee will remember the genesis of punitive damages in the common law is that they were to serve as a substitute punishment and deterrent for acts that would be difficult to criminalize. We are pleased that the Judiciary Committee is studying the issue. We hope the Committee will carefully weigh the arguments and conclude that the proposal to criminalize product liability as prepared today is not a good idea.

STATEMENT OF VICTOR E. SCHWARTZ, SHOOK, HARDY AND BACON, LLP, WASHINGTON, D.C.

In a nutshell, this is an idea that really does sound good. We don't want manufacturers to be killing people, but to put a crime based on the topic of defect is putting a crime based on a fog. And we don't want our Department of Justice to be there where instead of doing their job, you have good friends, like one who testified earlier, kind of waiting outside to see if there is going to be an indictment, because even if there was the slightest hint of an indictment, I assure you there would be a product liability pinata lawsuit following that no one has ever seen before.

STATEMENT OF DONALD L. MAYS, SENIOR DIRECTOR, PRODUCT SAFETY AND CONSUMER SCIENCES, CONSUMERS UNION, YONKERS, NEW YORK

My product safety work and expertise have led me to six overall conclusions that I would like to share with the Committee. No. 1, many injuries are avoidable if adequate pre-market safety testing is conducted. Two, manufacturers do not always react responsibly when informed that their products could potentially cause a repeated pattern of death or injury.

Three, due to changes in the global marketplace, consumers face increased risk from defective products. Four, there is a lack of compliance with voluntary safety standards. Five, there is inadequate enforcement authority, resources and activity by Federal agencies. And, six, civil penalties may not be an effective deterrent in preventing unsafe products from being in the marketplace. An example: a $750,000 civil penalty levied against Wal-Mart in 2003 for failing to report safety hazards with fitness machines cost the company an equivalent of their sales rung up in only 1 minute and 33 seconds.

So, clearly, Consumers Union strongly believes that the consumer marketplace does, in fact, need greater accountability. Consumers Union supports the introduction of legislation clearly designed to deter company employees with decisionmaking authority from knowingly jeopardizing consumer safety. And on this point, please let me be clear. We understand that any company can make a mistake, but it is what companies do after they have taken the time to do their due diligence and establish that they have a defect that could likely cause bodily injury or death that should be the focus of this bill. If companies don't go public and they continue to sell their defective products, then the individuals responsible should be punished to the fullest extent possible.

. . .

Chairman *SPECTER*: Mr. Schwartz, do you think that the possibility of a criminal sanction would have any effect at all on judgments of corporate officials in evaluating safety precautions which are expensive, contrasted with the evaluation of what their damages would be if the safety precautions are not undertaken?

Mr. *SCHWARTZ*: That is a good question and it does call for speculation, but I don't think so. I think that right now they can lose their jobs and they can lose their market share completely on a product once it is branded in the product liability system as being bad. It takes some time, and that threat, potentially millions and billions of dollars, is sufficient.

I think if there are additional penalties . . . that may be needed. That is a different question as to whether you introduce something that is very vague, very hard to understand, and illusory to kind of grab onto. So I don't think it will. Specific penalties, sir, that would be very clear and easy to understand might be needed in some areas, and they may help proper decisionmaking.

. . .

Chairman *SPECTER:* You think there would be no difference between an impact of a decisionmaker, say a chief executive officer, if he or she faced criminal sanctions, contrasted with the punitive damages in a civil case which would be awarded against the company and a cost really to the shareholders?

Mr. *SCHWARTZ*: As the appendix to my testimony shows, there are criminal sanctions for very serious acts by individual executives, and State attorneys general have power, which you would know, to go after people personally if they have the evidence that they have done something criminally wrong.

Chairman *SPECTER*: On defects in products?

Mr. *SCHWARTZ*: Well, not on defects in the products, and that is, I guess, the core of my testimony. "Defect" is one of those words that we think we know what it means, but not when it gets down to actually defining it, it is hard enough to define it in tort law. It is one of those words that we think, ah, I know what that means, like we may think we know what a reasonable person is in tort law.

Chairman *SPECTER*: I take it your answer is no.

Mr. *SCHWARTZ*: Well, I began with "no," but then you wanted to get me to "yes," so I went back to "no."

Chairman *SPECTER*: I didn't hear a "no." If I had heard a "no," I would have moved on to the next question. The question isn't whether there are some penalties scattered through the State law books. The question is whether there is any real program which deals with defects. And I will use that word; I think we can define it. I think there are many terms that are difficult to define. You started to move on to the definition of "reasonable." There are tens of thousands, hundreds of thousands of cases written on it, but on individual cases we deal with it.

That is why, Mr. Schwartz, I come back to the question as to whether the existing laws which you refer to involve products, and your answer to that was no.

Mr. *SCHWARTZ:* Well, the product liability laws are amazingly strong, over-strong, in my view, and this separation of somehow an executive, because he may not feel personally that he is going to go to jail, needs additional deterrence I have answered. I think when people are working in the companies—I work with them every single day of my life—they are thinking carefully about what decisions they are making, what warnings are to be on products. I have spent hundreds of hours on this and I don't see the need for any additional criminal deterrence to get to the right decision. That is just based on my experience.

Chairman *SPECTER:* Well, summarize for us again what are existing criminal deterrents.

Mr. *SCHWARTZ:* Well, there are existing criminal laws on manslaughter, negligent homicide and other provisions, and they are spelled out more carefully in the appendix to my statement. But I think that the power of—

Chairman *SPECTER:* But those don't refer specifically to products.

Mr. *SCHWARTZ:* No, they don't, but they can capture somebody who has knowingly and willfully tried to intentionally kill another person. I mean, those words we understand. We know what those words mean. We have always been kind to one another and we just happen to differ here, but the tort law classes—I was thinking of Fleming James, who may have been your teacher back at Yale.

Chairman *SPECTER:* He was.

Mr. *SCHWARTZ:* In tort law classes, they will say, "Well, what about this? What about that?" It is all vague. You step over into the criminal law and then there are very precise rules that govern conduct, and I think the two worlds shouldn't be put together.

NOTES

1. Donald Mays commented on the "inadequate enforcement authority, resources and activity by Federal agencies." For more on the limitations of agencies, see Chapter 3.

2. One of the main sticky issues is whether the concept of "defect" is sufficiently distinct so that criminal liability is not too uncertain. Senator Specter believes "defect" can be defined, but Mr. Schwartz thinks that criminal statutes should be more precise than the word allows. For more on the issue of precision in criminal statutes, see Chapter 2.

Hidden Defects in Software

Defects in software can cause personal injury, for example, if the software in an airline is defective and causes a crash. To date, society has not utilized the penal instrument to deal with this problem. However, in an ongoing project on software contracts, the American Law Institute has drafted rules that make software manufacturers strictly liable for known, serious hidden defects. The rule states that "The transferor [manufacturer] warrants to any party in the normal chain of distribution that the software contains no material hidden defects of which the transferor was aware at the time of the transfer. This warranty may not be excluded. In addition, this warranty does not displace an action for misrepresentation or its remedies." ALI Principles of the Law of Software Contracts §3.05(b) (Final Draft, 2009). Common law supports this approach as liability would surely arise for failure to disclose a known material hidden defect in goods under tort or contract law. Imagine if the manufacturers of a car included a component that it knew, but no one else could find out, was defective and would make the car dangerous. We saw that in 2006 the U.S. Senate considered making such conduct criminal.

SPECIFIC CRIMINAL STATUTES

Criminal prosecution under specific criminal statutes rather than general criminal statutes has been more common and more successful.

For example, the Chicago Tribune, Jan. 6, 1985, §4, at 1, reported that SmithKline Beckman Corporation, the manufacturer of Selacryn, a drug used for hypertension, and its doctors in charge of reporting information to the Food and Drug Administration pleaded guilty to criminal misdemeanor charges. Selacryn was linked to 36 deaths and 500 serious injuries while it was on the market.

The defendants violated FDA regulations requiring timely reports to the FDA of information acquired by SmithKline on liver damage and deaths caused by the drug, as well as regulations involving accurate labeling. Among information withheld beyond the FDA's 15-day timely notification requirement was information that the French company that had sold SmithKline the license to manufacture Selacryn in the United States had linked the drug to liver damage, and information from doctors "across the country" that their patients were "developing hepatitis, falling into . . . coma[s] and dying." In addition, SmithKline had labeled the drug inaccurately with a statement that no "cause and effect relationship" existed between Selacryn and liver disease.

Violations of these regulations are misdemeanors. SmithKline and its doctors pleaded guilty to 34 counts, each punishable by a $1,000 fine and one year of prison. Thus, the maximum fine against SmithKline was $34,000. The company's 1983 profits, according to the article, were $490 million.

Punitive Damages in Civil Actions

Punitive damages are a means of punishing vendors who put dangerous products in the stream of commerce. The goal of such awards is in part to punish the wrongdoer and in part to deter the conduct, so many of the underlying themes of the criminal law apply to the civil award of punitive damages.

Punitive damages in product safety cases are quite controversial for several reasons. First, critics claim that they are increasing rapidly in number and amount, with the result being fewer products, less innovation, and higher prices. But others say there is little empirical evidence, either of the increase in numbers and generosity of awards or of the reduction in new products. Second, critics also worry about the randomness of the awards—juries have little guidance and seem to award or not award punitive damages arbitrarily. Third, some critics quarrel with the validity of *ever* awarding such damages. Along with adverse effects of the awards just mentioned, they point out that other instruments of the law should deal with product safety. And they further say that the vendor's conduct is rarely blameworthy and worthy of punishment. The proponents of this last position make many of the same arguments found in the Wheeler excerpts above.

The notoriety of particular cases inflame the controversy. For example, in 1999, a jury awarded more than $4.9 billion to the passengers in a General Motors Malibu car who were severely burned when their car burst into flames after being hit in the rear by a drunk driver. The jury found that GM placed the gas tank in a precarious position to save money. The case received front-page publicity, although the press did not cover with the same notoriety the later reduction in the award by the trial court to $1.09 billion or the parties' subsequent settlement for less.

In analyzing whether punitive damages in civil actions violate due process under our Constitution, the Supreme Court applied three tests: the conduct of the defendant (the degree of reprehensibleness), the relationship of actual harm and the punitive damages award, and the relationship of comparable civil penalties and the jury award. See State Farm Mut. Auto. Ins. Co. v. Campbell, 538 U.S. 408, 418, 123 S. Ct. 1513, 1520 (2003).

Section Six
PRODUCT SAFETY AND THE PUBLIC-BENEFIT INSTRUMENT

We learned in Chapter 4 that another basic legal instrument involves conferring on individuals various substantive governmental benefits, such as education, health programs, and welfare payments. Our government also allocates vast amounts of resources to protect people from dangerous products. For example, the Consumer Product Safety Commission not only issues safety standards, brings actions, and so forth, but also provides the public with information through the National Injury Information Clearinghouse. According to its website, http://www.cpsc.gov/about/clrnghse.html, "The Clearinghouse disseminates statistics and information relating to the prevention of death and injury associated with consumer products. Each year the Clearinghouse responds to 6,000 requests for information from the American public. Information specialists search agency data bases to tailor responses to each customer's needs." In addition, the Commission issues safety alerts to the public about unsafe products.

Beware: The National Injury Information Clearinghouse's site listed the following products as subject to recalls in October 2007: certain razors, air purifiers, aluminum water bottles, bookmarks, key chains, children's decorating sets, tumblers, flashlights, color blocks, gas valves in fireplaces and stoves, rattles, electric toasters, and steel toe boots.

Our government obviously could do more to protect us. But would the costs outweigh the benefits? One area in which the debate continues on this point deals with imported products. For example, the New York Times in 2008 reported that the Food and Drug Administration has announced that heparin, an imported blood thinner from China, was contaminated and "associated" with 81 U.S. deaths. (The article also reported that "China has in recent years exported poisonous toothpaste, lead painted toys, toxic pet food, tainted fish" and other contaminated medicine.) In response, the U.S. Congress has considered new laws to increase inspections of imported goods. However, the New York Times article reported that the Government Accountability Office's report "show[ed] that the F.D.A. would need to spend at least $56 million more [in 2009] to begin full inspections of foreign plants. It would need to spend at least $15 million annually to inspect China's drug plants every two years, which is the domestic standard." The article concludes that "President Bush's budget does not provide the F.D.A. with funds to hire more inspectors." Gardiner Harris, F.D.A. Identifies Tainted Heparin in 11 Countries, N.Y. Times, Apr. 22, 2008, at A1.

But do not despair. Some people have suggested that product liability lawsuits against American distributors of Chinese defective products create incentives for the distributors to inspect imported products. See, e.g., Lorraine Woellert, Made in China. Sued Here, Bus. Week, July 9, 2007, available at http://www.businessweek.com/magazine/content/07_28/c4042003.htm#ZZZKQQKVG3F/.

Section Seven
SUMMARY

This chapter focused on a particular goal of society—product safety—to illustrate how the five instruments of the law studied in Part One contribute to achieving a societal goal. Product safety is a useful tool for this study because of our familiarity with the problem of defective products and our inclination to believe that law should help solve the problem. But a threshold issue is whether the law should step in at all. If so, which instruments of the law in what combination can be most effective? We saw that people have widely different views on these issues. For example, recall that Epstein believes the law ultimately may have gone too far in protecting people, whereas Shapo justifies legal intervention because the uncertain dangers of defective products means that people cannot protect themselves.

We have seen that private-arrangement law contributes to product safety by creating express and implied warranties of the quality of products. However, often these warranties do not amount to much protection because manufacturers can easily disclaim them or can limit remedies for their breach. Partly as a result, "strict tort liability" arose as a remedial instrument, which made manufacturers liable for defective products regardless of their fault in producing them. And manufacturers could not disclaim this liability. But we saw that faultless liability is very controversial. In part because of this wariness, the drafters of the Restatement (Third) of Torts reintroduced the manufacturer's blameworthiness as a component of a users claim that the design of a product was defective.

Perhaps the threat of strict-tort lawsuits with multiple plaintiffs can increase the incentive for manufacturers to make safer products. At least until recently, the availability of class action lawsuits arguably had this potential. But these actions may increase unmeritorious claims and create pressure for manufacturers to settle them. Accordingly, we have seen that the trend is towards narrowing the availability of class actions.

We have also sampled how the administrative instrument of the law treats the problem of product safety. As we saw in Chapter 3, regulation is an important avenue for dealing with the problem because of its potential to stop dangerous products from ever reaching the market. But the the challenge of promulgating reasonable and effective safety standards and the task of reviewing them effectively in the courts raises doubts about the instrument's effectiveness. Additional problems with regulation are the potential for agency corruption and capture by industry.

We have also introduced the complexity of the relationship between the administrative instrument and state strict tort and warranty law. In this regard, a recurring issue of great importance is whether a manufacturer that satisfies agency safety standards can still be liable under state law or whether the latter law is preempted by the federal regulation. The rules in this regard are complex and depend on whether Congress intended to bar the state law when it delegated to an agency the task of creating safety standards.

Chapter 6 then moved to the question of whether manufacturers of defective products should ever be punished criminally and, if so, under what conditions. The answer should depend on whether any of the reasons for punishment discussed in Chapter 2—retribution, deterrence, rehabilitation, or incapacitation— apply to manufacturers of defective products. At least when the manufacturer is a large company, none of the reasons for punishment seem compelling. We are left with the question of whether the moral outrage of the community should be enough to support criminality. We have seen that this ground for punishment has had little success. Another important and more specific issue in this regard is whether manufacturers' use of cost-benefit analysis to determine the level of safety of products should ever be punished criminally. The wide use of cost-benefit analysis in everyday decisionmaking of all kinds casts doubt on such an approach.

Finally, Chapter 6 considers how the public-benefit instrument contributes to product safety. The material revisits the issue of cost-benefit analysis this time with regard to whether the costs of governmental inspection of imported goods outweigh its benefits, especially when there may be other ways to protect the public from defective imported goods.

For further general reading, a useful book is Mark Geistfeld, Principles of Products Liability (2006). For a treatment of the relationship of insurance and tort liability, see Kenneth S. Abraham, The Liability Century: Insurance and Tort Law from the Progressive Era to 9/11 (2008). Furthermore, James A. Henderson, Jr., Why Negligence Dominates Tort, 50 UCLA L. Rev. 377 (2002), and James A. Henderson, Jr. & Aaron Twersky, Closing the American Products Liability Frontier: The Rejection of Liability Without Defect, 66 N.Y.U. L. Rev. 1263 (1991), are useful discussions of the strict tort and negligence standards in product liability cases.

Chapter 7

LAW CAN HELP

PROMOTE EQUALITY

But, with such inequality as ours, a perfect civilization is impossible.
MATTHEW ARNOLD

Equality is thus the beginning, not the end.
SIR ERNEST BARKER

Section One
INTRODUCTION

This chapter concerns how the law functions to promote equality. Just as the goal of the last chapter was not to teach product safety law but to provide an example of how each of the five instrumentalities of law can help achieve a specific, concrete societal objective, the goal of this chapter is not to teach the law of the Fourteenth Amendment or the civil rights statutes. Instead, this chapter aims to illustrate the use of the various instrumentalities to further the other kind of societal objective: a broad, abstract principle.

We shall focus on the objective of racial equality for two reasons: first, because the struggle for racial equality in this country has been long and hard; second, because that struggle has provided the model for those seeking to eliminate other kinds of inequality, such as discrimination based on gender, age, or sexual preference. The materials in this chapter, therefore, address when law should be used to promote racial equality, which instrumentality of the law should be used, and how that instrumentality should be used. Although the text occasionally explicitly includes materials addressing other forms of equality, you will learn the most from this chapter, if, even in the absence of such materials, you pause after each selection to consider the extent to which the constitutional principles and statutory policies that evolved to promote racial equality should be used to promote equality between men and women, between the old and the young, and between heterosexuals and homosexuals.

In the United States, law furthers equality by acting as both a shield and a sword. The Fourteenth Amendment to our Constitution provides: "No State shall . . . deny to any person within its jurisdiction the equal protection of the laws." As you probably know, this Amendment was adopted after the Civil War primarily to protect the rights of former slaves. Notice that the Amendment does not assure African Americans (or anyone else) that they will be treated equally by private persons; by its terms, the Amendment applies only to actions taken by a state. Although the Supreme Court has interpreted the Fifth Amendment's Due Process Clause, which applies to actions taken by the federal government, to embody a guarantee of equal protection of the laws analogous to that contained in the Fourteenth Amendment, no provision of the Constitution has been interpreted to mandate equal treatment by private citizens. The Constitution thus shields the individual from *governmental* actions that discriminate unfairly between people of different races. The state and federal governments may pursue a wide variety of goals other than racial equality, but the constitutional provisions concerning race limit the means by which these goals may be pursued.

Law also furthers equality aggressively, as a sword. Statutes are passed and regulations are promulgated with the goal of increasing racial equality. These statutes and regulations may attempt to prevent private persons from discriminating on the basis of race, or they may seek to eliminate the effects of past discrimination. Just as the constitutional provisions concerning equality limit the government's pursuit of other societal objectives, statutes and regulations aimed at increasing equality interfere with individuals' pursuit of their personal objectives. Both kinds of law will, therefore, reflect a balancing of racial equality with other competing values as well as a judgment of how effective various measures are in achieving racial equality.

The remaining sections of this chapter concern how each of the five instrumentalities of law promotes or fails to promote racial equality. For each instrumentality, we shall first consider the extent to which the constitutional provisions concerning racial equality limit the pursuit of other societal goals through that instrumentality. We shall then consider some examples of how that instrumentality has been or could be used to promote the goal of racial equality.

Section Two
RACIAL EQUALITY AND THE PENAL INSTRUMENT

A. Equality as a Limit

Early in this country's history, a crime sometimes depended upon the defendant's race. Some actions were illegal only if taken by an African or Native American. In this century, few statutes have singled out one race as the object of criminal prohibitions. Anti-miscegenation statutes, to which we shall turn at the end of this section, were one notable exception, and the Supreme Court eventually struck them down as unconstitutional. The other prominent exception involved the drastic restrictions placed on the freedom of Japanese Americans during World War II, which were upheld in the following case.

KOREMATSU v. UNITED STATES

Supreme Court of the United States, 1944
323 U.S. 214, 65 S. Ct. 193

MR. JUSTICE BLACK delivered the opinion of the Court:

The petitioner, an American citizen of Japanese descent, was convicted in a federal district court for remaining in San Leandro, California, a "Military Area," contrary to Civilian Exclusion Order No. 34 of the Commanding General of the Western Command, U.S. Army, which directed that after May 9, 1942, all persons of Japanese ancestry should be excluded from that area. No question was raised as to petitioner's loyalty to the United States. The Circuit Court of Appeals affirmed, and the importance of the constitutional question involved caused us to grant certiorari.

It should be noted, to begin with, that all legal restrictions which curtail the civil rights of a single racial group are immediately suspect. That is not to say that all such restrictions are unconstitutional. It is to say that courts must subject them to the most rigid scrutiny. Pressing public necessity may sometimes justify the existence of such restrictions; racial antagonism never can.

In the instant case prosecution of the petitioner was begun by information charging violation of an Act of Congress, of March 21, 1942, 56 Stat. 173, 18 U.S.C. §97a, which provides that

> ... whoever shall enter, remain in, leave, or commit any act in any military area or military zone prescribed, under the authority of an Executive order of the President, by the Secretary of War, or by any military commander designated by the Secretary of War, contrary to the restrictions applicable to any such area or zone or contrary to the order of the Secretary of War or any such military commander, shall, if it appears that he knew or should have known of the existence and extent of the restrictions or order and that his act was in violation thereof, be guilty of a misdemeanor and upon conviction shall be liable to a fine of not to exceed $5,000 or to imprisonment for not more than one year, or both, for each offense.

Exclusion Order No. 34, which the petitioner knowingly and admittedly violated was one of a number of military orders and proclamations, all of which were substantially based upon Executive Order No. 9066, 7 Fed. Reg. 1407. That order, issued after we were at war with Japan, declared that "the successful prosecution of the war requires every possible protection against espionage and against sabotage to national-defense material, national-defense premises, and national-defense utilities...."

One of the series of orders and proclamations, a curfew order, which like the exclusion order here was promulgated pursuant to Executive Order 9066, subjected all persons of Japanese ancestry in prescribed West Coast military areas to remain in their residences from 8 P.M. to 6 A.M. As is the case with the exclusion order here, that prior curfew order was designed as a "protection against espionage and against sabotage." In Kiyoshi Hirabayashi v. United States, 320 U.S. 81, 63 S. Ct. 1375, we sustained a conviction obtained for violation of the curfew order....

Like curfew, exclusion of those of Japanese origin was deemed necessary because of the presence of an unascertained number of disloyal members of the group, most of whom we have no doubt were loyal to this country. It was because we could not reject the finding of the military authorities that it was impossible to bring about an immediate segregation of the disloyal from the loyal that we sustained the validity of the curfew order as applying to the whole group. In the instant case, temporary exclusion of the entire group was rested by the military on the same ground. The judgment that exclusion of the whole group was for the same reason a military imperative answers the contention that the exclusion was in the nature of group punishment based on antagonism to those of Japanese origin. That there were members of the group who retained loyalties to Japan has been confirmed by investigations made subsequent to the exclusion. Approximately five thousand American citizens of Japanese ancestry refused to swear unqualified allegiance to the United States and to renounce allegiance to the Japanese Emperor, and several thousand evacuees requested repatriation to Japan.

We uphold the exclusion order as of the time it was made and when the petitioner violated it. In doing so, we are not unmindful of the hardships imposed by it upon a large group of American citizens. Cf. Ex parte Kumezo Kawato, 317 U.S. 69, 73, 63 S. Ct. 115, 117. But hardships are part of war, and war is an aggregation of hardships. All citizens alike, both in and out of uniform, feel the impact of war in greater or lesser measure. Citizenship has its responsibilities as well as its privileges, and in time of war the burden is always heavier. Compulsory exclusion of large groups of citizens from their homes, except under circumstances of direst emergency and peril, is inconsistent with our basic governmental institutions. But when under conditions of modern warfare our shores are threatened by hostile forces, the power to protect must be commensurate with the threatened danger....

It is said that we are dealing here with the case of imprisonment of a citizen in a concentration camp solely because of his ancestry, without evidence or inquiry concerning his loyalty and good disposition towards the United States. Our task would be simple, our duty clear, were this a case involving the imprisonment of a loyal citizen in a concentration camp because of racial prejudice. Regardless of the true nature of the assembly and relocation centers — and we deem it unjustifiable to call them concentration camps with all the ugly connotations that term implies — we are dealing specifically with nothing but an exclusion order. To cast this case into outlines of racial prejudice, without reference to the real military dangers which were presented, merely confuses the issue. Korematsu was not excluded from the Military Area because of hostility to him or his race. He was excluded because we are at war with the Japanese Empire, because the properly constituted military authorities feared an invasion of our West Coast and felt constrained to take proper security measures, because they decided that the military urgency of the situation demanded that all citizens of Japanese ancestry be segregated from the West Coast temporarily, and finally, because Congress, reposing its confidence in this time of war in our military leaders — as inevitably it must — determined that they should have the power to do just this. There was evidence of disloyalty on the part of some, the military authorities considered that the need for action was great, and time was short. We cannot — by availing ourselves of the calm perspective of hindsight — now say that at that time these actions were unjustified.

Affirmed.

[A concurring opinion by Justice Frankfurter and a dissenting opinion by Justice Roberts are omitted.]

Mr. Justice Murphy, dissenting:

This exclusion of "all persons of Japanese ancestry, both alien and non-alien," from the Pacific Coast area on a plea of military necessity in the absence of martial law ought not to be approved. Such exclusion goes over "the very brink of constitutional power" and falls into the ugly abyss of racism....

It must be conceded that the military and naval situation in the spring of 1942 was such as to generate a very real fear of invasion of the Pacific Coast, accompanied by fears of sabotage and espionage in that area. The military command was therefore justified in adopting all reasonable means necessary to combat these dangers. In adjudging the military action taken in light of the then apparent dangers, we must not erect too high or too meticulous standards; it is necessary only that the action have some reasonable relation to the removal of the dangers of invasion, sabotage and espionage. But the exclusion, either temporarily or permanently, of all persons with Japanese blood in their veins has no such reasonable relation. And that relation is lacking because the exclusion order necessarily must rely for its reasonableness upon the assumption that *all* persons of Japanese ancestry may have a dangerous tendency to commit sabotage and espionage and to aid our Japanese enemy in other ways. It is difficult to believe that reason, logic or experience could be marshalled in support of such an assumption. . . .

The military necessity which is essential to the validity of the evacuation order thus resolves itself into a few intimations that certain individuals actively aided the enemy, from which it is inferred that the entire group of Japanese Americans could not be trusted to be or remain loyal to the United States. No one denies, of course, that there were some disloyal persons of Japanese descent on the Pacific Coast who did all in their power to aid their ancestral land. Similar disloyal activities have been engaged in by many persons of German, Italian and even more pioneer stock in our country. But to infer that examples of individual disloyalty prove group disloyalty and justify discriminatory action against the entire group is to deny that under our system of law individual guilt is the sole basis for deprivation of rights. Moreover, this inference, which is at the very heart of the evacuation orders, has been used in support of the abhorrent and despicable treatment of minority groups by the dictatorial tyrannies which this nation is now pledged to destroy. To give constitutional sanction to that inference in this case, however well-intentioned may have been the military command on the Pacific Coast, is to adopt one of the cruelest of the rationales used by our enemies to destroy the dignity of the individual and to encourage and open the door to discriminatory actions against other minority groups in the passions of tomorrow.

No adequate reason is given for the failure to treat these Japanese Americans on an individual basis by holding investigations and hearings to separate the loyal from the disloyal, as was done in the case of persons of German and Italian ancestry. . . .

I dissent, therefore, from this legalization of racism. Racial discrimination in any form and in any degree has no justifiable part whatever in our democratic way of life. It is unattractive in any setting but it is utterly revolting among a free people who have embraced the principles set forth in the Constitution of the United States. All residents of this nation are kin in some way by blood or culture to a foreign land. Yet they are primarily and necessarily a part of the new and distinct civilization of the United States. They must accordingly be treated at all times as the heirs of the American experiment and as entitled to all the rights and freedoms guaranteed by the Constitution.

Mr. Justice Jackson, dissenting:

. . . Had Korematsu been one of four — the others being, say, a German alien enemy, an Italian alien enemy, and a citizen of American-born ancestors, convicted of treason but out on parole — only Korematsu's presence would have violated the order. The difference between their innocence and his crime would result, not from anything he did, said, or thought, different than they, but only in that he was born of different racial stock. . . .

Much is said of the danger to liberty from the Army program for deporting and detaining these citizens of Japanese extraction. But a judicial construction of the due process clause that will sustain this order is a far more subtle blow to liberty than the promulgation of the order itself. A military order, however unconstitutional, is not apt to last longer than the military emergency. Even during that period a succeeding commander may revoke it all. But once a judicial opinion rationalizes such an order to show that it conforms to the Constitution, or rather rationalizes the Constitution to show that the Constitution sanctions such an order, the Court for all time has validated the principle of racial discrimination in criminal procedure and of transplanting American citizens. The principle then lies about like a loaded weapon ready for the hand of any authority that can bring forward a plausible claim of an urgent need. Every repetition imbeds that principle more deeply in our law and thinking and expands it to new purposes. All who observe the work of courts are familiar with what Judge Cardozo described as "the tendency of a principle to expand itself to the limit of its logic." A military commander may overstep the bounds of constitutionality, and it is an incident. But if we review and approve, that passing incident becomes the doctrine of the Constitution. There it has a generative power of its own, and all that it creates will be in its own image. Nothing better illustrates this danger than does that Court's opinion in this case. . . .

American Concentration Camps

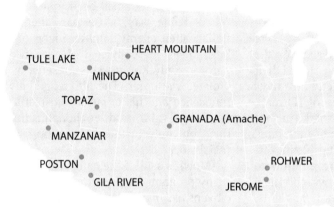

The WRA Relocation Camps, 1942–1946

On December 7, 1941, Fred Korematsu was picnicking with his girlfriend in Oakland, California, as news of the bombing at Pearl Harbor began coming over the radio — news that would change his life, as well as the history of our nation, forever. A welder from San Francisco, Korematsu was living a typical American life until February 19, 1942, when President Roosevelt issued Executive Order No. 9066 ordering the internment of all people of Japanese ancestry. His family complied with the order, but Korematsu decided to stay behind to be with his Italian–American girlfriend.

The order affected all those of Japanese ancestry, regardless of their United States citizenry. Italy and Germany were enemy nations during WWII as well, and subsequently the civil liberties of some Italian and German Americans were also restricted, though not nearly as severely as Japanese Americans.

Korematsu did all he could to avoid internment by moving to Nevada, changing his name, and even getting plastic surgery on his eyes at the suggestion of his girlfriend, but he was soon discovered and arrested. The executive director of the American Civil Liberties Union (ACLU) convinced Korematsu to file a lawsuit against the United States, claiming violations of his constitutional rights based on racial discrimination. Nearly two and a half years later, the Supreme Court denied his claim.

Unsatisfied, Korematsu vowed, "If there is a chance of reopening the case, I will do it." He explained, "As long as my record stands in federal court, any American citizen can be held in prison or concentration camps without trial or hearing." In 1983, with the help of a law school professor, Peter Irons, Korematsu got his chance. Irons had uncovered documents from the FBI and other federal agencies stating that Japanese

Americans were not a threat — documents that the Justice Department had concealed during their case to the Supreme Court. A federal court in San Francisco overturned the conviction, spurring an apology from President Reagan, as well as limited monetary compensation for the surviving internment camp residents. Korematsu v. United States, 584 F. Supp. 1406 (N.D. Cal. 1984).

Fred Korematsu remained an influential civil rights advocate for the remainder of his life. In 1998, President Clinton awarded him the Presidential Medal of Freedom for his accomplishments. In 2003, concerned that history would repeat itself, Korematsu filed an amicus curiae brief on behalf of three men detained after 9/11. He argued, "As in the past, the issues these cases raise involve a direct conflict between our civil liberties and a threat to our safety and security. That we have made mistakes in the past does not mean we should make another, perhaps more serious, mistake now. We should learn from our experience." Fred Korematsu died on March 30, 2005, of respiratory failure.

Korematsu upholds the use of a racial classification in a criminal statute. It may be criticized in two different ways. First, one may disagree with the standard employed by the Court. *Korematsu* describes the standard it employs as "the most rigid scrutiny." Then the Court goes on to say that "[p]ressing public necessity may sometimes justify the existence of such restrictions," and adds that "racial antagonism never can." More recent cases describe the standard of review for racial classifications as "strict scrutiny," phrasing the test as requiring that the racial classification be a "necessary means" to further a "compelling governmental [or state] interest." Thus, the more modern test requires not only a very important goal, but that the goal cannot be accomplished by means other than a racial classification. It seems unlikely that the exclusion order challenged in *Korematsu* would be upheld under this standard. For many years, as acceptance of this new test increased, support for the decision in *Korematsu* decreased. However, the events of September 11, 2001, have resulted in greater public support for race-based national security restrictions. Some commentators believe that an exception to the newer test should be made when national security is at stake, while others would argue that the danger of race-based antagonism is highest when national security is threatened, and that the protection of a strict standard in most important at such times.

Korematsu may also be criticized for misapplication of the standard it articulates. That is, even if the Court was right to select a relatively lenient standard, it may have been wrong in finding that standard satisfied by the facts underlying the exclusion orders. Although the Court states that "racial antagonism never can [justify a racial classification]," at least in hindsight, the Court seems to have overlooked available evidence of racial antagonism. In particular, Americans of Italian and German descent were never placed in concentration camps. Some people argue that it would be reasonable to expect more disloyalty from Japanese Americans than from Italian or German Americans because of the extensive prior discrimination against Japanese Americans. In fact, however, when Japanese Americans were later permitted to serve in the United States armed forces, they were repeatedly decorated for heroism.

RACIAL PROFILING

Although the consequences are less drastic, racial profiling is in some sense similar to the relocation of persons based upon their race. Racial profiling of African Americans has long been a problem in our country. In the last part of the twentieth century, a consensus was growing that the use of race in decisions by law-enforcement personnel was improper.

However, racial profiling in this century has taken a new form. After September 11, 2001, people of Middle Eastern appearance or ancestry have been subject to discrimination from both private and governmental sources. Many people have advocated the use of profiling at airports and in other national security contexts, while others warn that this would provoke a deplorable return to the *Korematsu* era. The articles below give examples of the varied opinions on racial profiling in a post–9/11 United States.

BARRY D. FRIEDMAN, POLICY POINT-COUNTERPOINT: PROFILING AT AIRPORTS
79 Int'l Soc. Sci. Rev. 152, 152–53 (2004)

The United States is confronted with a dilemma: Should federal authorities utilize profiling at the security check-in point at airports? If so, they might mistreat members of certain minority groups, particularly individuals of Middle Eastern descent. "Distinctions between citizens solely because of their ancestry," the U.S. Supreme Court declared in 1943, "are by their very nature odious to a free people whose institutions are founded upon the doctrine of equality."[1] Yet, if federal authorities fail to do so, they risk the admission of a hijacker or someone who is willing to cause a mid-air explosion. This dilemma is best described by Herbert London, humanities professor at New York University, who writes: "In the freedom-security equation, we have to ask ourselves: If we interrogate or detain one person inappropriately, but in the process save 1 million lives, is it worth the trade-off?"[2]

. . . .

Some Americans consider the practice of subjecting Grandma to a wand search and even a pat-down search to be demeaning as well as a waste of time. They argue that since all of the nineteen terrorists who carried out the 9/11 atrocity were men of Middle Eastern descent between the ages of twenty and forty-five,[3] a search of Grandma is likely to do nothing to thwart terrorism. As Los Angeles Times editorial page editor Michael Kinsley has stated: "Today we're at war with a terror network that just killed [3,000] innocents and has anonymous agents in our country planning more slaughter. Are we really supposed to ignore the one identifiable fact we know about them?"[4] Even worse, the argument goes, the time and effort spent patting down Grandma represent resources that are squandered and that could have been utilized to screen more likely candidates.

Others fear the damage that profiling may do to the values of American society; they see limited benefit in profiling in so far as terrorist organizations like al Qaeda will simply deploy individuals who do not resemble men of Middle Eastern descent if screening procedures target such

---

1. Hirabayashi v. United States, 320 U.S. 81, 100-101 (1943); emphasis added.
2. Herbert London, "Profiling as Needed," Albany Law Review 66:2 (2003):346.
3. R. Spencer Macdonald, "Rational Profiling in America's Airports," BYU Journal of Public Law 17 (Fall 2002):113.
4. Quoted in Ibid., 115.

individuals. Such profiling may also complicate other law enforcement efforts. "Racial profiling poisons the water. It's one of the things that makes racial minorities distrust the police and that makes their work more difficult," writes Harvard law professor Randall Kennedy.[5] Furthermore, these critics fear the possible effects of expanded government powers to invade the privacy of innocent Americans. Brief cases, pocketbooks, and carry-on luggage often contain address books, cosmetics, underwear, and other items that individuals would just as soon keep private rather than seeing them scattered on a table as hundreds of travelers pass by.

Another opinion suggests the use of a combination of screening criteria: country of origin, age, sex, and travel patterns.[6] R. Spencer Macdonald, a business-law specialist, argues:

"Of middle eastern appearance" is a rather broad category, and one susceptible to mistakes in judgment. However, a profile that considers race and gender and age and other factors (when the ticket was purchased, if the passenger paid cash,

etc.) substantially mitigates the chances of error.... Narrowing the pool of potential terrorist suspects at airports by profiling race, gender, age, and other considerations could significantly improve our chances of apprehending terrorists before they act.[7]

On 9/11, the United States discovered that Islamic fundamentalists associated with al Qaeda were at war with it. President George W. Bush responded by declaring war against al Qaeda. The war continues. Terrorists are of a new variety: They "do not value their own lives."[8] Decisions concerning passenger screening at airports are, inevitably, matters of life and death.

---

5. Quoted in Ibid., 125.
6. Nelson Lund, "The Conservative Case Against Racial Profiling in the War on Terrorism," Albany Law Review 66:2 (2003):338–39.
7. Macdonald, "Rational Profiling in America's Airports," 137.
8. James Yetman, "Suicidal Terrorism and Discriminatory Screening: An Efficiency–Equity Trade–Off," Defense and Peace Economics 15 (June 2004):222.

HERBERT LONDON, PROFILING AS NEEDED
66 Alb. L. Rev. 343, 344–47 (2003)

Common sense would dictate that some form of profiling goes on all of the time in the area of law enforcement even if it is not formal....

Is profiling always a matter of prejudice? It would hardly seem to be the case. Governments are prone to excessive activity.... But governments are prone to excessive activity in the direction of political correctness as much as in the excesses that may occur with profiling. All one has to do is look at affirmative action policies to see that a government that was attempting to engage in a temporary policy to redress the wrongs of the past has engaged in a policy with no likelihood of change....

This is not a war like wars of the past. We are not mobilizing millions of Americans to fight, but there is a clear enemy. The enemy is made up of radical Islamists, who not only detest the United States;

they detest our culture and they detest modernity. They are at war with America. It is important to understand the nature of the enemy. This is not Bonnie and Clyde robbing some banks. These people are intent on destroying a significant segment of American life. Are we willing to engage in racial profiling in order to maintain some sense of order and understanding of the American way of life — even if in the process we violate some civil liberties?

The problem, as I see it, is that the violation of rights is always visible, but saving lives might not be. How do you make a judgment about what is appropriate? If the government goes too far in violating our understanding of Constitutional provisions, we may say it was an inappropriate act. However, if the government goes too far by our standards, but in the process saves a million lives, is that an appropriate trade-off? I ask the question because I think that it is the question for all Americans to ask at this time even though there is no obvious answer....

...September 11th represents a significant departure from anything that we have known in our lifetime.... This is a different period during which we have to employ every means at our disposal to foil the efforts of those who are intent on destroying the United States.... Do we suspend freedoms in order to take care of ourselves and to defend ourselves? Well, certainly I am not in favor of that. But at the same time, I think that we have to recognize that in the freedom-security exchange, there might be times when we violate someone's civil liberties in order to protect the welfare of this Country.

AMERICAN CIVIL LIBERTIES UNION, SANCTIONED BIAS: RACIAL PROFILING SINCE 9/11
14–16 (2004)

Syed Wasim Abbas

Syed Wasim Abbas came to the United States from Pakistan to attend college. "It was 1992, March 27 when I first landed in New York. I went there as a student on an F–1 visa. I went to Brooklyn College and I worked in between." At the time of his arrest Abbas had a temporary work authorization card and was in the process of applying for a green card. He was running his own business: "I had a gas station, a Sunoco gas station right on Route 30 West. And I had my apartment there and I wanted to settle down there, bring my wife to Pennsylvania. But the circumstances didn't give me a chance to do it."

On June 11, 2002 Abbas was driving home to Pennsylvania when he was pulled over by an INS agent. "When he pulled me over he came and said to turn the car off. He got the key from me and said, 'I'm from INS.' Then he showed me the paper in his hand and he said, 'Is this you, a-hole?' I said, 'Yeah. That's me.' He used really bad language, so I was scared because this was the first time ever I faced somebody pulling me over like that. He said, 'You have a deportation order.' Then he handcuffed me and he searched my car. He took my passport, my license, my social security card, my wallet and everything. He searched the back of the car, the trunk and then they left my car right there and took me to the INS office in Newark."

Abbas was shackled at the INS office: "They put chains on my legs and real tight handcuffs and stuff. I told them that it's really hurting, you know? Can you just open it up and you can handcuff me in front? But they said, 'We can't do it. This is how we do it.' It was very hard to walk and I wasn't a criminal. I never, you know, was involved in any crime or anything but I was like suddenly I just broke down, I cried. I can't express how I felt at that time."

After 29 days in the Bergen County Jail, Abbas, who had spent his entire adult life in America, was deported to Pakistan. His gas station is gone, and his wife, an American citizen, is living with relatives in New York. He now lives in London in a state of limbo. When we met him in Pakistan, he told us, "I could not and cannot take this out of my mind the fact that I've been to jail, I've been handcuffed and I've been chained. I do get nightmares sometimes and I get scared and when I wake up I'm all sweaty and scared and that stays there. Another thing is financially. Although my dad he's pretty good; I can't ask him for money because I'm 32 years old and those days are gone when I asked money from my parents. Unfortunately there aren't much opportunities here to work."

Banafsheh Akhlaghi

In September of 2001, law school professor Banafsheh Akhlaghi abandoned her position teaching the Constitution to work overtime defending it. As an activist attorney fighting for the civil liberties of Arabs, Muslims and South Asians, Akhlaghi had represented hundreds of men targeted by the government solely because of their ethnicity and religion. She was still swamped with clients over a year later, when the first round of Special Registration began. On Dec. 16, the deadline for the first call-in group, she spent all day at the San Francisco District INS Office, providing free legal counsel for registrants. By the end of the day, Akhlaghi watched, helpless, as dozens of her newly retained clients found themselves detained. Shackled at the hands and feet, 12 of the men were shoved onto a bus to Oakland, Calif., then flown around the country. Akhlaghi explains, "They are the very faces that our government and the media continue to feed us with as the faces of terror. They are Stanford students, they are business owners, they are shoe salesmen, they are working for high technology firms as engineers, they are in the food industry, they are just normal, normal folks."

Two days passed before one of Akhlaghi's clients was able to contact her. He told her that the men, blindfolded and shackled, had been flown from California to Arizona, to Kentucky, to Chicago, then back to Arizona, then to Bakersfield, Calif., then back to Oakland, before crossing the state again to end up in San Diego — all over the course of 36 hours. Federal officials had been looking for vacant jail cells. The men had not eaten, showered or slept at any point during the 72 hours in which they had been held.

When she learned what had happened, Akhlaghi immediately jumped in her car and drove 10 hours south to San Diego to get in front of the immigration court and secure release dates for her clients who had yet to see an immigration judge. But she was unsuccessful because her clients had not yet been processed into the system that would allow them to have an immigration hearing. To make matters worse, the judges were on vacation and not coming back until after New Year's Day. Despite these setbacks, Akhlaghi was able to convince a district director to issue bonds to her clients, releasing most of them on Dec. 23 and one man on the 24th. Their cases were finally heard on Feb. 17. But for Akhlaghi's extraordinary efforts, these men would have remained in detention until that date. Unfortunately, there were many other men who did not have access to such an advocate. Akhlaghi remains hopeful despite the present crises before her. "After September 11, we all lost our minds here in America, we numbed ourselves out to what is just and what is fair. Hopefully, since time has passed we have started to come back to what is just."

In the weeks following 9/11, there were incidents of airlines' removing people of Middle Eastern descent from planes because of perceived threats to security. One of these people was Ashraf Kahn, a United States citizen born in Pakistan. The captain of the aircraft told Kahn that the crew did not feel safe with him onboard, causing him to miss his three connecting flights taking him to his brother's wedding in Pakistan.

After the Ashraf Kahn incident, the airline involved issued an internal memo instructing employees to consider suspicious behavior — and not skin color — when removing passengers. In addition to behavior, airlines are supposed to use data such as one-way tickets, checking baggage, or paying in cash to detect security threats. Whether the employees are following these instructions is difficult to know; compliance is complicated by the possibility that an employee may be unaware that his or her level of suspicion is being influenced by the skin color of the passenger.

Many people find reliance on race or ethnicity especially problematic when the person subjected to detention is an American citizen. One approach would be to permit the use of *nationality* but not the use of *ancestry* in assessing the suspiciousness of a person's behavior. Those persons focused on national security tend to see this compromise as too restrictive, while those advocating the importance of civil liberties may find it insufficiently solicitous of the rights of noncitizens. Moreover, it seems likely that giving law enforcement personnel permission to consider nationality will lead them to focus on the appearance that corresponds to a particular nationality — which in turn will sweep in citizens as well as noncitizens. Thus, a workable compromise in this arena seems unlikely; a choice of priorities seems necessary.

B. Equality as the Goal

The penal instrument has often been needed to protect the most basic rights of racial minorities. Sometimes ordinary criminal statutes, such as those prohibiting assault and murder, function to promote racial equality. At times when these have failed to provide racial minorities with even the minimal right to physical safety, specialized criminal statutes such as the Ku Klux Klan Act have been enacted. In addition, comprehensive civil and voting rights legislation has utilized criminal penalties as well as civil remedies for enforcement of the rights they confer. The effectiveness of these statutes has varied widely.

Hate crimes, such as the high profile murder of Matthew Shephard in 1998, have spurred legislatures to adopt laws increasing the penalties for bias-motivated crimes. Congress enacted the Hate Crime Sentencing Enhancement Act in 1994. The Act increases the penalties for crimes motivated by actual or perceived race, color, religion, national origin, ethnicity, gender, disability, or sexual orientation. Although these sentencing guidelines apply only to federal crimes, 45 states and the District of Columbia have enacted similar hate crime statutes. Such hate crime legislation is somewhat controversial. Chief Justice Rehnquist explained the reasoning behind hate crime legislation on the bases that "this conduct is thought to inflict greater individual and societal harm" and "bias-motivated crimes are more likely to provoke retaliatory crimes, inflict distinct emotional harms on their victims, and incite community unrest." Wisconsin v. Mitchell, 508 U.S. 476, 487–88, 113 S. Ct. 2194, 2201 (1993). Some critics, however, argue that the increased penalties offer protection to some groups over others, creating a type of reverse discrimination. Moreover, although hate crime enhancement is applicable only in situations where conduct that is otherwise criminal has occurred, other critics worry that these statutes will create a slippery slope toward favored and disfavored viewpoints. They argue that the laws attempt to control thought and will result in a chilling effect on speech espousing views on race, religion, or sexual orientation.

Even more controversial is the criminalization of speech expressing group hatred *in the absence of conduct that would otherwise be a crime*. Criminal sanctions attempting to promote racial equality by direct curtailment of speech have often run afoul of the First Amendment: "Congress shall make no law respecting an establishment of religion, or prohibiting the free exercise thereof; or abridging the freedom of speech, or of the press; or the right of the people peaceably to assemble, and to petition the Government for a redress of grievances."

Even though the First Amendment restrains the government from restricting freedom of speech, the freedom guaranteed by the First Amendment is not

Anti-Miscegenation Statutes

The Supreme Court held in Loving v. Virginia, 388 U.S. 1, 87 S. Ct. 1817 (1967), that anti-miscegenation statutes were unconstitutional. Mildred Jeter (a black woman) and Richard Perry Loving (a white man), lived in Virginia, but moved to the District of Columbia to get married and avoid Virginia's race-based marriage restrictions. When they returned to Virginia, they were arrested under Virginia's statute prohibiting the marriage of a white person to any non-white person. They were sentenced to one year in prison, with the sentence suspended for 25 years if the couple left the state. The trial judge explained, "Almighty God created the races white, black, yellow, Malay and red, and he placed them on separate continents. And but for the interference with his arrangement there would be no cause for such marriages. The fact that he separated the races shows that he did not intend for the races to mix."

After moving back to Washington, D.C., the couple appealed their conviction, and eventually the Supreme Court of the United States agreed to review the case. The Court found Virginia's statute unconstitutional, and proclaimed, "The Fourteenth Amendment requires that the freedom of choice to marry not be restricted by invidious racial discrimination. Under our Constitution, the freedom to marry, or not marry, a person of another race resides with the individual and cannot be infringed by the State."

Despite the ruling, racially discriminatory marriage statutes remained on the books in many states, but were simply not enforced. In 2000, Alabama became the last state to repeal its anti-miscegenation statute. In 1996, the story of the aptly named Lovings was turned into a movie entitled, "Mr. and Mrs. Loving." Forty years after the Supreme Court decision, Mildred Loving issued a statement commemorating the case:

Surrounded as I am now by wonderful children and grandchildren, not a day goes by that I don't think of Richard and our love, our right to marry, and how much it meant to me to have that freedom to marry the person precious to me, even if others thought he was the "wrong kind of person" for me to marry. I believe all Americans, no matter their race, no matter their sex, no matter their sexual orientation, should have that same freedom to marry. Government has no business imposing some people's religious beliefs over others. Especially if it denies people's civil rights.

Rates of interracial marriage have continued to rise since the Loving decision. In 1960 only 0.4 percent of marriages were interracial; by 1992 this had risen to 2.2 percent of all marriages, or about 1,161,000 total marriages.

In Loving v. Virginia, the Supreme Court cited both the Due Process Clause and the Equal Protection Clause in the course of holding that criminal prohibitions on interracial marriage are unconstitutional. The resulting ambiguity is of some significance. If the Due Process Clause is a sufficient basis for the holding, it might be thought that any restrictions on who may marry bear a heavy burden of justification, thus making it harder (but not impossible) to distinguish between prohibitions on interracial marriage and prohibitions on gay marriage. In contrast, if the Equal Protection Clause is a basis for the holding, there are fewer implications for nonracial restrictions on marriage, including prohibitions on gay marriage. This is because the Equal Protection Clause was designed to remedy problems relating to slavery, and has therefore imposed the highest burden of justification when a statute contains a classification based upon race. At the time Loving was decided, no equal protection case had suggested that classifications based upon sexual orientation required any significant justification, and even today no case has suggested that sexual-orientation classifications bear as high a burden of justification as do racial classifications. Thus, if the holding in *Loving* depends on the fact that a racial classification was used, and therefore upon the Equal Protection Clause, it says virtually nothing about the permissibility of other classifications that limit who may marry.

absolute, and a variety of justifications for restraining speech have been accepted by the Supreme Court. We consider below three possible justifications for regulating speech with racial content: advocacy of illegal action, fighting words, and group libel. This section explores the legitimacy of such restrictions on speech that are aimed at the prevention of race-based violence or the promotion of racial equality.

In order to understand the legitimacy of regulating racist speech, we have to begin with some understanding of the constitutional framework for regulating speech of any sort. Regulating speech, even racist speech, lies on a slippery slope of government intervention. As Justice Robert Jackson stated in his Supreme Court opinion overturning a mandatory flag salute regulation in a public school: "Those who begin coercive elimination of dissent soon find themselves exterminating dissenters. Compulsory unification of opinion achieves only the unanimity of the graveyard." West Virginia State Board of Education v. Barnette, 319 U.S. 624, 641, 63 S. Ct. 1178, 1187 (1943). While there is a great interest in social order and morality in general, and in the promotion of equal opportunity in particular, any regulation of speech risks a "chilling effect" on speech outside common morals or ideology. Recognizing these concerns, courts and sometimes even legislatures have been wary of the regulation of speech, even when the speech is generally agreed to be of little or negative value. The bar is set very high for speech that is completely banned before its utterance, and lower when only the time, place, or manner of the speech is restricted.

Speech statutes may be overturned as either overbroad or vague, or both. Overbroad statutes include constitutionally protected speech within the reach of their prohibitions. Vague statutes may be interpreted to reach a substantial amount of constitutionally protected speech. It is important for legislatures to express speech prohibitions or regulations clearly in order to give citizens adequate notice of whether or not they are breaking a law. Clear regulations also discourage arbitrary, and potentially discriminatory, enforcement by police or prosecutors.

ADVOCACY OF ILLEGAL ACTION

One might begin by asking why the advocacy of illegal action should ever be punishable: why not just punish the illegal action itself, should that action take place? A short answer is that some illegal actions cause great damage or even loss of life, and the state should not be required to incur that damage or to stand idly by while its citizens suffer losses. Most people accept the premise that on some occasions speech urging illegal action poses a sufficiently large risk to justify its punishment, but there is much disagreement over how to describe those occasions or that speech. Over time, the Supreme Court has narrowed the test for restricting advocacy of illegal action.

BRANDENBURG v. OHIO
Supreme Court of the United States, 1969
395 U.S. 444, 89 S. Ct. 1827

PER CURIAM:

The appellant, a leader of a Ku Klux Klan group, was convicted under the Ohio Criminal Syndicalism statute for "advocat[ing] . . . the duty, necessity, or propriety of crime, sabotage, violence, or unlawful methods of terrorism as a means of accomplishing industrial or political reform" and for "voluntarily assembl[ing] with any society, group, or assemblage of persons formed to teach or advocate the doctrines of criminal syndicalism." Ohio Rev. Code Ann. §2923.13. He was fined $1,000 and sentenced to one to 10 years' imprisonment. The appellant challenged the constitutionality of the criminal syndicalism statute under the First and Fourteenth Amendments to the United States Constitution, but the intermediate appellate court of Ohio affirmed his conviction without opinion. The Supreme Court of Ohio dismissed his appeal . . . . We reverse.

The record shows that a man, identified at trial as the appellant, telephoned an announcer-reporter on the staff of a Cincinnati television station and invited him to come to a Ku Klux Klan "rally" to be held at a farm in Hamilton County. With the cooperation of the organizers, the reporter and a cameraman attended the meeting and filmed the events. Portions of the films were later broadcast on the local station and on a national network.

The prosecution's case rested on the films and on testimony identifying the appellant as the person who communicated with the reporter and who spoke at the rally. The State also introduced into evidence several articles appearing in the film, including a pistol, a rifle, a shotgun, ammunition, a Bible, and a red hood worn by the speaker in the films.

One film showed 12 hooded figures, some of whom carried firearms. They were gathered around a large wooden cross, which they burned. No one was present other than the participants and the newsmen who made the film. Most of the words uttered during the scene were incomprehensible when the film was projected, but scattered phrases could be understood that were derogatory of Negroes and, in one instance, of Jews.[9] Another scene on the same film showed the appellant, in Klan regalia, making a speech. The speech, in full, was as follows:

> This is an organizers' meeting. We have had quite a few members here today which are — we have hundreds, hundreds of members throughout the State of Ohio. I can quote from a newspaper clipping from the Columbus, Ohio Dispatch, five weeks ago Sunday morning. The Klan has more members in the State of Ohio than does any other organization. We're not a revengent organization, but if our President, our Congress, our Supreme Court, continues to suppress the white, Caucasian race, it's possible that there might have to be some revengeance taken.

---

9. The significant portions that could be understood were:
"How far is the nigger going to — yeah."
"This is what we are going to do to the niggers."
"A dirty nigger."
"Send the Jews back to Israel."
"Let's give them back to the dark garden."
"Save America."
"Let's go back to constitutional betterment."
"Bury the niggers."
"We intend to do our part."
"Give us our state rights."
"Freedom for the whites."
"Nigger will have to fight for every inch he gets from now on."

We are marching on Congress July the Fourth, four hundred thousand strong. From there we are dividing into two groups, one group to march on St. Augustine, Florida, the other group to march into Mississippi. Thank you.

The second film showed six hooded figures one of whom, later identified as the appellant, repeated a speech very similar to that recorded on the first film. The reference to the possibility of "revengeance" was omitted, and one sentence was added: "Personally, I believe the nigger should be returned to Africa, the Jew returned to Israel." Though some of the figures in the films carried weapons, the speaker did not.

The Ohio Criminal Syndicalism Statute was enacted in 1919. From 1917 to 1920, identical or quite similar laws were adopted by 20 States and two territories. E. Dowell, A History of Criminal Syndicalism Legislation in the United States 21 (1939). In 1927, this Court sustained the constitutionality of California's Criminal Syndicalism Act, Cal. Penal Code §§11400–11402, the text of which is quite similar to that of the laws of Ohio. Whitney v. California, 274 U.S. 357, 47 S. Ct. 641 (1927). The Court upheld the statute on the ground that, without more, "advocating" violent means to effect political and economic change involves such danger to the security of the State that the State may outlaw it. But *Whitney* has been thoroughly discredited by later decisions. See Dennis v. United States, 341 U.S. 494, at 507, 71 S. Ct. 857, at 866 (1951). These later decisions have fashioned the principle that the constitutional guarantees of free speech and free press do not permit a State to forbid or proscribe advocacy of the use of force or of law violation except where such advocacy is directed to inciting or producing imminent lawless action and is likely to incite or

produce such action. As we said in Noto v. United States, 367 U.S. 290, 297-298, 81 S. Ct. 1517, 1520-1521 (1961), "the mere abstract teaching . . . of the moral propriety or even moral necessity for a resort to force and violence, is not the same as preparing a group for violent action and steeling it to such action." A statute which fails to draw this distinction impermissibly intrudes upon the freedoms guaranteed by the First and Fourteenth Amendments. It sweeps within its condemnation speech which our Constitution has immunized from governmental control.

Measured by this test, Ohio's Criminal Syndicalism Act cannot be sustained. The Act punishes persons who "advocate or teach the duty, necessity, or propriety" of violence "as a means of accomplishing industrial or political reform"; or who publish or circulate or display any book or paper containing such advocacy; or who "justify" the commission of violent acts "with intent to exemplify, spread or advocate the propriety of the doctrines of criminal syndicalism"; or who "voluntarily assemble" with a group formed "to teach or advocate the doctrines of criminal syndicalism." Neither the indictment nor the trial judge's instructions to the jury in any way refined the statute's bald definition of the crime in terms of mere advocacy not distinguished from incitement to imminent lawless action.

Accordingly, we are here confronted with a statute which, by its own words and as applied, purports to punish mere advocacy and to forbid, on pain of criminal punishment, assembly with others merely to advocate the described type of action. Such a statute falls within the condemnation of the First and Fourteenth Amendments. The contrary teaching of Whitney v. California, supra, cannot be supported, and that decision is therefore overruled.

After *Brandenburg*, one might wonder if it is possible to write a statute proscribing advocacy of race-based violence that would survive constitutional scrutiny? The opinion does not discuss the possibility that a statute might regulate groups like the Ku Klux Klan by name. In an earlier case, the Supreme Court upheld broader restrictions on advocacy of illegal action by members of the

Communist Party, justifying the greater leniency as warranted by the extraordinary danger posed by the Communist Party. Certainly as a practical matter, the Communist Party has caused far less damage in the United States than has the KKK. Observing this disparity between danger or the possibility of prohibition might lead you to disagree with *Brandenburg*'s applying the general rule to the KKK — or it might lead you instead to disagree with the more lenient treatment of regulation of the speech of Communist Party members.

FIGHTING WORDS

Like advocacy of illegal action, the category of "fighting words" has narrowed over time, as we explained in connection with the *Skokie* case at the beginning of this book. In the first fighting words case, Chaplinsky v. New Hampshire, 315 U.S. 568, 62 S. Ct. 766 (1942), the subsequent punishment of a Jehovah's Witness was upheld when he had called a police officer "a goddamned racketeer" and a fascist. The state statute had forbidden addressing anyone in a public place with offensive, derisive, or annoying words or calling them any offensive or derisive name. The Court explained that the slight value of Chaplinsky's speech was outweighed by the social interest in order and morality. Fighting words were defined as words which, by their very utterance, inflict injury or tend to incite an immediate breach of the peace.

It is interesting to consider, in a society that values order and morality, exactly what kind of insult would be so offensive as to incite a reasonable man to commit an immediate breach of the peace. Accordingly, over time the category has been limited in various ways. Terminiello v. City of Chicago, 337 U.S. 1, 69 S. Ct. 894 (1949), is such a limitation. The city ordinance was overturned as overbroad because it prohibited speech that "stirs the public to anger or invites dispute." The Court stated that inviting dispute was an important function of free speech, and that statutes could not bar the functions of free speech unless there was a clear and present danger of a substantial public evil. Politically dissident speech will inevitably invite dispute, which creates a "marketplace of ideas" that benefits society and should not be regulated. Perhaps in response to these considerations, in Texas v. Johnson, 491 U.S. 397, 109 S. Ct. 2533 (1989), the Court expressed the fighting words standard more narrowly, apparently limiting the category to direct personal insults that are "invitations to exchange fisticuffs."

Fifty years ago, it appeared that the presence of a "hostile audience" would justify punishment of speech — even if the speaker did not resort to fighting words. In Feiner v. New York, 340 U.S. 315, 71 S. Ct. 303 (1951), a man criticized the government for what he considered the mistreatment of African Americans, and called the mayor a "champagne sipping bum." The Court upheld his conviction because there had been muttering and pushing in the crowd around him, and the Justices agreed that the police were only acting to prevent a fight. However, in Edwards v. South Carolina, 372 U.S. 229, 83 S. Ct. 680 (1963), the Court reversed a breach of peace conviction for a group of civil rights demonstrators, concluding that there was no threat of violence from the protestors, despite a vigorous dissent that argued that 300 angry counterdemonstrators posed just such a threat. *Edwards* may suggest disapproval of the hostile audience category — or it may simply reflect that between 1951 and 1963, speech arguing for civil rights for African Americans had become more commonplace and received increasing approval from the public. Probably, the government no longer has the power to suppress speech in advance based on the audience's distaste, but instead must control the crowd and protect the speaker.

R.A.V. v. CITY OF ST. PAUL
Supreme Court of the United States, 1992
505 U.S. 377, 112 S. Ct. 2538

Justice Scalia delivered the opinion of the Court:

In the predawn hours of June 21, 1990, petitioner and several other teenagers allegedly assembled a crudely made cross by taping together broken chair legs. They then allegedly burned the cross inside the fenced yard of a black family that lived across the street from the house where petitioner was staying. Although this conduct could have been punished under any of a number of laws, one of the two provisions under which respondent city of St. Paul chose to charge petitioner (then a juvenile) was the St. Paul Bias–Motivated Crime Ordinance, St. Paul, Minn., Legis. Code §292.02 (1990), which provides:

"Whoever places on public or private property a symbol, object, appellation, characterization or graffiti, including, but not limited to, a burning cross or Nazi swastika, which one knows or has reasonable grounds to know arouses anger, alarm or resentment in others on the basis of race, color, creed, religion or gender commits disorderly conduct and shall be guilty of a misdemeanor."

Petitioner moved to dismiss this count on the ground that the St. Paul ordinance was substantially overbroad and impermissibly content based and therefore facially invalid under the First Amendment. The trial court granted this motion, but the Minnesota Supreme Court reversed.... The court...concluded that the ordinance was not impermissibly content based because, in its view, "the ordinance is a narrowly tailored means toward accomplishing the compelling governmental interest in protecting the community against bias-motivated threats to public safety and order." We granted certiorari.

...Assuming, arguendo, that all of the expression reached by the ordinance is proscribable under the "fighting words" doctrine, we nonetheless conclude that the ordinance is facially unconstitutional in that it prohibits otherwise permitted speech solely on the basis of the subjects the speech addresses.

The First Amendment generally prevents government from proscribing speech, because of disapproval of the ideas expressed. Content-based regulations are presumptively invalid. From 1791 to the present, however, our society, like other free but civilized societies, has permitted restrictions upon the content of speech in a few limited areas, which are "of such slight social value as a step to truth that any benefit that may be derived from them is clearly outweighed by the social interest in order and morality." *Chaplinsky*, 315 U.S. at 572, 62 S. Ct. at 762. We have recognized that "the freedom of speech" referred to by the First Amendment does not include a freedom to disregard these traditional limitations. Our decisions since the 1960's have narrowed the scope of the traditional categorical exceptions for defamation, but a limited categorical approach has remained an important part of our First Amendment jurisprudence.

...We have long held, for example, that nonverbal expressive activity can be banned because of the action it entails, but not because of the ideas it expresses — so that burning a flag in violation of an ordinance against outdoor fires could be punishable, whereas burning a flag in violation of an ordinance against dishonoring the flag is not. Similarly, we have upheld reasonable "time, place, or manner" restrictions, but only if they are "justified without reference to the content of the regulated speech." Ward v. Rock Against Racism, 491 U.S. 781, 791, 109 S. Ct. 2746, 2753-2754 (1989). And just as the power to proscribe particular speech on the basis of a noncontent element (e.g., noise) does not entail the power to proscribe the same speech on the basis of a content element; so also, the power to proscribe it on the basis of one content element (e.g., obscenity) does not entail the power to proscribe it on the basis of other content elements....

Even the prohibition against content discrimination that we assert the First Amendment requires is not absolute. It applies differently in the context of proscribable speech than in the area of fully protected speech. The rationale of the general prohibition, after all, is that content discrimination "raises the specter that the Government may effectively drive certain ideas or viewpoints from the marketplace," Simon & Schuster, [Inc. v. Members of New York State Crime Victims Bd., 502 U.S. 105, 116, 112 S. Ct. 501, 508 (1991)]. But content discrimination among various instances of a class of proscribable speech often does not pose this threat.

When the basis for the content discrimination consists entirely of the very reason the entire class of speech at issue is proscribable, no significant danger of idea or viewpoint discrimination exists. Such a reason, having been adjudged neutral enough to support exclusion of the entire class of speech from First Amendment protection, is also neutral enough to form the basis of distinction within the class. To illustrate: A State might choose to prohibit only that obscenity which is the most patently offensive in its prurience — i.e., that which involves the most lascivious displays of sexual activity. But it may not prohibit, for example, only that obscenity which includes offensive political messages. See Kucharek v. Hanaway, 902 F.2d 513, 517 (CA7 1990), cert. denied, 498 U.S. 1041, 111 S. Ct. 713 (1991). And the Federal Government can criminalize only those threats of violence that are directed against the President, see 18 U.S.C. §871 — since the reasons why threats of violence are outside the First Amendment (protecting individuals from the fear of violence, from the disruption that fear engenders, and from the possibility that the threatened violence will occur) have special force when applied to the person of the President. See Watts v. United States, 394 U.S. 705, 707, 89 S. Ct. 1399

(1969) (upholding the facial validity of §871 because of the "overwhelming interest in protecting the safety of [the] Chief Executive and in allowing him to perform his duties without interference from threats of physical violence"). But the Federal Government may not criminalize only those threats against the President that mention his policy on aid to inner cities.

Another valid basis for according differential treatment to even a content-defined subclass of proscribable speech is that the subclass happens to be associated with particular "secondary effects" of the speech, so that the regulation is "justified without reference to the content of the speech," Renton v. Playtime Theatres, Inc., 475 U.S. 41, 48, 106 S. Ct. 925, 929 (1986). A State could, for example, permit all obscene live performances except those involving minors....

...There may be other such bases as well. Indeed, to validate such selectivity (where totally proscribable speech is at issue) it may not even be necessary to identify any particular "neutral" basis, so long as the nature of the content discrimination is such that there is no realistic possibility that official suppression of ideas is afoot. (We cannot think of any First Amendment interest that would stand in the way of a State's prohibiting only those obscene motion pictures with blue-eyed actresses.) Save for that limitation, the regulation of "fighting words," like the regulation of noisy speech, may address some offensive instances and leave other, equally offensive, instances alone.

Applying these principles to the St. Paul ordinance, we conclude that, even as narrowly construed by the Minnesota Supreme Court, the ordinance is facially unconstitutional. Although the phrase in the ordinance, "arouses anger, alarm or resentment in others," has been limited by the Minnesota Supreme Court's construction to reach only those symbols or displays that amount to "fighting words," the remaining, unmodified terms make clear that the ordinance applies only to "fighting words" that insult, or provoke violence, "on the basis of race, color, creed, religion or gender." Displays containing abusive invective, no matter how vicious or severe, are permissible unless they are addressed to one of the specified disfavored topics. Those who wish to use "fighting words" in connection with other ideas — to express hostility, for example, on the basis of political affiliation, union membership, or homosexuality — are not covered. The First Amendment does not permit St. Paul to impose special prohibitions on those speakers who express views on disfavored subjects.

In its practical operation, moreover, the ordinance goes even beyond mere content discrimination, to actual viewpoint discrimination. Displays containing some words — odious racial epithets, for example — would be prohibited to proponents of all views. But "fighting words" that do not themselves invoke race, color, creed, religion, or gender — aspersions upon a person's mother, for example — would seemingly be usable ad libitum in the placards of those arguing *in favor* of racial, color, etc., tolerance and equality, but could not be used by those speakers' opponents....

...One must wholeheartedly agree with the Minnesota Supreme Court that "it is the responsibility, even the obligation, of diverse communities to confront such notions in whatever form they appear," but the manner of that confrontation cannot consist of selective limitations upon speech.... The point of the First Amendment is that majority preferences must be expressed in some fashion other than silencing speech on the basis of its content....

Finally, St. Paul and its amici defend the conclusion of the Minnesota Supreme Court that, even if the ordinance regulates expression based on hostility towards its protected ideological content, this discrimination is nonetheless justified because it is narrowly tailored to serve compelling state interests. Specifically, they assert that the ordinance helps to ensure the basic human rights of members of groups that have historically been subjected to discrimination, including the right of such group members to live in peace where they wish. We do not doubt that these interests are compelling, and that the ordinance can be said to promote them. But the "danger of censorship" presented by a facially content-based statute, Leathers v. Medlock, [499 U.S. 439, 448, 111 S. Ct. 1438, 1444 (1991)], requires that that

weapon be employed only where it is "*necessary* to serve the asserted [compelling] interest," Burson v. Freeman, 504 U.S. 191, 199, 112 S. Ct. 1846, 1852 (1992) (plurality opinion) (emphasis added). The existence of adequate content-neutral alternatives thus "undercut[s] significantly" any defense of such a statute, Boos v. Barry, [485 U.S. 312, 329, 108 S. Ct. 1157, 1168 (1988)], casting considerable doubt on the government's protestations that "the asserted justification is in fact an accurate description of the purpose and effect of the law," Burson, supra, 504 U.S., at 213, 112 S. Ct., at 1859 (Kennedy, J., concurring). The dispositive question in this case, therefore, is whether content discrimination is reasonably necessary to achieve St. Paul's compelling interests; it plainly is not....

Let there be no mistake about our belief that burning a cross in someone's front yard is reprehensible. But St. Paul has sufficient means at its disposal to prevent such behavior without adding the First Amendment to the fire.

The judgment of the Minnesota Supreme Court is reversed, and the case is remanded for proceedings not inconsistent with this opinion.

It is so ordered.

[Justices White, Blackmun, O'Connor, and Stevens merely concurred in the judgment. They would have relied on the grounds of overbreadth to overturn the statute, as opposed to the viewpoint discrimination framework used by the majority. Justice White argued that the ordinance, "in reaching expressive conduct that causes only hurt feelings, offense, or resentment, criminalized expression protected by the First Amendment and thus was overbroad," but maintained that, if the ordinance had not been overbroad, it would have been a valid statute. Justice Blackmun also wrote separately to warn that the majority's approach either would, if broadly applied, eventually result in relaxing the strict-scrutiny review of content-based laws or would, if narrowly read, seem like a manipulation of First Amendment doctrine to overturn an ordinance the majority opposed. Justice Stevens added that not all content-based speech statutes are "equally infirm and presumptively invalid."]

GROUP LIBEL

In Beauharnais v. Illinois, 343 U.S. 250, 72 S. Ct. 725 (1952), a man was convicted under an Illinois statute prohibiting publication of material portraying the "depravity, criminality, unchastity or lack of virtue of a class of citizens" and exposing "citizens of any race . . . to contempt, derision or obloquy." The man, Beauharnais, published an advertisement to urge joining the White Circle League of America to fight the ban on racially restrictive neighborhood covenants. The advertisement advocated a petition to the mayor of Chicago "to halt the further encroachment, harassment and invasion of white people, their property, neighborhoods and persons, by the Negro." It added: "If the persuasion and the need to prevent the white race from becoming mongrelized by the negro will not unite us, then the aggressions . . . rapes, robberies, knives, guns and marijuana of the negro, surely will." Beauharnais argued that the statute violated his freedom of speech and was too vague.

The Supreme Court upheld the conviction and the statute. The Court noted that all American jurisdictions had laws against libel directed at individuals, and that fighting words were not protected speech. The Court decided that the statements would be considered libelous against an individual, and so could be considered libel against a collective group. Emphasizing historical episodes of violence spurred by "willful purveyors of falsehood" in Illinois, the Court concluded that it would "deny experience to say that the Illinois legislature was without reason [in prohibiting the speech], made in public places and by means calculated to have a powerful emotional impact on those to whom it was presented."

Justice Douglas dissented from the *Beauharnais* decision. He argued that to ban speech under the First Amendment, "the peril of the speech must be clear and present, leaving no room for argument, raising no doubts as to the necessity of curbing speech in order to prevent disaster." Arguments, especially those involving unpopular minority viewpoints, can be emotional and passionate. Douglas cited the framers of the Constitution and said that when faced with the choice between the reasons for constraining speech and the potential abuses of liberty, "[t]hey chose liberty."

NOTES

1. Although *Beauharnais* has never been overruled or expressly limited by the Supreme Court, lower courts and commentators have questioned whether *Beauharnais* is still "good law" in light of new developments in First Amendment doctrine. Turn back to the *Skokie* case. Can the decision in that case be reconciled with *Beauharnais*? Do you think that the *Skokie* decision reflects a weakening commitment to racial equality?

2. If you think *Beauharnais* was wrongly decided, do you think the only flaw in the statute was the use of the penal instrument? Are racist acts better controlled by other instruments? For example, in Bob Jones University v. United

States, 461 U.S. 574, 103 S. Ct. 2017 (1983), the administrative instrument was used to control racial discrimination. That fundamentalist Christian university denied admission to applicants who had married interracially, or who promoted interracial marriage or dating. Because of this policy, the IRS revoked the tax-exempt status of the educational institution, stating that because of the racially discriminatory nature of the policies, the university was not "charitable" under the definition of the exemption in §501(c)(3) of the Internal Revenue Code. The Supreme Court upheld the revocation, holding that institutions seeking tax exemptions must serve a public purpose and must not be contrary to established public policy. The Court found that the admissions policies constituted racial discrimination, and thus were contrary to public policy. The Court held that the goal of racial equality outweighed any burden that the taxes placed on the university's exercise of its religious beliefs. The case set an important precedent: that the government would not support institutions violating important public policy goals like racial equality, even where petitioners claimed they were exercising religious beliefs.

3. Section 130 of the German Criminal Code sets forth regulations regarding "agitation of the people" and bans incitement of hatred against a minority of the population. The concept is called *Volksverhetzung*. For example, §130(1) of that Code provides:

> Whoever, in a manner that is capable of disturbing the public peace: 1. incites hatred against segments of the population or calls for violent or arbitrary measures against them; or 2. assaults the human dignity of others by insulting, maliciously maligning, or defaming segments of the population, shall be punished with imprisonment from three months to five years.

In the 1990s, the German government added criminal provisions for holocaust denial and for speech justifying or glorifying the Nazi government. The German government felt that the atrocities committed in their country's past justified the passage of these statutes. Should the United States be willing to enforce regulations against racist speech because of our history of slavery and racial discrimination?

Section Three
RACIAL EQUALITY AND THE REMEDIAL INSTRUMENT

A. Equality as a Limit

Unlike the criminal law, substantive tort law never made many distinctions based upon race. This does not mean that issues of racial equality as a limit on the remedial instrument have never been litigated. Prior to the Civil War, slaves — but not all African Americans — were generally unable to seek redress of grievances from the state courts. Moreover, in the infamous *Dred Scott* decision, the Supreme Court held that blacks were not citizens of the United

States, thus sharply limiting the right of blacks — slave or free — to seek redress of their grievances in the federal courts. Dred Scott v. Sandford, 60 U.S. (19 How.) 393 (1857).

The Thirteenth and Fourteenth Amendments ended slavery and granted equal citizenship rights to all races, thus eliminating these formal sources of inequality. Nevertheless, the question of whether the remedial instrument is equally applied to litigants of all races remains. Recall the discussion in Chapter 1 concerning the role of the jury in resolving factual issues. We noted there that there is no way of knowing whether the jury decided on the basis of some irrelevancy. One such irrelevancy might be the race of the litigants. How can law protect minority-race litigants from unfair application of the remedial instrument?

The power of trial court judges to set aside an unreasonable verdict and the power of appellate courts to review the trial judge's decision constitute checks on prejudiced fact-finding, but it can provide no remedy in close cases. One other way to check prejudiced verdicts is to control the composition of the jury in the first place.

Would it be most fair to make the jury half black and half white when one litigant is black and one is white? The Supreme Court has rejected the argument that a litigant has the right to any particular composition of his or her jury. This does not mean, however, that a state may deliberately rig the system so that all juries exclude persons of one race. In Strauder v. West Virginia, 100 U.S. 303 (1880), the Court overturned a black criminal defendant's conviction, ruling that the West Virginia statute excluding blacks from jury service was unconstitutional. In Thiel v. Southern Pacific Co., 328 U.S. 217, 66 S. Ct. 984 (1946), a personal injury case, the Court made it clear that racial groups could not be excluded from civil juries either.

Suppose that persons of all races are included in the jury rolls but that only white jurors happen to be called for a particular case involving a minority-race plaintiff and a white defendant. Is the plaintiff out of luck? Would it be desirable to guarantee the presence of members of the plaintiff's ethnic or racial group? The following case discusses a more modest means of controlling prejudice in the jury box.

EDMONSON v. LEESVILLE CONCRETE CO.
Supreme Court of the United States, 1991
500 U.S. 614, 111 S. Ct. 2077

JUSTICE KENNEDY delivered the opinion of the Court:

We must decide in the case before us whether a private litigant in a civil case may use peremptory challenges to exclude jurors on account of their race. Recognizing the impropriety of racial bias in the courtroom, we hold the race-based exclusion violates the equal protection rights of the challenged jurors.

Thaddeus Donald Edmonson, a construction worker, was injured in a jobsite accident at Fort Polk, Louisiana, a federal enclave. Edmonson sued Leesville Concrete Company for negligence in the United States District Court for the Western District of Louisiana, claiming that a Leesville employee permitted one of the company's trucks to roll backward and pin him against some construction equipment. Edmonson invoked his Seventh Amendment right to a trial by jury.

During voir dire, Leesville used two of its three peremptory challenges authorized by statute to remove black persons from the prospective jury. Citing our decision in Batson v. Kentucky, 476 U.S. 79, 106 S. Ct. 1712 (1986), Edmonson, who is himself black, requested that the District Court require Leesville to articulate a race-neutral explanation for striking the two jurors. The District Court denied the request on the ground that *Batson* does not apply in civil proceedings. As empaneled, the jury included 11 white persons and 1 black person. The jury rendered a verdict for Edmonson, assessing his total damages at $90,000. It also attributed 80% of the fault to Edmonson's contributory negligence, however, and awarded him the sum of $18,000.

... The court [of appeals affirmed and] concluded that the use of peremptories by private litigants does not constitute state action and, as a result, does not implicate constitutional guarantees. . . .

... [I]n determining whether a particular action or course of conduct is governmental in character, it is relevant to examine the following: the extent to which the actor relies on governmental assistance and benefits; whether the actor is performing a traditional governmental function; and whether the injury caused is aggravated in a unique way by the incidents of governmental authority. Based on our application of these three principles to the circumstances here, we hold that the exercise of peremptory challenges by the defendant in the District Court was pursuant to a course of state action.

Although private use of state-sanctioned private remedies or procedures does not rise, by itself, to the level of state action, our cases have found state action when private parties make extensive use of state procedures with "the overt, significant assistance of state officials." [Tulsa Professional Collection Services, Inc. v. Pope, 485 U.S. 478, 485, 108 S. Ct. 1340, 1345 (1988)] . . . .

... The government summons jurors, constrains their freedom of movement, and subjects them to public scrutiny and examination. The party who exercises a challenge invokes the formal authority of the court, which must discharge the prospective juror, thus effecting the

"final and practical denial" of the excluded individual's opportunity to serve on the petit jury. Virginia v. Rives, 100 U.S. 313, 322 (1880). Without the direct and indispensable participation of the judge, who beyond all question is a state actor, the peremptory challenge system would serve no purpose. By enforcing a discriminatory peremptory challenge, the court "has not only made itself a party to the [biased act], but has elected to place its power, property and prestige behind the [alleged] discrimination." Burton v. Wilmington Parking Authority, 365 U.S. [715, 725, 81 S. Ct. 856, 862 (1961)] . . . .

... A traditional function of government is evident here. The peremptory challenge is used in selecting an entity that is a quintessential governmental body, having no attributes of a private actor. . . .

If a government confers on a private body the power to choose the government's employees or officials, the private body will be bound by the constitutional mandate of race neutrality. . . .

... If peremptory challenges based on race were permitted, persons could be required by summons to be put at risk of open and public discrimination as a condition of their participation in the justice system. The injury to excluded jurors would be the direct result of governmental delegation and participation.

Finally, we note that the injury caused by the discrimination is made more severe because the government permits it to occur within the courthouse itself. Few places are a more real expression of the constitutional authority of the government than a courtroom, where the law itself unfolds. . . .

The judgment is reversed, and the case is remanded for further proceedings consistent with our opinion.

It is so ordered.

O'CONNOR, J., joined by REHNQUIST, C.J., and SCALIA, J., dissenting:

... It is the nature of a peremptory that its exercise is left wholly within the discretion of the litigant. . . . In both criminal and civil trials, the peremptory challenge is a mechanism for the exercise of *private* choice in the pursuit of fairness. The peremptory is, by design, an enclave of private action in a government-managed proceeding.

The Court amasses much ostensible evidence of the Federal Government's "overt, significant assistance" in the peremptory process.... All of this government action is in furtherance of the Government's distinct obligation to provide a qualified jury; the Government would do these things even if there were no peremptory challenges....

...The government "normally can be held responsible for a private decision only when it has exercised coercive power or has provided such significant encouragement, either overt or covert, that the choice must in law be deemed to be that of the State." Blum [v. Yaretsky, 457 U.S. 991, 1004, 102 S. Ct. 2777, 2786 (1982)].

...A judge does not "significantly encourage" discrimination by the mere act of excusing a juror in response to an unexplained request....

In *Edmonson*, the Court does not determine whether the challenges were in fact based upon race, but remands the case for "further proceedings" consistent with its opinion. What are those proceedings? Batson v. Kentucky, 476 U.S. 79, 106 S. Ct. 1712 (1986), cited in *Edmonson*, forbade the racially motivated exercise of peremptory challenges by prosecutors in criminal cases. It also established a procedure for determining whether the prosecutor has acted with racial motivation: After the defendant establishes a prima facie case of discrimination, the prosecutor must offer a racially neutral explanation for the challenged strikes. If he does not do so, discrimination is established. If he does offer another reason, the trial court must determine whether the reasons he has offered are the true reason for the strike.

B. Equality as the Goal

Following the Civil War, the Reconstruction Congress attempted to use the remedial instrument to block efforts to force blacks into a condition of de facto slavery. The Civil Rights Act of 1866 provided that all citizens would have the same right as a white person to make and enforce contracts and to own or lease property. The Civil Rights Act of 1870 extended federal protection to black voting rights. The Civil Rights Act of 1871 provided civil remedies and criminal penalties for violating constitutional rights. Finally, the Civil Rights Act of 1875 prohibited racial discrimination in public accommodations. But these statutes proved to be of little practical significance, in part because of Supreme Court decisions striking down key provisions and in part because in 1894 Congress repealed the most effective provisions — those protecting voting rights.

Not until the second half of the twentieth century did the remedial instrument begin to play an important role in promoting racial equality. A number of new civil rights statutes, combined with Supreme Court decisions resurrecting some of the older statutes, resulted in a reasonably comprehensive — and correspondingly controversial — package of protections. The Civil Rights Acts of 1957 and 1960 improved remedies against racial discrimination in voting; the Civil Rights Act of 1964 added remedies for discrimination in private employment, public accommodations, and federally assisted programs; the Voting Rights Act of 1965 addressed discrimination in voting; and the Civil Rights Act of 1968 outlawed

Title VII

Title VII addresses workplace discrimination based on race, color, religion, sex, and national origin. The picture shows President Johnson signing the Civil Rights Act of 1964, with guest Martin Luther King, Jr., behind him. All private employers, except those who employ fewer than 15 people, are subject to Title VII. Discrimination based on the protected factors is prohibited in any aspect of employment, including, for example, hiring, firing, recruitment, job advertisements, promotions, retirement plans, and benefits. Title VII also protects against harassment in the workplace, retaliatory firings, employment decisions based on stereotypes, and decisions based on marriage to someone of a protected class. Intentional discrimination is illegal, as is any practice having the effect of discrimination that does not actually improve an employee's performance of the job. For example, English-only rules may be illegal where the employer cannot show that speaking English is necessary to conducting its business.

Title VII is enforced by the Equal Employment Opportunity Commission (EEOC), a federal agency created in 1964. The EEOC has field offices in all 50 states and requires that employers subject to Title VII post fliers on site to notify employees of their rights. To protect the employee's legal rights under the statute, complaints must be filed within 180 days of the alleged discriminatory incident. Individuals may file complaints with the EEOC either on their own behalf or on the behalf of another individual who wishes to remain anonymous. The EEOC then investigates the complaint and may aid in the parties' settlement of the claim at any time during the investigation. If the EEOC does not find a violation, it will give the employee the "right to sue" on his or her own but will not continue the investigation. If the EEOC does find a violation, it may choose to either settle the claim or bring suit against the employer itself. Remedies from settlements and lawsuits may include back pay, reinstatement, promotion, or any other reasonable accommodation. If the complaint goes to trial, the employee may also be able to recover trial costs and attorney's fees. Punitive damages are usually available only where intentional discrimination is found and the employer has acted recklessly or maliciously.

most private discrimination in housing. Some of the key employment provisions of the 1964 Act are referred to as "Title VII." Other important federal laws prohibiting workplace discrimination include the Equal Pay Act of 1963, protecting men and women from sex-based wage discrimination; the Age Discrimination in Employment Act of 1967, protecting individuals age 40 and older; Titles I and V of the Americans with Disabilities Act of 1990, protecting individuals with disabilities; and the Civil Rights Act of 1991, providing monetary damages in cases of intentional discrimination in employment.

Public interest groups, along with private citizens, have brought various suits against the Ku Klux Klan to remedy private wrongs suffered at the hands of the organization. The remedial instrument awards damages to citizens, as opposed to criminal sanctions imposed by the state. Civil cases not only compensate the victims of racially motivated crimes but also can bankrupt and disable racist groups.

WILLIAM CLAIBORNE, KLAN CHAPTERS HELD LIABLE IN CHURCH FIRE; JURY AWARDS $37.8 MILLION IN DAMAGES
Wash. Post, July 25, 1998, at A14

A South Carolina jury ordered two Ku Klux Klan chapters and five Klansmen yesterday to pay $37.8 million for creating an atmosphere of hate that led to the torching of a black church in 1995.

The verdict exceeded by more than $10 million the amount of damages sought by the Macedonia Baptist Church in Manning, S.C., 55 miles southeast of Columbia, the capital. It represented the largest-ever civil award for damages in a hate crime case.

"The verdict shows that there are still some things sacred in this country, still some lines that no one can cross," said Morris Dees, co-founder of the Southern Poverty Law Center, who argued the case for the church.

The jury of nine blacks and three whites in Manning deliberated just 45 minutes before awarding $300,000 in actual damages and $37.5 million in punitive damages against KKK organizations in North Carolina and South Carolina and their leaders.

Mark Potok, spokesman for the Montgomery, Ala.-based SPLC, said the size of the award was unprecedented in hate crime cases. However, even if the verdict withstands an expected appeal, it is doubtful that the church will be able to collect much.

Three of the Klansmen held liable are serving prison sentences for the church burning, and the lawyer for Horace King, the 65–year-old grand dragon of the North Carolina-based Christian Knights of the Ku Klux Klan, said his client is a poor chicken farmer living on disability payments. Another defendant, Virgil Griffin, an imperial wizard of the South Carolina Klan chapter, also was reported unable to substantially meet the verdict.

Nonetheless, Dees, in a telephone interview, asked, "If we put the Christian Knights out of business, what's that worth? We don't look at what we can collect. It's what the jury thinks this egregious conduct is worth that matters, along with the message it sends."

Two of the men in prison for the Macedonia Baptist Church fire implicated the Klan during the week-long trial, with Timothy Adron Welch testifying, "The church fire was Klan business, and we were told we would not go to jail."

However, King, even after confronted in court with a videotape showing him in robes, exhorting whites to take back their country from blacks, testified that he "never told anyone to go out there and fight blacks." His lawyer, Gary White, said the men who were convicted of setting the fire acted on their own and that "this whole suit is about shutting down the Ku Klux Klan."

The church fire came at a time when the nation's attention was focused on a series of church burnings across the South, many of which occurred in old wooden frame buildings virtually hidden off rural roads. Another fire was set a day earlier at the nearby Mount Zion AME Church.

At least 32 suspicious fires were reported at black churches just between January 1995 and June 1996, the largest number in South Carolina. Although at the time there were reports of Klan links to some of the fires and occasional arrests of whites with ties to racist groups, federal investigators were unable to find any pattern of organized involvement.

However, Dees has made a career of beating the Klan in civil cases, including an $8 million verdict last year against the United Klans of America for inciting the 1981 lynch-style slaying of a black teenager in Mobile, Ala., that bankrupted that Klan faction. Dees's group also won a $1 million judgment against two Klan groups and 11 followers in 1997 after an interracial march in Forsyth County, Ga., was attacked by rock-throwers, and a $12.5 million judgment against the White Aryan Resistance for inciting the killing of an Ethiopian student by Portland, Ore., skinheads.

Hate crime experts said that while large jury awards against Klan and other such groups are rarely collected, the verdicts still serve a purpose by sending a message to similar groups across the country.

"What they [the awards] have done has changed the way hate groups do business. They have had to turn to what they call 'leaderless resistance' and try to inspire acts of violence in such a way they will not be held liable," said Brian Levin, director of the Center on Hate and Extremism at Stockton College in Pomona, N.J. "So they lighten up and it kills their credibility with their constituents."

Pornography as Discrimination

In the 1980s, feminists and moralists in several cities joined together to support passage of an ordinance that would make the production and distribution of pornography a violation of women's civil rights. Under the ordinance, women could use the remedial instrument to bring civil suits against producers or distributors of harmful pornography. The ordinance would ban pornography that objectifies women, places them in situations where they enjoy pain or humiliation, or presents them in violent, torturous, or submissive positions.

The anti-pornography ordinance was developed and drafted by feminist scholars Catherine MacKinnon and Andrea Dworkin. They believed that degrading, violent pornography objectified and glorified violence toward women. They were convinced that exposure to this material would make men more likely to commit sexual assault or violent acts on women. The ordinance would utilize the remedial instrument as a preventative measure, to stop the domino effect before the criminal consequences were realized.

The ordinance was passed in various cities, including Minneapolis and Indianapolis. Ultimately, the Seventh Circuit struck down the ordinance passed in Indianapolis as unconstitutional in American Booksellers Association v. Hudnut, 771 F.2d 323 (7th Cir. 1985), aff'd mem., 475 U.S. 1001, 106 S. Ct. 1172 (1986). The court decided that while pornography might lead to dangerous effects, this was not enough under the First Amendment to ban the speech. The *Hudnut* decision has outraged many feminists, who feel strongly that pornography is not only degrading to women in general, but that it causes actual harm to the women coerced into making the material and to all women from the way that men learn to sexualize violence against women. But the debate is complex: there are factions of feminists who disagree with the ordinances in favor of free speech; there are feminists who warn against coalitions with the conservative right for fear of its condemnation of reproductive rights and homosexuality; and there is disagreement about the definition of violent sexual material within the gay community.

Below are various viewpoints on this movement against pornography. As you read the excerpts, keep in mind the goals of free speech from the previous section.

Feminists' View of Pornography

Catherine A. MacKinnon, Not a Moral Issue, in Feminism Unmodified: Discourse on Life and Law 146–62 (1987):

"Pornography, in the feminist view, is a form of forced sex, a practice of sexual politics, an institution of gender inequality. In this perspective, pornography is not harmless fantasy or a corrupt and confused misrepresentation of an otherwise natural and healthy sexuality. Along with the rape and prostitution in which it participates, pornography institutionalizes the sexuality of male supremacy, which fuses the erotization of dominance and submission with the social construction of male and female. Gender is sexual. Pornography constitutes the meaning of that sexuality. Men treat women as who they see women as being. Pornography constructs who that is. Men's power over women means that the way men see women defines who women can be. Pornography is that way.

"Men are scared to make it possible for some men to tell other men what they can and cannot have sexual access to because men have power. If you don't let them have theirs, they might not let you have yours. This is why the *indefinability* of pornography, all the 'one man's this is another man's that', is so central to pornography's *definition*. It is not because they are such great liberals, but because some men might be able to do to them whatever they can do to those other men, and this is more why the liberal principle is what it is. Because the fought-over are invisible in this, it obscures the fact that the fight over a definition of obscenity is a fight among men over the best means to guarantee male power as a system.

"... Sometimes I think that the real issue [of what is ultimately found obscene] is how male sexuality is presented, so that anything can be done to a woman, but obscenity is sex that makes male sexuality look bad."

Diana E.H. Russell, Making Violence Sexy: Feminist Views on Pornography (1993):

"Although rape is illegal, the showing and distribution of actual rapes on film is protected as free speech. As Dworkin and MacKinnon so aptly question: 'If lynchings were done in order to make photographs, on a ten-billion-dollar-a-year scale, would that make them protected speech?' And later they ask: 'What would it say about the seriousness with which society regards lynching if actual lynching is illegal but pictures of actual lynching are protected and highly profitable and defended as a form of freedom and a constitutional right? What would it say about the seriousness and effectiveness of laws against lynching if people paid good money to see it and the law looked the other way, so long as they saw it in mass-produced form?'"

"Although it is disturbing that so many people ignore the harm done to the women who are used in making pornography, this kind of harm should be distinguished from the harm that occurs to the consumer and their victims. Either harm can occur, with or without the other."

Social Learning Through Pornography

Diana E.H. Russell, Making Violence Sexy: Feminist Views on Pornography (1993):

"Dolf Zillmann and Jennings Bryant have studied the effects of what they refer to as 'massive exposure' to pornography. (In fact, it was not that massive: 4 hours and 48 minutes per week over a period of 6 weeks.) These researchers . . . focus on trying to ascertain the effects of *non-violent* pornography and, in the study to be described, they use a sample drawn from a non-student adult population.

"Subjects in the *massive exposure* condition saw 36 nonviolent pornographic films, 6 per session per week; subjects in the *intermediate* condition saw 18 such movies, 3 per session per week. Subjects in the control group saw 36 nonpornographic movies. Various measures were taken after 1 week, 2 weeks, and 3 weeks of exposure.

"Zillmann and Bryant found that an appetite for stronger material was fostered in their subjects, presumably, Zillmann suggests, 'because familiar material becomes unexciting as a result of habituation.' Hence, 'consumers graduate from common to less common forms of pornography,' that is, to more violent and more degrading materials.

"According to this research, then, pornography can transform a male who was not previously interested in the ore abusive types of pornography, into one who *is* turned on by such material. In turn, [another researcher named Neil] Malamuth has shown that males who did not previously find rape sexually arousing, generate such fantasies after being exposed to a typical example of violent pornography. And men who have rape fantasies are more likely to act them out than men who do not.

"I have argued that the laws of social learning apply to pornography, just as they apply to other media. As [Edward] Donnerstein testified at the hearings in Minneapolis: 'If you assume that your child can learn from Sesame Street how to count one, two, three, four, five, believe me, they can learn how to pick up a gun.' Presumably, males can learn equally well how to rape, beat, sexually abuse, and degrade females."

Pornography as a Defense?

Serial sex murderer Ted Bundy blamed his murders on an addiction to pornography. He claimed that his addiction to sadomasochistic pornography encouraged him to kill, as he repeatedly sought a higher "dose" of sexual violence. If there is empirical evidence to support the causal connection between pornography and sex, and a convicted sex murderer admits that this was the cause of his crimes, does this lend support to an ordinance banning violent, degrading pornography? The excerpts below discuss the ramifications of accepting this testimony as part of the feminist argument.

Catherine A. MacKinnon, Pornography: An Exchange, N.Y. Rev. Books, Mar. 3, 1994, at 47–48: "In *Schiro v. Clark*, expert evidence supported the lower court's finding that Thomas Schiro, convicted of rape and murder, could not appreciate the wrongfulness of his acts, due to his extensive consumption of sadomasochistic pornography and snuff films. Whether he can be executed turned in part on whether this conclusion can be drawn from this evidence. The reviewing court, which included the author of *Hudnut*, faced a dilemma: having decided that pornography causes rapes but must be permitted, must it also permit the rapes pornography causes, because it causes them? The court stated that '*the recognition in* Hudnut *that pornography leads to violence against women* does not require Indiana to establish a defense of insanity by pornography' (emphasis added). It refused 'to tell Indiana that it can neither ban pornography nor hold criminally responsible persons who are encouraged to commit violent acts because of pornography!' To repeat: *Hudnut* held that pornography 'leads to' violence against women. *Schiro* recognized that persons like Schiro exist, who 'are encouraged to' commit violent acts because of pornography. Both are causal connections."

Deborah Cameron & Elizabeth Frazer, On the Question of Pornography and Sexual Violence: Moving Beyond Cause and Effect, in Pornography: Woman, Violence and Civil Liberties 395–471 (Catherine Itzin ed., 1994):

"Where does a sex killer's account of himself come from? Not, we suggest, from some privileged personal insight, but from a finite repertoire of cultural clichés which the murderer, like everyone else, has come across in case histories, pop-psychology, newspapers, films and ordinary gossip with family, friends and workmates. At any given time the clichés available are a heterogeneous and contradictory collection; some may carry more authority than others (for instance, we no longer think much of a killer who tells us he was possessed by the devil, though traces of this ancient supernatural account can be seen in the tabloid label 'fiend' used for sex murderers); new clichés may enter the repertoire, challenging or providing alternatives to the existing explanations. Porn-blaming is a recent example.

"Let us examine how cultural clichés work by examining one that feminists are in no danger of confusing with 'the truth': the mother-blaming explanation of sexual murder. The idea that sexual killers are revenging themselves on dominating or inadequate mothers is a relatively recent cliché. Although it was found in expert discourse (i.e. forensic psychiatry, criminology) much

earlier — its source, in fact, is psychoanalytic theory — it entered popular awareness only in the 1950s and 1960s, by way of cultural products like the Hitchcock movie *Psycho*. At this point, not untypically, the popularized version 'fed back' into the expert pronouncements in a circular, reinforcing process. Police in the Boston Strangler case in the 1960s announced that they were looking for someone like Norman Bates, the mother-fixated character in *Psycho*. The actual strangler, Albert DeSalvo, in fact bore little resemblance to this stereotype. But the perception of sexual murder as a consequence of pathological mother-son relations persisted and during the 1970s became a theme in the testimony of some real-life killers (a striking example is Edmund Kemper, the 'Co-ed Killer' of Santa Cruz) — whereupon it re-entered expert discourse in case-history form. The circle was completed once again.

"By the time of Ted Bundy's confession in 1989, a new account had become culturally available: the porn blaming explanation. This one entered popular awareness in a relatively unusual way, through organized political activity on the part of the feminists during the 1970s.

"If feminists follow through with the logic of the addiction model, they risk adding to an already depressing catalogue of defences and excuses. The truly novel thing about porn-blaming explanations may turn out to be that a feminist, as opposed to misogynist, account is being co-opted for use in the interests of violent men and against those of women.

"Humans are not like billiard balls — of indeed like animals, whose behaviour can be described in terms of a stimulus-response model. Humans have the capacity for symbolization and language, which enables us — and perhaps even obliges us — to impose meaning on the stimuli we encounter, and to respond in ways which also carry meaning. Human 'behavior,' therefore, is not determined by laws analogous to those of physics. It is not deterministically 'caused.' It needs to be explained in a different way, by interpretation of what it means and elucidation of the beliefs or understandings that make it possible and intelligible."

Section Four
RACIAL EQUALITY AND THE PRIVATE-ARRANGEMENT INSTRUMENT

A. Equality as a Limit

As explained in the introduction to this chapter, the constitutional provisions concerning racial equality do not speak to individuals but to the government. A natural assumption, therefore, would be that these provisions do not limit the private-arrangement instrument. This assumption, however, would be erroneous. This instrument facilitates private arrangements by legitimizing and enforcing them, but it can also shape these arrangements by disapproving or refusing to enforce certain variations. Recall *Loving v. Virginia* from the penal section. While marriage is a private arrangement, the government had sought to regulate interracial marriages using criminal sanctions — unconstitutionally.

The first case in this subsection involves racially discriminatory governmental action favoring some private arrangements, and the issue is whether the discrimination can be justified under the strict-scrutiny standard. The second case is different in that the issue is whether the government's role in enforcing a discriminatory private arrangement is significant enough to require application of the strict-scrutiny standard.

PALMORE v. SIDOTI
Supreme Court of the United States, 1984
466 U.S. 429, 104 S. Ct. 1879

CHIEF JUSTICE BURGER delivered the opinion of the Court:

We granted certiorari to review a judgment of a state court divesting a natural mother of the custody of her infant child because of her remarriage to a person of a different race.

I

When petitioner Linda Sidoti Palmore and respondent Anthony J. Sidoti, both Caucasians, were divorced in May 1980 in Florida, the mother was awarded custody of their three-year-old daughter.

In September 1981 the father sought custody of the child by filing a petition to modify the prior judgment because of changed conditions. The change was that the child's mother was then cohabiting with a Negro, Clarence Palmore, Jr., whom she married two months later. Additionally, the

father made several allegations of instances in which the mother had not properly cared for the child.

After hearing testimony from both parties and considering a court counselor's investigative report, the court noted that the father had made allegations about the' child's care, but the court made no findings with respect to these allegations. On the contrary, the court made a finding that "there is no issue as to either party's devotion to the child, adequacy of housing facilities, or respect[a]bility of the new spouse of either parent."

The court then addressed the recommendations of the court counselor, who had made an earlier report "in [another] case coming out of this circuit also involving the social consequences of an interracial marriage. Niles v. Niles, 299 So. 2d 162." From this vague reference to that earlier case, the court turned to the present case and noted the counselor's recommendation for a change in custody because "[t]he wife [petitioner] has chosen for herself and for her child, a life-style unacceptable to her father *and to society....* The child...is, or at school age will be, subject to environmental pressures not of choice." (emphasis added)

The court then concluded that the best interests of the child would be served by awarding custody to the father. The court's rationale is contained in the following:

> The father's evident resentment of the mother's choice of a black partner is not sufficient to wrest custody from the mother. It is of some significance, however, that the mother did see fit to bring a man into her home and carry on a sexual relationship with him without being married to him. Such action tended to place gratification of her own desires ahead of her concern for the child's future welfare. *This Court feels that despite the strides that have been made in bettering relations between the races in this country, it is inevitable that Melanie will, if allowed to remain in her present situation and attains school age and thus more vulnerable to peer pressures, suffer from the social stigmatization that is sure to come.* (emphasis added)

[The decision was affirmed in the state court system, and certiorari was granted.]

II

The judgment of a state court determining or reviewing a child custody decision is not ordinarily a likely candidate for review by this Court. However, the court's opinion, after stating that the "father's evident resentment of the mother's choice of a black partner is not sufficient" to deprive her of custody, then turns to what it regarded as the damaging impact on the child from remaining in a racially-mixed household. This raises important federal concerns arising from the Constitution's commitment to eradicating discrimination based on race....

The court correctly stated that the child's welfare was the controlling factor. But that court was entirely candid and made no effort to place its holding on any ground other than race. Taking the court's findings and rationale at face value, it is clear that the outcome would have been different had petitioner married a Caucasian male of similar respectability.

A core purpose of the Fourteenth Amendment was to do away with all governmentally-imposed discrimination based on race. Classifying persons according to their race is more likely to reflect racial prejudice than legitimate public concerns; the race, not the person, dictates the category. Such classifications are subject to the most exacting scrutiny; to pass constitutional muster, they must be justified by a compelling governmental interest and must be "necessary...to the accomplishment" of its legitimate purpose, McLaughlin v. Florida, 379 U.S. 184, 196, 85 S. Ct. 283, 290 (1964). See Loving v. Virginia, 388 U.S. 1, 11, 87 S. Ct. 1817, 1823 (1967).

The State, of course, has a duty of the highest order to protect the interests of minor children, particularly those of tender years. In common with most states, Florida law mandates that custody determinations be made in the best interests of the children involved. Fla. Stat. §61.13(2)(b)(1) (1983). The goal of granting custody based on the best interests of the child is indisputably a substantial governmental interest for purposes of the Equal Protection Clause.

It would ignore reality to suggest that racial and ethnic prejudices do not exist or that all manifestations of those prejudices have been eliminated. There is a risk that a child living with a step-parent of a different race may be subject to a variety of pressures and stresses not present if the child were living with parents of the same racial or ethnic origin.

The question, however, is whether the reality of private biases and the possible injury they might inflict are permissible considerations for removal of an infant child from the custody of its natural mother. We have little difficulty concluding that they are not. The Constitution cannot control such prejudices but neither can it tolerate them. Private biases may be outside the reach of the law, but the law cannot, directly or indirectly, give them effect. "Public officials sworn to uphold the Constitution may not avoid a constitutional duty by bowing to the hypothetical effects of private racial prejudice that they assume to be both widely and deeply held." Palmer v. Thompson, 403 U.S. 217, 260–261, 91 S. Ct. 1940, 1962–1963 (1971) (White, J., dissenting).

This is by no means the first time that acknowledged racial prejudice has been invoked to justify racial classifications. In Buchanan v. Warley, 245 U.S. 60, 38 S. Ct. 16 (1917), for example, this Court invalidated a Kentucky law forbidding Negroes from buying homes in white neighborhoods.

> It is urged that this proposed segregation will promote the public peace by preventing race conflicts. Desirable as this is, and important as is the preservation of the public peace, this aim cannot be accomplished by laws or ordinances which deny rights created or protected by the Federal Constitution.

Id., at 81, 38 S. Ct., at 20. Whatever problems racially-mixed households may pose for children in 1984 can no more support a denial of constitutional rights than could the stresses that residential integration was thought to entail in 1917. The effects of racial prejudice, however real, cannot justify a racial classification removing an infant child from the custody of its natural mother found to be an appropriate person to have such custody.[3]

The judgment of the District Court of Appeal is reversed.

It is so ordered.

---

3. This conclusion finds support in other cases as well. For instance, in Watson v. City of Memphis, 373 U.S. 526, 83 S. Ct. 1314 (1963), city officials claimed that desegregation of city parks had to proceed slowly to "prevent interracial disturbances, violence, riots, and community confusion and turmoil." Id., at 535, 83 S. Ct., at 1319. The Court found such predictions no more than "personal speculations or vague disquietudes," id., at 536, 83 S. Ct., at 1320, and held that "constitutional rights may not be denied simply because of hostility to their assertion or exercise," id., at 535, 83 S. Ct., at 1319–1320. In Wright v. Georgia, 373 U.S. 284, 83 S. Ct. 1240 (1963), the Court reversed a Negro defendant's breach-of-peace conviction, holding that "the possibility of disorder by others cannot justify exclusion of persons from a place if they otherwise have a constitutional right (founded upon the Equal Protection Clause) to be present." Id., at 293, 83 S. Ct., at 1246.

The *Palmore* opinion says that the existence of private bias can never justify racially discriminatory public actions, but other Supreme Court cases cast doubt on this broad assertion. In Lee v. Washington, 390 U.S. 333, 88 S. Ct. 994 (1968), the Court issued a per curiam affirmance of a federal court order holding Alabama's segregated prison system unconstitutional. The opinion noted Alabama's argument that the lower court order had made no allowance for the necessities of prison security and discipline, commenting that "we do not so read" the order. In a separate concurring paragraph, three Justices explained: "[W]e wish to make explicit [that] prison authorities have the right, acting in good faith and in particularized circumstances, to take into account racial tensions in maintaining security, discipline, and good order in jails." Perhaps the problem is not taking account of private bias, but *assuming* that such biases exist. That is, it was improper for Alabama to segregate its prison system on a theory that racial bias would cause riots or the like, but not improper to respond to a concrete instance of racial violence. If that is correct, then it would be acceptable for a family court to hear and consider testimony that a child was in fact enduring ostracism or threats based his interracial family, but improper to assume that he would do so, and improper to assume that any negative effects of an interracial family would outweigh positive benefits.

Custody, Adoption, and Sexual Orientation

Approximately 14 million gays and lesbians in the United States are currently parenting children. The vast majority of these children were born when the gay or lesbian parent was in a heterosexual relationship, but in the last dozen years, an increasing number of gays and lesbians have adopted or attempted to adopt children. Gay and lesbian adoptions occur in at least three different situations: a gay or lesbian person adopts the biological child of his or her same sex partner; a gay or lesbian person legally adopts a child as a single parent; or both persons in a gay or lesbian couple adopt a child to which neither has a biological relationship, either at the same time, or sequentially.

Only one state, Florida, by statute prohibits all adoptions by "homosexuals." New Hampshire had a similar statute, but it was amended in 1999 to delete the sexual orientation restriction. In many states, however, a gay or lesbian *couple* is unable to adopt a child because the adoption statute permits only adoptions by a single person or by married couples. Courts in Colorado, Wisconsin, Georgia, New Hampshire, Arizona and Nebraska have upheld such statutes as applied to gays and lesbians. On the other hand, gays and lesbians in Vermont, New Jersey, California, the District of Columbia, Illinois, Massachusetts, Connecticut, and Ohio permit adoption by same sex couples. Pennsylvania permits such adoptions on a case by case basis, requiring the applicants to show cause why the statutory requirement of marriage should be waived. Most of the remaining states permit adoption by any single person or by a married couple but have not yet addressed the application of the statute to same sex couples. Even in states where adoption by a same sex couple is possible, many private agencies openly refuse to accept gay and lesbian couples as applicants.

Experts on parenting reported on several long-term studies of gay and lesbian biological parents. In general — though not universally — these studies found that gays and lesbians were neither better nor worse parents than heterosexuals, and that their children were no more likely to become gay or lesbian than the general population. There is however, no extensive data on gay and lesbian *adoptive* parents or their children.

Do gays and lesbians have a right to be considered as adoptive parents? *Palmore v. Sidoti* is not directly on point for two reasons. First, it concerns "divesting a natural mother of the custody of her infant child," which is not at stake in adoption. Second, *Palmore* involves the use of a racial classification, which is, as we have seen, subjected to a higher level of scrutiny than are other forms of discrimination. What level of scrutiny should be accorded decisions based on sexual orientation?

SHELLEY v. KRAEMER

Supreme Court of the United States, 1948
334 U.S. 1, 68 S. Ct. 836

Mr. Chief Justice Vinson delivered the opinion of the Court:

These cases present for our consideration questions relating to the validity of court enforcement of private agreements, generally described as restrictive covenants, which have as their purpose the exclusion of persons of designated race or color from the ownership or occupancy of real property. Basic constitutional issues of obvious importance have been raised.

The first of these cases comes to this Court on certiorari to the Supreme Court of Missouri. On February 16, 1911, thirty out of a total of thirty-nine owners of property fronting both sides of Labadie Avenue between Taylor Avenue and

Cora Avenue in the city of St. Louis, signed an agreement, which was subsequently recorded, providing in part:

> ...the said property is hereby restricted to the use and occupancy for the term of Fifty (50) years from this date, so that it shall be a condition all the time and whether recited and referred to as [sic] not in subsequent conveyances and shall attach to the land, as a condition precedent to the sale of the same, that hereafter no part of said property or any portion thereof shall be, for said term of Fifty-years, occupied by any person not of the Caucasian race, it being intended hereby to restrict the use of said property for said period of time against the occupancy as owners or tenants of any portion of said property for resident or other purpose by people of the Negro or Mongolian Race.

The entire district described in the agreement included fifty-seven parcels of land. The thirty owners who signed the agreement held title to forty-seven parcels, including the particular parcel involved in this case. At the time the agreement was signed, five of the parcels in the district were owned by Negroes. One of those had been occupied by Negro families since 1882, nearly thirty years before the restrictive agreement was executed. The trial court found that owners of seven out of nine homes on the south side of Labadie Avenue, within the restricted district and "in the immediate vicinity" of the premises in question, had failed to sign the restrictive agreement in 1911. At the time this action was brought, four of the premises were occupied by Negroes, and had been so occupied for periods ranging from twenty-three to sixty-three years. A fifth parcel had been occupied by Negroes until a year before this suit was instituted.

On August 11, 1945, pursuant to a contract of sale, petitioners Shelley, who are Negroes, for valuable consideration received from one Fitzgerald a warranty deed to the parcel in question. The trial court found that petitioners had no actual knowledge of the restrictive agreement at the time of the purchase.

On October 9, 1945, respondents, as owners of other property subject to the terms of the restrictive covenant, brought suit in the Circuit Court of the city of St. Louis praying that petitioners Shelley be restrained from taking possession of the property and that judgment be entered divesting title out of petitioners Shelley and revesting title in the immediate grantor or in such other person as the court should direct. The trial court denied the requested relief on the ground that the restrictive agreement, upon which respondents based their action, had never become final and complete because it was the intention of the parties to that agreement that it was not to become effective until signed by all property owners in the district, and signatures of all the owners had never been obtained.

The Supreme Court of Missouri sitting en banc reversed and directed the trial court to grant the relief for which respondents had prayed. That court held the agreement effective and concluded that enforcement of its provisions violated no rights guaranteed to petitioners by the Federal Constitution. At the time the court rendered its decision, petitioners were occupying the property in question.

The second of the cases under consideration comes to this Court from the Supreme Court of Michigan. The circumstances presented do not differ materially from the Missouri case....

Whether the equal protection clause of the Fourteenth Amendment inhibits judicial enforcement by state courts of restrictive covenants based on race or color is a question which this Court has not heretofore been called upon to consider....

Since the decision of this Court in the Civil Rights Cases, 1883, 109 U.S. 3, 3 S. Ct. 18, the principle has become firmly embedded in our constitutional law, that the action inhibited by the first section of the Fourteenth Amendment is only such action as may fairly be said to be that of the States. That Amendment erects no shield against merely private conduct, however discriminatory or wrongful.

We conclude, therefore, that the restrictive agreements standing alone cannot be regarded as a violation of any rights guaranteed to petitioners by the Fourteenth Amendment. So long as the purposes of those agreements are effectuated by voluntary adherence to their terms, it would appear clear that there has been no action by the State and the provisions of the Amendment have not been violated.

But here there was more. These are cases in which the purposes of the agreements were secured only by judicial enforcement by state courts of the restrictive terms of the agreements. The respondents urge that judicial enforcement of private agreements does not amount to state action; or, in any event, the participation of the State is so attenuated in character as not to amount to state action within the meaning of the Fourteenth Amendment. Finally, it is suggested, even if the States in these cases may be deemed to have acted in the constitutional sense, their action did not deprive petitioners of rights guaranteed by the Fourteenth Amendment. We move to a consideration of these matters.

That the action of state courts and of judicial officers in their official capacities is to be regarded as action of the State within the meaning of the Fourteenth Amendment, is a proposition which has long been established by decisions of this Court. That principle was given expression in the earliest cases involving the construction of the terms of the Fourteenth Amendment. Thus, in Commonwealth of Virginia v. Rives, 1880, 100 U.S. 313, 318, this Court stated: "It is doubtless true that a State may act through different agencies, — either by its legislative, its executive, or its judicial authorities; and the prohibitions of the amendment extend to all action of the State denying equal protection of the laws, whether it be action by one of these agencies or by another." ...

We have no doubt that there has been state action in these cases in the full and complete sense of the phrase. The undisputed facts disclose that petitioners were willing purchasers of properties upon which they desired to establish homes. The owners of the properties were willing sellers; and contracts of sale were accordingly consummated. It is clear that but for the active intervention of the state courts, supported by the full panoply of state power, petitioners would have been free to occupy the properties in question without restraint.

These are not cases, as has been suggested, in which the States have merely abstained from action, leaving private individuals free to impose such discriminations as they see fit. Rather, these are cases in which the States have made available to such individuals the full coercive power of government to deny to petitioners, on the grounds of race or color, the enjoyment of property rights in premises which petitioners are willing and financially able to acquire and which the grantors are willing to sell. The difference between judicial enforcement and nonenforcement of the restrictive covenants is the difference to petitioners between being denied rights of property available to other members of the community and being accorded full enjoyment of those rights on an equal footing.

The enforcement of the restrictive agreements by the state courts in these cases was directed pursuant to the common-law policy of the States as formulated by those courts in earlier decisions. In the Missouri case, enforcement of the covenant was directed in the first instance by the highest court of the State after the trial court had determined the agreement to be invalid for want of the requisite number of signatures. In the Michigan case, the order of enforcement by the trial court was affirmed by the highest state court. The judicial action in each case bears the clear and unmistakable imprimatur of the State. We have noted that previous decisions of this Court have established the proposition that judicial action is not immunized from the operation of the Fourteenth Amendment simply because it is taken pursuant to the state's common-law policy. Nor is the Amendment ineffective simply because the particular pattern of discrimination, which the State has enforced, was defined initially by the terms of a private agreement. State action, as that phrase is understood for the purposes of the Fourteenth Amendment, refers to exertions of state power in all forms. And when the effect of that action is to deny rights subject to the protection of the Fourteenth Amendment, it is the obligation of this Court to enforce the constitutional commands.

We hold that in granting judicial enforcement of the restrictive agreements in these cases, the States have denied petitioners the equal protection of the laws and that, therefore, the action of the state courts cannot stand. ...

For the reasons stated, the judgment of the Supreme Court of Missouri and the judgment of the Supreme Court of Michigan must be reversed.

Reversed.

Mr. Justice Reed, Mr. Justice Jackson, and Mr. Justice Rutledge took no part in the consideration or decision of these cases.

After reading *Shelley v. Kraemer*, you might imagine that any state *enforcement* of private racial bias is forbidden by the Constitution, but its holding has been pretty much limited to restrictive covenants. If, for example, your great-aunt leaves a will providing that you shall receive $10,000 a year unless and until you marry a person of the white race, at which time the money will be donated to her favorite charity, a court will generally enforce the provisions of her will. Although the Court in *Shelley* held that 'state action,' which is subject to the Fourteenth Amendment, includes "exertions of state power in all forms," and the level of judicial involvement may be the same in the enforcement of a will as in the enforcement of a restrictive covenant, the size of the public effect may be different because of the relative prevalence of the two private arrangements. Moreover, while it might be thought that everyone should be able to purchase land, it is hard to argue that everyone has a right to inherit property from his or her relative.

B. Equality as the Goal

On the one hand, the law does not attempt to coerce racial equality in the most intimate of private arrangements. Why are there no laws prohibiting discrimination on the basis of race in decisions concerning marriage or adoption? Is it merely because enforcement would be impossible? On the other hand, private arrangements that do not involve family matters are sometimes regulated to promote racial equality — for example, education or employment. Here enforcement is feasible, and the only question is the desirability of intruding upon private choices.

EL-HAKEM v. BJY, INC.

United States Court of Appeals, Ninth Circuit, 2005
415 F.3d 1068, cert. denied, 547 U.S. 1004, 126 S. Ct. 1470 (2006)

Before T.G. Nelson, Rawlinson, Circuit Judges, and Schwarzer, District Judge.

Rawlinson, Circuit Judge:

Plaintiff Mamdouh El-Hakem, who is of Arabic heritage, brought this action against his former employer BJY, Inc., and Gregg Young, BJY's Chief Executive Officer, for employment discrimination, wrongful termination, and failure to pay wages.

El-Hakem's racial discrimination claims stemmed from Young's repeated references to El-Hakem as "Manny." Despite El-Hakem's strenuous objections, Young insisted on using the non-Arabic name rather than "Mamdouh," El-Hakem's given name. In Young's expressed view, a "Western" name would increase El-Hakem's chances for success and would be more acceptable to BJY's clientele. El-Hakem's wage claims were predicated upon assertions that BJY failed to pay El-Hakem regular and overtime wages during his employment and after his employment with BJY ended, which occurred when BJY closed the office where El-Hakem worked.

After a five-day trial, the jury completed interrogatories on separate special verdict forms for each of the Defendants. The jury found that Young intentionally discriminated against El-Hakem on the basis of his race in violation of 42 U.S.C. §1981 by creating a hostile work environment, and awarded $15,000 in compensatory damages and $15,000 in punitive damages. In addition, the jury found that BJY failed to pay El-Hakem regular wages in the amount of $11,051.64 due at the time El-Hakem's employment ended. Young contended that he could not be held liable for racial discrimination in violation of §1981 because his conduct was not race-based.

Defendants argue that they could not be held liable for intentionally discriminating on the basis of race under §1981, because the name "Manny" is not a racial epithet. We disagree with Defendants' premise. Their contention that actionable race discrimination must be based on physical or "genetically determined characteristics such as skin color" ignores the broad reach of §1981. In Saint Francis Coll. v. Al-Khazraji, 481 U.S. 604, 613, 107 S. Ct. 2022 (1987), the United States Supreme Court explained that "a distinctive physiognomy is not essential to qualify for §1981 protection." Rather, the section was "intended to protect from discrimination identifiable classes of persons who are subjected to intentional discrimination solely because of their ancestry or ethnic characteristics." Id.

A group's ethnic characteristics encompass more than its members' skin color and physical traits. Names are often a proxy for race and ethnicity. See Orhorhaghe v. INS, 38 F.3d 488, 498 (9th Cir. 1994) (recognizing that "discrimination against people who possess surnames identified with particular racial or national groups is discrimination on the basis of race or national origin.") (citation omitted).

In Manatt v. Bank of America, 339 F.3d 792, 794–95 (9th Cir. 2003), we identified two incidents

of racial derogation directed at a Chinese woman. One instance occurred when other employees ridiculed the woman for mispronouncing "Lima," and the other consisted of employees pulling their eyes back with their fingers in mocking imitation of the appearance of Asians. Id. at 798. Although the second instance is an example of discrimination directed at a genetically-determined physical trait, the first is not. In the first instance, the coworkers were ridiculing the woman's language and pronunciation rather than a physical characteristic. Thus, Defendants misread Manatt when they cite it for the proposition that racial discrimination must be based solely on physical traits.

We also reject Defendants' contention that Young's conduct was not frequent or pervasive enough to create a hostile work environment. It is true that "[c]onduct that is not severe or pervasive enough to create an objectively hostile or abusive work environment...is beyond Title VII's purview." Harris v. Forklift Sys., Inc., 510 U.S. 17, 21, 114 S. Ct. 367 (1993). It is also correct that this standard applies to the §1981 claim at issue in this case, because we evaluate §1981 claims the same as we do Title VII claims. See Manatt, 339 F.3d at 797. However, as the district court noted, "rational jurors could find [that] Young's intentional conduct created a hostile work environment because his conduct was sufficiently pervasive to alter the conditions of Plaintiff's employment and to create a work environment racially hostile to a reasonable Arab." (case citations omitted).

"The required level of severity or seriousness varies inversely with the pervasiveness or frequency of the conduct." Nichols v. Azteca Rest. Enters., Inc., 256 F.3d 864, 872 (9th Cir. 2001) (citation and internal quotation marks omitted). Although Young's conduct may not have been especially severe, there was unrefuted evidence of its frequency and pervasiveness. The jury heard testimony that Young continued to use the name "Manny" over El-Hakem's repeated objections. El-Hakem first objected to Young's use of "Manny" in a marketing meeting. Despite El-Hakem's objection, Young insisted on calling him "Manny" in a subsequent telephone conversation and e-mail. Approximately one month later, El-Hakem proposed in an e-mail that Young use Hakem, his last name, if he found Mamdouh difficult to pronounce. Rather than call him Hakem, Young suggested in his reply e-mail that El-Hakem be called "Hank." El-Hakem objected again. Despite El-Hakem's continued objections, Young persisted in calling El-Hakem "Manny" once a week in the Monday marketing meeting for approximately two months, and in e-mails at least twice a month thereafter. The conduct continued for almost a year, from May, 1999 to April, 2000. Because these incidents were frequent and consistent rather than isolated, a reasonable juror could conclude that El-Hakem's work environment was hostile.

Finally, we disagree with Defendants' contention that El-Hakem failed to present evidence of Young's discriminatory intent. In Defendants' view, there was no evidence of intent because "even if plaintiff felt the name 'Manny' had racial implications, there is no indication Mr. Young felt that way." However, the record is clear that Young intended to discriminate against El-Hakem's Arabic name in favor of a non-Arabic name, first by altering Mamdouh to "Manny" and then by changing Hakem to "Hank." Therefore, there was sufficient evidence of discriminatory intent to support the jury's verdict, and the district court properly denied Young's motion for judgment as a matter of law. . . .

The district court properly denied Young's motion for judgment as a matter of law on El-Hakem's intentional discrimination claim. Young's persistent reference to El-Hakem by a racially-motivated nickname supported the jury's finding of discrimination. The court also properly amended the judgment to hold BJY vicariously liable for racial discrimination, and acted within its discretion in declining to apportion the attorney's fees.

The statute that this case discusses, §1981, is part of the Civil Rights Act of 1866. The Act states:

> All persons within the jurisdiction of the United States shall have the same right in every State and Territory to make and enforce contracts, to sue, be parties, give evidence, and to the full and equal benefit of all laws and proceedings for the security of persons and property as is enjoyed by white citizens, and shall be subject to the like punishment, pains, penalties, taxes, licenses, and exactions of every kind, and to no other.

In 1989, the Supreme Court limited the applicability of this Act to the formation and enforcement of contracts, thus severely limiting employment discrimination suits where most of the discriminatory conduct occurs after the formation of the employment contract. Patterson v. McLean Credit Union, 491 U.S. 164, 109 S. Ct. 2363 (1989). Congress did not like this result and passed the Civil Rights Act of 1991, which expanded the scope of §1981. Section 1981(b) now states:

> For purposes of this section, the term "make and enforce contracts" includes the making, performance, modification, and termination of contacts, and the enjoyment of all benefits, privileges, terms, and condition of the contractual relationship.

Congress thus allowed employees to sue for wrongful termination and other discriminatory actions taken after the formation of the employment contract. Section 1981, unlike Title VII, discussed in the remedial section, does not have exceptions for employers with fewer than 15 employees.

This legislation reflects a strong concern with equal employment opportunity, and it is easy to see why: "private" discrimination in the employment context can have very onerous effects on minority groups. Private discrimination that does not involve employment, such as is common in clubs, might or might not have significant economic consequences, depending on the nature of the club. A Minnesota statute prohibiting sex discrimination in "places of public accommodation" had been applied to the Jaycees, a civic organization that restricted voting membership to men between the ages of 18 and 35. The Jaycees

Segregated Proms

Consider the article by Sara Corbett, A Prom Divided, N.Y. Times, May 24, 2009 (Magazine), at 24:

About now, high-school seniors everywhere slip into a glorious sort of limbo. Waiting out the final weeks of the school year, they begin rightfully to revel in the shared thrill of moving on. It is no different in south-central Georgia's Montgomery County, made up of a few small towns set between fields of wire grass and sweet onion. The music is turned up. Homework languishes. The future looms large. But for the 54 students in the class of 2009 at Montgomery County High School, so, too, does the past. On May 1 — a balmy Friday evening — the white students held their senior prom. And the following night — a balmy Saturday — the black students had theirs.

Racially segregated proms have been held in Montgomery County — where about two-thirds of the population is white — almost every year since its schools were integrated in 1971. Such proms are, by many accounts, longstanding traditions in towns across the rural South, though in recent years a number of communities have successfully pushed for change. When the actor Morgan Freeman offered to pay for last year's first-of-its-kind integrated prom at Charleston High School in Mississippi, his home state, the idea was quickly embraced by students — and rejected by a group of white parents, who held a competing "private" prom.... The senior proms held by Montgomery County High School students — referred to by many students as "the black-folks prom" and "the white-folks prom" — are organized outside school through student committees with the help of parents. All students are welcome at the black prom, though generally few if any white students show up. The white prom, students say, remains governed by a largely unspoken set of rules about who may come. Black members of the student council say they have asked school administrators about holding a single school-sponsored prom, but that, along with efforts to collaborate with white prom planners, has failed. According to Timothy Wiggs, the outgoing student council president and one of 21 black students graduating this year, "We just never get anywhere with it." Principal Luke Smith says the school has no plans to sponsor a prom, noting that when it did so in 1995, attendance was poor.

As discussed earlier, the law does not attempt to compel racial equality in friendships, marriages, or small social groups. Should it intervene when, as here, an entire school engages in a racially segregated activity?

argued that this statute interfered with their members' free association rights. In Roberts v. United States Jaycees, 468 U.S. 609, 104 S. Ct. 3244 (1984), the Supreme Court upheld application of the statute to the Jaycees. The Court reasoned that the core of the right of free association was marriage and family relationships, and if it extended to other relationships, they would have to be relatively small, selective, and secluded from others. Because the Jaycees had none of these traits, their constitutional rights had not been violated. Although the Court's rationale in the Jaycees case did not depend upon the economic consequences of discrimination by a club, it is interesting to notice that limiting protection of free association rights to marriage and family relationships, and possibly small, selective, and secluded clubs, corresponds to protecting discrimination decisions only when made by organizations unlikely to have significant economic effects.

Section Five
RACIAL EQUALITY AND THE ADMINISTRATIVE INSTRUMENT

A. Equality as a Limit

It is easy to see why the constitutional limits on racial discrimination must apply to the administrative instrument. If they did not, legislatures would be free to pass laws that were facially fair and then delegate their application to biased agencies. For this reason, early Supreme Court opinions made it clear that racial discrimination by administrative agencies was subject to the strict-scrutiny standard. Nevertheless, controversy concerning racial equality constraints frequently arises in the administrative instrument. At least in part, this results from the increasing significance of the administrative instrument.

YICK WO v. HOPKINS
Supreme Court of the United States, 1886
118 U.S. 356, 6 S. Ct. 1064

. . . The plaintiff in error, Yick Wo, on August 24, 1885, petitioned the supreme court of California for the writ of habeas corpus, alleging that he was illegally deprived of his personal liberty by the defendant as sheriff of the city and county of San Francisco. The sheriff made return to the writ that he held the petitioner in custody by virtue of a sentence of the police judge's court No. 2 of the city and county of San Francisco, whereby he was found guilty of a violation of certain ordinances of the board of supervisors of that county, and adjudged to pay a fine of $10, and, in default of payment, be imprisoned in the county jail at the rate of one day for each dollar of fine until said fine should be satisfied; and a commitment in consequence of non-payment of said fine.

The ordinances for the violation of which he had been found guilty are set out as follows:

Order No. 1,569, passed May 26, 1880, prescribing the kind of buildings in which laundries may be located.

"The people of the city and county of San Francisco do ordain as follows:

"Section 1. It shall be unlawful, from and after the passage of this order, for any person or persons to establish, maintain, or carry on a laundry, within the corporate limits of the city and county of San Francisco, without having first obtained the consent of the board of supervisors, except the same be located in a building constructed either of brick or stone."

"Sec. 2. It shall be unlawful for any person to erect, build, or maintain, or cause to be erected, built, or maintained, over or upon the roof of any building now erected, or which may hereafter be erected, within the limits of said city and county, any scaffolding, without first obtaining the written permission of the board of supervisors, which permit shall state fully for what purpose said scaffolding is to be erected and used, and such scaffolding shall not be used for any other purpose than that designated in such permit."

"Sec. 3. Any person who shall violate any of the provisions of this order shall be deemed guilty of a misdemeanor, and upon conviction thereof shall be punished by a fine of not more than one thousand dollars, or by imprisonment in the county jail not more than six months, or by both such fine and imprisonment."

Order No. 1,587, passed July 28, 1880, the following section:

"Sec. 68. It shall be unlawful, from and after the passage of this order, for any person or persons to establish, maintain, or carry on a laundry within the corporate limits of the city and county of San Francisco without having first obtained the consent of the board of supervisors, except the same be located in a building constructed either of brick or stone."

The following facts are also admitted on the record: That petitioner is a native of China, and came to California in 1861, and is still a subject of the emperor of China; that he has been engaged in the laundry business in the same premises and building for 22 years last past; that he had a license from the board of fire-wardens, dated March 3, 1884, from which it appeared "that the above-described premises have been inspected by the board of fire-wardens, and upon such inspection

said board found all proper arrangements for carrying on the business; that the stoves, washing and drying apparatus, and the appliances for heating smoothing-irons, are in good condition, and that their use is not dangerous to the surrounding property from fire, and that all proper precautions have been taken to comply with the provisions of order No. 1,617, defining 'the fire limits of the city and county of San Francisco, and making regulations concerning the erection and use of buildings in said city and county,' and of order No. 1,670, 'prohibiting the kindling, maintenance, and use of open fires in houses'; that he had a certificate from the health officer that the same premises had been inspected by him, and that he found that they were properly and sufficiently drained, and that all proper arrangements for carrying on the business of a laundry, without injury to the sanitary condition of the neighborhood, had been complied with; that the city license of the petitioner was in force, and expired October 1, 1885; and that the petitioner applied to the board of supervisors, June 1, 1885, for consent of said board to maintain and carry on his laundry, but that said board, on July 1, 1885, refused said consent." It is also admitted to be true, as alleged in the petition, that on February 24, 1880, "there were about 320 laundries in the city and county of San Francisco, of which about 240 were owned and conducted by subjects of China, and of the whole number, viz., 320, about 310 were constructed of wood, the same material that constitutes nine-tenths of the houses in the city of San Francisco. The capital thus invested by the subjects of China was not less than two hundred thousand dollars, and they paid annually for rent, license, taxes, gas, and water about one hundred and eighty thousand dollars." It is alleged in the petition that "your petitioner, and more than one hundred and fifty of his countrymen, have been arrested upon the charge of carrying on business without having such special consent, while those who are not subjects of China, and who are conducting eighty odd laundries under similar conditions, are left unmolested, and free to enjoy the enhanced trade and profits arising from this hurtful and unfair discrimination. The business of your petitioner, and of those of his countrymen similarly situated, is greatly impaired, and in many cases practically ruined, by this system of oppression to one kind of men, and favoritism to all others."

The statement therein contained as to the arrest, etc., is admitted to be true, with the qualification only that the 80–odd laundries referred to are in wooden buildings without scaffolds on the roofs. It is also admitted "that petitioner and 200 of his countrymen similarly situated petitioned the board of supervisors for permission to continue their business in the various houses which they had been occupying and using for laundries for more than twenty years, and such petitions were denied, and all the petitions of those who were not Chinese, with one exception of Mrs. Mary Meagles, were granted." . . .

MATTHEWS, J.: . . .

In the present cases, we are not obliged to reason from the probable to the actual, and pass upon the validity of the ordinances complained of, as tried merely by the opportunities which their terms afford, of unequal and unjust discrimination in their administration; for the cases present the ordinances in actual operation, and the facts shown establish an administration directed so exclusively against a particular class of persons as to warrant and require the conclusion that, whatever may have been the intent of the ordinances as adopted, they are applied by the public authorities charged with their administration, and thus representing the state itself, with a mind so unequal and oppressive as to amount to a practical denial by the state of that equal protection of the laws which is secured to the petitioners, as to all other persons, by the broad and benign provisions of the fourteenth amendment to the constitution of the United States. Though the law itself be fair on its face, and impartial in appliance, yet, if it is applied and administered by public authority with an evil eye and an unequal hand, so as practically to make unjust and illegal discriminations between persons in similar circumstances,

material to their rights, the denial of equal justice is still within the prohibition of the constitution. This principle of interpretation has been sanctioned by this court in Henderson v. Mayor of New York, 92 U.S. 259; Chy Luny v. Freeman, 92 U.S. 275; Ex parte Virginia, 100 U.S. 339; Neal v. Delaware, 103 U.S. 370; and Soon Hing v. Crowley, 113 U.S. 703; S.C. 5 Sup. Ct. Rep. 730.

The present cases, as shown by the facts disclosed in the record, are within this class. It appears that both petitioners have complied with every requisite deemed by the law, or by the public officers charged with its administration, necessary for the protection of neighboring property from fire, or as a precaution against injury to the public health. No reason whatever, except the will of the supervisors, is assigned why they should not be permitted to carry on, in the accustomed manner, their harmless and useful occupation, on which they depend for a livelihood; and while this consent of the supervisors is withheld from them, and from 200 others who have also petitioned, all of whom happen to be Chinese subjects, 80 others, not Chinese subjects, are permitted to carry on the same business under similar conditions. The fact of this discrimination is admitted. No reason for it is shown, and the conclusion cannot be resisted that no reason for it exists except hostility to the race and nationality to which the petitioners belong, and which, in the eye of the law, is not justified. The discrimination is therefore illegal, and the public administration which enforces it is a denial of the equal protection of the laws, and a violation of the fourteenth amendment of the constitution. The imprisonment of the petitioners is therefore illegal, and they must be discharged. To this end the judgment of the supreme court of California in the *Case of Yick Wo*, and that of the circuit court of the United States for the district of California in the *Case of Wo Lee*, are severally reversed, and the cases remanded, each to the proper court, with directions to discharge the petitioners from custody and imprisonment.

In *Yick Wo*, the administrative board followed a blatant course of discrimination and did not deny that it had done so. Presumably, most modern agencies would attempt to hide discriminatory actions. This means that a person who believes that racial discrimination is taking place may have difficulty proving its existence. The Supreme Court has held that simply showing disproportionate impact — that a greater percentage of whites were granted permits, received favorable rulings, or benefited from the adopted regulation — is not enough to warrant application of the strict-scrutiny standard. Instead, discriminatory purpose, or the *intent* to discriminate on the basis of race, must be shown before the agency is called upon to justify its actions. In Arlington Heights v. Metropolitan Housing Development Corp., 429 U.S. 252, 97 S. Ct. 555 (1977), the Court explained that a variety of factors could be used to show discriminatory purpose, including disproportionate impact, the historical background of the decision, the specific sequence of events leading up to the decision, procedural irregularities, unexpected or unusual decisions, and explanatory statements by members of the decisionmaking body.

Since *Arlington Heights*, few litigants have cleared the hurdle of showing discriminatory purpose. Two quite different explanations can be offered for the paucity of winning race discrimination claims: that very little discrimination persists, or that the legal standard for proving discrimination is too high.

MOOSE LODGE NO. 107 v. IRVIS
Supreme Court of the United States, 1972
407 U.S. 163, 92 S. Ct. 1965

Mr. Justice Rehnquist delivered the opinion of the Court:

Appellee Irvis, a Negro (hereafter appellee), was refused service by appellant Moose Lodge, a local branch of the national fraternal organization located in Harrisburg, Pennsylvania. Appellee then brought this action under 42 U.S.C. §1983 for injunctive relief in the United States District Court for the Middle District of Pennsylvania. He claimed that because the Pennsylvania liquor board had issued appellant Moose Lodge a private club license that authorized the sale of alcoholic beverages on its premises, the refusal of service to him was "state action" for the purposes of the Equal Protection Clause of the Fourteenth Amendment. He named both Moose Lodge and the Pennsylvania Liquor Authority as defendants, seeking injunctive relief that would have required the defendant liquor board to revoke Moose Lodge's license so long as it continued its discriminatory practices. Appellee sought no damages. . . .

Moose Lodge is a private club in the ordinary meaning of that term. It is a local chapter of a national fraternal organization having well-defined

requirements for membership. It conducts all of its activities in a building that is owned by it. It is not publicly funded. Only members and guests are permitted in any lodge of the order; one may become a guest only by invitation of a member or upon invitation of the house committee.

Appellee, while conceding the right of private clubs to choose members upon a discriminatory basis, asserts that the licensing of Moose Lodge to serve liquor by the Pennsylvania Liquor Control Board amounts to such state involvement with the club's activities as to make its discriminatory practices forbidden by the Equal Protection Clause of the Fourteenth Amendment. The relief sought and obtained by appellee in the District Court was an injunction forbidding the licensing by the liquor authority of Moose Lodge until it ceased its discriminatory practices. We conclude that Moose Lodge's refusal to serve food and beverages to a guest by reason of the fact that he was a Negro does not, under the circumstances here presented, violate the Fourteenth Amendment.

In 1883, this Court in The Civil Rights Cases, 109 U.S. 3, 3 S. Ct. 18, set forth the essential dichotomy between discriminatory action by the State, which is prohibited by the Equal Protection Clause, and private conduct, "however discriminatory or wrongful," against which that clause "erects no shield," Shelley v. Kraemer, 334 U.S. 1, 13, 68 S. Ct. 836, 842 (1948). That dichotomy has been subsequently reaffirmed in *Shelley v. Kraemer*, supra, and in Burton v. Wilmington Parking Authority, 365 U.S. 715, 81 S. Ct. 856 (1961).

While the principle is easily stated, the question of whether particular discriminatory conduct is private, on the one hand, or amounts to "state action," on the other hand, frequently admits of no easy answer. "Only by sifting facts and weighing circumstances can the nonobvious involvement of the State in private conduct be attributed its true significance." Burton v. Wilmington Parking Authority, supra, at 722, 81 S. Ct., at 860.

Our cases make clear that the impetus for the forbidden discrimination need not originate with the State if it is state action that enforces privately originated discrimination. *Shelley v. Kraemer*, supra. The Court held in *Burton v. Wilmington Parking Authority*, supra, that a private restaurant owner who refused service because of a customer's race violated the Fourteenth Amendment, where the restaurant was located in a building owned by a state-created parking authority and leased from the authority. The Court, after a comprehensive review of the relationship between the lessee and the parking authority concluded that the latter had "so far insinuated itself into a position of interdependence with Eagle [the restaurant owner] that it must be recognized as a joint participant in the challenged activity, which, on that account, cannot be considered to have been so 'purely private' as to fall without the scope of the Fourteenth Amendment." 365 U.S., at 725, 81 S. Ct., at 862.

The Court has never held, of course, that discrimination by an otherwise private entity would be violative of the Equal Protection Clause if the private entity receives any sort of benefit or service at all from the State, or if it is subject to state regulation in any degree whatever. Since state-furnished services include such necessities of life as electricity, water, and police and fire protection, such a holding would utterly emasculate the distinction between private as distinguished from

state conduct set forth in The Civil Rights Cases, supra, and adhered to in subsequent decisions. Our holdings indicate that where the impetus for the discrimination is private, the State must have "significantly involved itself with invidious discriminations," Reitman v. Mulkey, 387 U.S. 369, 380, 87 S. Ct. 1627, 1634 (1967), in order for the discriminatory action to fall within the ambit of the constitutional prohibition.

Our prior decisions dealing with discriminatory refusal of service in public eating places are significantly different factually from the case now before us. Peterson v. City of Greenville, 373 U.S. 244, 83 S. Ct. 1119 (1963), dealt with the trespass prosecution of persons who "sat in" at a restaurant to protest its refusal of service to Negroes. There the Court held that although the ostensible initiative for the trespass prosecution came from the proprietor, the existence of a local ordinance requiring segregation of races in such places was tantamount to the State having "commanded a particular result," 373 U.S., at 248, 83 S. Ct., at 1121. With one exception, which is discussed infra, there is no suggestion in this record that the Pennsylvania statutes and regulations governing the sale of liquor are intended either overtly or covertly to encourage discrimination. . . .

Here there is nothing approaching the symbiotic relationship between lessor and lessee that was present in *Burton*, where the private lessee obtained the benefit of locating in a building owned by the state-created parking authority, and the parking authority was enabled to carry out its primary public purpose of furnishing parking space by advantageously leasing portions of the building constructed for that purpose to commercial lessees such as the owner of the Eagle Restaurant. Unlike *Burton*, the Moose Lodge building is located on land owned by it, not by any public authority. Far from apparently holding itself out as a place of public accommodation, Moose Lodge quite ostentatiously proclaims the fact that it is not open to the public at large. Nor is it located and operated in such surroundings that although private in name, it discharges a function or performs a service that would otherwise in all likelihood be performed by the State. In short, while Eagle was a public restaurant in a public building, Moose Lodge is a private social club in a private building.

With the exception hereafter noted, the Pennsylvania Liquor Control Board plays absolutely no part in establishing or enforcing the membership or guest policies of the club that it licenses to serve liquor. There is no suggestion in this record that Pennsylvania law, either as written or as applied, discriminates against minority groups either in their right to apply for club licenses themselves or in their right to purchase and be served liquor in places of public accommodation. The only effect that the state licensing of Moose Lodge to serve liquor can be said to have on the right of any other Pennsylvanian to buy or be served liquor on premises other than those of Moose Lodge is that for some purposes club licenses are counted in the maximum number of licenses that may be issued in a given municipality. Basically each municipality has a quota of one retail license for each 1,500 inhabitants. Licenses issued to hotels, municipal golf courses, and airport restaurants are not counted in this quota, nor are club licenses until the maximum number of retail licenses is reached. Beyond that point, neither additional retail licenses nor additional club licenses may be issued so long as the number of issued and outstanding retail licenses remains at or above the statutory maximum.

The District Court was at pains to point out in its opinion what it considered to be the "pervasive" nature of the regulation of private clubs by the Pennsylvania Liquor Control Board. As that court noted, an applicant for a club license must make such physical alterations in its premises as the board may require, must file a list of the names and addresses of its members and employees, and must keep extensive financial records. The board is granted the right to inspect the licensed premises at any time when patrons, guests, or members are present.

However detailed this type of regulation may be in some particulars, it cannot be said to in any way foster or encourage racial discrimination. Nor can it be said to make the State in any realistic sense a partner or even a joint venturer in the club's enterprise. The limited effect of the prohibition against obtaining additional club licenses

when the maximum number of retail licenses allotted to a municipality has been issued, when considered together with the availability of liquor from hotel, restaurant, and retail licensees, falls far short of conferring upon club licensees a monopoly in the dispensing of liquor in any given municipality or in the State as a whole. We therefore hold that, with the exception hereafter noted, the operation of the regulatory scheme enforced by the Pennsylvania Liquor Control Board does not sufficiently implicate the State in the discriminatory guest policies of Moose Lodge to make the latter "state action" within the ambit of the Equal Protection Clause of the Fourteenth Amendment.

The District Court found that the regulations of the Liquor Control Board adopted pursuant to statute affirmatively require that "[e]very club licensee shall adhere to all of the provisions of its Constitution and By-Laws." Appellant argues that the purpose of this provision "is purely and simply and plainly the prevention of subterfuge," pointing out that the bona fides of a private club, as opposed to a place of public accommodation masquerading as a private club, is a matter with which the State Liquor Control Board may legitimately concern itself. Appellee concedes this to be the case, and expresses disagreement with the District Court on this point. There can be no doubt that the label "private club" can be and has been used to evade both regulations of state and local liquor authorities, and statutes requiring places of public accommodation to serve all persons without regard to race, color, religion, or national origin. This Court in Daniel v. Paul, 395 U.S. 298, 89 S. Ct. 1697 (1969), had occasion to address this issue in connection with the application of Title II of the Civil Rights Act of 1964, 78 Stat. 243, 42 U.S.C. §2000a et seq. . . .

Even though the Liquor Control Board regulation in question is neutral in its terms, the result of its application in a case where the constitution and bylaws of a club required racial discrimination would be to invoke the sanctions of the State to enforce a concededly discriminatory private rule. State action, for purposes of the Equal Protection Clause, may emanate from rulings of administrative and regulatory agencies as well as from legislative or judicial action. Robinson v. Florida, 378 U.S. 153, 156, 84 S. Ct. 1693, 1695 (1964). Shelley v. Kraemer, 334 U.S. 1, 68 S. Ct. 836 (1948), makes it clear that the application of state sanctions to enforce such a rule would violate the Fourteenth Amendment. Although the record before us is not as clear as one would like, appellant has not persuaded us that the District Court should have denied any and all relief.

Appellee was entitled to a decree enjoining the enforcement of §113.09 of the regulations promulgated by the Pennsylvania Liquor Control Board insofar as that regulation requires compliance by Moose Lodge with provisions of its constitution and bylaws containing racially discriminatory provisions. He was entitled to no more. The judgment of the District Court is reversed, and the cause remanded with instructions to enter a decree in conformity with this opinion.

Reversed and remanded.

MR. JUSTICE DOUGLAS, with whom MR. JUSTICE MARSHALL joins, dissenting:

My view of the First Amendment and the related guarantees of the Bill of Rights is that they create a zone of privacy which precludes government from interfering with private clubs or groups. The associational rights which our system honors permit all white, all black, all brown, and all yellow clubs to be formed. They also permit all Catholic, all Jewish, or all agnostic clubs to be established. Government may not tell a man or woman who his or her associates must be. The individual can be as selective as he desires. So the fact that the Moose Lodge allows only Caucasians to join or come as guests is constitutionally irrelevant, as is the decision of the Black Muslims to admit to their services only members of their race.

The problem is different, however, where the public domain is concerned. I have indicated in Garner v. Louisiana, 368 U.S. 157, 82 S. Ct. 248, and Lombard v. Louisiana, 373 U.S. 267, 83 S. Ct. 1122, that where restaurants or other facilities serving the public are concerned and licenses are obtained from the State for operating the business, the "public" may not be defined by the

proprietor to include only people of his choice; nor may a state or municipal service be granted only to some.

Those cases are not precisely apposite, however, for a private club, by definition, is not in the public domain. And the fact that a private club gets some kind of permit from the State or municipality does not make it ipso facto a public enterprise or undertaking, any more than the grant to a householder of a permit to operate an incinerator puts the householder in the public domain. We must, therefore, examine whether there are special circumstances involved in the Pennsylvania scheme which differentiate the liquor license possessed by Moose Lodge from the incinerator permit.

Pennsylvania has a state store system of alcohol distribution. Resale is permitted by hotels, restaurants, and private clubs which all must obtain licenses from the Liquor Control Board. The scheme of regulation is complete and pervasive; and the state courts have sustained many restrictions on the licensees. See Tahiti Bar Inc. Liquor License Case, 395 Pa. 355, 150 A.2d 112. Once a license is issued the licensee must comply with many detailed requirements or risk suspension or revocation of the license. Among these requirements is Regulation §113.09 which says: "Every club licensee shall adhere to all of the provisions of its Constitution and By-laws." This regulation means, as applied to Moose Lodge, that it must adhere to the racially discriminatory provision of the Constitution of its Supreme Lodge that "[t]he membership of lodges shall be composed of male persons of the Caucasian or White race above the age of twenty-one years, and not married to someone of any other than the Caucasian or White race, who are of good moral character, physically and mentally normal, who shall profess a belief in a Supreme Being."

It is argued that this regulation only aims at the prevention of subterfuge and at enforcing Pennsylvania's differentiation between places of public accommodation and bona fide private clubs. It is also argued that the regulation only gives effect to the constitutionally protected rights of privacy and of association. But I cannot so read the regulation. While those other purposes are embraced in it, so is the restrictive membership clause. And we have held that "a State is responsible for the discriminatory act of a private party when the State, by its law, has compelled the act." Adickes v. S.H. Kress & Co., 398 U.S. 144, 170, 90 S. Ct. 1598, 1615. See Peterson v. City of Greenville, 373 U.S. 244, 248, 83 S. Ct. 1119, 1121. It is irrelevant whether the law is statutory, or an administrative regulation. Robinson v. Florida, 378 U.S. 153, 156, 84 S. Ct. 1693, 1695. And it is irrelevant whether the discriminatory act was instigated by the regulation, or was independent of it. Peterson v. City of Greenville, supra. The result, as I see it, is the same as though Pennsylvania had put into its liquor licenses a provision that the license may not be used to dispense liquor to blacks, browns, yellows — or atheists or agnostics. Regulation §113.09 is thus an invidious form of state action.

Were this regulation the only infirmity in Pennsylvania's licensing scheme, I would perhaps agree with the majority that the appropriate relief would be a decree enjoining its enforcement. But there is another flaw in the scheme not so easily cured. Liquor licenses in Pennsylvania, unlike driver's licenses, or marriage licenses, are not freely available to those who meet racially neutral qualifications. There is a complex quota system, which the majority accurately describes. What the majority neglects to say is that the quota for Harrisburg, where Moose Lodge No. 107 is located, has been full for many years. No more club licenses may be issued in that city.

This state-enforced scarcity of licenses restricts the ability of blacks to obtain liquor, for liquor is commercially available *only* at private clubs for a significant portion of each week. Access by blacks to places that serve liquor is further limited by the fact that the state quota is filled. A group desiring to form a nondiscriminatory club which would serve blacks must purchase a license held by an existing club, which can exact a monopoly price for the transfer. The availability of such a license is speculative at best, however, for, as Moose Lodge itself concedes, without a liquor license a fraternal organization would be hard pressed to survive.

Thus, the State of Pennsylvania is putting the weight of its liquor license, concededly a valued and important adjunct to a private club, behind racial discrimination. . . .

I would affirm the judgment below.

[Justice Brennan, joined by Justice Marshall, also filed a dissenting opinion.]

If an administrative body could issue only one license — perhaps to decide what company should operate a natural monopoly such as a public utility — it seems clear that a decision to issue the license to a racially discriminatory company would not be constitutional. Put differently, if a governmental body knowingly chooses to deprive a racial minority of all access to some significant good or service, that seems intolerably close to delegating discrimination desired by the state to a private party. The majority opinion does not suggest otherwise. But this poses a question of line drawing. If the same governmental body can issue only *two* licenses, and chooses to issue *one* to a discriminatory company, that seems like vicarious discrimination as well. It is hard to see how the line drawn by the Court — or any line other than that of scarce versus infinite licenses — can be defended.

One reason the Supreme Court may have balked at the dissent's seemingly logical conclusion is that if the dissent's view had prevailed, other constitutional limitations may also have been argued to apply to Moose Lodge? The Fourteenth Amendment, in addition to assuring "equal protection of the law," also provides that no state shall "deprive any person of life, liberty, or property, without due process of law." Under the approach of the dissent, Moose Lodge might have been subject to the due process clause as well. That in turn might have meant that Moose Lodge would have to hold hearings before firing an employee or fining a member. Some commentators and lower courts have tried to solve this problem by being very generous in finding "state action" when the equal protection clause is at stake, but much more strict when a due process challenge is raised to a private party's action. The Supreme Court, however, has never endorsed different standards for the different clauses.

B. Equality as the Goal

In Chapter 3, we saw that the administrative instrument operates to prevent grievances from arising and to resolve disputes before they reach a court. Most of the examples of the administrative instrument we have thus far examined involve the setting of regulatory standards or the enforcement of those standards. Although these techniques of the administrative instrument are often used to promote racial equality (for example, by the Equal Employment Opportunity Commission), we shall not consider them here. You may recall that the administrative instrument also has less overtly coercive techniques, including the power to investigate, the power to publicize unfavorable findings, and the power to encourage self-regulation. These we shall consider.

The United States Civil Rights Commission exemplifies the use of these techniques because it has no power to adjudicate or take any action that will affect an individual's rights. Established in 1957, the Commission was designed to terminate two years later upon the submission of a final report, but amendments have repeatedly extended its life. Below is an example of the work that the Civil Rights Commission does. The Commission regularly publishes informational studies on the state of equal protection and of discrimination in the United States. The Commission not only studies race discrimination but also issues relating to religion, sex, age, handicap, and national origin.

THE ECONOMIC STAGNATION OF THE BLACK MIDDLE CLASS

Briefing Before the United States Commission on Civil Rights
Held in Washington, D.C., July 15, 2005
On July 15, 2005, a panel of experts briefed members of the U.S. Commission on Civil Rights on explanations for and consequences of stagnation in the growth of America's black middle class. Professor Douglas Besharov from the University of Maryland School of Public Affairs and Senior Scholar at the American Enterprise Institute led the discussion. Dr. Harry Holzer, Professor of Public Policy, Georgetown Public Policy Institute, and Dr. Bart Landry, Professor of Sociology, University of Maryland, College Park and author of *The New Black Middle Class*, also made presentations and offered their expertise. The briefing was held in Room 2226 of the Rayburn House Office Building in Washington, D.C., and was televised by C–SPAN.

Expanding the African-American Middle Class:
Improving Labor Market Outcomes
By Harry J. Holzer

The data presented by Doug Besharov shows that, despite some progress during the 1990s, the share of African-Americans joining the middle class in the U.S. has stagnated over the past 20 to 30 years. At least some of these trends are closely tied to changes in the labor market for Americans with different levels of educational attainment in that time period. What opportunities currently exist for blacks in the labor market, and how do these vary with their level of education? What explains the remaining gaps between whites and blacks, and how might the opportunities for blacks be improved over time?

The strong effects of education on employment and earnings reflect a labor market that puts a much greater premium on education, and skills more broadly, than in the past; indeed, the differences in earnings across education groups have grown greatly over time for all workers in the U.S. The continuing education gaps between young blacks and whites clearly contribute to earnings gaps between them as well. Blacks continue to drop out of high school in greater numbers than whites, and they enroll and complete college less frequently.

The gaps in earnings between black and white men, even with the same education levels, partly reflect gaps in cognitive skills (as measured by test scores); but other factors are also relevant. A lack of early work experience, persistent discrimination, weak informal networks, and geographic mismatches between jobs and workers contribute to the poor employment experience of black men. Among other effects, these factors limit their access to the better-paying jobs in construction, manufacturing, transportation and some parts of the service sector that will continue to be available to those without college diplomas.

Employment and earnings trends for black females have been much more positive since the 1990's than for males; indeed, the employment of black women is similar to or higher than that of white women in each educational category, while their annual earnings are fairly comparable as well. Only the fact that their educational attainment lags behind that of whites prevents them from achieving parity.

The positive employment trends since the 1990's for less-educated females reflect welfare reform, the growth of work supports (such as the Earned Income Tax Credit) and a strong economy during that time period. In contrast, the continuing decline in work activity for less educated black men reflects, among other factors, the explosive growth in the number of young men with criminal records in the 1990's, and perhaps the tendency of the child support enforcement system to deter regular employment among low-income black men. These forces mostly impact men and women well below the middle-class threshold; but they also will limit the chances of *children* in lower-income black families to enter the middle class in the future.

But, even at higher levels of education, black women have achieved greater parity in earnings and employment with whites than have black men. The fact that young black women are now completing high school and enrolling in college at substantially higher rates than black men also raises concerns about future trends in the growth of the black middle class. The employment difficulties of black men likely contribute to the growth of female-headed families over the past few decades. Scholars still debate the extent to which the shrinking pool of "marriageable men" contributes to the growth of female headship in the black community, though few doubt that it plays some role. Clearly, the growth of families with only one potential earner in the black community limits the ability of many black families today, and their children tomorrow, to join the middle class.

Statement of Commissioner Michael J. Yaki on The Stagnation of the Black Middle Class

It remains a fact that today, more than 50 years after the *Brown* decision, and 40 years after the passage of the landmark Civil Rights and Voting Rights Acts, the African–American community has still not reached the economic parity and equality promised when the legal walls separating them from economic prosperity were torn down. What remains, therefore, is a lesson in what our government and society must continue to do to remedy past discrimination and combat present discrimination.

Unfortunately, our government, particularly the Administration, seeks to simply start from the premise that we are all equal — a noble sentiment in spirit — without accounting for the history of discrimination and the impact that it has had on the African-American community. Yet the mere fact that we have a briefing on the stagnation of the African-American middle class must suggest that barriers — whether they are economic or educational — remain for this community and that equality, while in spirit true, is in fact more elusive than we care to admit.

But we must ask more than the question of the stagnation of the middle class. We must also ask what we can do to lift more out of the middle class and into the highest socioeconomic strata of our society. It is not enough to say we need better guidance counselors in our high schools to facilitate the growth of the African-American middle class. In fact, I become suspicious that the guidance counselors that the Administration and their conservative shock troops talk about are people who will divert African-American students into what they believe are more "realistic" or "achievable" colleges and trade schools. Perhaps it is my natural suspicion as a public official, yet it comes on the heels of several "academic" reports claiming that the elite major universities should not engage in affirmative action because it sets unrealistic standards for African-American students. "Guidance counselors" is not an adequate answer to a complex problem with roots over two hundred years old in the history of this country.

I would submit, instead, that it should be our urgent and solemn duty, as a country, to continue such programs and create and innovate new programs that are aimed at enhancing the economic prosperity of African-Americans, particularly African-American business owners. Rather than terminate, as the Administration proposes, we should expand affirmative action programs in federal contracting; rather than weaken, we should reinvigorate Community Reinvestment Act obligations of financial institutions to create better access

> to capital and credit for the African-American small businesses and to assist in efforts to rebuild neighborhoods through aggressive home lending; and instead of cutting block grant funding for our cities and communities, we need to recognize that we must continue to invest in programs that enrich and expand the opportunities for youth.
>
> Talking about a problem and acting upon a problem are two different things altogether. It is a hallmark of this Administration that it has chosen to do the former, and ignored the policy mandates of the latter.

This report is critical of the Bush Administration and even uses the term "conservative shock troops" to describe the Administration's supporters. Some critics have argued that this is not an appropriate way for an administrative agency to act, while defenders have argued that the Commission is necessary to check and balance the party in power. Not surprisingly, at times, membership in the Commission has been controversial. Members of the Commission are appointed by the President, the President pro tempore of the Senate, and the Speaker of the House of Representatives; of the eight members, no more than four may be from the same political party. The membership guidelines for the Commission thus specifically address the potential for partisan appointments, though they may not eliminate it.

In addition to being criticized for partisanship, the Commission has also been criticized for not representing a full array of racial and ethnic backgrounds, which many argue may affect the direction and legitimacy of the Commission's work. From a quite different perspective, others have argued that it is time to disband the Civil Rights Commission because it has served its purpose. Such views are not new, as the following quote illustrates:

> When a man has emerged from slavery, and by the aid of beneficent legislation has shaken off the inseparable concomitants of that state, there must be some stage in the progress of his elevation when he takes the rank of a mere citizen, and ceases to be the special favorite of the laws.

This statement appears in The Civil Rights Cases, 109 U.S. 3, 25, 3 S. Ct. 18, 31 (1883). Certainly it was a ludicrous description of the time when written.

Section Six
RACIAL EQUALITY AND THE PUBLIC-BENEFIT INSTRUMENT

A. Racial Equality as a Limit

You do not have to take a course about law to know that a state could not decide to provide education only for white students — or even provide separate education systems for white and black students. Virtually all Americans are aware of the Supreme Court's decision in *Brown v. Board of Education*, which you read in Chapter 4 and which outlawed segregated schools.

By now you can guess that restricting to whites other pubic benefits, such as social security, job programs, or police services, would also be unconstitutional. Statutes restricting public benefits based on racial classifications are inherently suspect. The Supreme Court recognized that "[d]istinctions between citizens solely because of their ancestry are by their very nature odious to a free people whose institutions are founded upon the doctrine of equality." Hirabayashi v. United States, 320 U.S. 81, 100, 63 S. Ct. 1375, 1385 (1943). Classifications based on race will receive the highest standard of judicial review, strict scrutiny. (This heightened standard was first mentioned in what is probably the most famous footnote in constitutional law, footnote four of United States v. Carolene Products Co., 304 U.S. 144, 152 n.4, 58 S. Ct. 778, 783 n.4 (1938). The *Carolene Products* footnote suggested that statutes involving "discrete and insular minorities" receive a "more searching judicial inquiry.")

The more difficult question, on which the Court has charted a less than even course, is whether racial equality limits the public-benefit instrument even when the goal of unequal treatment is the remedying of prior disadvantage.

REMEDYING RACIAL DISCRIMINATION IN INDUSTRY

Fullilove v. Klutznick, 448 U.S. 448, 100 S. Ct. 2758 (1980), was the first Supreme Court case to address a statute designed to remedy racial discrimination in private industry. The statute at issue in *Fullilove* was a federal spending bill from 1977 that required 10 percent of federal funding for public works to go to minority-owned companies. The "minority business enterprise" (MBE) provision defined a minority-owned business as "a business at least 50 per centum of which is owned by minority group members [and] minority group members are citizens of the United States who are Negroes, Spanish-speaking, Orientals, Indians, Eskimos, and Aleuts." The MBE provision was aimed at remedying the longstanding barriers preventing minority-owned businesses from accessing public works contracts. The Supreme Court found that both the objectives and the means used to accomplish these objectives were constitutional exercises of the legislative and remedial power of Congress. The Court held that, when acting in the remedial context, Congress did not have to be "color-blind," but could make "limited" use of set-aside provisions. In response to the charge that innocent nonminority businesses were burdened by the statute, the Court stated:

> The actual "burden" shouldered by nonminority firms is relatively light in this connection when we consider the scope of this public works program as compared with overall construction contracting opportunities. Moreover, although we may assume that the complaining parties are innocent of any past

discriminatory conduct, it was within the congressional power to act on the assumption that in the past some nonminority businesses may have reaped competitive benefit over the years from the virtual exclusion of minority firms from these contracting opportunities.

The dissenters in *Fullilove* would have found this an impermissible classification based on race.

Nearly a decade later, in City of Richmond v. J.A. Croson Co., 488 U.S. 469, 109 S. Ct. 706 (1989), the Supreme Court rejected the city of Richmond's minority set-aside program. Richmond's program required nonminority-owned primary contractors awarded municipal contracts to subcontract out at least 30 percent of their contract price to MBEs. The language defining "minority" was exactly the same as that in *Fullilove*. While there was no direct evidence of past racial discrimination by the city, 50 percent of the city was African American, but only 0.67 percent of the city's construction contracts had previously been awarded to MBEs. This vast discrepancy was argued to be the result of discrimination within the construction industry as a whole, as well as within the city, state, and across the nation. Nevertheless, the Supreme Court found the program unconstitutional under the Equal Protection Clause. The Court applied the strict-scrutiny standard—which it had not done in *Fullilove*—and concluded that the program failed that standard because the city had failed to show a compelling interest supporting the racial classification. In the majority's view, remedying past discrimination *by the city itself* would have constituted a compelling interest, but there was no evidence of wrongdoing by the city. While there was evidence of a desire to remedy the effects of past industry-wide discrimination, as well as general societal discrimination, that motivation was not, according to the majority, a compelling interest:

> To accept Richmond's claim that past societal discrimination alone can serve as the basis for rigid racial preferences would be to open the door to competing claims for "remedial relief" for every disadvantaged group. The dream of a Nation of equal citizens in a society where race is irrelevant to personal opportunity and achievement would be lost in a mosaic of shifting preferences based on inherently unmeasurable claims of past wrongs. "Courts would be asked to evaluate the extent of the prejudice and consequent harm suffered by various minority groups. Those whose societal injury is thought to exceed some arbitrary level of tolerability then would be entitled to preferential classifications ...." [Regents of University of California v. Bakke, 438 U.S. 265, 296–97, 98 S. Ct. 2733, 2751 (1978)] (Powell, J.). We think such a result would be contrary to both the letter and spirit of a constitutional provision whose central command is equality.

The Court also found that the program failed the second prong of the strict-scrutiny test, narrow tailoring. In the Court's view, the program was not narrowly tailored because the 30 percent goal "rests upon the 'completely unrealistic' assumption that minorities will choose a particular trade in lockstep proportion to their representation in the local population." The Court also criticized the determination of which groups to include within the program, noting that there was no evidence of past discrimination against any of the other racial groups included, such as Eskimos or Aleuts. The dissents to the decision expressed concerns that the *Croson* decision was a step backward in the Court's affirmative action jurisprudence.

The following case of *Adarand Constructors, Inc. v. Pena* answers a question that *Croson*, read with *Fullilove*, left open: should federal remedial programs be judged by a more lenient standard than are state remedial programs? One reason to think the standards might be different is that the Fourteenth Amendment's Equal Protection Clause is aimed at the states; there is no analogous provision constraining the federal government, although even prior to *Adarand*, the Court had held that the Fifth Amendment's Due Process Clause (which is aimed at the federal government) does have "an equal protection component." Moreover, the federal government is given power in Section Five of the Fourteenth Amendment to enforce the provisions of the Amendment; some commentators had argued that this power should give the federal government more leeway when it acts for remedial purposes. *Adarand* rejects these possible distinctions.

ADARAND CONSTRUCTORS, INC. v. PENA

Supreme Court of the United States, 1995
515 U.S. 200, 115 S. Ct. 2097

JUSTICE O'CONNOR delivered the opinion of the Court in part:

Petitioner Adarand Constructors, Inc., claims that the Federal Government's practice of giving general contractors on Government projects a financial incentive to hire subcontractors controlled by "socially and economically disadvantaged individuals," and in particular, the Government's use of race-based presumptions in identifying such individuals, violates the equal protection component of the Fifth Amendment's Due Process Clause. The Court of Appeals rejected Adarand's claim. We conclude, however, that courts should analyze cases of this kind under a different standard of review than the one the Court of Appeals applied. We therefore vacate the Court of Appeals' judgment and remand the case for further proceedings.

In 1989, the Central Federal Lands Highway Division (CFLHD), which is part of the United States Department of Transportation (DOT), awarded the prime contract for a highway construction project in Colorado to Mountain Gravel & Construction Company. Mountain Gravel then solicited bids from subcontractors for the guardrail portion of the contract. Adarand, a Colorado-based highway construction company specializing in guardrail work, submitted the low bid. Gonzales Construction Company also submitted a bid.

The prime contract's terms provide that Mountain Gravel would receive additional compensation if it hired subcontractors certified as small businesses controlled by "socially and economically disadvantaged individuals," App. 24. Gonzales is certified as such a business; Adarand is not. Mountain Gravel awarded the subcontract to Gonzales, despite Adarand's low bid, and Mountain Gravel's Chief Estimator has submitted an affidavit stating that Mountain Gravel would have accepted Adarand's bid, had it not been for the additional payment it received by hiring Gonzales instead. Id., at 28–31. Federal law requires that a subcontracting clause similar to the one used here must appear in most federal agency contracts . . . .

Respondents urge that "the Subcontracting Compensation Clause program is . . . a program based on *disadvantage*, not on race," and thus that it is subject only to "the most relaxed judicial scrutiny." Brief for Respondents 26. To the extent that the statutes and regulations involved in this case are race neutral, we agree. Respondents concede, however, that "the race-based rebuttable presumption used in some certification determinations under the Subcontracting Compensation Clause" is subject to some heightened level of scrutiny. Id., at 27. The parties disagree as to what that level should be. . . .

Adarand's claim arises under the Fifth Amendment to the Constitution, which provides that "No person shall . . . be deprived of life, liberty, or property, without due process of law." Although this Court has always understood that Clause to provide some measure of protection against *arbitrary* treatment by the Federal Government, it is not as explicit a guarantee of *equal* treatment as the Fourteenth Amendment, which provides that "No *State* shall . . . deny to any person within its jurisdiction the equal protection of the laws" (emphasis added). Our cases have accorded varying degrees of significance to the difference in the language of those two Clauses. We think it necessary to revisit the issue here.

Through the 1940's, this Court had routinely taken the view in non-race-related cases that, "unlike the Fourteenth Amendment, the Fifth contains no equal protection clause and it provides no guaranty against discriminatory legislation by Congress." [The Court discussed the history of the standard used in cases brought under the Fifth Amendment and the Fourteenth Amendment, which had increasingly used the same standard.] Thus, in 1975, the Court stated explicitly that "this Court's approach to Fifth Amendment equal protection claims has always been precisely the same as to equal protection claims under the Fourteenth Amendment." . . .

. . . A majority of the Court in *Croson* held that "the standard of review under the Equal Protection Clause is not dependent on the race of those

burdened or benefited by a particular classification," and that the single standard of review for racial classifications should be "strict scrutiny." . . .

With *Croson*, the Court finally agreed that the Fourteenth Amendment requires strict scrutiny of all race-based action by state and local governments. But *Croson* of course had no occasion to declare what standard of review the Fifth Amendment requires for such action taken by the Federal Government. . . .

Despite lingering uncertainty in the details, however, the Court's cases through *Croson* had established three general propositions with respect to governmental racial classifications. First, skepticism: " 'Any preference based on racial or ethnic criteria must necessarily receive a most searching examination.' " Second, consistency: "The standard of review under the Equal Protection Clause is not dependent on the race of those burdened or benefited by a particular classification." And third, congruence: "Equal protection analysis in the Fifth Amendment area is the same as that under the Fourteenth Amendment." Taken together, these three propositions lead to the conclusion that any person, of whatever race, has the right to demand that any governmental actor subject to the Constitution justify any racial classification subjecting that person to unequal treatment under the strictest judicial scrutiny. . . .

. . . Accordingly, we hold today that all racial classifications, imposed by whatever federal, state, or local governmental actor, must be analyzed by a reviewing court under strict scrutiny. In other words, such classifications are constitutional only if they are narrowly tailored measures that further compelling governmental interests. . . .

Accordingly, the judgment of the Court of Appeals is vacated, and the case is remanded for further proceedings consistent with this opinion.

JUSTICE SCALIA, concurring in part and concurring in the judgment:

In my view, government can never have a "compelling interest" in discriminating on the basis of race in order to "make up" for past racial discrimination in the opposite direction. Individuals who have been wronged by unlawful racial discrimination should be made whole; but under our Constitution there can be no such thing as either a creditor or a debtor race. That concept is alien to the Constitution's focus upon the individual . . . . To pursue the concept of racial entitlement — even for the most admirable and benign of purposes — is to reinforce and preserve for future mischief the way of thinking that produced race slavery, race privilege and race hatred. In the eyes of government, we are just one race here. It is American.

It is unlikely, if not impossible, that the challenged program would survive under this understanding of strict scrutiny, but I am content to leave that to be decided on remand.

[Justices Stevens, Souter, Ginsburg, and Breyer dissented.]

Given the history of racial discrimination, the question arises whether African Americans (or Latinos or Native Americans) can ever catch up with whites without some kind of compensatory programs. Some writers have drawn an analogy to a foot race: if certain runners are forced to carry heavy weights for the first half of the race, removing those weights in the middle of the race does not equalize the chances of all the runners. Opponents of affirmative action argue that America should be a meritocracy, where rewards and admission are based on individual achievement. But the skills that are rewarded are mainly tied to the family the child is born into. This makes racial discrimination a more difficult problem to remedy than gender discrimination. If we could end all discrimination, the problem of gender inequality would disappear within one generation;

Required
No Legislation
Optional / limited
Forbidden

Educational Segregation in the US Prior to Brown v. Board of Education

The Persistence of Racial Associations in the Absence of Racial Hostility

Sheri Lynn Johnson, Litigating for Racial Fairness After *McCleskey v. Kemp*, 39 Colum. Hum. Rts. L. Rev. 178, 191-92 (2007) (footnotes omitted), observed:

The new research on implicit attitudes is designed to bypass the normal screening that a person who recognizes racial prejudice as bad — or at least socially undesirable — so that attitudes can be accurately measured. The biggest collection of data here has been gathered using the implicit attitudes test, or "IAT," which more than a million Americans have taken. IATs are premised on the fact that if a person "automatically" associates one thing with another, then it will be easier for him or her to pair those two things; put differently, we can measure how long it takes a person to pair two things, and how many mistakes he or she makes, and then compare it to how long it takes that person to pair two other things. So the classical measurement is: How long does it take a person to pair black and good on the one hand, and white and bad on the other, *as compared to* the amount of time it takes that person to pair white and good, and black and bad. It turns out that, measured by those response times, about 80 percent of white Americans have a moderate or strong association of black with bad. Education doesn't matter; law students

do the same. Georgia defense lawyers and habeas lawyers also show the same pattern, as do the judges we have tested. Interestingly enough, these patterns are only weakly correlated with explicit attitudes, meaning the attitudes a person would consciously endorse. I should add that as a whole, African Americans are neutral in their associations between black or white and good or bad, though there is individual variation. Asian Americans look similar to white Americans in their responses and Latinos are in between white and black Americans.

A second form of measuring automatic reactions comes from what are called "the shooter studies." These come in a couple of forms, but basically, the subject sees a black or white person with either a gun or a tool in his hand and has to decide very quickly whether or not to shoot. It turns out that most people shoot black targets too often — they mistake tools for guns. And they also shoot too *few* white targets — they mistake guns for tools. Interestingly, both black and white subjects show these tendencies.

How can the law take account of these persistent racial biases? On the other hand, if the law ignores such biases, will that delay the achievement of racial equality?

women now in the workforce might never "catch up," but those entering the workforce after gender discrimination had been eliminated would suffer no handicap. Racial inequality is more resistant to change because the effects of discrimination against an African American are passed on to his or her children.

B. Equality as the Goal

Croson and *Adarand* held that classifications based on race — whether remedial or not — must be narrowly tailored (or necessary to) the furtherance of a compelling governmental interest to survive strict scrutiny. Lawsuits attempting to overturn affirmative action plans have forced the Court to specify which state interests qualify as compelling enough to justify the use of affirmative action programs. As you read in the last section, affirmative action programs necessary to remedy identified, specific past discrimination by a particular governmental entity are constitutionally permissible. Programs remedying generalized, long-term societal discrimination are not permissible.

In this section we shall discuss remedies for discrimination in education. As reflected in the map, almost half of the United States engaged in segregated education in the past. The transition from segregation has been an ongoing battle, with educational opportunities for minorities still lagging behind those for whites. The cases in this section consider possible justifications for affirmative action programs in education, and in doing so will demonstrate what the Court means by "narrowly tailored."

WYGANT v. JACKSON BOARD OF EDUCATION
Supreme Court of the United States, 1986
476 U.S. 267, 106 S. Ct. 1842

JUSTICE POWELL announced the judgment of the Court:

This case presents the question whether a school board, consistent with the Equal Protection Clause, may extend preferential protection against layoffs to some of its employees because of their race or national origin.

In 1972 the Jackson Board of Education, because of racial tension in the community that extended to its schools, considered adding a layoff provision to the Collective Bargaining Agreement (CBA) between the Board and the Jackson Education Association (Union) that would protect employees who were members of certain minority groups against layoffs. The Board and the Union eventually approved a new provision, Article XII of the CBA, covering layoffs. It stated:

In the event that it becomes necessary to reduce the number of teachers through layoff from employment by the Board, teachers with the most seniority in the district shall be retained, except that at no time will there be a greater percentage of minority personnel laid off than the current percentage of minority personnel employed at the time of the layoff. In no event will the

number given notice of possible layoff be greater than the number of positions to be eliminated. Each teacher so affected will be called back in reverse order for positions for which he is certificated maintaining the above minority balance.

When layoffs became necessary in 1974, it was evident that adherence to the CBA would result in the layoff of tenured nonminority teachers while minority teachers on probationary status were retained. Rather than complying with Article XII, the Board retained the tenured teachers and laid off probationary minority teachers, thus failing to maintain the percentage of minority personnel that existed at the time of the layoff. The Union, together with two minority teachers who had been laid off, brought suit in federal court, claiming that the Board's failure to adhere to the layoff provision violated the Equal Protection Clause of the Fourteenth Amendment and Title VII of the Civil Rights Act of 1964....

... [T]he court held that Article XII was permissible, despite its discriminatory effect on nonminority teachers, as an attempt to remedy the effects of societal discrimination.

After [that court decision], the Board adhered to Article XII. As a result, during the 1976–1977 and 1981–1982 school years, nonminority teachers were laid off, while minority teachers with less seniority were retained. The displaced nonminority teachers, petitioners here, brought suit in Federal District Court, alleging violations of the Equal Protection Clause, Title VII, 42 U.S.C. §1983, and other federal and state statutes.... [T]he court decided that the racial preferences were permissible under the Equal Protection Clause as an attempt to remedy societal discrimination by providing "role models" for minority schoolchildren, and upheld the constitutionality of the layoff provision.

The Court of Appeals for the Sixth Circuit affirmed, largely adopting the reasoning and language of the District Court. 746 F.2d 1152 (1984). We granted certiorari to resolve the important issue of the constitutionality of race-based layoffs by public employers. We now reverse.

Petitioners' central claim is that they were laid off because of their race in violation of the Equal Protection Clause of the Fourteenth Amendment. Decisions by faculties and administrators of public schools based on race or ethnic origin are reviewable under the Fourteenth Amendment. This Court has "consistently repudiated '[distinctions] between citizens solely because of their ancestry' as being 'odious to a free people whose institutions are founded upon the doctrine of equality,'" Loving v. Virginia, 388 U.S. 1, 11, 87 S. Ct. 1817, 1823 (1967), quoting Hirabayashi v. United States, 320 U.S. 81, 100, 63 S. Ct. 1375, 1385 (1943). "Racial and ethnic distinctions of any sort are inherently suspect and thus call for the most exacting judicial examination." University of California Regents v. Bakke, 438 U.S. 265, 291, 98 S. Ct. 2733, 2748 (1978).

The Court has recognized that the level of scrutiny does not change merely because the challenged classification operates against a group that historically has not been subject to governmental discrimination.... "Any preference based on racial or ethnic criteria must necessarily receive a most searching examination to make sure that it does not conflict with constitutional guarantees." Fullilove v. Klutznick, 448 U.S. 448, 491, 100 S. Ct. 2758, 2781 (1980) (opinion of Burger, C.J.). There are two prongs to this examination. First, any racial classification "must be justified by a compelling governmental interest." Palmore v. Sidoti, 466 U.S. 429, 432, 104 S. Ct. 1879, 1882

(1984). Second, the means chosen by the State to effectuate its purpose must be "narrowly tailored to the achievement of that goal." Fullilove, supra, 448 U.S., at 480, 100 S. Ct., at 2776....

This Court never has held that societal discrimination alone is sufficient to justify a racial classification. Rather, the Court has insisted upon some showing of prior discrimination by the governmental unit involved before allowing limited use of racial classifications in order to remedy such discrimination....

... [T]he role model theory employed by the District Court has no logical stopping point. The role model theory allows the Board to engage in discriminatory hiring and layoff practices long past the point required by any legitimate remedial purpose....

Societal discrimination, without more, is too amorphous a basis for imposing a racially classified remedy. The role model theory announced by the District Court and the resultant holding typify this indefiniteness.... No one doubts that there has been serious racial discrimination in this country. But as the basis for imposing discriminatory *legal* remedies that work against innocent people, societal discrimination is insufficient and over-expansive. In the absence of particularized findings, a court could uphold remedies that are ageless in their reach into the past, and timeless in their ability to affect the future.

[The Court said: "The term 'narrowly tailored,' so frequently used in our cases, has acquired a secondary meaning. More specifically, as commentators have indicated, the term maybe used to require consideration of whether lawful alternative and less restrictive means could have been used." It quoted *Fullilove*: "When effectuating a limited and properly tailored remedy to cure the effects of prior discrimination, such a 'sharing of the burden' by innocent parties is not impermissible." But it then noted that none of the cases previously decided involving racially motivated employment policies included layoffs.] Here, by contrast, the means chosen to achieve the Board's asserted purposes is that of laying off nonminority teachers with greater seniority in order to retain minority teachers with less seniority. We have previously expressed concern over the burden that a preferential-layoffs scheme imposes on innocent parties. See Firefighters v. Stotts, 467 U.S. 561, 574–576, 578–579, 104 S. Ct. 2576, 2585–2586, 2587–2588 (1984); see also Steelworkers v. Weber, 443 U.S. 193, 208, 99 S. Ct. 2721, 2730 (1979) ("The plan does not require the discharge of white workers and their replacement with new black hires"). In cases involving valid *hiring* goals, the burden to be borne by innocent individuals is diffused to a considerable extent among society generally. Though hiring goals may burden some innocent individuals, they simply do not impose the same kind of injury that layoffs impose. Denial of a future employment opportunity is not as intrusive as loss of an existing job. . . .

While hiring goals impose a diffuse burden, often foreclosing only one of several opportunities, layoffs impose the entire burden of achieving racial equality on particular individuals, often resulting in serious disruption of their lives. That burden is too intrusive. We therefore hold that, as a means of accomplishing purposes that otherwise may be legitimate, the Board's layoff plan is not sufficiently narrowly tailored. Other, less intrusive means of accomplishing similar purposes — such as the adoption of hiring goals — are available. For these reasons, the Board's selection of layoffs as the means to accomplish even a valid purpose cannot satisfy the demands of the Equal Protection Clause.

We accordingly reverse the judgment of the Court of Appeals for the Sixth Circuit.

[Justice White concurred in the judgment.]

JUSTICE MARSHALL, with whom JUSTICE BRENNAN and JUSTICE BLACKMUN join, dissenting: . . .

I, too, believe that layoffs are unfair. But unfairness ought not be confused with constitutional injury. Paying no heed to the true circumstances of petitioners' plight, the plurality would nullify years of negotiation and compromise designed to solve serious educational problems in the public schools of Jackson, Michigan. Because I believe that a public employer, with the full agreement of its employees, should be permitted to preserve the benefits of a legitimate and constitutional affirmative-action hiring plan even while reducing its work force, I dissent. . . .

[There is,] at the very least, a wealth of plausible evidence supporting the Board's position that Article XII was a legitimate and necessary response both to racial discrimination and to educational imperatives. To attempt to resolve the constitutional issue either with no historical context whatever, as the plurality has done, or on the basis of a record devoid of established facts, is to do a grave injustice not only to the Board and teachers of Jackson and to the State of Michigan, but also to individuals and governments committed to the goal of eliminating all traces of segregation throughout the country. Most of all, it does an injustice to the aspirations embodied in the Fourteenth Amendment itself. I would vacate the judgment of the Court of Appeals and remand with instructions that the case be remanded to the District Court for further proceedings consistent with the views I have expressed.

JUSTICE STEVENS, dissenting:

In my opinion, it is not necessary to find that the Board of Education has been guilty of racial discrimination in the past to support the conclusion that it has a legitimate interest in employing more black teachers in the future. Rather than analyzing a case of this kind by asking whether minority teachers have some sort of special entitlement to jobs as a remedy for sins that were committed in the past, I believe that we should first ask whether the Board's action advances the public interest in educating children for the future. If so, I believe we should consider whether that public interest, and the manner in which it is pursued, justifies any adverse effects on the disadvantaged group. . . .

In this case, the collective-bargaining agreement between the Union and the Board of Education succinctly stated a valid public purpose — "recognition of the desirability of multi-ethnic representation on the teaching faculty," and thus "a policy of actively seeking minority group personnel." App. to Pet. for Cert. 22a. Nothing in the record — not a shred of evidence — contradicts the view that the Board's attempt to employ, and to retain, more minority teachers in the Jackson public school system served this completely sound educational purpose. Thus, there was a rational and unquestionably legitimate basis for the Board's decision to enter into the collective-bargaining agreement that petitioners have challenged, even though the agreement required special efforts to recruit and retain minority teachers. . . .

In this case, there can be no question about either the fairness of the procedures used to adopt the race-conscious provision, or the propriety of its breadth. As Justice Marshall has demonstrated, the procedures for adopting this provision were scrupulously fair. The Union that represents petitioners negotiated the provision and agreed to it; the agreement was put to a vote of the membership, and overwhelmingly approved. Again, not a shred of evidence in the record suggests *any* procedural unfairness in the adoption of the agreement. Similarly, the provision is specifically designed to achieve its objective—retaining the minority teachers that have been specially recruited to give the Jackson schools, after a period of racial unrest, an integrated faculty. Thus, in striking contrast to the procedural inadequacy

and unjustified breadth of the race-based classification in Fullilove v. Klutznick, 448 U.S. 448, 100 S. Ct. 2758 (1980), the race-conscious layoff policy here was adopted with full participation of the disadvantaged individuals and with a narrowly circumscribed berth for the policy's operation. . . .

We should not lightly approve the government's use of a race-based distinction. History teaches the obvious dangers of such classifications. Our ultimate goal must, of course, be "to eliminate entirely from governmental decisionmaking such irrelevant factors as a human being's race." In this case, however, I am persuaded that the decision to include more minority teachers in the Jackson, Michigan, school system served a valid public purpose, that it was adopted with fair procedures and given a narrow breadth, that it transcends the harm to petitioners, and that it is a step toward that ultimate goal of eliminating entirely from governmental decisionmaking such irrelevant factors as a human being's race. I would therefore affirm the judgment of the Court of Appeals.

In *Wygant*, the Court mandates that states must prove past discrimination within their system in order to implement an affirmative action scheme and rejects a history of broad societal discrimination as sufficient justification for such a program in the educational sphere. The Court also dismisses the "role model" justification for the plan as indefinite and amorphous. The two most recent affirmative action cases in higher education, *Gratz v. Bollinger* (2003) and *Grutter v. Bollinger* (2003) — both brought by students who were denied admission to the University of Michigan — consider yet another justification for remedial action.

GRATZ v. BOLLINGER

Supreme Court of the United States, 2003
539 U.S. 244, 123 S. Ct. 2411

Chief Justice Rehnquist delivered the opinion of the Court:

We granted certiorari in this case to decide whether "the University of Michigan's use of racial preferences in undergraduate admissions violates the Equal Protection Clause of the Fourteenth Amendment . . . . Because we find that the manner in which the University considers the race

of applicants in its undergraduate admissions guidelines violates these constitutional and statutory provisions, we reverse that portion of the District Court's decision upholding the guidelines.

Petitioners Jennifer Gratz and Patrick Hamacher both applied for admission to the University of Michigan's (University) College of Literature, Science, and the Arts (LSA) as residents of the State of Michigan. Both petitioners are Caucasian. Gratz, who applied for admission for the fall of 1995, was notified in January of that year that a final decision regarding her admission had been delayed until April. This delay was based upon the University's determination that, although Gratz was " 'well qualified,' " she was " 'less competitive than the students who had been admitted on first review.' " App. to Pet. for Cert. 109a. Gratz was notified in April that the LSA was unable to offer her admission. She enrolled in the University of Michigan at Dearborn, from which she graduated in the spring of 1999.

Hamacher applied for admission to the LSA for the fall of 1997. A final decision as to his application was also postponed because, though his " 'academic credentials [were] in the qualified range, they [were] not at the level needed for first review admission.' " Ibid. Hamacher's application was subsequently denied in April 1997, and he enrolled at Michigan State University. . . .

[The office of undergraduate admissions, OUA,] considers a number of factors in making admissions decisions, including high school grades, standardized test scores, high school quality, curriculum strength, geography, alumni relationships, and leadership. OUA also considers race. During all periods relevant to this litigation, the University has considered African–Americans, Hispanics, and Native Americans to be "underrepresented minorities," and it is undisputed that the University admits "virtually every qualified . . . applicant" from these groups. App. to Pet. for Cert. 111a.

During 1995 and 1996, OUA counselors evaluated applications according to grade point average combined with what were referred to as the "SCUGA" factors. These factors included the quality of an applicant's high school (S), the strength of an applicant's high school curriculum (C), an applicant's unusual circumstances (U), an applicant's geographical residence (G), and an applicant's alumni relationships (A). After these scores were combined to produce an applicant's "GPA 2" score, the reviewing admissions counselors referenced a set of "Guidelines" tables, which listed GPA 2 ranges on the vertical axis, and American College Test/Scholastic Aptitude Test (ACT/SAT) scores on the horizontal axis. Each table was divided into cells that included one or more courses of action to be taken, including

admit, reject, delay for additional information, or postpone for reconsideration.

In both years, applicants with the same GPA 2 score and ACT/SAT score were subject to different admissions outcomes based upon their racial or ethnic status. For example, as a Caucasian in-state applicant, Gratz's GPA 2 score and ACT score placed her within a cell calling for a postponed decision on her application. An in-state or out-of-state minority applicant with Gratz's scores would have fallen within a cell calling for admission.

In 1997, the University modified its admissions procedure. Specifically, the formula for calculating an applicant's GPA 2 score was restructured to include additional point values under the "U" category in the SCUGA factors. Under this new system, applicants could receive points for underrepresented minority status, socioeconomic disadvantage, or attendance at a high school with a predominantly underrepresented minority population, or underrepresentation in the unit to which the student was applying (for example, men who sought to pursue a career in nursing). Under the 1997 procedures, Hamacher's GPA 2 score and ACT score placed him in a cell on the in-state applicant table calling for postponement of a final admissions decision. An underrepresented minority applicant placed in the same cell would generally have been admitted.

Each application received points based on high school grade point average, standardized test scores, academic quality of an applicant's high school, strength or weakness of high school curriculum, in-state residency, alumni relationship, personal essay, and personal achievement or leadership. Of particular significance here, under a "miscellaneous" category, an applicant was entitled to 20 points based upon his or her membership in an underrepresented racial or ethnic minority group. The University explained that the " 'development of the selection index for admissions in 1998 changed only the mechanics, not the substance of how race and ethnicity were considered in admissions.' " App. to Pet. for Cert. 116a.

In all application years from 1995 to 1998, the guidelines provided that qualified applicants from underrepresented minority groups be admitted as soon as possible in light of the University's belief that such applicants were more likely to enroll if promptly notified of their admission. Also from 1995 through 1998, the University carefully managed its rolling admissions system to permit consideration of certain applications submitted later in the academic year through the use of "protected seats." Specific groups — including athletes, foreign students, ROTC candidates, and underrepresented minorities — were "protected categories" eligible for these seats. A committee called the Enrollment Working Group (EWG) projected how many applicants from each of these protected categories the University was likely to receive after a given date and then paced admissions decisions to permit full consideration of expected applications from these groups. If this space was not filled by qualified candidates from the designated groups toward the end of the admissions season, it was then used to admit qualified candidates remaining in the applicant pool, including those on the waiting list. . . .

. . . Respondents contended that the LSA has just such an interest in the educational benefits that result from having a racially and ethnically diverse student body and that its program is narrowly tailored to serve that interest. Respondent-intervenors asserted that the LSA had a compelling interest in remedying the University's past and current discrimination against minorities. . . .

Petitioners argue, first and foremost, that the University's use of race in undergraduate admissions violates the Fourteenth Amendment. Specifically, they contend that this Court has only sanctioned the use of racial classifications to remedy identified discrimination, a justification on which respondents have never relied. . . .

Petitioners alternatively argue that even if the University's interest in diversity can constitute a compelling state interest, the District Court erroneously concluded that the University's use of race in its current freshman admissions policy is narrowly tailored to achieve such an interest. . . .

It is by now well established that "all racial classifications reviewable under the Equal Protection Clause must be strictly scrutinized." Adarand Constructors, Inc. v. Pena, 515 U.S. 200, 224, 115

S. Ct. 2097 (1995). This " 'standard of review . . . is not dependent on the race of those burdened or benefited by a particular classification.' " Ibid. (quoting Richmond v. J. A. Croson Co., 488 U.S. 469, 494, 109 S. Ct. 706 (1989) (plurality opinion)). . . .

To withstand our strict scrutiny analysis, respondents must demonstrate that the University's use of race in its current admission program employs "narrowly tailored measures that further compelling governmental interests." Id., at 227, 115 S. Ct. 2097. . . . We find that the University's policy, which automatically distributes 20 points, or one-fifth of the points needed to guarantee admission, to every single "underrepresented minority" applicant solely because of race, is not narrowly tailored to achieve the interest in educational diversity that respondents claim justifies their program. . . .

Justice Powell's opinion in [Regents of University of California v. Bakke, 438 U.S. 265, 98 S. Ct. 2733 (1978),] emphasized the importance of considering each particular applicant as an individual, assessing all of the qualities that individual possesses, and in turn, evaluating that individual's ability to contribute to the unique setting of higher education. The admissions program Justice Powell described, however, did not contemplate that any single characteristic automatically ensured a specific and identifiable contribution to a university's diversity. Instead, under the approach Justice Powell described, each characteristic of a particular applicant was to be considered in assessing the applicant's entire application.

The current LSA policy does not provide such individualized consideration. The LSA's policy automatically distributes 20 points to every single applicant from an "underrepresented minority" group, as defined by the University. The only consideration that accompanies this distribution of points is a factual review of an application to determine whether an individual is a member of one of these minority groups. Moreover, unlike Justice Powell's example, where the race of a "particular black applicant" could be considered without being decisive, see Bakke, 438 U.S., at 317, 98 S. Ct. 2733, the LSA's automatic distribution of 20 points has the effect of making "the factor of race...decisive" for virtually every minimally qualified underrepresented minority applicant. Ibid....

We conclude, therefore, that because the University's use of race in its current freshman admissions policy is not narrowly tailored to achieve respondents' asserted compelling interest in diversity, the admissions policy violates the Equal Protection Clause of the Fourteenth Amendment.... Accordingly, we reverse ....

[Justices Stevens, Souter, and Ginsburg dissented, and Justice Breyer dissented in part.]

GRUTTER v. BOLLINGER

Supreme Court of the United States, 2003
539 U.S. 306, 123 S. Ct. 2325

JUSTICE O'CONNOR delivered the opinion of the Court:

This case requires us to decide whether the use of race as a factor in student admissions by the University of Michigan Law School (Law School) is unlawful.

The Law School ranks among the Nation's top law schools. It receives more than 3,500 applications each year for a class of around 350 students. Seeking to "admit a group of students who individually and collectively are among the most capable," the Law School looks for individuals with "substantial promise for success in law school" and "a strong likelihood of succeeding in the practice of law and contributing in diverse ways to the well-being of others." App. 110. More broadly, the Law School seeks "a mix of students with varying backgrounds and experiences who will respect and learn from each other." Ibid. In 1992, the dean of the Law School charged a faculty committee with crafting a written admissions policy to implement these goals. In particular, the Law School sought to ensure that its efforts to achieve student body diversity complied with this Court's most recent ruling on the use of race in university admissions. See Regents of Univ. of Cal. v. Bakke, 438 U.S. 265, 98 S. Ct. 2733 (1978). Upon the unanimous adoption of the committee's report by the Law School faculty, it became the Law School's official admissions policy.

The hallmark of that policy is its focus on academic ability coupled with a flexible assessment of applicants' talents, experiences, and potential "to contribute to the learning of those around them." App. 111....

The policy makes clear, however, that even the highest possible score does not guarantee admission to the Law School. Id., at 113. Nor does a low score automatically disqualify an applicant. Ibid. Rather, the policy requires admissions officials to look beyond grades and test scores to other criteria that are important to the Law School's educational objectives....

The policy aspires to "achieve that diversity which has the potential to enrich everyone's education and thus make a law school class stronger than the sum of its parts." Id., at 118. The policy does not restrict the types of diversity contributions eligible for "substantial weight" in the admissions process, but instead recognizes "many possible bases for diversity admissions." Id., at 118, 120. The policy does, however, reaffirm the Law School's longstanding commitment to "one particular type of diversity," that is, "racial and ethnic diversity with special reference to the inclusion of students from groups which have been historically discriminated against, like African–Americans, Hispanics and Native Americans, who without this commitment might not be represented in our student body in meaningful numbers." Id., at 120. By enrolling a " 'critical mass' of [underrepresented] minority students," the Law School seeks to "ensure their ability to make unique contributions to the character of the Law School." Id., at 120–121....

Petitioner Barbara Grutter is a white Michigan resident who applied to the Law School in 1996 with a 3.8 grade point average and 161 LSAT score. The Law School initially placed petitioner on a waiting list, but subsequently rejected her application. In December 1997, petitioner filed suit in the United States District Court for the Eastern District of Michigan against the Law School [and others]. Petitioner alleged that respondents discriminated against her on the basis of race in violation of the Fourteenth Amendment . . . .

Petitioner further alleged that her application was rejected because the Law School uses race as a "predominant" factor, giving applicants who belong to certain minority groups "a significantly greater chance of admission than students with similar credentials from disfavored racial groups." App. 33–34. Petitioner also alleged that respondents "had no compelling interest to justify their use of race in the admissions process." Id., at 34. . . .

During the 15–day bench trial, the parties introduced extensive evidence concerning the Law School's use of race in the admissions process. Dennis Shields, Director of Admissions when petitioner applied to the Law School, testified that he did not direct his staff to admit a particular percentage or number of minority students, but rather to consider an applicant's race along with all other factors. Id., at 206a. Shields testified that at the height of the admissions season, he would frequently consult the so-called "daily reports" that kept track of the racial and ethnic composition of the class (along with other information such as residency status and gender). Id., at 207a. This was done, Shields testified, to ensure that a critical mass of underrepresented minority students would be reached so as to realize the educational benefits of a diverse student body. Ibid. Shields stressed, however, that he did not seek to admit any particular number or percentage of underrepresented minority students. Ibid.

Erica Munzel, who succeeded Shields as Director of Admissions, testified that " 'critical mass' " means " 'meaningful numbers' " or " 'meaningful representation,' " which she understood to mean a number that encourages underrepresented minority students to participate in the classroom and not feel isolated. Id., at 208a–209a. Munzel stated there is no number, percentage, or range of numbers or percentages that constitute critical mass. Id., at 209a. Munzel also asserted that she must

consider the race of applicants because a critical mass of underrepresented minority students could not be enrolled if admissions decisions were based primarily on undergraduate GPAs and LSAT scores. . . .

In the end, the District Court concluded that the Law School's use of race as a factor in admissions decisions was unlawful. . . .

Sitting en banc, the Court of Appeals reversed the District Court's judgment and vacated the injunction. The Court of Appeals first held that Justice Powell's opinion in *Bakke* was binding precedent establishing diversity as a compelling state interest. . . . The Court of Appeals also held that the Law School's use of race was narrowly tailored because race was merely a "potential 'plus' factor" . . . .

. . . We apply strict scrutiny to all racial classifications to " 'smoke out' illegitimate uses of race by assuring that [government] is pursuing a goal important enough to warrant use of a highly suspect tool." [City of Richmond v. J.A. Croson Co., 488 U.S. 469, 493, 109 S. Ct. 706 (1989)].

Strict scrutiny is not "strict in theory, but fatal in fact." Adarand Constructors, Inc. v. Pena [,515 U.S. 200, 237, 115 S. Ct. 2097 (1995)] (internal quotation marks and citation omitted). Although all governmental uses of race are subject to strict scrutiny, not all are invalidated by it. . . .

With these principles in mind, we turn to the question whether the Law School's use of race is justified by a compelling state interest. . . . [T]he Law School asks us to recognize, in the context of higher education, a compelling state interest in student body diversity. . . .

The Law School's educational judgment that such diversity is essential to its educational mission is one to which we defer. The Law School's assessment that diversity will, in fact, yield educational benefits is substantiated by respondents and their amici. Our scrutiny of the interest asserted by the Law School is no less strict for taking into account complex educational judgments in an area that lies primarily within the expertise of the university. Our holding today is in keeping with our tradition of giving a degree of deference to a university's academic decisions, within constitutionally prescribed limits.

...In announcing the principle of student body diversity as a compelling state interest, Justice Powell invoked our cases recognizing a constitutional dimension, grounded in the First Amendment, of educational autonomy: "The freedom of a university to make its own judgments as to education includes the selection of its student body." *Bakke*, supra, at 312, 98 S. Ct. 2733. From this premise, Justice Powell reasoned that by claiming "the right to select those students who will contribute the most to the 'robust exchange of ideas,'" a university "seek[s] to achieve a goal that is of paramount importance in the fulfillment of its mission." Our conclusion that the Law School has a compelling interest in a diverse student body is informed by our view that attaining a diverse student body is at the heart of the Law School's proper institutional mission, and that "good faith" on the part of a university is "presumed" absent "a showing to the contrary." 438 U.S., at 318–319, 98 S. Ct. 2733.

As part of its goal of "assembling a class that is both exceptionally academically qualified and broadly diverse," the Law School seeks to "enroll a 'critical mass' of minority students." Brief for Respondents Bollinger et al. 13. The Law School's interest is not simply "to assure within its student body some specified percentage of a particular group merely because of its race or ethnic origin." *Bakke*, 438 U.S., at 307, 98 S. Ct. 2733 (opinion of Powell, J.). That would amount to outright racial balancing, which is patently unconstitutional. Rather, the Law School's concept of critical mass is defined by reference to the educational benefits that diversity is designed to produce.

These benefits are substantial. As the District Court emphasized, the Law School's admissions policy promotes "cross-racial understanding," helps to break down racial stereotypes, and "enables [students] to better understand persons of different races."...

...In addition to the expert studies and reports entered into evidence at trial, numerous studies show that student body diversity promotes learning outcomes, and "better prepares students for an increasingly diverse workforce and society, and better prepares them as professionals."...

...Effective participation by members of all racial and ethnic groups in the civic life of our Nation is essential if the dream of one Nation, indivisible, is to be realized.

Moreover, universities, and in particular, law schools, represent the training ground for a large number of our Nation's leaders....

In order to cultivate a set of leaders with legitimacy in the eyes of the citizenry, it is necessary that the path to leadership be visibly open to talented and qualified individuals of every race and ethnicity....

...The Law School has determined, based on its experience and expertise, that a "critical mass" of underrepresented minorities is necessary to further its compelling interest in securing the educational benefits of a diverse student body.

Even in the limited circumstance when drawing racial distinctions is permissible to further a compelling state interest, government is still "constrained in how it may pursue that end: [T]he means chosen to accomplish the [government's] asserted purpose must be specifically and narrowly framed to accomplish that purpose." Shaw v. Hunt, 517 U.S. 899, 908, 116 S. Ct. 1894 (1996)....

To be narrowly tailored, a race-conscious admissions program cannot use a quota system — it cannot "insulate each category of applicants with certain desired qualifications from competition with all other applicants." *Bakke*, supra, at 315, 98 S. Ct. 2733 (opinion of Powell, J.). Instead, a university may consider race or ethnicity only as a "'plus' in a particular applicant's file," without "insulating the individual from comparison with all other candidates for the available seats." Id., at 317, 57 L. Ed. 2d 750, 98 S. Ct. 2733. In other words, an admissions program must be "flexible enough to consider all pertinent elements of diversity in light of the particular qualifications of each applicant, and to place them on the same footing for consideration, although not necessarily according them the same weight." Ibid.

We find that the Law School's admissions program bears the hallmarks of a narrowly tailored plan....Universities can...consider race or ethnicity more flexibly as a "plus" factor in the context of individualized consideration of each and every applicant....

That a race-conscious admissions program does not operate as a quota does not, by itself, satisfy the requirement of individualized consideration. When using race as a "plus" factor in university admissions, a university's admissions program must remain flexible enough to ensure that each applicant is evaluated as an individual and not in a way that makes an applicant's race or ethnicity the defining feature of his or her application. The importance of this individualized consideration in the context of a race-conscious admissions program is paramount.

Here, the Law School engages in a highly individualized, holistic review of each applicant's file, giving serious consideration to all the ways an applicant might contribute to a diverse educational environment. The Law School affords this individualized consideration to applicants of all races. There is no policy, either de jure or de facto, of automatic acceptance or rejection based on any single "soft" variable. . . .

We are mindful, however, that "[a] core purpose of the Fourteenth Amendment was to do away with all governmentally imposed discrimination based on race." Palmore v. Sidoti, 466 U.S. 429, 432, 104 S. Ct. 1879 (1984). Accordingly, race-conscious admissions policies must be limited in time. The Law School, too, concedes that all "race-conscious programs must have reasonable durational limits." Brief for Respondent Bollinger et al. 32. . . .

We take the Law School at its word that it would "like nothing better than to find a race-neutral admissions formula" and will terminate its race-conscious admissions program as soon as practicable. See id. at 34. It has been 25 years since Justice Powell first approved the use of race to further an interest in student body diversity in the context of public higher education. Since that time, the number of minority applicants with high grades and test scores has indeed increased. See Tr. of Oral Arg. 43. We expect that 25 years from now, the use of racial preferences will no longer be necessary to further the interest approved today.

In summary, the Equal Protection Clause does not prohibit the Law School's narrowly tailored use of race in admissions decisions to further a compelling interest in obtaining the educational benefits that flow from a diverse student body. . . . The judgment of the Court of Appeals for the Sixth Circuit, accordingly, is affirmed.

It is so ordered.

JUSTICE SCALIA, with whom JUSTICE THOMAS joins, concurring in part and dissenting in part:

. . . The "educational benefit" that the University of Michigan seeks to achieve by racial discrimination consists, according to the Court, of " 'cross-racial understanding,' " and " 'better par[ation of] students for an increasingly diverse workforce and society,' " all of which is necessary not only for work, but also for good "citizenship." This is not, of course, an "educational benefit" on which students will be graded on their Law School transcript (Works and Plays Well with Others: B+) or tested by the bar examiners (Q: Describe in 500 words or less your cross-racial understanding). For it is a lesson of life rather than law — essentially the same lesson taught to (or rather learned by, for it cannot be "taught" in the usual sense) people three feet shorter and twenty years younger than the full-grown adults at the University of Michigan Law School, in institutions ranging from Boy Scout troops to public-school kindergartens. If properly considered an "educational benefit" at all, it is surely not one that is either uniquely relevant to law school or uniquely "teachable" in a formal educational setting. *And therefore:* If it is appropriate for the University of Michigan Law School to use racial discrimination for the purpose of putting together a "critical mass" that will convey generic lessons in socialization and good citizenship, surely it is no less appropriate — indeed, *particularly* appropriate — for the civil service system of the State of Michigan to do so. There, also, those exposed to "critical masses" of certain races will presumably become better Americans, better Michiganders, better civil servants. And surely private employers cannot be criticized — indeed, should be praised — if they also "teach" good citizenship to their adult employees through a patriotic, all-American system of racial discrimination in hiring. The nonminority individuals who are deprived of a legal education, a civil service job, or any job at all by reason of their skin color will surely understand. . . .

JUSTICE THOMAS, with whom JUSTICE SCALIA joins . . . , concurring in part and dissenting in part:

Frederick Douglass, speaking to a group of abolitionists almost 140 years ago, delivered a message lost on today's majority:

[I]n regard to the colored people, there is always more that is benevolent, I perceive, than just, manifested towards us. What I ask for the negro is not benevolence, not pity, not sympathy, but simply *justice*. The American people have always been anxious to know what they shall do with us.... I have had but one answer from the beginning. Do nothing with us! Your doing with us has already played the mischief with us. Do nothing with us! If the apples will not remain on the tree of their own strength, if they are worm-eaten at the core, if they are early ripe and disposed to fall, let them fall!... And if the negro cannot stand on his own legs, let him fall also. All I ask is, give him a chance to stand on his own legs! Let him alone!... Your interference is doing him positive injury. What the Black Man Wants: An Address Delivered in Boston, Massachusetts, on 26 January 1865, reprinted in 4 The Frederick Douglass Papers 59, 68 (J. Blassingame & J. McKivigan eds. 1991) (emphasis in original).

Like Douglass, I believe blacks can achieve in every avenue of American life without the meddling of university administrators....

No one would argue that a university could set up a lower general admission standard and then impose heightened requirements only on black applicants. Similarly, a university may not maintain a high admission standard and grant exemptions to favored races. The Law School, of its own choosing, and for its own purposes, maintains an exclusionary admissions system that it knows produces racially disproportionate results. Racial discrimination is not a permissible solution to the self-inflicted wounds of this elitist admissions policy.

...First, I agree with the Court insofar as its decision, which approves of only one racial classification, confirms that further use of race in admissions remains unlawful. Second, I agree with the Court's holding that racial discrimination

in higher education admissions will be illegal in 25 years. I respectfully dissent from the remainder of the Court's opinion and the judgment, however, because I believe that the Law School's current use of race violates the Equal Protection Clause and that the Constitution means the same thing today as it will in 300 months....

Undoubtedly there are other ways to "better" the education of law students aside from ensuring that the student body contains a "critical mass" of underrepresented minority students. Attaining "diversity," whatever it means, is the mechanism by which the Law School obtains educational benefits, not an end of itself. The Law School, however, apparently believes that only a racially mixed student body can lead to the educational benefits it seeks. How, then, is the Law School's interest in these allegedly unique educational "benefits" *not* simply the forbidden interest in "racial balancing" that the majority expressly rejects?

...I believe what lies beneath the Court's decision today are the benighted notions that one can tell when racial discrimination benefits (rather than hurts) minority groups, see *Adarand*, 515 U.S., at 239, 115 S. Ct. 2097 (Scalia, J., concurring in part and concurring in judgment), and that racial discrimination is necessary to remedy general societal ills....

Putting aside what I take to be the Court's implicit rejection of *Adarand*'s holding that beneficial and burdensome racial classifications are equally invalid, I must contest the notion that the Law School's discrimination benefits those admitted as a result of it. The Court spends considerable time discussing the impressive display of amicus support for the Law School in this case from all corners of society. But nowhere in any of the filings in this Court is any evidence that the purported "beneficiaries" of this racial discrimination prove themselves by performing at (or even near) the same level as those students who receive no preferences.

... The Law School is not looking for those students who, despite a lower LSAT score or undergraduate grade point average, will succeed in the study of law. The Law School seeks only a facade — it is sufficient that the class looks right, even if it does not perform right.

The Law School tantalizes unprepared students with the promise of a University of Michigan degree and all of the opportunities that it offers. These overmatched students take the bait, only to find that they cannot succeed in the cauldron of competition....

Beyond the harm the Law School's racial discrimination visits upon its test subjects, no social science has disproved the notion that this discrimination "engender[s] attitudes of superiority or, alternatively, provoke[s] resentment among those who believe that they have been wronged by the government's use of race.... These programs stamp minorities with a badge of inferiority and may cause them to develop dependencies or to adopt an attitude that they are 'entitled' to preferences." *Adarand*, 515 U.S., at 241, 115 S. Ct. 2097 (Thomas, J., concurring in part and concurring in judgment).

It is uncontested that each year, the Law School admits a handful of blacks who would be admitted in the absence of racial discrimination. See Brief for Respondents Bollinger et al. 6. Who can differ-entiate between those who belong and those who do not? The majority of blacks are admitted to the Law School because of discrimination, and because of this policy all are tarred as undeserving. This problem of stigma does not depend on determinacy as to whether those stigmatized are actually the "beneficiaries" of racial discrimination. When blacks take positions in the highest places of government, industry, or academia, it is an open question today whether their skin color played a part in their advancement. The question itself is the stigma — because either racial discrimination did play a role, in which case the person may be deemed "otherwise unqualified," or it did not, in which case asking the question itself unfairly marks those blacks who would succeed without discrimination. Is this what the Court means by "visibly open"?...

As the foregoing makes clear, I believe the Court's opinion to be, in most respects, erroneous....

[Chief Justice Rehnquist and Justice Kennedy dissented.]

NOTES

1. The undergraduate admissions committee said that it could not implement the program of individualized review utilized by the law school, but the Court was not swayed:

> Respondents contend that "the volume of applications and the presentation of applicant information make it impractical for [the undergraduate college] to use the... admissions system" upheld by the Court today in *Grutter*. But the fact that the implementation of a program capable of providing individualized consideration might present administrative challenges does not render constitutional an otherwise problematic system.

In his dissent, Justice Souter disagreed:

> The very nature of a college's permissible practice of awarding value to racial diversity means that race must be considered in a way that increases some applicants' chances for admission. Since college admission is not left entirely to inarticulate intuition, it is hard to see what is inappropriate in assigning some stated value to a relevant characteristic, whether it be reasoning ability, writing style, running speed, or minority race. The college simply does by a numbered scale what the law school accomplishes in its "holistic review"; the distinction

does not imply that applicants to the undergraduate college are denied individualized consideration or a fair chance to compete on the basis of all the various merits their applications may disclose.

How can a large undergraduate institution give individualized attention to every applicant? Instead, some states, such as California, Texas, and Florida, have adopted "percentage plans." In Texas, the top 10 percent of graduates from every high school in the state are allowed to attend any Texas school of their choosing. Proponents of this plan say that it allows minority enrollment without considering race, while critics warn that the numbers of minorities at state schools is slipping. Consider:

> "The top 10 percent plan is not producing the ethnic and racial composition that the affirmative-action plan produced, and the numbers are big enough to really be noticeable," says Kevin Leicht, a sociology professor at the University of Iowa in Iowa City and a coauthor of [*Closing the Gap? Admissions & Enrollments at the Texas Public Flagships Before and After Affirmative Action*]. Those numbers are especially troubling given that Texas is fast becoming a majority-minority state. In fact, say opponents of the percentage plan, the only reason it works at all is that Texas still has segregated high schools. At Milby High School, for instance, 95 percent of students are Hispanic — guaranteeing that the majority who qualify for the top 10 percent plan will be Hispanic.

Kris Axtman, Affirmative Action, Texas Style, Stirs Criticism, Christian Sci. Monitor, Feb. 12, 2003, available at http://www.csmonitor.com/2003/0212/p03s01-usgn.html.

2. At the end of his dissent, Justice Thomas discusses his views on the stigma that affirmative action places upon all African Americans. The stigma argument is essentially that affirmative action increases discriminatory stereotypes, and therefore affirmative action — itself a program aimed at reducing discriminatory stereotypes — should be banned. Notice why this argument is attractive — or maybe even necessary — to opponents of affirmative action: because the intent of the framers of the Fourteenth Amendment clearly was to protect *African Americans* from race-based harms imposed by government, if only whites were harmed by affirmative action, then it would be hard to justify judicial interference on their behalf. One might question whether hypothesizing the existence of such stigma is sufficient, or whether some empirical showing of the frequency with which minorities suffer from such stigma (and/or that the costs of the stigma outweigh the benefits of the affirmative action program) should be required before departing from the historical view of the sort of discrimination encompassed by the Fourteenth Amendment prohibition.

3. The affirmative action debate did not end with the *Gratz* and *Grutter* cases. Opponents of affirmative action programs decided to shift their focus to state-based referendums, beginning with Michigan. Voters in Michigan approved the ban.

SCOTT JASCHIK, MICHIGAN VOTES DOWN AFFIRMATIVE ACTION

InsideHigherEd.com (Nov. 8, 2006)

Michigan voters on Tuesday approved a ban on affirmative action at the state's public colleges and in government contracting. The vote came despite opposition to the ban from most academic and business leaders in the state — and the history in which the University of Michigan played a key role in preserving the right of colleges to consider race as a factor in admissions.

Defenders of affirmative action had been encouraged in the campaign's closing days by polls suggesting growing skepticism for the ban. But in the end, the ban won support from more than 58 percent of voters, according to unofficial results. Michigan thus followed a pattern in which some voters appear reluctant to tell pollsters of their opposition to affirmative action.

. . . .

Donn M. Fresard, editor in chief of *The Michigan Daily*, which opposed the ban, said he didn't expect major student unrest over the vote. "You are not going to see rioting on the Diag," he said. "The average student isn't overly upset about this, and you'd be surprised how many students support it. Especially among white students, support was pretty high."

The Michigan Civil Rights Initiative was the brainchild of Ward Connerly, who as a regent of the University of California led that system and then the state to bar affirmative action, with statewide action coming in 1996 vote. A similar vote two years later banned affirmative action in Washington State, but efforts by affirmative action foes then shifted largely to the courts, leading to the landmark 2003 Supreme Court decisions in two cases involving the University of Michigan.

Those decisions — one about the system used by Michigan to admit undergraduates and one about the system used by its law school — effectively said that colleges could continue to use affirmative action, but couldn't have separate systems in which extra points were awarded across the board specifically for race and ethnicity. Many critics of affirmative action had high hopes that the Michigan cases would be used by the Supreme Court to roll back its 1978 ruling in the *Bakke* case, which upheld the right of colleges to consider race in admissions. When *Bakke* largely survived, Connerly and others shifted back to the referendum approach, with a focus on Michigan.

The Michigan law, Proposition 2, was implemented mid-admission cycle, on December 28, 2006. Prior to this date 39.6 percent of minority applicants to the University of Michigan Law School were accepted, and after this date only 5.5 percent of minority applicants were admitted. Put differently, 157 minorities were admitted prior to Proposition 2, and 26 were admitted after. Those in favor of the Proposition 2 saw this decline as evidence that affirmative action had unfairly admitted students based on racial preference, while critics saw it as evidence of the damage the ordinance would cause. The admissions committee disputed both interpretations, contending that these numbers were simply the result of the fact that they had encouraged the more qualified applicants to apply earlier in the rolling admissions cycle. In response to the Detroit public interest group "By Any Means Necessary," which sued to overturn Proposition 2, the assistant dean and director of admissions, Sarah C. Zearfoss, explained:

> [By Any Means Necessary] says what this means is we won't be able to admit anyone who's a minority under Prop 2 and it's catastrophic. That's not what it

means. What it means is a lot of the people in the 157 group [of minorities admitted by late December] are people who might have been in the 26 group [of minority students admitted after that] too. That's not going to be 100 percent of it; some of the people I admitted pre-Prop 2 were people I wouldn't have been able to admit after. Realistically, Prop 2 is going to have some effect on the overall number of minorities that we admit, but there's a couple reasons why it's pretty hard to know exactly what kind of effect and whether it's reasonable to think the proportion will be more like the post-Prop 2 activity this year or more like the overall percentage this year. I think that it's going to be more like the overall percentage.

Elizabeth Redden, Now and Then: Minorities and Michigan, http://www. insidehighered.com/layout/set/print/news/2007/06/19/michigan.

Many groups have legally challenged the implementation of Proposition 2, but none have been successful. The latest request for a delay in implementation was denied review by the Supreme Court on January 19, 2007. The petition was made by three Michigan universities and the public interest group By Any Means Necessary. The universities claimed that because Proposition 2 went into effect halfway through the admissions cycle, there may have been unfair treatment to students applying after it went into effect. While there are some legal challenges remaining in state and district courts, Michigan schools have been ordered to immediately comply with the law.

Recall the quote from this chapter's administrative section: "When a man has emerged from slavery, and by the aid of beneficent legislation has shaken off the inseparable concomitants of that state, there must be some stage in the progress of his elevation when he takes the rank of a mere citizen, and ceases to be the special favorite of the laws." Compare this idea with the foot-race analogy from the beginning of this public-benefit section. Which idea do you find most convincing? Discrimination is not limited to intentional, visible discrimination, but also includes discrimination inherent in the system, for example, the so-called good-old-boys network present in many industries or de facto segregation in

The First Black President

In 2008, the United States elected its first black President, Barack Obama. While it is obvious that this marks a historic moment, it is not clear what the overall impact of this event will be upon race relations in this country. Will his success make it harder for some whites to see the problem of racism? Will the image of a black man as President daily challenge anti-black stereotypes? Will Obama be viewed as an "exception," and therefore permit whites to maintain the belief that African Americans are dangerous and inferior? Will children be the most affected and grow up less likely to make assumptions based on race because Obama was President? Will racist groups gain in adherents in response to the perceived threat of a black President? The preliminary answer to each of these questions appears to be yes.

neighborhoods and schools. Consider the differences between educational opportunities in the primarily minority inner cities and primarily white suburbs. Is it fair to judge college applicants by the same standard when they have not received the same quality of education? Moreover, there is a growing body of psychological literature that documents unconscious prejudice and associations. How should the law respond to these varied sources of inequality?

Section Seven
SUMMARY

This chapter focused on a particular aim of society — equality — to illustrate how the five instruments of the law studied in Part One can contribute to achieving a societal goal. Equality is an especially interesting aim to consider because the normative consensus on equality is wide — but not very deep. Which groups are entitled to equality? Equal distribution of what resources? Equal treatment by whom? And so on. Because of the enormous variety of questions relating to equality, we have focused on racial equality since few would dispute that racial equality (unlike, for example, equality between felons and nonfelons) is desirable. We have seen that with respect to each of the five instruments, racial equality may pose a limit on the operation of the instrument, or it may serve as the goal of that instrument. In this chapter we have seen that people have widely divergent views on whether, in some spheres, law should intervene at all to further equality, and in other spheres, more modest disagreement about which instrument will be the most likely to produce racial equality, or the most likely to produce racial equality without damaging other goals that are important.

We have seen the penal law used in ways that threaten racial equality. Although the Japanese-American concentration camps of World War II are now largely reviled, the war on terror has revived debates about the appropriateness of using race or ethnicity as an indicator of criminal propensity. We have also seen attempts to use the penal law to promote racial equality. Hate crime legislation is one example of such an attempt that has survived constitutional scrutiny, but many other attempts to control the expression of racial bias have foundered as violations of the First Amendment.

Prior to the Civil War, the remedial instrument was unavailable to slaves, but after the Thirteenth and Fourteenth Amendments were passed, there were no formal racial barriers to using the remedial instrument. As we saw, this does not mean that the biases of jurors may not have led to unequal application of the instrument, a risk the Supreme Court attempted to diminish by prohibiting racial discrimination in jury selection. A variety of federal statutes, beginning with the Civil Rights Act of 1866, have provided remedies for racial discrimination in various areas. Most important today are Congressional enactments of the

1960s that outlaw racial discrimination in private employment, public accommodation, voting, federally assisted programs, and housing.

Equality limits openly expressed governmental discrimination against interracial family units. It also limits governmental enforcement of private racial biases — at least where racially restrictive covenants are at stake. In general, the private arrangement mode is not used to compel equality because of the intimacy of the choices involved. An exception is employment arrangements, which are regulated by federal statute, in large part because private discrimination in employment may have significant economic consequences for minority groups.

We saw that constitutional prohibitions against racial discrimination extend to the administrative instrument, but that in the modern era, it is difficult to prove discrimination by administrative bodies. Historically, the Civil Rights Commission provides an excellent example of how the administrative instrument may, through factfinding and recommendations, serve to promote racial equality. More recently, however, the Commission has been quite divided and divisive.

Finally, we examined the role of racial equality in the public-benefit instrument. What is the best way to remedy the legacy of racial equality? There is much heated disagreement on this question. Ironically, attempts to use the public benefit instrument to further racial equality as a goal have in recent times been thwarted by the assertion of racial equality as a limit on the public benefit instrument. Currently, a majority of the Supreme Court agrees that, to survive constitutional scrutiny, attempts to remedy past discrimination must meet the same strict standard as must traditional forms of race discrimination.

For a general historical treatment of the legal struggle for equality in the schools, see Richard Kluger, Simple Justice (1976). For a broader history of the NAACP Legal Defense Fund, see Jack Greenberg, Crusaders in the Courts (1994). For a review of many of the findings related to implicit racial bias, see Jerry Kang, The Trojan Horses of Race, 118 Harv. L. Rev. 1489 (2005). For the reader interested in Critical Race Theory, see Richard Delgado & Jean Stefancic. Critical Race Theory: An Annotated Bibliography, 79 Va. L. Rev. 461 (1993).

THE CONSTITUTION OF THE UNITED STATES OF AMERICA

We the people of the United States, in order to form a more perfect Union, establish Justice, insure domestic Tranquility, provide for the common defense, promote the general Welfare, and secure the Blessing of Liberty to ourselves and our Posterity, do ordain and establish this constitution for the United States of America.

Article I

Section 1. All legislative Powers herein granted shall be vested in a Congress of the United States, which shall consist of a Senate and House of Representatives.

Section 2. The House of Representatives shall be composed of Members chosen every second Year by the People of the several States, and the Electors in each State shall have the Qualifications requisite for Electors of the most numerous Branch of the State Legislature.

No Person shall be a Representative who shall not have attained to the Age of twenty-five Years, and been seven Years a Citizen of the United States, and who shall not, when elected, be an Inhabitant of that State in which he shall be chosen.

Representatives and direct Taxes shall be apportioned among the several States which may be included within this Union, according to their respective Numbers, which shall be determined by adding to the whole Number of free Persons, including those bound to Service for a Term of Years, and excluding Indians not taxed, three fifths of all other persons.[a] The actual Enumeration shall be made within three Years after the first Meeting of the Congress of the United States, and within every subsequent Term of ten Years, in such Manner as they shall by Law direct. The Number of Representatives shall not exceed one for every thirty thousand, but each State shall have at Least one Representative; and until such enumeration shall be made, the State of New Hampshire shall be entitled to chuse three, Massachusetts eight, Rhode Island and Providence Plantations one, Connecticut five, New York six, New Jersey four, Pennsylvania eight, Delaware one, Maryland six, Virginia ten, North Carolina five, South Carolina five, and Georgia three.

When vacancies happen in the Representation from any State, the Executive Authority thereof shall issue Writs of Election to fill such Vacancies.

The House of Representatives shall chuse their Speaker and other Officers; and shall have the sole Power of Impeachment.

Section 3. The Senate of the United States shall be composed of two Senators from each State, chosen by the Legislature thereof,[b] for six Years; and each Senator shall have one Vote.

Immediately after they shall be assembled in Consequence of the first Election, they shall be divided as equally as may be into three Classes. The Seats of the Senators of the first Class shall be vacated at the Expiration of the second Year, of the second Class at the Expiration of the fourth Year, and of the third Class at the Expiration of the sixth Year, so that one-third may be chosen every second Year; and if Vacancies happen by Resignation, or otherwise, during the Recess of the Legislature of any State, the Executive thereof may make temporary Appointments until the next Meeting of the Legislature, which shall then fill such Vacancies.

No Person shall be a Senator who shall not have attained to the Age of thirty Years, and been nine Years a Citizen of the United States, and who shall not, when elected, be an Inhabitant of that State for which he shall be chosen.

---

a. This provision was modified by the Sixteenth Amendment. The three-fifths reference to slaves was rendered obsolete by the Thirteenth and Fourteenth Amendments.
b. See the Seventeenth Amendment.

The Vice-President of the United States shall be President of the Senate, but shall have no Vote, unless they be equally divided.

The Senate shall chuse their other Officers, and also a President pro tempore, in the absence of the Vice-President, or when he shall exercise the Office of President of the United States.

The Senate shall have the sole Power to try all Impeachments. When sitting for that Purpose, they shall be on Oath or Affirmation. When the President of the United States is tried, the Chief Justice shall preside; And no Person shall be convicted without the Concurrence of two thirds of the Members present.

Judgment in Cases of Impeachment shall not extend further than to removal from Office, and disqualification to hold and enjoy any Office of honor, Trust or Profit under the United States; but the Party convicted shall nevertheless be liable and subject to Indictment, Trial, Judgment and Punishment, according to Law.

Section 4. The Times, Places and Manner of holding Elections for Senators and Representatives, shall be prescribed in each State by the Legislature thereof; but the Congress may at any time by Law make or alter such Regulations, except as to the Places of chusing Senators.

The Congress shall assemble at least once in every Year, and such Meeting shall be on the first Monday in December, unless they shall by Law appoint a different Day.[c]

Section 5. Each House shall be the Judge of the Elections, Returns and Qualifications of its own Members, and a Majority of each shall constitute a Quorum to do Business; but a smaller Number may adjourn from day to day, and may be authorized to compel the Attendance of absent Members, in such Manner, and under such Penalties as each House may provide.

Each House may determine the Rules of its Proceedings, punish its Members for disorderly Behavior, and, with the Concurrence of two thirds, expel a Member.

Each House shall keep a Journal of its Proceedings and from time to time publish the same, excepting such Parts as may in their Judgment require Secrecy; and the Yeas and Nays of the Members of either House on any question shall, at the Desire of one fifth of those Present, be entered on the Journal.

Neither House, during the Session of Congress, shall without the Consent of the other, adjourn for more than three days, nor to any other Place than that in which the two Houses shall be sitting.

Section 6. The Senators and Representatives shall receive a Compensation for their Services, to be ascertained by Law, and paid out of the Treasury of the United States. They shall in all Cases, except Treason, Felony, and Breach of the peace, be privileged from Arrest during their Attendance at the Session of their respective Houses, and in going to and returning from the same; and for any Speech or Debate in either House, they shall not be questioned in any other Place.

No Senator or Representative shall, during the Time for which he was elected, be appointed to any civil Office under the Authority of the United States, which shall have been created, or the Emoluments whereof shall have been encreased during such time; and no Person holding any Office under the United States, shall be a Member of either House during his Continuance in Office.

Section 7. All Bills for raising Revenue shall originate in the House of Representatives; but the Senate may propose or concur with Amendments as on other Bills.

Every Bill which shall have passed the House of Representatives and the Senate, shall, before it becomes a Law, be presented to the President of the United States; If he approve he shall sign it, but if not he shall return it, with his Objections to that House in which it shall have originated, who shall enter the Objections at large on their Journal, and proceed to reconsider it. If after such Reconsideration two thirds of that House shall agree to pass the Bill it shall be sent, together with the Objections, to the other House, by which it shall likewise be reconsidered, and if approved by two thirds of that House, it shall become a Law. But in all such Cases the Votes of both Houses shall be determined by Yeas and Nays, and the Names of the Persons voting for and against the Bill shall be entered on the Journal of each House respectively. If any Bill shall not be returned by the President

---

c. See the Twentieth Amendment.

within ten Days (Sundays excepted) after it shall have been presented to him, the Same shall be a Law, in like Manner as if he had signed it, unless the Congress by their Adjournment prevent its Return, in which Case it shall not be a Law.

Every Order, Resolution, or Vote to which the Concurrence of the Senate and House of Representatives may be necessary (except on a question of Adjournment) shall be presented to the President of the United States: and before the Same shall take Effect, shall be approved by him, or being disapproved by him, shall be repassed by two thirds of the Senate and House of Representatives, according to the Rules and Limitations prescribed in the Case of a Bill.

Section 8. The Congress shall have Power To lay and collect Taxes, Duties, Imposts and Excises, to pay the Debts and provide for the common Defence and general Welfare of the United States; but all Duties, Imposts and Excises shall be uniform throughout the United States;

To borrow money on the Credit of the United States;

To regulate Commerce with foreign Nations, and among the several States, and with the Indian Tribes;

To establish an uniform Rule of Naturalization, and uniform Laws on the subject of Bankruptcies throughout the United States;

To coin Money, regulate the Value thereof, and of foreign Coin, and fix the Standard of Weights and Measures;

To provide for the Punishment of counterfeiting the Securities and current Coin of the United States;

To establish Post Officers and post Roads;

To promote the Progress of Science and useful arts, by securing for limited Times to Authors and Inventors the exclusive Right to their respective Writings and Discoveries;

To constitute Tribunals inferior to the supreme Court;

To define and punish Piracies and Felonies committed on the high Seas, and Offenses against the Law of Nations;

To declare War, grant Letters of Marque and Reprisal, and make Rules concerning Captures on Land and Water;

To raise and support Armies, but no Appropriation of Money to that Use shall be for a longer Term than two Years;

To provide and maintain a Navy;

To make Rules for the Government and Regulation of the land and naval Forces;

To provide for calling forth the Militia to execute the Laws of the Union, suppress Insurrections and repel Invasions;

To provide for organizing, arming, and disciplining the Militia, and for governing such Part of them as may be employed in the Service of the United States, reserving to the States respectively, the Appointment of the Officers, and the Authority of training the Militia according to the discipline prescribed by Congress;

To exercise exclusive Legislation in all Cases whatsoever, over such District (not exceeding ten Miles square) as may, by Cession of particular States, and the acceptance of Congress, become the Seat of the Government of the United States, and to exercise like Authority over all Places purchased, by the Consent of the Legislature of the State in which the Same shall be, for the Erection of Forts, Magazines, Arsenals, dock-Yards, and other needful Buildings;—And

To make all Laws which shall be necessary and proper for carrying into Execution the foregoing Powers, and all other Powers vested by this Constitution in the Government of the United States, or in any Department or Officer thereof.

Section 9. The Migration or Importation of such Persons as any of the States now existing shall think proper to admit, shall not be prohibited by the Congress prior to the Year one thousand eight hundred and eight, but a tax or duty may be imposed on such Importation, not exceeding ten dollars for each Person.

The privilege of the Writ of Habeas Corpus shall not be suspended, unless when in Cases of Rebellion or Invasion the public Safety may require it.

No Bill of Attainder or ex post facto Law shall be passed.

No capitation, or other direct Tax shall be laid, unless in Proportion to the Census or Enumeration herein before directed to be taken.[d]

d. See the Sixteenth Amendment.

No Tax or Duty shall be laid on Articles exported from any State.

No Preference shall be given by any Regulation of Commerce or Revenue to the Ports of one State over those of another: nor shall Vessels bound to, or from one State, be obliged to enter, clear, or pay Duties in another.

No Money shall be drawn from the Treasury, but in Consequence of Appropriations made by Law; and a regular Statement and Account of the Receipts and Expenditures of all public Money shall be published from time to time.

No Title of Nobility shall be granted by the United States: And no Person holding any Office of Profit or Trust under them, shall, without the Consent of the Congress, accept of any present, Emolument, Office, or Title, of any kind whatever, from any King, Prince, or foreign State.

Section 10. No State shall enter into any Treaty, Alliance, or Confederation; grant Letters of Marque and Reprisal; coin Money; emit Bills of Credit; make any Thing but gold and silver Coin a Tender in Payment of Debts; pass any Bill of Attainder, ex post facto Law, or Law impairing the Obligation of Contracts, or grant any Title of Nobility.

No State shall, without the Consent of the Congress, lay any Imposts or Duties on Imports or Exports, except what may be absolutely necessary for executing its inspection Laws: and the net Produce of all Duties and Imposts, laid by any State on Imports or Exports, shall be for the Use of the Treasury of the United States and all such Laws shall be subject to the Revision and Control of the Congress.

No State shall, without the Consent of Congress, lay any duty of Tonnage, keep Troops, or Ships of War in time of Peace, enter into any Agreement or Compact with another State, or with a foreign Power, or engage in War, unless actually invaded, or in such imminent Danger as will not admit of delay.

Article II

Section 1. The executive Power shall be vested in a President of the United States of America. He shall hold his Office during the Term of four Years, and, together with the Vice-President, chosen for the same Term, be elected, as follows.

Each State shall appoint, in such Manner as the Legislature thereof may direct, a Number of Electors, equal to the whole number of Senators and Representatives to which the State may be entitled in the Congress; but no Senator or Representative, or Person holding an Office of Trust or Profit under the United States, shall be appointed an Elector.

The Electors shall meet in their respective States, and vote by Ballot for two persons, of whom one at least shall not be an Inhabitant of the same State with themselves. And they shall make a List of all the Persons voted for, and of the Number of Votes for each; which List they shall sign and certify, and transmit sealed to the Seat of the Government of the United States, directed to the President of the Senate. The President of the Senate shall, in the Presence of the Senate and House of Representatives, open all the Certificates, and the Votes shall then be counted. The Person having the greatest Number of Votes shall be the President, if such Number be a Majority of the whole Number of Electors appointed; and if there be more than one who have such Majority, and have an Equal Number of Votes, then the House of Representatives shall immediately chuse by Ballot one of them for President; and if no Person have a Majority, then from the five highest on the List the said House shall in like Manner chuse the President, but in chusing the President, the Votes shall be taken by States, the Representation from each State having one Vote; A quorum for this Purpose shall consist of a Member or Members from two-thirds of the States, and a Majority of all the States shall be necessary to a Choice. In every Case, after the Choice of the President, the Person having the greatest Number of Votes of the Electors shall be the Vice-President. But if there should remain two or more who have equal Votes, the Senate shall chuse from them by Ballot the Vice-President.[e]

The Congress may determine the Time of chusing the Electors, and the Day on which they shall give their Vote; which Day shall be the same throughout the United States.

No person except a natural born Citizen, or a Citizen of the United States, at the time of the

e. This paragraph was superseded by the Twelfth Amendment.

Adoption of this Constitution, shall be eligible to the Office of President; neither shall any Person be eligible to that Office who shall not have attained to the Age of thirty-five Years, and been fourteen Years a Resident within the United States.

In Case of the Removal of the President from Office, or of his Death, Resignation, or Inability to discharge the Powers and Duties of the said office, the same devolve on the Vice-President,[f] and the Congress may by Law provide for the Case of Removal, Death, Resignation or Inability, both of the President and Vice-President, declaring what Officer shall then act as President, and such Officer shall act accordingly, until the Disability be removed, or a President shall be elected.

The President shall, at stated Times, receive for his Services, a Compensation, which shall neither be encreased nor diminished during the Period for which he shall have been elected, and he shall not receive within that Period any other Emolument from the United States, or any of them.

Before he enter on the Execution of his Office, he shall take the following Oath or Affirmation:— "I do solemnly swear (or affirm) that I will faithfully execute the Office of President of the United States, and will to the best of my Ability, preserve, protect and defend the Constitution of the United States."

Section 2. The President shall be Commander in Chief of the Army and Navy of the United States, and of the Militia of the several States, when called into the actual Service of the United States; he may require the Opinion in writing, of the principal Officer in each of the executive Departments, upon any subject relating to the Duties of their respective Offices, and he shall have Power to Grant Reprieves and Pardons for Offenses against the United States, except in Cases of Impeachment.

He shall have Power, by and with the Advice and Consent of the Senate, to make Treaties, provided two-thirds of the Senators present concur; and he shall nominate, and by and with the Advice and Consent of the Senate, shall appoint Ambassadors, other public Ministers and Consuls, Judges of the supreme Court, and all other Officers of the United States, whose Appointments are not herein otherwise provided for, and which shall be established by Law: but the Congress may by Law vest the Appointment of such inferior Officers, as they think proper, in the President alone, in the Courts of Law, or in the Heads of Departments.

The President shall have Power to fill up all Vacancies that may happen during the Recess of the Senate by granting Commissions which shall expire at the End of their next Session.

Section 3. He shall from time to time give to the Congress Information of the State of the Union, and recommend to their Consideration such Measures as he shall judge necessary and expedient; he may, on extraordinary Occasions, convene both Houses, or either of them, and in Cases of Disagreement between them, with Respect to the Time of Adjournment, he may adjourn them to such Time as he shall think proper; he shall receive Ambassadors and other public Ministers; he shall take Care that the Laws be faithfully executed, and shall Commission all the Officers of the United States.

Section 4. The President, Vice-President and all civil Officers of the United States, shall be removed from Office on Impeachment for, and conviction of, Treason, Bribery, or other high Crimes and Misdemeanors.

Article III

Section 1. The judicial Power of the United States shall be vested in one supreme Court, and in such inferior Courts as the Congress may from time to time ordain and establish. The Judges, both of the supreme and inferior Courts, shall hold their offices during good Behaviour, and shall, at stated Times, receive for their Services a Compensation which shall not be diminished during their Continuance in Office.

Section 2. The judicial Power shall extend to all Cases, in Law and Equity, arising under this Constitution, the Laws of the United States and Treaties made, or which shall be made, under their Authority;—to all Cases affecting Ambassadors, other public Ministers and Consuls;—to all Cases of admiralty and maritime Jurisdiction;—to Controversies to which the United States shall be a Party;—to Controversies between two or more

---

f. See the Twenty-fifth Amendment.

States;—between a State and Citizens of another State;—Between Citizens of different States;—between Citizens of the same State claiming Lands under Grants of different States, and between a State, or the Citizens thereof, and foreign States, Citizens or Subjects.[g]

In all Cases affecting Ambassadors, other public Ministers and Consuls, and those in which a State shall be Party, the supreme Court shall have original Jurisdiction. In all the other Cases before mentioned, the supreme Court shall have appellate Jurisdiction, both as to Law and Fact, with such Exceptions, and under such Regulations as the Congress shall make.

The trial of all Crimes, except in Cases of Impeachment, shall be by Jury, and such Trial shall be held in the State where the said Crimes shall have been committed; but when not committed within any State, the Trial shall be at such Place or Places as the Congress may by Law have directed.

Section 3. Treason against the United States, shall consist only in levying War against them, or in adhering to their Enemies, giving them Aid and Comfort. No Person shall be convicted of Treason unless on the Testimony of two Witnesses to the same overt Act, or on Confession in open Court.

The Congress shall have power to declare the Punishment of Treason, but no Attainder of Treason shall work Corruption of Blood, or Forfeiture except during the Life of the Person attainted.

Article IV

Section 1. Full Faith and Credit shall be given in each State to the public acts, Records, and judicial Proceedings of every other State. And the Congress may by general Laws prescribe the Manner in which such Acts, Records and Proceedings shall be proved, and the Effect thereof.

Section 2. The Citizens of each State shall be entitled to all Privileges and Immunities of Citizens in the several States.

A Person charged in any State with Treason, Felony, or other Crime, who shall flee from Justice, and be found in another State, shall on demand of the executive Authority of the State from which he fled, be delivered up, to be removed to the State having Jurisdiction of the Crime.

No Person held to Service or Labour in one State, under the Laws thereof, escaping into another, shall in Consequence of any Law or Regulation therein, be discharged from such Service or Labour, but shall be delivered up on Claim of the Party to whom such Service or Labour may be due.[h]

Section 3. New States may be admitted by the Congress into this Union; but no new States shall be formed or erected within the Jurisdiction of any other State; nor any State be formed by the Junction of two or more States, or parts of States, without the Consent of the Legislatures of the States concerned as well as of the Congress.

The Congress shall have Power to dispose of and make all needful Rules and Regulations respecting the Territory or other Property belonging to the United States; and nothing in this Constitution shall be so constructed as to Prejudice any Claims of the United States, or of any particular State.

Section 4. The United States shall guarantee to every State in this Union a Republican Form of Government, and shall protect each of them against Invasion; and on Application of the Legislature, or of the Executive (when the Legislature cannot be convened) against domestic Violence.

Article V

The Congress whenever two-thirds of both Houses shall deem it necessary, shall propose Amendments to this Constitution, or, on the Application of the Legislatures of two-thirds of the several States, shall call a Convention for proposing Amendments, which, in either Case, shall be valid to all Intents and Purposes, as part of this Constitution, when ratified by the Legislatures of three-fourths of the several States, or by Conventions in three-fourths thereof, as the one or the other Mode of Ratification may be proposed by the Congress; Provided that no Amendment which may be made prior to the Year One thousand eight hundred and eight shall in any Manner affect the first and fourth Clauses in the Ninth Section of the first Article; and that no State, without its Consent, shall be deprived of its equal Suffrage in the Senate.

---

g. See the Eleventh Amendment.

h This provision was rendered obsolete by the Thirteenth Amendment.

Article VI

All Debts contracted and Engagements entered into, before the Adoption of this Constitution, shall be as valid against the United States under this Constitution, as under the Confederation.

This Constitution, and the Laws of the United States which shall be made in Pursuance thereof; and all Treaties made, or which shall be made, under the Authority of the United States, shall be the supreme Law of the Land; and the Judges in every State shall be bound thereby, any Thing in the Constitution or Laws of any State to the Contrary notwithstanding.

The Senators and Representatives before mentioned, and the Members of the several State Legislatures, and all executive and judicial Officers, both of the United States and of the several States, shall be bound by Oath or Affirmation, to support this Constitution; but no religious Test shall ever be required as a Qualification to any Office or public Trust under the United States.

Article VII

The Ratification of the Conventions of nine States shall be sufficient for the Establishment of this Constitution between the States so ratifying the Same.

Done in Convention by the Unanimous Consent of the States Present the Seventeenth Day of September in the Year of our Lord one thousand seven hundred and Eighty seven and of the Independence of the United States of America the Twelfth. In Witness whereof We have hereunto subscribed our Names.

Go. WASHINGTON
Presid't and deputy from Virginia

Delaware
Geo: Read
John Dickinson
Jaco: Broom
Gunning Bedford jun
Richard Bassett

Maryland
James McHenry
Danl Carroll
Dan: of St. Thos Jenifer

South Carolina
J. Rutledge
Charles Pinckney
Charles Cotesworth Pinckney
Pierce Butler

Georgia
William Few
Abr Baldwin

New York
Alexander Hamilton

New Jersey
Wil: Livingston
David Brearley
Wm. Patterson
Jona: Dayton

New Hampshire
John Langdon
Nicholas Gilman

Massachusetts
Nathaniel Gorham
Rufus King

Connecticut
Wm Saml Johnson
Roger Sherman

Virginia
John Blair
James Madison, Jr.

North Carolina
Wm Blount
Hu Williamson

Pennsylvania
B. Franklin
Robt. Morris
Thos. Fitzsimons
James Wilson

Richd Dobbs Spaight
Thomas Mifflin
Geo. Clymer
Jared Ingersoll
Gouv Morris

Attest:
WILLIAM JACKSON, Secretary.

AMENDMENTS[i]

Amendment I

Congress shall make no law respecting an establishment of religion, or prohibiting the free exercise thereof; or abridging the freedom of speech, or of the press; or the right of the people peaceably to assemble, and to petition the Government for a redress of grievances.

Amendment II

A well regulated Militia, being necessary to the security of a free State, the right of the people to keep and bear Arms, shall not be infringed.

Amendment III

No Soldier shall, in time of peace be quartered in any house, without the consent of the Owner, nor in time of war, but in a manner to be prescribed by law.

Amendment IV

The right of the people to be secure in their persons, houses, papers, and effects, against unreasonable searches and seizures, shall not be violated, and no Warrants shall issue, but upon probable cause, supported by Oath or affirmation, and particularly describing the place to be searched, and the persons or things to be seized.

Amendment V

No person shall be held to answer for a capital, or otherwise infamous crime, unless on a presentment or indictment of a Grand Jury, except in cases arising in the land or naval forces, or in the Militia, when in actual service in time of War or public danger; nor shall any person be subject for the same offense to be twice put in jeopardy of life or limb, nor shall be compelled in any criminal case to be a witness against himself, nor be deprived of life, liberty, or property, without due process of law; nor shall private property be taken for public use, without just compensation.

Amendment VI

In all criminal prosecutions, the accused shall enjoy the right to a speedy and public trial, by an impartial jury of the State and district wherein the crime shall have been committed, which district shall have been previously ascertained by law, and to be informed of the nature and cause of the accusation; to be confronted with the witnesses against him; to have the compulsory process for obtaining witnesses in his favor, and to have the Assistance of Counsel for his defence.

Amendment VII

In suits at common law, where the value in controversy shall exceed twenty dollars, the right of trial by jury shall be preserved, and no fact tried by a jury, shall be otherwise reexamined in any Court of the United States, than according to the rules of the common law.

Amendment VIII

Excessive bail shall not be required, nor excessive fines imposed, nor cruel and unusual punishments inflicted.

---

i. The first ten Amendments were adopted in 1791, as the Bill of Rights.

Amendment IX

The enumeration in the Constitution, of certain rights shall not be construed to deny or disparage others retained by the people.

Amendment X

The powers not delegated to the United States by the Constitution, nor prohibited by it to the States, are reserved to the States respectively, or to the people.

Amendment XI[j]

The Judicial power of the United States shall not be construed to extend to any suit in law or equity, commenced or prosecuted against one of the United States by Citizens of another State, or by Citizens or Subjects of any Foreign States.

Amendment XII[k]

The Electors shall meet in their respective states and vote by ballot for President and Vice-President, one of whom, at least, shall not be an inhabitant of the same state with themselves; they shall name in their ballots the person voted for as President and in distinct ballots the person voted for as Vice-President, and they shall make distinct lists of all persons voted for as President, and of all persons voted for as Vice-Presidents, and of the number of votes for each, which lists they shall sign and certify, and transmit sealed to the seat of the government of the United States, directed to the President of the Senate;—The President of the Senate shall, in the presence of the Senate and House of Representatives, open all the certificates and the votes shall then be counted;—The person having the greatest number of votes for President, shall be the President, if such number be a majority of the whole number of Electors appointed; and if no person have such majority, then from the persons having the highest numbers not exceeding three on the list of those voted for as President, the House of Representatives shall choose immediately, by ballot, the President. But in choosing the President, the votes shall be taken by states, the representation from each state having one vote; a quorum for this purpose shall consist of a member or members from two-thirds of the states, and a majority of all the states shall be necessary to a choice. And if the House of Representatives shall not choose a President whenever the right of choice shall devolve upon them, before the fourth day of March next following, then the Vice-President shall act as President, as in the case of the death or other constitutional disability of the President.—The person having the greatest number of votes as Vice-President, shall be the Vice-President, if such number be a majority of the whole number of Electors appointed, and if no person have a majority, then from the two highest numbers on the list, the Senate shall choose the Vice-President; a quorum for the purpose shall consist of two-thirds of the whole number of Senators, and a majority of the whole number shall be necessary to a choice. But no person constitutionally ineligible to the office of President shall be eligible to that of Vice-President of the United States.

Amendment XIII[l]

Section 1. Neither slavery nor involuntary servitude, except as a punishment for crime whereof the party shall have been duly convicted, shall exist within the United States, or any place subject to their jurisdiction.

Section 2. Congress shall have power to enforce this article by appropriate legislation.

Amendment XIV[m]

Section 1. All persons born or naturalized in the United States, and subject to the jurisdiction thereof, are citizens of the United States and of the State wherein they reside. No State shall make or enforce any law which shall abridge the privileges or immunities of citizens of the United States; nor shall any State deprive any person of life, liberty, or property, without due process of law; nor deny to any person within its jurisdiction the equal protection of the laws.

j Adopted in 1798.
k. Adopted in 1804.
l. Adopted in 1865.
m. Adopted in 1868.

Section 2. Representatives shall be apportioned among the several States according to their respective numbers, counting the whole number of persons in each State, excluding Indians not taxed. But when the right to vote at any election for the choice of electors for President and Vice President of the United States, Representatives in Congress, the Executive and Judicial Officers of a State, or the members of the Legislature thereof, is denied to any of the male inhabitants of such State, being twenty-one years of age, and citizens of the United States, or in any way abridged, except for participation in rebellion, or other crime, the basis of representation therein shall be reduced in the proportion which the number of such male citizens shall bear to the whole number of male citizens twenty-one years of age in such State.

Section 3. No person shall be a Senator or Representative in Congress, or elector of President and Vice President, or hold any office, civil or military, under the United States, or under any State, who, having previously taken an oath, as a member of Congress, or as an officer of the United States, or as a member of any State legislature, or as an executive or judicial officer of any State, to support the Constitution of the United States, shall have engaged in insurrection or rebellion against the same, or given aid or comfort to the enemies thereof. But Congress may by a vote of two-thirds of each House, remove such disability.

Section 4. The validity of the public debt of the United States, authorized by law, including debts incurred for payment of pensions and bounties for services in suppressing insurrection or rebellion, shall not be questioned. But neither the United States nor any State shall assume or pay any debt or obligation incurred in aid of insurrection or rebellion against the United States, or any claim for the loss or emancipation of any slave; but all such debts, obligations and claims shall be held illegal and void.

Section 5. The Congress shall have power to enforce, by appropriate legislation, the provisions of this article.

Amendment XV[n]

Section 1. The right of citizens of the United States to vote shall not be denied or abridged by the United States or by any State on account of race, color, or previous condition of servitude.

Section 2. The Congress shall have power to enforce this article by appropriate legislation.

Amendment XVI[o]

The Congress shall have power to lay and collect taxes on incomes, from whatever source derived, without apportionment among the several States, and without regard to any census or enumeration.

Amendment XVII[p]

The Senate of the United States shall be composed of two Senators from each State, elected by the people thereof, for six years, and each Senator shall have one vote. The electors in each State shall have the qualifications requisite for electors of the most numerous branch of the State legislatures.

When vacancies happen in the representation of any State in the Senate, the executive authority of such State shall issue writs of election to fill such vacancies: Provided, That the legislature of any State may empower the executive thereof to make temporary appointments until the people fill the vacancies by election as the legislature may direct.

This amendment shall not be so construed as to affect the election or term of any Senator chosen before it becomes valid as part of the Constitution.

Amendment XVIII[q]

Section 1. After one year from the ratification of this article the manufacture, sale, or transportation of intoxicating liquors within, the importation thereof into, or the exportation thereof from the United States and all territory subject to the jurisdiction thereof for beverage purposes is hereby prohibited.

---

n. Adopted in 1870.
o. Adopted in 1913.
p. Adopted in 1913.
q. Adopted in 1919. Repealed by the Twenty-first Amendment.

Section 2. The Congress and the several States shall have concurrent power to enforce this article by appropriate legislation.

Section 3. This article shall be inoperative unless it shall have been ratified as an amendment to the Constitution by the legislatures of the several States, as provided in the Constitution, within seven years from the date of the submission hereof to the States by the Congress.

Amendment XIX[r]

The right of citizens of the United States to vote shall not be denied or abridged by the United States or by any State on account of sex.

Congress shall have power to enforce this article by appropriate legislation.

Amendment XX[s]

Section 1. The terms of the President and Vice President shall end at noon on the 20th day of January, and the terms of Senators and Representatives at noon on the 3d day of January, of the years in which such terms would have ended if this article had not been ratified; and the terms of their successors shall then begin.

Section 2. The Congress shall assemble at least once in every year, and such meeting shall begin at noon on the 3rd day of January, unless they shall by law appoint a different day.

Section 3. If, at the time fixed for the beginning of the term of the President, the President elect shall have died, the Vice President elect shall become President. If a President shall not have been chosen before the time fixed for the beginning of his term, or if the President elect shall have failed to qualify, then the Vice President elect shall act as President until a President shall have qualified; and the Congress may by law provide for the case wherein neither a President elect nor a Vice President elect shall have qualified, declaring who shall then act as President, or the manner in which one who is to act shall be selected, and such person shall act accordingly until a President or Vice President shall have qualified.

Section 4. The Congress may by law provide for the case of the death of any of the persons from whom the House of Representatives may choose a President whenever the right of choice shall have devolved upon them, and for the case of the death of any of the persons from whom the Senate may choose a Vice President whenever the right of choice shall have devolved upon them.

Section 5. Sections 1 and 2 shall take effect on the 15th day of October following the ratification of this article.

Section 6. This article shall be inoperative unless it shall have been ratified as an amendment to the Constitution by the legislatures of three-fourths of the several States within seven years from the date of its submission.

Amendment XXI[t]

Section 1. The eighteenth article of amendment to the Constitution of the United States is hereby repealed.

Section 2. The transportation or importation into any State, Territory, or possession of the United States for delivery or use therein of intoxicating liquors, in violation of the laws thereof, is hereby prohibited.

Section 3. This article shall be inoperative unless it shall have been ratified as an amendment to the Constitution by conventions in the several States, as provided in the Constitution, within seven years from the date of the submission hereof to the States by the Congress.

Amendment XXII[u]

Section 1. No person shall be elected to the office of the President more than twice, and no person who has held the office of President, or acted as President, for more than two years of a term to which some other person was elected President shall be elected to the office of the President more than once. But this article shall not apply to any person holding the office of President when this article was proposed by the Congress, and shall not prevent any person who may be holding the office of President, or acting as President,

---

r. Adopted in 1920.
s. Adopted in 1933.
t. Adopted in 1933.
u. Adopted in 1951.

during the term within which this article becomes operative from holding the office of President or acting as President during the remainder of such term.

Section 2. This article shall be inoperative unless it shall have been ratified as an amendment to the Constitution by the legislatures of three-fourths of the several States within seven years from the date of its submission to the States by the Congress.

Amendment XXIII[v]

Section 1. The District constituting the seat of Government of the United States shall appoint in such manner as the Congress may direct:

A number of electors of President and Vice President equal to the whole number of Senators and Representatives in Congress to which the District would be entitled if it were a State, but in no event more than the least populous State; they shall be in addition to those appointed by the States, but they shall be considered, for the purposes of the election of President and Vice President, to be electors appointed by a State; and they shall meet in the District and perform such duties as provided by the twelfth article of amendment.

Section 2. The Congress shall have power to enforce this article by appropriate legislation.

Amendment XXIV[w]

Section 1. The right of citizens of the United States to vote in any primary or other election for President or Vice President, for electors for President or Vice President, or for Senator or Representative in Congress, shall not be denied or abridged by the United States or any State by reason of failure to pay any poll tax or other tax.

Section 2. The Congress shall have power to enforce this article by appropriate legislation.

Amendment XXV[x]

Section 1. In case of the removal of the President from office or of his death or resignation, the Vice President shall become President.

Section 2. Whenever there is a vacancy in the office of the Vice President, the President shall nominate a Vice President who shall take office upon confirmation by a majority vote of both Houses of Congress.

Section 3. Whenever the President transmits to the President pro tempore of the Senate and the Speaker of the House of Representatives his written declaration that he is unable to discharge the powers and duties of his office, and until he transmits to them a written declaration to the contrary, such powers and duties shall be discharged by the Vice President as Acting President.

Section 4. Whenever the Vice President and a majority of either the principal officers of the executive departments or of such other body as Congress may by law provide, transmit to the President pro tempore of the Senate and the Speaker of the House of Representatives their written declaration that the President is unable to discharge the powers and duties of his office, the Vice President shall immediately assume the powers and duties of the office as Acting President.

Thereafter, when the President transmits to the President pro tempore of the Senate and the Speaker of the House of Representatives his written declaration that no inability exists, he shall resume the powers and duties of his office unless the Vice President and a majority of either the principal officers of the executive department or of such other body as Congress may by law provide, transmit within four days to the President pro tempore of the Senate and the Speaker of the House of Representatives their written declaration that the President is unable to discharge the powers and duties of his office. Thereupon Congress shall decide the issue, assembling within forty-eight hours for that purpose if not in session. If the Congress, within twenty-one days after receipt of the latter written declaration, or, if Congress is not in session, within twenty-one days after Congress is required to assemble, determines by two-thirds vote of both Houses that the President is unable to discharge the powers and duties of his office, the Vice President shall continue to discharge the same as Acting President; otherwise, the President shall resume the powers and duties of his office.

---

v. Adopted in 1961.

w. Adopted in 1964.

x. Adopted in 1967.

Amendment XXVI[y]

Section 1. The right of citizens of the United States, who are eighteen years of age or older, to vote shall not be denied or abridged by the United States or by any State on account of age.

Section 2. The Congress shall have power to enforce this article by appropriate legislation.

Amendment XXVII[z]

No law varying the compensation for the services of the Senators and Representatives shall take effect until an election of Representatives shall have intervened.

---

y. Adopted in 1971.
z. Adopted in 1992.

Table of Cases

Principal cases are in italics. Cases cited or discussed within the authors' text are in roman type.

605